THE CAMBRIDGE HISTORY OF

THE FIRST WORLD WAR

This first volume of *The Cambridge History of the First World War* provides a comprehensive account of the war's military history. An international team of leading historians chart how a war made possible by globalisation and imperial expansion unfolded into catastrophe, growing year by year in scale and destructive power far beyond what anyone had anticipated in 1914.

Adopting a global perspective, the volume analyses the spatial impact of the war and the subsequent ripple effects that occurred both regionally and across the world. It explores how imperial powers devoted vast reserves of manpower and material to their war efforts, and how, by doing so, they changed the political landscape of the world order. It also charts the moral, political and legal implications of the changing character of war and, in particular, the collapse of the distinction between civilian and military targets.

Jay Winter is Charles J. Stille Professor of History at Yale University and Distinguished Visiting Professor at Monash University. He is one of the founders of the Historial de la Grande Guerre, the International Museum of the Great War, in Péronne, Somme, France. In 1997 he received an Emmy award for the best documentary series of the year as co-producer and co-writer of *The Great War and the Shaping of the Twentieth Century*, an eight-hour series broadcast on PBS and the BBC, shown subsequently in twenty-eight countries. His previous publications include *Sites of Memory, Sites of Mourning: The Great War in European Cultural History* (1995); *Remembering War* (2006) and *Dreams of Peace and Freedom* (2006).

THE HISTORIAL MUSEUM OF THE

GREAT WAR

PÉRONNE, SOMME

The Historial is an internationally acclaimed museum that presents the First World War in a unique way. Located on the battlefields of the Somme, the museum presents and compares the presence of the three main belligerent nations on the Western Front – Great Britain, France and Germany. It unfolds the story both of the front and of civilians under the pressure of war. The Battle of the Somme in 1916 caused over a million casualties in less than five months of fighting. The ground would be fought over again in 1918. By the end of the war, combatants from well over twenty-five nations had fought on the Somme, making it the place where the war truly became a World War.

Historial de la Grande Guerre / Thiepval
Château de Péronne
B. P. 20063
80201 Péronne Cedex
www.historial.org

THE CAMBRIDGE HISTORY OF THE FIRST WORLD WAR

*

VOLUME I

Global War

*

Edited by

JAY WINTER
Charles J. Stille Professor of History, Yale University

and

The Editorial Committee of the International Research Centre
of the Historial de la Grande Guerre

CAMBRIDGE
UNIVERSITY PRESS

CAMBRIDGE
UNIVERSITY PRESS

University Printing House, Cambridge CB2 8BS, United Kingdom

Cambridge University Press is part of the University of Cambridge.

It furthers the University's mission by disseminating knowledge in the pursuit of education, learning, and research at the highest international levels of excellence.

www.cambridge.org
Information on this title: www.cambridge.org/9780521763851

First published 2014
Reprinted 2014

Printed in the United Kingdom by TJ International Ltd. Padstow Cornwall

A catalogue record for this publication is available from the British Library

Library of Congress Cataloguing in Publication data
The Cambridge History of the First World War / general editor, Jay Winter, Charles J. Stille Professor of History, Yale University.
pages cm
Includes bibliographical references and index.
ISBN 978-0-521-76385-1 (v. 1) – ISBN 978-0-521-76653-1 (v. 2) – ISBN 978-0-521-76684-5 (v. 3)
1. World War, 1914–1918. 2. World War, 1914–1918 – Political aspects. 3. World War, 1914–1918 – Social aspects. I. Winter, J. M., editor. II. Title: History of the First World War.
D521.C36 2013
940.3–dc23
2013007649

ISBN 978-0-521-76385-1 Hardback

Contents

PART III
WORLD WAR

PART IV
RULES OF ENGAGEMENT, LAWS OF WAR AND WAR CRIMES

Illustrations

Plate section I

All illustrations are from the Collection of the Historial de la Grande Guerre, Péronne (Somme), unless otherwise stated.

Photography: Yazid Medmoun (Conseil Général de la Somme), unless otherwise stated.

Plate section II

Every effort has been made to contact the relevant copyright-holders for the images reproduced in this book. In the event of any error, the publisher will be pleased to make corrections in any reprints or future editions.

The colour pages can be found between pages 334 and 335 and pages 622 and 623.

Maps

Contributors

Holger Afflerbach is Professor of Central European History at the University of Leeds.

Mustafa Aksakal is Associate Professor of History and Modern Turkish Studies at Georgetown University.

Stéphane Audoin-Rouzeau is Directeur d'études at the École des Hautes Études en Sciences Sociales (EHESS), Paris, and President of the Centre International de Recherche de l'Historial de la Grande Guerre at Péronne.

Stephen Badsey is Professor of Conflict Studies at the University of Wolverhampton.

Annette Becker is Professor of Modern History at the University of Paris Ouest Nanterre La Défense and a senior member of the Institut Universitaire de France. She is Vice-President of the Centre International de Recherche de l'Historial de la Grande Guerre at Péronne.

Jean-Jacques Becker is Professor Emeritus at the Université Paris Ouest Nanterre La Défense and founding President of the International Research Centre of the Historial de la Grande Guerre, Péronne, Somme.

Volker R. Berghahn is Seth Low Professor of History at Columbia University.

Donald Bloxham is Richard Pares Professor of European History at the University of Edinburgh.

Bruno Cabanes is Associate Professor in the Department of History at Yale University.

Olivier Compagnon is Professor of Contemporary Latin American History at Université Sorbonne Nouvelle – Paris 3.

Annie Deperchin is Professor of Law at the Centre d'Histoire Judiciaire, Université de Lille 2.

John Horne is Professor of Modern European History at Trinity College Dublin, where he was the first Director of the Centre for War Studies, 2008–10.

Jennifer D. Keene is Professor of History and Chair of the History Department at Chapman University, Orange, California.

PAUL KENNEDY is J. Richardson Dilworth Professor of History and Director of International Security Studies at Yale University.

HANS-LUKAS KIESER is adjunct Professor of Modern History at the Universität Zürich, specialising in the late Ottoman Empire and the Republic of Turkey, and on interactions between the Near East and the transatlantic world in general.

GERD KRUMEICH is Professor Emeritus of Contemporary History at the Heinrich Heine Universität Düsseldorf and Vice-President of the International Research Centre of the Historial de la Grande Guerre, Péronne, Somme.

NICOLA LABANCA is Professor of Contemporary History in the Department of Historical Sciences at the Università degli Studi di Siena.

CHRISTOPH MICK is Associate Professor of History at the University of Warwick.

JOHN H. MORROW, JR. is Franklin Professor and Chairman of the History Department at the University of Georgia.

BILL NASSON is Professor of History at the University of Stellenbosch.

MICHAEL S. NEIBERG is Professor of History in the Department of National Security and Strategy at the US Army War College in Carlisle, Pennsylvania.

ROBIN PRIOR has been Visiting Professorial Fellow at the School of History and Politics at the University of Adelaide since 2007.

GARY SHEFFIELD is Professor of War Studies at the University of Wolverhampton.

JAY WINTER is Charles J. Stille Professor of History at Yale University and Distinguished Visiting Professor at Monash University.

GUOQI XU is Professor of History at the University of Hong Kong.

Acknowledgements

The completion of this three-volume history of the First World War would not have been possible without the support and assistance of the staff of the Historial de la Grand Guerre, Péronne, Somme, France. This museum, opened in 1992, was the first international museum of the 1914–18 conflict to give equal treatment to both sides and to its global character. The fruit of a generation of work in cultural history, the Historial was designed and its museography developed through its Research Centre, which began its work in 1989. We historians were at the heart of the project throughout its inception and remain so today.

The Historial is funded by the Conseil Général de la Somme. It reflects local pride and a commitment to the preservation of the traces of the Great War embedded in the landscape and cultural life of the Department of the Somme and of the wider world that shared the catastrophe of the Great War. In the Conseil Général, we are indebted to Christian Manable, Président, and Marc Pellan, Directeur de la Culture. At the Historial itself, thanks are due to Pierre Linéatte, Président, Historial de la Grande Guerre; Marie-Pascale Prévost-Bault, Conservateur en chef; Hervé François, Directeur; and the following staff members: Christine Cazé (a very large vote of thanks); Frederick Hadley; Catherine Mouquet; Séverine Lavallard. In addition, Yazid Medmoun was of essential help in providing us with photographs of the Historial's unique collection, visible in the illustrations selected for this three-volume history.

This transnational account of the history of the Great War was assembled through an editorial board composed of the members of the Comité directeur of the Research Centre of the Historial. As editor-in-chief of this project, I simply could not have even begun the task of creating this history without being part of a collective of historians with whom I have worked for more than two decades. Their shared vision is at the heart of these three volumes, and it is to these people and numerous other colleagues in the field of Great War studies working alongside us that the deepest vote of thanks is due. May I add a special note of gratitude for Rebecca Wheatley for her help in preparing the maps we have used?

Our work took the following form. After the table of contents was set, and authors' assignments distributed, each section of the book was placed in the hands of section editors, who were responsible for the development and completion of individual chapters and bibliographical essays for each chapter in their sections. The chapters they approved were sent to the editorial board as a whole, and I, as editor-in-chief, ensured their completeness, and the compatibility of their style and approach with our global and transnational objective. Helen McPhail and Harvey Mendelsohn did yeoman's work and more in translating French and German draft chapters into English, respectively. An essential part of the coordination of this vast project rested on the shoulders of Caroline Fontaine, Director of the International Research Centre of the Historial de la Grande Guerre at Péronne. For any errors that still remain, I take full responsibility.

General Introduction

JAY WINTER

Writing history is always a dialogue. When historians put pen to paper, they carry with them the accumulated interpretations their colleagues have developed over time. Frequently, it is against the grain of these interpretations, in opposition to them, in exasperation with them, that historians decide to write. To be sure, there are many occasions when historians concur with their colleagues or draw their attention to previously untapped sources on matters of common interest. But most of the time historians argue, make objections, and present through their writing a portrait of the past different from those available in print.

This is true both within a generation of historians and between generations. Today's scholars engage with colleagues still at work, and they do so dialogically. The critical point, though, it that the dialogue is also with those historians in the past whose works still inspire reflection, confirmation, elaboration and, on occasion, refutation. We historians are part of a very long engagement with the Great War, an engagement that will continue long after we cease to practise our profession.

The dialogic nature of historical practice therefore makes it necessary to place one generation's thinking about the Great War alongside those of early generations. And we are now the fourth generation of historians who have approached the history of the war of 1914–18.

There have been three earlier generations of writing to which current scholars refer, sometimes explicitly, most times, implicitly.[1] The first was what I will term 'the Great War generation'. These were scholars, former soldiers and public officials who had direct knowledge of the war either through their own military service or through alternative service to their

1 For a fuller elaboration of this interpretation see Jay Winter and Antoine Prost, *The Great War in History: Debates and Controversies, 1914 to the Present* (Cambridge University Press, 2005); and Jay Winter (ed.), *The Legacy of the Great War: Ninety Years On* (Columbia, MO: University of Missouri Press, 2009).

country's war effort. They wrote history from the top down, by and large through direct experience of the events they described. The central actor portrayed in these books was the state, either in its *dirigiste* forms at home or at the front. The most voluminous of these efforts was the 133-book effort to write the economic and social history of the war, sponsored by the Carnegie Endowment for International Peace. Most of these tomes were penned by men who helped run the war or who had to deal with its aftershocks.

This first generation was also composed of men whose memoirs went over the ground again for evident purposes of self-justification. This took many forms, from books by generals and cabinet ministers about their contributions to victory, to exculpatory reminiscences about those trying to evade responsibility for defeat. There were also official histories, many of which were written by former soldiers for the benefit of the various national staff colleges, trying one at a time to frame 'lessons' for the future. These works were frequently highly technical and so detailed that they took decades to appear. The delay diminished their significance for planning the next war in more efficient ways.

The second generation may be termed the generation 'fifty years on'. This group of historians wrote in the late 1950s and 1960s, and wrote not only the history of politics and decision-making at the top, but also the history of society, defined as the history of social structures and social movements. Of course the two kinds of history, political and social, went together, but they were braided together in different ways than in the interwar years. Many of these scholars had the benefit of sources unknown or unavailable before the Second World War. The 'fifty year rule' enabling scholars to consult state papers meant that all kinds of documents could be exploited by those writing in the 1960s, which threw new light on the history of the war.

In the 1960s, there was much more use of film and visual evidence than in the first generation, though in the interwar years battlefield guides and collections of photographs of devastation and weaponry were produced in abundance. After the Second World War, the age of television history began, and attracted an audience to historical narratives greater than ever before. This became evident in the size of the audience for new and powerful television documentaries about the war. In 1964 the BBC launched its second channel with the monumental twenty-six-part history of the war, exhaustively researched in film archives and vetted by an impressive group of military historians. Many of the millions of people who saw this series had lived through the war. In 1964, the young men who had fought and survived were mostly above the age of seventy, but what made the series a major cultural event was that the families of the survivors, and of those who did not come back, integrated these war stories into their own family narratives. The Great War thus escaped from the academy into the much more lucrative and populous field of public history, represented by museums, special exhibitions, films and now television. By the 1960s, the Imperial War Museum in London had surpassed many other sites as the premier destination of visitors to London. It remains to this day a major attraction in the capital, just as does the Australian War Memorial, an equally impressive museum and site of remembrance in the Australian capital, Canberra.

There was more than a little nostalgia in the celebration by survivors of 'fifty years on'. By 1964, the European world that went to war in 1914 no longer existed. All the major imperial powers that joined the struggle had been radically transformed. The British Empire was a thing of the past; so was *Algérie française*, and the French *mission civilisatrice* in Africa and South Asia. The German Empire was gone, and so were most of its eastern territories, ceded to Poland and Russia after 1945. Austria, Hungary and Yugoslavia were small independent states. And while the Soviet Union resembled Tsarist Russia in some respects, these continuities were dwarfed by the massive transformation of Soviet society since 1917.

The nostalgia of 1964 was, therefore, for a world which had fallen apart in the Great War. For many people, the blemishes and ugliness of much of that world were hidden by a kind of sepia-toned reverence for the days before the conflict. 'Never such innocence, / Never before or since', wrote Philip Larkin in a poem whose title referred not to 1914, but to the more archaic 'MCMXIV'. This poem was published in 1964.

In much historical writing, as much as in historical documentaries, the dramatic tension derived from juxtaposing this set of pre-lapsarian images with the devastation and horror of the Western Front, and with the sense of decline, a loss of greatness, which marked the post-1945 decades in Britain and beyond. Whatever was wrong with the world seemed to be linked to 1914, to the time when a multitude of decent men went off to fight one war and wound up fighting a much more terrible one.

Decencies were betrayed, some argued, by a blind elite prepared to sacrifice the lives of the masses for vapid generalisations like 'glory' or 'honour'. This populist strain may be detected in much writing about the war in the 1960s, and in the study of social movements which arose out of it. The fiftieth anniversary of the Gallipoli landing provoked a surge of interest in the Great War in Australia and New Zealand, where the loss of the battle was eclipsed by the birth of these two nations. Similarly heroic were narratives of the Bolshevik Revolution, celebrating its fiftieth anniversary in 1967. It is hardly surprising, therefore, that many scholars told us much more about the history of labour, of women, of ordinary people during the conflict than had scholars working in the interwar years.

The third generation may be termed the 'Vietnam generation'. Its practitioners started writing in the 1970s and 1980s, when a general reaction against military adventures like the war in Vietnam took place in Britain and Europe as well as in the United States. This was also the period in Europe when public opinion turned against the nuclear deterrent, and when the 1973 Middle Eastern war had dangerous effects on the economies of the developed world. The glow of the 'just war' of 1939–45 had faded, and a new generation was more open to a view that war was a catastrophe to both winners and losers alike.

This was the environment in which darker histories of the Great War emerged. There were still scholars who insisted that the Great War was a noble cause, won by those who had right on their side. But there were others who came to portray the Great War as a futile exercise, a tragedy, a stupid, horrendous waste of lives, producing nothing of great value aside from the ordinary decencies and dignities thrown away by blind and arrogant leaders.

The most influential works were written by three very different scholars. Paul Fussell, a veteran of the Second World War who was wounded in combat, produced a classic literary study, *The Great War and Modern Memory*, in 1975.[2] He was a professor of literature, who fashioned an interpretation of how soldiers came to understand the war they found in 1914–18 as an ironic event, one in which anticipation and outcome were wildly different. It was a time when the old romantic language of battle seemed to lose its meaning. Writers twisted older forms to suit the new world of trench warfare, one in which mass death was dominant and where, under artillery and gas bombardment, soldiers lost any sense that war was a glorious thing. Fussell termed this style the 'ironic' style and challenged us to see war writing throughout the twentieth century as built upon the foundations laid by the British soldier writers of the Great War.

Sir John Keegan produced a book a year later which paralleled Fussell's. An instructor in the Royal Military College at Sandhurst, but a man whose childhood infirmities ensured he would never go to war, Keegan asked the disarmingly simple question: 'Is battle possible?' The answer, published in *The Face of Battle* in 1976,[3] was perhaps yes, long ago, but now in the twentieth

2 Paul Fussell, *The Great War and Modern Memory* (New York: Oxford University Press, 1975).
3 John Keegan, *The Face of Battle* (London: Allen Lane, 1976).

century, battle presented men with terrifying challenges. The men who fought at the Battle of Agincourt in 1415 could run to the next hill to save their lives. Foot soldiers converging on Waterloo four centuries later could arrive a day late. But in 1916, at the Battle of the Somme, there was no way out. Given the industrialisation of warfare, the air above the trenches on the Somme was filled with lethal projectiles from which there was no escape. Mass death in that battle and in the other great conflict of 1916 at Verdun, pushed soldiers beyond the limits of human endurance. Nothing like the set battles of the First World War followed in the 1939–45 war, though Stalingrad came close to replicating the horror of the Somme and Verdun. Here was a military historian's book, but one whose starting point was humane and to a degree psychological. The soldiers' breaking point was Keegan's subject, and with power, subtlety and technical authority, he opened a new chapter in the study of military history as a humane discipline.

In 1979, Eric Leed, a historian steeped in the literature of anthropology, wrote a similarly path-breaking book. *No Man's Land: Combat and Identity in World War I*[4] borrowed subtly from the work of the anthropologist Victor Turner. He had examined people in a liminal condition, no longer part of an older world from which they had come, and unable to escape from the midpoint, the no-man's-land, in which they found themselves. Here is the emotional landscape of the trench soldiers of the Great War. They were men who could never come home again, for whom war was their home, and who recreated it in the years following the Armistice. Here was the world of shell-shocked men, but also that of the *Freikorps*, militarised freebooters of the immediate post-war period, who prepared the ground for the Nazis.

In all three cases, and by reference to very different sources, the subject at hand was the tragedy of the millions of men who went into the trenches and who came out, if at all, permanently marked by the experience. They bore what some observers of the survivors of Hiroshima termed the 'death imprint'; the knowledge that their survival was a purely arbitrary accident. Here we may see some traces of the anti-nuclear movement, putting alongside one another Japanese civilians and Great War soldiers. The moral and political differences between the two cases are evident, but the wreckage of war, so these writers seemed to say, is at the heart of the civilisation in which we live. It is probably not an exaggeration to say that these three books, alongside others of the time, helped create a tragic interpretation of the Great War, one in which victimhood

4 Eric Leed, *No Man's Land: Combat and Identity in World War I* (Cambridge University Press, 1979).

and violence were braided together in such a way as to tell a fully European story of the war, one to which the founders of the European Union clearly reacted. From the 1970s on, European integration was an attempt to move away from the notion of the nation-state as that institution which had the right to go to war, as Raymond Aron put it. The result has been a progressive diminution of the role of the military in the political and social life of most European countries. James Sheehan asked the question in a recent book, *Where Have All the Soldiers Gone?*[5] The answer is, they and most (though not all) of their leaders have fled from the landscape of war so devastatingly presented in the works of Fussell, Keegan, Leed and others.

Now we are in a fourth generation of writing on the Great War. I would like to term it the 'transnational generation'. This generation has a global outlook. The term 'global' describes both the tendency to write about the war in more than European terms and to see the conflict as trans-European, transatlantic and beyond. Here was the first war among industrialised countries, reaching the Middle East and Africa, the Falkland Islands and China, drawing soldiers into the epicentre in Europe from Vancouver to Capetown to Bombay and to Adelaide. Here was a war that gave birth to the Turkey of Atatürk and to the Soviet Union of Lenin and Stalin. Demands for decolonisation arose from a war that had promised self-determination and had produced very little of the kind. Economic troubles arose directly out of the war, and these were sufficiently serious to undermine the capacity of the older imperial powers to pay for their imperial and quasi-imperial footholds around the world.

A word or two may be useful to distinguish the international approach, common to many of the older Cambridge histories, from what I have termed the transnational approach to the history of the Great War. For nearly a century, the Great War was framed in terms of a system of international relations in which the national and imperial levels of conflict and cooperation were taken as given. Transnational history does not start with one state and move on to others, but takes multiple levels of historical experience as given, levels which are both below and above the national level.[6] Thus the history of

5 James Keegan, *Where Have All the Soldiers Gone?* (Cambridge, MA: Harvard University Press, 2008).

6 For some discussions of the emergence of transnational history, see Akira Iriye, 'Transnational history', *Contemporary European History*, 13 (2004), pp. 211–22; John Heilbron *et al.*, 'Towards a transnational history of the social sciences', *Journal of the History of the Behavioral Sciences*, 44:2 (2008), pp. 146–60; and C. A. Bayly, Sven Beckert, Matthew Connelly, Isabel Hofmeyr, Wendy Kozol and Patricia Seed, 'AHR conversation: on transnational history', *American Historical Review*, 111:5 (2006), pp. 1441–64.

mutiny, developed in Volume II, is transnational, in that it happened in different armies for different reasons, some of which are strikingly similar to the sources of protest and refusal in other armies. So is the history of finance, technology, war economies, logistics and command. The history of commemoration, cited in the discussion on remembrance in Volume III, also happened on many levels, and the national is not necessarily the most significant, not the most enduring. The peace treaties following the Great War, discussed in Volume II, show the meaning of the transnational in other ways. Now we can see that the war was both the apogee and the beginning of the end of imperial power, spanning and eroding national and imperial boundaries. Erez Manela's work on 'the Wilsonian moment' is a case in point. He reconfigures the meaning of the Versailles settlement by exploring its unintended consequences in stimulating movements of national liberation in Egypt, India, Korea and China. Instead of telling us about the interplay of Great Power politics, he shows how non-Europeans invented their own version of Wilson in their search for a kind of self-determination that he, alongside Lloyd George, Clemenceau and Orlando, was unprepared to offer to them. Who could have imagined that the decision these men took to award rights to Shandong province, formerly held by Germany, not to China but to Japan would lead to major rioting and the formation of the Chinese Communist Party?[7]

Historians of the revolutionary moment in Europe itself between 1917 and 1921 have approached their subject more and more as a transnational phenomenon, as we can see in Volume II. After all, both revolutionaries and the forces of order who worked to destroy them were well aware of what may be termed the cultural transfer of revolutionary (and counter-revolutionary) strategy, tactics and violence. In recent years, these exchanges have been analysed at the urban and regional levels, helping us to see the complexity of a story somewhat obscured by treating it solely in national terms. Comparative urban history has established the striking parallels between the challenges urban populations faced in different warring states. Now we can answer in the affirmative the question as to whether there is a metropolitan history of warfare. In important respects, the residents of Paris, London and Berlin shared more with one another than they did with their respective rural compatriots. These experienced communities had a visceral reality somewhat lacking even in the imagined communities of the nation.

7 Erez Manela, *The Wilsonian Moment: Self-Determination and the International Origins of Anticolonial Nationalism* (New York: Oxford University Press, 2007).

Here we must be sensitive to the way contemporaries used the language of nation and empire to describe loyalties and affiliations of a much smaller level of aggregation. A journalist asking British troops on the Western Front whether they were fighting for the Empire, got a 'yes' from one soldier. His mates asked him what he meant. The answer was that he was fighting for the Empire Music Hall in Hackney, a working-class district of London. This attachment to the local and the familiar was utterly transnational.[8]

Another subject now understood more in transnational than in international terms is the history of women in wartime, discussed in Volume III. Patriarchy, family formation and the persistence of gender inequality were transnational realities in the period of the Great War. Furthermore, the war's massive effects on civilian life precipitated a movement of populations of staggering proportions, discussed in Volume III. Refugees in France, the Netherlands and Britain from the area occupied by the Western Front numbered in the millions. So did those fleeing the fighting in the borderlands spanning the old German, Austro-Hungarian and Russian Empires. One scholar has estimated that perhaps 20 per cent of the population of Russia was on the move, heading for safety wherever it could be found during the Great War. And that population current turned into a torrent throughout Eastern Europe during the period of chaos surrounding the Armistice. What made it worse was that the United States closed its gates to such immigrants, ending one of the most extraordinary periods of transcontinental migration in history. Thus population transfer, forced or precipitated by war, transformed the ethnic character of many parts of Greece, Turkey, the Balkans and the vast tract of land from the Baltic states to the Caucasus. Such movements antedated the war, but they grew exponentially after 1914. This is why it makes sense to see the Great War as having occasioned the emergence of that icon of transnational history in the twentieth century, the refugee, with his or her pitiful belongings slung over shoulders or carts. The photographic evidence of this phenomenon is immense, as we see in the photographic essays accompanying all three volumes.

This three-volume project is transnational in yet another respect. We live in a world where historians born in one country have been able to migrate to follow their historical studies and either to stay in their adopted homes or to migrate again, when necessary, to obtain a university post. Many of the authors of chapters in these volumes are transnational scholars, practising

8 Jay Winter, 'British popular culture in the First World War', in R. Stites and A. Roshwald (eds.), *Popular Culture in the First World War* (Cambridge University Press, 1999), pp. 138–59.

history far from their place of birth and enriching the world of scholarship thereby. Seeing the world in which we live at a tangent, in the words of the Greek poet Kafavy, opens up insights harder to identify from within a settled order. The world of scholarship today may be described in many ways, but the term 'settled' is not one of them. This unsettledness is a major advantage, one which someday will enable more transnational histories to emerge alongside national histories, and for each to enrich the other.

It is important to repeat that these new initiatives in transnational history have built on the work of the three generations of scholars that preceded them. The history of the Great War that has emerged in recent years is additive, cumulative and multi-faceted. National histories have a symbiotic relationship with transnational histories; the richer the one, the deeper the other. No cultural historian of any standing ignores the history of the state, or of the social movements which at times have overthrown them; to do so would be absurd. No military historian ignores the language in which commands turn into movements on the field of battle. War is such a protean event that it touches every facet of human life. Earlier scholars pointed the way; we who have collectively constructed this three-volume history acknowledge their presence among us in our effort to take stock of the current state of knowledge in this field.

The potential imbedded in this transnational approach is reflected as well in one institution explicitly committed to going beyond the strictly national confines of the history of the war: the Historial de la Grande Guerre at Péronne, France. The Historial is a museum of the war, designed by historians and presented in three languages – English, French and German – located at the site of German Headquarters during the Battle of the Somme, that vast bloodletting in 1916, which the German writer Ernst Jünger termed the birthplace of the twentieth century. Together with four historians of the Great War from France and Germany – Jean-Jacques Becker, Gerd Krumeich, Stéphane Audoin-Rouzeau and Annette Becker – I joined a collective which reached out across national frontiers to create a new kind of museum, one which treated the Great War as a transnational catastrophe.[9] This blending of different national viewpoints and emphases suited the new Europe of the 1990s, when it became apparent that to understand the integration of Europe at

9 For the story of the creation of the Historial, see *Collections de l'Historial de la grande guerre* (Péronne, Somme: Département de la Somme, 2010); and Jay Winter, 'Designing a war museum: some reflections on representations of war and combat', in Elizabeth Anderson, Avril Maddrell, Kate McLoughlin and Alana Vincent (eds.), *Memory, Mourning, Landscape* (Amsterdam and New York: Rodolfi, 2010), pp. 10–30.

the end of the twentieth century, you had to understand the disintegration of Europe at its beginning. It is this optic which guides these three volumes, as it has guided the Historial in the first generation of its existence.

The board of directors of the International Research Centre of the Historial de la Grande Guerre served as the editorial committee which guided this book through its long gestation. We note that all authors and editors have foregone payment in order to direct the royalties these volumes earn into a fund for postgraduate work in First World War studies anywhere in the world. It is to the young scholars whose work we have supported and to those still to come, those whose perspectives are still unfolding, that this transnational project is dedicated.

Introduction to Volume I

JAY WINTER

A global war needs global history to bring out in high relief its conduct, its character and its manifold repercussions. The first volume of this global history of the 1914–18 conflict focuses on the war in time and space. First, we present a narrative of the war as an unfolding catastrophe, growing year by year in scale and in destructive power far beyond what anyone had anticipated in 1914. Secondly, this volume considers the war in spatial terms, and shows the ripple effect of the conflict throughout the world. We explore how imperial powers devoted huge reserves of manpower and materiel to their war efforts, and how, by doing so, they unintentionally transformed the global world order of 1914 into something radically different four years later. Emphasising the Eastern European and the extra-European character of the conflict enables us to escape from a narrow definition of the war as that which took place on the Western Front alone.

By a global war, we mean the engagement in a conflict of fifty months' duration of the world's great empires and industrialised or industrialising economies. Historians of globalisation point to 1914 as the moment of rupture of the first phase of globalisation, entailing the movement of goods, capital and people on an order of magnitude the world had never seen before. It was only after 1945 that this first phase of globalisation was succeeded by another, which is still in motion today. Our approach to global war is therefore one which is dialectical in character: it examines the way the war ended one of the most remarkable periods of the expansion of capitalism, and the way it channelled the remarkable energies of the world's economies into the greatest destructive campaign to date. Innovation and structural change compensated to a degree for the destruction of capital, land and lives in wartime, and created new forms of state capitalism and communism which came to govern economic and political life for the rest of the century. The history of the war in time and space in Volume I thus prepares the ground for Volume II, where we focus primarily on the wartime transformation of the institutions of the state.

The war we present has a history that cannot stop at the confines of the European continent. Our intention is to introduce readers to a war made possible by globalisation and imperial expansion, a war which left its unmistakable imprint on the way global affairs have developed ever since. We conclude this volume with a discussion of the moral, political and legal implications of the changing character of war, and in particular of the collapse of the distinction between civilian and military targets, reaching its nadir in genocide.

PART I

★

A NARRATIVE HISTORY

Introduction to Part I

JAY WINTER

There is little doubt as to when the Great War began, but much more doubt as to when it ended. The reason for the shift in perspective is that the revolutionary character of a war beginning with a set of formal declarations of hostilities set in motion forces which broke through the conventional moment of the eleventh hour of the eleventh day of November 1918 as the time when the conflict came to an end. It did no such thing in Eastern Europe or in Russia, in Turkey, nor in colonial or semi-colonial settings ranging from Egypt to India to Korea to China.

The primary reason we still celebrate 11 November as Armistice day is that on that day the great European powers accepted the formal capitulation of Germany in a railway carriage in a forest near Compiègne. But even then, it took six months to settle the terms of the peace treaty with Germany, during which interval the Allied blockade of Germany and Central Europe continued. And it took longer to settle terms with Germany's allies, the successor states of the Austro-Hungarian Empire, Bulgaria and Turkey. Terms were agreed with the Ottoman Empire in 1920 at Sèvres, and then renegotiated after considerable fighting, and to Turkey's advantage, in 1923 at Lausanne.

A global history of the Great War thus needs a chronological narrative that sets the outbreak of war and the end of the conflict in a framework starting before 1914 and ending after 1918. This we provide in seven chapters. The first two focus on the long-term and immediate origins of the conflict. The chapters on 1915 and 1916 unfold the story of stalemate and slaughter which, as we see in chapters on 1917 and 1918, both continued and took on new forms on account of the entry of the United States and the withdrawal of Russia from the war. On balance, the Central Powers were in a stronger position than the Allied Powers in the first two years of the war, but after 1916, the balance of forces shifted the strategic balance in favour of the Allies. In 1919 more chaos than order emerged from the effort to construct a lasting peace. The rest of these three volumes tell us in a host of ways how, where and why this general narrative unfolded.

I

Origins

VOLKER R. BERGHAHN

Introduction

While the immediate origins of the First World War are being analysed in the next chapter of this book, this one will examine the more long-term and deeper causes of what has rightly been called by George F. Kennan and others 'the primordial catastrophe' of the twentieth century.

In trying to identify these causes, historians have traditionally taken a chronological approach and written detailed narratives, some of which are very readable to this day; others are somewhat less riveting. The drawback of this approach is that, in light of the complexities of international politics and economics in the decades before 1914, readers could easily lose their way in the thickets of events and actors in the historical drama that ended in the outbreak of a world war in 1914.

The alternative is to take a thematic approach to the subject with individual sections devoted to one of the major issues of the time, such as European colonialism and imperialism, domestic politics, cultural developments and armaments. The advantage of this approach is its relatively greater clarity and accessibility. At the same time it is inevitably more difficult to provide a sense of the constant inter-relatedness of events. The best example of this approach is James Joll's *The Origins of the First World War.*[1] To be sure, Joll was too sophisticated a scholar to keep all his themes in a finely calibrated balance. Instead he raised the question of which of his various themes was, in his view, in the end the most important one. Although his rankings are not very explicit, he does highlight one theme that, he believes, is the key to an understanding of the war's origins and deeper causes. He called this factor, discussed significantly enough at the very end of his book, 'the mood of 1914', and defines it as follows:

1 James Joll, *The Origins of the First World War* (London: Longman, 1984).

> This mood can only be assessed approximately and impressionistically. The more we study it in detail, the more we see how it differed from country to country or from class to class. Yet at each level there was a willingness to risk or to accept war as a solution to a whole range of problems, political, social, international, to say nothing of war as apparently the only way of resisting a direct physical threat. It is these attitudes which made war possible; and it is still in an investigation of the mentalities of the rulers of Europe and their subjects that the explanation of the causes of the war will ultimately lie.[2]

This chapter is also very much concerned with 'moods' and mentalities and the bearing that these had on the outbreak of war in 1914. But it is sociologically quite specific in that it focuses on the role of the military in the decision-making processes that led to war and relates it to the dynamics of one major factor, the pre-1914 arms race. This means that other factors relevant to the origins of the First World War will be discussed first before turning to the one that in my view must take first place in a ranking of causes. Organised like a funnel, it ultimately homes in on the key to understanding what happened in Europe in July and August 1914.

Industrialisation, demographic change and urbanisation

To grasp the highly dynamic developments that the societies of Europe underwent in the three or four decades before 1914, the impact of industrialisation, demography and urbanisation must be considered as major background factors. It is in this period that much of continental Europe experienced two Industrial Revolutions following closely upon each other. The first Industrial Revolution began in Britain in the eighteenth century, driven by the manufacture of soft weaving materials and textiles as well as by coal mining and iron-making. In the second half of the nineteenth century it was followed by what is generally termed the Second Industrial Revolution, characterised by the development of electrical and non-electrical engineering and chemicals. For both these revolutions it should also be remembered that production initially took place in quite small units, many of which began as craftsmen's workshops. However, before the end of the nineteenth century there occurred a merger and concentration movement, resulting in the emergence of large corporations with hundreds and thousands of workers. And with their increased numbers

2 *Ibid.*, p. 196.

also came the rise of white-collar employees, white-coated scientists and the female white-blouse professions.

Secondly, from the eighteenth century Europe had also seen a very rapid population growth. Sooner or later, many men and women no longer found employment in agriculture, the mainstay of the pre-industrial economies. They began to move to regional or faraway towns, many of which grew into cities. In fact, there were many urban communities by the late nineteenth century that had trebled or quadrupled their populations within a decade. Most of the migrants who did not emigrate to North America, South America or Australia in those years, found employment in manufacturing industry, and although pay and work conditions were better than in agriculture that they had left behind, the levels of poverty were still shocking to contemporaries. With, on average, three or four children, many working-class families lived in very cramped apartment blocks, known as rental barracks. Medical and dental care was minimal and often unaffordable for blue-collar workers and their families. Charities were overburdened and underfunded. Unemployment benefits and social security programmes developed slowly in some European states, but were never adequate.

At the same time, industry and commerce created new wealth, promoting the rise of a well-to-do commercial and professional middle class, including white-collar employees. The growth of local regional and national bureaucracies and of systems of primary, secondary and tertiary education also provided better-paid and more secure jobs. The gap between the wealthy and the poor was particularly visible in residential segregation, dress and shopping habits. Accordingly, the industrial societies of pre-1914 Europe became more rigidly stratified in terms of socio-economic position and cultural habitus.

Political mobilisation and domestic politics

Since the political systems outside Eastern Europe had begun to open up and tried to integrate as citizens those who had been born into a particular nation-state, socio-economic conditions and divisions contributed to an awakening of a political consciousness, but this time not merely among the liberal bourgeoisie or the upper classes who tended to hold on to the positions of power they had gained within the state, but increasingly also among industrial workers. With the spread of suffrage systems and the rise of the printing press, the lower classes, too, were able to articulate their hopes and expectations vis-à-vis their local and national governments. Like the middle and upper classes, they founded political parties and associations to represent them in public.

Although many suffrage systems remained restricted and unfairly skewed against the working class, by the later nineteenth century there were a growing number of deputies in the local, regional and national assemblies who had been elected by those at the bottom of the pile. It did not take long for the other parties and classes to see them as a threat. It did not matter whether they were running a republic, like in Italy or France, or a constitutional monarchy; they all were faced with growing numbers of citizens living in the cities under conditions that were crying out for improvement. Perceiving a threat to the established order, politicians and bureaucrats relied on and refined several means by which they tried to stabilise political conditions. One of these was social appeasement, the attempt to satisfy the hopes and expectations of the working class with tangible concessions or promises of a better life in the future. But there was also reliance on the repressive power of the police and, as a last resort, on the army.

A third method was to mobilise nationalist feelings and to win over citizens by appealing to the integrating force of patriotism. There are two examples of how these processes worked in the 1880s under the French Republic led by Jules Ferry, on the one hand, and in the Prusso-German monarchy during the period of Reich Chancellor Otto von Bismarck, on the other. Both of them faced stiff opposition in the national parliament and were anxious to stabilise their support among the parties. National elections were coming up, Bismarck found himself in a situation similar to Ferry's, who had successfully pushed back the monarchist opposition, whereas Bismarck had curbed the threat that the German Social Democrats posed to retaining his conservative majorities in the national parliament by outlawing their party, trade unions and related organisations.

Imperialism and colonialism

There was yet another device by which – so politicians calculated – patriotic pride and support for the national state could be fostered: the lure of expansion into overseas territories and the quest for a colonial empire. The British elites had already practised this policy by mobilising 'working-class Tories' who cheered the Empire that they had been told would bring both material and immaterial benefits to all Britons. Bismarck, the conservative Prussian landowner, was personally unenthusiastic about Germany joining the scramble for colonies that was in full swing in the final decades of the nineteenth century. At the 1884 Congo Conference in Berlin, where the Great Powers discussed the distribution of territories in Africa, Leopold II, King of the Belgians, had been given for his personal exploitation the huge Congo Basin with its rich mineral resources.[3]

Soon sceptical Bismarck began to change his tune, significantly enough just prior to the upcoming Reichstag elections. He was not concerned about a few German working-class Tories, if they existed at all, but about powerful interest groups among the commercial bourgeoisie who were clamouring for the acquisition of colonies. As the Reich Chancellor once put it rather cynically, he knew that the quest for colonies was a hoax but that he needed it for creating majorities that supported his government.[4]

The notion that imperialism was a useful tool not only to respond to commercial pressures but also to divert and ease domestic tensions and to promise material gains for more than a few businessmen involved in international trade, had by the 1890s become popular among politicians and intellectuals all over Europe. In Britain, Cecil Rhodes, the tycoon, stated that

> my cherished idea is a solution for the social problem, i.e., in order to save the 40,000,000 inhabitants of the United Kingdom from a bloody civil war, we colonial statesmen must acquire new lands to settle the surplus population, to provide new markets for the goods produced by them in the factories and mines. The empire . . . is a bread and butter question. If you want to avoid civil war, you must become imperialists.[5]

Alfred von Tirpitz, a German naval officer soon to become the naval secretary of Kaiser Wilhelm II, wrote in 1895: 'In my view, Germany will in the coming century rapidly drop from her position as a great power unless we begin to develop our maritime interests energetically, systematically and without delay.'[6] This expansion, he added, was necessary 'to no small degree also because the great patriotic task and the economic benefits to be derived from it will offer a strong palliative against educated and uneducated Social Democrats'. The importance of this factor to international politics and ultimately to the origins of the First World War may also be gauged from the statement by Enrico Corradini, an Italian intellectual who opined: 'Social

3 See Adam Hochschild, *King Leopold's Ghost* (Boston: Houghton Mifflin, 1999).

4 See, e.g., Hartmut Pogge von Strandmann, 'Domestic origins of Germany's colonial expansion under Bismarck', *Past and Present*, 42:1 (1969), pp. 140–59; see also Sebastian Conrad, *German Colonialism: A Short History* (Cambridge University Press, 2011).

5 Quoted in Edward Tannenbaum, *1900: The Generation before the Great War* (Garden City, NJ: Anchor Press, 1976), p. 349.

6 Quoted in Alfred von Tirpitz, *Erinnerungen* (Leipzig: Hase and Koehler, 1919), p. 52.

imperialism was designed to draw all classes together in defence of the nation and empire and aimed to prove to the least well-to-do class that its interests were inseparable from those of the nation. It aimed at undermining the argument of the socialists and demonstrating that, contrary to the Marxist allegation, the workers *had* more to lose than their chains.'[7]

As the jockeying for colonies continued among the Great Powers up to 1914, research also turned to studying the impact of European colonialism on the non-European world. While Ferry had claimed quite unabashedly that France was on a civilising mission that the Europeans had gone out to fulfil, scholars today are generally agreed that European colonialism brought few benefits to the colonised peoples and was by and large extremely destructive to local economies, social structures and cultural traditions. In Leopold's Congo it is estimated that some 11 million indigenous men, women and children died either of diseases and malnutrition or through killing sprees that colonial troops perpetrated. It was no better in Asia where revolts, however insignificant, against the colonial masters were, like in Africa, brutally repressed. This has led students of imperialism to raise the question of what this massive violence in turn did to the European psyche. Some have gone so far as to see in this violence the precursors of the Nazi Holocaust of the Second World War. Others have had no hesitation to call, for example, Germany's war against the Herero and Nama in colonial South West Africa a genocide. Isabel Hull, in her book *Absolute Destruction*, has argued that the violence practised in this war became part of German military culture.[8] In other words, it became so deeply ingrained in the ethos of the officer corps that it came to see a future European war in the same terms of complete annihilation, a concept that will be discussed in more detail below.

The economies of pre-1914 European colonialism

Colonialism was dangerous and, indeed, self-defeating in the sense that it exacerbated economic tensions and rivalries that were inherent in the economic systems of an increasingly industrialised Europe. Economic constitutions were essentially capitalist and hence based on the principle of competition in the national and international marketplace. However, and as we have seen above, late-nineteenth-century colonialism was not an

7 Quoted in Tannenbaum, *1900: The Generation*, p. 348.
8 Isabel Hull, *Absolute Destruction: Military Culture and the Practices of War in Imperial Germany* (Ithaca, NY: Cornell University Press, 2003).

exclusively private enterprise. National governments had made the conquest and possession of colonies their own project. They stationed troops abroad and sent bureaucrats to administer these territories. The trouble was that there were several international crises in the decade before 1914 that involved both European governments and certain business interests.

These crises in turn impacted on the trade among the Great Powers within Europe in which the United States had meanwhile also made an appearance. In the late nineteenth century America had witnessed a process of industrialisation and urbanisation at least as dramatic as that of Britain or Germany. By 1900, trade within the Anglo-American-German triangle had become very lucrative, although there had been a few diplomatic crises around 1900 when Britain and Germany appeared in Latin America and upset the US government that, pointing to the Monroe Doctrine, considered these European efforts an intrusion into its 'backyard'. But by the mid decade, peaceful trade among the three nations and also in the rest of Europe had intensified. They were making direct investments by setting up agencies and subsidiaries. Some firms even built factories abroad. Other companies concluded patent agreements and other forms of cooperation. However, for reasons to be examined below, from around 1910 the business communities on both sides of the Atlantic became increasingly nervous about the international diplomatic and military situation. Before going into this topic, an analysis of cultural developments in Europe before 1914 provides yet another clue for understanding why the Great Powers ended up in the First World War.

European culture between optimism and pessimism

An evaluation of the press around New Year's Day 1900 will reveal that the mood in most of Europe was overwhelmingly celebratory – with splendid fireworks and church bells ringing in the twentieth century.[9] The nations looked back on a century that had not only brought industrialisation and urbanisation but also relative peace and prosperity. The wars that had taken place in mid century had been quite short. After the Franco-Prussian War of 1870 that had led to the founding of the German Empire, much further progress had been made, especially in the fields of science and technology. The achievements in the arts, humanities and social sciences had been no

9 See Volker R. Berghahn, *Sarajewo, 28. Juni 1914: Der Untergang des Alten Europa* (Munich: Deutscher Taschenbuch Verlag, 1997), pp. 16ff.

less impressive. Conservative agrarian newspapers in Germany, it is true, were not quite so enthusiastic about the new century as was the bourgeois-liberal press. The agrarians warned of the growing threat that the industrial working class posed, thought to have fallen under the spell of Marxian socialism. Meanwhile British conservative papers wondered about the future viability of the Empire after the difficulties that the army had encountered during the war against the South African Boers.

Overall, though, European culture, broadly defined so as to include the sciences, education and popular culture, was divided into optimists and pessimists when it came to looking into the future. The optimists could be found among the professional middle classes and among the engineering and laboratory professions in particular. They confidently expected further breakthroughs and successes to emerge from the centres of research and learning in the universities, academies and Research & Development departments that the big corporations had added to their operations, especially in the chemical and electrical engineering branches. The cities that had come into wealth through rising tax revenues tackled the major task of building a modem infrastructure such as gas, electricity and water works, as well as sewage plants. They proudly also funded concert halls, theatres and opera houses as well as recreational parks, playgrounds and public swimming pools. The Arts and Crafts movement in Britain and the *Werkbund* in Germany became typical expressions of this optimism. There were also the architects who designed modern housing, garden cities and spacious and light factories. They were searching for an 'international style' that transcended national borders and experimented with new building materials such as glass and concrete. The transatlantic connections of these movements were embodied by American architects such as Frank Lloyd Wright, whose visions of modern housing left a deep impression on his European counterparts. Finally, there were the World Exhibitions that had started in London in 1851 and reached a high point at the Paris Exhibition in 1900, where the nations of the world presented themselves in their architectural tastes and the display of industrial machinery and artistic creations.

However, all the while there were also the cultural pessimists. They worried not merely about a political radicalisation of the 'masses' in the age of universal manhood suffrage. Nor was it just radical Marxists who believed that industrial capitalism and the bourgeois age were bound to collapse under the weight of their inner contradictions. There were also non-Marxist intellectuals and social critics who foresaw a period of conflict and instability. Among them was the German sociologist Max Weber who, while acknowledging the wealth-creating and rational capacities of capitalism, nevertheless warned of the growth of large and ever more pervasive public and private organisations that promoted the bureaucratisation of the world.[10] To him this trend was so powerful that he feared humanity would end up in what he called an 'iron cage of serfdom'. It was a world in which the *Fachmensch* (expert) ruled from the top, regulating all aspects of individuals' lives. Meanwhile in Vienna, Sigmund Freud probed the darker and irrational corners of the human soul.

Perhaps the most intriguing development in the field of European culture was a shift that took place in the arts. Classical music, theatre and painting had highlighted the uplifting aspects of human experience. Good invariably triumphed over evil. The stage was devoted to portraying such values as beauty, heroism and generosity. A new generation of artists now insisted that the mission of modern art was different; it confronted its audiences and viewers with the sordid and disharmonious sides of the human predicament. Soon realism was overtaken by expressionism, with its creations that reflected not what the eye captured in the real world but what an inner eye was making of it. Life to these artists appeared fragmented, de-centred, subjective. It was full of contradictions and disharmonies. For some cultural producers it was but a small step from these positions and their implicit or explicit criticism of the world to believing that European civilisation as a whole was rotten and heading towards the rocks.

Significantly, such predictions of the last days of mankind could most frequently be heard in Central Europe. A few intellectuals and artists even began to see its end in a huge cataclysm from which a thoroughly rejuvenated society would emerge, freed of its outmoded traditions and values and its stuffy bourgeois conformism. For orthodox Marxists, this cataclysm would come in the shape of a violent social revolution. For some artists who were not radical socialists, rejuvenation would come in a major war. In Germany, these pessimists received lateral support from more political popular writers such as Friedrich von Bernhardi, who in 1912 published his bestselling *Germany and the Next War*.[11] But as 1914 drew closer there were also other voices. With tensions rising both inside the nations of Europe and in international politics, partly stimulated – as has been seen – by colonial rivalries, there were those who warned against just such a war. Among them was the Polish banker Ivan

10 For a very good digest of Weber's ideas see Wolfgang J. Mommsen, *The Age of Bureaucracy* (Oxford: Blackwell, 1974).

11 Friedrich von Bernhardi, *Deutschland und der nächste Krieg* (Stuttgart: J. G. Cotta, 1912), English trans., Allen H. Powell, *Germany and the Next War* (New York: Longmans, 1914).

Bloch, who published a six-volume study on *The Future of War in its Technical, Economic and Political Relations* as early as 1898 (Russian edition).[12] It contained disturbingly accurate descriptions of what this war would be like, i.e., a mass slaughter of the kind that occurred for real in the trenches of the First World War. War between industrialised nations was for him tantamount to the destruction of civil and civilised society. In 1909 Bloch's dire predictions were complemented by a bestseller written by another businessman, Norman Angell, entitled *The Great Illusion*.[13] He postulated that with the rise of industry and peaceful commerce around the world the future was potentially bright. But it was threatened, at least for the time being, by militaristic and chauvinistic elements in modern society. Consequently, Angell became another writer to warn against the self-destructive danger that hovered over Europe. To him, major wars among Great Powers had become a loss for all participants, even for those who formally won, and the drain on resources would be so great that the region might never recover.

Looking at cultural developments in pre-1914 Europe, the situation had become curiously schizophrenic. On the one hand, large sections of the population and their intellectual and political leaders saw a bright future ahead. If to them the nineteenth century had been one of socio-economic, technological, political and human progress, the twentieth century would be no less one of further improvement and gradual reform. On the other side were the cultural pessimists whose numbers were growing towards 1914. They were sceptical of the viability of the liberal-capitalist societies of Europe. Some of them predicted not only a great upheaval but actively prepared it. The artists among them, though often unpolitical, also interpreted recent trends as harbingers of a huge crisis to come. While popular culture continued in its traditional tracks of folk festivals, folk music, folk art and folklore, analysts of high culture and avant-garde artists saw themselves as seismographs registering the early rumblings of an impending violent eruption that would bury European society. To be sure, none of the writers, painters or composers who celebrated disharmony, gloom and decadence had the power and influence to unleash the catastrophe that they predicted. It was army and naval officers who devoted their careers to the preparation of a major war and who would then unleash it in August 1914 with ferocious force.

12 Ivan Bloch, *The Future of War in its Technical, Economic and Political Relations: Is War Now Impossible?*, trans. R. C. Long, with a prefatory conversation with the author by W. T. Stead (New York: Doubleday & McClure, 1899).

13 Norman Angell, *The Great Illusion* (London: Putnam's Sons, 1910).

The German naval challenge to British hegemony

During the late nineteenth century, the Great Powers on the European continent eyed the armament policies of their rivals with much suspicion. Perhaps one of them would achieve military superiority and then use this advantage to start a preventive war. At the same time there was the question of naval armaments after the scramble for colonies had shifted the balance: now it was thought to be naval power that would determine the course of power relations in the twentieth century. Up to 1900 Britain had occupied the first rank by maintaining the Two-Power Standard, i.e., a navy large enough to be capable of confronting the next two strongest sea powers together and thus able to protect both the British homeland and her overseas possessions.[14] In the 1890s, technological developments generated a debate among naval strategists. The orthodoxies of contemporary naval warfare envisioned prolonged raids by fast-moving cruisers against enemy ports and overseas settlements. Along came an alternative strategy that demanded the building of very large, slow battleships that would face their opponent in the European waters in a do-or-die battle.

By 1897, Tirpitz, by now the Kaiser's naval secretary, had opted for the latter strategy. He was convinced that the only way to gain sufficient power-political leverage against Britain, the first sea power, was to expand the hitherto modest Imperial Navy into a major tool that could be used to wring territorial concessions from the British at the conference table when another 'division of the world' was being negotiated. However, should Britain not only refuse to make such concessions, but also steam across the North Sea to destroy the German battle fleet at Wilhelmshaven, the latter would be strong and well-trained enough to defeat the Royal Navy in a battle of annihilation. It is interesting how this idea of annihilation and total victory that had gained currency in the Prusso-German army inspired Tirpitz's concept of a *Vernichtungsschlacht* in the North Sea. A victory would have shifted the international balance of power virtually in one afternoon. The German naval files contain the evidence for this preposterous idea that, according to the German historian Klaus Hildebrand, would have revolutionised the international system.[15]

14 See, e.g., Arthur Marder, *The Anatomy of British Sea Power* (London: Putnam & Co., 1940).

15 Klaus Hildebrand, 'Imperialismus, Wettrüsten und Kriegsausbruch 1914', *Neue Politische Literatur*, 2 (1975), pp. 160–94.

As Tirpitz explained to Wilhelm II in September 1899, 'thanks to our geographic position, our system of military service, mobilization, torpedo boats, tactical training, organizational structure [and] our uniform leadership by the Monarch we shall no doubt have [a] good chance against England'.[16] In another secret document, he added that all of Germany's efforts should concentrate on the creation of a battle fleet 'which alone will give us a maritime influence vis-à-vis England'. Of course, 'the battle must first have taken place and have been won before one can think of exploiting it'. Indeed, 'without a victorious battle' the sea lanes to the Atlantic could not be kept open for Germany: '"Victorious" is the decisive word. Hence let us concentrate our resources on this victory.' After all, 'the bear's skin' could not be cut up 'before the bear has been killed'.[17]

After Wilhelm II, himself an enthusiast of German overseas expansion and naval power, had given his approval, Tirpitz and his fellow-officers in the Reich Navy Office began to implement a long-term building plan. They envisioned an expansion of the German battle fleet in several stages at the end of which Germany would have sixty big battleships, capable of defeating the Royal Navy. A file note of February 1900 assumed

> that the enlargement of the British fleet cannot proceed at the same rate as ours because the size of their fleet requires a considerably larger number of replacements. The [attached] table ... demonstrates that England ... will have to construct and replace a fleet almost three times as large as the German one as envisaged by the Navy Law [of 1900], if she expects to have an efficient fleet ... in 1920 [!]. The inferior tonnage which our battle-fleet will continue to have vis-à-vis Britain's shall be compensated for by particularly good training of our personnel and better tactical manoeuverability of large battle formations. ... The [enclosed] figures ... on the tonnage which both battle fleets keep in service amount to a superiority of Germany. In view of the notorious difficulties in England to recruit enough personnel, it is unlikely that this favorable position will change.

These quotations should be telling enough about what was being planned in Berlin. By adopting a building tempo of three big ships per annum up to 1920, Tirpitz would not only have gained his sixty battleships, but would also have provided the German steel and shipbuilding industry with regular orders, protecting them against the vagaries of the market. A further

16 Quoted in Volker R. Berghahn, *Germany and the Approach of War in 1914* (Basingstoke: Macmillan, 1993), p. 51.
17 *Ibid.*, pp. 50ff.

advantage was that the building tempo looked quite modest in its early stages and was therefore unlikely to alarm the Royal Navy. In other words, at the turn of the century Germany started a unilateral arms build-up against Britain, and Germany's long-term ambition of defeating the Royal Navy had to be kept secret. Tirpitz was therefore very conscious of the need to keep this secret and of the 'danger zone', as he called it, that the Imperial Navy would be passing through. For, if London discovered the ultimate aims, it was likely that it would try to destroy the embryonic Imperial Navy in a coup reminiscent of the preventive strike Britain had launched against the Danish fleet in 1805 outside Copenhagen. To avoid such a 'Copenhagening', German diplomacy had to be aligned with the Tirpitz Plan, and indeed this is what Reich Chancellor Bernhard von Bülow tried to do after 1900.[18]

However, the future is always unpredictable and German diplomacy failed to give the necessary cover by keeping Germany aloof from international troubles. First, Britain began to wonder about the relentless building tempo across the Channel, and concluded the Entente Cordiale with France, Germany's arch-enemy on the continent. It was not quite as solid as the Franco-Russian alliance treaty of 1893 that would involve Germany in a nightmarish war on two fronts. But the Entente of 1904 rattled the German Foreign Office and caused it to test its firmness by challenging France in North Africa a year later. The Moroccan test proved to be a very bad miscalculation, and the international conference that followed left Germany without the gains she had expected. At exactly the same moment there arose an even greater threat to Tirpitz's grand design, i.e., the decision of the British to begin building a much bigger battleship, the *Dreadnought*. Having observed German shipbuilding activity very closely, Sir John Fisher, the First Sea Lord, had been suspecting for some time that the Germans were up to something sinister and were hoping to win a veiled quantitative naval arms build-up. Fisher now escalated the competition by adding a *qualitative* dimension to it, i.e., by building ships with bigger displacements and bigger guns against which German ships had insufficient armour.[19]

When Tirpitz, unwilling to concede that his ambitious plan was failing, also began to build dreadnoughts, Fisher stepped up the building tempo. Against the three ships per annum envisaged by Tirpitz he decided to build four dreadnoughts per annum. Still refusing to give up, Tirpitz again followed suit.

18 Jonathan Steinberg, 'The Copenhagen complex', *Journal of Contemporary History*, 1 (1966), pp. 23–40.

19 See Volker R. Berghahn, *Der Tirpitz-Plan* (Düsseldorf: Droste, 1971), pp. 419ff.

But by 1908/9 it was becoming clear that he could not sustain this accelerated arms race in dreadnoughts. The additional costs were throwing the careful budgetary calculations on which the original plan had been based into disarray.

There are two telling statements that put the story of what happened in 1908/9 nicely into focus. The first one is by Lord Richard Haldane, a member of the Liberal Cabinet in London. The Liberals had won the elections of 1906 with promises of reducing the armament burdens through international negotiations at The Hague. The savings were to be used for a new social security and insurance programme to attract the votes of the British working class. Faced with the failure of the disarmament talks (largely because Germany refused to be part of any armament reduction) and with the need to fulfil election promises, the Liberal Cabinet decided to finance both stepped-up naval armaments and social programmes. As Haldane declared on 8 August 1908:[20] 'We should boldly take our stand on the facts and proclaim a policy of taking, mainly by direct taxation, such a toll from the increase and growth of this wealth as will enable us to provide for (1) the increasing costs of social reform, (2) national defence [and] (3) a margin in aid of the sinking fund.' Knowing that the wealthy in Britain would not welcome higher direct taxes on their incomes, Haldane tapped into middle-class fears of the labour movement by adding that this policy 'will commend itself to many timid people as a bulwark against the nationalisation of wealth'.

Meanwhile in Germany, Reich Chancellor Bülow was facing exactly the same dilemma. There were the increased costs of the dreadnoughts. At the same time, he continued to hope that increasing the social insurance benefits that Bismarck had first introduced in the 1880s would woo the industrial workers away from the Social Democrats and the Social Democratic trade unions. The SPD had greatly increased their votes in the 1903 national elections, but had lost seats in 1907, partly because of stepped-up nationalist agitation. Thanks to this agitation it had been relatively easy in the past to get enough Reichstag votes for increased naval armaments. However, when in a follow-up finance bill it came to distributing the costs of naval expansion onto different shoulders, the well-to-do, and the agrarians in particular, had rejected higher income and inheritance taxes. Instead they

20 Quoted in H. V. Emy, *Liberals, Radicals and Social Politics, 1892–1914* (Cambridge University Press, 1973), p. 201.

voted for increased indirect taxes on food and other daily needs that disproportionately hit the lower-income groups. The medicine that Haldane prescribed for the British was therefore not available to Bülow. He was under pressure from the Conservatives and no higher direct taxes were in the end approved. The SPD having been kept out of the government and not having enough votes to reverse the trend, only had its press organs and speakers to protest against this unequal distribution of tax burdens imposed for military expenditures that they had been opposed to from the beginning. Their supporters, well aware of the rising cost of living in their weekly budget felt that these protests were perfectly justified.

It is against this background that Albert Ballin, the Hamburg shipping magnate and friend of Wilhelm II, made the other telling statement. He warned the Kaiser and his Reich Chancellor in July 1908 that 'we cannot enter into a race in Dreadnoughts with the much wealthier British'.[21] He might have added that the British did not have a system of taxation as unfair and conflict-ridden as that of Imperial Germany. Of course, Ballin was also opposed to a continuation of the Anglo-German naval arms race because he feared a further escalation of tensions that the building of battleships had already produced. A major war, he felt, would be a disaster for his shipping empire and for world trade, as indeed it turned out to be in 1914.

There was yet another and in this case very powerful group that began to get restive in the face of a costly naval arms race that Germany now increasingly looked like losing: the Prusso-German army. Partly in order to allow Tirpitz to have the first call on the Reich's financial resources, but also because the top brass feared that an expansion of the army beyond its 1890s size would undermine the social exclusivity and reliability of the armed forces, the officer corps had decided at the turn of the century to refrain from submitting fresh increases to the size of the land forces. The existing shortage of officers of noble background was thought to undermine the esprit de corps if more men of bourgeois background had to be taken in. There was also the problem of a growing number of ordinary draftees who came from an urban working-class background and were suspected of having been influenced by socialist ideas. In the late 1890s, the army had initiated a programme of patriotic indoctrination to counter this threat. Soldiers were not allowed to frequent certain pubs in the vicinity of their barracks, and time and again their lockers were searched for socialist literature. In short, no more working-class recruits either.

21 Quoted in *Die Grosse Politik der Europäischen Kabinette, 1871–1914*, 40 vols. (Berlin 1922–), vol. XXIV, no. 8216, letter from Bülow to Wilhelm II, 15 July 1908.

The shift towards the pre-1914 European arms race on land

In 1907 Britain and Russia had settled their longstanding differences in Afghanistan, which had facilitated the formation of the Triple Entente of France, Britain and Russia. Thereupon the spectre of 'encirclement' took root in the thinking of the German general staff and of the Kaiser. The scales were finally tipping against further naval expenditures in favour of rearmament on land. This became very visible in the wake of the Second Moroccan Crisis of the summer 1911. This confrontation over North African territories further strengthened the determination of France and Britain to stand together. Berlin was forced into a humiliating retreat. As Helmuth von Moltke, the Chief of the general staff, wrote very angrily to his wife on 19 August 1911:

> I am beginning to get sick and tired of this unhappy Moroccan affair . . . If we again slip away from this affair with our tail between our legs and if we cannot bring ourselves to put forward a determined claim which we are prepared to force through with the sword, I shall despair of the future of the German Empire. I shall then resign. But before handing in my resignation, I shall move to abolish the Army and to place ourselves under Japanese protectorate, we shall then be in a position to make money without interference and develop into ninnies.[22]

While these lines reflected the mood of this key army officer bluntly enough, the first signs of a revolt against the Imperial Navy could be detected as early as 1909. In March of that year, the influential and semi-official *Militaerwochenblatt* published an article with the title 'Army in Chains'. By the summer of 1910 dissatisfaction had become so strong that Colonel Erich Ludendorff made the army's case even more insistently: 'Any state that is involved in a struggle for its survival must use, with utmost energy, all its forces and resources if it wants to live up to its highest duties.'[23] The number of Germany's enemies, he added, had now become 'so great that it could become our inescapable duty' to use 'in certain cases' and from the first moment every available soldier. Thenceforth everything depended 'on our winning the first battles'.

22 Helmuth von Moltke, *Erinnerungen, Briefe, Dokumente* (Stuttgart: Der Kommende Tag, 1922), p. 362.

23 Quoted in Gerhard Ritter, *Staatskunst und Kriegshandwerk*, 4 vols. (Munich: R. Oldenbourg Verlag, 1954–68), vol. II, p. 274.

This evaluation is significant for two reasons. First of all, Ludendorff, himself of non-noble background, advocated dropping all limits on recruitment that had guided earlier policies of freezing the size of the army. Secondly, it indicated that sooner or later the general staff would insist on the introduction of a bill to enlarge the country's land forces. Accordingly War Minister Josias von Heeringen, announced in November 1911 that the 'political-strategic situation' had 'shifted to Germany's disadvantage'.[24] Appropriations for the army had to be increased without delay. Tirpitz immediately averred what was at stake: the army was to be used as the 'battering ram' against his naval plan. No less awkward for him was that the Reich Treasury had meanwhile collated figures to show that Germany could not afford both a powerful navy and an army large enough to face the Franco-Russian alliance. With the Treasury also putting its political weight behind a reorientation of the nation's armaments policy, it was clear that Tirpitz had already lost the interdepartmental struggle that raged in Berlin in late 1911, and of course he had lost the naval competition against Britain that had thwarted his plan to out-build the Royal Navy.[25] Meanwhile, subverted by Slav and particularly Serbian nationalist independence movements within its boundaries, Vienna was also getting more and more agitated.

Against the backdrop of these developments both within the structures of the imperial courts and the governments in Berlin and Vienna, it is no longer surprising that the army's demand for 29,000 more soldiers and 'manifold technical improvements' became law very quickly in 1912. There were also enough Reichstag votes to approve the subsequent finance bills, but only with a good deal of manipulation and the appendix of the so-called Lex Bassermann-Erzberger, which required that the Reich government introduce before 30 April 1913 'a general property tax that takes account of the various forms of property'.[26] By the winter of 1912/13 the debate over taxes that revolved around the same questions that Haldane had asked in Britain in 1908 was in full swing. By autumn 1912 a regional war had broken out in which the Balkan League of Bulgaria and Serbia (with Greece joining a few months later) challenged the possessions of the Ottoman Empire in Europe. The Ottoman Turks were soundly defeated, with Serbia gaining many of the territorial spoils of the League's victory. After this the government in Vienna was even

24 See Berghahn, *Germany and the Approach of War in 1914*, pp. 126ff.

25 Isabel Hull, *The Entourage of Kaiser Wilhelm II: 1888–1918* (Cambridge University Press, 1982).

26 Quoted in Fritz Fischer, *Krieg der Illusionen* (Düsseldorf: Droste, 1969), p. 257.

more alarmed about the future of its own position in the Balkans. In 1908 the Habsburgs had tried to bolster their territorial position by annexing Bosnia-Herzegovina. However, this move backfired because it angered the Russians who now saw themselves more than ever as the protectors of the Slavs in the Balkans.

The alarm spilled over into Berlin where the army was now drawing up plans for a second expansion of its land forces. As in the previous year, this bill was also passed by a Reichstag majority in a mood of determined patriotism. Again the funding question had been postponed. It was clear that more money had to be found, and there was also the Lex Bassermann-Erzberger of the previous year to be implemented. There is no space here to discuss the very complicated tax bill that, apart from the usual higher indirect taxes, this time did include, in the face of the fierce opposition of the Conservatives, an income tax, the *Wehrbeitrag*, though it was limited to one year.

In terms of the origins of the First World War, the more important development was the reaction of France and Russia.[27] They promptly introduced army bills themselves so that the abandoned Anglo-German naval arms race was now being replaced by an even more dangerous military competition on land. Next to the push for the 1913 army bill, the German generals also reacted to the First Balkan War with a growing sense that a war was bound to break out soon. It seems that Wilhelm II, under the influence of his *maison militaire*, had been reaching a similar conclusion.

Thus, when he received news from London that the British position was also hardening towards his policies, the pressure was rising, also from Vienna, to launch an early war against Serbia in an effort to strengthen the position of Austria-Hungary against Slav nationalism. To the Kaiser the life-or-death question had been raised for his realm:[28] 'The eventual struggle for existence which the Germans (Austria, Germany) will have to fight in Europe against the Slavs (Russia) supported by the Romans (Gauls) will find the Anglo-Saxons on the side of the Slavs.' In pursuit of this strategic assessment, Wilhelm II called a conference with his top naval and army advisers on 8 December 1912.[29] The monarch opened the discussions by urging that Austria should, without delay, take a stand against Serbia, lest 'she lost control over the Serbs

27 See Peter-Christian Witt, *Die Finanzpolitik des Deutschen Reiches von 1903 bis 1913* (Lubeck: Matthiesen, 1970), pp. 356ff.

28 See John C. G. Röhl, 'An der Schwelle zum Weltkrieg: Eine Dokumentation über den "Kriegsrat" vom 8. Dezember 1912', *Militärgeschichtliche Mitteilungen*, 21 (1977), pp. 77–134.

29 *Ibid.*

inside the Austro-Hungarian monarchy'. Moltke also took the view that a war was inevitable. The sooner it took place the better it would be. Tirpitz argued for a postponement by eighteen months because the widening of the Kiel Canal to allow for the movement of German dreadnoughts between the Baltic and the North Seas would not be completed before the summer of 1914. Moltke voiced his impatience at Tirpitz by interjecting that 'the Navy would not be ready then either and the Army's position would become less and less favourable'. The country's enemies 'were arming more rapidly than we do, as we were short of money'. In the end no decision to unleash a war was taken, not only because of Tirpitz's opposition and the Kaiser's vacillations, but also because it was found that the German 'nation' had not yet been sufficiently enlightened about the 'great national interests' that were at stake in the event of a war between Austria-Hungary and Serbia.

Preparing for a preventive war in 1914

This chapter began with an examination of the non-military factors that have to be studied when trying to understand the deeper origins of the First World War. Accordingly, we discussed industrialisation, demographic change, electoral politics, cultural optimism and cultural pessimism. However, the most dangerous development that pointed towards an outbreak of a major war was, after the collapse of Tirpitz's naval ambitions to challenge Britain's power, the incipient arms race on land between Russia and France on the one hand, and Germany and Austria-Hungary on the other. Moreover, the army professionals who, in the wake of these developments, had moved to the centres of decision-making in Berlin and Vienna, not only shared the gloomy sense that a great clash of arms would come in any case, but were also increasingly attracted by the concept of a preventive war. Not knowing the future, the generals became inclined to hit before it was too late and while victory still seemed possible. When the 'mood of 1914' is therefore invoked, it is important to remember that a preventive strike was very prevalent among the military in Berlin and Vienna.

There are two key documents that date from the spring of 1914 after the international and domestic situation in Germany and Austria-Hungary had deteriorated further in 1913. There is first of all an exchange that the Austrian Chief of the general staff, Franz Conrad von Hötzendorf, had with Colonel Josef Metzger, the head of the Operations Department. On this occasion, the former had been wondering aloud 'if one should wait until France and Russia were prepared to invade us jointly or if it were more desirable to settle the inevitable conflict at an earlier date'.[30] He added that 'the Slav question was becoming more and more difficult and dangerous for us'.

Having summarised his worries, in particular about the size of the Russian armament programme, in a memorandum to the German Foreign Office on 24 February 1914, Moltke decided to meet Conrad at Karlsbad in the middle of May. The meeting merely confirmed both of them in their conviction that time was running out. Moltke was by now firmly convinced that 'to wait any longer meant a diminishing of our chances; as far as manpower was concerned, one cannot enter into a competition with Russia'. Upon his return to Berlin, Moltke went to see Foreign Secretary Gottlieb von Jagow, who made the following record of the meeting:

> The prospects of the future seriously worried him [Moltke]. Russia will have completed her armaments in 2 to 3 years. The military superiority of our enemies would be so great then that he did not know how we might cope with them. Now we could still be more or less a match for them. In his view, there was no alternative to waging a preventive war in order to defeat the enemy as long as we could still more or less pass the test. The Chief of the general staff left it at my discretion to gear our policy to an early unleashing of a war.[31]

In all these discussions the industrial and commercial elites of Europe played no active part and most of them were nervous onlookers. They knew that a major war would not only have terrible consequences for their own businesses, but also for the region and its populations as a whole. This is why some of them with connections to the inner political circles tried to dissuade the two emperors from using their exclusive constitutional right to declare a war. In the end, they were sidelined and this also applied to the business communities in France and Britain, once the German invasion of Belgium and France had begun.[32]

The 'masses' of ordinary Europeans, many of whom were organised by 1914 into large socialist parties and trade unions, found themselves in a similar situation. Their leaders, though not privy to government thinking, had an inkling of what would happen if several industrial powers clashed, that were

30 Franz Conrad von Hötzendorf, *Aus meiner Dienstzeit, 1906–1918*, 5 vols. (Vienna: Rikola, 1921–5), vol. III, p. 597. For an excellent analysis of Austro-Hungarian policy in 1913/14 see Samuel R. Williamson, Jr., *Austria-Hungary and the Origins of the First World War* (New York: St Martin's Press, 1991), esp. pp. 143ff., 164ff.

31 Quoted in Fischer, *Krieg der Illusionen*, p. 584.

32 On the attitudes of business and finance see Niall Ferguson, *The Pity of War: 1914–1918* (New York: Basic Books, 1998), pp. 193f.

now so frantically arming themselves to the teeth irrespective of the financial costs. They sensed that there would be a blood bath, in which their own members would be the first victims. As the threat of war loomed larger following the armament bills, the leaders of the European left made desperate efforts to stop the march towards the abyss. Jean Jaurès, the French socialist leader, sent out a call to hold a congress of the Second International in Brussels. On 31 July he was shot and killed by a right-wing nationalist fanatic. Meanwhile, after the delivery of the Austro-Hungarian ultimatum to Serbia on 23 July 1914, the German Social Democrats, fearing the outbreak of war, held demonstrations in major cities to warn Vienna against an invasion of Serbia.[33]

These demonstrations made Reich Chancellor Theobald von Bethmann Hollweg realise that Germany could not possibly join an Austro-Hungarian war, unless the population could be convinced that they were being called up to defend the fatherland against the autocratic tsarist juggernaut. He promptly initiated negotiations with moderate SPD leaders to obtain their support if the country found itself in a defensive war against Russia. This explains why the Kaiser waited for Russia to announce her mobilisation order first. When the deadline of the German ultimatum to rescind the order passed without a Russian response, Wilhelm II proclaimed Germany's mobilisation. But instead of moving against the Tsarist Empire, Moltke invaded France and Belgium as envisaged by a revised Schlieffen Plan. It was his only option. All Eastern operations' plans had been dropped in previous years. Still there was great relief once the trains had been ordered to roll West. As Georg Alexander von Mueller, the Chief of the Naval Cabinet, recorded in his diary on 1 August 1914: 'Brilliant mood. The government has succeeded very well in making us appear as the attacked.'[34]

As these developments put the two monarchs and the military entourage so glaringly into the limelight, we must take a final look at their 'mood', also in order to build a bridge to the next chapter that will discuss the last weeks and days of peace in greater detail, including the question of whether Berlin and Vienna thought at first in terms of a localisation of the conflict to the Balkans or whether, as Fritz Fischer has argued, the Reich government and

33 See Wolfgang Schieder (ed.), *Erster Weltkrieg* (Cologne: Kiepenheuer & Witsch, 1969), pp. 174ff. For the moves of the Austro-Hungarian government in July, see Williamson, Jr., *Austria-Hungary and the Origins of the First World War*, pp. 190ff.

34 Quoted in John C. G. Röhl, 'Admiral von Müller and the approach of war', *Historische Zeitschrift*, 4 (1969), pp. 610ff.

the military aimed at an all-out war from early July onwards.[35] The issue on which to conclude this chapter is therefore what Lancelot Farrar has called 'The Short War Illusion'.[36] To understand this phenomenon, the warnings of Helmuth von Moltke the Elder, the uncle of the namesake who in 1 August 1914 got the Kaiser to order the attack in the West, are highly germane. Pondering in his years of retirement the lessons of the Franco-Prussian War in which he had led Prussia to victory against Napoleon III, he came to the conclusion that a future war could no longer be fought among the Great Powers of Europe. Such a war, he was convinced, would be a *Volkskrieg*, a people's war, that no belligerent could hope to win. Everything should therefore be done to avoid a major European war.[37]

The problem was that if this insight of an old war horse had been followed by his successors it would have made large armies and the planning of a major war superfluous. Although his nephew and his comrades never openly refuted Moltke the Elder's wisdom, it seems that for their own profession's sake they wanted to make great wars fightable and winnable again. Hence they adopted Schlieffen's idea of annihilation and added to it the notion of a lightning war. Brutal attack, swift advances into enemy territory and total defeat within weeks had become the way out of the military-professional dilemma that they faced in the era of People's Wars. This explains the illusory claim that circulated among the soldiers on the Western Front, that victory would be achieved within months and that they would be home again by Christmas 1914. It is against the background of the feeling that a preventive war could be won by the Central Powers that a fatal decision was taken by a few men in Berlin and Vienna that pushed Europe over the brink. This means that there is no need for scholars to go on a roundtrip through the capitals of Europe with the aim of finding out that other decision-makers were more responsible for the First World War than the two emperors and their advisers. Berlin and Vienna continue to be the best places for historians to look closely for clues as to why war broke out in 1914.[38]

35 Fritz Fischer, *Griff nach der Weltmacht: Die Kriegszielpolitik des Kaiserlichen Deutschland (1914–1918)* (Düsseldorf: Droste, 1964 [1961]).

36 Lancelot L. Farrar, *The Short War Illusion* (Santa Barbara, CA: ABC-Clio, 1973).

37 See Stig Förster, 'Facing people's war', *Journal of Strategic Studies*, 2 (1987), pp. 209–30.

38 Many years ago L. F. C. Turner, *The Origins of the First World War* (London: Edward Arnold, 1970), held Russia primarily responsible for the outbreak of war in July / August 1914. This argument has most recently been taken up again by Sean McMeekin, *The Russian Origins of the First World War* (Cambridge, MA: Harvard University Press, 2011). The most recent work (2013) that also raises the question of Russian responsibility is Christopher Clark's *The Sleepwalkers: How Europe Went to War in 1914* (New York: HarperCollins, 2012). Clark also examines the role of Serbia and her ambitions in the

There is also likely to be more work on the so-called 'unspoken assumptions' – a notion that T. G. Otte has revived with reference to the attitudes and mentalities prevailing in the British Foreign Office before 1914 below the top ministerial and Cabinet level.[39] This chapter, it is true, has focused on the 'outspoken assumptions' that flowed from the mentalities, dispositions and decision-making processes in Berlin and Vienna. While often but opaquely articulated perceptions and assumptions of international politics are no doubt worth exploring, the moves of Sir Edward Grey in London, through which the decision to go to war was delayed until 4 August, were largely imposed by the split in the British Cabinet about whether to enter the war at all. Only when it became absolutely clear that the main thrust of the German invasion was head on through Belgium and not further south against France, was he able to sway his Cabinet colleagues. Like London, Paris similarly took a more 'attentiste' position and not the proactive one of the decision-makers in Berlin and Vienna.

There can be little doubt that the debate is likely to continue on what share of the responsibility not only Russia, but also the other powers have to bear in the origins of the First World War. However, as this chapter has been arguing, these shares will be secondary in comparison to the aggressive diplomacy and armament policies that the German monarchy, with Vienna increasingly in its wake, pursued from the turn of the century, and that for the reasons examined here, culminated in the idea of the Central Powers launching a preventive war in 1914.

Balkans. It is to be hoped that the research that is likely to be published in connection with the centenary of 1914 will yield a more definitive weighting among the three governments that have also been at the centre of this analysis.

39 T. G. Otte, *The Foreign Office Mind: The Making of British Foreign Policy, 1865–1914* (Cambridge University Press, 2011).

2

1914: Outbreak

JEAN-JACQUES BECKER AND GERD KRUMEICH

On 28 July 1914, Austria-Hungary declared war on Serbia. On 30 July, Russia ordered general mobilisation. During the night of 30–31 July, Austria-Hungary decided to mobilise, followed on 1 August by Germany and France at approximately the same time. Also on 1 August, Germany declared war on Russia, and on France on 3 August. On 4 August the United Kingdom declared war on Germany, and on 6 August Austria-Hungary declared war on Russia. Within a few days virtually all the great European powers were at war (with the exception of Italy at this stage, which did not declare war on Austria-Hungary until 23 May 1915).

From the very beginning of a European war such as had not been seen for nearly a century, it was impossible to compare it to any other conflict: by reason of the general mobilisations at its outbreak, and the call for mass volunteers in Britain, this time millions of men would be involved in the war. How did all this come about?

It seems that no other historic event has ever aroused so many questions, controversies or so much research – and so it has continued for nearly a century. First, there was the bitter argument over 'responsibility', which began in August 1914, and which led to the first official white, blue, yellow and orange books prepared by the foreign offices of the various nations at war. These documents are to some extent still useful today, but are partially undermined by falsifications, counter-truths and omissions. It was later, after 1918, that the debate became equally political and historiographic, concentrating on the clauses of the Treaty of Versailles and in particular the clause which unilaterally declared Germany and her allies responsible for starting the war. The discussion was intensified by the need to justify to public opinion the deaths of the 10 million soldiers who were killed in the war. In addition there were the tens of millions more who suffered the consequences of wounds or

Helen McPhail translated this chapter from French into English.

exposure to gas, including incalculable numbers of permanently handicapped and mutilated men. This discussion, led by Sydney Fay, Bernadotte Schmitt and Pierre Renouvin, continued until the early 1930s, when historians of the different nationalities agreed that none of the Great Powers could be considered entirely free from some degree of responsibility. 'Willy-nilly, along with the great majority of historians (even though the number is irrelevant), the (unequal) division of responsibility must be accepted.'[1]

The colossal total sum calculated by the Italian journalist Luigi Albertini (published in 1940, but debated and accepted as an authoritative work of reference since its publication in English in 1953)[2] reflects this trend in the interwar years to deepen knowledge of the actions of all the leaders in the crisis of July 1914 through comparative study. The general impression of this approach had already been stated by Lloyd George in his *War Memoirs*,[3] that all the Powers 'slithered into the War'. Nonetheless, it may have been the particular intransigence of the German government which initiated the final explosion, or perhaps Russia above all should take the blame: in the view of Jules Isaac, it was Russia's general mobilisation on 30 July which made war inevitable.[4]

This relative equilibrium in the historiography of the Great War was disturbed in 1961 by the German historian Fritz Fischer, in his publication *Griff nach der Weltmacht*.[5] Using all the documentation known at that time, he accused the German government of having intended and prepared for this war since 1912 as a conflict from which Germany was to emerge as a world power – in other words, a power of world supremacy. The result was an outcry, above all in Germany, with profound opposition between the 'Fischerites' and their opponents. In the longer term, however, the controversy was valuable: it instigated an entirely fresh and wholehearted approach to the historiography of the Great War – despite the general opinion in the 1950s that it had broadly reached saturation point. Concentration was focused far more closely than before on specific actions or behaviour in July 1914. This was the moment when 'mentalities' began to appear in historiographical works on the origins of the war and of fateful

1 Jules Isaac, *Un débat historique: 1914, le problème des origines de la guerre* (Paris: Rieder, 1933), p. 227.

2 Luigi Albertini, *The Origins of the War of 1914*, 3 vols. (London: Oxford University Press, 1953).

3 David Lloyd George, *War Memoirs* (London: Nicholson & Watson, 1936).

4 Isaac, *Un débat historique*, p. 21.

5 Fritz Fischer, *Griff nach der Weltmacht: Die Kriegszielpolitik des kaiserlichen Deutschland (1914–1918)* (Düsseldorf: Droste, 1961), translated into French as *Les buts de guerre de l'Allemagne impériale*, preface by Jacques Droz (Paris: Éditions de Trévise, 1970) and into English as *Germany's Aims in the First World War* (London: Chatto & Windus, 1967).

decisions. From this perspective, the inaugural lecture at the London School of Economics by James Joll, *1914: The Unspoken Assumptions*, remains a beacon for research on July 1914.[6] For France, we have the book by Jean-Jacques Becker[7] on French public opinion and the mentalities of those taking the decisions, and of the French in general – since then we have learned that, for example, the 'enthusiasm' of August 1914 is either ephemeral or a myth. In the case of Germany, we have Wolfgang Mommsen's fundamental article, 'The topos of inevitable war in Germany in the decade before 1914',[8] which established a solid link between 'mentalities' in general and the spirit of decision-makers in the approach to war, particularly in July 1914.

This historiographical list could be extended further but, to remain strictly with the 'July crisis', several quite recent studies by Samuel Williamson, Annika Mombauer,[9] Antoine Prost and Jay Winter[10] have amplified our knowledge. For Samuel Williamson,[11] who has personally revived research on military agreements before the war of 1914–18,[12] the role of Austria-Hungary was primordial in the genesis of the international crisis in July 1914. Williamson's study is of particular value since the role of Austria-Hungary was long overlooked in historiography. For Fritz Fischer and his followers, it merely followed in the wake of Germany's aggressive designs, yet for the past twenty years research into the role of Austria-Hungary has been increasingly important.[13] The least that can be said is that the Emperor and his entourage, together with the enigmatic Chief of the general staff, Conrad von Hötzendorf, played an active and aggressive role both before and after the attack in Sarajevo. This applies particularly to the Foreign Minister, Berchtold, while General Conrad was unrestrained in his demands for a

6 James Joll, *1914: The Unspoken Assumptions* (London: Weidenfeld & Nicolson, 1968).

7 Jean-Jacques Becker, *1914, Comment les français sont entrés dans la guerre: contribution à l'étude de l'opinion publique, printemps-été 1914* (Paris: Presses de la Fondation Nationale des Sciences Politiques, 1977).

8 Wolfgang J. Mommsen, 'The topos of inevitable war in Germany in the decade before 1914', in Volker Berghahn and Martin Kitchen (eds.), *Germany in the Age of Total War: Essays in Honour of Francis Carsten* (London: Croom Helm, 1981).

9 Annika Mombauer, *The Origins of the Great War: Controversies and Consensus* (London: Longman, 2002).

10 Antoine Prost and Jay Winter, *Penser la grande Guerre, un essai d'historiographie* (Paris: Éditions du Seuil, 2004); English translation, *The Great War in History: Debates and Controversies, 1914 to the Present* (Cambridge University Press, 2005).

11 Samuel R. Williamson, *Austria-Hungary and the Origins of the First World War* (London: Macmillan, 1993).

12 Samuel R. Williamson, *The Politics of Grand Strategy: France and Britain Prepare for War* (Cambridge, MA: Harvard University Press, 1969).

13 Manfried Rauchensteiner, *Der Tod des Doppeladlers: Österreich-Ungarn und der Erste Weltkrieg* (Graz: Styria Verlag, 1993).

'good' war against Serbia: in the aftermath of the Balkan wars this 'minor power' had expanded greatly and taken an increasingly aggressive attitude towards Austria-Hungary in order to instigate the outbreak of such a war. Had not Conrad demanded, at least three times since December 1912, that this disturbing neighbour be disposed of by means of a preventive war?

The Sarajevo attack would supply Austria-Hungary's political and military leaders with a convenient reason for dealing conclusively with the Serbian (and pan-Slav) threat. Whatever the more or less remote origins of the conflict (as discussed in Chapter 1), the assassination in Sarajevo on 28 June 1914, which killed the heir to the Austro-Hungarian Empire, Archduke Franz-Ferdinand, and his wife, in effect gave the signal. This assassination was a 'Serb' affair. From the Congress of Berlin in 1878 until their final annexation by Austria-Hungary in 1908, the provinces of Bosnia-Herzegovina – which in law were always Ottoman – came under Austro-Hungarian annexation. Russia, protector of the Slavs, was unable to respond to this situation: it had been weakened by the combination of its defeat against Japan in 1905 and the revolutionary movements of 1905 – and, further, its French ally had indicated that it was not to be called on in an affair which did not concern France's vital interests.

The population of Bosnia-Herzegovina was not solely Serbian since it also included Catholic Croats and Muslims. In reality the great majority of these Muslims were Serbs who had converted to Islam. Overall, however, Orthodox Serbs represented the most numerous ethnicity, and despite the advances introduced by the Austro-Hungarian authorities the young Serbs resented foreign domination. Many plots had been fomented to assassinate one or another significant person without ever coming to the point of action, and Franz-Ferdinand's announced visit provoked a new conspiracy in which the chief figure was a 19-year-old Bosniac, Gavrilo Princip. Surprisingly, this conspiracy came to fruition through a series of accidents, even exceeding the intentions of its plotters: the car bearing Franz-Ferdinand stopped in front of Princip, who used his revolver to kill both the Archduke and his wife, the Duchess of Hohenberg, a second murder which had not been part of the conspirators' plan.

The attack immediately posed the question of who was behind the plot. In Austria-Hungary, all eyes turned immediately towards Serbia: had the attack genuinely been fomented in Serbia with the knowledge of the Serb government? Princip was a student in Belgrade, in independent Serbia, when he learned of the Archduke's visit to Sarajevo. The idea of the assault came to him almost at once, but he had three problems to solve. The task of assembling a certain number of fellow conspirators from Bosniac students in Belgrade and Sarajevo did not seem very difficult; in addition, weapons had to be found and transported to Sarajevo. Weapons were provided by a Serb nationalist group, Ujedinjenje ili Smrt (Union or Death), better known under the name used by its enemies, Crna Ruka (The Black Hand), and it was also branches of the Black Hand which enabled Princip and two of his comrades to reach Sarajevo with the weapons. At the same time, the Black Hand had connections in the Serb army: its leader, Colonel Dragutin Dimitrievic, was also head of intelligence for the Serb army's general staff. It should not be inferred from this that the Serb government was implicated in preparing the attack. For the directors of the Black Hand (who thought that this attack would fail like all others before it), it was above all a means of applying pressure to the Prime Minister, Nikola Pašić; having personified the Serb nationalist current, Pašić was now accused of passivity and complaisancy towards Austria-Hungary. Clearly he found the situation far from easy and understood immediately that this attack would be exploited against Serbia by its powerful neighbour. The following day he established his political strategy: the Serb government declared that it was not concerned by an event that was 'internal' to Austria-Hungary because the authors of the attack were all Bosniacs and thus Austro-Hungarian subjects. However, as Pašić also knew that members of the Serb army and frontier officials had helped Princip and his companions, supplying them with weapons and allowing them to cross the frontier, it was easy to see that Austria-Hungary would hold Serbia responsible. Although Pašić and his entourage expressed their condolences and displayed (more or less sincere) alarm, the very different attitude taken by other members of the government was echoed in the press, which represented the nationalist and pan-Serb opposition. It exulted whole-heartedly and congratulated Princip and his companions, who were raised to hero status, even martyrs, in the 'Yugoslav' cause.

Pašić had every reason to maintain his stance because it was evident that Russia had not the slightest interest in adding oil to the fire at that moment. When on 3 July Pašić sought advice from Sazonov, the Russian Minister for Foreign Affairs, the reply was the same as that already given by the French Président du Conseil, René Viviani, on 1 July: everything must be done to keep calm. This was easier said than done, but Pašić, without any great conviction, made the effort. However, to say to the Austro-Hungarians that Serbia regretted this incident but was not unduly concerned by it was one thing, but it was another matter entirely to claim that it could not muzzle the free Serb press and that to do so would undermine the 'difficult balance of restraint and cooperation' between officials and the press. No one took this latter argument seriously.[14]

Without going further into these subtleties, Austro-Hungarian opinion immediately expressed great indignation towards Serbia. The Austro-Hungarian government considered that the incident must be put to good use to tame Serbia, whose aggressive behaviour, and indeed its very existence, were a danger to the stability of the 'multi-national' Empire. The imperial court in Vienna immediately decided to seize the occasion to settle the question of Serbia once and for all. On 7 July, the Imperial Council of Ministers took offence at this Serbian lack of genuine cooperation in which certain circles of officials and the mainstream press persisted in applauding the attack – a reproach which was expressed again in the ultimatum of 23 July. German 'nationalist' historiography also recorded this ultimatum as severe – but not exaggerated, in view of the events. In reality, at this Council of 7 July the participants had favoured sending an unacceptable ultimatum to Serbia in order to trigger a punitive war, even though Berchtold, the Minister for Foreign Affairs, had pointed out the inherent risk of provoking war with Russia and that the Prime Minister of the Hungarian Council, Tisza, was openly opposed to it:

> In return, all participants with the exception of the President of the Council of the Kingdom of Hungary consider that a success of a purely diplomatic nature would be without value, even if it led to dazzling humiliation for Serbia. It would thus be necessary to bring Serbia face to face with claims so considerable that rejection could be expected and a radical military intervention can be undertaken.[15]

Nonetheless, Austria-Hungary could not act without German acquiescence, particularly because in the preceding year Austria-Hungary and Italy had categorically objected to Serbia becoming a maritime power by extending its territory as far as the Adriatic Sea, and had achieved this through the creation of Albania. Austria-Hungary would have liked to take further advantage of these circumstances to eliminate the Serb danger once and for all, but Germany had restrained them from acting to do so.

14 Apart from the works of Williamson and Rauchensteiner, see the clarification by Mark Cornwall, 'Serbia', in Keith Wilson (ed.), *Decisions for War, 1914* (London: UCL Press, 1995), pp. 55–96.

15 See Immanuel Geiss (ed.), *Julikrise und Kriegsausbruch Eine Dokumentensammlung*, 2 vols. (Hanover: Verlag für Literatur und Zeitgeschehen, 1963), vol. 1, no. 39: Protokoll des Gemeinsamen Ministerrates . . . 7 July 1914; *cit. ibid.* p. 110.

The eventual outcome of events therefore depended on Germany, where the attack had been felt more powerfully than in most other European countries. It had stirred feelings everywhere and sometimes, but rarely, anxiety. In France, for example, Clemenceau was almost alone in expressing concern, in his journal *L'Homme libre*, over the potentially far-reaching consequences of the attack. In Bavaria, long allied to Austria, feelings had been particularly strong. The same was true of Kaiser Wilhelm II, to whom Franz-Ferdinand had been close.

The Kaiser's feelings were reflected in remarks which have become famous, written in the margins of a report from the German ambassador to Vienna, Count Heinrich von Tschirschky. The ambassador later recounted his first conversation with the Austro-Hungarian Foreign Minister, Berchtold, on 30 June, in a report addressed to Chancellor Bethmann Hollweg but also read and annotated by the Kaiser. Among other points, Tschirschky explained that in Vienna, even among 'serious people', many voices explicitly wanted the Serb question to be dealt with conclusively, and he took pains to assure the Chancellor that he would not stop preaching caution to all concerned. The Kaiser commented in the margin:

> Who authorised him to speak like that? It is very stupid! And this is no concern of his because it is Austria alone which will decide what it sees best to do. Otherwise, it will be said later, if the affair goes off the rails, that it was Germany which did not wish it. Tschirschky must imperatively stop saying such absurd things. Austria-Hungary must finish with Serbia, and finish soon.

It is unlikely that debate about the real impact of the Kaiser's remarks on German foreign policy over the July crisis will ever end. His ministers were used to his temperamental outbursts, and it does not seem that Tschirschky suffered any sanction; nonetheless, it should be noted that in this case German policy followed the Kaiser's directions quite closely. It is even possible that the genesis of the doctrine of 'localisation' of the conflict may lie in these marginal notes. It was not a sophisticated calculation, but simply Germany's wish not to be reproached by Austria-Hungary with having prevented it taking action against the Serbs (as had happened in 1909, 1912 and 1913). The thinking of the Kaiser was thus simple and doubtless quite widely shared: the opportunity offered by the assassination attack must be used to tame Serbia – the affair must also remain the work of the double monarchy alone and, if the Austro-Hungarian action were to fail, Germany must not be held responsible for this fresh setback suffered by its Austrian allies.

This obsession was shared by the entire German government and had heavy consequences for later events. It was the result of a major fact, which has frequently been overlooked in the relevant historiography – namely, that Germany had only one reliable ally in Europe, Austria-Hungary. Although Italy was also linked to Germany within the Triple Alliance, its lack of reliability as an ally was already felt strongly and would soon be confirmed. If Austria-Hungry were to remain an important ally it must not be weakened. When an Austrian diplomat, Count Hoyos, came to Berlin on 5 July to discuss reprisals against Serbia, he therefore received full German support – what came to be called 'the blank cheque'. The British military historian Hew Strachan, whose analysis of 'July 1914' is perhaps the most complete ever achieved, has expressed understandable surprise: 'What is striking about the "blank cheque" is not that it was issued but that it was indeed blank.'[16] Certainly what happened at this moment was an unexpected 'extraordinary abdication of responsibility'[17] on the part of the German government. Far from pressing the Austrians to take action against Serbia even at the risk of a war with Russia (this, in summary, was the thesis of Fritz Fischer and his school[18]), the German government simply let them go ahead. Hoyos brought a letter to Berlin from the Emperor Franz-Joseph (in reality, a very long memorandum), explaining the situation of Austria-Hungary faced with the Balkan states and Russia, and above all sketching out a general policy designed to weaken the Balkan League, attract Bulgaria and totally undermine the entire pan-Slavist movement, while frustrating Russia's clear intention to 'encircle' Austria-Hungary by means of its French alliance. But this long-term strategy would only be possible if Serbia, at that time the linchpin of the pan-Slav policy, were eliminated as a Balkan political power, and the Emperor Franz-Joseph asked his ally the Kaiser to support him in a 'common counter-attack of the members of the Triple Alliance, above all Austria-Hungary and the German Empire'. It would be in the interest of the two powers to strike down agitations 'systematically conceived and nourished by Russia'. The assault in Sarajevo – and this was the conclusion of the memorandum – demanded a response from the double monarchy, to achieve a decisive break in the threads which the adversaries were in the course of 'weaving into a web around them'.[19]

16 Hew Strachan, *The First World War*, vol. 1: *To Arms* (Oxford University Press, 2001), p. 95.

17 *Ibid.*

18 See Geiss (ed.), *Julikrise*, vol. 1, p. 119: Fischer, *Griff nach der Weltmacht*, p. 71 and *passim*.

19 *Die österreich-ungarischen Dokumente zum Kriegsausbruch* (Berlin: National-Verlag, 1923), p. 12.

This Austro-Hungarian memorandum referred only secondarily to action by Germany, insisting all the while that Austria-Hungary must use the crisis to decapitate the pan-Slav movement and defend itself against its originator, Russia. This document was delivered by Hoyos through the Austro-Hungarian ambassador, Szőgyény-Marich, and on 5 July the Kaiser assembled his entourage of political and military figures of authority. Much was said in the 1920s of a 'Council of the Crown' set up for this purpose, but this was not the case. The meeting brought together the Chancellor, Bethmann Hollweg, the Under-Secretary of State, Arthur Zimmermann (instead of the Minister for Foreign Affairs, Jagow, who, remarkably, was on holiday), the Prussian War Minister, Falkenhayn, Moriz von Lynker, the Prussian military *chef de cabinet* and General Hans von Plessen, who was close to the Kaiser. Moltke and Tirpitz were both also on holiday and therefore absent. The decision was taken, apparently quite quickly, to support the Austro-Hungarian intentions, even in the case of a Russian intervention. No record of the meeting exists. In 1919 General von Falkenhayn affirmed to the commission of enquiry of the German Parliament that nothing had been discussed, and that the Kaiser had simply asked him whether, if it so required, the army would be ready. He had confirmed this.

On 6 July, Chancellor Bethmann Hollweg summarised for the Austrian ambassador the opinion of this group at the Kaiser's meeting. Germany would accept fully whatever action Austria-Hungary considered useful to take against Serbia, given that the German policy, which until then had consisted of seeking a compromise with that country, had been rendered null and void by the Sarajevo attack. The Chancellor again gave assurances that Austria-Hungary would be supported by Germany in whatever action they decided on; but he also repeated the advice to take action quickly against Serbia.[20]

The German government has been heavily criticised for the risk of a far-reaching war. Fritz Fischer and his school have dramatised this concession, maintaining that the double monarchy would not have been capable on its own of taking any serious decision: it was German consent alone which opened the way for the actions which followed. The risks, in truth, had not been great: the only one, Russian intervention, was unlikely, specifically because of the origins of the situation and the existence of a certain monarchical solidarity. Above all the risks were if any reprisals were swift and brief.

20 Szogyeny, report on the meeting, 6 July, *ibid.*, p. 19.

Nonetheless, there are problems in analysing the German Chancellor's situation. Reference to Bethmann Hollweg as 'the enigmatic chancellor'[21] is well-founded, and since German diplomatic and political correspondence show that he very rarely took a stance before the ultimatum of 23 July, it is not easy to define his policy during the July crisis. It seems likely that at the very beginning of the crisis, Bethmann Hollweg, whose policy since taking office had not been warlike or even included any risk of war, was still trying to calm the situation. In the interests of maintaining European peace, he considered that it would be useful, and possible, to 'localise' the conflict – to prevent it from spreading beyond the single point at issue between Austria-Hungary and Serbia. Germany should therefore remain in the background. But, and this is a major 'but', Bethmann Hollweg was fundamentally convinced of the 'Russian danger' and this since at least the armaments crisis of 1913 when he had spoken in the Reichstag about an inevitable conflagration in the long run between 'the Slavs and the Germans'. The press campaign between Russia and Germany in the spring of 1914, following the appointment of a German general, Liman von Sanders, as head of the Ottoman army,[22] had noticeably intensified his fatalism. In addition, he was deeply concerned at information transmitted by a German spy, Siebert, at the heart of the Russian embassy in London, concerning Anglo-Russian negotiations over a possible maritime treaty between them. This concern was aggravated by the British government's denial, on several occasions, that such conversations had taken place, despite Siebert's detailed reports. Before July 1914 Bethmann Hollweg was increasingly convinced that the encirclement so much feared by the Germans since the Franco-British treaty of 1904, the Moroccan crises of 1905 and 1911, the exchange of letters of support between Grey (the British Minister for Foreign Affairs) and Paul Cambon (French ambassador in the United Kingdom) at the end of 1912, had now become reality.[23] From these suspicions he became convinced that something extremely serious was in the making, to the detriment of Germany. On 24 June, four days before the assassination in Sarajevo, he was again showing signs of extreme anxiety over Russia's behaviour.[24]

21 Konrad Jarausch, *The Enigmatic Chancellor: Bethmann Hollweg and the Hubris of Imperial Germany* (New Haven, CT: Yale University Press, 1973).

22 See particularly Klaus Wernecke, *Der Wille zur Weltgeltung* (Düsseldorf: Droste, 1970).

23 See particularly Stephen Schröder, *Die englisch-russische Marinekonvention: Das Deutsche Reich und die Flottenverhandlungen der Tripelentente am Vorabend des Ersten Weltkriegs* (Göttingen: Vandenhoeck & Ruprecht, 2006).

24 See Geiss (ed.), *Julikrise*, no. 6 (Hoyos report), vol. 1, n.1.

Whether or not this was well-founded is of little importance: the important point was what the German authorities thought.

Bethmann Hollweg's personal pessimism was further intensified in May 1914 by the death of his wife. Kurt Riezler, his secretary and confidant, expressed this clearly in his diary which, despite its deficiencies and the cuts that it has suffered, has become one of the key sources for the July crisis. On 7 July, for example, Bethmann Hollweg commented to Riezler that for him the Russo-British negotiations on a maritime convention were very worrying and formed 'the final link in the chain'. Russia's military strength was growing rapidly; Austria was increasingly weakened by pressures from north and south, and would be incapable of following Germany into a war. On 8 July Riezler noted the Chancellor's opinion that if war came from the East, Germany would go to war to support Austria-Hungary. It was always possible that Germany would win. 'If war does not come, if the Tsar does not wish it or if France, in confusion, counsels peace, we will still have the prospect of making the Entente collapse through this action [i.e., war by Austria against Serbia].' A week later, on 14 July, Riezler's notes show that for the Chancellor the intervention of Austria-Hungary and its support by Germany was 'like a jump into the unknown, and that is the supreme duty'. The Chancellor considered, however, that it would be convenient for the Austro-Hungarian ultimatum not to be sent before Poincaré's visit to Russia, so that 'France in anguish' over a potential war would ask Russia to maintain the peace.

On 20 July, informed that the ultimatum would not be sent before 23 July, Bethmann Hollweg showed himself to be 'resolute and silent'. However, he spoke to Riezler of Russia's growing ambitions and its impressive expansion, which in a few years would be beyond restraint. On 23 July Riezler noted that 'the opinion of the Chancellor is that if war comes, it will be the consequence of a Russian mobilisation undertaken in the heat of the moment, that is, ahead of any preliminary negotiations. In that case negotiations would hardly be possible, because we would have to attack immediately. The entire nation would recognise the danger and would rise.'

Overall, the German rulers were convinced that rapid action would prevent the other powers from intervening in the conflict between Serbia and Austria-Hungary. Bethmann Hollweg told Riezler of his opinion that 'to strike rapidly and then be friendly towards the Powers – this was how to soften the blow'.[25] Jagow, Secretary of State for Foreign Affairs, referred to this attitude as the

25 Kurt Riezler, *Tagebücher – Aufsätze Dokumente*, ed. Karl-Dietrich Erdmann (Göttingen: Vandenhoeck & Ruprecht, 1972), p. 190.

'localisation' of the conflict. He explained his plan in a long memorandum dated 15 July: 'localisation' also meant that Germany would require the other powers to stand back from getting mixed up in this conflict in any way. Because of the rigidity of the system of alliances, and purely through their operation, the risk would exist in the continuing situation of being led into a European war. In consequence, the British were asked to abstain when, in line with the custom of the Concert of Europe, they proposed to unite the 'non-interested powers' in order to find a friendly solution. Jagow and his collaborators then made every effort to avoid such a meeting of ambassadors, asserting that if the Serb question was not 'localised' in this way, there was a risk of a general war. For, it was added, if Russia did not fall in with this wish for 'localisation' and acted militarily in support of Serbia, it would show proof of its war-mongering and pan-Slavist aims. In this case – and this was an old argument, but updated during the 'July crisis' – it would be convenient to go to war immediately, before the Russian army could draw on its numerical superiority and the completion of its 'strategic' railway lines. These developments, which could be expected around 1916, would enable it to undertake a rapid offensive and mark the death of the Schlieffen Plan.

In the end, the 'localisation' of the conflict thus formulated was an adventurous political tactic. As described by Wolfgang Mommsen, it would mean a deliberately high-risk 'all or nothing' scheme – but with the genuine risk of plunging into major catastrophe.[26] Yet, did this political calculation reflect a spirit of moderation, as has often been asked? Of course when it is asserted, as do Fischer and his school, that Germany's all-out insistence on war was in the interests of imperialism, this wish for the 'localisation' of the conflict between Austria-Hungary and Serbia alone could indicate that it was truly a spirit of moderation which ruled in Berlin. Gerhard Ritter and many others have confirmed this – it was even one of the salient points of the 'Fritz Fischer controversy' in the 1960s.[27] In reality, above all in the minds of Bethmann Hollweg, Jagow and the Kaiser, localisation was a test of what Russia and its allies wanted. The conviction of Russian aggressive intent, and the prospect of its military superiority within a few years was such that this fear had overwhelmed calmer and more balanced political reasoning.

26 Wolfgang J. Mommsen, *Die Urkatastrophe Deutschlands: der Erste Weltkrieg 1914–1918* (Stuttgart: Klett-Cotta, 2004), p. 18.

27 See Gerhard Ritter, *Staatskunst und Kriegshandwerk*, 4 vols. (Munich: R. Oldenbourg Verlag, 1965), vol. II, p. 314; Hans Herzfeld, *Der Erste Weltkrieg* (Munich: Deutscher Taschenbuch Verlag, 1974), p. 38; Karl-Dietrich Erdmann, *Der Erste Weltkrieg* (Stuttgart: Klett-Cotta, 1918), p. 80.

No one in Berlin, apparently, had wondered whether or not this strict concept of the localisation of the war – which was not taken up by any of the other Great Powers – might push the situation further towards war. To demand that this conflict remain limited between Austria-Hungary and Serbia meant that no mediation was acceptable. To demand that Russia should let Austria-Hungary act against Serbia was not a test, but genuine blackmail on a grand scale and a self-fulfilling prophecy in respect of Russian behaviour. This was the attitude that struck Chancellor Bethmann Hollweg, according to Riezler's notes, as 'our heaviest duty'. German policy in July 1914 cannot be stated more clearly. It was the reflection of behaviour which was entirely speculative, even irresponsible.

In an interview with a politician friend, the liberal deputy Conrad Haussman, in 1918, and despite his recognition of the terrible slaughter in the war since August 1914, Bethmann Hollweg summarised his way of thinking and attitude to his responsibilities at the time of the July crisis: 'Yes, by God, in a way it was a preventive war. But if war was in any case hovering over us; if it had come in two years' time, but even more dangerously and even more unavoidably, and if the military leaders declared that now it was still possible without being defeated, in two years' time no longer . . . ! Yes, the military!'[28]

The final straw that was to change everything was the slowness of the Austrian reactions: in letting affairs drag on for nearly a month they modified behaviour elsewhere, in particular in Russia. The Austrian government was generally slow to act – but this time it was slow for a particular reason. The most active protagonists in favour of an Austrian intervention against Serbia were the Foreign Minister, Count Leopold Berchtold, who lacked both experience and character and was a man of a 'disturbing lightness', according to Pierre Renouvin,[29] and General Franz Conrad von Hötzendorf, Chief of the general staff to the army. Hötzendorf had been a protégé and friend of Franz-Ferdinand and had succeeded at least partially in overcoming the distrust of the Emperor Franz-Joseph, who was now 84 years old and recovering from an operation. But there was a sizeable obstacle in the form of the Hungarian Prime Minister, Count István Tisza, a firm and energetic spirit who had no wish for a war which could possibly lead to an increase in the number of Slavs in the Empire – a number which he already considered excessive. It was not

28 English translation by Annika Mombauer, *Helmuth von Moltke and the Origins of the First World War* (Cambridge University Press, 2001), p. 189.

29 Pierre Renouvin, *Histoire des relations internationales*, 6 vols. (Paris: Hachette, 1955), vol. VI, p. 378.

until 14 July that he accepted the plan to intervene against the Serbs. The reasons for his change of mind remained mysterious for a long time, but recent research has shown how he was influenced by Istvan Burian, Minister responsible for Bosnia-Herzegovina affairs between 1903 and 1912. Burian seems to have convinced him that only military intervention against the Serbs could prevent the power of Austria-Hungary being permanently undermined in these regions. Whatever the circumstances may have been, after 14 July Tisza became 'a relentless supporter of the military solution'.[30]

The decisions to attack Serbia were not settled until 19 July. On 23 July an ultimatum was sent to Serbia which, as shown above, had been designed to be unacceptable. Serbia had forty-eight hours to accept the conditions, which would turn the country into a sort of Austro-Hungarian protectorate. Anti-Austrian propaganda would be forbidden, nationalist associations dissolved and, as a supplementary condition, Austro-Hungarian officials would take part in repression of the 'subversive' movement. The Serb government showed great prudence and accepted all the conditions – except the final one. To the Austro-Hungarian government this proviso represented a rejection of its ultimatum: it declared war on Serbia on 28 July and Austro-Hungarian artillery opened fire on Belgrade from the opposite bank of the Danube.

The German government had complained continually at the slowness of the Austro-Hungarian reaction, but to Wilhelm II the conciliatory response from Serbia was a great success, and there was no longer any reason for war: at most, Austria-Hungary could demand a pledge that the commitments would be fulfilled. But the hitherto docile ally, Austria-Hungary, rejected the Kaiser's counsels of moderation – encouraged by Chancellor Bethmann Hollweg's extremely tardy transmission of the Kaiser's thinking, for reasons which still remain unclear. Further, at the same time Moltke let it be known to his Austrian analogue, Conrad, that Germany would continue to support the action of Austria-Hungary without alteration: a military intrusion into politics, no doubt, which gave rise to the famous exclamation by the Austro-Hungarian Foreign Minister, Berchtold: 'So who is governing in Berlin, Bethmann or Moltke?'[31]

30 Samual R. Williamson and Ernest R. May, 'An identity of opinion: historians and July 1914', *Journal of Modern History*, 79 (2007), p. 357; with reference to the works of Leslie, and the biography of Tisza by Gabor Vermes, *Istvan Tisza: The Liberal Vision and Conservative Statescraft of a Magyar Nationalist* (New York: Columbia University Press, 1985).

31 Isaac, *Un débat historique*, p. 165; for the Berchtold–Conrad interview in full, see Geiss (ed.), *Julikrise*, vol. II, no. 858.

The great question now became, what was Russia going to do? As in 1908 at the time of the annexation of Bosnia-Herzegovina, would it accept the fait accompli or would it claim to fulfil its role as protector of the Balkan Slavs? The conditions were no longer the same. The effects of the defeat against Japan and the events of 1905 were fading, and Raymond Poincaré, France's Président du Conseil at the time of the Balkan wars and now President of the Republic, had held back from restraining Russia's action out of fear of losing the alliance. As a result, the Russian government could imagine that no matter how France behaved, Russia had no reason to fear Clemenceau's crisp warning of 1908.

This hypothesis was supported by the presence in Russia of the French Presidents – Président du Conseil, René Viviani, and President of the Republic, Poincaré – in the days before the Austrian ultimatum. In the prevailing circumstances this visit, in theory a routine encounter between two great allies, held consequences of two kinds. Leaving from Dunkirk on 15 July, Viviani and Poincaré stayed in Saint Petersburg between 21 and 23 July. They did not yet know of the ultimatum, but French diplomats in Vienna had an idea that something was in the wind. In this context, Poincaré's reference to the 'indissoluble alliance' did not appear to be purely routine, and his warning to the Austrian ambassador affirming that 'Serbia has very warm friends in the Russian people and Russia has an ally, France. How many complications there are to be feared!' was heard particularly clearly in Russia.

It may be added that after the departure of the Presidents, the French ambassador, Maurice Paléologue, was to add to this inclination and, further, kept his government very poorly informed about what was happening in Russia. It was only after an appreciable delay, therefore, that the French government learned of the Russian move to general mobilisation – but none of this had any apparent effect on the course of events. The second consequence of the French Presidents' visit to Russia was that, not without reason, the ultimatum was sent on 23 July, while the French Presidents were at sea and where they remained until 29 July, at the mercy of unreliable communications. The role of France was naturally affected.

Both the Russian Minister for Foreign Affairs, Sergei Sazonov, and Tsar Nicholas II were peaceable. Neither the Sarajevo attack nor the death of Franz-Ferdinand, who was seen as broadly hostile to Russia, had provoked any great emotion. A warning of some kind could have been tolerated, or sanctions against Serbia, but an ultimatum sent so late was to change the situation, to the extent that the attack had not immediately led to limited reprisals in terms of area or time. Russia could not let Serbia be overwhelmed without reacting:

what would have been felt as a new national humiliation would be unacceptable to the army leaders and public opinion alike (urban opinion at least – the vast mass of peasants remained indifferent to all of this). Nor would it be acceptable to a government dominated by its Minister of the Interior, the somewhat outspoken nationalist, Nicolai Maklakov. The only question was how to react without provoking German intervention. The first thought was to launch a merely partial mobilisation clearly directed against Austria alone – but this turned out to be technically impossible. It should, however, be stressed that in the end Russia was the first of all the Powers to call on the army, with the decision on 24 July to mobilise four military districts (the district of Warsaw was avoided for this mobilisation as it would have been a direct threat to Germany). Hew Strachan considers that for Sazonov this mobilisation did not exclude the possibility of opening political negotiations. But he also suggests that it was naive to think of it as being insignificant. Could not this be considered a sort of 'blank cheque' for Serbia?[32]

It was of course known that in the case of war the German plans were based on the Russian army mobilising slowly, and that Germany could not accept being caught out by speed of action. Matters became more urgent when on 30 July Russia decided on general mobilisation, ignoring Bethmann Hollweg's warning to Russia that general mobilisation there would lead to general mobilisation in Germany, and would mean certain war. It is not known precisely when the German government learned of the Russian decision for general mobilisation, but with this decision the dice were thrown. As Jules Isaac has written: 'Would the war have been avoided if the order for [Russian] general mobilisation had not been issued on 30 July? Very probably not. Did the Russian general mobilisation render war inevitable? Certainly, yes.'[33]

The second idea was an exchange of messages between the two cousins – the emperors of Germany and of Russia – which took place on 29 July but which ended inconclusively. Following Austria-Hungary's declaration of war on Serbia, the Russian Minister for Foreign Affairs, Sazonov, shifted his position and abandoned his earlier pacific stance. Tsar Nicholas was submitted to such pressure that, after several refusals, on 30 July he allowed himself to give the order for Russian general mobilisation.

This Russian decision, taken without consulting France but with the conviction of French support following the declarations of Poincaré and the ambassador Paléologue, was extremely serious. It should be emphasised that Austria-Hungary, which had so far hoped for a local conflict, decreed its

32 Strachan, *The First World War*, vol. I, pp. 104–6. 33 Isaac, *Un débat historique*, p. 217.

own general mobilisation on 31 July, some eighteen hours after the Russian decision. Contrary to what has frequently been said, and was believed at the time, Russian mobilisation preceded Austrian mobilisation.

The first great question had been what would Russia do? The question now was what would Germany do? Russia's action settled the matter. Taking into account its extreme technical superiority, Germany had no need to be excessively anxious over a mobilisation which was bound to be slow, but this was not the opinion of the generals nor, to some extent, of public opinion. Kaiser Wilhelm II and the civil powers, still hesitant, were insistently driven by the generals who had hitherto remained reserved. The generals considered – rightly – that in order to carry out the Schlieffen Plan, this very bold plan which was designed to finish with France before turning to deal with Russia, every day counted.

This applied above all to the head of the German army, Moltke. Like Conrad von Hötzendorf, Moltke had insisted for some years that matters must come to a head in a preventive war to save the position of Austria-Hungary in the face of Slav nationalist movements. He had said this in 1909, 1911 and 1912. His biographer Annika Mombauer, with whom we agree on this point, has rightly pointed out this semi-obsessional conviction held by the nephew of Moltke the Elder. He felt, and expressed this repeatedly to his political leaders, that the war was necessary and that Germany and its ally had still every chance of winning – but not for long. Did Moltke exceed the limits of his functions in trying to impose his beliefs? Annika Mombauer thinks so, but she is contradicted by, among others, Samuel Williamson, who considers that Moltke acted correctly in sharing his observations and wishes with his political leaders. In 1917, Bethmann Hollweg, as mentioned above, confirmed that the generals' warnings had to be followed, but were they followed throughout the July crisis? This raises the question of knowing who led decision-making in Berlin. It was obvious on 28 July when, faced with the Serbian response to Austria-Hungary's ultimatum, Kaiser Wilhelm II showed signs of hesitation and was in favour of halting the action undertaken: the slogan was 'Stop at Belgrade.'

Undoubtedly at this moment Moltke wished to impose the military point of view. On 30 July he demanded urgently to proceed to mobilisation, while Bethmann Hollweg wanted at any price to wait for the Russian general mobilisation. As he had said repeatedly since 28 July, this was in order to be forced to act in the interests of national defence, and thus obtain the support of the Social Democrats. But Moltke was so impatient that at around 2.00 p.m. on 30 July he took the initiative and asked the Austrian military representative in Berlin for general mobilisation to take place immediately in Austria-Hungary – a move which would force the German government to follow suit.[34]

A further question arises: would agreement on German mobilisation have been reached on 31 July, even if Russia had not mobilised first? This is what Fritz Fischer and his followers assert, but it remains very doubtful. It has by no means been shown that Germany would indeed have mobilised if Russia had not made the first move, if only because Bethmann Hollweg was convinced of the importance of national consensus for 'national defence'.

Russia was called on to halt its mobilisation. On receiving its negative reply at around 7.00 p.m. on 1 August, Germany declared war on Russia. Another question arose in Germany. As Poincaré had recalled, Russia had an ally in the form of France. Although France was not directly concerned in events, the German generals considered that they could not take the risk of a war on two fronts. The Schlieffen Plan must be put into action without delay; as described above, the plan provided for the use of all possible force against France to eliminate it in a few weeks before redirecting all German forces against a Russia which was slow to mobilise. Understandably, in these circumstances it was necessary to act as fast as possible. On 2 August, German troops crossed the frontier into Luxembourg, while Belgium was summoned to allow them free passage. On 3 August, Germany declared war on France.

What had France been doing during this time? Not very much: as the British historian John Keiger has written, it followed a 'policy of going with the flow of the stream' and was one of the most 'passive' of the Great Powers. At least two or three reasons explain this. The two French Presidents had left Dunkirk only on 29 July, even if Poincaré, who was punctilious about courtesies, had resigned himself with difficulty to hasten through certain Scandinavian stages of their travels. French opinion, including among politicians, was largely drawn away from international affairs by the vagaries of the case of Madame Caillaux, whose husband Joseph Caillaux was leader of the Radical party and one of the most powerful men in France; a few weeks earlier she had assassinated the editor of *Le Figaro*, Joseph Calmette. Further, the evolution of the crisis, and the fact that Russia had been the first to mobilise, did not oblige France to go to war automatically in support of Russia. In

34 See Geiss (ed.), *Julikrise*, vol. II, no. 858; David Stevenson, *The First World War and International Politics* (Oxford University Press, 1988), p. 28 for mention of an 'act of military insubordination'. See in particular Mombauer, *Helmuth von Moltke*, pp. 203ff.

practice, general mobilisation in France began at approximately the same time as in Germany; the German 'aggression' had left France no option.

And Britain? Under the leadership of the Liberal H. H. Asquith, who along with the business circles of the City was strongly against war despite the Entente with France and Russia, there was no question of joining in automatically, particularly since it was initially a Balkan affair, concerning the Serbs. As a supplementary reason, Serbia was held in very low esteem in Britain. This was indeed the main error in the calculations of the German leaders, who hoped that the United Kingdom would not intervene; to add to this, in the phrase made famous by the Kaiser, the British army immediately available was said to be 'contemptible'. Traditionally, it is said that it was the invasion of Belgium which sharply overturned the British attitude. In reality it was not, properly speaking, for Belgium that Britain was to go to war, but because a German victory in Western Europe implied a disturbance in the European equilibrium which would be unacceptable to the British, and because such a victory would put Germany in control of the Channel ports. On 4 August, Britain declared war on Germany.

It is, however, useful to understand why Germany was mistaken over the British attitude. For his part, Wilhelm II was convinced that the British would hold back from any war because of the close relationship between the two royal families. Not all German leaders shared this view – according to the study by Volker Ullrich,[35] Bethmann Hollweg's opinion was the complete opposite. He seems to have been fundamentally convinced that Britain 'would march' in line with France, and this since well before the 'July crisis'. Had not Grey, the British Foreign Minister, replied to a message from Bethmann Hollweg dated 24 June (four days before the assassination in Sarajevo), expressing German anxieties over a possible maritime alliance with Russia, that Britain in fact had very strong links with France and Russia? In return, the opinion of the German Foreign Secretary, Jagow, wavered during the crisis. Zimmermann, the Under-Secretary for Foreign Affairs, shared Bethmann Hollweg's opinion, while Wilhelm von Stumm, the political leader at the Ministry for Foreign Affairs, and considered the expert on British questions, tended to agree with the Kaiser that Britain would hold firm.

It is true that the behaviour of Grey, who had been leading foreign affairs in Britain since 1905, changed a great deal during the course of the crisis – for which he was bitterly reproached after the war. It has been suggested that a

35 Volker Ullrich, 'Das deutsche Kalkül in der Julikrise 1914 und die Frage der englischen Neutralität', *Geschichte in Wissenschaft und Unterricht*, 34 (1983), pp. 79–97.

firmer attitude from Britain could have led Germany towards negotiation. In fact, Grey's behaviour was extremely complex, as a number of studies have underlined,[36] and he avoided taking any firm position until the moment of the Austro-Hungarian ultimatum. Diplomatic documents reveal only a remarkably few sparse and insignificant remarks from Great Britain's senior diplomat.[37] At the beginning of the crisis, the British government considered letting Austria punish Serbia – and that it would remain a 'local' affair – which supported the German strategy. On 27 July, Grey stated his opinion that it was appropriate for Austria to deal with Serbia, and that Russia should keep out of the matter.[38]

The attitude of Grey and his advisers changed fundamentally with the Austrian ultimatum against Serbia on 23 July. Grey was greatly angered by this, although without adopting a firm position. This was demanded of him by an important diplomat, Eyre Crowe, on 25 July: to the extent that France and Russia were very close to each other and that France would not halt Russia, it was necessary for the United Kingdom to prove its solidarity with its usual partners. Grey judged that this could lead to war, and for this reason on 27 July he proposed to call a meeting of the powers which had no interest in the war, a proposal which surprised his partners. Germany persisted in its wish for 'localisation'. Bethmann Hollweg replied to this proposal, which fell within the framework of customary European diplomacy, that it seemed to him unsuitable to expose Austria to being 'judged' by the powers. After accepting for too long the German demand for 'localisation', Grey thus persisted in hoping that the matter could be settled along traditional diplomatic lines. But after 28 July the behaviour of the British government was less equivocal: on 29 July it refused to accept Bethmann Hollweg's demand that Britain should remain neutral in the case of war if Germany promised not to touch French possessions. On 30 July, Bethmann Hollweg declared to the authorities of the Prussian Ministry of State that the hope of keeping Britain neutral was 'nil'.

Was the British entry into the war already certain? Poincaré was very doubtful of this when he wrote to the King of England. And if we follow the study of Herbert Butterfield, on 31 July British opinion was still very deeply divided between neutrality and participation in the war, as it was among

36 For the details, see the historiographical study by Williamson and May, 'An identity of opinion'.

37 See the classic study by Herbert Butterfield, 'Sir Edward Grey and the July crisis of 1914', *Historical Studies*, 5 (1965), pp. 1–25.

38 George B. Gooch (ed.), *British Documents on the Origins of the War*, vol. xi: *The Outbreak of War: Foreign Office Documents June 28th–August 4th, 1914* (London: HMSO, 1926), p. 130.

members of the Cabinet and of Parliament. This was so marked that Butterfield concluded – in 1965 – that it is still not known in our time what Britain would have done if Germany had not violated Belgian neutrality.

In less than seven days, Europe was launched into what would be the greatest war ever known to date. Only Italy broke its alliance with Austria-Hungary and Germany and chose neutrality. It was not a casual decision. In broad terms 'the right', including Roman Catholics, was in favour of respecting commitments, while 'the left', including socialists, preferred neutrality. General opinion also broadly favoured neutrality, which Italy kept until 1915.

How can we explain such a brutal descent into this war between Europeans, particularly since in preceding years negotiation had resolved some serious crises? Looking elsewhere, we can see that the Second World War in particular, despite its unforeseen later developments, was deliberately triggered by Hitler. The Great War had no Hitler figure; virtually none of the European leaders, monarchs or civil governments wished to go to war. But there were no statesmen energetic or capable enough to find the means to block or delay the mechanism which led to the war, not least because the origin of the crisis seemed marginal. Only Austria-Hungary and Russia had a direct interest in this Balkan affair. Despite everything, it was a disturbing sign that the great European nations split into two camps, the Triple Alliance and the Triple Entente, particularly because adherence to these two groups did not in any way signify automatic participation in a war. The best proof of this came from Italy, which found itself in the opposing camp. On 1 August the British government still refused to assure France of its support in the event of war. The French situation was the most ambiguous, to the extent that a figure like Poincaré, who as an individual was not in favour of war, was very clearly obsessed by the need to avoid losing the Russian alliance.

Apart from the leaders, were the nations champing at the bit for war? In this respect, not all the nations were in the same situation. There would have been general stupefaction if the Belgians had been told that they would soon be drawn into a European war, and the same applies to the British. It is more difficult to describe in a single phrase the attitude of the French faced with a potential war, although one at least can be put into words. The idea of 'la Revanche' had largely faded, although this should not be confused (as frequently happens) with enduring regret at having lost the two provinces of Alsace and northern Lorraine. Fear of war existed, however, for international relations had not been calm in the early years of the twentieth century. It explains France's return to three years of compulsory military service in 1913, a question on which the nation was sharply divided. The law of three years was still a major theme in the election of 1914, won mainly by those hostile to the law and thus the least war-like. Moreover, the Socialists and their main leader, Jean Jaurès, campaigned tirelessly to maintain peace. It goes without saying, however, that continual discussion in favour of peace and the organising of pacifist meetings meant that at least part of society saw war as a possibility.

The situation of Germany and the German people was different, if only for geographical reasons. For a Germany located between the two allies, France to the west and Russia to the east, the concept and fear of encirclement were sensitive matters. Further, as is often the case, opinions did not always reflect realities. German opinion, for example, believed quite strongly – and entirely wrongly – that France was preparing to attack Germany at the first opportunity. Speeches over the three years' law, military propaganda in France, French pressure for Russia to develop its strategic lines in relation to Germany which, for lack of economic interest, held only military interests, had together convinced many Germans that France still held thoughts of revenge and was even preparing to realise them with the help of Russia and its huge numerical advantage over Germany. The fear was strengthened by the knowledge that, following its defeats, the Russian army was rebuilding and would not take long to reach its optimum level.

A consequence highlighted by the German historian Wolfgang Mommsen[39] is that 'the idea of the inevitable war developed in Germany'. But also for Mommsen, who took his inspiration from the works of Max Weber, semi-constitutional systems like the German political model were more sensitive than parliamentary systems to the pressures of public opinion. Large sections of opinion were convinced that Germany was threatened, even 'encircled by ill-disposed neighbours'. While Germany was seen as the aggressor by most European nations, this did not apply to German opinion: in taking the initiative, Germany felt, it was simply acting in self-defence, and indeed young German soldiers set off for the war with the conviction that they were defending their country. Moreover, Mommsen thought that this syndrome of 'the inevitable war' existed not only in Germany but could be seen in many countries, including France – at least among the leaders who were incapable of seeing the performative element in this precipitate march towards war.

The German Chancellor Bethmann Hollweg, who had tried to block the idea of war and then been forced to renounce this stance, declared on 27 July 1914 that: 'A fate beyond the power of mankind hovers over Europe and the

39 Mommsen, 'The topos of inevitable war in Germany', pp. 23–45.

German people.'[40] This was expressed by the British historian James Joll in the following way: 'Again and again, in the crisis of July 1914, we are confronted by men who suddenly felt themselves caught in a trap and from it called for a destiny that they were incapable of controlling.'[41]

Not everything, however, was the result of fate or impotence. From a certain moment on, and for simple reasons, military circles played a decisive role in launching the war. All the European armies were convinced that any potential war would be terrible, but it would be based on offensive tactics: after one or several large-scale battles everything would be settled in a few weeks. The essential point was not to be left behind by any potential adversary. Apart from Conrad von Hötzendorf, the Chief of Staff of the Austro-Hungarian army – who, as partisan of a preventive war against Serbia and by laying siege to Franz-Joseph until the old man gave way, had largely set fire to the powder-keg – there were three large military forces in Europe: German, French and Russian. The leaders of these armies were warriors by trade, for this was still the period when making war was in the natural order of things, and from the moment when they felt it was their turn to speak, they leaned on the civilian governments as heavily as possible. In France, General Joffre, Chief of Staff since 1911, was not as peaceable as he seemed from his genial appearance. To an interlocutor who, in 1912, said to him, 'you are not thinking of war', he retorted briskly, 'No, I am thinking of it. Indeed I am always thinking of it . . . we will have it. I will wage it. I will win it.'[42] During the crisis he redoubled his warnings to the government over the risk of a potential delay, and was entirely opposed to the governmental decision on 20 July to keep the troops at a distance of ten kilometres from the frontier, to show French goodwill and avoid chance incidents. Finally, at 3.30 p.m. on 31 July he jumped at the order for general mobilisation.

On the Russian side, it was also Headquarters (with the help of Sazonov who, as we have seen, had switched camp), which seized the order for general mobilisation from the very hesitant Tsar. It was first obtained on 29 July; the Tsar then cancelled the order – and reconfirmed it on 30 July. At this point, Headquarters acted to cut communications, to avoid any possible further change.

The decisive role, however, was played by the German Chief of Staff, General Helmuth von Moltke, the nephew of the victor of 1871 and head of

40 Quoted by Raymond Poidevin in *Les origines de la Première guerre mondiale* (Paris: Documents d'histoire PUF, 1975), p. 97.

41 Joll, *1914: The Unspoken Assumptions*, p. 6.

42 Quoted by Henry Contamine, *La victoire de la Marne* (Paris: Gallimard, 1970), p. 58.

the German army since 1906. Moltke was a convinced partisan of the war, at least since 1912 after the Agadir Crisis. For him 'war was inevitable' and 'the sooner the better'. Since the beginning of the crisis, German Headquarters had been pressing its Austro-Hungarian equivalents to reject any compromise and put pressure on the civilian authorities, that is on the Chancellor Bethmann Hollweg, to take measures against Russia. They made no secret of the fact that it was essential not to have the French army at their heels and they must therefore start by getting it out of the way.

The role played by Moltke nonetheless requires some further nuance. It is known that *in extremis* he sought to impose the military point of view: on 28 July itself, he addressed a long memorandum to Chancellor Bethmann Hollweg[43] which opened with an explanation of the general political situation. For five years Serbia had been 'the cause of European troubles': Austria had tolerated this for too long; it was only since Sarajevo that Austria had decided to 'burst this abscess', an action for which Europe should, in normal times, be grateful. But Russia had chosen 'to take the part of this criminal nation', which had disturbed the situation in Europe. After this political section, Moltke proceeded to strictly military explanations. Austria's mobilisation against Serbia concerned only eight army corps and was thus negligible, while Russia was preparing at short notice to mobilise four military districts. For this reason, Austria would be obliged to mobilise completely if it wished to tackle Russia. Once Austria had decided on general mobilisation, the conflagration with Russia would be inevitable and the terms of alliance relationships would draw Germany into the decision. If Germany mobilised, however, Russia would mobilise completely, alleging its own defence, which would bring in French support. Russia denies to this day having mobilised, but its preparations were advanced to the extent that once the mobilisation began it was able to proceed in a few days to the deployment of its forces. The memorandum concluded:

> To realise the military measures that we envisage, it is extremely important to know as soon as possible if Russia and France are ready to go to war with Germany. In the event that our neighbours' preparations continue, their mobilisation will be quickly accomplished. For this reason, our military situation can be seen day by day in a less advantageous light, which could have harmful consequences if our potential enemies are in a position to make their preparations in tranquillity.

43 Geiss, *Julikrise*, vol. 1, no. 659.

This text has given rise to numerous interpretations and in particular that it reflected a seizure of power by the army when the 'July crisis' reached its peak. In reality, is it not possible to argue, with Hew Strachan and Samuel Williamson, that Moltke's only concern in this case, what he had to do, was to explain to the government the potential military consequences of the situation? In fact the success of the Schlieffen Plan, as is known, depended on Russian tardiness in mobilisation, which explains very well the anxiety of the German generals. Finally, the essential problem lay elsewhere. It was that Germany depended entirely on such an inflexible military plan and had given priority to strictly military considerations. 'Military needs' had hampered possible political discussions. As we have seen, Moltke's anxiety was such that at around 2.00 p.m. on 30 July he even dared to ask the Austrian military representative in Berlin to start the general mobilisation of Austria-Hungary immediately, in order to force the German government to order mobilisation in response. But there is no proof that this appeal from Moltke had any effect on the decision of the Austrian government, which knew nothing of this intervention until the morning of 31 July.[44] On 30 July, Moltke urgently sought to proceed finally to an inevitable mobilisation; but, as we know, Bethmann Hollweg wished at any cost to await the Russian general mobilisation.

But can one say that the German mobilisation would have been confirmed on 31 July, even if Russia had not mobilised first? This is what Fritz Fischer and his school assert, but it may be doubted, as has already been shown by Jules Isaac, established in detail by Luigi Albertini and demonstrated again with precision by Marc Trachtenberg.[45] There is no certainty at all that Germany would indeed have mobilised if Russia had not moved first: the contrary appears to be true. Moltke did not succeed in making Bethmann Hollweg 'capitulate' before military exigencies: 'Von Moltke was not able to get Bethmann to agree even to the *Kriegsgefahrzustand* ("threatening danger of war") until the news of the Russian general mobilization reached Berlin.'[46] It is, however, true and noteworthy that, once he had been informed of the Russian decision to proceed to general mobilisation, Bethmann Hollweg had no further cards to play, and that he was completely resigned to the situation.

44 *Ibid.*, p. 270; but compare this with Gerhard Ritter, *The Sword and the Scepter*, 4 vols. (Coral Gables, FL: University of Miami Press, 1970), vol. II, p. 258, quoted by Marc Trachtenberg, 'The coming of the First World War: a reassessment', in Trachtenberg, *History and Strategy* (Princeton University Press, 1991), pp. 47–99 (this chapter is an extended version of the frequently cited article by this author: 'The meaning of mobilization in 1914', *International Security*, 15 (1990), p. 89).

45 Trachtenberg, 'The coming of the First World War', pp. 120ff.

46 *Ibid.*, p. 89.

And we follow Marc Trachtenberg again: 'There had been no "loss of control", only an abdication of control.'[47] Since the Russian mobilization, Bethmann Hollweg remained set in his habitual pessimism and held suddenly to a single idea: to do everything to convince the Social Democrats and the nation that Germany was in a defensive situation. Bethmann Hollweg knew that the prize of 'national consensus' lay here.

In reality, the German military men were not the masters of political decisions at the severest moment of the crisis – but in practice it is not realistic to reject the view that the political decision-makers were heavily influenced by the military warnings. In the end, if a climate of risk of war had developed, it was indeed the army leaders who provoked the outbreak of the war, applying pressure on hesitant or paralysed civilian powers.

A careful study of the July crisis shows that the eventual outcome was not inevitable. It is clear that most of the European leaders harboured no wish for this war, and that actors as central as Tsar Nicholas II and Kaiser Wilhelm II hesitated greatly at certain moments. The July crisis could have been concluded like many other earlier crises and the fate of the world would have been different. Why did this not happen? Because certain elements – which were not new – came together and took the lead. This also applied to national feelings which, in Russia just as in Germany, could not be ignored. Although important elements of public opinion and political forces, in particular the socialists, who represented a growing force in the various nations, included a struggle for peace in their plans, international attitudes in general still did not regard war as an absolute evil. And even if the reality of war was increasingly rejected, recourse to armed conflict was a legal and undeniable historical fact, a habit. When all solutions were exhausted, or judged to be exhausted, war remained the solution.

A final feature was substantial. It was said, and accepted, that a European war would be terrible, but no one, either in the armed forces or civilians, had any idea of how terrible it could be. It took more than four years of war for this lesson to be grasped.

47 *Ibid.* p. 91.

3
1915: Stalemate

STÉPHANE AUDOIN-ROUZEAU

The European war which broke out in 1914 acquired its enduring name in the following year: in France it became the *Grande Guerre*, or 'Great War', in Germany it was the *Weltkrieg*, or 'World War'. Here was final confirmation of a genuine awareness at the time that this was indeed a new kind of war which required an appropriate new title. The very considerable interest of this second year of the conflict lies here, in the shift from one form of war to another. Yet collective historical memory now seems to overlook 1915, which has been somewhat neglected: caught between the vast events of the war of movement in the summer and autumn of 1914 and the great wars of materiel in 1916, the second year of the war appears to lack an identity of its own.

Rediscovering 1915 means returning to the sources of the strategic impasse from which the war of position emerged. It also means a return to the comprehensive mobilisation of the societies at war, the essential basis for the prolongation of this new kind of war. This in turn involves examination of the way in which war activity extended its roots into every sector of cultural life. Although mobilisation of every resource – demographic of course, but also economic, moral and cultural – was developing by the end of 1914, its effects only came to be felt during the course of 1915. Only then did European societies, at war since the summer of 1914, tend to become 'societies-for-war'. The year 1915 saw the gradual invention of a new kind of war activity which, in return, permanently transformed the actual image of the war.

Apprenticeship for a static war

The 'map of the war' which defined the general evolution of the conflict is a useful starting place. In this respect, 1915 was a year of strong contrasts. On the 'decisive front', the Western Front – decisive in the sense that, like defeat,

Helen McPhail translated this chapter from French into English.

victory on this front would lead to the defeat or victory of one of the two coalitions engaged – 1915 confirmed and even reinforced the strategic deadlock which was apparent from the autumn of 1914. Yet the war of movement did not cease in 1915. It was still the aim of the belligerents and met with some success where the confrontation was less dense than on the Western Front: in the theatres of the Eastern Front, the Balkans and even more visibly in the Near East, the war of movement alternated with a war of position which imposed its pattern only partially and temporarily.

The long-term digging in along the lines on the Western Front and the slide into static warfare grew out of a strategic and tactical situation which was characteristic of military operations in the First World War, and which established the whole of its evolution: the superiority of the defence over assault. Added to this was the extreme difficulty for the High Command to fully understand this new factor, which had appeared for the first time exactly ten years before 1915 but on a much smaller scale and over a much shorter period: specifically, at the Battle of Mukden in February–March 1905 during the Russo-Japanese War.

At the beginning of 1915 the troops dug into trenches in somewhat summary style. Initially the network of defences dug into the ground, in a mirror image of stone walling, which transformed open warfare into a vast siege war under open skies along a front of 700 kilometres, was not laid out in depth. Behind the front line, along deliberately wavy lines in order to avoid enfilading fire, the trenches were protected by banks of barbed wire, parapets, sandbags and crenellations. Dugouts were set into the sides, designed to protect soldiers from shelling, but as yet no one dreamed of organising more solid reserve positions to the rear. In most cases the front line was linked by a few hundred metres of communication trench to a simple support trench. This turning point of the front line was characteristic of a battle tactic leading to long-term survival: a rigid reading of the principle of defence. This meant holding the front positions in such a way that in case of enemy attack there was no danger of having to retake the line. Further, there was no question of abandoning any particular stretch of front line that was too exposed, or of shortening the lines in the interests of easier defence: the position remained where battle had established it.

Nonetheless, however rigid and relatively provisional, from the beginning of 1915, this defence system showed its superiority over offensive tactics. Several elements contributed to this – barbed wire, which prevented any simple crossing of no-man's-land; infantry rifle fire, above all machine-gun fire, setting up a virtually impassable wall of bullets; and barrages of artillery shells, which shattered assault troops as soon as they left their trench. In 1915 this link between barbed wire and fire from both artillery and machine guns, set up an equation which was impossible for any attacking force to resolve on the Western Front. Some factors intensified this situation: with the prevailing somewhat simple techniques of attack, the temptation was strong to launch troops into an assault without adequate artillery preparation. Without any hope of achieving the essential preliminary destruction of enemy defences, they were doomed to failure from the start and had no hope of reaching the enemy positions. Infantry tactics for crossing no-man's-land were also generally unsophisticated in the first months of 1915.

The major offensives of 1915 – Allied and particularly French, because with the exception of the assault on Ypres in April 1915 the Germans concentrated all their offensive efforts on the Eastern Front – added impetus to defensive planning. Techniques of attack also made progress, notably with the French infantry development of advancing in short rushes behind a rolling artillery barrage, which was dependent on extremely tight coordination between the two military branches. But the development of artillery in the trenches and the widespread use of grenades reinforced the combatants' defensive capacity as much as their offensive strength. At the same time, techniques of defensive organisation of the lines made greater advances. On several occasions the Germans observed the collapse of their front-line position under the blows of the great Allied attacks (as in Artois and Champagne) and learned from this: support trenches were strengthened and supplementary lines of defence were laid out well to the rear. In October 1915, the French High Command in its turn codified the principles of defence in depth, based on the spacing out of several successive lines of trenches. By the end of 1915, therefore, even where the enemy front line was pierced, no one could hope to exploit the initial success. The stopping power of the rear lines, combined with the prompt availability of reserves, enabled enemy advances to be blocked and breaches to be filled.

No one on either side was resigned to a purely defensive war: fearing a collapse in the troops' offensive spirit, Headquarters sought to maintain it by maintaining a permanent state of attack, notably through repeated raids on the enemy lines. Similarly, in an instruction of September 1915, Falkenhayn decreed that rear trenches must not be designated 'fall-back trenches', 'counter-attack trenches', 'defensive trenches' or 'protective trenches'.[1] The very heavy losses on the Western Front during 1915 can be explained largely

1 Anne Duménil, 'De la guerre de mouvement à la guerre de positions: les combattants allemands', in John Horne (ed.), *Vers la guerre totale: le tournant de 1914–1915* (Paris: Tallandier, 2010), p. 59.

by this gap between the cult of the offensive, sustained towards and against everything, a hope of decisive breakthrough which was not eliminated by the digging in of the lines, and a flagrant inability to achieve such a programme of assault. 1915 was not the year of a paradigm shift, and it was the soldiers who paid the price of this ideological rigidity of command.

In this strategic and tactical context, all the great offensives of 1915 on the Western Front ended in bloody setbacks. Although the German army remained essentially in defensive positions in order to to concentrate its attacking powers on the Eastern Front, the Allied offensives rested principally on the shoulders of the French army: despite Kitchener's army's gradual entry into the lines, in 1915 the British Expeditionary Force was still far from being on equal terms with the French and German forces.

The French army first pursued a series of attacks on a moderate scale. In Champagne, following a start in December 1914 which was broken off in mid January, it took the offensive again from mid February to mid March while the British army launched its brief parallel attack at Neuve Chapelle (10–12 March 1915). Then, between 9 May and 18 June, the combined French and British forces launched a massive attack in Artois: in some places this achieved penetration of up to four kilometres in depth along a front of around fifteen kilometres, but without achieving a decisive breakthrough – in static warfare, this breach was too narrow for lasting exploitation. From 25 September, while the British were playing an important role around Loos, the offensive began again in Artois. This time the front, at thirty-five kilometres, was much broader; at the same time, the greatest offensive of the year was launched in Champagne, along a forty-kilometre front. Despite the increased density of field artillery and the mobilisation of heavy artillery for the first time in the French forces, the hoped-for breakthrough was not achieved. Although the German front line was taken and the second line reached in a few places, the arc of field artillery fire had not inflicted sufficient damage on the enemy defensive positions; the German machine guns remained intact and decimated the waves of attack while their batteries, also undamaged, proved the force of their firepower as a barrage or in support of counter-attacks. The two offensives continued until mid October, however, in a pattern characteristic of a war which was slow to learn from an initial setback. Both sides suffered massive losses but, following the logic of static warfare, the numbers of Allied dead and wounded were twice as heavy as those among the defending Germans.

The gap between an offensive effort sustained on both sides and the superiority of defence over attack; the great attempts at breakthrough on one side, but the proliferation of small-scale attacks on the other (the murderous 'nibbling away' of the winter of 1914–15 promoted by the head of the French general staff, Joffre); a doctrine of pushing forward to recover lost positions at any cost; finally, the particularly challenging living conditions of the first year in the trenches, all these were elements which, cumulatively, explain the scale of casualties in 1915. The figures were lower than those for losses in the second half of 1914, proving, from one point of view, the effectiveness of the trenches in providing protection from modern firepower: for both the French and the Germans, 1915 showed a spectacular reduction in the monthly mortality rate of the previous year. Nonetheless, the French army, by far the worst affected, lost 392,000 men during this single year of 1915 – a higher total of violent death and wounding than was to be recorded in any of the three following years.[2]

Casualty figures are not the whole story. In particular, they do not show clearly how levels of brutality in battle increased steadily in the battles of 1915. The long-term installation of the war of position, a defining feature of the second year of the war, also contributed to the institutionalisation of a full range of practices which radicalised the inherent violence of the battlefield. Gradual increases in explosive charges expanded the scale of the mining war and other growing forms of violence also became institutionalised: with a range of around seventy metres, grenades were used increasingly and became one of the infantry's essential fighting tools for attack as well as defence. The enemy drew even closer as weapons for hand-to-hand fighting became more widespread:[3] daggers and bludgeons were distributed to the soldiers, while they often took the initiative in creating such weapons for their own needs. For the offensive in Champagne in September 1915, knives were liberally distributed to the French assault troops. In October, German directives specified in their turn the use of daggers and shovels sharpened on both edges. There is no doubt that during the great offensives of 1916, both sides turned to extreme methods of putting prisoners to death.

The introduction of gas and flamethrowers in the same year marked an inflection in violence of a different order, inflicting death or wounds without breaking the anatomical barrier of the skin, and thus without spilling blood. The flamethrower, originally a German invention which made an occasional appearance from the autumn of 1914, was used by waves of assault troops

2 This represents more than a quarter of French losses for the whole of the war. *Ibid.*, p. 79.

3 Stéphane Audoin-Rouzeau, *Les armes et la chair: trois objets de mort en 1914–1918* (Paris: A. Colin, 2009).

from mid 1915 before coming into general use in the French army. The appearance of gas as a battlefield weapon was on a much greater range. A first threshold was breached early in 1915, when asphyxiating forms of gas – chlorine, at this stage – replaced tear gas and suffocating gas products used in the autumn of 1914. Their first use at the end of January 1915 on the Vistula was a failure due to the wind and cold, but the second trial, at Ypres on 22 April, during the only German offensive on the Western Front, was a shock. The attack, which took the form of a drifting wave of chlorine released into the atmosphere from gas cylinders, brought to the site and hidden in the front lines, caused massive panic among Allied troops: a three-kilometre-wide breakthrough was achieved, the right bank of the Yser had to be abandoned and liaison between the French and British forces was broken in a front zone of high strategic sensitivity. But the Germans, surprised by their own success and by changes in wind patterns, failed to exploit the breakthrough, and from 26 April the front was stabilised once more.

Then the escalation began. By early June the French artillery was already capable of responding, using gas shells during the offensive in Artois. On 25 September it was the turn of the British to use gas for the first time, at Loos. In October, in Champagne, the 'race to toxicity'[4] crossed a first threshold with the German use of chlorine with added phosgene.

At Ypres, despite the panic among the French troops caused by the attack of 22 April, the British and Canadian counter-attacks managed to close the breach: in the end, the terrain lost at the end of May remained limited and the Ypres salient, although broached, was intact. Elsewhere, defensive measures such as gas masks advanced more rapidly than the means of assault and reduced the anticipated effectiveness of gas as a weapon of attack. Although it was seen at the time as a major rupture, for which the Allies immediately cast the blame firmly on Germany, nonetheless in this domain too defence overcame attack: in December 1915 a fresh gas attack at Ypres was a complete failure.

This superiority of defence over attack was repeated all the more easily elsewhere because the experience of static warfare was broadly valid on other fronts. This applied to the Germans on the Eastern Front, in the Near East and at Gallipoli.

The principle of the operation in the Dardanelles – driven politically by Winston Churchill, First Lord of the Admiralty, and imposed on the military forces – was accepted by the British and French governments in January and

4 Olivier Lepick, *La Grande Guerre chimique, 1914–1918* (Paris: PUF, 1998).

February respectively. Designed to take control of the Dardanelles Straits and Constantinople while simultaneously creating solid and direct liaison with Russia, the plan for the operation was an interesting attempt to get round the strategic blockade in the West, supported by the British navy. But it was precisely the offensive move which failed when the British and French fleets were unable to force their passage through the Dardanelles on 18 March. The laborious landing of British, New Zealand, Australian and French troops on the Gallipoli peninsula, which began on 25 April, was also a failure: the troops were pinned down on the beaches and dominated by Ottoman defensive positions. In August, fresh landings by night further to the north also failed to break the stalemate. By the end of the summer all the troops present on the peninsula were immobilised in a dense network of trenches, similar to those on the Western Front but concentrated into a much smaller area. In November, evacuation was agreed on, and was carried out in masterly fashion from the end of December. The end of 1915 thus saw the failure of a strategically imaginative undertaking, which had been broken on insurmountable tactical obstacles and a series of errors in the preparing and carrying out of the operation.

When Italy entered the war on the side of the Allies in May 1915, the Austro-Italian front presented an even more sharply defined state of stalemate. Because of the mountainous terrain, the Isonzo front provided the only possible terrain where an offensive strategy could be envisaged. But from June to November 1915 the four Italian offensives on the Isonzo, with inadequate artillery support, failed one after the other, gaining only minimal territorial advances at the cost of increasingly heavy losses. By the end of the year, losses in the Italian army had reached over 200,000 men killed and wounded, against an Austrian figure of 165,000. The unfolding of operations on the Austro-Italian front brought fresh proof of the impossibility of any breach in a defensive front line that was solidly established, above all when the terrain added to the difficulties inherent in any attack.

Maintaining momentum

Even so, the war of movement was not dead in 1915. The warring nations continued to believe in it, particularly as the German High Command turned its main efforts to the East in the hope of then being able to concentrate fully on the Western Front. In the East, in fact, movement could still be achieved between long periods of immobility: lacking the manpower and the defensive network in terms of artillery and logistics, the Eastern Front was less dense than its equivalent in the West. Despite extremely severe weather conditions, the Austro-German High Commands launched a double offensive in mid January, in a pincer movement against the Russian wings, starting in the Carpathians and East Prussia. The first failed to recapture Galicia from the Russians as they advanced in the Carpathians and also forced the Germans to capitulate at Przemyśl on 22 March. The second German offensive was successful, however, and the Russian front gave way early in February. The winter battle of the Masurian Lakes left more than 90,000 prisoners in German hands together with a vast quantity of materiel. The Russian retreat covered nearly 130 kilometres.

In April the German High Command went on the offensive again in Galicia. The Austro-German attack broke through for the first time early in May at Gorlice-Tarnów, forcing the Russians into an initial retreat on a 160-kilometre front: Przemyśl first, then Lemberg, fell in June. The next German move was northwards, a thrust towards the Warsaw salient: the Russian lines were broken on 13 July to the north of the city, which fell on 4 August, while the German armies continued their frontal assault. Brest-Litovsk was taken on 26 August, Grodno and Vilna in September, while the advance on a very broad front continued towards Minsk.

By the end of the month, the German and Austro-Hungarian forces, exhausted by five months of uninterrupted and murderous fighting, could go no further. And yet the 'great advance' of the Germans was the chief military victory in 1915: Russia lost Galicia, Poland, Lithuania and Courland in their 'Great Retreat', representing a withdrawal of 250 kilometres between January and September, provoking the decision of the Tsar to take over the military High Command in person. Since May, the Russian army had lost 2 million men, including a million prisoners.[5] It did not collapse, however, and resisted any separate peace with Germany.

The Austro-German success on the Eastern Front was matched by parallel success on the Balkan front, at the same time establishing liaison between the Central Powers, Ottoman Turkey and Bulgaria. While the latter took its place alongside the Central Powers on 1 September, two German and Austro-Hungarian armies attacked on the Sava and the Danube on 6 October, just as Anglo-French forces were landing at Salonica, too late to come to the help of Serbia. Belgrade fell on 9 October, while Bulgaria in its turn entered the stage on 14 October, outflanking the Serbian army from the south. At the beginning of December, with Serbia entirely occupied, the remains of its army had no

5 Norman Stone, *The Eastern Front, 1914–1917* (London: Penguin, 1998), p. 191.

alternative but to set off for the Adriatic at the cost of a murderous winter march through the Albanian mountains, while the Allied troops had no choice but to withdraw to the Greek frontier.

In the Near East, military operations were even more dominated by movement. The beginning of the year was initially marked by fruitless Ottoman Turkish attacks on the defences of the Suez Canal. From April to November 1915, the British forces moved up the River Tigris to a distance of around thirty kilometres from Baghdad before clashing with Ottoman Turkish resistance at Ctesiphon, forcing them into a difficult retreat of 160 kilometres to Kut-al-Amara, which was encircled in December.

Thus by the end of 1915, not only had movement continued to be the order of the day everywhere except on the Western Front, but even there, the end of 1915 showed that there was still hope of a breakthrough followed by a return to manoeuvre. Indeed, by the end of 1915 vast battles of materiel were being planned for the following year: at the turn of the year the Germans had not yet decided on the project to attack Verdun, but the inter-Allied conference at Chantilly on 6–8 December 1915 made the decision in principle to plan for a general simultaneous offensive on all fronts. Substantial breakthroughs were expected in Galicia on one side, on the Somme on the other. For the Allies, this was the first real attempt at combined strategic coordination.

Violence against unarmed populations

The events of 1914 had established mass attacks on unarmed civilians as the order of the day. The '1914 invasions' had been accompanied by serial atrocities, more numerous, however, in the West by Germans than in the East by Russians: civilians massacred, but also soldiers wounded after laying down their weapons, villages or whole towns burned, women raped, and so on.[6] All these practices stimulated movements of mass exodus: the effects of the refugee phenomenon, a central feature of the outbreak of war, continued to be felt throughout 1915, upsetting the fragile equilibrium of the home fronts.

Although in the West the attacks on unarmed populations were limited to 1914, it was in 1915 that *awareness* of the attacks spread through the warring nations: the commissions set up by all the nations at war to enquire into failings affecting 'human rights' made their reports from the beginning of the

6 John Horne and Alan Kramer, *German Atrocities, 1914: A History of Denial* (New Haven, CT: Yale University Press, 2001).

second year of the war. Their content was then widely taken up by the press, in popular literature, caricature, posters, film and so on. This moment of 'revelation' of the violence of the 'Other', accompanied by written and pictorial records, themselves very violent, constitutes an essential phase in the fixation of mutual hatreds. During 1915, for example, the 'war cultures' became enduringly crystallised around a body of mobilising themes, words and images which confirmed the meaning initially attributed to the war itself – both in justifying its continuation and the new sacrifices that this implied. This was particularly the case when atrocities continued to feature in powerful replays of memory: for the Allies, the sinking of the *Lusitania*, which caused the death of 1,198 civilians on 7 May 1915, or the execution of Edith Cavell in Belgium in October,[7] forcefully revived memories of the atrocities of invasion the year before. The bombing of civilian targets – in south-east England, London and also Paris – created very few victims and did very little material damage, but nonetheless indicated a further major rupture: without true strategic objective, they signalled that enemy populations in their entirety were henceforward considered enemies and were therefore now a legitimate target. The extension of institutionalised concentration – with the prolonged internment, on both sides, of non-national individuals present on national soil at the time of the outbreak of war – was fundamentally part of the same logic.

All the same, 1915 brought a certain degree of stabilisation in the West: although it led to a logic of repression in the case of the occupied population, the establishment of a regime of occupation meant an end to the straightforward brutality of the summer and autumn of 1914. In the Balkans, on the other hand, the assaults of the invasion remained part of daily life during the second year of the war. In this way the third invasion of Serbia by German, Austro-Hungarian and Bulgarian troops during the second half of 1915 involved ferocious treatment of civilians. Violent assaults were inflicted on the Serbian and Greek populations of Kosovo and Macedonia when they were invaded in October by Bulgarian troops. On the Eastern Front, the situation was different again: civilian populations there suffered from a long war of movement throughout 1915. The war provoked massive movements of exodus – 4 million people in all, fleeing the German armies, but also from May onwards the Russian authorities' 'scorched earth' policy; above all the assaults took the form of deportations operated by Russian civilian and military authorities related to ethnic nationality and origin. They were

7 The nurse Edith Cavell belonged to a clandestine Brussels organisation which helped Allied prisoners to escape to the Netherlands.

aimed at Austro-Hungarian and German subjects and Russian subjects of German origin, as well as a large fraction of the Jews of the Russian Empire who were seen as 'unreliable elements' and thus likely to aid the invader. The great Russian retreat between May and September accentuated the process; in 1915 alone, 134,000 German and Austrian civilians were deported and assigned to live in the Russian interior. From the summer, the process began to expropriate and deport most of the 700,000 German settlers from Western Ukraine. Although direct physical violence was not entirely absent from this exercise, it remained occasional, as in the great anti-German pogrom in Moscow on 26–29 May 1915. In the case of the Jewish population of Galicia, on the other hand, the procedure was one of deportation and extreme brutality accompanied by systematic pogroms and physical elimination (see below).[8]

The regimes of occupation which were established in the West from the end of 1914, and during the following year in the East and in the Balkans, are evidence of the significance of the territory conquered by the Central Powers during 1915 – territory which also grew larger month by month. At the beginning of the year the German forces occupied almost all of Belgium (7 million inhabitants) and nine departments of the regions of the north and east of France (3 million); but in October it was the entire population of Russia's Polish territories (6 million) which was living under German and Austro-Hungarian occupying forces. Belgrade also fell in October, and before the end of 1915 it was the turn of Serbia to fall under a regime of occupation. In all, at the end of the year 19 million people were living under German, Austro-Hungarian or Bulgarian occupation.[9]

A very varied range of mechanisms was established for the supervision of occupied territories, themselves in widely contrasting conditions by the end of the invasion period with its associated forms of violence. For the occupying powers, the primary concern was the material exploitation of resources; the local occupied population was itself an important local resource, to be put to active use as part of the invaders' war effort. Violence was part of this process, less in relation to the German occupation in Belgium and the north and east of France than to the Austro-Hungarian presence in Serbia and above all the Bulgarians in Macedonia; in these latter regions, instead of the occupation bringing an end to the violence of the invasion it created a new situation which allowed it to continue.

8 Peter Holquist, 'Les violences de l'armée russe à l'encontre des Juifs en 1915: causes et limites', in Horne (ed.), *Vers la guerre totale*, pp. 191–219.

9 Sophie de Schaepdrijver, 'L'Europe occupée en 1915: entre violence et exploitation', in Horne (ed.), *Vers la guerre totale*, pp. 121–51.

On the other hand, the German and Austro-Hungarian occupations of the second year of the war, however severe, constituted a stage designed to re-establish order. Military engagements, the Russian scorched earth policy and depopulation as a result of the massive exodus had inflicted terrible suffering on the occupied territories. Epidemics of typhus, malaria and cholera were rife. Several occupation regimes developed in this space characterised by a mosaic of complex ethnicities regarded as 'uncivilised' by the Germans: the Russian areas of Poland were divided between an Austro-Hungarian administration around Lublin on the one hand and a German zone with Warsaw at its centre on the other. Combining northern Poland, Lithuania, part of Belorussia and Courland, the Ober Ost represented a veritable German military colony.[10]

Although the reorganised regions of Central and Eastern Europe were not yet settled by the end of 1915, the occupation was clearly visible in the establishment of a certain degree of appeasement and legitimation of the occupying power. It was in this sense that one can speak of a 'long' 1915,[11] characterised by relatively moderate regimes of occupation, before their radicalisation in 1916.

With the massacre of part of their own population by certain warring states – Russian Jews, Assyrian Christians and above all Armenians in the Ottoman Empire – 1915 was also characterised by an unprecedented radicalisation of violence towards populations seen as too unreliable to be left alive in their towns and villages. It was in this sense that the second year of the war played a central role in the process of totalisation and 'brutalisation' of the war.

The first mass expulsions of Jewish communities by the Russian army occurred in the autumn of 1914 in Poland, and from the start were accompanied by acts of violence committed by the troops: to the traditional anti-Jewish prejudice was added here a new form of anti-Semitism, focused on a population seen as politically and militarily 'dangerous'. It was repeated early in 1915 in Austrian Galicia, this time in a region under temporary occupation. From the end of April expulsion turned into deportation on a massive scale. While assaults developed in parallel with the reverses suffered by the Russian army from May, the deportations expanded with the 'Great Retreat', henceforward touching communities located well beyond the front line and forcing abolition of the residential restrictions hitherto imposed on

10 Vejas Gabriel Liulevicius, *War Land on the Eastern Front: Culture, National Identity and German Occupation in World War I* (Cambridge University Press, 2000).

11 *Ibid.*, p. 150.

Jews in Russia. In this way a million Jews in all were forcibly displaced during 1915.

Apart from the heavy death toll resulting from the hunger and exhaustion which accompanied these measures, pogroms were part of the mass deportations. Here the army played a major role, unlike the anti-Jewish assaults of pre-1914, which were condemned by the authorities. Nonetheless, programmes of deportation were broken off in the autumn and the anti-Jewish measures of 1915 ceased to follow a rising curve. At the same time, there was no move to a policy of generalised massacre.[12]

A precisely opposite process occurred with the Armenians of the Ottoman Empire, whose genocide was one of the major events of 1915.[13] Without entering into deterministic detail, it appears that the Armenians of the Empire had been targeted well before the outbreak of war, as seen in the widespread plundering and large-scale massacres of 1894–6 and 1909. In addition, although the war should not be seen as the principal rationale for the genocide, the reading of the war by the Young Turks movement was undoubtedly significant in the designation of Armenian communities as 'the internal enemy'. The jihad proclaimed in November 1914 thus placed the Christians of the East (like the Syrian Christians, who were also massacred) in the position of legitimate victims of the Muslims. The setting of a pan-Turkish ethnicity designated the Armenians as potential enemies of the 'Turkish race' destined to regenerate the Empire. Finally, the vicissitudes of the war also contributed to setting a cumulative genocidal spiral in motion. The anti-Armenian policy thus grew more intense with each new military threat: in January, at the time of the Russian victory of Sarkamish in the Caucasus; in March, with the Russian victories in Persia and the Franco-British attack on the strongpoints of the Dardanelles; in April, at the time of the Allied landings on the Gallipoli peninsula and the fresh Ottoman setbacks in Persia; in May–June, during the Van uprising (a defensive movement which escaped the massacre) and the Russian advance in Anatolia. Against the setback to their external military projects, the Young Turks' leadership to some extent turned to the destruction of the designated internal enemy.

The first massacres began in January 1915. On 24 April came the arrest followed by the killing of more than 2,300 Armenian intellectuals and distinguished figures of Constantinople. Mass deportation orders aimed at the

12 Holquist, 'Les violences de l'armée russe', pp. 191–219.

13 Donald Bloxham, 'Les causes immédiates de la destruction des Arméniens ottomans', in Horne (ed.), *Vers la guerre totale*, pp. 247–70.

eastern provinces of the Empire were not launched as such until the end of May: it was these which signalled the intention to eradicate the Armenian community. From June onwards the forced displacement was accompanied by systematic massacres carried out by the Kurdish tribes, unionist agents, the police and the Turkish people themselves. The use of forms of cruelty was systematic; in the camps established in Mesopotamia and Syria, the survivors who had not died on the journey (that is, a fifth of those deported) were to die of hunger, thirst and sickness, or would later be massacred within the camps themselves. This process of elimination, 'improvised along the way'[14] and according to a 'cumulative logic'[15] of eradication, brought about the death of more than a million individuals out of a total of between 1.8 and 2 million Armenians living in the Empire before 1914.

These applications of extreme violence, which culminated in genocide in the case of the Armenians and the many variations – on the battlefields in respect of wounded men and prisoners, or focused on civilian populations, or again in indirect and invisible forms of blockade (see below) – were all central to the establishment on both sides of the warring societies of a powerfully mobilising logic of justification. In this context, the year of 1915 can be seen as the moment of full flowering of the different national 'war cultures', transmitting diverse ways in which contemporaries represented, and represented to themselves, a conflict in which they were, directly or indirectly, simultaneously victims and actors. All of them transmitted extreme hostility to the enemy. In such conditions, challenges to the validity of the war existed but were extremely minor. Self-censorship in the media was largely complicit in the universally established management of information; few intellectuals, writers, scientists or artists escaped self-mobilisation in the service of their own country. Forms of political rallying round the existing powers – the '*union sacrée*' in France, *Burgfrieden* in Germany, the Asquith coalition Cabinet in Great Britain in May 1915, the Duma–government alliance on the Russian economic management of the war in August – were universally absorbed and even deepened, leaving minimal space for any forces of dispute over the war.

This was the case of the 'national' claims at the heart of the Austro-Hungarian and Russian Empires: the mutiny of certain Czechoslovak regiments sounded a disturbing forewarning in April 1915, but only in retrospect would the creation in London of the Czech National Committee in November, looking towards a future Czecho-Slovak state, gain its full stature. The same applies to the first breaches at the heart of the working world.

14 *Ibid.*, p. 266. 15 *Ibid.*, p. 270.

Russia's first strikes broke out in the winter of 1914. In Western Europe, the first protest movements came in February 1915 in Glasgow and the Clyde valley, followed by a strike of Welsh miners in July: nonetheless, the Munitions of War Act, of the same month, which set up special tribunals to settle work disputes and to set wage and skill levels in war industries, showed that worker participation in the British industrial effort had to be negotiated with the trade unions. In fact, social conflict in 1915 was averted by rent control and other measures of accommodation of workers' grievances. Inflation was very noticeable from 1915 because of the distribution of paper money and the various bottlenecks that strangled production (notably agricultural); but in the Entente powers food supplies remained acceptable and standards of living were stabilised. In addition, strikes, frequent at the outbreak of the war, disappeared with industrial mobilisation. Although the situation was from the first more difficult in the Central Powers, where the blockade meant that problems in the food supply were felt very quickly (bread was rationed in Germany from January 1915), real social difficulties and ruptures in the consensus were not seen until after 1915.

At the time, direct opposition to the war had little popular support on either side. The socialist minority in Germany, which showed its opposition to the pursuit of the war from the beginning of 1915 and dared to vote against the military credits in December, remained restrained. In September, the denunciation of the war by minority socialists at their Zimmerwald gathering in Switzerland found no further echo, any more than the 'address to warring peoples and to their governments' from Pope Benedict XV at the end of July. In this second year of the war, appeals of this nature still fell on deaf ears.

Development of the war logic and the process of totalisation

On 24 January 1915, a brief naval encounter on the Dogger Bank in the North Sea proved that any major offensive by the German fleet against the British navy was doomed to failure. Thereafter, naval surface warfare remained of very limited significance. Still, the question of control of the seas was of central importance during the course of 1915. The blockade imposed on the Central Powers, and the submarine war designed in response to unlock its grip, were thus determining elements in totalisation of the conflict. The consequences of the blockade, in terms of food supply and the economy on the one hand and of military and diplomatic matters on the other – and, finally, of morale – were indeed considerable. They were to be an enduring burden throughout the rest of the war.

The blockade began in the autumn of 1914, with the British declaration that the North Sea was now a 'war zone'. This statement was open to challenge in international law, but it resulted in the blockade of the neutral ports and shipping used for a large proportion of German imports. Early in February 1915 this embargo elicited a protest in which it was described as a barbarous way of undertaking a form of war designed to overcome the enemy through hunger. Here lay the origins of the submarine war, launched as a legitimate response through the affirmation of a violation of human rights. In return, the classification of the waters surrounding Great Britain as a 'war zone' and the proclamation of submarine warfare provoked the British Reprisals Order of early March 1915, which radicalised the economic war by allowing the seizure of *any* merchandise of German origin, or destined for Germany, via inspection of all neutral shipping.

Early in 1915, the German submarine war was based on a very limited body of submariners. From the beginning of February, with the German declaration of British coasts as a 'war zone', these men, who had hitherto been engaged in regular warfare against enemy shipping, changed their practices: German submarines were now authorised to sink civilian shipping of the French and British merchant fleets without warning – nearly 580 ships were sunk in this way between February and September. This was the context, early in May, in which the British merchant ship *Lusitania* was torpedoed. Around 1,198 passengers died, including 128 Americans, and the shock produced by this direct attack on civilian life was exploited intensively in Allied propaganda. Faced with the force of the American reaction, the German government gave up a style of submarine warfare in which international diplomatic risks were all too obvious, limiting itself thereafter to targeting British shipping as it transported troops to the continent. The political powers then resisted the demands of the High Command which wished to use the undersea arm to an unlimited extent, that is, against any ship without restriction and whatever its nationality.

The gradual totalisation of the war evidently did not always proceed according to cumulative logic in 1915: despite the serious situation in getting supplies into Germany, certain steps back remained possible during this second year of the war. However, the effects of the blockade very soon made themselves felt in the treatment of occupied populations and of soldiers in prisoner-of-war camps. In this respect the blockade and Germany's early food-supply problems legitimised the requisitions operated in the occupied territories and the rationing system imposed on their civilian populations: total exploitation (ameliorated to some extent by the Commission of Relief for Belgium) was established. But the blockade also legitimised the harsh food regime imposed on French and British prisoners of war: in clear breach of Article 7 of the Hague Conventions prescribing food supplies for military prisoners equal to that of soldiers in the captor country, supplies in their camps declined considerably in both quantity and quality.[16] In mid 1915 the situation in the camps deteriorated still further with the interruption of food aid supplies sent via Switzerland from warring and neutral countries.

In 1915 the nations of the Entente established a system of drawing on international resources – principally American, thanks to Morgan's Bank – in the service of the war effort.[17] Meanwhile, the measures for the comprehensive naval blockade of Germany and their stiffening, together with the German reaction on the other, both at sea and on land in the occupied territories and the prisoners' camps, showed the extent to which from 1915 onwards the blockade helped to extend and intensify the violence of the war.[18] Through restrictions, above all nutritional – still relatively limited in 1915, unlike the following years – suffered by the German and Austro-Hungarian populations, the societies of the Central Powers became more clearly integrated into the logic of a war in the course of radicalisation. The consequences in terms of representations of the war are significant: as a powerful reinforcement of a besieged fortress mentality, already apparent in 1914, the blockade effectively contributed to the growing totalisation of the war.[19]

With two new belligerent nations joining the war (Italy in May in support of the Entente, Bulgaria in October on the side of the Central Powers), 1915 would see only a limited extension of the war's territorial hold in Europe. On the other hand, the conflict steadily continued to plunge its roots ever deeper into the very heart of the societies at war.

From 1915 the prolongation of such a murderous and costly war constituted a demographic challenge. Although nations with universal conscription such

16 Uta Hinz, *Gefanen im Grossen Krieg: Kreigsgefangenschaft in Deutschland, 1914–1921* (Essen: Klartext Verlag, 2006). Heather Jones, *Violence against Prisoners of War: Britain, France and Germany, 1919–1920* (Cambridge University Press, 2011).

17 Kathleen Burk, *Britain, America and the Sinews of War, 1914–1918* (London: Allen & Unwin, 1985).

18 Gerd Krumeich, 'Le blocus maritime et la guerre sous-marine', in Horne (ed.), *Vers la guerre totale*, pp. 175–90.

19 *Ibid.*, p. 177.

as Germany, France or Russia remained capable of filling the gaps resulting from battles without any need to change their system of recruitment,[20] the United Kingdom was differently placed: despite the massive volunteer movement of 1914 and the recruitment of a million further men for the Kitchener army in 1915, such numbers did not provide a demographic base capable of meeting the demands of the British war effort. July 1915 saw the introduction of a compulsory census of all adult males (the National Registration Act) followed at the end of 1915 with the shift to compulsory conscription from 1 January 1916.

The demographic effort also drew directly on Empire territories, and 1915 saw the quasi-completion of the conquest of the German colonies with the capitulation of South West Africa in July.[21] Great Britain mobilised her colonies, with India in the lead (particularly in sending troops to the Middle East), and the Dominions sent large numbers of volunteers to Gallipoli (Australians, New Zealanders) and the Western Front (Canadians). For the French, it was North Africa and sub-Saharan Africa (French West Africa) which constituted the main source of recruitment of troops destined to be used against the Germans. From November 1914 and continuing for nine months, this pressure from the colonial force provoked the largest African revolt stirred up by forced recruitment throughout the modern states of west Burkina and south-east Mali.

The challenge of 1915 was also economic. The background to the organisation of war economies was a net drop in industrial and agricultural production in all the warring nations, with the possible exception of the United Kingdom.[22] Originally, this industrial mobilisation was linked, fundamentally, to the consumption of munitions on all the fronts that were active during the first months of the war, and to the grave supply crisis which followed in all the belligerent nations. In this respect, although the first measures of industrial mobilisation were taken in 1914, it was during 1915 that their principal consequences became apparent.

20 Searching all the while, however, to pick up the largest possible number of men available, as in the Dalbiez Law in France, voted in August 1915.

21 The struggle continued only in South West Africa, although it continued there until the end of the war.

22 In relation to 1913, the drop in production was calculated at 25 per cent in France in 1915, 15 per cent in Germany, 10 per cent in Austria-Hungary and 5 per cent in Russia. This reduction was not made up for through imports. (Theo Balderston, 'Industrial mobilization and war economies', in John Horne (ed.), *A Companion to World War I* (Chichester: Wiley-Blackwell, 2010), pp. 227–249.)

Even so they sometimes appeared gradually. Great Britain's turn towards a true war economy, for example, had barely begun by the end of 1914 and developed only slowly. Without direct territorial threat and without general mobilisation capable of upsetting agricultural and industrial production, the measures of setting a war economy in hand were initially limited in scale. However, a turning point can be identified during 1915, in the context of a scandal connected to the munitions crisis, as revealed in the battles which involved the British Expeditionary Force. A new ministry extending state control over a vital industrial sector was set up in May 1915: in the hands of Lloyd George, the Ministry of Munitions was now empowered to act decisively in supervising the production and management of armaments, machinery, raw materials and prices. Further, with the law of July 1915 giving full powers of economic mobilisation to the executive, several vital sectors passed into state supervision by means of requisitioning – without, however, going so far as direct administration. In a government/industry confrontation, the state thus established firmly its oversight of the distribution of raw materials and food supplies, at the same time maintaining an overall liberal framework, which included a degree of profit motive to encourage entrepreneurs.

In the case of France,[23] the decisive moment in industrial mobilisation can be located in 1914 – more precisely on 20 September, at the time of the Bordeaux Conference which brought the main French industrialists together with the War Ministry as it sought to make good the shortages of shells and guns. Contrary to the situation in Britain, the launch of a war industry in France came up against a double stranglehold: shortage of workforce and loss of the industrial regions of the north and the east. These lay behind a massive fall (50 per cent or more) in the production of coal, iron and steel. In 1915 the state deliberately and wisely gave priority to industry in enabling half a million mobilised workers to return from the army to the factory. At the same time, a large-scale appeal was made to foreign and colonial workers and also to women. Faced with the heavy deficit in raw materials, the planning of imports began in November 1915. A decisive role was played by the Comité des Forges, which was rewarded with a monopoly of import and distribution. In managing supplies to metallurgy in this way, French industry developed its own organisation independent of the state, through its organisation into manufacturing groups under a major business 'group leader'. The system – a form of

23 Patrick Fridenson (ed.), *The French Home Front, 1914–1918* (Oxford: Berg, 1993).

cartel of large armaments firms enabling coordination and centralisation – was launched in 1914 and developed effectively in 1915. From the second year of the war, as Paris and its region became a major industrial centre, armaments production made a great leap forward: although demand exceeded supply, from the summer of 1915 the production of rifles was multiplied five-fold, that of shells ten-fold and that of explosives six-fold.

At the core of the French state's armaments programme was the Directorate of Artillery located in the War Ministry. In May 1915 this Directorate became an autonomous Under-secretariat of State for Artillery (led by the socialist, Albert Thomas). In July 1915, the title of the responsible authority was changed to that of an Under-secretariat of State for Artillery and Munitions, again with Thomas at its head. The latter played a decisive role in coordination between the High Command, the state and industry, as well as in the planning of armaments production, while still maintaining a liberal framework which respected private initiative and authorised the search for profit.

Similarly in Germany, the effects of the blockade and mobilisation of the workforce in terms of a large conscripted army forced the establishment of economic mobilisation, and in 1914 the industrialist, Walther Rathenau, proposed the necessary plan at the War Ministry. On this basis, an 'Office of Raw Materials of War' (Kriegsrohstoffabteilung or KRA) was created, prepared to undertake the first measures of economic planning; large companies were brought together to work for the national defence in compulsory cartels (*Kriegsgesellschaften*) which were dominated by the largest *Konzern* but directed jointly by entrepreneurs and civil servants. Stocks of raw materials were requisitioned and distributed appropriately, with priority of delivery to factories involved in war production. Research into substitute products was encouraged. From the beginning of 1915 this system offered a solution to the German war economy at least temporarily, characterised by an army/industry face-to-face management based on the Office of Raw Materials of War, under military direction. In fact the preconditions were now in place for a segmented war economy in which the army had every opportunity of gaining priority for supplies. This was contrary to the war economies established on the French and British model, in which the state remained capable of arbitrating as necessary between the needs of the two fronts – military and domestic – and thus between war industries and domestic supply industries. Nonetheless, after 1915 the superiority of the second model emerged fully.

Among the Great Powers, it was in Russia that the crisis of shell supplies, clearly evident from September 1914 onwards, reached its peak at the beginning of 1915. It was also in Russia that it lasted the longest, in large part due to transportation problems: in May 1915, which marked the beginning of the great Russian retreat, at the time of the break in the front, it could even be considered dramatic. From January to April the Russian army received fewer than 2 million shells, at a point when the same quantity *per month* would have been far from adequate.

No more than any other power had Russia foreseen the need for a production and distribution system organised 'in depth' in the case of war: as elsewhere, the accent had been on the accumulation of stocks. But it was the Russian delay in building a war economy in 1915 that defines its particular place among the leading nations at war. The combination of the Russian War Ministry's unjustified resistance over the nation's capacity to develop its own production, and its equally unjustified confidence in the Allies' capacity to provide aid, led to considerable delay in the establishment of a home-based industrial production system. Thus the massive orders passed to external production at the beginning of 1915 resulted in due course in very disappointing deliveries, aggravated by material difficulties of supply in Russia, problems of transport and a chain of distrust between the principal actors – Headquarters, War Ministry, entrepreneurs and government. This over-tardy development of a war economy resulted in inadequate armaments production being maintained to a much later stage than in the other warring economies.

And yet, in May, Russia's greatest industrialists came together in a 'special council for the examination and harmonisation of measures required for the defence of the nation', in order to take control of the war effort. In June, this structure included the local Committees of War Industries allied to the union of zemstvos local authorities. From this moment, the framework for a war economy was established. The special council, dominated by large entrepreneurs and monopolies, had 2 million workers under its wing. It divided the country into eleven regions, each one with a plenipotentiary official at its head to set prices and wages and if necessary to arrange requisitions to their best advantage.

The year 1915 was thus identified as a first point of take-off for production,[24] even though it continued to be hampered by multiple pinch-points characteristic of an accelerated crisis of growth. No matter: at the cost of this gigantic industrial effort launched in 1915 and sustained in the following year, the superiority in materiel, and no longer simply in men, was to tip in favour of the Russian army in 1916.

24 Stone, *The Eastern Front*, p. 209.

In return, the financing of the war – in 1915 this absorbed around a quarter of the expenditure of the various warring states[25] – did not produce a tipping point of the same kind. In this respect, it was Great Britain which initially made the greatest innovations. With an effective tax system already in place before 1914, the United Kingdom chose to apply intensified fiscal pressure: beginning with the first wartime budget, the number of those subject to income tax was increased, and on 1 December 1914 the rate was increased. The British government was also the first to tax war profits with a special tax of 50 per cent.

The other powers retained more classic policies. France was already in a state of full fiscal reorganisation on the eve of war; in addition, the occupation of part of its most productive territory sharply reduced its resources. Initially, it therefore refused to increase existing taxes and create new ones. Income tax (introduced on 15 July 1914) would not be applied until 1 January 1916. As a result, the resources of the French state continued to diminish in 1915 (as also happened in Russia). Germany, where the budget was also poorly adapted to modern warfare, announced in March 1915 that in order to avoid increasing the burden of charges weighing upon its population, no new taxes would be imposed. Military costs would be taken into a special budget provisionally fed by borrowing ahead of payment on the understanding that it would be repaid by the future losing side. The income from indirect taxation would not enable the Reich to do more than maintain the stability of its tax receipts during 1915, not to increase them.

None of the nations at war had a fiscal system capable of meeting the costs of the war; all had recourse to credit – in France, this applied from the beginning of 1915, in the form of Treasury Bonds and long-term war loans. In March and again in June, the British government launched two large loans, as did Germany in the same year. France, after its success with 'Bonds of National Defence' in September 1914, launched its first large loan in November 1915. At the same time, external credits were underwritten by the Allies with American banks: in mid October, a banking consortium under the aegis of Morgan's Bank lent $500 million to the British and French governments. Finally, apart from the tax on war profits introduced very early in Britain, 1915 did not see the emergence of true innovations designed to finance the costs of the war. Similarly, the change of scale in fiscal pressure

25 This included 25 per cent for Great Britain and France, 27 per cent for Germany, 22 per cent for Austria-Hungary and 24 per cent for Russia (Balderston, 'Industrial mobilization and war economies', p. 222).

and public borrowing would be effective at a later stage. In this respect, 1915 can be recorded as a relatively gentle transition between the financial norms of peacetime and the new demands of modern warfare.

Conclusion

As the historian John Horne has rightly written, it was in 1915 that 'the war [became] a world in itself'.[26] Nonetheless, the second year of the war can be seen in a complex and ambiguous light. Rather than a brisk turning point in the history of conflict, it can perhaps be described as a curve. On certain points, of course, the rupture is clear. It was in 1915 that the first great attempts at breakthrough were launched against an organised defensive front, and it was also in 1915 that they failed at the cost of bloody sacrifices which foreshadowed the immense battles of materiel of the following year; it was in 1915 that completely new forms of combat – such as gas – were introduced, giving contemporaries a clear sense of historic rupture; it was in 1915 that the Allied blockade, destined to create a later and tragic excess death rate at the heart of the Central Powers, was tightened, while initially provoking a type of counter-measure – submarine warfare – of extreme brutality; 1915 was the year when civilian populations were first shelled without military objective, and suspect populations deported. After the atrocities of the invasions of 1914 – which tended to continue into 1915 on fronts which remained mobile – these acts of war, of a new kind, signalled a depth of hostility to the 'Other' in which no part of the 'enemy' population within would be spared: it was in 1915, finally, that the first genocide of the twentieth century was committed.[27] In a context of extreme 'negative mobilisation',[28] 1915 confirms that the totality of the enemy population – and sometimes a part of one's own people – was now *the enemy*, and not only the nation's armed and fighting fraction.

But the year 1915 cannot be summed up solely in terms of these undeniable developments, so clearly felt as such by contemporaries. These twelve months saw the survival of the warfare of earlier times, at least in certain respects. The great strategic movements, in which the cavalry continued to play its part, played a key role in the unfolding of the war on all fronts other than the Western Front. Complete demographic mobilisation was not imposed everywhere, as can be seen in the important place of volunteering in the United

26 John Horne, 'Introduction', in Horne (ed.), *Vers la guerre totale*, p. 17.

27 On condition of excluding from this heading the massacre of the Herero, in modern Namibia, ten years before the Great War.

28 Horne, 'Introduction', p. 24.

Kingdom and the Dominions of the British Empire; the occupations of 1915, however severe, became established as a phase of normalisation following the anomaly of the invasion rather than as a form of exploitation of a new kind. As for the industrial, social and financial mobilisations, they unquestionably made their effects felt, without, however, rendering the belligerent societies henceforward fully prepared for war.

The year 1915 was the one in which totalisation of the war was substantially set in motion. But it was still some way from reaching its full destructive potential. That was soon to come.

4
1916: Impasse

ROBIN PRIOR

The year 1915 had proved barren for the cause of the Entente. The French, with some British assistance, tried to blast their way through the Western Front by enormous offensives in the spring and autumn. They failed with heavy casualties and no useful ground gained. The British, with some French assistance, tried to go around the Western Front by their adventure against the Ottoman Turks at Gallipoli. They failed even to take the ridges overlooking their landing places. Italy joined the Entente in May to no effect whatsoever. The least of the Great Powers would not, it was soon realised, alter the balance.

The Germans were no more successful on the Western Front. They tried a new measure of frightfulness – poison gas – at Ypres but it had little impact except as a boost to Allied propaganda. In the East they were more successful. Their armies made great gains at the Battle of Gorlice-Tarnów, capturing all of Russian Poland. In the Balkans they assisted their struggling ally, Austria-Hungary, by eliminating Serbia. But they also knew that these gains meant little while the armies of France and Britain remained undefeated in the West.

In 1916 the major powers sought to increase their production of armaments before they made additional attempts to break this stalemate. Germany was the most successful in this endeavour. It had entered the war with a considerable munitions industry. But in 1915 it was still only able to produce thirty-eight pieces of heavy artillery per month. By the autumn of 1916 this figure had increased almost ten-fold to 330. Shell production rose in due proportion.

France was not as well placed. The army had called up an undue number of munitions workers and was slow to release them. Moreover, some of the French industrial heartland in the north-east was now under German occupation. Despite these difficulties the French made some headway. By mid year its production of heavy guns showed a five-fold increase over the previous year.

Even Russia, contrary to popular belief, had made some progress. Its munitions industries were no match for those of Western Europe but by

1916 it was starting to produce guns and shells in the quantities that the huge size of its army had always required.

Britain entered the war with a munitions industry designed almost exclusively for the use of the navy. In 1915 Lloyd George had been appointed Minister of Munitions to create a similar industry for the army. He was spectacularly successful. In 1914 Britain produced just ninety guns of all types. By mid 1916 this number had increased to 3,200. And increasingly the types being produced were the heavy weapons needed to batter down the ever more complex trench systems on the Western Front.

The transformation of Britain into a major military – as against naval – power, was looked on with consternation by the decision-makers in Berlin. The longer the war, they reasoned, the less chance Germany would have of winning it. This especially troubled the German Commander-in-Chief, Falkenhayn. Falkenhayn had always been a Westerner. He had looked on with impatience during 1915 while his rivals, Hindenberg and Ludendorff had won great victories in the East. At the end of the year he wrote a paper on Grand Strategy, always a dangerous matter when entrusted to the military. Not surprisingly he identified the Western Front as the area for decisive action in 1916. He also identified Britain as the ultimate enemy, the glue which held the Entente together. At first sight the logic of Falkenhayn's paper seemed to point towards an attack in the West on the British armies, not yet fully trained and not yet fully formed. But as with many papers with a grand strategic sweep, logic was not its strongpoint. With some ingenuity, Falkenhayn concluded that France was 'Britain's best sword' in the West and therefore it should be the French who should bear the brunt of the German offensive. To defeat the British therefore it was essential to defeat the French. It seems idle to point out that to defeat the British the most direct and obvious method was to attack the British. But the fact is that the new conception of war being hatched by Falkenhayn precluded such an operation. His new idea was to attack at a point that was bound to be defended and then use his superiority in artillery to batter the defenders into submission. The British were not bound to defend any particular locality in France or Flanders. The French would better fit the bill if a locality on French soil could be found that they would defend to the last man. Falkenhayn thought he had identified such a place – and events would prove that he was correct – in Verdun.

It is true that the fortress of Verdun had played a role in the military history of the French since at the least the time of Charlemagne. But it was also true that whenever Verdun had been besieged by a hostile army, it had fallen. This was true in the Napoleonic Wars and in the Franco-Prussian War. Why then was Falkenhayn correct in assuming that the French would see its fall in 1916 as something catastrophic – something indeed that might end the Third Republic? The fact is that given the military doctrine prevalent among the French in 1916, almost any point on French soil that was subjected to attack would be defended to the utmost. They would defend Verdun but they would almost certainly have defended Belfort or Reims or anywhere else with equal tenacity. Falkenhayn would achieve his purpose, not so much because he was attacking Verdun but because he was attacking France.

It should go without saying that the French were not obliged to defend Verdun to the last. Its fall would have meant little. Behind it stood no large strategic objectives such as munitions factories or important railway junctions. If the Germans had captured Verdun nothing would have followed. They had no means of exploiting such a victory and the hills to the west of the city might easily have proved too strong for an increasingly exhausted army to assail. As for the Third Republic, there is no reason to suppose that it would not have survived the fall of Verdun. It survived worse disasters in 1917 and 1918. In truth the sacred nature of Verdun is largely a post-war construct – a symbol of the sacrifice that had to be paid for victory. At the time to the *poilu*, Verdun was 'the mill on the Meuse', a grinding machine of appalling proportions. A withdrawal from the salient around Verdun might actually have raised French morale, not led to the fall of the Republic.

Falkenhayn would therefore attack at Verdun. But his ultimate goal still lies shrouded in mystery. Did he intend to capture the city? Or was his purpose to bleed the French army white? In his paper he has a bet each way. If the French stand and fight he will grind them down. If they collapse he will have scored a great victory. In short, however the plan unfolds, Falkenhayn emerges as a winner. All this is very convenient as is the fact that the only copy of Falkenhayn's paper that can be found is that published in his memoirs. It seems possible that Falkenhayn always intended to capture Verdun but wrote a post-war justification for the nature of the battle into his paper.

By what means did Falkenhayn seek to achieve victory – however that is defined? What he proposed was to assemble the largest amount of artillery yet seen in war, about 1,200 guns of which 500 were heavy calibre, and in relatively short but devastating bombardments destroy the French defenders until the ground could be occupied with modest infantry resources. To this end 2 million shells were stockpiled for the battle. Operations would be entrusted to the German Fifth Army commanded by the Crown Prince but actually directed by his Chief of Staff General Knobelsdorf.

The Allies were also making plans. Joffre called a conference at Chantilly, north of Paris in December 1915. One conclusion reached there was that in 1915 the Entente had not coordinated its actions, which allowed the Central Powers to transfer troops from one front to another. To rectify this in 1916 it was decided that all powers – Russia, Italy, France and Britain should mount simultaneous attacks. But given the munitions shortages such operations could not be carried out until mid year. The centrepiece of the proposed operations was an attack by the Russians against the Germans on the northern part of the Eastern Front around Lake Naroch and a combined Anglo-French operation astride the River Somme in Picardy. These operations looked very different from those being devised by Falkenhayn. They were not designed to be attritional battles. Great masses of cavalry would sweep through gaps made in the enemy defences and roll up the German positions. However, the gaps in the enemy line would be achieved by the same means put forward by Falkenhayn – that is, huge amounts of artillery and shells would be used to eliminate the dominance of defensive trench positions.

These plans were destined to be disrupted by the speed of the German preparations. Just a conception in December, Falkenhayn had by mid February assembled his guns and shells and concentrated 500,000 troops opposite Verdun. Only bad weather delayed the opening of the attack until 21 February.

The defences Falkenhayn would be assailing looked formidable. The city was defended by twelve main forts. In the outer ring lay the formidable Douaumont, Thiaumont and Vaux; the inner contained Vacherauville, Belleville, Souville and others. There were also eight smaller forts, many redoubts and trench lines to be overcome. Just before the war many of the forts had been strengthened. Douaumont had received a three-and-a-half-metre concrete reinforcement, supplemented by four metres of earth. In the event this reinforcement kept out even the largest German shells. But the forts were not as formidable in practice as they seemed on paper. The destruction of the Antwerp forts by heavy German mortars and howitzers in 1914 had convinced many in the French High Command that the days of such defences were over. Consequently many of the largest guns had been removed from the Verdun forts and deployed on more active sectors of the front. And as the manpower crisis deepened in France, many of the garrisons of the forts were also removed. So in 1916 Douaumont had been reduced to just one 155 mm and four 75 mm guns and a garrison of sixty. Vaux had no heavy guns at all and a similarly meagre garrison. Pleas from local commanders for reinforcement fell on deaf ears. But continued pressure finally brought Joffre to Verdun on 24

January. He conceded that the defences needed reinforcement and offered two additional infantry divisions. There was to be no reinforcement in guns, either for the forts or the field artillery.

Contrary to some accounts, the French were not unaware of the impending German attack. Despite German air superiority, some French reconnaissance aircraft managed to obtain some photographs of German concentrations of guns and men. Deserters from the German army confirmed that a great attack was imminent. They even told of fearful new weapons – flamethrowers and a new and more deadly poison gas. This intelligence produced another corps of troops from Joffre for Verdun but no more guns.

Amid some controversy, Falkenhayn had decided to confine his attack to a ten-kilometre section on the right bank of the Meuse. The Crown Prince (or Knobelsdorf) pointed out that this would lay the attackers open to French artillery fire from the unattacked left bank. Falkenhayn was not swayed. He reckoned, not without reason, that to sufficiently devastate the French defenders his artillery fire must be as concentrated as possible. Spreading its fire across both banks of the Meuse might weaken it everywhere. In the event, however, the success or failure of his endeavour would turn on the question of whether he had sufficient artillery even to achieve success on the right. Whether he ever made any calculations on this matter is open to doubt. In the Great War, generals on both sides proved astonishingly averse to calculating whether the guns and shells they had at hand were sufficient for their purpose. What most of them did instead was merely assemble an amount of guns heretofore unprecedented and assume that this would be enough. In Falkenhayn's case this lack of precision is particularly egregious considering that the whole basis of his plan turned on artillery concentration. And at Verdun Falkenhayn was not just taking on lines of trench defences. There were also numerous forts and fortified villages to be overcome. In fact what was required at Verdun was the bombardment of the entire area of ground between the front line and the city, a formidable undertaking indeed.

The weather improved in the latter half of February and on the 21st the bombardment began (Map 4.1). Nothing approaching its ferocity had been seen before. Every hour for nine hours 2,400 shells landed on the French defences. They destroyed train lines, uprooted trees and obliterated troops in trenches or caught in the open. Some French defenders were too shell-shocked to respond, others fled to the rear, but as the Germans sent forward their probing patrols, they found to their consternation that many French defenders had survived the bombardment and were manning their weapons. Soon the sparse numbers of assaulting troops were stopped in their tracks, and

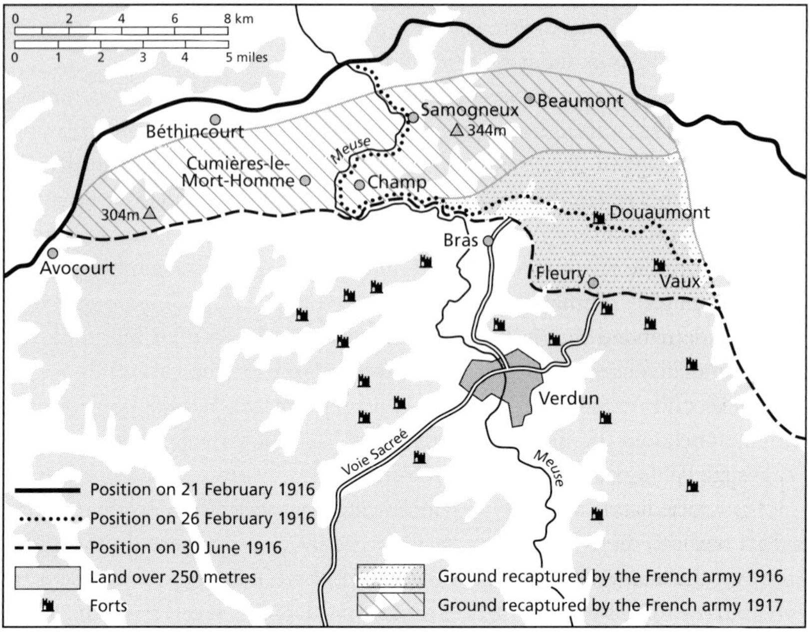

Map 4.1 The Battle of Verdun and its aftermath.

even, in a few areas, driven back by spirited French counter-attacks. In all, gains on the first day were minimal.

The next four days, however, were to tell a different story. Each German attack was again preceded by an intense bombardment and the attackers now committed more troops. They also committed a new weapon – flamethrowers. These devices sprayed troops with fire from cylinders filled with petrol. Being burnt to death as well as being gassed or blown to pieces became an added horror to fighting on the Western Front. No doubt the introduction of flamethrowers was one reason that the French defence gradually wilted. One division broke entirely; others were worn down by the bombardments. The XXX Corps, so recently committed by Joffre to Verdun, had ceased to exist as a fighting unit by the evening of the 24th. Key defended localities which had resisted on the first day fell one by one. By the 24th, Bois des Caures, defended to the death by Colonel Briant and his men, was captured, as were the villages of Beaumont, Samogneux and Haumont. Then on the 25th disaster struck – Fort Douaumont was captured by a handful of German troops who infiltrated into the underground galleries and overpowered the garrison. To those who knew of the true state of Douaumont, defended by few guns and a score of weary men, its capture would have come as no surprise. But for many the fort represented the last word in French fortification and its fall produced a shock throughout the country. More shocking in fact was the feeble and uncoordinated response of the French artillery on the left bank. Individual batteries did their best to hamper the Germans, but their fire was sporadic and random.

Even before the fall of Douaumont however, the French were responding. At French High Command (*Grand Quartier Général*, or GQG) General de Castelnau demanded that Joffre send a new commander to Verdun. Pétain, the master of defensive warfare, was selected and told to proceed to the Meuse with his Second Army at once. In the meantime Castelnau rushed to Verdun himself, concluded that it was still possible to defend the right bank, and on Pétain's arrival handed him an order to that effect.

Pétain immediately came down with double pneumonia and was forced for the first week to direct the battle from his sickbed. He did so to some effect, helped by the arrival of Balfourier's XX Corps, one of the best in the French army. One of Pétain's first acts was to insist that the left-bank artillery coordinate their response. There would be no more sporadic fire. Batteries were grouped and given specific targets. He requested many more batteries and this time there was no hesitation – 155 mm and 75 mm guns soon began to arrive in numbers.

Just as importantly, Pétain had to ensure that the increased numbers of guns and men being requested were adequately supplied. This was a difficult feat. Of the two railways that had supplied Verdun before the war, one was in German hands and the other was under regular German artillery fire. This left a road which ran from Verdun to Bar-le-Duc. The question was, could motor transport, then in its infancy, supply an entire army? Pétain was fortunate to have on his staff an engineer of genius, Major Richard. Richard calculated how many trucks would be required to support the Verdun army and went about gathering them. In no time he had assembled a fleet of astonishing size – no fewer than 3,500 assorted vehicles. By 28 February, 25,000 tons of supplies and 190,000 men were brought along the road. By June a vehicle passed every fourteen seconds. Those which broke down were pushed into a side ditch and left for repair. Troops marched to Verdun in the fields parallel to the road. A division of men was diverted simply to keep the road in constant repair. Two-thirds of the entire French army in 1916 would arrive at Verdun by this road. After the war it became known as the *Voie Sacrée*. During the war it was called 'the road' and to the troops who marched along it during the battle, we can speculate that its post-war beatification would have been greeted with astonishment or derision or both.

Pétain also reorganised the defensive arrangements in the Verdun salient. The area was divided into four and each placed under a Corps Commander. Divisions were to spend just fifteen days in the line before being rested. (This arrangement explains why such a high proportion of the French army fought at Verdun. It may be contrasted to the German system of leaving divisions in the line and replacing casualties with new drafts.)

After 25 February the intensity of the German offensive certainly fell away. No doubt Pétain's reforms, especially concerning the French artillery, had much to do with this. However, the Germans were having artillery problems of their own. Before the great attack on the 21st they had developed plans for moving their guns forward to support the next phase of the attack. These plans now came undone. The earlier bombardments had ploughed up the ground over which the Germans needed to move their guns. The weather conditions at Verdun in February – rain and sleet – ensured that the ploughed-up ground was reduced to glutinous mud. Even though exact positions had been designated for each gun, the German command found it impossible to move them forward over this ground. The super-heavy howitzers and mortars proved especially difficult. Some were moved but no stable platform could be found. Others sank into the mire and because of their great weight could not quickly be dug out. For these reasons the fire support received by the German troops suffered a savage diminution and as a result the first phase of the Verdun operation fizzled out.

This failure led to an agonising reappraisal on the German side. The Crown Prince had always wanted to attack the left bank. Now the devastating French artillery response in that area suggested to him that the time had come to do it. With some misgivings Falkenhayn agreed. The left bank of the Meuse is in some ways an easier proposition to attack than the right. The original attack had to contend with ravines and gullies, with steep ridges covered by woods. The left bank consists of more open country with gently rolling slopes and grasslands. There is, however, a ridge that dominates the entire area. At one end is the ominously titled Mort Homme, at the other Côte 304, a name which also measures its height in metres.

On 6 March the German preliminary bombardment began. It was devastating. One French division broke; the others conceded ground. Mort Homme was in danger. A counter-attack was ordered, with the most drastic consequences threatened should it fail. It went in on the 8th and did not fail. Most of the ground lost was regained. On the right bank the Germans had also attacked but made no gains. Interest returned to the left.

In fact for the next two months on the left the positions hardly moved. Some of the most intensive fighting of the whole Verdun campaign was to take place around the shattered slopes of the Mort Homme and Côte 304. The line swayed back and forth some metres and then was re-established. The terrible flamethrowers, introduced by the Germans on the first day, were now marked by the French as targets of especial importance. For the Germans wielding them they became suicide weapons. They were used less and less. The terror had passed. The fighting went on throughout April and into May. At stake were the prime French artillery concentrations behind the ridge. On 3 May the Germans brought up fresh divisions and made one last effort, their attack supported by 500 heavy guns. This time there was partial success – Côte 304 was lost. This in fact proved the key to the ridge which was rolled up from left to right. Mort Homme fell in this manner at the end of the month. The Crown Prince now had the artillery observation areas he had wanted. But his success had come at a fearful price. In this fighting, German losses probably exceeded the French. It was a good question by the end of May as to which army was being bled white.

The fighting also saw the end of Pétain's intimate association with the battle. Perhaps because of the losses on the left bank, perhaps because of his success in stabilising the front, Joffre kicked him upstairs to command the Central Group of Armies. The commanders on the spot would now be General Robert Nivelle and his favourite Corps Commander, General Mangin – nicknamed the Butcher. Their efforts to retake Douaumont at the end of May were bloody fiascos. One suicidal counter-attack after another was launched against the fort. The Germans were prepared. On one occasion the French troops briefly held the top of the fort but they were driven back. Mangin was sacked, Nivelle reined in.

The fighting at Verdun had by this point lost all sensible purpose. It should have been obvious to the Germans that the price to be paid to gain the additional seven kilometres of ground that they needed to take the city was too high. There were obviously no easy victories to be had on the Meuse. Nivelle and Mangin had at least demonstrated that the French army was far from broken. Yet the failure of the French efforts and the additional knowledge that the British were preparing a great offensive on the Somme, led Falkenhayn into making another attempt on the right bank.

The offensive opened on 1 June. Much ground was gained by the Germans. They had blanketed the French artillery with a new gas – phosgene or Green

Cross gas – against which existing gas masks were not effective. The Germans were now able to approach Fort Vaux. The fort was in fact a shell. It had no large guns at all and was defended under Major Raynal by the remnants of a few companies. Nevertheless it held. Raynal's ragged garrison inflicted thousands of casualties on the Germans for little cost. Lack of water supplies, criminally neglected in the pre-battle period, eventually forced its surrender. The Germans inched towards Fort Souville, one of the ring of forts that defended Verdun itself.

On 11 July, Souville was assaulted. But by now the French gunners were equipped with more efficient gas masks. The Germans reached the fort but were wiped out by French artillery fire. There would be no follow-up. The Somme offensive had now opened and Falkenhayn had diverted ammunition supplies to that area. Events in the East, as we will see, also drained divisions away from the Western Front. Falkenhayn had in any case seemed to grow tired of his own conception. Losses for both sides approached 250,000. There would be no more German offensives at Verdun.

This did not apply to the French. Nivelle was still there and Mangin had returned. But this time Pétain was also involved in the planning. The former commander insisted that any counter-attack be accompanied by the heaviest of artillery bombardments. Super-heavy French guns were brought up. The bombardment only began after 300,000 shells had been stockpiled. They were employed on a narrow five-kilometre front to increase the concentration of shells that would rain down on the Germans. The troops would also advance behind a slowly moving curtain of shells fired by the lighter guns. This was the creeping barrage, introduced at Verdun from lessons learned at the Somme. The preliminary bombardment started on 19 October. On the 24th the infantry followed. The French had regained air superiority, thereby blinding the German artillery. The attack was a success. Fort Douaumont was regained. On 2 November Fort Vaux was taken. The Germans were now back within a few kilometres from where they had launched their offensive in February.

Although sporadic fighting broke out around the front at Verdun for several months, the battle was in fact over. Losses, as far as they can be established, were staggering. The French had lost 351,000, of whom probably 150,000 were dead. If this did not amount to 'bleeding white', it at least meant progress had been made by Falkenhayn towards that goal. The problem was that he had bled his own army white as well. The Germans had suffered almost as severely as the French; their casualties being 330,000, of whom 143,000 were dead or missing. Given that Germany now faced two great military powers on the Western Front, it was not at all certain that Falkenhayn had brought the balance of loss out on the correct side.

The other great army to confront the Germans was that of the British. But it was the lesser ally of the French – Tsarist Russia – which first responded to the cry for help sent out by the French President (Poincaré) in May, at the height of the fighting at Verdun. Russia was not yet ready to launch its northern offensive against the Germans around Lake Naroch. But it was prepared to consider an opportunistic attack against the Austro-Hungarians on the southern section of the Eastern Front. In fact the Russians had been preparing this attack even before Verdun, but they gained the maximum kudos by seeming to respond to Poincaré. The commander on this section of the front was General Brusilov, and he carefully noted the removal of some veteran Austrian divisions for a new offensive against Italy. This attack, which was launched on 15 May 1916, enjoyed considerable early success. Two Italian defensive lines fell to the Austro-Hungarian commander (Conrad) and 400,000 Italians were taken prisoner. For a moment it seemed that Conrad would break out into the Venetian plain. Now the Italians also appealed to Brusilov to commence his offensive. As they did so it just happened that Conrad's offensive was running out of steam because, as was often the case in the Great War, his troops had outrun their artillery support.

Brusilov's manner of attack defied the conventional methods. He did not concentrate his forces against a particular centre but attacked on 6 June along the whole southern front. Remarkably, he broke through. The Austro-Hungarian forces, denuded by Conrad's operations against Italy, collapsed. In a month Brusilov had advanced ninety-six kilometres along the entire front, capturing 300,000 prisoners along the way. No doubt if Brusilov had attacked the Germans the result would have been very different. But he did force the Germans to rush reinforcements from the Western Front to help sustain their ally. However, like many another offensive Brusilov's began to lose momentum. Once again it was the lack of artillery support and in this case supplies of all kinds that slowed his advance. In addition the Austro-Hungarians had recovered from the surprise and were increasingly shored up by German troops.

Meanwhile, the Russian High Command was uncertain how to respond to Brusilov's initial success. Should it divert troops to maintain the momentum of the offensive or should it carry through its northern offensive as promised to its Allies? Late in July the decision was taken to proceed with the northern operation. This proved to be a mistake. In short order the Germans stopped the offensive in its tracks. There would be no more Russian offensives in 1916.

Thanks to Romania, however, there would be a renewed German attack. At the very time that the Brusilov offensive was slowing, the rulers of Romania – which was just to the south of the Russian advance – considered that their hour had come. In Churchill's words, it had not only come, it had gone. Romania entered the war on the Allied side just in time to encounter the armies of Germany – commanded by Falkenhayn – who had been replaced by the Kaiser as Commander-in-Chief by the combination of Hindenburg and Ludendorff. The Romanians were defeated with astonishing rapidity, Falkenhayn winning back all the ground gained by Brusilov in the process. Great reserves of oil and wheat fell into German hands as a result. With these vital raw materials secured, Germany was able to continue the war indefinitely. Such was Romania's contribution to the Allied cause.

Meanwhile back on the Western Front, where the war would be won or lost, the British army was slowly building to a size where a considerable offensive could be launched. It should be noted that this was a radical departure from Britain's previous wars. Rarely had Britain devoted such large resources to ground forces in Europe. Now, with the French and Russians under pressure, they were clearly required. By the summer British forces in the West totalled around a million men. Where would their great offensive be launched? The answer was astride the River Somme, with the French to the south (and just to the north) and the British extending the front further northward by twenty-three kilometres. Because of the strong German defences in this area the choice of site for the new battle has attracted much derision. Why launch an attack in an area just because it was the joining point of the British and French armies? Yet it is not easy to find another promising area for an offensive. Flanders was too low-lying, south of that lay the industrial area around Lens – where a failed offensive had been launched in 1915. Just to the north of the Somme front stood the formidable fortifications around Vimy Ridge. Further south from the Somme lay hilly and wooded slopes. In short, if the Somme seemed to have many disadvantages so did everywhere else. At least a joint attack by the Allies would force the Germans to defend a very wide front of attack.

But as the killing at Verdun proceeded, it became clear that the Allies' front of attack would be narrower than at first thought. The continued fighting at Verdun gradually leached away the French divisions that were to have been committed to the Somme. In March the French were to have thirty-nine divisions on the Somme, compared to the British fourteen, by the end of April the French number had been reduced to thirty, by 20 May the number was twenty-six, by the end of the month twenty. After that Joffre refrained from estimating how many French divisions would assist the British. The British by their own deductions correctly assumed that by the time the offensive was launched there would be no more than twelve French divisions to their south. In this way the Somme became mainly a British campaign.

Not that any of this fazed the British commander Sir Douglas Haig. This was to be Haig's first battle in his new position. He had replaced Sir John French after the failure at Loos. Since December 1915 he had been gradually accumulating men and guns for the 'big push'.

Haig's notion, that he would launch his attack on a wide front, was soundly based. In this way, the central troops at least, would be protected from flanking enemy fire. But to attack on a wide front (in this case eleven kilometres) it was necessary to accumulate massive amounts of ammunition and guns to demolish the extensive German trench lines and fortified villages faced by the British. Having accumulated all these munitions it was also essential to ensure that the British artillerymen had sufficient skill to deliver the shells with some accuracy onto the German defences. It would be pleasing to report that Haig and his associates made the most exacting calculations about shell numbers and conducted the most thorough review of artillery methods to ensure that the artillery could and would do its job. It would be pleasing but incorrect. Haig, rather like Falkenhayn at Verdun, merely accumulated a number of guns and shells heretofore unprecedented in the British army and assumed they would be sufficient.

And it was not just in numbers that the artillery would prove to be insufficient. There were serious inadequacies in quality, type and manner of delivery. In Britain, in order to fulfil Haig's needs, the Ministry of Munitions had made a number of dubious decisions. To increase output they abandoned quality control, with the consequence that many shells either failed to explode or exploded prematurely, thus destroying the gun that was firing them. Moreover, it so happened that the majority of shells supplied to Haig were shrapnel – that is they were excellent shells with which to cut barbed wire entanglements or for dealing with troops in the open. They were useless against deep trench defences and the dugouts beneath them in which the majority of the German defenders on the Somme lurked. The British were well informed by offensive patrols of these deep dugouts, but they failed to grasp the implications for a bombardment consisting largely of shrapnel.

At one point in the planning of the operation, the army commander who was to carry it out, General Rawlinson, seemed to grasp that the British destructive efforts would be inadequate. He implored Haig to limit his objective in the first instance to the first German defensive position. Haig was having none of this. He planned to capture all three German lines. How else could the four divisions of cavalry he had massed just behind the front break through and gallop towards the coast, thus rolling up the German defences in the northern sector of the Western Front?

Rawlinson could have suggested that such an operation on the Western Front in 1916 was quite chimerical. He could have noted that massed cavalry in the open were ideal targets for German machine gunners and artillerymen and in the war so far no bombardment, including Falkenhayn's at Verdun, had managed to eliminate anything like the entire enemy defences. He could have gone on to note that in any case there would be German weaponry of the type that could devastate cavalry situated well behind the front and out of range of the most ferocious of bombardments. He could have done these things but he did not. When challenged by Haig, he retreated into convoluted arguments about the difficulties green troops would have in advancing the distances suggested by Haig's plan. This was the wrong tack. Dead troops whether green or experienced would not advance anywhere. This was the issue and no one on the British side tackled it.

Consequently when the great offensive opened on 1 July it met with disaster on a scale not yet seen on any opening day of any offensive on the Western Front. (It would keep this dubious distinction for the remainder of the war.) By the end of the day 57,000 British troops had become casualties – about 40 per cent of all those engaged on that day. There was a time when these horrific casualties were attributed to unimaginative infantry tactics which had the troops advancing at a slow walk, shoulder to shoulder with the view that these tactics had been imposed on the men by an unreasoning command. In fact battalion commanders seem to have ignored any tactical instructions from above and adopted their own measures, most of which were very imaginative indeed. However, the type of infantry tactics employed was supremely irrelevant in the face of unsubdued German machine guns and artillery. In the face of this storm of fire it mattered little if men walked or ran or did the Highland fling across no-man's-land. What mattered was that the inadequate and inaccurate artillery bombardment had missed much of the German defensive systems and most of the German batteries ranged on no-man's-land. This left machine gunners (who took the heaviest toll that day) free to emerge from the safety of their deep dugouts and mow down the advancing troops at will. It is a melancholy fact that about 10,000 British troops became casualties before they reached their own front line. In the centre an entire division from III Corps hardly came to grips with the enemy at all before they were slaughtered. The end result was that by nightfall the British had gained a little ground on the south of their front – where they were fighting alongside the French who were more lavishly supplied with artillery and where the creeping barrage was employed by some divisions for the first time – but no ground at all in the centre or the north. To the south of the river the French made modest gains but their efforts were always a side-show to Haig's.

There was never any doubt that despite these losses the battle would be continued. The French were still under pressure at Verdun and the lengthy preparations made by Haig could hardly be broken off after twenty-four hours. Joffre met with the British commander and ordered Haig to make a second attempt to capture ground in the north, that is, to persist in an area that had cost him 13,000 casualties on 1 July. Haig demurred and told Joffre plainly that he did not take orders from him. Instead Haig proposed to keep making ground in the south until he was in striking distance of the German second defensive position. Joffre had no alternative but to agree.

Haig's decision to reinforce success was sensible. The way he went about these operations was, however, anything but sensible. During the next two weeks Rawlinson's Fourth Army made a series of narrow-front, small-scale attacks which saw them inching forward. But they inched forward at great cost because the tactics employed allowed the Germans to concentrate the maximum amount of artillery against the small areas of the front under threat. By these means several divisions – a notable one was the 38th Welsh Division, raised due to the enthusiasm of Lloyd George – ceased to exist as fighting forces.

On 14 July, however, Rawlinson scored a success. He was finally close enough to the German second line to launch an attack. For this operation, however, he adopted the expedient of a night advance. It caught the Germans by surprise and a whole section of the German second line fell into British hands. This augured well, but an attempt to push the cavalry through to exploit the victory did not. The few troops from an Indian cavalry division unlucky enough to get into position to charge the Germans were swept away by machine gun and artillery fire. The idea that cavalry had a place on a battlefield such as the Somme died hard.

To interpret what happened in the next two months on the Somme is one of the hardest tasks in modern military history. On the left or north of the front the Reserve Army, under General Gough and employing the Australian Corps, after it had captured the German second position around Pozières, made repeated attempts to move further north against a German strongpoint called Mouquet Farm. This strongpoint was without real tactical significance and was not eventually captured until September. Its fall, as could have been predicted, meant nothing. The campaign, however, cost the Australian Corps some 23,000 casualties and at the end it had to withdraw from the Somme battle. Here was a good example of how to fritter away a strong fighting unit for no purpose.

The Mouquet Farm operations had another peculiar feature. The direction of advance towards the farm took the troops of the Reserve Army away from the direction that the Fourth Army was attempting to advance. If either of these armies made significant gains they would have separated themselves from their companions. In the event the tactics employed by Haig and Rawlinson saw to it that no great gains – or indeed gains that could even be seen on a large-scale map – were made. The same miserable, small-scale, narrow-front attacks that had characterised the period from 2 to 13 July were used between 15 July and 14 September. But there was an added twist to the story in this latter period. The Fourth Army itself was trying to advance in two different directions at once. The left of the army was attempting to proceed almost due north, while the right of the army was attempting to advance east. Once again, any great forward move by either section of the army would have seen it separate from the other. Once again the penny-packet attack methods employed ensured that neither section moved at all. Haig eventually noticed what was happening and endeavoured to persuade Rawlinson to cease attacking in one sector until the other sector came into line. He failed. Rawlinson seemed to be listening but kept on as though Haig had not spoken. Haig then relapsed into silence. Meanwhile the battle spiralled out of control. It cost the British around 100,000 casualties even to capture one wood along the front (High Wood) because it was repeatedly attacked by inadequate numbers of men supported by derisory amounts of artillery. Only towards the end of the period were sufficient gains made on the right to ensure that something like an adequate start line was reached in time for Haig's large attack on 15 September.

But this is only one side of the story. The Somme should not be looked upon as a contest between British donkeys and an intelligent German defence. There were donkeys on both sides. Falkenhayn had decreed that any ground lost was immediately to be recaptured by counter-attack. So small advances by small numbers of British troops were countered by similar attacks by small numbers of German troops. In this manner Falkenhayn, against the odds, managed to restore some kind of balance to the casualty lists.

Moreover, the German troops were undergoing their own kind of hell. When they were not exacting a toll on the ill-thought-out British attacks, they were under continuous bombardment from the British artillery. The Somme, despite the crude tactics used by Haig, reflected the arrival of Britain as a major military power. This fact shocked the Germans, as did the 7 million artillery shells fired at them by the British between 2 July and mid September. By 1916 Britain had assembled a mass army on a continental scale and it was backed by what was soon to become the largest munitions effort in the world. In addition, Britain's financial connections and the fact that its fleet could cut Germany off from the financial markets of the world, gave it unimpeded access to the wealth of the United States. It is true that some British assets had to be liquidated to pay for American raw materials and financial support, but Britain had very deep pockets (4,000 million pounds were available to it in foreign investments in 1914) and the Germans could only watch as British war production reached new heights with American help.

Meanwhile back at the front Haig had a surprise in store for the Germans. The British had developed in secret a new weapon of war. This was the tank, and Haig wished to employ it as soon as possible. For this he has been castigated. It is claimed that had he waited until the new weapon was available in the hundreds he might have scored a stunning victory, instead of going off half-cocked with the fifty available to him in September. But in using the tank in small numbers Haig was almost certainly correct. The weapon was untried and to base a war-winning campaign on an untested weapon would have involved the utmost peril. As it was, 50 per cent of the tanks broke down before they reached the front line. If this had occurred on a large scale a fiasco might have ensued.

In the event it was not the small numbers of tanks that ensured the battle of 15 September would have only a very limited success, it was the way Haig employed them. Sensibly, he concentrated his tanks opposite the strongest section of the German front. Less sensibly, he decided not to fire a creeping barrage, which by this time had become the standard form of infantry protection in an attack, for fear of hitting the tanks. Yet even the Mark I tank – employed here – could withstand some shrapnel and it would therefore have been possible to fire the barrage across the entire front. What happened during the battle was that some tanks failed to arrive due to mechanical failure, so the enemy strongpoints opposite them were not subject to any artillery fire at all. And as these points tended to hold nests of German machine gunners, the defenders were able to take a fearful toll on the attacking British troops. Only in the centre, where all the tanks arrived, were they able to advance against the Germans with impunity. This area saw German troops stream towards the rear in panic, and as a result some small villages such as

Flers fell into British hands. So some ground was gained with the help of the tanks but at high cost.

In any case a subsequent battle on 25 September proved that on occasion more ground could be gained without tanks if the traditional methods of infantry protection were reinstated. By the 25th most tanks were out of action. So, accompanied by a creeping barrage fired across the whole front, the Fourth Army subdued the German defence and made reasonable ground (in Great War terms) at modest cost.

Haig had now reached the crest of a ridge. Below lay more German defences. But it was late in the campaigning season. Rain was sure to come and the prospect of advancing into the valley before him, which must turn into a sea of mud if the seasons remained true, was hardly appealing. But Haig never hesitated to consider such matters. As he had often remarked (and been proved wrong) German morale was teetering on the brink of collapse. Why stop now when victory beckoned?

Victory of course made no such gesture. But Haig was stiffened in his resolve to pursue the offensive by the support he was receiving from the politicians in Britain. This is surprising. The small number of politicians which made up the War Committee that ran the war was not filled with unintelligent men. Asquith, Lloyd George, Arthur Balfour and the rest were some of the most prominent politicians of their age. Certainly, in Kitchener, the Minister of War, they had a relic from the days of colonial warfare who knew little about the industrial war developing on the Western Front, and in General Robertson, Chief of the Imperial general staff (CIGS), they had an adviser who saw it as his duty to support Haig whatever the circumstances. Nevertheless, the civilians were not ciphers; they were well able to make up their own minds on any issue. Yet before the Battle of the Somme they did not ask and were not told about the type of offensive Haig had in mind or exactly how he was going to use the munitions that had been supplied to him by Lloyd George's ministry. Once battle was joined, it might have been expected that some kind of outcry would ensue from these civilised men over the great slaughter on the first day. At their first meeting after 1 July there is silence, partly because the full horror of the casualties had not yet been revealed. But at subsequent meetings when the truth was apparent, there followed only more silence. It is clear from the diaries of the secretary to the War Committee (Hankey) that many members of it were uneasy about the high casualty bill and the lack of substantial progress. Yet in Committee the civilian members sat supine while Robertson assured them with blatantly false figures that while it was true that Haig was suffering casualties, he was inflicting a greater number on the Germans. When Winston Churchill, who was then outside the Cabinet, produced a memorandum which refuted Robertson's figures and demonstrated that for every two casualties suffered by the Germans the British suffered three, the response of the War Committee was to send their congratulations to Haig on the splendid job he was doing.

But as Haig paused in late September he made what could have been a serious mistake. In early October he wrote to the War Committee and sought permission to continue the offensive. Here was a chance for the civilians to reassert their authority. It was not necessary for them to sack Haig. All that would have been required was to thank him for the splendid results achieved so far and order the battle closed because the campaigning season was drawing to an end. By that time most members of the Committee were thoroughly alarmed at the casualty total and perplexed that Romania could be overrun when they had been assured that at the very least the Somme offensive was pinning German troops to the Western Front. But in the event they not only passed up this opportunity, they did not even discuss Haig's request in Committee. They had totally lost the will to question their chief military adviser or their Commander-in-Chief in the West. The offensive would continue. Haig could do what he liked.

Haig did precisely that. Despite the rain which had begun to fall on cue in October, he made preparations for another gigantic offensive. This time the objectives were around Arras, some 112 kilometres distant. Though Haig had only managed to advance his front a little more than 16 kilometres in three months, no one sought to question this aspiration. Five divisions of cavalry were duly massed to exploit the victory, even though the horsed-soldiers had found it difficult to wade through the mire even to get into position. The artillery bombardment which accompanied this offensive was a woeful failure. In the gloom and rain, guns could not be registered with any certainty on distant targets. The creeping barrage could not be followed by the troops for the simple reason that many of them found themselves stuck in their muddy trenches. They could only stagger forward with the assistance of their comrades. Meanwhile the creeping barrage had crept off into the distance. Not only was Arras not in sight, but the German front trenches still were. Ground gained started to be measured in feet, and on some sections of the front even that proved too large a scale.

Then, in November, Haig was summoned to an Allied conference at Chantilly. He was desperate to appear before this gathering with a victory – any victory – under his belt. He therefore reactivated the long-forgotten Reserve Army, now rebranded as the Fifth Army. Their objective was

Beaumont Hamel. No one pointed out that it had also been an objective way back in July for the first day of the battle. Gough leapt at the chance. Despite the weather, to which fog now added an additional impairment, due preparations were made. Artillery support would be considerable despite the difficulty the gunners would have in distinguishing the distant targets or even friend from foe among the infantry. The battle has been considered a success because after many travails Beaumont Hamel was taken. There are two things to be said about this. First, it mattered little at this stage of campaigning whether an insignificant village near the British front line remained in German hands. Secondly, the cost of capturing this place was considerable. About 10,000 men became casualties so that Haig could hold his head high at Chantilly. This was not the price of glory; it was the price of ignominy.

The Somme saw the martyrdom of the volunteer armies raised in Britain between 1914 and 1916. During the campaign some 432,000 of them became casualties. Of these probably 150,000 died and 100,000 were wounded so severely as to never fight again. In all, twenty-five divisions of British troops, about half of all those on the Western Front, were wiped out. For this terrible price, Haig managed to inflict only 230,000 casualties on the Germans. In addition, on the Allied side, the French suffered 200,000 casualties as they kept flank guard on Haig's futile endeavours. In terms of numbers alone then, there is no doubt who won the Battle of the Somme. It was the Germans. Yet it is a reasonable assumption that this is not how it felt to the enemy armies. They had suffered withering artillery attacks for some five months from a quite unexpected source – the British. And added to their casualties at Verdun, 500,000 men had been removed from the great engine of the war for the Central Powers. In August, this accumulation of loss for no apparent gain cost Falkenhayn his job. Nor were his successors, Hindenberg and Ludendorff, in a position to go over to the offensive for another fifteen months. Despite their casualties, the initiative at the end of 1916 still lay with the Entente.

The battles in 1916 were some of the largest seen in the melancholy tale of men at war. Total casualties for the Verdun campaign were probably close to 700,000 men; for the Somme they were over 1 million. In the East and in Italy the total bill was probably not far short of 1 million. The munitions effort was also immense. The British alone at the Somme threw some 15 million shells at the Germans. Added to the French effort, the Allied total for the Somme is probably around 20 million shells. Add to this an unknown total of German shells and all those fired by all sides in the East, and some idea of the enormous munitions effort expended by the European powers in this period can be gauged.

Yet in other ways, to call the battles of 1916 episodes of total war is misleading. Probably the maximum number of divisions employed in action on any one day was that by the British on the first day of the Somme – that is, fourteen divisions. The Germans probably employed ten divisions on the same day and the French six. Thus on the most intensive day of fighting in the West in 1916 just thirty divisions out of the two hundred deployed along the Western Front were locked in battle. Yet even this picture overstates the overall pattern of the fighting. The first day of the Somme and the first day of Verdun (when far fewer than thirty divisions fought it out) were not typical of either battle. On an average day on the Somme and at Verdun just a handful of divisions were engaged in an attack, large battles being followed by a rapid diminution in intensity. For most of the time, along most of the Western Front, most divisions were not involved in an attack. The mens' lives were hardly comfortable as they could at any time be subjected to artillery bombardments or trench raids of varying size and intensity. Yet the picture hardly adds up to total war. What it does add up to is attrition, in that the armies of all the combatants were being worn down. Of course this was not what their commanders were trying to achieve. At Verdun it has been suggested that Falkenhayn's objective was really the city itself and his 'bleeding white' strategy a convenient fallback position. In all Haig's major offensives on the Somme, he aimed at rupturing the German line and sending through the cavalry. This was his aim on 1 July, 14 July, 15 September and in the various battles of October. Attrition was what eventuated when these overly ambitious plans failed. But attrition was never a major aim of Haig's, though he has become known as the attritional general par excellence. He was not in fact a modern reincarnation of Ulysses S. Grant, he was much more a Napoleonic romantic, who dreamt of moving battlefronts, subjected to enormous cavalry sweeps. His men paid the price for this romanticism in 1916. They would pay it again in the year that was about to dawn.

5

1917: Global war

MICHAEL S. NEIBERG

A purgatory of souls

Sitting in the trenches of the Western Front on 30 December 1916 and struggling to keep warm as he wrote a letter home, French soldier Marc Boasson told his family that 'life is a terrible burden. Never has the baseness of human thought weighed on me so deeply. Life is an immense responsibility.' Although he did not know what 1917 might bring, Boasson was certain that it would mean more senseless killing and more suffering in the 'hell of flesh and the purgatory of souls' that the war had made out of Europe.[1] For soldiers the suffering was immense and seemingly without end, but those on the home front suffered as well. The privations of that winter were so intense that people remembered it, especially in Germany, as the 'turnip winter' and as one of the worst seasons of its kind in European history.

As 1917 dawned, the logic of total war dictated that societies had no choice but to fight on. Winning the war would require further monumental sacrifices, but losing the war would mean accepting the devastating terms that the enemy demanded. The war was now about survival, not ideals. Looking at 1917 through the narrow lens of the war itself, the dominant pattern is one of strategic futility and an inability by both sides to convert their national power into victory. The year meant more blood and treasure wasted to no greater strategic purpose, unless one accepts the cold logic of attrition, which dictated that one side had to wear the other down through large-scale battles before it could achieve victory. Although some historians have attempted to find in attrition a war-winning strategy, none of the battles of 1917 had attrition as its primary strategic purpose.[2]

1 Quoted in Benoist Méchin, *Ce qui demeure: lettres de soldats tombés au champ d'honneur, 1914–1918* (Paris: Bartillat, 2000), pp. 254–5.

2 See David French, 'The meaning of attrition, 1914–1916', *English Historical Review*, 103 (1988), pp. 385–405.

With a few notable exceptions, therefore, the campaigns of 1917 were strategic failures. Even those that achieved operational success, such as the Canadian/British seizure of Vimy Ridge in April or the German/Austro-Hungarian shattering of the Italian line at Caporetto in October, failed to achieve any long-lasting strategic success. Although these battles previewed what might be possible with proper planning and a bit of good fortune, the larger story of the year revolved around the continuing inability to break enemy lines then sustain that breakthrough. Both the French on the Chemin des Dames and the British in Belgium fought battles that ground their armies down without materially changing the situation in the West. That they also ground down the German army is undeniable, but it does not change the fact that at the end of the year the Allies believed themselves no closer to victory than at the start. Indeed, many highly placed Allied generals believed themselves to be much worse off in December than they had been in January. None of them dared even to dream that victory might be attainable in the year to come. Many more worried about defeat.

With a greater degree of perspective, one can see 1917 as a major watershed in military history. The year began an important transition on the battlefield; the battles of Cambrai, Riga and Caporetto represented the start of a shift from the infantry-based age of mass assaults to the mechanical, combined-arms approach that featured infantry working with aviation, artillery and armour in various combinations. This transition showed the fulfilment of the Industrial Revolution and its impacts on war. The second transition marked the growth of the United States and Russia to superpowers. Although few could have seen it at the time, 1917 represented the beginning of the end of the European imperial system and the start of a new system that, a generation later, would place the United States and the Soviet Union in a position of power over Europe.

In January (or even December) 1917, the idea of America or Russia rising looked like nonsense. Russia began the year as a badly weakened and stumbling colossus, unable to use its enormous human and natural resources to achieve victory. Although it had had some notable success on the battlefield in 1916, it was nowhere near forcing Germany or the Ottoman Empire out of the war, nor was it close to achieving any of its major war aims. Instead, it was coming apart at the seams as the tsarist regime lost legitimacy and the loyalty of its people. In February 1917, three centuries of Romanov rule came to an ignominious end, replaced by a fragile provisional government that, despite massive French and British aid, did not survive the year. Rocked by revolution and on the verge of civil war, Russia in 1917 was far from the great power that it would soon become.

Nor did the United States appear to be a rising superpower. When Woodrow Wilson took his nation to war in April it had an army so pitiful that it ranked behind that of Portugal. It had no tanks, no fully equipped divisions, no experienced commanders, no modern training system and just fifty-five airplanes. The army was also humbled by its failure to find the Mexican bandit, Pancho Villa, despite the dispatch of 12,000 soldiers to do the job. The Americans had no combat experience and, owing to Wilson's strict definition of neutrality, had sent no observers to the Western Front to learn about the war first-hand. The Americans were also wracked by organisational problems, endemic corruption in their arms industries and a divided populace.[3] The military was so unprepared for war that Senate Finance Committee chairman Thomas S. Martin of Virginia replied to an army major's request for military funding with a horrified 'Good Lord! You're not going to send soldiers over there, are you?'[4] Martin and others had expected the American contribution to Allied victory to be financial and naval. Even he didn't expect the American army to do much to influence the outcome.

Nevertheless, 1917 marked changes so massive for both nations that it is difficult to overstate them. Russia experienced two revolutions, the latter arguably the most important revolution in European history since the fall of the Bastille in 1789. Bolshevik Russia may have been no less authoritarian or brutal than the aristocratic regime it violently overthrew, but it eventually found a way to harness the energies and resources of the lands under its control. In doing so, it both inspired and terrified millions of people across the globe and set up a rivalry with the other beneficiary of 1917, the United States.

For their part the Americans spent 1917 inconsistently and, at times, unwillingly, becoming a world power. Although it demobilised its army after the war, the United States emerged as the world's unquestioned financial power and industrial giant. The nation spent the interwar years reluctantly lurching towards Great Power status. Although large sections of the American population remained isolationist and the Great Depression dented America's global influence, after 1941 its leaders enthusiastically embraced the vision Woodrow Wilson had set out in 1917 to use American power to promote its own vision of democracy and freedom. That this vision contained contradictions and self-serving aims has not stopped succeeding generations from

3 For an introduction into these problems see Linda Robertson, *The Dream of Civilized Warfare* (Minneapolis: University of Minnesota Press, 2005).

4 Quoted in David Kennedy, *Over Here: The First World War and American Society* (New York: Oxford University Press, 1980), p. 144.

embracing it with a vigour that would have stunned the Americans who set it in motion in the fateful year of 1917.[5]

A wasteland

The war was, of course, the primary catalyst of these changes. At the start of 1917, both sides remained mired in strategic paralysis. Contrary to the assumptions of many strategists in 1914, neither side had broken financially or morally under the stresses and strains of three years of modern war. The pre-war beliefs of men like Norman Angell and Ivan Bloch that societies could not stand prolonged war proved to be tragically false.[6] Although at tremendous human and financial cost, both alliances had remained determined and capable of maintaining powerful armies in the field and functioning economies to support them. New weapons had increased the lethality of the battlefield, but not even tanks or new generations of airplanes had made important strategic differences. By the beginning of 1917 neither side appeared close to breaking, and there seemed to be no end in sight to the war.

German strategists had still not found a solution to the essential two-front dilemma that had haunted their general staff for decades. In 1916 they had put their main effort in the West at Verdun while holding on to a defensive posture in the East. The surprising success of the Russians in the Brusilov offensive that summer put significant pressure on the Germans and, perhaps more importantly, on their faltering Austro-Hungarian allies. The German strategy was evidently not working, and German planners knew that a long war put pressures on the German home front that it might not be able to withstand for long. It was, after all, in Germany that the moniker 'the turnip winter' had stuck.

The Germans therefore decided on a new command team and a new strategy. In 1916, they had replaced General Erich von Falkenhayn, the chief architect of the Verdun catastrophe, with Generals Paul von Hindenburg and Erich Ludendorff, the successful duumvirate from the Eastern Front. With them came what Holger Herwig called 'a new spirit and a new concept of war'. The new German leadership envisioned not just hanging on, but changing the momentum of the war and winning a complete victory to

5 For a wonderfully eloquent introduction to the limitations of that vision see Erez Manela, *The Wilsonian Moment: Self-Determination and the International Origins of Anticolonial Nationalism* (New York: Oxford University Press, 2007).

6 See Norman Angell, *The Great Illusion* (London: Putnam's Sons, 1910), which argued that modern economies would break quickly under the strain of war.

provide Germany 'monetary indemnities and vast territorial annexations' to justify the high German casualties of 1914–16.[7]

Their strategy depended on finding a way to buy some time to allow Germany to recover from its losses and to shift its focus east once again. Hindenburg and Ludendorff abandoned the previous concept of holding every square metre of territory that the German army had captured since 1914. Instead, they sensibly evacuated exposed salients and terrain that was difficult to hold. Doing so made the line easier to defend and required fewer soldiers, an important consideration after the bloodletting of 1916. The German army thus retreated to a straighter line protected by powerful fortifications known collectively as the Hindenburg or Siegfried Line, itself an impressive achievement of military engineering.

The new defences were formidable. Built largely with the forced labour of prisoners of war, the line was in fact five different prepared positions that covered 300 miles of the Western Front. Each set of defences ideally began with a forward anti-tank ditch three yards deep and four yards wide, followed by no fewer than five belts of barbed wire each four yards deep, behind which sat the main killing section of the line. It contained steel-reinforced concrete blockhouses that protected machine guns. Should any enemy troops manage to get past these lines, they would have to face modern trenches dug in zigzag fashion and virtually immune from howitzers or grenades. They were linked to one another by communication trenches, telegraphs and electrical lines and they contained field hospitals, command posts and ammunition storage. Behind them stood artillery units to break up attacking enemy formations from a distance.

The new plan required the Germans to cede more than 1,000 square miles of hard-won territory in France, but it made strategic sense. The Germans then devastated the land they abandoned, taking away everything they could carry and destroying what they could not. As Ernst Jünger recalled, 'every village was reduced to rubble, every tree felled, every street mined, every well poisoned, every creek dammed up, every cellar blown up or studded with hidden bombs, all metals and supplies taken back to our lines . . . in short, we transformed the land into which the enemy would advance into a wasteland'.[8] The French did not forget this intentional devastation when they drew up peace terms the following year.

7 Holger Herwig, *The First World War: Germany and Austria-Hungary, 1914–1918* (London: Edward Arnold, 1997), p. 229.

8 Jünger quoted in *ibid.*, p. 251.

The Hindenburg Line further demonstrated the pattern that the defence was much more powerful than the offence in 1917. Still, the Allies knew that to win the war and to recover lost French and Belgian territory, they would have to attack. Although the major Allied offensives of 1917 proved to be failures, it is important to keep in mind that Allied generals did not have the luxury of remaining on the defensive. Doing so would have given Germany the time it needed to finish off the Russians and improve even further on the defences they had created in the West. This essential dilemma does not excuse the poor planning of the Allies in 1917, but it must be a factor in explaining the failures in the battles of the Chemin des Dames (also called the Nivelle offensive) and at the Third Battle of Ypres (also called Passchendaele).

The Germans hoped that the new plan would buy them time and allow them to blunt any major Allied offensive in 1917 in the West. They also turned up the pressure on the British by resuming unrestricted submarine warfare in January. They knew that the move risked antagonising the world's most powerful neutral nation, the United States, but they determined that the gamble was worth it. Submarines could cut the British Isles from badly needed imports and, they hoped, without Britain the French could not continue the war. At first the gamble seemed to pay off as the Americans responded not with a declaration of war but with the far lighter measure of severing diplomatic relations. Tensions continued to build, however, and the publication of the Zimmermann Telegram in March seemed to demonstrate to the Americans that the Germans did indeed pose a clear and present danger to the United States. President Woodrow Wilson asked the American Congress for a declaration of war in April, with disastrous consequences for the Germans.[9]

The small numbers of U-boats severely limited German effectiveness, although their potential to cause harm continued to strike fear into Allied maritime officials. In the words of the French official history, the Germans had too few U-boats to win the war but had just enough to 'permit discussion of peace terms based on a "map of the war" increasingly favorable to them'.[10] Defeating the U-boats was thus a serious problem. The Allied navies

9 Jennifer D. Keene, *World War I: The American Soldier Experience* (Lincoln: University of Nebraska Press, 2011), p. 10. In March 1917, the American people learned of the Zimmermann Telegram. It promised Mexico generous financial help and the return of Texas, Arizona and New Mexico if Mexico joined Germany in any future war between Germany and the United States. It also posited a future anti-American alliance of Germany, Mexico and Japan that terrified many Americans. The Mexican government disavowed any interest in a German alliance, but the damage was done.

10 Ministère de la Guerre, État-Major, Service Historique, *Les armées françaises dans la Grande Guerre*, Tome v, vol. II (Paris: Imprimerie nationale, 1936), p. 32.

responded by implementing a convoy plan that ended the practice of sending merchant ships across the Atlantic individually and with little protection except the mercantile rights that the Germans were ignoring in any case. Instead, the Allies sent the ships in groups, each of which received protection from destroyers, which were fast and nimble enough to hunt down submarines. After American entry into the war, the American and British navies worked together to ensure the safety of transatlantic shipping. In the end, North American goods and American soldiers crossed the Atlantic safely throughout 1917 and 1918. The German submarine gamble had failed.

Another German gamble, however, succeeded beyond anyone's expectations. In March, Russian Tsar Nicholas II abdicated his throne as his reactionary regime proved far too brittle to survive the demands of modern war.[11] A few weeks later, the Germans put thirty-two Russian radicals, most notably V. I. Lenin, in a special train bound for Petrograd to foment a full-scale revolution. Although he had not been in his native country for more than a decade, Lenin's rhetoric appealed to a segment of the Russian populace that wanted change and an end to the war under almost any circumstances.

The leader of the provisional Russian government, Alexander Kerensky, hoped to prove Lenin wrong. Supported by the Allies and arguing that Russian soldiers should continue to fight, Kerensky implored the Russian army to remain loyal. He turned to General Alexei Brusilov, who had led Russia's successful offensives in 1916, in the hopes that Brusilov could perform the trick once again. In July he led two Russian armies in a massive offensive that enjoyed some early success but then fizzled out with men deserting from the army by the thousands. The failure of the Kerensky offensive led to a sharp decline in Russian morale and the virtual end of Russian support for continuing the war. Russia's middle class and moderates soon found themselves assailed by radicals like Lenin's Bolsheviks, who promised to end the war and reform Russian society amid cries of 'Peace, Land and Bread'.

The Germans took advantage of the chaos inside Russia by pushing east as far as their supply lines would take them. Nevertheless, the Austro-Hungarian army was showing signs of weakness, the German leadership refused to send men or materiel from the West and the nightmarish vision of repeating Napoleon's mistake always remained vivid in the eyes of German planners. By the end of the year the Bolsheviks had control of the Russian government

11 For a recent interpretation of the events that led to the Tsar's downfall, see Sean McMeekin, *The Russian Origins of the First World War* (Cambridge, MA: Harvard University Press, 2011), especially chapter 9.

and the Germans decided that they could gain more from negotiation than by enduring another Russian winter on the battlefield. In December, they opened negotiations from a position of strength and in the ensuing Treaty of Brest-Litovsk they seized more than 1 million square miles of Russian territory, along with enough raw materials to compensate for some of the losses suffered from the British blockade.

The German leadership hoped to realise great benefits from eliminating its largest front, but events turned out to be more complicated than it had anticipated. Political upheaval in Russia and in Ukraine made the Eastern Front unstable, and resistance on the part of the local populace to German seizures of grain threatened to prevent the Germans from taking everything that they wanted. As a result, the Germans had to deploy more men in the East than they had originally planned, even if major combat there had ended. Perhaps more surprisingly, the same Bolshevik virus that they had injected into the Russian body politic infected German soldiers, contributing to the radicalisation of the once-loyal German left, which had now 'found a new model in the Bolshevik revolution'.[12]

On the Western Front, Allied strategy also took a new turn with a new commander. The tired French commander General Joseph Joffre, long out of ideas and having burned one too many bridges with his political masters, was shipped off to the United States to encourage and advise the Americans. His former protégé, the more energetic and intellectual Ferdinand Foch, also went into eclipse, and received the largely pointless assignment to develop war plans in the extremely unlikely event of a German invasion of France through Switzerland.[13] Both men were associated with the failed strategies of 1915 and 1916. Joffre, who had fired dozens of French commanders in 1914, now found himself on the receiving end of such treatment. Foch spent 1917 dealing with the largely make-believe Swiss problem before going to Italy in the wake of the Caporetto disaster in Italy, then returning to become the French Chief of Staff by the end of the year.

Joffre's replacement as the commander of the French army was the confident and smooth-tongued General Robert Nivelle. A Protestant and fluent English speaker (both rarities in the French High Command), Nivelle and his innovative artillery methods received much of the credit for French successes

12 Roger Chickering, *Imperial Germany and the Great War, 1914–1918*, 2nd edn (Cambridge University Press, 2005), p. 157.

13 Elizabeth Greenhalgh sees the Switzerland assignment in more positive terms. She covers the dismissal of Joffre and Foch in *Foch in Command: The Forging of a First World War General* (Cambridge University Press, 2011), pp. 200–7.

at the end of the Verdun campaign the previous year. His scientific and aggressive methods seemed to stand in marked contrast to the slow, slogging approach that Joffre, Foch and Henri-Philippe Pétain preferred. Nivelle was not shy about the supposed superiority of his methods, claiming 'The experience is conclusive; our method has proved itself.'[14]

Nivelle's optimism was infectious among politicians who wanted desperately to believe that he really had unlocked the secret to modern warfare. Among those he charmed was the British Prime Minister, David Lloyd George, who saw Nivelle as a viable alternative to British Field Marshal Sir Douglas Haig, in whom Lloyd George was rapidly losing faith. Lloyd George therefore agreed to Nivelle's overall strategic direction for 1917 and forced Haig to conform to it in lieu of Haig's preference for an operation in Flanders. In mid January, Nivelle presented a plan to target the giant salient from Arras in the north to Reims in the south that jutted towards Paris. He sought 'to fix the enemy at one point and then to attack another point where we will penetrate and will march toward his reserves in order to destroy them'.[15] The British and French would jointly attack in the north as soon as spring weather permitted, drawing German attention towards Arras and the strategic heights nearby. The French would then use the methods Nivelle had allegedly perfected at Verdun to open a hole in the difficult terrain along the River Aisne. The rising ground around the river would pose a challenge but, Nivelle supposed, the Germans would not be prepared to face a determined attack there.

The politicians fell for Nivelle's bravado, but most of his fellow generals did not. Haig objected to being treated as a subordinate when he was, in point of fact, senior to Nivelle. More importantly, French generals objected to Nivelle's operational plan, his lack of secrecy and the location of his attack. The ridge Nivelle planned to assault was a veritable cliff topped by a road, the Chemin des Dames, which afforded the Germans excellent visibility into the valley below. There would thus be no chance of achieving surprise. The ridge, moreover, featured two powerful defensive formations, the Malmaison fortress on the western edge, and a stone quarry, the Caverne du Dragon, that the Germans had converted into a subterranean stronghold.[16] Professionals knew that the ridge would likely resist any attack because the Germans had

14 Quoted in Robert Doughty, *Pyrrhic Victory: French Strategy and Operations in the Great War* (Cambridge, MA: Harvard University Press, 2005), p. 324.

15 Quoted in *ibid.*, pp. 329–30.

16 There is a wonderful website on the Caverne that affords a terrific look at its role in 1917: www.caverne-du-dragon.com/en/default.aspx. The Caverne is also open for tours.

the advantage of exceptional high ground and positions that were invulnerable to the kinds of tactical artillery bombardments that had worked at Verdun.

More importantly, the German withdrawal to the Hindenburg Line removed any strategic reason to attack the Chemin des Dames. Why attack an area that the enemy was planning to evacuate voluntarily? Nivelle protested that the aerial evidence showing the construction of the new German lines proved nothing about German intent and that the Germans would not under any circumstances evacuate positions that sat just seventy-five miles from Paris. The French government was concerned enough about the disagreement of many of Nivelle's senior subordinates to start asking questions. The new French War Minister, Paul Painlevé, who took office in March, owed his new job to the fact that his predecessor, France's legendary imperial soldier General Hubert Lyautey, had resigned rather than assume responsibility for a plan that he thought was amateurish and destined for disaster. Painlevé, confused about the mixed signals he was hearing, even took the unusual step of seeking out Haig to get his views on Nivelle.[17]

Painlevé did confront Nivelle, who defended his plan, despite the fact that key details of it were well-known in circles that should not have been in the loop. Nivelle pledged to achieve success in forty-eight hours or, he promised, he would shut the offensive down. He also threatened to resign if the French government did not back him, thereby creating a military crisis as well as a diplomatic crisis because Nivelle had Lloyd George's support. Painlevé reluctantly gave in, and the offensive went ahead.

The first phase of the offensive involved an attack on a series of hills known as Vimy Ridge. Overlooking the city of Arras, these hills were the key to holding the entire sector. The Germans had spared little expense improving upon the natural position that the high ground afforded. They had dug deep defensive positions that German generals considered unbreakable. The hills had also become symbolically important following a series of bloody failures by the French army to take them in 1915. Although Nivelle saw it largely in

17 Gary Sheffield and John Bourne (eds.), *Douglas Haig: War Diaries and Letters, 1914–1918* (London: Weidenfeld & Nicolson, 2005), p. 277, entry for 24 March 1917. Haig had his doubts about Nivelle but did not express them to Painlevé, possibly because he did not want to speak badly about a fellow soldier to a politician. Foch had done the same service for him when Lloyd George had asked his opinion of Haig's performance on the Somme. Haig wrote then that 'Unless I had been told of this conversation personally by General Foch I would not have believed that a British Minister could be so ungentlemanly as to go to a foreigner and put such questions regarding his subordinates.' Entry for 17 September 1916 quoted in *ibid.*, p. 232.

terms of a diversion from his own attack in the Chemin des Dames, the attack on Vimy Ridge proved to be the only bright spot in an otherwise dismal campaign.

The task fell to the British army and, through it, to the Canadian Corps. Its commander was a relative amateur, a militia officer once under a cloud of suspicion for alleged embezzlement of regimental funds, named Arthur Currie. Portly and clean shaven, he did not fit in well with his aristocratic and mustachioed British colleagues. Currie sought neither to emulate British appearance nor methods. He had spent more time studying the successful French methods at the end of the Verdun campaign than he had studying British failures on the Somme. Inquisitive, independent to the point of insubordination and meticulous, Currie emerged as one of the best Corps Commanders of the war.[18]

Nivelle may have seen the Vimy Ridge attack as a diversion, but Currie did not. Learning from Nivelle's artillery methods and improving upon them, Currie was able to give his troops adequate cover for the attack. He relied on an artillery plan devised largely by the future British Chief of the Imperial general staff in the Second World War, Lord Alanbrooke. Currie had trained his men in their specific tasks and, in part because his own aims were limited, he could match what he asked of them to the resources available. As a result the Canadian attack on Vimy Ridge on 9–12 April 1917 was an astonishing success. As Currie himself wrote to the Premier of British Columbia, 'We penetrated over six miles into the enemy's defenses, capturing all our objectives, and what is considered more remarkable still, captured them all on time.' Currie took particular pride in having a German prisoner of war tell him that the Germans had considered Vimy 'impregnable' and a British general calling his corps 'the wonder of the British Army'.[19] By any standard, the Canadian accomplishment was one of the most impressive of the entire war.

The success at Vimy and the official announcement that the United States had declared war on Germany raised both spirits and expectations for the main part of Nivelle's operation, the attack on the Chemin des Dames. Launched on 17 April, despite poor weather and strong indications that the

18 See Tim Cook, *The Madman and the Butcher: The Sensational Wars of Sam Hughes and General Arthur Currie* (Toronto: Allen Lane, 2010).

19 Currie to Harlan Brewster, 31 May 1917, in Mark Osbourne Humphries (ed.), *The Selected Papers of Sir Arthur Currie: Diaries, Letters, and Report to the Ministry, 1917–1933* (Waterloo, ON: Laurier Centre for Military and Disarmament Studies, Wilfrid Laurier University Press, 2008), p. 40.

Germans were fully expecting the attack, it gained some ground, but manifestly failed to deliver what Nivelle had so loftily promised (Map 5.1). Nivelle had expected tanks and airplanes to help make his artillery more effective, but the cloudy, rainy weather grounded the planes and most of the tanks broke down in the difficult terrain. As a result, German machine guns remained virtually intact and they inflicted murderous casualties on attacking French units. Nivelle continued to send in reinforcements in hopes of breaking the lines, but that decision only increased the bloodshed. Instead of gaining six miles, as Nivelle had promised, his attack gained less than 600 yards. Even combat-hardened units, like the elite Senegalese regiments, broke and ran.

Rather than stop the offensive after forty-eight hours as he had pledged to Painlevé, Nivelle kept going. He may have believed overly optimistic reports coming into his Headquarters that the Germans were ready to break, or he may just have been intellectually incapable of stopping after having invested so much into the offensive's success. Whatever the reason, casualties mounted to no apparent purpose. Having planned for 15,000 casualties, French medical services instead had to deal with more than 100,000. With Nivelle still unwilling to call a halt, the French government stepped in and ordered the offensive stopped.

The failure of the Nivelle offensive carried with it important consequences. It severely damaged French relations with the British, in part because the British felt compelled to renew attacks around Arras to relieve pressure from the French, and in part because Nivelle, who had once been so free with information, refused to share critical details of the failure with Haig's headquarters. The disaster also undermined British support for French proposals to create a unified command for the Western Front. British generals were understandably reluctant to place their troops under foreign command even before the catastrophe on the Chemin des Dames; after it, they dug their heels in even deeper, with important consequences for 1918.

But the most important ramification of the failure of Nivelle's grand plan occurred among the French troops themselves. Furious at the gross incompetence of their own leaders, thousands of them refused to attack. A small but vocal few advocated revolution or mutiny, but most sought some third option beyond outright rebellion and senseless slaughter.[20] Exact numbers remain hard to calculate, but it is clear that tens of thousands of men refused to obey their officers' orders to attack. Most of them remained in their trenches,

20 The starting point for a study of this topic should be Leonard V. Smith, *Between Mutiny and Obedience: The Case of the French Fifth Infantry Division during World War I* (Princeton University Press, 1994).

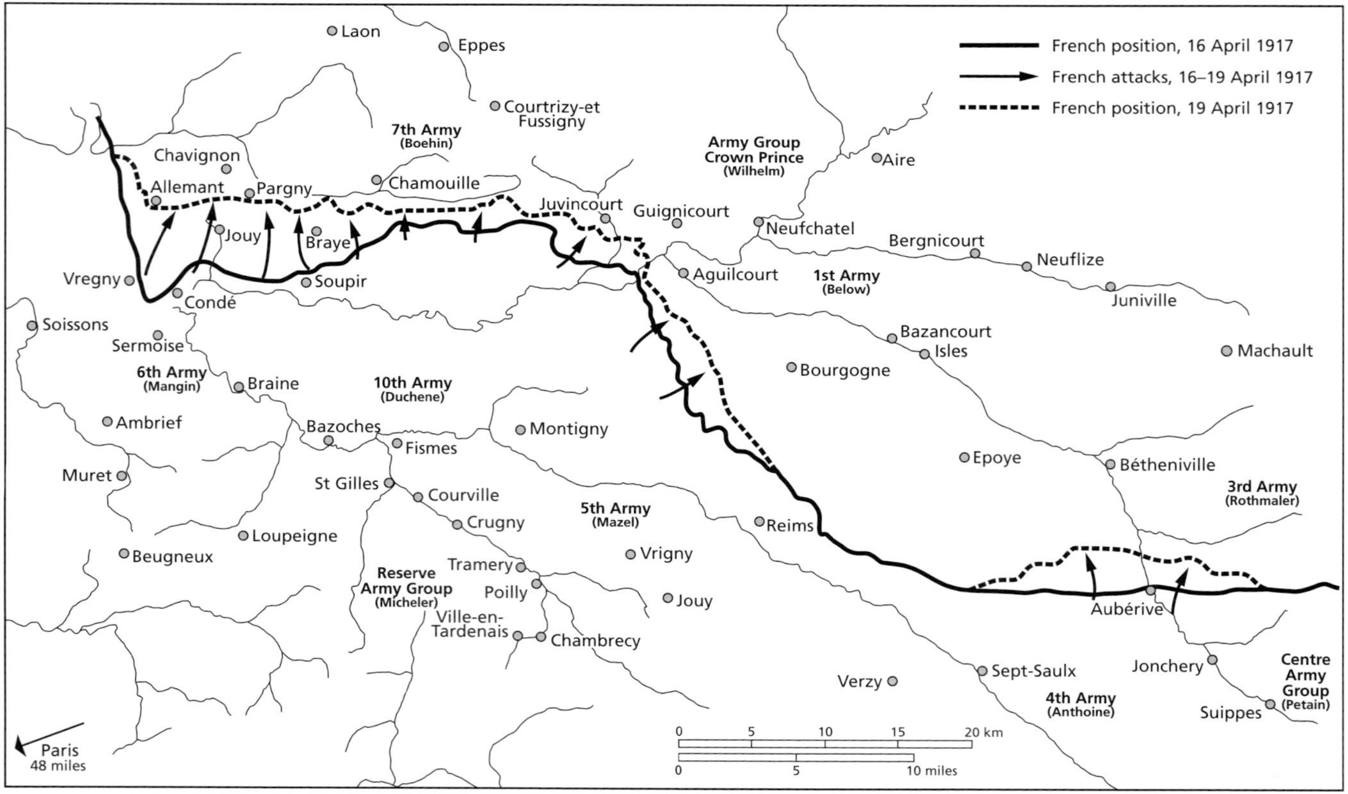

Map 5.1 The Nivelle offensive, April 1917.

however, and pledged that they would still defend French soil, but that they would no longer attack under such murderous circumstances. They were also careful enough not to let the Germans opposite them get a clear picture of what was happening just a few hundred yards away.

At the same time, a wave of strikes hit French cities, with French workers protesting inflation and their general lack of a voice in the wartime industrial system.[21] Although there were no direct causal connections between the two movements, the strikes heightened fears inside the French army's leadership that pacifism, defeatism or, worse yet, communism, was spreading through France. Initial beliefs by French leaders that the mutinies were the work of a few malcontents and poor soldiers prodded by the far left proved unfounded. Even excellent units and soldiers participated. One soldier, a future winner of the Croix de Guerre, remained dedicated to France, but was deeply disillusioned by its generals. 'It is shameful', he wrote home, 'to see how we are being led; I believe that they have no thought of finishing the war until every man is dead.'[22]

The crisis demanded swift action. Nivelle was replaced by another hero of Verdun, the taciturn General Henri-Philippe Pétain. Known as a defensively minded general, he was a good choice and reasonably popular among the men. He dealt harshly with soldiers who had threatened officers or encouraged rebellion, but he also knew that the men had legitimate complaints. He instituted major reforms in the French army, ranging from better food and more leave to ordering French officers to spend more time in the trenches with their men. He also began a reform of the French army designed to make it a modern force that fought with artillery, armour and aviation all working together to reduce casualties. As the French army itself put it, 'New Chief, New Plan, New Methods.'[23]

Pétain's strategic vision aimed to use more force, mostly with artillery and tanks, aimed at smaller goals. He wanted his offensives limited in both space and time; if an offensive showed signs of failure, he would shut it down and look elsewhere. Above all, he wanted to avoid long, attritional campaigns on the 1915 and 1916 models. He ordered an end to all large-scale offensives until his new tactical system was in place, although he did order smaller-scale attacks in strategic areas, including Verdun and against the Malmaison fortress

21 See several of the essays in Patrick Fridenson (ed.), *The French Home Front, 1914–1918* (Oxford: Berg, 1992).

22 Quoted in Martha Hanna, *Your Death Would Be Mine: Paul and Marie Pireaud in the Great War* (Cambridge, MA: Harvard University Press, 2006), p. 205.

23 *Les armées françaises dans la Grande Guerre*, Tome V, vol. II, p. v.

on the Chemin des Dames. Most of these attacks were successful and caused casualties that by 1917 standards were proportionate to their accomplishments. Pétain thus brought calm to the French army and implemented some of the important changes that made the army a fighting force once again in 1918. He knew, however, that French manpower was a dwindling resource and that the arrival of the Americans would be critical to Allied success.

The mutinies in France and Russia proved that all armies, even those defending their own homeland, had a breaking point. The Germans were to learn this lesson a year later. They also proved, at least in the French case, that even in circumstances as desperate as those of April and May 1917, soldiers and the societies that supported them were unwilling to surrender. In the 1930s, many observers argued that the First World War had broken French martial spirit, but there was no irrefutable evidence that French morale had broken in 1917. It was clear, however, that the French army was unlikely to launch another major offensive for many months to come. It needed time to rest, to regain military discipline and to learn Pétain's new system.

Failure in Flanders

Douglas Haig, the British commander, had received discouraging reports about the French army, including some that suggested that French soldiers were demanding peace and refusing to salute their officers. These reports convinced Haig that the French army might not survive a German attack against it. Without the French army, which occupied the majority of the Allied line, the British could not hope to win. Haig concluded that his long-desired offensive in Flanders offered the best way to draw the Germans away from the French and give his ally the time it desperately needed.[24] In point of fact, the French army was not in as dire a position as Haig believed it to be, but given the seriousness of the situation and the lack of information forthcoming from French Headquarters, his fears were well founded. Haig was also gaining confidence in his army, now better trained and more battle-tested after its long weeks of fighting on the Somme in 1916. That army, once filled with inexperienced civilians with no prior history of military service, was now a larger, better-led force that Haig hoped could win the war before the end of the year.

British politicians did not always share his optimism. David Lloyd George in particular doubted whether the offensive would work and seriously

24 Gary Sheffield, *The Chief: Douglas Haig and the British Army* (London: Aurum Press, 2011), p. 230.

doubted whether Haig was the man to lead it. Lloyd George made noises about his disapproval of the plan and threatened to divert resources needed for it to other theatres, most notably Italy and Palestine. In the end, however, neither the Prime Minister nor the War Cabinet did anything other than note their disapproval of Haig's plans and request that he not fight another long and protracted campaign like the Somme.

The campaign to be known as Passchendaele or the Third Battle of Ypres began auspiciously enough on 7 June when the British detonated a massive and painstakingly dug set of mines under the Messines Ridge on the south face of the Ypres salient. A tremendous explosion literally removed the ridge from the Belgian landscape; people as far away as London heard and felt the blast. Thousands of Germans were buried under the debris or killed by the concussion. The offensive was off to an unexpected start that seemed to augur success.

Thereafter, however, little went as Haig had planned. The British were slow to exploit the shock of Messines, allowing the Germans to move reinforcements into the area. Haig had placed in command of one of the armies one of his protégés, Sir Hubert Gough. Gough came from a distinguished military family, but he was completely unprepared for the tasks Haig gave him. Haig's intelligence officers also consistently misread the situation, especially in their repeated assertions that German morale was close to breaking.

Command confusion, strong German defences that better protected soldiers from the effects of artillery and almost unprecedented levels of rain further slowed British advances. Massive casualties mounted from both the British and the French who fought in support, belying the notion that the French army was incapable of combat operations. The small gains of muddy Belgian fields did not come close to redeeming those losses, nor did they match Haig's ambitious goals for a breakthrough. German defences in depth, arranged around pillboxes laid out in a checkerboard pattern, proved effective (Map 5.2).

The British adapted and scored local successes at places like Menin Road, Polygon Wood and Broodseinde, but the campaign as a whole failed to achieve Haig's goals. As autumn brought worsening weather and shorter days, British gains slowed to a halt. In one attack in late October the British lost 2,000 men to move the line a mere 500 yards. In November Haig called a halt to an offensive that had done little to improve the Allies' strategic situation. Nor had it attrited the Germans in proportion to British losses. Recent estimates place British losses at 275,000 men against 200,000 Germans. Not

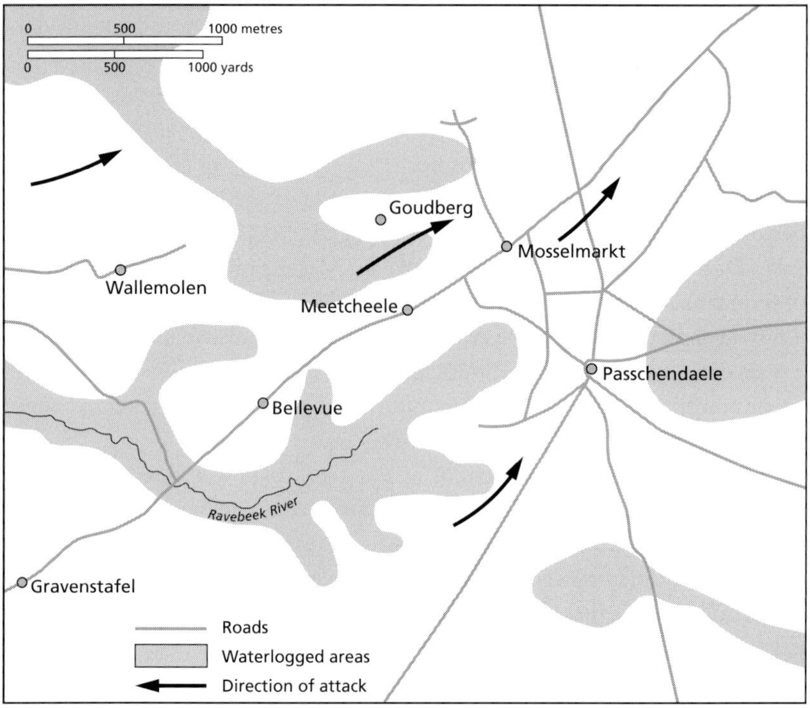

Map 5.2 Passchendaele: waterlogged areas.

only had the British failed to break through, they were actually in a worse geographic position than they had been in July. They also had fewer reserves with which to meet any future German offensives, such as the one that came the following spring.[25]

A glimpse of the future

Three smaller battles of 1917 clearly looked forward and gave a glimpse of warfare's future. The first two were designed and executed by the Germans, although the French and Italians had also been moving in similar directions. Changes in the use of artillery were at the heart of the new methods. Designed

25 Sheffield, *The Chief*, presents a relatively positive interpretation of these events. A more critical perspective is in Robin Prior and Trevor Wilson, *Passchendaele: The Untold Story* (New Haven, CT: Yale University Press, 1996).

in large part by Germany's Colonel Georg Bruchmüller, the new artillery system used shorter and sharper barrages and included heavier concentrations of poison gas. Bruchmüller's system also emphasised shorter barrages delivered with little advance warning in order to maintain surprise and prevent the enemy from rushing reserves into the target area. These new methods aimed more to disorient than to overwhelm.[26] Into the breaches thus created the Germans sent specially trained soldiers who would bypass the enemy's forward trenches in order to target the command and control centres behind them. Once the enemy's command system had been disabled, German artillery could target the enemy's reinforcements as they arrived and regular German infantry could attack the enemy's front lines with the odds more in their favour.

This new system of infiltration tactics required highly trained infantry and a new approach to artillery. It sought to win not by trading punches as in a heavyweight fight, but by exploiting enemy weaknesses in something more akin to a judo match. In September, in the first of the three battles, the Germans used the new system to capture Riga. The operation was a spectacular success, inflicting casualties at a six to one ratio and instilling widespread panic in Russian ranks. The victory at Riga was enough to convince the Germans to try again on a larger scale, setting up the second forward-looking battle of 1917, Caporetto on the Italian Front.

That front had been mired in a bloody stalemate that cost both sides enormous casualties without moving the lines much at all. Although the Austro-Hungarian defenders managed to hold off repeated Italian offensives, difficult fighting in mountainous terrain had taken its toll. The Germans decided to test the methods used at Riga on the Italian Front, in the hopes of helping their Austro-Hungarian ally and buying them time to regroup and refit.

Launched on 24 October, the Caporetto offensive succeeded beyond the Germans' wildest imagination. Artillery destroyed Italian positions and the rapid collapse of Italian lines caused a panic and rout that sent 1.5 million Italian soldiers fleeing in disorder towards the presumed safety of the Piave river. Italy lost an estimated 280,000 prisoners of war on top of thousands of pieces of heavy equipment that soldiers could not take with them. Bad as it was, the Italian defeat would have been even worse but for the fact that even the Germans were surprised by their success and had made no plans to pursue deep into Italian territory. Now, having seen the new system work twice, the

26 See David Zabecki, *Steel Wind: Colonel Georg Bruchmüller and the Birth of Modern Artillery* (Westport, CT: Greenwood Press, 1994).

Germans exported it to the Western Front where it would demonstrate tactical success once more in 1918.[27]

In the third battle, at Cambrai on the Western Front, the British sought to exploit the one technological advantage they possessed over the Germans: tanks. Both the British and the French had invested heavily in tanks but thus far they had proven to be a disappointment due to mechanical problems and a poor doctrine for using them. A group of young and innovative British officers believed that the problem lay mainly in the unimaginative use the British High Command had made of tanks. They argued that tanks could supplement artillery barrages by using their strengths of surprise and mobility; tanks, moreover, did not chew up the ground for the infantry as artillery shells did. At the same time, British artillery had improved its effectiveness through scientific advancements in targeting and accuracy.

At Cambrai on 20 November, the British used 476 tanks massed in teams of three. They caused surprise and panic on the German side of the line in large part because the Germans had no effective anti-tank weapons. The tanks experienced mechanical problems but provided much-needed direct fire support to infantry. A gap of five miles soon opened up in the German lines, presenting Haig and the British command with exactly the scenario they had worked so hard to create for three years. Tragically, though, they had too few reserves to push through the gap and the British planners had erred by not leaving any tanks in reserve to help keep the gap open. Even if they had, the tanks did not have the ability to sustain such a breakthrough. The British thus had a tantalising opportunity, but no tools with which to exploit it.

Cambrai had thus been an enormous operational success, but one that the British could not turn into a strategic success. Haig ordered the offensive to continue despite diminishing returns and signs that the Germans were preparing a counter-offensive to attack the badly exposed flanks of the British lines. A furious German attack came on 30 November, catching the British off guard and recovering almost all British gains from the previous ten days. They even captured some ground that had been British on 20 November. The quick reversal of British fortunes prompted a court of enquiry into the British defeat. Despite the failures, Cambrai pointed the way to a future method of war based around armour. Men on both sides of the lines internalised that lesson and used it in the interwar years to rewrite the doctrines of land warfare.

27 See Mario Morselli, *Caporetto 1917: Victory or Defeat?* (London: Routledge, 2001). Among the most successful young German officers at Caporetto was Lieutenant Erwin Rommel.

The end of yet another frustrating year of war set up a race of sorts. The key to 1918, most planners believed, was whether the Germans could move men from the Eastern Front to the Western Front faster than the Americans could land their fresh but hastily trained soldiers in France. If the Germans won that race, and managed to implement their new artillery and infiltration tactics on a wide scale, then they had a chance to win the war before the Americans could make much difference. If, however, they failed, the arrival of hundreds of thousands of fresh bodies would buy the Allies all the time they would need to grind the Germans down through attrition, superior firepower and the ongoing naval blockade that continued to cut deeply into German food and fuel supplies.

Economics and the pressures that the war brought to bear on the German people played a critical role in ending the war. Strikes, shortages and accusations of profiteering were rampant in France and (to a lesser extent) in Britain as well, but the democracies managed to keep the problem manageable. In part, their ability to keep their economies functioning was a function of determined and skilled civilians like France's Minister of Munitions, Albert Thomas, and Britain's Chancellor of the Exchequer (and later Prime Minister), David Lloyd George.[28] The Western Allies also benefited tremendously from access to American credit and other forms of financial assistance as well as raw materials from Asia, Africa and the Americas.

By 1917, as America came formally into the war and the U-boat crisis abated, the French and British could take maximum advantage of such access. The Germans, by contrast, were reduced to taking resources from an already impoverished Eastern Front.[29] Moreover, rather than being able to pool resources with allies as the British, French and Americans were doing, the Germans had the additional responsibility of trying to prop up their faltering Austro-Hungarian and Ottoman allies. The German economy was simply incapable of meeting such a monumental challenge.

In Germany, furthermore, the military took over more and more of the economic planning, with disastrous results. To planners in Berlin, much more than to their counterparts in Paris or London, the civilian economy became little more than an engine for providing resources to the army. In the words of Jay Winter, once Hindenburg and Ludendorff took effective control over the reins of the German government, 'a different order of priorities existed . . . The military

28 For more on Thomas and the French economy, see Leonard V. Smith, Stéphane Audoin-Rouzeau and Annette Becker, *France and the Great War, 1914–1918* (Cambridge University Press, 2003), chapter 2.

29 For more see Vejas Liulevicius, *War Land on the Eastern Front: Culture, National Identity and German Occupation in World War I* (Cambridge University Press, 2000).

came first, and the economy created to service it completely distorted the delicate economic system at home.'[30] Inflation ran rampant, robbing Germans of both purchasing power and savings. A German war bond purchased for 1,000 marks in 1914 was, by 1917, worth just 300 marks. Consumer goods and foodstuffs disappeared from German shelves as the mismanagement of the German economy continued apace.[31]

Indeed the extent of the economic crisis in Germany raised serious doubts about the ability of Germany to win the war in any meaningful sense, regardless of what its armies did on the battlefield. Just as bread riots were the proximate cause of the outbreak of revolution in Russia, the rise of strikes and urban unrest in Germany raised a spectre of revolution at home that terrified German leaders as much, if not more, than did defeat on the battlefield.[32] The events of 1917 proved that, in Winter's words, 'the price civilians believed they could and should pay for victory or peace was not limitless'.[33] The superior ability of the French and British to manage their home fronts thus played a critical role in delivering victory.

1917 in global perspective

As we look back on 1917 from the perspective of almost a century, global patterns emerge and the events on the Western Front in that year seem less important. Indeed, when seen through a wider and broader lens, 1917 appears less as the start of the final phase of the First World War and more as the starting point of the wars that would shape the rest of the twentieth century and beyond. Although 1917 marked the end of large-scale combat operations in the East for the Germans, for the Russians it merely meant the end of one war and the start of another. That war, the Russian civil war which lasted until 1921, led to more deaths from combat and disease than did the fighting of 1914–18. It ended with the triumph of the Bolsheviks, a war between Russia and Poland that took Bolshevik armies to the gates of Warsaw and the creation of a new

30 Jay Winter, 'Paris, London, Berlin, 1914–1919: capital cities at war', in Jay Winter and Jean-Louis Robert (eds.), *Capital Cities at War: Paris, London, and Berlin 1914–1919* (Cambridge University Press, 1997), pp. 10–11.

31 For much more on the German economy, see Chickering, *Imperial Germany and the Great War*, pp. 102–7.

32 It is worth noting that the only term of the Armistice of 11 November 1918 that the German delegation tried to modify was the requirement to turn over machine guns. They argued, successfully, that they would need the machine guns to put down an expected revolution at home. In other words, they wanted the machine guns to kill their own people.

33 Winter, 'Paris, London, Berlin', p. 17.

colossus in Europe and in Asia, the Soviet Union. Forged out of the crucible of two major wars, the USSR radically changed the nature of global politics for most of what remained of the twentieth century. The Cold War may not have begun in 1917, but it is easy enough to see the seeds of it in that year.

Events in the Middle East in 1917 received far less attention at the time, but in retrospect we can see the importance of the year for this troubled region's history. Looking for an alternative to the Western Front and anxious to edge out France and Russia as imperial rivals, David Lloyd George committed precious British assets to the conquest of the Middle East. British forces advanced through Mesopotamia, avenging a horrible defeat suffered in 1915 and taking Baghdad in March 1917. They also began an advance through Sinai and Gaza, armed with tanks, airplanes and reinforcements that Douglas Haig badly wanted in Europe. A rapid campaign utilising artillery and cavalry to great effect led to the British capture of Beersheba in October and Jaffa in November. Then, two weeks before Christmas, British forces marched into Jerusalem. More than 400 years of Ottoman rule in the Arab world was effectively over, even if, nearly a century of bloodshed in the region later, no one has yet been able to form a consensus on what should follow it.

The year 1917 did lead to an end to most of the fighting in another part of the world, although that year in sub-Saharan Africa can hardly be called peaceful. In November, the remaining African and German troops under General Paul von Lettow-Vorbeck left German-controlled territory. They continued to evade British efforts until the end of the war. At the time, people in both Britain and Germany saw his actions as heroic, leading as he did a small band of dedicated men who evaded much larger forces through very difficult terrain. But all he really did was extend a campaign that had long lost its strategic purpose. Men (as well as women and children, because African units often travelled as families) continued to die of disease and exhaustion for no real reason. Casualty estimates for Africa are difficult to obtain, but they surely reached into the hundreds of thousands. In the end, Africans traded their German masters for new, often British, ones, ushering in what some scholars call the second partition of the continent, and furthering the transition into the final phase of European imperialism.[34]

Thus to understand 1917 we need to see the global impacts of a war that left behind it the seeds of future conflicts around the world. From a military

34 For a general introduction see Edward Paice, *World War I: The African Front* (New York: Pegasus, 2008); Hew Strachan, *The First World War in Africa* (Oxford University Press, 2004); and Giles Foden's quirky but enjoyable *Mimi and Toutou's Big Adventure: The Bizarre Battle of Lake Tanganyika* (New York: Vintage, 2006).

perspective, the war both looked forwards, as in the use of armour and new infantry tactics, and backwards, as evidenced at the Chemin des Dames and at Passchendaele. If today we generally recall the latter more than the former, it is largely because of the modern associations of the First World War with futility and failure, much of it (fairly or unfairly) tied to the events of 1917.

6

1918: Endgame

CHRISTOPH MICK

Introduction

Ach, ich bin des Treibens müde,
Was soll all der Schmerz und Lust?
Süßer Friede,
Komm, ach komm in meine Brust!

On 1 January 1918, the liberal Austrian newspaper *Neue Freie Presse* in Vienna began its leader with the second part of Johann Wolfgang von Goethe's *Wandrers Nachtlied* (1776). The article was titled 'Dem Frieden entgegen' ('Towards peace'). A peace treaty with Soviet Russia was imminent and the author hoped that Britain and France would be forced to make peace with the Central Powers. The newspaper did not expect a triumphal victory but prepared the Austrian population for a peace without reparations. It warned of difficult times ahead. After the war the peoples of Austria-Hungary could expect to face a long period of austerity. The article reflected the war weariness in Austria while at the same time it entertained hopes that some sort of victory was still possible.[1]

German newspapers were more optimistic, as *The Times* also noticed. On the front page of its first edition of 1918 it quoted the *Frankfurter Zeitung*:

> Thus the prospect is that in the next six months, the decisive period during which the Central Powers will with absolute certainty have the strategic superiority, the eminently important period during which the hopes which the Western Powers set upon America's masses cannot in any circumstances be fulfilled – in these coming months the Central Powers will be enabled to concentrate almost their whole strength on the Western front . . . This means the collapse of any hope on the part of the Western Powers of success in a

1 'Dem Frieden entgegen', *Neue Freie Presse*, 1 January 1918, p. 1. 'I am weary with contending / why this rapture and unrest / peace descending / come ah, come into my breast'.

> new offensive of their own on the Western front ... Thus the strategic conditions on the Western front have been completely reversed. The war is turning against France.[2]

The *Frankfurter Zeitung* was not alone in expecting victory in 1918. Regional newspapers such as the *Freiburger Zeitung* also hoped the tide would turn in favour of the Central Powers, and christened the coming year *Friedensjahr* (year of peace). Hopes for peace, not for victory, dominated the front pages of German newspapers, but the envisaged peace was after a German victory, not as the result of defeat.[3]

The two newspapers shared the optimism of Kaiser Wilhelm and the Third Supreme Army Command (*Oberste-Heeresleitung*, or OHL) headed by Chief of Staff, Field Marshal Paul von Hindenburg but effectively led by the First Quartermaster General Erich Ludendorff. Recent events on the Eastern Front had lifted the spirits of the military and of the public. After three years of heavy fighting, Russia had been defeated and was now in revolutionary turmoil.

A peace treaty with Soviet Russia was signed in the Belorussian town of Brest-Litovsk on 3 March 1918, but the treaty only confirmed what everybody had known since autumn 1917: that the Central Powers had won the war on the Eastern Front. Since the armistice with Soviet Russia on 17 December 1917, it was only a question of time when more German divisions would be directed to the Western Front. But there were problems of ambition and of timing. Ludendorff shared the imperialist dreams of some of the military, political and economic elite, and wanted to fully exploit the collapse of the Russian Empire and the power vacuum it created by expanding borders, promoting colonisation and securing German dominance in Eastern Europe for the foreseeable future. These plans committed approximately 1 million German soldiers to the western borderlands of the Russian Empire. They were needed there to control and exploit the occupied territory and – last but not least – for further advances into the Crimea and the Caucasus.[4] German ambitions and the volatile situation in the former Russian Empire prevented the full weight of German military power from being directed to the Western Front.

The timing was also crucial. The United States of America had entered the war in April 1917, but the US army was still small and not yet ready for battle. The entry into the war of the world's largest economy had boosted the Allies'

2 *Frankfurter Zeitung*, quoted in *The Times*, 'Through German eyes', 1 January 1918, p. 5.

3 P. W., 'Vor dem Tore der Jahre', *Freiburger Zeitung – Zweites Abendblatt*, 31 December 1917, p. 1.

4 Winfried Baumgart, *Deutsche Ostpolitik 1918: Von Brest-Litowsk bis zum Ende des Ersten Weltkrieges* (Vienna and Munich: R. Oldenbourg Verlag, 1966), pp. 93–207.

confidence. In its first edition in 1918, the Parisian daily newspaper, *Le Matin*, published a collage of the Statue of Liberty and a ship with waving American soldiers arriving in France. The collage was headed '1918 – L'Année Décisive – 1918'. *Le Matin* hoped that their new 'brothers in arms' would sound the death knell for 'German tyranny'.[5] This optimism was not shared by political and military leaders. While the German OHL was hoping for victory in 1918, the Allies were expecting to defeat Germany only in 1919 with the help of fresh US troops. The endgame of the war had begun.[6]

Ludendorff was right that the war could only be won on the Western Front, but the war could be lost on other fronts. The Austrian army needed to hold the Italian Front otherwise Germany itself would be in danger. In 1917 Austria-Hungary was poised economically and politically on the brink of collapse, but the conclusive victory in the Battle of Caporetto (Twelfth Battle of the Isonzo) in October–November 1917 – achieved with the support of several German divisions – gave the Austrian army some respite. A collapse of the Macedonian (Salonica) front would force Bulgaria out of the war and cut the connection between Germany and its Ottoman ally. A loss of the Arabian Peninsula and Palestine would put further pressure on the Ottoman Empire. Ludendorff took the risk, removed German troops from these fronts and thus made them vulnerable to Allied offensives. He took a gamble, placing all his hopes on the success of the spring offensive.

At first glance, the spring offensive was very successful. Never since 1914 had an offensive or better, a series of offensives, gained more territory. For a moment military victory for Germany was close. Contemporaries and military historians have debated why Germany's superiority in materiel and manpower in the spring of 1918 was not sufficient to defeat the Allies. The German troops had been especially trained for this offensive, with their best and strongest soldiers concentrated in attack divisions led by the best officers and non-commissioned officers, whose abilities were seen as one of the German army's major strengths. The infiltration tactics, which made use of specially trained shock (storm) troops (*Sturmtruppen*) and a much-improved deployment of artillery, seemed to give Germany the edge. Moreover, the plan had been devised and the offensive supervised by Erich Ludendorff himself, who had made his name as the man behind the great victories on

5 *Le Matin*, 1 January 1918, p. 1.

6 Bruno Thoss, 'Militärische Entscheidung und politisch-gesellschaftlicher Umbruch. Das Jahr 1918 in der neueren Weltkriegsforschung', in Jörg Duppler and Gerhard P. Gross (eds.), *Kriegsende 1918* (Munich: R. Oldenbourg Verlag, 1999), pp. 17–40.

the Eastern Front. So why did Germany not win the war in the spring of 1918? We will come back to this question at the end of the chapter.

War aims and peace treaties

After Germany and Austria-Hungary had lost the war they placed their hopes on the programme outlined by the American President Woodrow Wilson at the beginning of the year. In his speech to Congress on 8 January 1918, Wilson listed Fourteen Points as the basis for a future peace. Wilson wanted to counter the efforts of the Central Powers and win the support of stateless nations in Eastern Europe. One of the underlying principles of his speech was the right of self-determination of all nations. There was a certain tension between this principle and some of the Fourteen Points. Wilson did not apply the right of self-determination to Russia, as he still saw Russia as a potential ally, and applied the concept only in part to the Ottoman Empire and Austria-Hungary. Similarly to Lloyd George in his Caxton Hall speech of 5 January 1918, Wilson did not demand the dissolution of both empires but proposed autonomy for their nationalities. The speech disappointed the Italian government, as Wilson was quite vague about the Italian war aims.[7] He mentioned the restoration of Belgium and wanted to right the 'wrong done to France by Prussia in 1871 in the matter of Alsace-Lorraine', while stopping short of giving unconditional support to this central French war aim.

Point 13 referred to the creation of an independent Polish state with access to the sea. This proved to be an efficient counter-measure to the Polish policy (Polenpolitik) of the Central Powers. In 1916, they had promised independence to Poland but without stating where the borders of this future Polish state would be. A provisional Crown Council was installed in Warsaw, a sort of Polish proto-government, but it was given only very limited administrative powers. Germany never intended to give up the territory acquired during the partitions of Poland; there were even plans to expand it by annexing a strip along the border of Congress (Russian) Poland. The best the Polish national movement could hope for from a victory of the Central Powers was the unification of the Austrian crownland Galicia and Lodomeria with Russian Poland under an Austrian prince. While this was an attractive option for Polish patriots in 1915, this was no longer the case in 1918. After the two Russian Revolutions and Wilson's speech, an Allied victory guaranteed independence

7 Mark Thompson, *The White War: Life and Death on the Italian Front, 1915–1919* (London: Basic Books, 2008), pp. 336f.

for Poland – a Poland which included Congress Poland, Galicia and the Polish provinces of the German Empire.[8]

By 1918 Czechs and Slovaks were also hoping for an independent state. The vague promise of more autonomy if the Central Powers won the war was undercut by the very real possibility of independence in the event of an Allied victory. The numbers of desertions increased, and Slovak and Czech prisoners of war in Italy and Russia joined Czechoslovak legions formed to fight against the Central Powers. In the Balkans the attraction of switching sides was less obvious. There were quite a few supporters of the Yugoslav idea in Croatia, Slovenia, Bosnia and Herzegovina but the Slovenes and Croatians in particular feared Italian ambitions. The Italian government wanted to annex the north-eastern part of the Adriatic coast in return for Italy entering the war on the side of the Allies. Slovenian and Croatian soldiers therefore not only fought for the Habsburg Empire, they were also driven to hold off the Italian army by national motives.

The October Revolution in Russia had effectively ended the war in the East. The priorities of the revolutionary government were to remain in power and propagate world revolution. On 8 November 1917 the new government published its Decree on Peace, which called 'upon all the belligerent nations and their governments to start immediate negotiations for peace'. These negotiations should begin without conditions and be based on the principle of no annexations or reparations. The offer of peace also included the right of self-determination of nations which – as later became clear – opened up the possibility for manipulation. While the Western Allies rejected the offer, the Central Powers accepted the note as a starting point for negotiations. On 17 December 1917 an armistice took effect, and one week later peace negotiations began in Brest-Litovsk. The German delegation was not willing to return any of the occupied territory and justified their peace offer with the right of self-determination. On 9 February the leader of the Soviet Russian delegation, Leon D. Trotsky, walked out of the negotiations without signing the treaty. The Bolsheviks – at this point in time still in a coalition government with the left socialist revolutionaries – were in a dilemma. The chairman of the Council of People's Commissars, Vladimir I. Lenin, wanted to sign the treaty while the opposition, led by Nikolai I. Bukharin, wanted to start a revolutionary war and take a gamble on a revolution breaking out in Germany. Trotsky won the day with his formula of 'neither peace, nor war'. He was playing for time and

8 David Stevenson, *The First World War and International Politics* (Oxford University Press, 1988), pp. 192–8.

hoped that the German commanders would not dare to advance for fear of triggering a revolt by pro-Bolshevik workers in Germany or even a rebellion by rank-and-file soldiers.[9]

There was dissension in the German delegation, in the main between the Foreign Secretary, Richard von Kühlmann, and the Chief of Staff of the German armies on the Eastern Front (Oberkommando Ostfront, for short: Ober Ost), Major General Max Hoffmann. Kühlmann proposed more lenient conditions, which would have left the option open for a future alliance with Russia, but he lost out against Hoffmann who enjoyed the backing of the – at this point – most powerful man in Germany, Erich Ludendorff. On 13 February 1918 Kühlmann argued in the Crown Council in Bad Homburg against resuming fighting, but one day earlier the German army had crossed the armistice line.

Hoffmann wrote in his diary that this offensive was the 'most comical war' he had ever seen.[10] His troops advanced along the railway lines without meeting much resistance. Revolutionary Russia was in grave danger and Lenin finally won a majority in the party's central committee in support of his position. A new Soviet delegation travelled to Brest to accept terms which had been further sharpened. On 3 March 1918 a treaty was signed by Soviet Russia on the one side and the Central Powers on the other (Map 6.1). Russia lost most of its non-Russian western borderlands, including Congress Poland and Finland – about 1.3 million square miles – together with a quarter of the population and a quarter of the industry of the former Russian Empire. The Soviet government had to renounce all territorial claims on Finland, Poland, Lithuania, Courland and Ukraine, while Livonia and Estonia – formally still part of Russia – would stay occupied by German troops (Map 6.2). The Ottoman Empire received the territories which had been lost in the Russo-Turkish War of 1878, and Soviet Russia had to accept the independence of Transcaucasia. The Central Powers had already recognised the independence of Finland and Ukraine and concluded a separate treaty with the Ukrainian Rada even before signing the treaty with Soviet Russia.[11]

The German and Austrian public was elated by the peace treaty, and the political, military and economic elites discussed plans to colonise and

9 *Ibid.*, pp. 200ff. On the negotiations see Baumgart, *Deutsche Ostpolitik 1918*, pp. 13–29. On the discussions in Soviet Russia see Richard Pipes, *The Russian Revolution 1899–1919* (London: Fontana, 1992), pp. 576–605.

10 Max Hoffmann, *War Diaries and Other Papers*, 2 vols. (London: Secker & Warburg, 1929), vol. 1, p. 207.

11 Baumgart, *Deutsche Ostpolitik 1918*, pp. 27ff.; Stevenson, *The First World War and International Politics*, pp. 186–203.

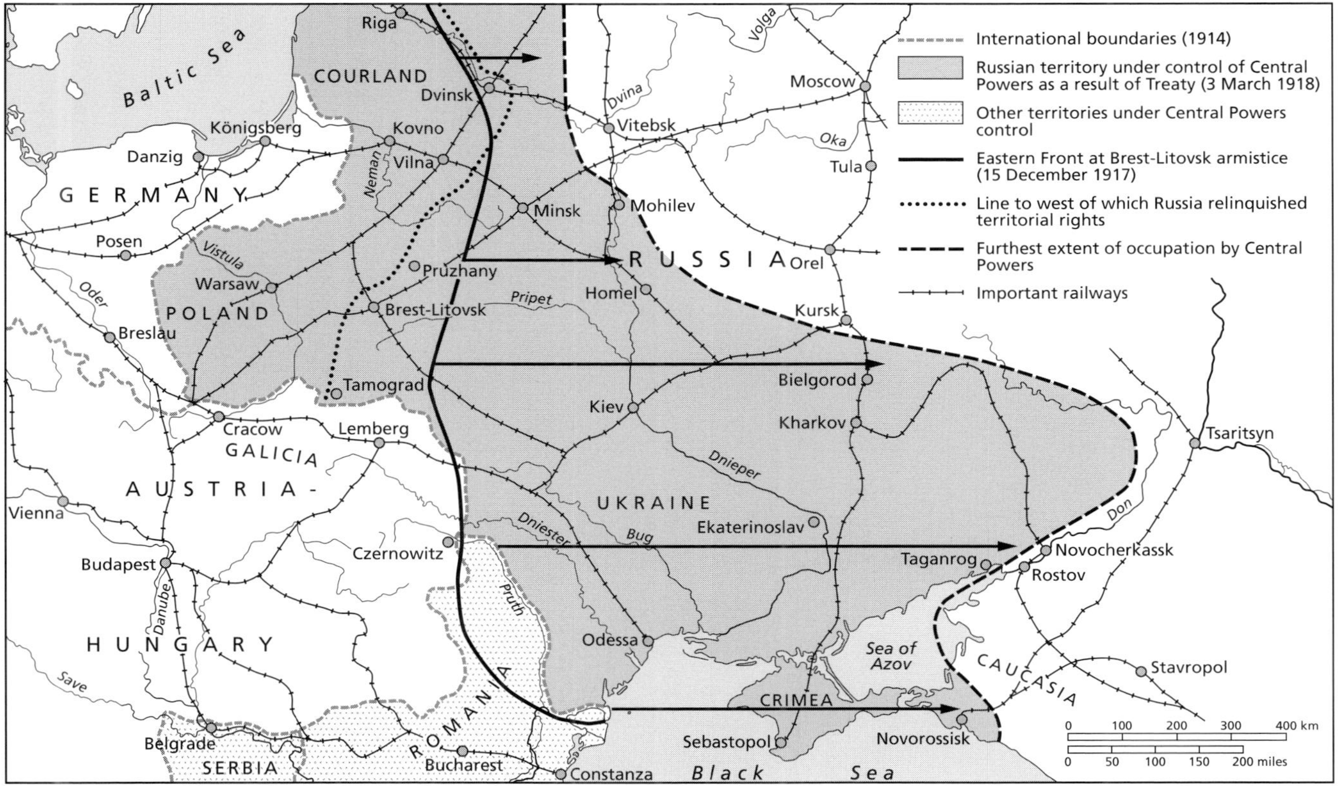

Map 6.1 Advances by the Central Powers on the Eastern Front, 1917–18.

Map 6.2 Territorial divisions under the Treaty of Brest-Litovsk, March 1918.

economically exploit Eastern Europe. Most Germans and Austrians hoped for Ukrainian grain as an end to hunger and, finally, for peace. The Social Democratic Party of Germany (SPD) criticised the inherently imperialist nature of the treaty but could not bring itself to vote against peace. Its deputies abstained from voting and only the Independent Social Democratic Party (USPD), which had split away from the SPD in April 1917, stuck to its principles and voted against it. In violation – at least of the spirit – of the treaty, German troops soon resumed their advance towards the Caucasus and the Crimea.

Historiography on Brest-Litovsk usually focuses on three aspects of the treaty: its meaning for the status of Russia as a Great Power, the tension between state interests and revolutionary ideology in Soviet Russia and, finally, the treaty as an indication of the overreaching nature of the German war aims and as evidence for the continuity between Ober Ost and the national-socialist Generalplan Ost. However, historians of the Great War, German imperialism or the Russian Revolution usually ignore what Brest-Litovsk meant for the nations involved. The defeat of the Russian Empire was the precondition for the independence of half a dozen nations. Soviet Russia lost territories where the majority of the populations were not keen to become part of a Russian state, irrespective of the type of government. A non-Bolshevik Russia might have been attractive to the Russian minority in this region, perhaps even for some Belorussians and Ukrainians, but it held no attraction for Poles, Lithuanians, Finns, Estonians or Latvians. In 1918 the political elites of these stateless nations were no longer satisfied with autonomy within a reformed Russia but wanted independence. Finland and Ukraine had proclaimed their independence soon after the Bolshevik Revolution, while the Central Powers allowed national organisations to develop in occupied Courland, Livonia, Lithuania and Estonia, albeit under strict German control.[12] After the war it was intended that these regions either be ruled by or be closely allied to the German Empire. They were intended to form a counterweight against Poland whose independence the Central Powers had promised. After the German defeat the national organisations either took power themselves or semi-legally delegated power to new national authorities. From the perspective of these nations the victory of the Central Powers thus did have its good side.[13]

Ukraine is an excellent example of the makeshift nature of German and Austrian policies in Eastern Europe. The occupation of Ukraine was not the

12 Vejas Gabriel Liulevicius, *War Land on the Eastern Front: Culture, National Identity and German Occupation in World War I* (Cambridge University Press, 2000), pp. 176ff.; Stevenson, *The First World War and International Politics*, p. 187; Abba Strazhas, *Deutsche Ostpolitik im Ersten Weltkrieg: Der Fall Ober Ost 1915–1917* (Wiesbaden: Harrassowitz, 1993); and Hans-Erich Volkmann, *Die deutsche Baltikumspolitik zwischen Brest-Litovsk und Compiègne: Ein Beitrag zur 'Kriegszieldiskussion'* (Cologne and Vienna: Böhlau Verlag, 1970).

13 In Ukrainian historiography Brest-Litovsk does not have such a negative connotation as in Russian, Soviet or Western historiography. For example, Orest Subtelny, *Ukraine: A History*, 3rd edn (University of Toronto, Press, 2000), 350ff.

result of a premeditated plan but a culmination of events into which the Central Powers more or less stumbled.[14] In January and February 1918 Russian and Ukrainian Red Guards tried to topple the Ukrainian government, while a delegation of the Rada negotiated a separate peace treaty with the Central Powers. The treaty was signed on 9 February 1918, one day after the Red Guards had taken Kiev. In exchange for food, especially grain, the Central Powers promised military aid. They divided Ukraine into two zones of influence and occupied the country with about 450,000 men. The Red Guards were forced to retreat. On 28 April 1918 Ober Ost interfered in Ukrainian domestic policy and replaced the powerless Rada by Hetman Pavlo Skoropadskyi, whose dictatorship depended entirely on German and Austrian military support. The Austrian government wanted to secure the Ukrainian crown for Archduke Wilhelm, hoping Ukraine could serve as a counterweight to German ambitions,[15] but the real power in Ukraine lay with Ober Ost. For the multi-ethnic population of Ukraine (Ukrainians, Russians, Jews, Poles and others) the occupation was ambivalent.

To a certain degree occupation restored order and protected the country from a Soviet Russian invasion or a Bolshevik coup d'état, but the population – after initially welcoming the German and Austrian soldiers – soon became dissatisfied with the occupation. As the occupiers could not rely on existing administrative structures, the transfer of resources had to be organised by the troops. The troops lived off the country and tried to extract more resources (especially food) from Ukraine. This led to local uprisings which were crushed by German and Austrian troops, generating even more disaffection.[16]

Jewish minorities suffered numerous hardships at the hands of Russian military and civil authorities. However, while before the Bolshevik Revolution Jews fared fairly well in the territories occupied by the Central Powers, increasing numbers of reports from the lands of Ober

14 On Germany's policy towards Ukraine see Frank Grelka, *Die ukrainische Nationalbewegung unter deutscher Besatzungsherrschaft 1918 und 1941/42* (Wiesbaden: Harrassowitz, 2005), pp. 75–92, 113; and Peter Borowsky, *Deutsche Ukrainepolitik 1918 unter besonderer Berücksichtigung der Wirtschaftsfragen* (Lubeck and Hamburg: Matthiesen, 1970).

15 On the policy of the Central Powers towards Ukraine and Poland see also Timothy Snyder, *The Red Prince: The Fall of a Dynasty and the Rise of Modern Europe* (London: Bodley Head, 2008), pp. 86–120; and Baumgart, *Deutsche Ostpolitik 1918*, pp. 123f.

16 For the German and Austrian occupation of Ukraine see Włodzimierz Mędrzecki, *Niemiecka interwencja militarna na Ukrainie w 1918 roku* (Warsaw: DiG, 2000) and Snyder, *The Red Prince*, pp. 108ff. Also Christian Westerhoff, *Zwangsarbeit im Ersten Weltkrieg* (Paderborn: Schöningh, 2012).

Ost linked the Jewish population to Bolshevism. This anti-Semitic stereotype of 'Jewish Bolshevism' poisoned the relationship between occupiers and Jewish minorities without this yet being translated into systematic discrimination.[17] In the interwar period, the imagination of the German political right transformed the lands of Ober Ost, where for a period of one to two years Germans had exercised nearly absolute power, into a Traumland Ost (dreamland east), just waiting to be colonised and ruled by Germans. There is a link between Ober Ost and the national-socialist Generalplan Ost, but this link should not be overstated or regarded as a simple continuity. The policy of Ober Ost was repressive, exploitative and imperialistic – but it was not genocidal.[18]

After dealing with Russia the Central Powers also defeated Romania, and on 7 May 1918 a peace treaty was signed in Bucharest. Bulgaria received Southern Dobrudja and part of Northern Dobrudja, while the rest of the province was placed under joint Romanian and Bulgarian administration.[19] Austria-Hungary was ceded control of the passes in the Carpathian Mountains. Romania had to lease its oil wells to Germany for ninety years and had to accept occupation for an indefinite period. The Central Powers consoled Romania by recognising its union with Bessarabia, which had previously belonged to the Russian Empire.[20] On 27 August the Treaty of Brest-Litovsk was amended by the Treaty of Berlin. It reflected the ideology of the German Fatherland Party and completely ignored more moderate views within Germany. Soviet Russia had to renounce any claims to the Baltic region, recognise the independence of Georgia, deliver all its gold reserves to Germany and pay 5 billion marks' compensation. Germany also got the right to exploit the coal mines in the Donetsk basin. The Soviet government never intended to honour the treaty, as it rightly expected that Germany would lose the war. While in Brest-Litovsk the OHL had used the right of self-determination as a fig leaf to cover its imperialist intentions, the Treaties of Berlin and Bucharest showed what the world would have looked like

17 Grelka, *Die ukrainische Nationalbewegung*, pp. 223–38.

18 Liulevicius, *War Land on the Eastern Front*, pp. 151–75; Manfred Nebelin, *Ludendorff: Diktator im Ersten Weltkrieg* (Munich: Siedler, 2011), pp. 193ff., 520; And Gregor Thum (ed.), *Traumland Osten: Deutsche Bilder vom östlichen Europa im 20. Jahrhundert* (Göttingen: Vandenhoeck & Ruprecht, 2006).

19 Bulgaria demanded the full control of the province, which was granted in a protocol dated 25 September 1918. This came to nothing, as four days later Bulgaria capitulated to the Allies.

20 Stevenson, *The First World War and International Politics*, pp. 203–5.

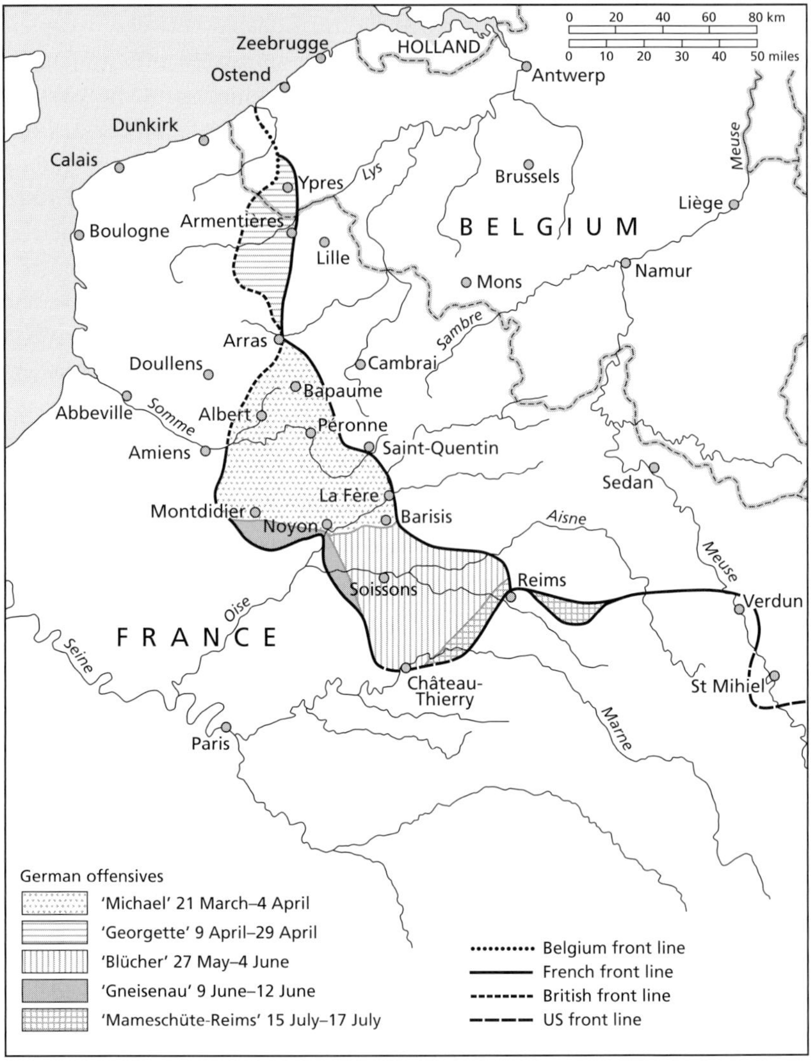

Map 6.3 German spring offensive, 1918.

according to the ideas of ruling German elites. In the end, even the German parliament had had enough of such open and reckless imperialism and voted against the Treaty of Berlin.[21]

21 Winfried Baumgart, 'Die "geschäftliche Behandlung" des Berliner Ergänzungsvertrags vom 27. August 1918', *Historisches Jahrbuch*, 89 (1969), pp. 116–52.

The spring offensive

Already prior to the Treaty of Brest-Litovsk the divisions on the Eastern Front were being combed for physically fit soldiers below the age of 35. Between November 1917 and the offensive on 21 March 1918, forty-four divisions arrived in Belgium and France. Ludendorff was criticised for leaving about 1.5 million soldiers, including large numbers of cavalry, in the East (Eastern Europe, the Balkans, Turkey and Russia). These divisions had less fighting value than the transferred divisions but could have freed up other divisions for the attack.[22] It could not be excluded, however, that either the Bolsheviks in the interests of promoting a German revolution or White forces supported by the Czechoslovak legions would resume fighting against the Central Powers. Winston Churchill, the British Minister of Munitions, even considered a possible new front against Germany in Russia, underpinned by Japanese troops which had just landed in the Russian Far East.[23]

But even without these additional divisions, in March 1918 the Central Powers had a significant advantage (Map 6.3). A total of 191 German divisions faced 175 Allied divisions. However, German divisions had fewer men than British or French divisions so in terms of absolute numbers the two sides were roughly equal: about 4 million soldiers.[24] The Germans also had superior numbers of artillery, even though this was less significant. The superiority was not the result of a massive numerical advantage but of a better fighting efficiency. This was not sufficient to launch a broad-scale offensive but enabled the OHL to concentrate troops and firepower on some portions of the front without dangerously weakening the rest of the front. The element of surprise was therefore crucial. The main problem for the German army was its lack of mobility. The Allies had ten times as many lorries and the German divisions were also desperately short of horses.[25]

22 Sir Douglas Haig once said that six divisions on 26 March at Amiens or on 10 April at Hazebrouck would have made all the difference. Also Hans-Ulrich Wehler, *Deutsche Gesellschaftsgeschichte*, vol. IV: *Vom Beginn des Ersten Weltkriegs bis zur Gründung der beiden deutschen Staaten 1914–1949* (Frankfurt am Main: C. H. Beck, 2003), pp. 154ff.

23 Winston Churchill, *The World Crisis 1911–1918*, 6 vols. (London: Odhams Press Ltd, 1939), vol. II, p. 1331. On the intervention of the Allies see Stevenson, *The First World War and International Politics*, pp. 205–16.

24 David T. Zabecki, *The German 1918 Offensives: A Case Study in the Operational Level of War* (Abingdon: Routledge, 2006), p. 91. David Stevenson, *With our Backs to the Wall: Victory and Defeat in 1918* (London: Allen Lane, 2011), p. 36.

25 Martin Kitchen, *The German Offensives of 1918* (Stroud: Tempus, 2005), pp. 14ff.; Stevenson, *With our Backs to the Wall*, p. 36.

The German army used combined-arms and infiltration tactics, which had been successfully applied by General Oskar von Hutier in the Battle of Riga and which were later tested at Caporetto and during the counter-attack at Cambrai. There was a relatively brief period of artillery preparation before attacks using hurricane bombardment with the aim of preventing the Allies from learning early on where the major blow would fall. Lieutenant Colonel Georg Bruchmüller, artillery commander of the Eighteenth Army, developed a new method of directing fire without ranging shots. The artillery aimed its fire at the enemy's batteries, Headquarters and lines of communication. Shortly before the infantry went over the top, shells with tear gas and poison gas (mustard, phosgene or diphosgene) were fired and a creeping barrage began, aimed not at destroying the enemy positions but at stunning the enemy soldiers. Ludendorff concentrated the best soldiers into shock/storm troops (*Sturmtruppen*). Organised in small units of between six and nine men, these storm troopers advanced as quickly as possible behind the creeping barrage, not bothering to destroy every fortified enemy position. The objective of these storm troopers was to reach the enemy's artillery positions and Headquarters and destroy the lines of communication, creating disorder and confusion among the defenders. Mobile troops, infantry battalions with light machine guns, mortars and flamethrowers followed and destroyed enemy strongholds. Finally, regular infantry was used to mop up any remaining resistance. In the rear, troops with less fighting value held the trenches and repulsed counter-attacks while the storm troops and mobile troops advanced.[26]

The question now was where to attack.[27] The German High Command had experienced the resilience of French soldiers and shrank back from taking on the French army at Verdun, the logical point for an offensive. Ludendorff expected that the morale of the British soldiers after the costly offensives of 1917 would be low, and decided to attack the BEF first. This was a sensible choice, as the British army had a severe problem with manpower. The Prime Minister, Lloyd George – possibly fearing that he could not prevent his Chief of Staff, General Douglas Haig, from starting a new offensive, held back reserves in Britain which were desperately needed in France and Belgium. The divisions of the BEF were under strength, the number of battalions per division was cut from twelve to nine.[28]

26 Zabecki, *The German 1918 Offensives*, pp. 63–72; Stevenson, *With our Backs to the Wall*, pp. 36ff.

27 On these discussions, see Kitchen, *The German Offensives of 1918*, pp. 24–49.

28 Gary Sheffield, 'Finest hour? British forces on the Western Front in 1918: an overview', in Ashley Ekins (ed.), *1918 – Year of Victory: The End of the Great War and the Shaping of History* (Titirangi, Auckland: Exisle Publishing, 2010), p. 56. See also Gary Sheffield, *Forgotten*

The Bavarian Crown Prince and Field Marshal Rupprecht and his Chief of Staff, General Hermann von Kuhl, favoured an attack on the portion of the front held by their army group. This would have meant an attack on the Ypres salient, but every year in early spring heavy rain transformed the battle-scarred landscape into a vast field of mud holes, making a quick advance impossible. Ludendorff finally decided to attack in Picardy between Arras and Saint Quentin where the ground dried out quicker after the winter and spring rains. Here the German troops would have to cross the old Somme battlefield. This was also very difficult terrain but not as muddy as 'Flanders fields'. On a tactical and operational level the plan was well thought out, but to win the war a clear strategic vision was necessary. That this strategic vision was 'blurred' became evident when Rupprecht challenged Ludendorff's plan to attack at the Somme. Asked by the Bavarian Crown Prince what his strategic objective was, Ludendorff referred to his experience on the Eastern Front: attack, find the weak spots, use the momentum and push forward. This gave the offensive a high degree of flexibility but the inherent flaw of this plan was that the attack could splinter into a number of advances without achieving a decisive victory.[29]

The first and main offensive was called Operation Michael after the Archangel Michael, the patron saint of Germany. The offensive was also dubbed the *Kaiserschlacht* (emperor's battle). Ludendorff gave it the clear strategic objective of breaking through the southern portion of the British front, turning north, and making the British positions impossible by simultaneously attacking the centre and the exposed southern flank. It could have worked, but Ludendorff then took steps which were incompatible with this strategy. Three German armies with sixty-seven divisions were in the assault sector. The three armies had 6,608 guns and howitzers (almost 50 per cent of all German guns on the Western Front), 3,534 mortars and 1,070 aircraft at their disposal. On the sixty-mile-long front the BEF only had 2,500 guns, 1,400 mortars and 579 aircraft.[30] The artillery preparation began on 21 March at

Victory: The First World War: Myths and Realities (London: Headline, 2001), pp. 224ff. and Dieter Storz, '"Aber was hätte anders geschehen sollen?"', in Duppler and Gross (eds.), *Kriegsende 1918*, pp. 165–82.

29 Kronprinz Rupprecht von Bayern, *Mein Kriegstagebuch*, 3 vols. (Berlin: Deutscher National Verlag, 1929), vol. II, p. 322; Zabecki, *The German 1918 Offensives*, pp. 97–123; And Kitchen, *The German Offensives of 1918*, pp. 38ff. See also Robert T. Foley, 'From victory to defeat: the German army in 1918', in Ekins (ed.), *1918 – Year of Victory*, pp. 69–88.

30 A detailed analysis of Operation 'Michael' is in Zabecki, *The German 1918 Offensives*, pp. 113–73. See also Kitchen, *The German Offensives of 1918*, pp. 66ff., Stevenson, *With our Backs to the Wall*, p. 42. See also *Der Weltkrieg 1914–1918: die militärischen Operationen zu*

4.40 a.m. and lasted only five hours. Shells with mustard, phosgene and tear gas were fired before the attack and thick fog disoriented the defenders. In the original plan, the German Eighteenth Army should have defended the left flank of the German Second and Seventeenth Armies, which were expected to turn north-west after having destroyed the Cambrai salient. The British Third Army's positions, however, were well manned.

A total of fourteen divisions were defending a mere twenty-eight miles of the front. The BEF held on to the strategically crucial Vimy Ridge and prevented the German troops from reaching their objectives. Progress was made but casualties on the German side were high. Haig had concentrated his strategic reserves behind this portion of the front, as he could not afford to lose much ground here.

The breakthrough came – unexpectedly – against the British Fifth Army on the southern section of the British front. Only twelve divisions with 976 heavy guns were defending forty-two miles against forty-three German divisions, which in turn were supported by 2,508 pieces of heavy artillery. As the British had just taken over part of the front from the French army, the principles of deep defence had not yet been fully applied. The rear positions were not ready and about one-third of the troops were concentrated in the front line. A considerable part of the Fifth Army was destroyed as a result of the artillery fire and the first German assault. On the first day of the offensive the Germans captured 21,000 British soldiers, and the total British casualties were 38,512. But the German casualties were even higher – 40,000 men – a figure that could have served as a warning signal for the OHL.[31]

Operation Michael had succeeded on one section of the front where a strategic victory was beyond the possibilities of the German army. Ludendorff, however, had the Eighteenth Army push on, not, as planned, in a north-westerly direction but south and south-west. One of the reasons for this was the stiff resistance of the British Third Army, but Ludendorff also seemed to believe that the BEF had been beaten and that it was now time to turn against the French army to prevent reinforcements being sent to the British. He saw the chance to drive a wedge between the BEF and the French army and inflict the deadly blow on the Allies he had hoped for.

Faced with this emergency, the opposition of Haig and Pétain against a unified High Command was finally overcome. On 26 March Ferdinand Foch

Lande. Bearbeitet im Reichsarchiv, 14 vols. (Berlin: E. S. Mittler, 1925–44), vol. XIV, p. 104 and Erich Ludendorff, *Meine Kriegserinnerungen, 1914–1918* (Berlin: E. S. Mittler, 1919), pp. 474ff.

31 Zabecki, *The German 1918 Offensives*, pp. 160ff.; Sheffield, *Forgotten Victory*, pp. 224ff.

was given the task of coordinating the actions of the British and French armies. His mandate was extended on 3 April to include the American Expeditionary Forces (AEF). Foch became Supreme Military Commander, first on the Western Front and later of all Allied troops. As a strategic reserve was missing, Haig and Pétain had previously agreed to help each other in the event of a massive German offensive at either part of the front. It is still a matter of dispute to what extent Pétain fulfilled his promises. Some historians have followed Haig, who complained that the support was slow and insufficient. Others have pointed to the fact that by the evening of 23 March, Pétain had sent fourteen divisions to repulse the German offensive. By the 28th half of the French army was on the move and on 31 March twenty-one French divisions were supporting the BEF. They helped stabilise the thirty-six miles of front between the Somme and Oise rivers. Pétain had refused to send even more troops as he expected a simultaneous German assault in Champagne.[32]

Operation Michael had cost the British 177,739, the French 77,000 and the Germans 239,800 casualties. Worrying for the Allies was the loss of 1,300 guns and the fact that 75,000 British and 15,000 French soldiers had been taken prisoner. The German army had overrun the British defence on a fifty-mile sector and gained 12,000 square miles of territory, but for Germany the failure to achieve a strategic victory was nothing short of a disaster.[33] The front was pushed back forty miles in some areas, but neither had the BEF and the French army permanently been separated nor had Amiens with its important railway hub been taken.[34] The German soldiers could see with their own eyes that the soldiers of the BEF were much better supplied. German soldiers often stopped to eat what they found in British trenches and depots. Many soldiers were drunk and discipline suffered. This was a recurring problem during the spring offensives. The British military historian, Liddell Hart, even believed that the abundance of food and alcohol found on the British side undermined the morale of the Germans and their will to resist the Allied offensives in summer and autumn.[35] It is highly unlikely, however, that the German troops would have been able – even if resistance had been weaker and less time had been

32 Hew Strachan, *The First World War* (Pocket Books: London, 2006), p. 300; Elizabeth Greenhalgh, 'A French victory, 1918', in Ekins (ed.), *1918 – Year of Victory*, pp. 89–98; Stevenson, *With our Backs to the Wall*, p. 58; Kitchen, *The German Offensives of 1918*, pp. 77, 87ff.

33 Stevenson, *With our Backs to the Wall*, pp. 67ff. Kitchen cites these casualty statistics: 230,000 German and 212,000 Allied soldiers: Kitchen, *The German Offensives of 1918*, p. 99.

34 Strachan, *The First World War*, pp. 288ff.

35 Basil H. Liddell Hart, *History of the First World War* (London: Papermac, 1970), pp. 396ff. Kitchen, *The German Offensives of 1918*, pp. 94ff., 100, 125ff.

spent on looting and drinking – to sustain the attack long enough to deal a resounding blow to either the French army or the BEF. The German troops were exhausted and too far from the railway heads. The lines were overstretched, there was insufficient motorised transportation and horses, and neither fresh troops nor supplies could be brought forward quickly enough. This gave the Allies enough time to reallocate resources, bring in reserve troops and stabilise the front.

Operation Michael was the first of several offensives. On 9 April Operation Georgette was launched, known in Britain as the Battle of Lys. The attack area ranged from six miles east of Ypres to six miles east of Béthune. The weakest portion of the front was defended by the British First Army, where two undermanned and tired Portuguese divisions were placed. The plan was to break through this portion of the front, take the important railway junction Hazebrouck, push the British Second Army north to the Channel ports and interrupt the British supply lines. On the first day the German Sixth Army broke through the British battle zone along a front of nine miles and advanced five miles. They were finally stopped by British reserve divisions. Further north on 10 April four divisions of the German Fourth Army pushed back the British Second Army which had sent its reserves to help the First Army. The Germans advanced two miles along a four-mile front and took Messines. On 11 April the British position had become so precarious that Haig gave his famous 'Backs to the wall' order. In a dramatic appeal to his troops he demanded that they defend every position as further retreat might end in defeat. In the days that followed, the Germans made further attempts to break through the British lines and achieved some territorial gains, but with the help of French reserves the front could be stabilised. Casualties were high, as here – where the BEF could not afford to lose much ground – the defences were deep and heavily fortified. Ludendorff stopped the offensive on 29 April. Since 21 March the German army had suffered 326,000, the BEF 260,000 and the French army 107,000 casualties.[36]

Ludendorff now turned against the French army. The Operations Blücher and Yorck, starting on 27 May, were meant to draw troops away from Flanders and prevent French reinforcements being sent to the BEF where – as before – it was intended that the major blow would fall. Pétain had expected an offensive but no longer expected it at the Chemin des Dames. Four exhausted British divisions had been transferred to this supposedly quiet sector of the

36 Zabecki, *The German 1918 Offensives*, pp. 174–205; Stevenson, *With our Backs to the Wall*, pp. 67ff.; Kitchen, *The German Offensives of 1918*, pp. 99–136.

front to rest. Forty-one German divisions with 3,719 guns at their disposal broke through the front held by the French Seventh Army and three British divisions. The advance reached the River Marne and German troops were now only fifty-six miles away from Paris. Ludendorff could again not resist the temptation and German divisions facing the British sector were sent in as reinforcements. On the evening of 28 May the British and French lines were, for a short period, separated by a wedge forty miles wide and fifteen miles deep. One day later German troops took Soissons. All in all the German troops captured more than 50,000 French soldiers, 630 guns and 2,000 machine guns. The German army had suffered 105,370 casualties, the Allies 127,337.[37] Paris was now within reach of artillery fire, and panic broke out. The French government even considered leaving the capital. The French Prime Minister, Georges Clemenceau, declared in the Chamber of Deputies that he would continue fighting even if Paris was lost: 'I shall fight before Paris, I shall fight in Paris, I shall fight behind Paris.'

Once again logistical, especially transportation problems prevented the German army from exploiting the strategic opportunities. The attack divisions were exhausted and supplies, artillery and fresh troops could not be brought forward quickly enough. Pétain was able to stabilise the front at the River Marne. Eight American divisions participated in this battle under French command. The relative success of Operation Blücher was sufficient to tempt Ludendorff to launch another attack between Noyon and Montdidier, Operation Gneisenau, on 9 June. The success was limited and was followed by a successful counter-attack in which American troops also took part. Some 1,000 German soldiers were captured.[38]

The days between 15 and 18 July represented the military turning point of the campaigns of 1918 and, in a way, of the war. On 15 July the German army attacked in Champagne. This time the French army had received previous intelligence of the attack and the French artillery fired shell after shell on the first line of the German trenches where the soldiers were crowded together, waiting to go over the top. On the French side the first line was only held by a few soldiers. The German fire was wasted on empty trenches and positions. When the Germans attacked they ran into a trap in the French battle zone and heavy casualties were inflicted on the attackers. French and a few American

37 Zabecki, *The German 1918 Offensives*, pp. 206–32; Stevenson, *With our Backs to the Wall*, p. 87; Liddell Hart, *History of the First World War* pp. 407–32; Martin Gilbert, *The First World War* (London: Henry Holt, 1994), pp. 425–7.

38 Zabecki, *The German 1918 Offensives*, pp. 233–45; Stevenson, *With our Backs to the Wall*, pp. 88–91; Kitchen, *The German Offensives of 1918*, pp. 158ff.

divisions launched a successful counter-attack – also using tanks – against the German Fifth and Seventh Armies on 18 July, which forced the Germans to retreat to Soissons on the River Aisne. In four days of fighting a total of 30,000 German soldiers had been killed.[39]

All in all, the German offensives had made considerable territorial gains, but none of the strategic objectives had been achieved. The BEF and the French army had neither been separated, nor had the British troops been pushed back to the Channel ports, nor had Paris been taken. Other important objectives such as the destruction of the Ypres salient or the capture of the crucial railway hub of Amiens were not realised. The German army had retaken old battlefields or territory which had been destroyed by its troops during the tactical retreat to the Hindenburg Line (referred to by the Germans as the Siegfried Line) in March–April 1917. The front had been extended from 390 to 510 miles (by 25 July) and the Germans held positions which still had to be fortified. The soldiers were much more vulnerable to Allied attacks than in the fortified positions they had held before the spring offensive. The German army had lost 800,000 men, including a high percentage of its best soldiers. The German army was also hit by the first wave of the Spanish influenza in June, three weeks earlier than the Allies, which further weakened the German troops. Taking all these factors into account, Churchill was right to state that the German army had been defeated in a defensive battle. The subsequent Allied offensives (starting with the counter-attack in Champagne in mid July) built on this defensive victory and finished off a weakened and demoralised enemy.[40]

The black days of the German army

The strategic position of Germany, which had seemed so good in January 1918, deteriorated rapidly. Ludendorff was out of his depth. On 2 August he ordered the German army to prepare for Allied attacks. He hoped that at least the repeated blows and the high number of casualties suffered by the defenders had made major Allied offensives impossible. He was not entirely wrong.

39 Zabecki, *The German 1918 Offensives*, pp. 246–79; Gilbert, *The First World War*, pp. 440–3.

40 Churchill, *The World Crisis*, vol. II; Wilhelm Deist, 'The military collapse of the German Empire: the reality behind the stab-in-the-back myth', *War in History*, 3 (1996), pp. 199–203; Sheffield, 'Finest hour?', pp. 54–68; André Bach, 'Die militärischen Operationen der französischen Armee an der Westfront Mitte 1917 bis 1918', in Duppler and Gross (eds.), *Kriegsende 1918*, pp. 135–44.

Foch, Pétain and Haig did not think that the war could be won in 1918, but they anticipated that counter-attacks and offensives with narrow objectives could be effective and break the morale of the German army.[41] The Allies now could draw on the experiences of their previous offensives and on lessons learned from the German successes and failures earlier in the year. Their superiority in terms of firepower was re-established in the summer of 1918. Rupprecht realised much earlier than Ludendorff that morale among the German soldiers was dropping. He heard about the growing number of field post letters demanding peace. Soldiers complained about the poor provision, the aerial superiority of the Allies and the growing number of American troops.[42] Even if desertion on the front was low it was very worrying that up to 20 per cent of the troops 'got lost' on the way from the Eastern to the Western Front.[43]

Foch devised a plan consisting of a series of attacks aimed at reaching important railway hubs and improving the lines of communication. The offensives were launched in rapid succession to prevent the OHL from directing reinforcements to critical points. In contrast to the German strategy of spring 1918 where storm troops advanced even without artillery support to exploit the momentum of a breakthrough, the Allied attacks did not go further than their artillery could reach. Only after the artillery had been brought forward and was ready to fire was the offensive resumed. The German tactics had resulted in quick territorial gains, but these tactics were also responsible for high casualty rates and the exhaustion of the troops. The Allied strategy was more suited to the conditions on the Western Front in 1918. On 4 August the French army retook Soissons and captured 35,000 German soldiers and 700 guns.[44] The BEF began with an offensive at Amiens, where the German troops had not had the time to build deep defensive positions. The artillery and aerial superiority was overwhelming and the assault troops were well equipped with Lewis guns and mortars. Every battalion was accompanied by six tanks. The result of the attack was an impressive victory. On 8 August, the first day of the

41 Strachan, *The First World War*, pp. 302ff.

42 Rupprecht, *Mein Kriegstagebuch*, vol. II, pp. 424–30; Strachan, *The First World War*, p. 311; and Kitchen, *The German Offensives of 1918*, p. 256. Also Benjamin Ziemann, *War Experiences in Rural Germany, 1914–1923* (Oxford and New York: Berg, 2007), pp. 97ff.

43 Kitchen, *The German Offensives of 1918*, p. 185, 198ff. On desertions in the German army and the BEF see Christoph Jahr, *Gewöhnliche Soldaten: Desertion und Deserteure im deutschen und britischen Heer 1914–1918* (Göttingen: Vandenhoeck & Ruprecht, 1998).

44 Gilbert, *The First World War*, pp. 447, 454.

offensive, the German army suffered 27,000 casualties. Some 15,000 soldiers, a very high percentage, surrendered. Ludendorff later called the day the 'Black Day of the German Army'.[45] A further series of successful attacks followed. The front did not collapse but collapse was near. Evidence for this is the unprecedented number of German soldiers taken prisoner. In August 1918, the German army had 228,000 casualties, 21,000 dead and 110,000 missing (most of them captured). It was a sign of the declining morale that it was now quite easy to take German soldiers prisoner.[46] The American army had the same experience. During their successful attack on the Saint-Mihiel salient on 13 September, they captured 13,000 German soldiers.[47] It was only now that the Allies realised how weakened the German army really was and that the end of the war was nearer than they had expected.

The Allies attacked with superior manpower, artillery fire and tanks, and a much higher morale. The failure of the spring offensive and the success of the Allied attacks were disastrous for the morale of German soldiers, and the effect on the morale of the High Command was even more disastrous. Ludendorff finally realised that the war could not be won but he still held hopes that a peace with favourable conditions was possible as German troops were standing in France and Belgium and controlled most of Eastern Europe.[48] Even now, neither the OHL nor the German government were willing to give up Alsace-Lorraine.[49] All the hopes of the OHL rested now on the Hindenburg (Siegfried) Line with its strongly fortified trenches and natural barriers.

The home front

While the armies on the Western Front prepared for the German spring offensive the home fronts held. Between February and December 1917 German submarines had destroyed more than 4 million tons of British shipping tonnage (world total losses: 6.238 million tons). But only for a short moment in late spring 1917 did it appear as if this could force Britain out of the

45 Strachan, *The First World War*, pp. 310ff.; Stevenson, *With our Backs to the Wall*, pp. 122ff.; J. P. Harris, 'Das britische Expeditionsheer in der Hundert-Tage-Schlacht vom 8. August bis 11. November 1918', in Duppler and Gross (eds.), *Kriegsende 1918*, pp. 115–34.

46 Stevenson, *With our Backs to the Wall*, pp. 122–33; Kitchen, *The German Offensives of 1918*, pp. 260–78; Gilbert, *The First World War*, pp. 452–5.

47 Gilbert, *The First World War*, pp. 452ff.

48 Deist, 'The military collapse of the German Empire'.

49 Stevenson, *The First World War and International Politics*, pp. 222ff.; Stevenson, *With our Backs to the Wall*, pp. 311–49.

war. The British shipbuilding industry had not fully replaced the lost capacity, but better organisation and the use of American and neutral ships allowed imports to rise by 8 per cent compared to 1916, and food production was expanded considerably by recultivating pastures, which reduced the volume of food imports.[50] The British navy had developed effective counter-measures against the threat of German submarines. Allied destroyers accompanied convoys of merchant ships and made them less vulnerable. In 1918 only 134 escorted merchant ships were sunk. Allied total losses still made up 3.9 million tons, but ships with a total of 5.4 million deadweight tons were built.[51] Technological devices were developed to detect submarines more easily and new ways were used to destroy them. Of the 320 submarines which saw battle, 200 were sunk. The submarine war was not able to starve Britain into submission nor did it prevent US troops from being brought to France. Only in 1918 did Britain have to move to full rationing, and bread was never rationed. In France, and even more so in Italy, the food situation was not as good as in Britain but it was still better than in Germany, not to speak of Austria, Bulgaria or the Ottoman Empire where people starved to death.[52]

The Allied naval blockade was much more effective than unrestricted submarine warfare had been. In 1918 ships from neutral countries were intercepted and German goods, or goods destined for Germany, were requisitioned. In 1916–17 the so-called 'turnip winter' had seen many Germans going hungry; the winter of 1917–18 was slightly better but many Germans were malnourished. It is difficult to tell how many Germans died as a result of the naval blockade. Alvin Jackson calculated that 750,000 civilians starved to death or died as a result of diseases their weakened bodies could not withstand. According to Richard Bessel and Gary Sheffield, in 1918 alone 293,000 German civilians died as a direct or indirect result of the naval blockade.[53] Niall Ferguson questions these calculations but without giving alternative numbers.[54]

50 On British society during the war see Jay Winter, *The Great War and the British People*, 2nd edn (Basingstoke: Palgrave Macmillan, 2003).

51 Stevenson, *With our Backs to the Wall*, p. 339.

52 Niall Ferguson, *The Pity of War, 1914–1918* (London: Basic Books, 1999), pp. 276f.

53 Alvin Jackson, 'Germany, the home front: blockade, government and revolution', in Hugh Cecil and Peter H. Liddle (eds.), *Facing Armageddon: The First World War Experienced* (London: Leo Cooper, 1996), p. 575; Richard Bessel, *Germany after the First World War* (Oxford: Clarendon Press, 1993), pp. 35–44; Gary Sheffield, *Forgotten Victory: The First World War: Myths and Realities* (London: Headline, 2001), p. 93.

54 Ferguson, *The Pity of War*, pp. 276–81; Sheffield, *Forgotten Victory*, pp. 102f.

Basil Liddell Hart believes that the naval blockade won the war for the Allies. He argues that the blockade would eventually have forced Germany to surrender, even without the costly offensives of 1916 and 1917. As some British historians have pointed out, it is a bit of an exaggeration to state that naval power had decided the war.[55] Without the defeat on the Western Front, Germany would have been able to continue fighting for a long period, as transfers of food, raw materials and labour from the occupied territories in Eastern Europe would have been organised more efficiently. It must not be forgotten that French and British resources, too, were strained to the utmost, and that there were moments when the governments of both countries feared they would no longer be able to meet the needs of the army or the population, and would have to seek a – probably unfavourable – peace. Strike activity in Britain was throughout the war higher than in Germany, but in critical moments the workers usually went back to work. In France, between 13 and 18 May 1918, 100,000 workers were on strike in Paris alone demonstrating for peace and and demanding clarity about the French war aims. When the Germans resumed their offensives the strike died down.[56]

As a result of the worsening living conditions, on 28 January 100,000 workers in Berlin went on strike. Hunger, cold, war weariness and solidarity with Soviet Russia – which was in a difficult situation after the temporary breakdown of the peace negotiations – had mobilised the workers. A couple of days later 400,000 workers were on the streets, demanding a peace without annexations and reparations and the presence of workers' representatives at the Peace Conference. Daily food consumption had fallen from 3,000 calories in 1914 to 1,400 in 1918. The official rations covered just 50 per cent of daily dietary requirements. The Berlin workers were supported by strikes and demonstrations in other cities. Politicians of the moderate Social Democratic Party of Germany (Sozialdemokratische Partei Deutschlands, SPD) joined the strike committees and tried to calm the workers. Finally, pressed by Ludendorff, the German Chancellor Georg von Hertling decided to end the strike by force. In Berlin, 150 ringleaders of the strike were arrested and between 3,500 and 6,000 strikers were sent to the front. The harsh crack-down by the government ended the strikes.[57]

55 Ferguson, *The Pity of War*, p. 253.

56 Stevenson, *With Our Backs to the Wall*, pp. 460–7.

57 Wehler, *Deutsche Gesellschaftsgeschichte*, vol. IV, pp. 83, 143ff.; Herwig, *The First World War*, pp. 378–81; Volker Ullrich, 'Zur inneren Revolutionierung der wilhelminischen Gesellschaft des Jahres 1918', in Duppler and Gross (eds.), *Kriegsende 1918*, pp. 273–84; Stevenson, *With Our Backs to the Wall*, pp. 468–77.

Over the following months the German home front remained quiet. While in 1917 667,229 workers had participated in 561 strikes, in 1918 before November only 531 strikes with 391,585 participants took place.[58] Everyone seemed to be waiting for the outcome of the spring offensive but reports from different regions of the Reich suggest that war weariness had grown and had been transformed into a general hatred of Prussian militarism, the junkers and war profiteers. The injustices of the provision system and the profits made by some had embittered many people. The black market flourished, but only the wealthy could afford to buy there. The unfair distribution of food increased class tensions. Members of the middle class in particular suffered. They were not – as part of the industrial workforce was – indispensable for the war effort and thus did not receive higher rations. The population felt that the burdens of the war were not being shared equally.[59]

The *Burgfrieden* (fortress truce) still held but everything depended on the success of the spring offensive. The political landscape was polarised. The reactionary German Fatherland Party, founded by Grand Admiral Alfred von Tirpitz in 1917, had become a mass party and united forces resisting democratic reform in Prussia and Germany. The party propagated war aims which made a compromise peace with the Allies impossible. On the other side of the political spectrum was the Independent Social Democratic Party (USPD) which had split from the Social Democratic Party in 1917 and advocated for a peace without annexations and reparations. The alliance between the SPD, the liberal Progressive People's Party (Fortschrittliche Volkspartei) and the Catholic Centre Party (Zentrum), which had supported the Reichstag peace resolution of 19 July 1917, had been undermined by disagreements about the Treaty of Brest-Litovsk. Zentrum and Fortschrittliche Volkspartei had supported the treaty while the SPD had abstained from voting. The Foreign Minister, Richard von Kühlmann, was forced to resign after he told the Reichstag on 24 June that it should not expect 'any definite end of the war based on a military decision alone'. He was accused of defeatism and was replaced by Admiral Paul von Hintze.

58 Wehler, *Deutsche Gesellschaftsgeschichte*, vol. IV, p. 135.

59 Jürgen Kocka, *Klassengesellschaft im Krieg: Deutsche Sozialgeschichte 1914–1918*, 2nd edn (Göttingen: Fischer, 1978); English translation: *Facing Total War: German Society 1914–1918* (Cambridge, MA: Harvard University Press, 1984); Wehler, *Deutsche Gesellschaftsgeschichte*, vol. IV, pp. 70–93; Ferguson, *The Pity of War*, pp. 278f.

Austria-Hungary and the Italian Front

While the German home front looked quite stable in spring and summer 1918, the situation in Austria-Hungary was different. The year 1917 had already been a very difficult one for the double monarchy. The peoples of the Empire were suffering from hunger. The war weariness had also infected the army. The number of mutinies and desertions had increased dramatically. On the plus side, the Austrian war aims had been mostly achieved: Russia was defeated, Serbia was occupied, Romania had been overrun. In 1917 and early 1918 the Foreign Minister, Count Czernin, and Emperor Karl approached the Allies through intermediaries. A couple of secret meetings took place, mostly in Switzerland. Karl even went so far as to hint that he would support the French claim to Alsace-Lorraine, but finally he shied away from risking the alliance with Germany. The German Kaiser and the Third OHL did not intend to restore Belgian independence or to return Alsace-Lorraine to France. And France and Britain would not make peace without these two conditions being met.[60]

The victory at Caporetto had bought Austria-Hungary time, but in 1918 the urban population, especially in the Austrian part of the Empire were suffering from hunger, industrial production was shrinking and the army in Italy was badly supplied with clothes, equipment, food and ammunition. The year 1918 brought even more internal turmoil, a radicalisation of the nations within the Empire and a weakening of their allegiance to the Habsburg dynasty. The economic situation had become desperate. Civilians in Austria consumed just 23g of meat and 70g of potatoes per person per day. When the government announced that it would cut the flour rations from 200g to 165g per day, Viennese workers went on strike. By 17 January, 200,000 workers were on strike. Two days later things had ground to a standstill in Bohemia and in other parts of Austria. The workers even created councils (soviets) following the Russian example. The government met some of the workers' main demands (at least on paper) and promised more food. As a result the strikes died down. But high hopes had rested on solving the food problem with supplies from Ukraine and Poland and this hope was disappointed. Requisitions in Congress Poland were intensified, but these supplies were far too little to meet the needs of the Austrian-Hungarian army and the urban population. Due mainly to a breakdown of transportation, in 1918 only 11,890

60 Strachan, *The First World War*, pp. 270–4.

of the expected 1 million wagons of grain from Ukraine arrived in Austria-Hungary.[61]

Supplies of rubber, aluminium, copper and zinc had almost dried up, and monthly coal supplies were down 40 per cent. It proved to be impossible to produce enough weapons and ammunition to replace those spent at the front. The production of machine-gun bullets, for example, fell from 6 million to 1.5 million per day between autumn 1916 and early 1918. Despite the return of Austrian prisoners of war from Russia, a manpower crisis weakened the army. The High Command of the Austrian-Hungarian army calculated that it was 600,000 men short, and the men-strength of many divisions had to be almost halved.[62] The food shortage in towns and cities in the Slavic provinces of the Empire was even worse than in the Austrian heartland and further undermined the loyalty to the state. All through the year, Austria-Hungary stood on the verge of internal collapse. As long as the Germans won victories the collapse could be avoided, but based on its own resources alone Austria-Hungary would not be able to stay in the war much longer.[63]

After the catastrophe of Caporetto, Britain and France had sent troops to stabilise the Italian Front. General Armando Diaz, who had succeeded General Luigi Cadorna as Chief of the general staff of the Italian army, was less reckless than his predecessor. He made sure that his soldiers were well fed and equipped and had fewer soldiers executed or severely punished. He was able to restore the morale of the Italian army.[64]

The Austrian offensive in June 1918 was started to prevent Allied troops from being transferred to the Western Front, but the attack was not well prepared and the way the offensive was executed did not make much sense. Not enough shells were available for a prolonged bombardment of the Italian positions, the Austrian soldiers were undernourished and many of them weakened by disease. The divisions were under strength. To make a bad situation worse, against the advice of the most able Austrian commander in Italy, Field Marshal Svetozar Boroević von Bojna, the firepower of the army was not concentrated on one portion of the front but divided between two offensives for which the Austrian-Hungarian army was not strong enough. The former Chief of the general staff, Franz Conrad von Hötzendorf, attacked from the Asiago plateau and Boroević was ordered to attack at the Piave river. Diaz had carefully ordered the defence and the Italian army fought well and

61 Herwig, *The First World War*, pp. 354, 357, 361–5. 62 *Ibid.*, pp. 356–60.
63 *Ibid.*, pp. 352–73. 64 Thompson, *The White War*, pp. 328–68.

lost very little ground. The offensive cost the Austrian army 118,000 casualties and boosted the morale of the Italian soldiers.[65]

In April 1918, as a secondary consequence of Karl's earlier secret attempts to negotiate a separate peace, his Foreign Minister, Count Czernin, had to resign. For a couple of months all contacts to the Allies broke down. From now on the fate of Austria-Hungary depended on a German victory.

Defeat on all fronts

Bulgaria was the first of the Central Powers to accept defeat. The concentration on the Western Front and the attempt to expand German rule far into the former Russian Empire had led to a weakening of other fronts. The population was war-weary, inflation was high and food scarce. In 1918 Germany reduced its financial and material support to Bulgaria. The morale of the Bulgarian soldiers deteriorated. Without substantial German help the Bulgarian ally was unable to defend the Salonica front against Serbian and Greek troops which were supported by French and British divisions. The Allies, led by the French General Franchet D'Esperey, attacked on 15 September, and two weeks later Bulgaria had to ask for an armistice.

The Ottoman Empire was under pressure from the successful offensives of the Commander of the (British) Egyptian Expeditionary Force (EEF), General Edmund Allenby, and his Arab allies. The best Turkish troops were operating in Transcaucasia and attempting to profit as much as possible from the fall of the Russian Empire. By the end of 1917 the Ottoman Empire was on the back foot in Palestine. Allenby took Jerusalem on 9 December while Arab partisans pushed up from the south.[66] The offensive only stopped after the EEF lost several divisions which had been sent to the Western Front. Reinforced by Indian, Canadian and Australian troops, Allenby resumed his offensive in September 1918. In the Battle of Megiddo (19–21 September) the Ottoman Turkish army was comprehensively beaten. In subsequent days 75,000 Ottoman Turkish soldiers were taken prisoner. The advancing EEF met with hardly any resistance. The low morale of the soldiers fighting far away from the Turkish heartlands corresponded to the worsening economic situation at home. Inflation was high and people in Constantinople were starving. Damascus fell on 1 October and Aleppo on 25 October. The Ottoman Empire capitulated five days later.[67]

65 *Ibid.*, pp. 356–78. 66 Strachan, *The First World War*, pp. 274–9.

67 Edward J. Erickson, *Ordered to Die: A History of the Ottoman Army in the First World War* (Westport, CT: Praeger, 2001), pp. 169–206, 237ff.

The Italian Chief of the general staff Diaz waited until October before he attacked. The morale of the Austrian army had been undermined by Italian propaganda and by learning about the Allied victories on the Western Front. Diaz started the attack knowing that the future borders of Italy would also depend on how far his troops would come. The Austrian army continued to struggle with supply problems and a rapidly declining morale. Polish, Slovenian, Croatian, Czech, Slovak and Ukrainian soldiers knew that new political options were available. Hungarian soldiers realised that the time of the double monarchy was over and some units refused to go to the front. The Italian army attacked on 24 October. The Battle of Vittorio Veneto ended after five days of heavy fighting with a decisive victory. The Austrian army was in dissolution. Many soldiers were killed while trying to escape. The soldiers of the multi-ethnic Empire just wanted to go home. Due to a tragic mistake by the Austrian High Command, which had failed to communicate the correct date of the armistice to the troops, Austrian soldiers stopped fighting twenty-four hours before the armistice took effect. In these twenty-four hours 350,000 soldiers of the Austrian army were taken prisoner. Of the 430,000 Habsburg prisoners held by Italy on 11 November, a minimum of 30,000 died in prisoner-of-war camps. The number might even be much higher. Alan Kramer states that the Italian army captured 468,000 Austrian-Hungarian soldiers, of whom at least 92,451 or 93,184 died in Italian camps.[68]

In September 1918 Emperor Karl and his new Foreign Minister, Count Stephan Burian, realised that Germany had lost the war on the Western Front. Burian and Karl contacted the Allies but their peace offer was rejected. The Allies had given up any hope of separating Austria-Hungary from Germany and no longer expected the Empire to survive the war. On 3 June Britain, France and Italy had expressed their full support for Polish, Czech and Yugoslav statehood. Karl desperately tried to save his throne, offering federalisation and democratisation of the Austrian part of his Empire, but it was too late for reforms. Czech, Slovak, Serbian, Croatian and Slovenian subjects of the Habsburg Empire declared their independence on 29 October. The Serbian army helped other South Slavs to secure the borders of future Yugoslavia.[69]

While Austria-Hungary was breaking down into its constituent parts, the German army was still fighting. Between 27 September and 4 October the Allies launched three successful offensives along the Western Front. The

68 Thompson, *The White War*, pp. 363ff. Alan Kramer, *Dynamic of Destruction: Culture and Mass Killing in the First World War* (Oxford University Press, 2007), p. 65.
69 Stevenson, *The First World War and International Politics*, pp. 228f.

strongly fortified Hindenburg Line could not be taken by surprise, but the material superiority of the Allies made the difference. Over a 10,000-yard front, 1,637 guns fired shells for fifty-six hours at the German defences. At the Saint-Quentin Canal nearly 50,000 shells rained on every fifty yards during the eight hours of the attack. Hardly any German soldier survived this bombardment. On 29 September the British 46th Division broke through the Hindenburg Line and the German positions further north were outflanked. The German troops had to withdraw.[70] Already in the days prior to this breach the OHL had realised that the war was lost. The front still held but the next attack could be the strategic breakthrough.

The news of the capitulation of Bulgaria was the final blow. Ludendorff and Hindenburg informed the German Kaiser on 29 September about the situation at the front. Ludendorff now believed that only an immediate ceasefire would prevent a catastrophe and urged the Kaiser to appoint a Chancellor who would have the support of the Reichstag. Ludendorff had not suddenly become a democrat. He hoped that a democratic Germany would get better terms but he also wanted the democrats, especially the Social Democrats, to take the responsibility for the defeat. He was looking for scapegoats for the disaster and blamed the lack of support the army had received from the home front. And so the myth that the German army had remained 'undefeated on the battlefield' was born – the myth that the army had been 'stabbed in the back' by its enemies in Germany.[71]

Ludendorff and the Foreign Minister, Paul von Hintze, proposed to contact the American President Woodrow Wilson, whose fourteen-point plan now – facing defeat – seemed much more attractive than it had in January. The new Chancellor appointed by the Kaiser was the more liberal Max von Baden, who included representatives of the SPD, the Zentrum and the Fortschrittliche Volkspartei in his coalition government. A few days later Germany became a parliamentary monarchy. Ludendorff still believed that the front could collapse any moment and urged the Chancellor to ask for an immediate armistice. The German army faced unrelenting pressure from the Allies but still held out. It withdrew where necessary but continued to fight.

What Ludendorff did not realise was that the Allied troops would have to stop soon and regroup as their lines of communication were becoming

70 Robin Priors, 'Stabbed in the front: the German defeat in 1918', in Ekins (ed.), *1918 – Year of Victory*, p. 50.

71 Wehler, *Deutsche Gesellschaftsgeschichte*, vol. IV, pp. 174–7. On the myth of the 'stab-in-the-back' see Boris Barth, *Dolchstosslegende und politische Desintegration: Das Trauma der deutschen Niederlage im Ersten Weltkrieg 1914–1933* (Düsseldorf: Droste, 2003).

overstretched. The negotiating position of the new German government was not good, but Ludendorff's insistence on an immediate ceasefire made it even weaker. In the night of 3 to 4 October, the German government sent a message to President Wilson asking him for his help in arranging an armistice based on the Fourteen Points. The Allies understood that the German government considered the war lost. A public exchange of notes between Wilson and the German government followed. In the first two notes Wilson only demanded the immediate evacuation of Belgium and France and an end to submarine warfare, but – after the intervention of Lloyd George, Clemenceau and Orlando – he informed Max von Baden in his third note dated 23 October about additional conditions. He strongly indicated that the Allies were not willing to negotiate with the OHL or the Kaiser. Without abdication and an end to the dictatorship of the OHL the Allies would insist on capitulation.

The intentions of the Allies were clear – the terms should make it impossible for the German army to resume hostilities. After learning about the conditions Ludendorff was suddenly more optimistic about the ability of the German army to continue fighting. He and Hindenburg sent – without informing the Chancellor or the Kaiser – a message to the troop commanders calling them to prepare for a final battle. Ideas of a *levée en masse* in Germany were floated, but it was too late. The new government was no longer willing to leave the fate of Germany and the lives of more young men in the hands of irresponsible military commanders. On 26 October Ludendorff was forced to resign and was replaced as First Quartermaster General by Wilhelm Groener. The primacy of politics was restored and the dictatorship of the Third OHL was finally over.[72]

As if to prove the point that German military leaders had acted irresponsibly and completely lost contact with reality, on 30 October the commanders of the German navy proposed sending the fleet to attack the Royal Navy as its last heroic deed. The sailors refused and extinguished the fires in the ships' boilers. They created councils of sailors and joined up with workers in Kiel. Soon councils of workers, sailors and soldiers (Arbeiter-, Matrosen- und Soldatenräte) were being created all over Germany. On 7 November the king of Bavaria abdicated in Munich and a soviet (Räte) republic was proclaimed. The German revolution had begun. After the mutiny of the Kiel sailors (which had spread like wildfire through Germany), the creation of

72 Stevenson, *The First World War and International Politics*, pp. 222–7; Michael Geyer, 'Insurrectionary warfare: the German debate about a levée en masse in October 1918', *Journal of Modern History*, 73 (2001), pp. 459–527.

workers' and soldiers' councils, strikes and mass demonstrations, it would have been irresponsible to delay the armistice any longer.[73]

On 8 November a German delegation led by the Zentrum politician Matthias Erzberger crossed the front and was brought to Foch's train in the forest of Compiègne. Marshal Foch had drafted the terms for the armistice which were handed to the German delegation. The Germans were given just seventy-two hours to accept or reject them. The German army would be partly disarmed, all occupied territory in the West would have to be returned within two weeks. The Rhineland would be demilitarised. The left bank of the Rhine would be occupied by the Allies, and the Allies would also establish several bridgeheads on the right bank of the Rhine. The German fleet should be interned in harbours of neutral countries or handed over to the British.[74]

The fighting continued during the exchange of notes between Max von Baden and Woodrow Wilson and the negotiations in Compiègne. The German troops still shot back and soldiers continued dying on both sides of the front up until the very last moment. Max von Baden had authorised the German delegation to accept any conditions and – unable to get new directives from the government – Erzberger signed the Armistice agreement on 11 November at 5 a.m. The Armistice took effect six hours later (Map 6.4).

In the meantime events in Germany followed thick and fast. Kaiser Wilhelm had escaped from revolutionary Berlin to the German army headquarters at Spa, and dreamt of returning at the head of his troops to quell the Revolution. There were now two power centres in Germany: the OHL and the Kaiser in Spa and the civil government supported by the old imperial and Prussian bureaucracy in Berlin. For a brief moment a military coup was a real possibility.[75] But after consulting with division commanders, Ludendorff's successor, Wilhelm Groener, had to inform Wilhelm that the army no longer stood behind him. The Kaiser was told that soldiers would follow their commanding officers 'but not Your Majesty'. Having lost the support of the military the Kaiser abdicated on 9 November for himself and for his sons and fled to neutral Holland. On the same day Max von Baden unceremoniously and unconstitutionally handed over the chancellorship to Friedrich Ebert, the

73 Heinrich August Winkler, *Von der Revolution zur Stabilisierung: Arbeiter und Arbeiterbewegung in der Weimarer Republik 1918–1924*, 2nd edn (Berlin: J. H. W. Dietz Nachf, 1985), pp. 34–61; Wilhelm Deist, 'Die Politik der Seekriegsleitung und die Rebellion der Flotte Ende Oktober 1918', *Vierteljahreshefte für Zeitgeschichte*, 14 (1966), pp. 325–43.

74 Stevenson, *The First World War and International Politics*, pp. 229–36. On the German revolution, the Armistice and the Treaty of Versailles see Klaus Schwabe, *Deutsche Revolution und Wilson-Friede* (Düsseldorf: Droste, 1971).

75 Wehler, *Deutsche Gesellschaftsgeschichte*, vol. IV, pp. 184–97.

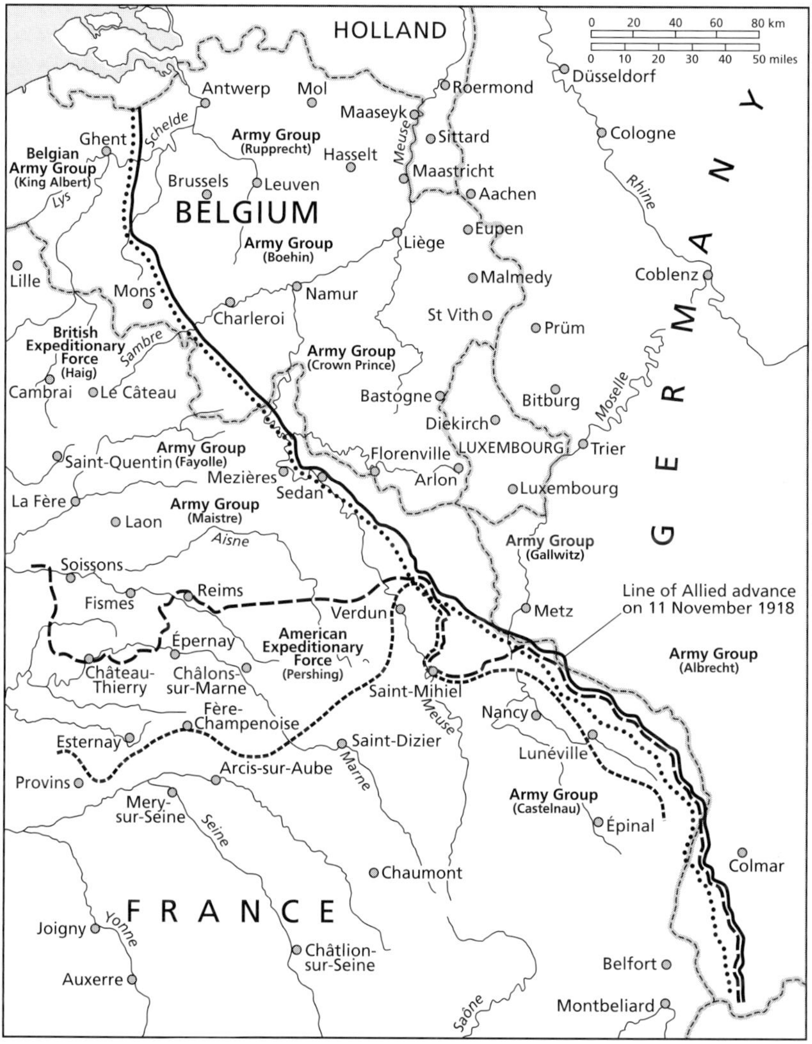

Map 6.4 The Armistice, 1918, and position of opposing forces in France and Belgium.

leader of the Social Democrats, while another prominent Social Democrat, Philipp Scheidemann, proclaimed a German republic, shortly before Karl Liebknecht, one of the leaders of the communist Spartakusbund, proclaimed a German Räterepublik. The power was with the new coalition government of SPD and USPD which could draw on the support of the military. Right-wing groups did not resist the German revolution as the military, politicians, junkers and heavy industrialists around the Fatherland Party entertained hopes that it would be easier to obtain tolerable armistice and peace conditions if democratically legitimised politicians were negotiating with the Allies. The old elite was paralysed by the defeat and reluctant to act, hoping that the moderate Social Democrats would at least prevent a Bolshevik-style revolution.[76]

The new government (which called itself the Rat der Volksbeauftragten) was confirmed by the Berlin Council of Workers and Soldiers, which strengthened its legitimacy and revolutionary credentials. Its main tasks were to negotiate the peace treaty with the Allies, to uphold public and economic life and to prevent a communist revolution. The government needed the help of the military for this last task. Both feared a communist revolution and the government used loyal troops to fight the threat from the radical left. While there was hardly any alternative to cooperating with the military and the old bureaucracy, the social-democratic Chancellor made the mistake of welcoming the returning troops as 'undefeated on the battlefield' (*unbesiegt im Schlachtfelde*). This gave fresh credence to the *Dolchstosslegende* (myth of the stab in the back). It helped the old elites to delegate the responsibility for the defeat to the young German democracy. According to this view, it was not the battlefront that had collapsed but the home front, and a plethora of 'Jews, Communists and Social Democrats' had stabbed the soldiers in the back. It was a lie but one that many Germans believed. At the end of the war Jews and Democrats were already made the scapegoats for the defeat.[77]

Why did the Central Powers lose the war, or, why did the Allies win?

Less than six months after the spring offensive which had begun with such high hopes, the German and the Austrian emperors had abdicated, Austria-Hungary was dissolved and the Ottoman Empire, with the exception of a small strip of land west of Constantinople, had been reduced to its territories in Asia Minor. But the Allied victory was not the result of the endemic

76 Winkler, *Von der Revolution zur Stabilisierung*, pp. 25–32.

77 Wehler, *Deutsche Gesellschaftsgeschichte*, vol. IV, pp. 128–34. On Hindenburg's role during and after the war and the cult of the 'victor of Tannenberg' see Wolfram Pyta, *Hindenburg: Herrschaft zwischen Hohenzollern und Hitler* (Munich: Siedler, 2009); Jesko von Hoegen, *Der Held von Tannenberg: Genese und Funktion des Hindenburg-Mythos (1914–1934)* (Cologne: Böhlau Verlag, 2007).

superiority of democracies over authoritarian regimes or a victory of the principle of liberalism over authoritarianism. Without assistance from the very authoritarian Russian Empire, the Western Allies would probably have lost the war. There were several moments when twenty or thirty divisions more would have made all the difference and a decisive German victory likely. The Russian army attacked when the pressure on the Western Front was highest. This was the case in late summer 1914, again in 1915 and during the Brusilov offensive in 1916. After the defeat of Russia the entry into the war of the United States saved the Allies.

Germany and Austria-Hungary were more disadvantaged by their federal structures. It was difficult to raise taxation in Germany where the states prevented the introduction of direct taxes on a national level, and in the Habsburg Empire, Hungary was run almost like an independent country. Hungarian politicians carefully guarded their prerogatives and were not always inclined to make sacrifices for the good of the Empire.[78]

Between 1916 and 1918, however, the disaster for Germany was that the Third OHL concentrated political and military power. Ludendorff may have been – at times – a good military leader but he was an inept and short-sighted politician. He did not realise the limits of German power and clung – as did his like-minded friends in the German Fatherland Party – to overreaching war aims even after the war had been lost. Given the Allied superiority in manpower and material resources in 1918, a compromise peace was the best the Central Powers could have hoped for. Defeat was inevitable after the failure of the spring offensive, but neither the OHL nor the political and economic elite were willing to accept the inevitable, which meant the return of all occupied territories, the restoration of Belgium and the loss of Alsace-Lorraine. They were full of illusions and clung to the unrealistic hope that one of the next offensives would bring victory.[79] On the Eastern Front either a moderate peace with Soviet Russia or the full application of the principle of the right to self-determination would have strengthened the position of the Central Powers more than reckless exploitation and plans for the region's colonisation and economic and political penetration.

The German political, economic and military leaders were convinced that Germany's future depended on becoming a world power and that only a *Siegfrieden* (peace after victory) would make it possible to achieve this goal. For

78 Stevenson, *With our Backs to the Wall*, pp. 416–19, 422.

79 Kitchen, *The German Offensives of 1918*, pp. 244ff.; and Michael Epkenhans, 'Die Politik der militärischen Führung 1918: "Kontinuität der Illusionen und das Dilemma der Wahrheit"', in Duppler and Gross (eds.), *Kriegsende 1918*, pp. 217–233.

them, Germany's security and very existence as a European power was at stake. They would not moderate their war aims or even concede territory as long as they could make themselves believe that the Allies would crack first.

Politicians on both sides faced the same problem. The loss of hundreds of thousands, even millions of lives could be easier justified if their own side won the war and if the peace treaty reflected this victory. Anything short of realising the key war aims would have destabilised the political system.[80] Only after the spring offensive had failed did some leading German politicians and military commanders come to the conclusion that Germany had to sue for peace before the Allies realised how weakened the German army really was.[81]

The ill-conceived military dictatorship Germany had become was also unable to strike a balance between the front and the home front.[82] The ambitious Hindenburg Programme succeeded in producing enough weapons and munitions but failed to provide enough motorised vehicles, aircraft or tanks and neglected the basic needs of the civilian population. Operation Michael had also failed because of a lack of horses and motorised transport. While at this point the French alone had 100,000 lorries along the Western Front, the German army had only 20,000. New weapons systems also played a role. Tanks did not win the war but they did help win some battles. In 1918 the French army had 3,000 tanks, the BEF even had 5,000. Germany had produced just twenty heavy tanks; most of the tanks used by the German army had been captured from the British.[83] Moreover, the German economy was not only producing for the German army. Without providing substantial financial and material aid, without sending weapons, munitions and soldiers to its allies, the various fronts would not have held. This meant straining German resources to the utmost, but when the German aid was reduced in 1918 it did not take much for Germany's allies to collapse. Once its allies had been defeated it was impossible for Germany to resist much longer.[84]

80 Storz, '"Aber was hätte anders geschehen sollen?"', pp. 51–97; Arno J. Meyer, *Politics and Diplomacy of Peacemaking: Containment and Counterrevolution at Versailles, 1918–1919* (New York: Knopf, 1967).

81 Kitchen, *The German Offensives of 1918*, pp. 48ff., 138, 161, 235, 244ff.

82 On the role of the military in German domestic policy during the war see Wilhelm Deist (ed.), *Militär und Innenpolitik im Weltkrieg 1914 bis 1918*, 2 vols. (Düsseldorf: Droste, 1970), vol. 1, part ii. Nebelin, *Ludendorff*, pp. 339ff.; Martin Kitchen, *The Silent Dictatorship: The Politics of the German High Command under Hindenburg and Ludendorff, 1916–1918* (London: Taylor & Francis, 1976).

83 Strachan, *The First World War*, pp. 305ff.

84 Stevenson, *With our Backs to the Wall*, pp. 404–19, 431ff.; Gerald D. Feldman, *Army, Industry and Labor in Germany 1914–1918* (Princeton University Press, 1966), pp. 513ff.; Nebelin, *Ludendorff*, pp. 245ff.

The most important contribution of the United States to victory had already started before the country entered the war. Lending money to Britain allowed Britain to provide financial support to her Allies on the continent. Food imports, especially imports of cereals from the USA and – also very important – from Canada, made it possible to keep the economy going and to feed the population. The Allies could draw on resources of manpower, raw materials and food from the British and French Empires. Soldiers from Australia, Canada, New Zealand, Newfoundland, India and other parts of the Empire helped to win the war. A total of 475,000 soldiers from the colonies fought in the French army. The Central Powers had to rely on their own manpower and material resources – imports from neutral European states were important but were insufficient to satisfy demand. While the Central Powers relied almost completely on land-based transportation, the American and British merchant fleets and most neutral ships were at the disposal of the Allies. While in 1918 there were some critical moments when food, coal or other supplies were running dangerously low in France, Britain and Italy, all these problems could be overcome or at least contained until the victory was secure.[85]

But why did the Allies win the war in 1918 and not one year later? Ludendorff has been disparaged for the way he handled the spring offensive in 1918. Military historians have criticised him for changing his war plans as soon as the opportunity arose instead of pursuing a coherent strategy.[86] The offensives were often tactically successful but did not achieve their strategic objectives, and the high casualty rates decisively weakened the German army. Neither the BEF nor the French army broke; the crisis in morale of 1916 and 1917 had been overcome, and the final successful defence of Amiens, Ypres and Arras and the victory in the Second Battle of the Marne had instilled new confidence in the Allied soldiers.

The contribution of the US army to the victory was important but its significance was more psychological than military. The arrival of American soldiers did do wonders for the morale of their British and French comrades. General John Pershing insisted on creating an autonomous US army but replied to urgent French and British requests by allowing 180,000 American infantry soldiers (organised in US units) in May and 150,000 in June to join the British and French armies. While the manpower resources of the Central

85 Strachan, *The First World War*, pp. 308ff.

86 For example Sheffield, *Forgotten Victory*, pp. 226ff. See also Storz '"Aber was hätte anders geschehen sollen?"', pp. 51–96.

Powers were almost exhausted and losses could no longer be compensated, the entry into the war of the United States guaranteed the Allies a seemingly limitless supply of new soldiers. At the time of the Armistice about 1.5 million American soldiers were stationed in France and forty-two divisions had been formed – divisions which had twice as many men as the British or French divisions. Twenty-nine divisions had already participated in the fighting.[87]

A further reason for Allied victory in 1918 was the manner in which their offensives were carried out. Pétain and Haig set limited objectives and made full use of their aerial and artillery superiority and the availability of tanks. A fully intact German army might have been more difficult to beat, but the German troops were battered, exhausted and no longer had a hope of victory. Allied troops continued to attack until the very day of the Armistice, putting the German front under permanent and relentless pressure. Within the space of 100 days the Allies took 363,000 German soldiers prisoner (25 per cent of the army in the field) and captured 6,400 guns (50 per cent of all German guns on the Western Front). These numbers show both the effectiveness of the Allied strategy and the low morale of the German soldiers.[88]

The disappointment on the German side was all the greater as soldiers and civilians had begun 1918 with such high hopes and had expected that the spring offensives would bring victory. Between March and May German newspapers were full of reports about German successes. Later reports were more sombre, but neither the general public nor the soldiers had been prepared for an eventual defeat. By the autumn of 1918 the morale on every level, from the military Headquarters to front-line soldiers, from politicians to workers, had reached rock bottom. Morale is crucial in war, including the morale of the High Command. Ludendorff's morale broke – it was not the reason for the collapse but reflected the mood in the German army. Ferguson argues that it was not superior tactics which brought victory but the decline in morale of the German soldiers.[89] In October and November 1918 the German front troops were still a fighting force even if discipline and morale had suffered and desertion had increased dramatically. The revolution had mostly affected the rear troops, where the authority of officers was being challenged and

87 Strachan, *The First World War*, p. 204.

88 Numbers taken from Gilbert, *The First World War*, p. 500.

89 Ferguson, *The Pity of War*, pp. 310–14; Gary D. Sheffield, 'The morale of the British army on the Western Front, 1914–1918', in Geoffrey Jensen and Andrew Wiest (eds.), *War in the Age of Technology: Myriad Faces of Modern Armed Conflict* (New York and London: New York University Press, 2001), pp. 105–31. See also Benjamin Ziemann, 'Enttäuschte Erwartung und kollektive Erschöpfung: Die deutschen Soldaten an der Westfront 1918 auf dem Weg zur Revolution', in Duppler and Gross (eds.), *Kriegsende 1918*, pp. 165–82.

councils of workers were being created.[90] Even if German soldiers had continued fighting, militarily this did not make sense. Germany was defeated, even before the mutiny by sailors of the German High Seas Fleet triggered the revolution. The home front collapsed after all hope of victory had vanished.

The Armistice of 11 November ended the killing along the Western Front, but in Eastern Europe the Great War was transmuted into a series of civil, state-building and revolutionary wars. The sudden withdrawal of German and Austrian-Hungarian troops left a power vacuum. Ukraine and Belarus became battlefields in the Russian civil war; in the Baltic region Estonians, Latvians and Lithuanians – supported by German *Freikorps* – defended their countries against the Red Army; in East Galicia war was raging between Poles and Western Ukrainians. The First World War was not the war 'which ended all wars', not even for a short time.

90 Scott Stephenson, *The Final Battle: Soldiers of the Western Front and the German Revolution of 1918* (Cambridge University Press, 2009).

7

1919: Aftermath

BRUNO CABANES

The end of the First World War cannot be easily demarcated by a specific date. The war's long-term effects were so devastating that it is fair to say no clear dividing-line separates the war itself from the post-war period; nearly 10 million men died, in other words, one in seven of all soldiers; 21 million were wounded; millions of widows, orphans and other grieving relatives were left behind to mourn their dead. The war's aftermath produced countless human tragedies; nearly every family continued to feel the emotional and psychological effects for years to come.[1] To take the single year of 1919 and consider it as a specific historical subject in its own right thus constitutes another way to question traditional chronology, which tends to view the Armistice of 11 November 1918 and the subsequent peace treaties as the two decisive markers in the return to peace. In reality, 1919 constitutes at most a step – but only a step – in what historians now call 'the transition from war to peace', in French, *la sortie de guerre*. This term refers to a transition period of several years, characterised by the return home of soldiers and prisoners of war, the pacification of the belligerent nations and the far slower demobilisation of minds and attitudes, or what is also called 'cultural demobilisation'.[2] This process was far from straightforward. It took place in a series of fits and starts, with periods of simultaneous demobilisation and remobilisation, gestures of peace and examples of the impossibility or refusal to demobilise.

Another difficulty in the complex transition from war to peace lay in the wide variety of national circumstances. In France and Great Britain, 1919 was a year of military demobilisation and rebuilding. Returning soldiers had to take

Helen McPhail translated this chapter from French into English.

1 Stéphane Audoin-Rouzeau and Christophe Prochasson (eds.), *Sortir de la Grande Guerre* (Paris: Tallandier, 2008).

2 John Horne (ed.), 'Démobilisations culturelles après la Grande Guerre', *14–18: Aujourd'hui, Today, Heute*, 5 (Paris: Noêsis, 2002), pp. 43–53.

up their civilian lives again, which was much more difficult for some than for others. The state and charitable organisations established aid programmes for victims of the war, while survivors tried to rebuild the ruins of regions devastated by the conflict. But in other countries, 1919 meant that outbreaks of violence were still occurring between armed factions and against civilians: the occupation of the Rhineland by Allied troops; confrontations between revolutionaries and counter-revolutionaries in Germany; civil war in Russia and in Ireland; frontier struggles between Greece and Turkey (1919–22), as well as Russia and Poland (1919–21), to name only a few. All these conflicts, each deadly to some degree, prolonged and magnified the effects of the First World War, to the extent that national histories sometimes associate the Great War with later confrontations as part of the same chronological sequence. The Greeks, for example, consider that a single period of war began with the Balkan wars in 1912 and ended ten years later, with the Greco-Turkish War. In 1919, some armies simply changed enemies. Roger Vercel's novel *Capitaine Conan* (1934), for example, portrays veterans of the French unit known as the *Armée d'Orient* engaging in the struggle against the Bolsheviks. In short, from the standpoint of a 'transition from war to peace', it is almost as if the year 1919 represents only the beginning of a larger phenomenon: a slow and chaotic demobilisation.

But 1919 was not only a step in an ongoing process: it was also a moment – in the way that Erez Manela has described a 'Wilsonian moment', a short period in which significant collective expectations coalesced. This occurred not just in the Western world, as has long been thought, but also on a global scale.[3] Seen as the dawn of a new era, the peace treaties embodied collective hopes for a profound change in international relations. New states were coming into being or were reborn out of the ruins of the Russian, Austro-Hungarian, German and Ottoman Empires. During the first six months of 1919, delegations from around the world came to Paris while everywhere else, the public generally followed the peace negotiations with great interest; they were major events in a globalised world. The signing of the Treaty of Versailles, on 28 June 1919, in the Hall of Mirrors, represented a kind of apotheosis. It was followed by the Treaty of Saint-Germain-en-Laye with Austria (10 September 1919), the Treaty of Neuilly-sur-Seine with Bulgaria (27 November 1919), then the Treaty of Trianon with Hungary (4 June 1920) and the Treaty of Sèvres with Turkey (10 August 1920), itself revised in the Treaty of Lausanne of 1923. In the autumn of 1919, the campaign began for the

3 Erez Manela, *The Wilsonian Moment: Self-Determination and the International Origins of Anticolonial Nationalism* (Oxford University Press, 2007).

ratification of the Treaty of Versailles in the United States Congress, but the American Senate ultimately rejected the treaty with a final vote in March 1920.[4]

The year 1919 to some extent symbolises all the hopes of the post-war era: a new diplomacy based on world peace and collective security; major transnational organisations like the ILO (International Labour Organisation) established in Geneva early in 1919; recognition of the right to self-determination. However, it was also a year of threats and disillusionment, which weakened the dynamics of demobilisation.

The Treaty of Versailles, or the disappointed dreams of Wilsonianism

On 28 June 1919, at 3.00 p.m. precisely, two German emissaries in ceremonial dress entered the great Hall of Mirrors in the château of Versailles and advanced to the centre of the room, escorted by Allied soldiers. The emissaries were Hermann Müller, the new German Minister for Foreign Affairs, and Johannes Bell, the Minister for Transport; they were there to sign the peace treaty that would bring the First World War to an end. 'The whole affair was elaborately staged and made as humiliating to the enemy as it well could be. To my mind it is out of keeping with the new era which we profess an ardent desire to promote', noted Colonel House, diplomatic adviser to the American President, Woodrow Wilson.[5] The French Président du Conseil, Georges Clemenceau, had designed a veritable Roman triumph. The two German emissaries had to proceed past a delegation of *gueules cassées*, men with permanently disfigured faces, who served as living reminders of the damage inflicted by the Central Powers.[6] In a historic first, cameras filmed the signing of the treaty. '[The two Germans] passed close to me. It was like seeing prisoners led in to hear the reading of their sentence', a British diplomat reported. Müller and Bell returned to Berlin the same evening, while in Paris, captured enemy guns were paraded through the streets.

The peace negotiations had opened five months earlier in the red and gold Salon de l'Horloge at the headquarters of the French Ministry for Foreign

4 John Milton Cooper, Jr., *Breaking the Heart of the World: Woodrow Wilson and the Fight for the League of Nations* (Cambridge University Press, 2001).

5 Edward M. House, *The Intimate Papers of Colonel House Arranged as a Narrative by Charles Seymour*, 4 vols. (Boston and New York: Houghton Mifflin, 1926–8), vol. IV, p. 487.

6 Stéphane Audoin-Rouzeau, 'Die Delegation der "Gueules cassées" in Versailles am 28. Juni 1919', in Gerd Krumeich *et al.* (eds.), *Versailles 1919: Ziele, Wirkung, Wahrnehmung* (Essen: Klartext Verlag, 2001), pp. 280–7.

Affairs, located on the Quai d'Orsay. Clemenceau had chosen the date of 18 January 1919, the anniversary of Kaiser Wilhelm I's 1871 coronation. He also insisted that the treaty be signed in the Hall of Mirrors, the very same place where the German Reich had been first proclaimed. John Maynard Keynes, a member of the British delegation, has left us a mordant portrait of Clemenceau: 'Silent ... throned, in his grey gloves, on the brocade chair, dry in soul and empty of hope, very old and tired, and surveying the scene with a cynical and almost impish air.'[7] In reality, recent historiography has largely done justice to Clemenceau and called into question the 'black legend' that tended to portray the French Président du Conseil ('who felt about France what Pericles felt about Athens', in Keynes's words) as the man responsible for all the defects of the peace treaty.

The vanquished imperial powers and their successors – Germany, Austria, Hungary, Bulgaria, Turkey – were not invited, nor was Russia. In this respect, the Paris Peace Conference differed significantly from the negotiations of 1815, the great European peace conference of the previous century. Another difference lay in the number of participating countries: five at the Congress of Vienna in 1815, but twenty-seven in Paris. The delegations themselves were far larger, comprising several hundred people on average, accompanied by chauffeurs and secretaries, and there were more than 500 journalists. In the words of Margaret Macmillan:

> Between January and June, Paris was at once the world's government, its court of appeal and its parliament, the focus of its fears and hopes. Officially, the Peace Conference lasted into 1920, but those first six months are the ones that counted, when the key decisions were taken and the crucial chain of events set in motion. The world has never seen anything quite like this and never will again.[8]

The Paris Peace Conference was a carefully structured hierarchical edifice in which the representatives of the Great Powers controlled the game. In January and February 1919, two members each from the French, British, Italian, American and Japanese delegations met under Clemenceau's chairmanship in the salons of the Quai d'Orsay. The Council of Ten, in which the representatives of smaller countries also participated, gave way to a Council of Four, with Clemenceau, the British and Italian Prime Ministers, David Lloyd

7 John Maynard Keynes, *The Economic Consequences of the Peace* (New York: Macmillan, 1919), p. 32.

8 Margaret Macmillan, *Paris 1919: Six Months That Changed the World* (New York: Random House, 2001), Introduction, p. xxv.

George and Vittorio Emanuele Orlando, and Woodrow Wilson, the first American head of state to travel abroad during his term in office. At the end of April 1919, it was mainly Clemenceau, Wilson and Lloyd George who decided on the essentials, often after lively discussions that revealed the tensions among the three men.[9] Here, the professional diplomats ceded their power to the politicians. Their influence was felt instead within the fifty-two commissions that worked on a wide range of technical issues: borders for the new states, the fate of ethnic minorities and questions of reparations.

The procedures of the conference remained nonetheless somewhat chaotic. No one had considered exactly how the negotiations would progress, nor at what speed. Important members had other obligations that required them to leave for long periods, such as President Wilson, who returned to the United States for nearly a month in mid February. It was not until mid April that an agenda was decided upon and minutes kept for each meeting. In the end, the Peace Treaty and its 440 articles were drawn up in great haste. The delegations of the victorious nations read over the text only a few hours before it was sent to representatives of the defeated countries.

Each delegation leader had come to Paris with his own objectives; he bore the weight of the expectations of public opinion in his own country. But all the delegations shared a common concern: the fate of Germany in post-war Europe. For France, both security and justice were at stake: ten French *départements* had suffered from direct experience of battle or occupation, and the entire nation had lost a quarter of its male population between the ages of 18 and 27. Faced with such large-scale sacrifices, endured by his nation for over four years, Clemenceau nonetheless showed himself to be a realist. He confided to Raymond Poincaré, President of the French Republic, 'We will perhaps not have the peace that you and I would wish for. France must make concessions, not to Germany but to her Allies.' For the British, who suspected the French of harbouring ambitions to annex the Rhineland, the reinforcement of French power in Europe was at least as alarming as the matter of German power. The Prime Minister, Lloyd George, sought to reconcile what he considered a just punishment for the war crimes committed by the Central Powers with maintaining economic harmony in Europe. Italy wanted to see the Allies keep the promises made during the London Conference in 1915, notably, to give up the irredentist territories of Trentino and Trieste, as well as Istria and Dalmatia. President Wilson, for his part, had always thought that the

9 Paul Mantoux, *Les délibérations du Conseil des Quatre*, 2 vols. (Paris: CNRS Éditions, 1955).

peace should be a 'just peace', based on a kind of moral pact that he called a 'covenant', that it should not take place at the price of a severely weakened Germany and that a distinction had to be made between the German people and their rulers, who alone were responsible for the war.[10]

After the treaty was signed, Articles 231 and 232 became the most frequent topics of debate. Article 231 assigned responsibility for the damages suffered by the Allies to Germany and the Central Powers, while Article 232 reached the conclusion that a guilty Germany owed reparations for the damages that it had caused. It made no difference that the great historian Pierre Renouvin, himself a veteran of the war, explained early on that the terms 'responsibility' and 'reparations' should be understood not in moral terms but in the terms of civil law.[11] The fact remains that for the Germans, and for most of the Allies, Articles 231 and 232 were seen as a form of moral condemnation – no doubt all the more unacceptable to Germany who itself had lost more than 2 million of its own soldiers. The sting of this moral condemnation was compounded by a sense of humiliation, shared by the Austrians, over their territorial losses and the end of imperial grandeur.

To understand the Allies' apparent harshness towards Germany, it is important to take into account the moral climate of the post-war period and especially the state of mind prevailing in Allied countries during the winter of 1918–19.[12] The discovery of the damage caused by the German troops during their withdrawal in the autumn of 1918,[13] the treatment meted out to civilians in occupied regions and the handling of prisoners of war[14] – in other words, the renewed energy in 1918–19 of the theme of 'German atrocities' – weighed heavily on the heads of state and diplomats at the Paris Conference. Another issue was the attitude towards Kaiser Wilhelm II, who had fled to the Netherlands and whom the Allies almost unanimously viewed as one of the worst war criminals in history. It is hardly surprising, then, that when French soldiers awaiting demobilisation first heard the terms of the peace treaties,

10 Manfred F. Boemeke, 'Woodrow Wilson's image of Germany, the war-guilt question and the Treaty of Versailles', in Manfred F. Boemeke, Gerald D. Feldman and Elisabeth Glaser (eds.), *The Treaty of Versailles: A Reassessment after 75 Years* (German Historical Institute and Cambridge University Press, 1998), pp. 603–14.

11 Pierre Renouvin, *Histoire des relations internationales*, 3 vols. (Paris: Hachette, 1958, republished 1994), vol. III, p. 446.

12 Gerd Krumeich *et al.*, *Versailles 1919: Ziele, Wirkung, Wahrnehmung* (Essen: Klartext Verlag, 2001).

13 Michael Geyer, 'Insurrectionary warfare: the German debate about a *levée en masse* in October 1918', *Journal of Modern History*, 73 (2001), pp. 459–527.

14 Annette Becker, *Oubliés de la Grande Guerre: humanitaire et culture de guerre, 1914–1918: populations occupées, déportés civils, prisonniers de guerre* (Paris: Éditions Noêsis, 1998).

they spoke of these terms in their letters home not as excessively harsh, but as not severe enough.[15]

The bibliography on the issue of reparations is vast. Beginning with John Maynard Keynes's pamphlet *The Economic Consequences of the Peace*, an instant bestseller published in the summer of 1919, an early tendency emphasised the disastrous consequences of the reparations on the German economy and the young Weimar Republic. Conversely, in the aftermath of the Second World War, Keynes found himself the subject of criticism, particularly in a famous text by Étienne Mantoux, who reproached him with simultaneously spreading the 'black legend' of the Treaty of Versailles, provoking the American Senate to reject the treaty and inspiring an attitude of appeasement towards Nazi Germany.[16] A long historiographical tradition resulted from this reversal of opinion,[17] continued today in the recent works of Niall Ferguson,[18] who has observed that between 1920 and 1932, from one negotiation to another, the reparations in fact paid by Germany never represented more than 8.3 per cent of the nation's gross national income – and not the 20–50 per cent recorded by Keynes. Did Germany have the means to pay? Certainly. Had Keynes allowed himself to be influenced by the propaganda of German bankers? Probably. Nonetheless, the question of reparations poisoned diplomatic relations throughout the interwar years; their cost was the subject of endless negotiations in numerous subsequent conferences and nurtured nationalist feeling in Germany.

In hindsight, the Treaty of Versailles, often presented as a victors' peace, was in fact a compromise peace: a compromise between Wilson's idealistic aspirations and a more realistic post-war approach; between the objectives of each nation and the need for each one to manage its allies; and between hatred for Germany, which reached its paroxysm at the end of the war, and the need for the gradual reintegration of the vanquished countries into the wider circle of nations. Indeed, the declared aim of the peace negotiations in Paris was not only to chastise the nations held responsible for the outbreak of war, it was also to implement the ideas advanced by Wilson in his 'Fourteen Points'

15 Bruno Cabanes, *La victoire endeuillée: la sortie de guerre des soldats français (1918–1920)* (Paris: Éditions du Seuil, 2004).

16 Étienne Mantoux, *La paix calomniée ou les conséquences économiques de Monsieur Keynes* (Paris: Gallimard, 1946). The first criticism came from Jacques Bainville, in his famous response to Keynes, *Les conséquences politiques de la paix* (Paris: Nouvelle Librairie Nationale, 1920).

17 Sally Marks, 'Smoke and mirrors, in smoke-filled rooms and the Galerie des Glaces', in Boemeke, Feldman and Glaser (eds.), *The Treaty of Versailles*, pp. 337–70.

18 Niall Ferguson, *The Pity of War* (London: Basic Books, 1998), chapter 14.

speech of 8 January 1918 and to banish war once and for all.[19] A young British diplomat, Harold Nicolson, noted: 'We were preparing not Peace only, but Eternal Peace. There was about us the halo of some divine mission.'[20] The presence of the American President on European soil gave birth to hopes in a way that no other foreign head of state had ever been able to stir. Throughout the journey that brought him to Paris, Wilson received an enthusiastic welcome. Upon his arrival in France, the Mayor of Brest, where the American President landed on 13 December 1919, greeted him as 'the Apostle of Liberty' who came to liberate the European peoples from their sufferings. In the words of the English writer H. G. Wells early in the 1930s, 'For a brief interval, Wilson . . . ceased to be a common statesman; he became a Messiah.'[21]

While scholars of the history of international relations have devoted a great deal of effort to exploring the European aspects of the peace negotiations, the repercussions these negotiations had beyond the Western world were neglected until recently.[22] And yet the beginning of 1919 was marked by the growing consciousness worldwide of a right to self-determination, which first emerged in 1917 in the writing by Lenin and Trotsky condemning the Russian Empire. Wilson later popularised this principle in 1918 when he saw it as the expression of government by consent.[23] In practice, Wilson had in mind the territories of the three empires – German, Austro-Hungarian and Ottoman – rather than Asian or African colonies.[24] Colonial soldiers were profoundly affected by their discovery of Europe and by the traumatic experience of the war; they were torn between pride at having fought, hope of seeing their situation improve on their return and disillusionment at the inertia of colonial society. 'When the survivors returned home in 1918 and 1919, they faced a new social phenomenon . . . the end of the myth of the invincibility and honesty of the white man', recalled Amadou Hampaté Bâ, a veteran of the Great War and a writer, originally from Mali. He added:

19 Jay Winter, *Dreams of Peace and Freedom: Utopian Moments in the 20th Century* (New Haven, CT and London: Yale University Press, 2006), chapter 2.
20 Harold Nicolson, *Peacemaking, 1919* (London: Constable, 1933), pp. 31–2.
21 H. G. Wells, *The Shape of Things to Come* (New York: Macmillan, 1933), p. 82.
22 Erez Manela, 'Imagining Woodrow Wilson in Asia: dreams of East-West harmony and the revolt against empire in 1919', *American Historical Review*, 111:5 (2006), pp. 1327–51.
23 Arno Mayer, *Wilson vs. Lenin: Political Origins of the New Democracy, 1917–1918* (New York: World Publishing Co., 1967).
24 Michla Pomerance, 'The United States and self determination: perspectives on the Wilsonian conception', *American Journal of International Law*, 70 (1976), pp. 1–27; William R. Keylor, 'Versailles and international diplomacy', in Boemeke, Feldman and Glaser (eds.), *The Treaty of Versailles*, pp. 469–506.

> Now, the black soldiers had experienced trench warfare alongside their white companions. They had seen heroes and courageous men, but they had also seen those men cry and scream with terror . . . And it was then, in 1919, that the spirit of emancipation and the voicing of demands began to appear.[25]

Messengers arrived at the Paris Peace Conference from almost everywhere, bearing petitions in favour of votes for women,[26] the rights of African Americans and workers' rights; there were spokesmen for those seeking recognition of their right to a state, including Zionists and Armenians among many others. A young *sous-chef* at the Ritz wrote to Woodrow Wilson to claim independence for his state and hired a suit in the hope of a private audience with him; this young man was the future Hô Chi Minh. Dressed in Eastern garb, T. E. Lawrence served as translator and adviser to Feisal, who had led the Arab uprising against Ottoman domination in June 1916 and would be the first King of Iraq after the war. Others had no opportunity to come to Paris to defend the rights of their people, such as Syngman Rhee, who had been refused a passport. In 1948, Rhee became the first President of South Korea.

Thanks to developments in journalism in Egypt, India and China, Wilson's speeches were translated and his message widely diffused and debated in nationalist circles, despite the censorship of colonial authorities. Extracts from the Fourteen Points speech were learned by heart in some Chinese schools.[27] Acknowledging the triumph of Wilson's ideas in India, V. S. Srinivasa Sastri imagined how the American President would have been welcomed in the Asian capitals: 'It would have been as though one of the great teachers of humanity, Christ or Buddha, had come back to his home, crowned with the glory that the centuries had brought him since he last walked the earth.'[28] In January 1919, many saw the Paris Peace Conference as a test of Western determination to see the right to self-determination put into practice. The Chinese delegation, consisting of young, westernised

25 Quoted in Thomas Compère-Morel (ed.), *Mémoires d'outre-mer: les colonies et la Première Guerre Mondiale* (Péronne: Historial de la Grande Guerre, 1996), p. 64. On African veterans, see also Marc Michel, *Les Africains et la Grande Guerre: l'appel à l'Afrique, 1914–1918* (Paris: Publications de la Sorbonne, 1982; republished, Paris: Karthala, 2003); and Joe Lunn, *Memoirs of the Maelstrom: A Senegalese Oral History of the First World War* (Portsmouth, NH: Heinemann, 1999).

26 In France, a law on votes for women was proposed in the *Chambre des Députés* in 1919, and then abandoned in 1922. British and German women won the right to vote in 1918.

27 Guoqi Xu, *China and the Great War: China's Pursuit of a New National Identity and Internationalization* (Cambridge University Press, 2005), p. 245.

28 V. S. Srinivasa Sastri, 'Woodrow Wilson's message for Eastern Nations', quoted by Manela, *The Wilsonian Moment*, p. 55.

diplomats (V. T. Wellington Koo studied at Columbia, C. T. Wang at Yale), advocated for the transfer to China of former German concessions. The setback in negotiations, which gave Japan control of the Shandong Peninsula, ruined the hopes of the Chinese nationalists, who refused to sign the peace treaty. Immediately, anti-Japanese demonstrations broke out throughout China, particularly on 4 May 1919, when 5,000 Chinese students marched through the streets of Beijing. In mid April, the Indian nationalist movement was repressed violently in the Amritsar massacre, when the troops of the British general Sir William Dyer fired on and killed several hundred demonstrators. Almost everywhere in Asia and Africa, the Versailles Treaty aroused dismay and revolution after the high hopes raised by Wilsonianism.

Recent studies of the Versailles Treaty have broadened our perspective to striking effect, showing the aftermath of the war no longer in strictly Western terms but on a worldwide scale. In the end, perhaps, the true failure of the Treaty of Versailles and the turning point of 1919 can be located beyond the borders of Europe and the battlefields of the Great War. By ignoring the hopes of colonised peoples, and by refusing to ratify equality between the races,[29] the negotiators in Paris ran the risk of disappointing all those who had placed their hopes in the doctrine of President Wilson. This course of action subsequently fuelled nationalism and stirred the first manifestations of Asian communism.[30]

A time for mourning and reflection

Internationally, the unfolding of the Peace Conference, its pitfalls and the ratification or non-ratification of the treaties all defined the year 1919. Nonetheless, the stakes of the immediate post-war period extended far beyond the context of international diplomacy. For many families, 1919 was above all a year of waiting – for the return home of soldiers or prisoners of war, for the identification of the bodies of missing soldiers, for the return of those bodies already identified but who could not yet be taken back to their family cemeteries, for the rebuilding of a house or a village destroyed in the fighting. Only at the end of the summer of 1920 did French law authorise the return of soldiers' bodies. This repatriation, in the form of entire trainloads of

29 Naoko Shimazu, *Japan, Race and Equality: The Racial Equality Proposal of 1919* (London and New York: Routledge, 1998).

30 Jonathan D. Spence, *The Search for Modern China* (New York: W. W. Norton, 1991), chapter 13.

coffins, over a few months, undoubtedly marked a major turning point in the life of many grieving families.

To better understand the chronology of 1919, we must therefore situate the survivors of the Great War, whether civilians or veterans, in the context of their domestic life. Demobilisation of the armies alone was a colossal task, if only because of the numbers of men involved: 5 million in the case of French survivors, 6 million Germans – many more than the number mobilised in the summer of 1914. In the case of Great Britain and the United States, demobilisation was a relatively straightforward process, even if the return home was never fast enough for the demobilised men. In his short story 'Soldier's home', published in 1923, Ernest Hemingway describes the varied types of welcome that greeted the waves of returning soldiers:

> By the time Krebs returned to his hometown in Oklahoma [in the summer of 1919], the greeting of heroes was over. He came back much too late. The men from the town who had been drafted had all been welcomed elaborately on their return. There had been a great deal of hysteria. Now the reaction had set in. People seemed to think it was rather ridiculous for Krebs to be getting back so late, years after the war was over.[31]

In Germany, in a context of defeat compounded by political revolution, the army literally fell apart in the space of two months. Nearly 500,000 German soldiers left their units as soon as they were across the Rhine and made their own way back to their families. Their homecoming was warmly celebrated, in contrast to the later claims of Nazi mythology of the 'stab in the back'.[32] It was mainly in France that demobilisation dragged on, an interminable process begun in November 1918, interrupted briefly in May–June 1919 and then relaunched and extended until early 1920. Following the principles of egalitarian, republican rule, French military authorities decided to demobilise according to age; but as the return of each age group depended on the demobilisation of the preceding group, it was impossible for the men to foresee exactly when they would return home. When reading their letters from that year, 1919 appears as a kind of suspended time, somewhere between war and peace. Some soldiers left to occupy the Rhineland, while others remained in the barracks, waiting to be demobilised, their morale worn away by boredom.

31 Ernest Hemingway, 'Soldier's home', 1923, in *The Complete Short Stories of Ernest Hemingway* (New York: Charles Scribner, 1987), pp. 109–16.

32 Richard Bessel, *Germany after the First World War* (Oxford: Clarendon Press, 1993).

At the outset of 1919, both plans and worries shaped the future. Demobilisation held the promise of a return to everyday life, but would veterans really be able to return to their pre-war lives? Rumours ran through the ranks of waiting soldiers about men who returned home to find themselves abandoned by unfaithful wives, or ignored by indifferent civilians. In France, the law of 22 November 1918 required each employer to rehire his former employees – but in order for that to happen, both the business and its owner had to have survived the war. Veterans originally from the areas of France destroyed by the fighting returned home only to find their houses in ruins. Sometimes their family home no longer existed, and everything had to be rebuilt.[33] It did not take long for the refugees who had fled during the war to return home: the town of Liévin in northern France, which had been entirely destroyed, already numbered 7,000 inhabitants by October 1919. In France, the *Charte des sinistrés* (Victims' charter) of 11 April 1919 opened the way to substantial reparations for victims of war damage. A true break with tradition in France's administrative history, this charter recognised the state's responsibility for the destruction caused by the war and established a form of national solidarity for the victims.

The very concept of 'war victims' thus had to be redefined and with it, rights to reparations. The Great War caused such vast losses that the entire system of legal categories, as well as the aid structures already in place, had to be brought up to date. In Great Britain it was mainly charitable organisations that came to the aid of wounded veterans and grieving families, while in Germany and France this role fell principally to the state, which modernised nineteenth-century pension laws in order to meet the new requirements of a conscript army.[34] In May 1920, the Weimar Republic voted in laws reforming the system for allocating pensions to disabled veterans, widows and orphans.[35] In France, the law of 31 March 1919 established a 'right to reparations' that accorded each disabled veteran, whatever his military rank, the status of 'war victim', along with a pension. Later, in 1923, jobs were reserved especially for disabled veterans. The jurist René Cassin, himself severely injured in the war,

33 Hugh Clout, *After the Ruins: Restoring the Countryside of Northern France after the Great War* (University of Exeter Press, 1996); Frédérique Pilleboue *et al.* (eds.), *Reconstructions en Picardie après 1919* (Paris: RMN, 2000); Eric Bussière, Patrice Marcilloux and Denis Varaschin (eds.), *La grande reconstruction: reconstruire le Pas-de-Calais après la Grande Guerre* (Archives départementales du Pas-de-Calais, 2000).

34 Deborah Cohen, *The War Come Home: Disabled Veterans in Britain and Germany, 1914–1939* (Berkeley and Los Angeles: University of California Press, 2001).

35 Sabine Kienitz, *Beschädigte Helden: Kriegsinvalidität und Körperbilder 1914–1923* (Paderborn: Schöningh, 2008).

was one of the leading advocates of disabled veterans' rights. At the same time, the United States, which was still spending $2 million a year in pensions for veterans of the American Civil War, sought to promote a new model based on the rehabilitation of wounded soldiers, the development of specialised hospitals (such as the Walter Reed Hospital in Washington, DC) and a rapid return to active life.[36] 'Rights, not charity' was the slogan on which veterans' organisations were based, a slogan that acquired increasing social significance. The year 1919 saw the first great conferences of veterans' associations, which subsequently joined forces with each other.

New rituals emerged in connection with the war memorials being built. These rituals linked former soldiers and civilians together in honouring the memory of the dead of the Great War.[37] This nationalisation of the memory of war very quickly came to hold a central place in national identities. In the case of Australia and New Zealand, the war experience of the Anzac troops became a true founding myth for these new nations.[38] The summer of 1919 saw a series of great victory parades organised in the Allied countries: 14 July in Paris; 19 July in London; 22 July in Brussels; 10 September in New York. On each occasion the ceremonies were associated with national symbols: in Paris, the procession passed beneath the Arc de Triomphe; in London, by way of denouncing enemy crimes, a wall was built consisting of thousands of pointed helmets along the route of the parade. In New York, where six successive parades were organised, thousands of wounded men from the 1st American Division took part in the procession. At the head of the column, soldiers on horseback carried banners such as: 'First Division: 4,899 killed; 21,433 wounded.' In Paris, 1,000 disabled veterans opened the victory parade down the Champs-Elysées – an overwhelming spectacle, illustrated by Jean Galtier-Boissière in his famous painting, *The Victory Parade*, where a blind soldier advances, leaning on the shoulder of a disabled veteran.

In every country, the construction of a national memory of the Great War was inseparable from the memory of the war dead. The Prix Goncourt for 1919 was awarded to Marcel Proust for *À l'ombre des jeunes filles en fleurs* instead of to the war novel by Roland Dorgelès, *Les croix de bois* ('The wooden

36 Beth Linker, *War's Waste: Rehabilitation in World War I America* (University of Chicago Press, 2011).

37 For a general approach, Stephen R. Ward (ed.), *The War Generation: Veterans of the First World War* (Port Washington, NY: Kennikat Press, 1975); in the case of France, Antoine Prost, *Les anciens combattants et la société française, 1914–1939* (Paris: Presses de la Fondation Nationale des Sciences Politiques, 1977).

38 Alistair Thomson, *ANZAC Memories: Living with the Legend* (Oxford University Press, 1994).

crosses'), a decision which could be seen as a sign of continuing 'cultural demobilisation' – i.e., people wanted to read about something other than the war. But 1919 was also the year of the great film *J'accuse,* which opened in April. With gripping realism, the director Abel Gance showed the dead of Verdun rising from the ground to return and haunt the living and to assert, in the face of civilian immorality, that their sacrifice had been in vain. Gance took up the theme of the 'return of the dead', which expressed perfectly the mindset of the immediate post-war period: societies tormented by the memory of the dead, and by a form of moral responsibility imposed on them by the sacrifice of so many soldiers.[39]

This demand for loyalty to the memory of the dead was responsible for the emergence of two contradictory kinds of discourse. Gance's film expressed a pacifist message that in the end became established as a kind of shared culture in the second half of the 1920s: '*nie wieder Krieg*', 'Never again war', '*Plus jamais ça*', in the former soldiers' words. At the same time, hatred of the enemy was still strong. A form of remobilisation can even be seen in the immediate post-war period, delaying and hindering the process of mourning: to turn the page on the war would be to betray the dead. In France, probably more than in other Allied countries, the desire for vengeance dominated public opinion. It was visible among the troops who occupied the Rhineland, through the full range of humiliations imposed on the German civilian population. In December 1918, the novelist Jacques Rivière, a former prisoner of war who had initially adopted the Wilsonian ideal of peace, published a text entitled *L'ennemi*. In his opening pages, Rivière described his feelings towards the Germans:

> What I reproach the Germans for is not primarily their deeds ... My complaint is more profound, it is their very being that I hate, or rather the void of their being. What I resent most in the Germans is that they are nothing.[40]

In how many grieving families did hatred of the enemy mark a large part of the interwar years? In 1925, the great mathematician Émile Picard, who had lost three sons during the war, argued that German scientists should continue to be excluded from the International Research Council. Six years since the

39 Jay Winter, *Sites of Memory, Sites of Mourning: The Great War in European Cultural History* (Cambridge University Press, 1995), chapter 1. On the presence of the war in German cinema in the 1920s, see also Anton Kaes, *Shell Shock Cinema: Weimar Culture and the Wounds of War* (Princeton University Press, 2009).

40 Jacques Rivière, *L'ennemi* (Paris: Gallimard, 1918).

end of the war represented 'a very short time to throw a veil over so many odious and criminal acts' he explained, 'especially when no regret was expressed'.[41]

Transnational stakes in the aftermath of war

In the eyes of many Westerners, however, the most serious threat came from the disintegration of the great empires of Central and Eastern Europe, and from the growth of communism. Fear of the 'Reds', Bolsheviks and revolutionaries profoundly affected many people. This fear was fed by the massive strikes that occurred in many countries after the war. In France, the Paris region witnessed the largest strikes in the history of the metalworking industry, in the spring of 1919.[42] The general strike in Winnipeg (15 May–25 June 1919) unleashed by the inflationary surge of the post-war period, was a major event in the history of the labour movement in Canada. In the United States, 1919 alone saw nearly 3,600 examples of social conflict. This 'fear of the Reds' could turn to madness, as when a bomb exploded on Wall Street on 16 September 1920, leaving thirty-eight dead and hundreds wounded.[43] The attack, which remains unexplained, was initially attributed to anarchists and later to Leninist agents.

Thus when Russian refugees flooded into Western Europe after the defeat of the White armies in the Russian civil war (1919–21), their presence inspired great anxiety. In the spring of 1919 more than 10,000 people, including 6,000 soldiers and officers from the White armies, fled to Turkey from Odessa. A total of 150,000 refugees followed after the defeat of General Wrangel's army in November 1920. The great majority of these refugees, completely destitute, settled into crowded camps on the outskirts of Constantinople, such as the camp installed near the battlefield of Gallipoli, or they ended up on ships moored in the Sea of Marmara. As Jean-Charles de Watteville of the

41 International Research Council, Third Assembly, Brussels, 1925, cited by Brigitte Schroeder-Gudehus, 'Pas de Locarno pour la science: la coopération scientifique internationale et la politique étrangère des États pendant l'entre-deux-guerres', *Relations Internationales*, 46 (1986), p. 183.

42 Jean-Louis Robert, *Les ouvriers, la patrie et la Révolution, 1914–1919* (Annales littéraires de l'Université de Besançon/Les Belles Lettres, 1995). On the birth of the French Communist Party, see Romain Ducoulombier, *Camarades: la naissance du parti communiste en France* (Paris: Perrin, 2010).

43 Beverly Gage, *The Day Wall Street Exploded: A Story of America in its First Age of Terror* (Oxford University Press, 2009).

International Committee of the Red Cross noted in the course of a humanitarian mission in 1921:

> The refugees could be compared to prisoners of war. Constantinople is a prison from which it is impossible to escape. [The refugees] are living in surroundings entirely strange to them, and this results in increased mental demoralisation and a growing incapacity to work.[44]

The governments that had supported the White armies, particularly France and Great Britain, sent food and aid before organising the evacuation of Russian refugees to the Balkans – including some Armenians who had escaped the genocide in 1915.

Other refugees crossed the Russo-Polish frontier, fleeing the wave of pogroms in which around 10 per cent of Ukrainian Jews disappeared in 1919. The war between Russia and Poland (1919–21) also resulted in vast population movements, initially of Polish citizens driven out of their homes by the fighting, then of individuals departing to the West and fleeing the famine gripping the valley of the Volga, Transcaucasia and the Ukraine in 1921. Two great floods of refugees, some from Poland and the others from the Baltic states, thus ended up in Germany, mainly in Berlin, where more than 500,000 refugees arrived in the autumn of 1920.[45] The most prosperous among them soon set off again, either to France, where 80,000 Russian immigrants settled in the early 1920s, or to Great Britain. For all these refugees, one of the major problems was the absence of immigration documents enabling them to cross borders. Some had identity papers from the Russian Empire, which no longer existed; others had lost everything in the civil war; and still others had lost their citizenship in a campaign undertaken by the Soviet authorities in December 1921 against their political enemies. A new legal category arose, that of the stateless person, who lacked any of the rights belonging to citizens with a country of their own.

The management of the refugee crisis consisted of several elements, one philanthropic (providing aid, often as a matter of emergency, to populations without any resources whatsoever) and the other legal (the rapid creation of a legal framework setting out a form of international recognition for stateless individuals was essential). The humanitarian element was undertaken by many organisations such as the International Committee of the Red Cross, which had played a major role in aid for prisoners of war in 1914–18, the

44 International Red Cross Archives, Geneva, CR 87 / SDN, 1921.

45 Annemarie H. Sammartino, *The Impossible Border: Germany and the East, 1914–1922* (Cornell University Press, 2010).

Quakers, the Save the Children Fund, founded in 1919 by the philanthropist Eglantyne Jebb, or Near East Relief. Humanitarian aid, rooted in a long Anglo-Saxon tradition dating back to the nineteenth century, expanded afresh at the end of the war. Nonetheless, action on the ground remained relatively improvised, even as it increasingly mobilised social activists and medical help.

At the legal level, the circulation of refugees clashed with identity controls that were much stricter for foreigners since the establishment of the international passport during the Great War. For stateless people, the only solution was the establishment of an internationally recognised document that would enable them to circulate freely and find work in other countries. In July 1922, the 'Nansen certificate' was created, from the name of the Norwegian diplomat Fridtjof Nansen who, since 1921, had served as the League of Nations' High Commissioner for Russian Refugees. This document was not a passport, since it did not allow its holder to return to the country that had granted it. Further, the beneficiaries of the Nansen certificate were subject to the same restrictive laws on immigration as others, such as the law on quotas adopted by the United States in 1921 and 1924. However, this document, soon extended to Armenians beginning in 1924 and then to Assyro-Chaldeans, represented a revolution in international law and solidified what Dzovinar Kévonian has called 'the institutionalisation of the international humanitarian field'.[46]

For many legal scholars in the 1920s, the transnational nature of the questions arising during the transition from war to peace required a profound redefinition of international law. The refugee problem, the return home of prisoners of war, economic reconstruction, epidemics and the distribution of humanitarian aid could no longer be dealt with solely within a national framework. In their work, Herbert Hoover, Fridtjof Nansen, Albert Thomas, René Cassin and Eglantyne Jebb, whether from a humanitarian or diplomatic background, best illustrate this surge in the spirit of internationalism.[47] 'We must deliberately and definitively reject the notion of sovereignty, for it is false and it is harmful', declared the jurist Georges Scelle, who considered the First World War to have been 'the greatest event recorded by History since the fall of the Roman Empire'.[48] Scelle, however, was one of the most radical voices among those thinkers who challenged not the

46 Dzovinar Kévonian, *Réfugiés et diplomatie humanitaire: les acteurs européens et la scène proche-orientale pendant l'entre-deux-guerres* (Paris: Publications de la Sorbonne, 2004).

47 Bruno Cabanes, *The Great War and the Origins of Humanitarianism, 1918–1924* (Cambridge University Press, forthcoming).

48 Georges Scelle, *Le pacte de la Société des Nations et sa liaison avec le traité de Paix* (Paris: Librairie du recueil Sirey, 1919).

sovereignty of states in itself but their *absolute sovereignty*. The birth of the League of Nations, 'the first dawn of an international judicial organisation' in his words, thus raised great hopes, even if international legal scholars were initially somewhat sceptical about the real range of the organisation. In the absence of any sanction against those who contravened international law, and in the absence of armed forces capable of imposing peace, the League of Nations could not 'attain the goal of high international morality, the aim with which it had been founded', in the words of Léon Duguit. The new history of international relations has studied extensively the limits of this new international order born of the war: 'The lights that failed', to use Zara Steiner's expression.[49] But this history has also stressed the breadth of the goals achieved towards better world governance under the sponsorship of the League of Nations, particularly in the social arena.[50]

From this point of view, one of the most dynamic organisations of the post-war world was undoubtedly the International Labour Organisation, established under Article 13 of the Treaty of Versailles and managed as of 1919 by the former French Minister for Munitions, Albert Thomas. His agenda was broad. Even a brief examination of the questions on the programme for the first labour conference in Washington, in October–November 1919, is impressive: the eight-hour workday, unemployment, protection for women before and after childbirth, no night work or unhealthy work by women and children, the minimum age for industrial work, etc., etc. Through the establishment of standards designed to improve the living conditions of workers and to protect their rights, the ILO gave substance to the belief in universal justice born from the ruins of the First World War. In the first issue of the *Revue Internationale du Travail*, published in 1921, Albert Thomas recalled that:

> It was the war that made the legislation of labour a matter of primordial importance. It was the war that forced governments to undertake to abolish poverty, injustice and the privations from which workers suffered. It was the war again that led organised workers to understand that the action of legal protection, in taking all its powers from the international field, was necessary to the realisation of some of their aspirations.

The ILO was not only the heir to the reformist movements established throughout Europe since the end of the nineteenth century; it also brought

49 Zara Steiner, *The Lights that Failed: European International History, 1919–1933* (New York: Oxford University Press, 2005).

50 Susan Pedersen, 'Back to the League of Nations: review essay', *American Historical Review*, 112:4 (2007), pp. 1091–117.

together aspirations towards a better world, which were to be supported by dialogue between unions and employers and the work of a new social group in full expansion after the war: international experts. Behind this quest for social justice lay the ambition for a world free from war. *Si vis pacem, cole justitiam* was the motto of the ILO – 'If you want peace, cultivate justice.'

For Albert Thomas and his team, coming from the 'reformist nebula' of pre-war years, 1919 was clearly a turning point, the dawn of a new era. Yet contemporary historians of the ILO increasingly tend to emphasise the tensions between transnational ideals and the persistent rivalries among nation-states, which deeply affected the inner workings of the institution. The fact that Germany and the other Central Powers quickly joined the ILO in 1919, did not mean that the painful memory of the war had faded. Meetings between veterans' groups from both sides were organised in the immediate post-war period, to discuss the rights of disabled veterans. At the first such meeting, Adrien Tixier of the ILO, himself severely wounded in the war, commented:

> I know from experience that it is not pleasant to meet people who not long ago were firing bullets and grenades at you while you were firing at them, but it is precisely in the interest of world peace that I judge such meetings necessary.[51]

The pacification of minds within the framework of international organisations was not self-evident, and in many countries, other kinds of conflict – border wars, civil wars, etc. – prolonged the violence of the First World War.

Post-war forms of violence: an experiment in typology

In recent years, a new field of research has gradually come to the forefront among specialists of the war: the Great War's place in the twentieth century and its impact on forms of violence after the war.[52] In the tradition of George

51 Archives of the International Labour Office, Geneva, A / B.I.T. / MU / 7 / 5 / 1, Tixier to Albert Thomas, letter dated 31 October 1922.

52 Mark Mazower, *Dark Continent: Europe's Twentieth Century* (New York: Knopf, 1998); Stéphane Audoin-Rouzeau, Annette Becker, Christian Ingrao and Henry Rousso (eds.), *La violence de guerre 1914–1945* (Brussels: Éditions Complexe, 2002); and Roger Chickering and Stig Förster (eds.), *The Shadows of Total War: Europe, East Asia and the United States, 1919–1939* (Cambridge University Press, 2003). For a study of recent historiography, see Robert Gerwarth and John Horne, 'The Great War and paramilitarism in Europe, 1917–23', *Contemporary European History*, 19:3 (2010), pp. 267–73.

Mosse,[53] some historians stress the process of 'brutalisation' that occurred after the war, although it is not clear whether this phenomenon mainly affects post-war societies and their political life, or former combatants as individuals, or whether it affects all countries in similar ways.[54] The transfer of wartime violence to the post-war period is in fact a complex mechanism and the terms 'violence' or 'forms of violence' are used to designate very different realities: battles between regular armies, for example, the Greco-Turkish War; ideological struggles against an 'inner enemy', as in the case of the Russian civil war; liquidation of the war's legacy, such as the purge of collaborators in Belgium; violence perpetrated by paramilitary groups, as seen in the counter-revolutionary repression in Germany; acts of ethnic or community violence, as in Poland, Ireland, etc. The specificity of these conflicts depended somewhat heavily on the experience of individual nations in the First World War (conquest, invasion or occupation? victory or defeat?), the ability of the state to channel or redirect the violence deployed during the war and the nation's place on the world stage. A resurgence of violence in the colonies thus characterises the post-war period, particularly in India, Egypt and Iraq in the case of the British,[55] and in Algeria and Indochina in the case of France.[56]

Several factors, sometimes working in concert, explain the violence of the post-war period, namely, the repercussions of the Russian Revolution in 1917 in Russia and other countries, and the frustrations born of defeat. In addition, national or ethnic tensions inherited from the disintegration of the four great empires (German, Russian, Austro-Hungarian and Ottoman), could take various forms: territorial claims, border tensions, populations on the move . . . In this extremely diverse and complicated climate, a clear delineation of any continuity between the 'cultures of war' in 1914–18 and post-war violence is therefore far from straightforward. Different approaches are often necessary:

53 George Mosse, *Fallen Soldiers: Reshaping the Memory of the World Wars* (Oxford University Press, 1990).

54 For a critical discussion of George Mosse's book, see Antoine Prost, 'The impact of war on French and German political cultures', *Historical Journal*, 37:1 (1994), pp. 209–17.

55 David M. Anderson and David Killingray (eds.), *Policing and Decolonisation: Politics, Nationalism and the Police, 1917–1965* (Manchester University Press, 1992).

56 This last area of research remains relatively unexplored at present, and much remains to be done on the links between colonial violence and war violence, both before and after the Great War. On the fear of the 'brutalisation' aroused by the Amritsar massacre, see Derek Sayer, 'British reaction to the Amritsar Massacre, 1919–1920', *Past and Present*, 131:1 (1991), pp. 130–64; Jon Lawrence, 'Forging a peaceable kingdom: war, violence and fear of brutalization in post First World War Britain', *Journal of Modern History*, 75 (2003), pp. 557–89; and Susan Kingsley Kent, *Aftershocks: Politics and Trauma in Britain, 1918–1931* (Basingstoke and New York: Palgrave Macmillan, 2009), pp. 64–90.

studies of local circumstances,[57] the progress of veterans and veterans' groups, civilians who refused to move on from the war,[58] the possible reuse of tactics and weapons first used on the battlefields and then in the 1920s, the gestures and language of violence, the ideological legacy of myths born during the war – for example, the 'myth of the War Experience' (George Mosse), the central element of the *völkisch* ideology in Germany or Italian fascism. The *Arditi* in Italy, the *Freikorps* in Germany and the Black and Tans in Ireland, all were veterans of the First World War, while Béla Kun's Republic of Councils in Hungary (March–July 1919) was based on former prisoners of war returning from captivity in Russia.

I will attempt a brief typology of post-war violence here. Certain forms of violence were a direct consequence of whether a country had been victorious or defeated in the war, and related to the implementation of the Armistice conventions. The year 1919 saw the liberation of countries occupied during the Great War and the occupation of the Rhineland by the victors, which gave rise in both cases to violence against individuals and property. Belgium witnessed the hunting down of collaborators, particularly war profiteers and 'shirkers'. In the spring of 1919, the Coppées, father and son, major employers in Hainaut, were accused of enriching themselves by supplying coal to the Germans. Their trial inflamed Belgian public opinion, which considered that the law was not dealing severely enough with collaborators. A similar emotion greeted the acquittal of several informers, especially Gaston Quien, brought to trial in 1919 for having betrayed Edith Cavell. In countries deeply divided by the war, as with the Flemings and Walloons in Belgium in 1914–18, the immediate post-war period was a time for settling accounts with wartime enemies. In Alsace, civilians of German descent were expelled to Germany in the winter of 1918–19, even if they no longer had any ties with that country.[59] In the Rhineland, occupying troops were known to play out, on a smaller scale, the confrontations of the First World War: brawls with German

57 A good example of comparative history can be found in Timothy Wilson, *Frontiers of Violence: Conflict and Identity in Ulster and Upper Silesia, 1918–1922* (Oxford University Press, 2010).

58 The micro-historical dimension appears particularly promising. See, for example, Christian Ingrao's study of the path taken by Oskar Dirlewanger, from infantry officer in the First World War to *Freikorps* leader to head of a Waffen-S.S. brigade made up of convicted criminals: *Les chasseurs noirs* (Paris: Perrin, 2006).

59 David Allen Harvey, 'Lost children or enemy aliens? Classifying the population of Alsace after the First World War', *Journal of Contemporary History*, 34 (1999), pp. 537–54; and Laird Boswell, 'From liberation to purge trials in the "mythic provinces": recasting French identities in Alsace and Lorraine, 1918–1920', *French Historical Studies*, 23:1 (2000), pp. 129–62.

civilians, destruction of the 1870 war memorial at Ems, insults and humiliations for the Rhineland population.

In other cases it was the collapse of the structure of the state, combined with material chaos, which lay behind the explosions of violence. In many countries, the end of the war brought with it a collective traumatic shock, and a reformulation of the 'culture of war' into the struggles between counter-revolutionary and revolutionary movements.[60] In Italy, the rise to power of the *Arditi* and the fascist movement can broadly be explained by the moral collapse of military and political elites during the Great War: the nation was victorious, but the victory was incomplete and ambiguous, insufficiently convincing to wipe out the humiliation of Caporetto.[61] The position of Germany was distinctive because here defeat was attributed to treason, which facilitated the transformation of foreign war into civil war.[62] In Berlin, 1919 opened with the Spartakist insurrection (5–11 January) and the particularly brutal assassination of Rosa Luxemburg and Karl Liebknecht by members of the *Freikorps* on 15 January. For several weeks the streets of the German capital were awash with the violence of war. A Berliner recorded in his diary that

> The combat ... began near the colonnade of the Belleallianceplatz, then spread out against the snipers hidden on rooftops, before reaching the strongly barricaded headquarters of the newspaper *Vorwärts*, with its network of interior courtyards. People were using large-calibre bombs and flame-throwers. The doors were blown open by hand grenades and the defenders surrendered only on the approach of assault troops. Three hundred prisoners were captured and one hundred machine guns seized.

The German state no longer held a monopoly on legitimate violence. Its army had been largely dismantled since the defeat. To deal with the revolutionary threat, it depended on recently demobilised veterans, on groups of students too young to have fought in the war but keen to use their strength in the struggle against the 'Reds'[63] and on local militias, who called for the

60 Wolfgang Schivelbusch, *The Culture of Defeat: On National Trauma, Mourning and Recovery* (London: Granta Books, 2000).

61 Adrian Lyttelton, 'Fascism and violence in post-war Italy: political strategy and social conflict', in Wolfgang Mommsen and Gerhard Hirschfeld (eds.), *Social Protest, Violence and Terror in Nineteenth and Twentieth-Century Europe* (New York: St Martin's Press, 1982), pp. 257–74; and Emilio Gentile, *Le origini dell'ideologia fascista, 1918–1925* (Rome and Bari: Laterza, 1975).

62 This is the theory that George Mosse develops in *Fallen Soldiers*.

63 Christian Ingrao, 'Etudiants allemands, mémoire de la guerre et militantisme nazi: étude de cas', *14–18: Aujourd'hui, Today, Heute*, 5 (2002), pp. 54–71.

destruction of the 'Bolshevik vermin'. Everything seemed to favour a radicalisation of political violence: the eschatological anguish aroused by the defeat, the fear of contamination by communists or Jews, the hope that the fraternity of soldiers in the trenches could be recreated against a common enemy. 'People told us that the war was over. That made us laugh. We ourselves are the war', declared a *Freikorps* volunteer.[64] In this climate, the government of the Weimar Republic renounced its pursuit of those guilty of the double crime of the Spartakist leaders. At the funerals of Karl Liebknecht and Rosa Luxemburg, nearly 300,000 activists shouted their anger against the Social Democratic government. The *Freikorps*, officially dissolved on 6 March 1919, proceeded two months later to crush the Munich 'Republic of Councils' in a bloody repression that resulted in 650 deaths. On the eastern margins of Germany, the Bolshevik threat was equally present, and the *Freikorps* were used to counter the risk of revolutionary expansion.

In Russia, the weakening of state power also opened the way for warlords to take control, with their private armies pillaging, terrorising the population and conducting repeated pogroms, such as in Ukraine.[65] The Allied intervention on the side of the White armies, in the context of the civil war, further contributed to the radicalisation of the violence of war. Faced with the intervention of a foreign force, which numbered nearly 20,000 men in 1919, and with the pressures of 'internal enemies' (White partisans of the armies of Kolchak, Denikin or Wrangel; *kulaks*, i.e., prosperous peasants, and ethnic minorities), the Bolshevik regime sensed that it was fighting for its survival. In this particular period of 'War Communism' (1918–21), political splits between communists and (real or supposed) counter-revolutionary opponents, currents of social antagonism between urban and rural societies and ethnic struggles and national confrontations all came together to sustain a climate of permanent and varied violence. One such war, between Russia and Poland in 1919–21, left 250,000 dead. In a speech at Rostov-on-Don in November 1919, the philosopher Piotr Struve, a former Bolshevik who rallied to the White movement, stated that

> The world war ended formally with the conclusion of the armistice . . . In fact, however, everything that we have experienced from that point

64 Quoted by Peter Gatrell, 'War after the war: conflicts, 1919–23', in John Horne (ed.), *A Companion to World War I* (Oxford: Blackwell, 2010), p. 568.

65 Joshua Sanborn, 'The genesis of Russian warlordism: violence and governance during the First World War and the civil war', *Contemporary European History*, 19:3 (2010), pp. 195–213.

> onward, and continue to experience, is a continuation and a transformation of the world war.[66]

During the so-called 'peasant wars' that broke out over the requisitions of grain crops, the special forces of the *Cheka*, the political police, used extreme brutality to crush rebellious peasants. Civilians massacred, villages shelled, the use of mustard gas – all demonstrate the full extent to which the practices of war inherited from the Great War were used on the home front, along with a radicalised perception of the enemy within.[67]

The fourth and final element in post-war violence was ethnic. The collapse of the Russian Empire first brought a surge in nationalist tensions in the Caucasus, in the new Baltic states and in Poland. These tensions tended to concentrate in smaller territories that carried symbolic weight, such as the city of Vilnius, disputed by Poland and Lithuania, or the port city of Memel, which the Treaty of Versailles put under the control of an Allied commission. Poland and Lithuania both claimed Memel, and Lithuania eventually took over the city in January 1923. The city of Fiume was another example of territorial struggle. Accorded to the Croats[68] under the Treaty of London on 26 April 1915, Italy subsequently staked a claim to Fiume during negotiations at the Paris Peace Conference, citing the presence of the city's sizeable Italian community. On 12 September 1919 the nationalist poet Gabriele D'Annunzio occupied Fiume illegally with a volunteer army, and for more than a year he headed a provisional government that favoured returning the city to Italian control.

In 1919–20, signatories of the peace treaties aimed to limit the risks of war by redistributing population groups, in the interests of building better ethnic homogeneity. However, the complexity of the intermingling languages, ethnicities and cultures, particularly in Central Europe and the Balkans, meant that things remained extremely confusing. In addition, the peace treaties set up clauses for the protection of minorities, which were guaranteed by the League of Nations. Furthermore, the treaties required each individual to settle in the country whose nationality he had adopted. In total, around 10 million people left territories that had passed into the hands of a third nation.

66 Quoted by Peter Holquist, *Making War, Forging Revolution: Russia's Continuum of Crisis, 1914–1921* (Cambridge, MA: Harvard University Press, 2002), p. 2.

67 Evan Mawdsley, *The Russian Civil War* (Boston: Allen & Unwin, 1987); and Vladimir N. Brovkin, *Behind the Front Lines of the Civil War* (Princeton University Press, 1994).

68 For a comparative approach to the question of minorities in relation to national identity, see Tara Zahra, 'The "minority problem": national classification in the French and Czechoslovak borderlands', *Contemporary European Review*, 17 (2008), pp. 137–65.

The Greco-Turkish war which broke out in May 1919, culminated in the capture of Smyrna by Kemalist troops, the burning of Armenian and Christian neighbourhoods and the massacre of nearly 30,000 civilians in September 1922. The forced transfer of populations between Greece and Turkey, undertaken under the auspices of the League of Nations in 1923, was the most dramatic consequence of the ethnic violence that broke out in the immediate post-war period, because it legalised an ethnicised definition of territory.

In this context as well, paramilitary groups appeared; they were responsible for much of the post-war violence. The distinctions between civilians and combatants, already vague during the First World War, completely vanished in this type of conflict. The Irish Civil War provides a good example of this; both the insurrection of 1919 against the British and the counter-insurrection were led by small groups that did not limit their targets to other armed combatants. The wives and families of militants fighting for independence were considered equally valid targets. British soldiers, supported by the Black and Tans, committed numerous atrocities against civilians. Conversely, the IRA conducted a policy of intimidation and revenge against those whom it saw as traitors. The bodies of those it executed were frequently left in a public place with the message: 'Spy. By Order of the IRA. Take Warning.' In the end, the Irish Civil War produced much heavier losses than the First World War did.[69] Several factors were at work here: the lack of compunction on the part of paramilitary troops, who attacked civilians more readily than regular troops might have done; the power of identity stakes in a war that radicalised positions on both sides; and surely the brutalisation that the Great War seems to have brought in its wake to the Europe of the 1920s.

Conclusion

The year 1919 did not mark the end of the cycle that began in 1914, nor, indeed, did it illustrate any shifts in the violence of war. In many countries the already strong tensions produced by the war seemed to expand in the immediate post-war period, at the very moment when the diplomats from all over the world were gathering together in Paris to negotiate the cessation of hostilities. In the ruins of four empires destroyed by the Great War, nationalism expanded.

69 Julia Eichenberg, 'The dark side of independence: paramilitary violence in Ireland and Poland after the First World War', *Contemporary European History*, 19:3 (2010), pp. 221–48.

Revolutionary fever spread across Central Europe, stirring counter-revolutionary movements of equal violence. Sometimes, the First World War simply continued. Armies and combat tactics that had been tested on the battlefields beginning in 1914 were transferred to the context of domestic warfare and used against civilians. Sometimes, various states of conflict coalesced. In the case of Russia, for example, four different kinds of wars interconnected and fuelled one another: the war against Poland; the war of the Bolshevik powers against the White armies and their Western allies; the class war against the *kulaks*; and the repression of ethnic minorities by the central powers in Moscow.

Was 1919 the year of peace or the year of an impossible transition from war to peace? An appropriate visual metaphor to describe 1919 would be an image of lines converging towards a vanishing point. Indeed, the year 1919 opens up various lines illustrating what would become, for several years, a difficult transition from war to peace: a world agitated by powerful ideological tensions between communism and liberalism; vast movements of populations, harried by civil war, hunger or religious persecution; hatreds inherited from the Great War ... But 1919 was also the year of the Paris Peace Conference, the founding of the League of Nations and the creation of the International Labour Organisation; it was a moment when those who lived through the war became aware that they were living in a globalised world, when they aspired to reframe international relations accordingly. For the survivors, 1919 was above all a time of waiting, grieving and disillusionment. This was a time when many veterans and civilians came to realise that they would never completely get away from war. In a letter written to his friend Robert Graves in 1922, that is, during the post-war transition period, T. E. Lawrence made this disturbing observation:

> What's the cause that you, and Siegfried Sassoon, and I ... can't get away from the war? Here are you riddled with thought like any old table-leg with worms; [Sassoon] yawing about like a ship aback: me in the ranks, finding squalor and maltreatment the only permitted experience: what's the matter with us all? It's like the malarial bugs in the blood, coming out months and years after in recurrent attacks.[70]

When did 1919 end? No one knows.

70 *T. E. Lawrence to His Biographer, Robert Graves: Information About Himself, in the Form of Letters, Notes, and Answers to Questions, Edited with a Critical Commentary* (London, Faber & Faber, 1938), p. 31.

PART II

★

THEATRES OF WAR

Introduction to Part II

ROBIN PRIOR

As the chapters in this volume demonstrate, the military history of the Great War is subject to national differences and differences between authors writing about the same events. Nevertheless, the chapters also show a new consensus which is far different from that prevailing at (say) the fiftieth anniversary of the war. Then the military performance of the participants would, in all probability, have been ranked in order of the so-called national characteristics. Germany and Britain would have been placed at the top of the list followed by France. The United States would rank highly with much disagreement on its performance because of its late entry. Italy and Austria-Hungary would come next followed by Russia and Romania with Ottoman Turkey somewhere near the bottom. A list created now would not rank by national characteristics but by levels of industrialisation. The list would not look substantially different from the earlier one but at least would have a foundation in hard statistics rather than stereotyping.

The chapters which follow reflect this new paradigm. For the war at sea the earlier handwringing over Britain's alleged failure to produce decent Dreadnoughts is replaced by a recognition of its overwhelming mastery at sea. Jutland, it now seems, was no close run thing. Whatever the comparative losses, there was only one fleet patrolling the North Sea the day after the battle and it was not the German. Nor did the Admiralty need the intervention of civilians to prod them into convoy to counter the U-boat campaign. The naval system worked and provided the solution.

As for the war in the air, it is no longer thought of as a 'duel of eagles' – of one group of fighter 'aces' trying to shoot down another. The Red Baron has given way to studies about the true purposes of air power in the Great War – aerial spotting to more accurately direct artillery fire and the taking of photographs to identify enemy defences and locate artillery positions.

In military matters the most marked increase in knowledge has come with at least the partial opening of the Russian archives. Although much remains to be done, the new information indicates that the armies of the Tsar fought and were equipped much better than previously thought. To some extent, what has emerged is that it was the lack of modern bureaucratic structures and management techniques and a decent political system that proved fatal to the Russian war effort.

The 'lesser' fronts are also being re-examined. Italy's and Austria's lack of industrial clout have been exposed as a major factor in the stalemate, but the lack of any available military techniques to achieve a decisive victory in the terrain in which the war was fought seem equally important. There also seems little doubt that had the major industrial powers of Europe fought in such conditions the outcome would have been much the same. The political structures of these two powers also clearly proved deficient to cope effectively with the demands of major war, although to some extent this view has been modified by the obvious but widely unappreciated fact that both powers kept armies in the field for three and four years without total disintegration.

A consensus also seems to have emerged about the war against Ottoman Turkey. It is no longer seen as having the potential to affect decisively the wider war. Moreover, the armies of the Ottoman Empire were not to be easily defeated by the scraps of soldiers that remained to the British after the demands of the Western Front had been met. Yet in the end the industrial might of Britain eventually wore down the Ottoman Turks, but it took four years and much effort to do it.

The major front and centre of attention remains the Western Front. The view that commanders were 'Donkeys' for fighting there has long been superseded. Few doubt that the war was won and lost on this front and attention has instead shifted to how it was fought. Here there is only partial consensus. Most scholars agree that the notion of the 'Chateau General' should be dismissed. Commanders were placed at appropriate locations at the end of unprecedented communication systems. Most scholars also agree that the generals were (perhaps) surprisingly good at logistical matters – armies very seldom ran out of food or ammunition – even if the quality of both commodities was highly variable. The role of weaponry in determining the outcome of battles, and indeed the war, has at last received its due, with the competence or otherwise of commanders judged by how they used the weapons available to them. Here any consensus breaks down. Was Verdun the first pure battle of attrition with the destruction of the French army as its only aim? Which army learned the most from past experience and how was that process applied to later battles? Who within an army proved capable of drawing the correct lessons from past mistakes? Did the commanders worry about the level of casualties that efforts such as Verdun, the Somme, Third Ypres and the Chemin des Dames were inflicting on their own armies? All that can be said about these matters is that the debate continues. Studies on particular generals at various levels (army, corps and lower) are welcome additions to the literature but have failed to have an impact on the weighty questions listed above. My view is that these debates will continue without resolution because of national perspectives, but also because of the widely different views about human nature that historians will inevitably bring to their subject.

What of the future? We can expect many further revelations from the Russian archives and also from the archives kept by the lesser powers of Austria and Italy and from those of the successor states in Eastern Europe. My hope is that future work on the Western Front concentrates more on technology rather than biography. Now we have a new biography of Haig there should be a moratorium on any more for at least ten years. It is extraordinary that although artillery inflicted about 60 per cent of all casualties in the war there has been no serious study of it. The British Ministry of Munitions (probably the determinant of victory on the Western Front) deserves serious study. The participation of the United States in the war could also come to maturity with some serious work on what contribution America made to the final victory. This would at least be a relief from books which start from the premise that the US won the war. It will be interesting to watch over the next decade to see if any of these challenges are taken up or if there will be new developments by academics in a field that has all too often been left to amateurs.

8

The Western Front

ROBIN PRIOR

The Western Front – the static line of trenches and trench systems that stretched from the Swiss frontier to the English Channel around Nieuport – became one of the defining images of the Great War. Yet had the war plans of the Great Powers come to fruition it would not have existed. The French, with Plan XVII, were supposed to sweep through Alsace-Lorraine and drive the German armies rapidly back into their own country – inflicting on them such massive defeats that capitulation would soon follow. The Germans, with the Schlieffen Plan, were to sweep through neutral Belgium, around Paris and drive the French armies back upon their own frontier defences. A rapid capitulation would also follow. These plans came to grief for a variety of reasons. The French, advancing in great numbers in the open, soon became victims of German machine gun and artillery fire. Their plan was based on Napoleonic élan and little else. It took no account of defensive firepower and within short order had ground to a halt. Over 300,000 casualties were suffered by the French in what became known as the Battle of the Frontiers.

The Germans came to grief for slightly different reasons. Their plan had been developed by the Chief of the general staff, General von Schlieffen, in 1905. Schlieffen had made it plain that his plan was a theoretical exercise only and that Germany did not possess the manpower to put it into practice. This major caveat became rather lost in the years after Schlieffen's retirement. The younger Moltke who replaced him modified the plan by reducing the number of divisions that would constitute the right flank sweeping through Belgium and increased the numbers who would defend the German–French border. This at least made the plan possible to put into effect because it took some notice of the capacity of the railway network to transport the troops to the front. But it did not make it feasible. The troops on the right wing had such large distances to cover that supply problems and exhaustion soon set in. The huge mass proved incapable of traversing Paris and slipped down to its east, pursuing what it thought to be the defeated French and British armies. This left it vulnerable to counter-attack by troops transferred by the French Commander-in-Chief General Joffre from his failed eastern offensive to the west and south of Paris. These troops were transferred by rail so arrived faster and fresher than the tired hordes of marching Germans. These reinforcements proved sufficient for the Allied forces to stop the Germans at the River Marne and even to drive them back.

Now began a new phase of the war that was popularly known as the race to the sea, because the sea (or the English Channel) was where they were forced to halt. In fact it was not the sea that the rival armies were racing for but the open flank of their respective opponents. Neither side proved capable of outdistancing the other to exploit an open flank. The last attempt had been made by the Germans in November 1914. Then General Falkenhayn, who had replaced Moltke – now deemed to have ruined Schlieffen's grand design – flung in his last troops in the form of masses of younger reservists. These inexperienced troops attacked in rather the same manner as the French had attempted in Alsace-Lorraine. They met the British army, concealed in rudimentary trenches around the Belgian village of Ypres. The outnumbered British stopped the German attack in its tracks with great slaughter. Defensive firepower had once again proved too formidable for troops attacking in the open to overcome. From this time lines of trenches were gradually extended to the north and south and became continuous from the Swiss border to the Channel. The Western Front had been created (Map 8.1).

The problem of the Western Front was simple; the answer fiendishly difficult. The problem was that to make ground men had to leave the security of their trenches and attack an entrenched enemy across a strip of ground that soon became known with some accuracy as no-man's-land. This narrow strip might vary in width from 10 to 1,000 yards. The enemy could bring to bear on men attacking across these distances a formidable amount of firepower. In the trenches themselves would lurk riflemen who could fire up to fifteen rounds per minute. Even more deadly trench-dwellers were the machine gunners. A modern machine gun could fire about 600 rounds per minute and machine gun positions might be protected by steel plate and eventually concreted dugouts. Further back – perhaps some 4,000 to 10,000 yards – would be placed the enemy artillery. For reasons that will soon be explained, guns were not sufficiently accurate to hit small targets. But they were accurate enough to fire shells with some degree of certainty into an area as large as no-man's-land, and this would be sufficient to wreak havoc on formations of tightly packed men attempting to advance across it. In contrast to this hail of fire from bullets, machine guns and artillery, the attacking infantry were armed

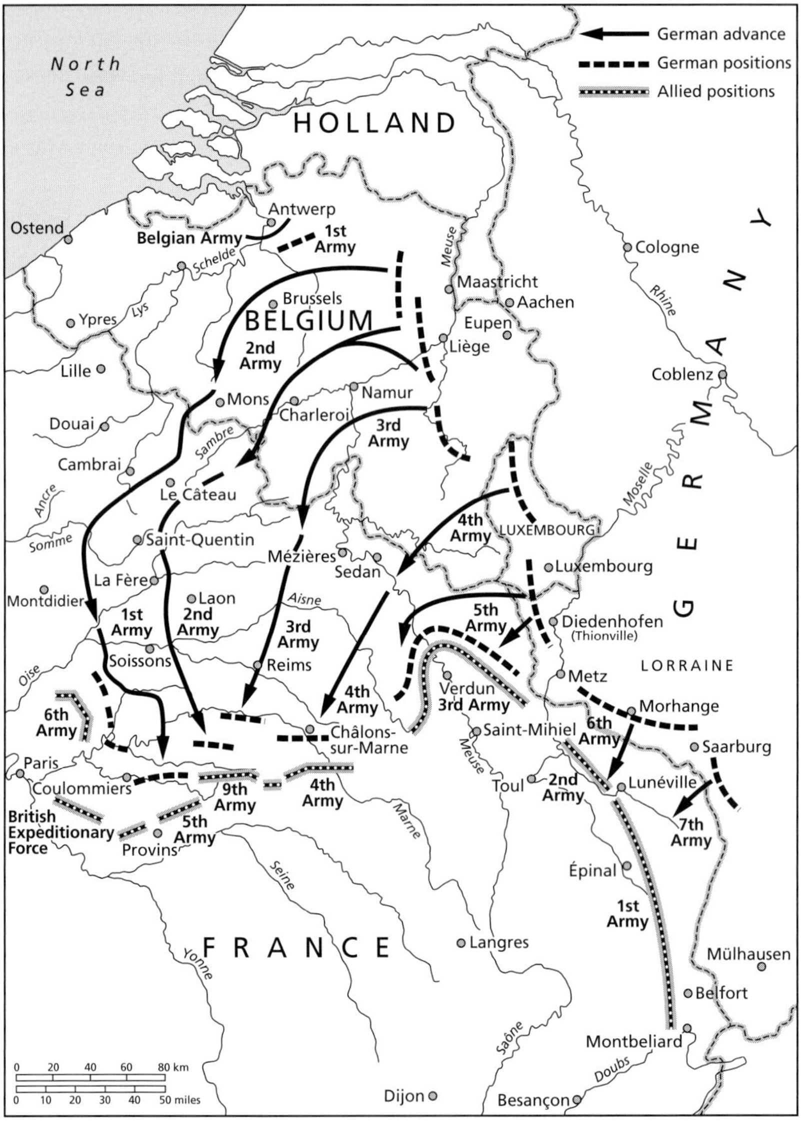

Map 8.1 German operations in France and Belgium, 1914.

with a service rifle and (in the early years of the war) a primitive hand grenade that was more likely to do damage to the thrower than his target. Moreover, in short order, the attacking soldiers would be required to face entanglements of barbed wire even before they arrived at the hostile trenches. This product of industrial society proved just as effective at keeping assaulting infantry out as it had previously been keeping cattle and sheep in.

Finding the answer to the question of the tactical problem that resulted in this firepower imbalance between attackers and defenders lay at the heart of warfare on the Western Front between the end of 1914 and November 1918. There was a solution that occurred surprisingly early to commanders on both sides. The main weapons of destruction were the artillery and the machine gun. The way to eliminate, or at least reduce to a tolerable level the fire from these weapons was to bombard them with shells from friendly artillery. This is what was attempted, especially by the British and the French, in the early battles of 1915. But while the solution sounded simple on paper, in practice there were many problems. The first was that neither the British nor the French had guns in sufficient numbers which had the power to batter down trench defences or fire the great distances that were necessary to eliminate enemy artillery. Their pre-war armies had been munitioned for a mobile type of warfare that required small guns that were highly manoeuvrable, short-range and now without the destructive power that the new warfare demanded.

But this was not the only problem with the artillery. At this period of their development guns were not precision instruments. Shells fired from a typical gun would not all land in the one place but be spread over an area of (say) 40 yards by 80 yards. This area was known as the 100 per cent zone of the gun. This sounds highly technical but all it means is that if 100 shells were fired from a gun under identical conditions all the shells could be expected to land within this zone. One difficulty with this is immediately apparent – the targets that the guns were required to hit were small. Trench lines were deliberately designed to be as narrow as possible to present small targets to enemy artillery. Single enemy guns at ranges of 10,000 yards or more were extremely small targets. One way of overcoming these difficulties was to possess a quantity of shells so huge that continuous firing from a gun must direct some of them onto their designated targets. But in 1914 and 1915 no munitions industry in the world was of sufficient size either to make this quantity of shells or to make the number of guns required to fire them. And by 1916, when the munitions industries of all the Great Powers were expanding, so were the trench defences that they were supposed to demolish. So in 1915, while an attacking army might have one main trench line and a few supporting lines to attack, by 1916 even the front defences would consist of whole systems of trenches of considerable strength all linked to each other by communications trenches. And some thousands of yards behind the front system there might be a second system and behind that yet another.

If quantity of shells and guns was not a practical proposition, did the answer lie in accuracy? If those shells that the attackers did possess could be delivered with some precision onto their targets, could not the enemy front be broken? But here too lay many difficulties. If we return to the 100 per cent zone of a gun it will be recalled that shells would only land within that zone if they were fired under *identical conditions*. But of course conditions on a battlefield could and did change. The most changeable factor was the weather. If a following wind sprang up during a bombardment the shells would travel beyond the 100 per cent zone. If there were a sudden head wind they would fall short. Shells would travel further on a hot day than when the weather was cold because the air through which they travelled was slightly thinner.

Numerous other factors affected the accuracy of a gun. There was the wear imposed upon it by continuous firing. Then as a gun barrel began to wear shells might wobble slightly as they passed through it, thus shortening their range. Alternatively, the heat generated inside the barrel by a heavy bombardment might cause the barrel to turn slightly upward and thus the shells would travel further. In addition, all shells were not exactly the same weight. In the case of an 18-pounder shell, the weight might vary by a fraction of an ounce either way. The heavier the shell, the shorter its range, and vice versa.

There was another problem with firing at distant targets. To fire with any accuracy, establishing the exact position of the target on the surface of the earth was critical. But in 1915 it was found that many maps of the battlefronts had been drawn in the time of Napoleon and not accurately. Even if the maps were only inaccurate by a few yards, this might nullify any attempt to hit a distant gun. Aerial photography was one imaginative answer to this problem. The battlefield could be mapped by aircraft carrying primitive cameras and the images then used to create maps. But this science was in its infancy. It was not fully realised that photographs taken from different heights would produce maps of widely differing scales. Moreover, a photograph of the earth was a flat image of a curved surface which introduced errors of parallax. As a result, accurate maps were difficult to produce and this had an inevitable effect on artillery accuracy.

Then there were problems of observation. If battles were fought in flat countryside it might be extremely difficult to estimate whether shells were hitting their targets or not. Distance imposed its own problem. Guns at great distances were vital targets but they could not be seen by the naked eye. Or, if the enemy had placed guns closer to the front they might conceal them behind the lee of a ridge to prevent direct observation. One way around this problem was to use aircraft equipped with radios. These planes could direct the fire of the artillery even against distant targets. Both sides soon realised that aerial observation was a vital matter. So if one side sent up aircraft to spot for the artillery, the other side would send against them fighter planes soon equipped with machine guns to shoot them down. Aerial battles known as dog fights soon developed around spotting activity, and if a combatant lost air superiority over a battlefield they lost their vital eye in the air.

Of course the weather could nullify all air activity. The Western Front was not located in an area noted for its sunshine. Even in summer, low cloud and rain could ruin observation, and yet battles had to be timed well in advance in order to assemble the required troops and munitions. The days before a battle were essential for the accuracy of a bombardment but were at the mercy of the weather. In winter, of course, fog, sleet and snow might prevent aircraft from even leaving the ground.

A battle of extraordinary interest illustrated the technical difficulties of artillery and to some extent demonstrated how they might be overcome. What makes the Battle of Neuve Chapelle even more exceptional is that it was one of the first trench warfare encounters to take place on the Western Front. In March 1915 the British IV Corps, led by General Rawlinson, were to take some low hills, called with some exaggeration, Aubers Ridge. It was originally to be a joint operation with the French but when Joffre declined to participate the British went ahead anyway. Confronting IV Corps was the small village of Neuve Chapelle, protected by a single trench and some rudimentary barbed wire barricades. Rawlinson considered the problem and sent raiding parties to examine closely the nature of the German trenches. He then dug trenches of a similar nature well behind the British front and bombarded them until they were destroyed. He then calculated exactly how many shells and of what calibre were required to demolish the 2,000 yards or so of trench that confronted him. The next step was to assemble the appropriate number of guns that could fire these shells in rapid bombardment, which would destroy the enemy trenches and not allow their defenders time to recover. All this took place on 10 March 1915 and by and large it worked. Except on the left of the line where there were observation difficulties, the German trenches were destroyed and British troops were able to capture them and consolidate their hold on the village. From then on the plan collapsed. Rawlinson's army commander General Haig insisted on massing the cavalry to exploit the capture of the village. But one matter had been beyond Rawlinson. His guns had not been able to locate or destroy most of the German artillery located out of sight behind Aubers Ridge. These guns began to take a toll on the soldiers and particularly the horsed-soldiers, who in any case were having difficulty making their way forward across ground intersected by trenches and littered with barbed wire entanglements. Eventually the cavalry was withdrawn but not before three days of futile endeavour and high casualties.

This battle provided clear lessons. After careful calculation it was possible to break trench defences and make advances of 1,000 to 2,000 yards at modest cost. But unless the enemy artillery had been neutralised, casualties would rise in the days ensuing the initial victory. Moreover, cavalry provided such large targets and were so difficult to manoeuvre across trench systems that their very utility on a modern battlefield had been brought into doubt.

But there was another lesson as well to be drawn from Neuve Chapelle. If gains could only be measured in distances of a mile, how many battles would be required to be fought before the Germans were expelled from French and Belgian soil? In the minds of the commanders this fact overruled all others including common sense. They had been raised in a period where defensive weaponry had not dominated battlefields. It was widely believed that France had lost the Franco-Prussian War through a lack of élan on the part of its infantry. If they looked back to any of the great commanders, it was not to Grant who had worn down the Confederate armies by tactics similar to those used on the first day at Neuve Chapelle; it was to Napoleon, the master of mobile warfare. Even then it was conveniently forgotten that Napoleon had lost his last battle because the British squares of infantry had proved impervious to his cavalry tactics. The war on the Western Front would therefore in its planning, although not in its execution, take a pre-industrial form where decisive encounters were sought that would decide the issue speedily.

So when Joffre came to make his plans for 1915 he sought grandiose objectives on a Napoleonic scale. He would attack in Artois on a front which extended from Vimy Ridge to Arras. If the ridge could be captured, he reasoned, he could unleash his cavalry across the plains of Douai. They would seize rail junctions vital to the supply of the German army in the West. The whole of the German front must be thrown into disarray and a spectacular victory – perhaps decisive – would follow. The British would make a modest contribution to the battle by attacking just to the north of the French.

The bombardment for the battle began on 9 May. There was some sophistication in the artillery arrangements. An unprecedented number of guns (over 1,000, 300 of them heavy calibre) had been assembled. They attacked the German trench lines and the German batteries gathered behind the ridge but revealed to the French by aerial observation. On the 16th the infantry went in. Initially gains were made. The German line in this area had been thinned of troops to assist the Austrians in the East. The Germans – despite the seven-day bombardment – had been caught by surprise. A French–Moroccan division even reached the summit of Vimy Ridge. Then the iron laws of trench warfare started to assert themselves. Despite their best efforts the French gunners had missed most of the enemy artillery behind the ridge. Their fire now began to take a toll on the Moroccans and eventually force them back. Further south the bombardment had missed large areas of the German trenches altogether. And here the Germans were well prepared. The French were driven back without securing a yard of ground. On the flanks the British – neglecting the lessons of Neuve Chapelle – used a lesser number of guns to attack stronger defences. Failure was total.

Joffre, against all reason, took heart from this battle. His troops had momentarily held Vimy, one of the strongest positions on the Western Front. He would try again. He did so later in May and again in June. In the latter battle the intrepid Moroccans once more took Vimy Ridge. Once more the untouched German guns drove them from it. The affair was over. Joffre's spring offensive had cost him 100,000 casualties. The Germans had suffered but to a lesser extent. They lost 60,000. The front remained more or less where it had been before the battle.

The losses incurred in this battle especially disturbed some politicians in Britain. Churchill had always counselled against giant offensives in the West where all that would be achieved would be 'men chewing barbed wire'. Now that his alternative plan at Gallipoli was under way, he wanted to divert even more troops away from the Western Front. But the French, who with the largest army continued to dictate strategy, thought otherwise. There would be an autumn offensive that would succeed where the one in the spring had not. Kitchener, British Secretary of State for War, reluctantly agreed, telling his colleagues that 'we must make war as we must, not as we would like'.

To make war as we must was more prophetic than Kitchener could have imagined. The enormous defeat inflicted on the Russians at Gorlice-Tarnów meant that some attempt must be made to divert troops away from them. Joffre's autumn offensive in the Champagne was the result. It was as barren as his earlier attempt. The French – with a British add-on at Loos – managed to bring sufficient artillery against the German front line to break it on a five-mile front. But defences were becoming more sophisticated. The Germans now had a second line of considerable strength some two to three thousand yards behind the first. This line was largely untouched by the French bombardment. Logic dictated that the French consolidate their gains and stop. Instead Joffre pressed on. Four days later he was forced to stop because of the enormous casualties inflicted on the French by fresh German troops and the untouched distant artillery. To the north the British had fared no better. Total Allied casualties in the autumn were 200,000 as against the Germans' 85,000. Attrition was working but hardly in the manner required by the Allied commanders. One of them paid a heavy price. Sir John French, who had led the BEF without distinction or imagination, was sacked. Sir Douglas Haig, who the political leadership in Britain thought would be an improvement, got the job.

There was a new weapon used by both sides which entered the fighting during 1915. Poison gas (chlorine) was used by the Germans in the Ypres salient in April. It had an immediate effect as the troops – deprived of the air that they needed to breathe – fled back. The Germans followed up but were stopped by unaffected troops and by the fact that they had run out of gas. They thus incurred the odium of introducing a frightful new weapon without having sufficient supplies to make it count. In any case their logic was dubious. For three days in four along most sections of the Western Front the wind blew from west to east – that is towards the German line. The Allies therefore retaliated in the autumn with poison gas of their own. It achieved little. Primitive gas masks were beginning to appear which filtered most of the gas out of the air. In other areas the gas was dispersed by the wind. The British managed the feat of releasing their gas when the wind was blowing the wrong way, thus gassing their own troops instead of the Germans. Gas would be used for the remainder of the war but it would never prove a decisive weapon.

In some ways 1916 marked the apogee of the war on the Western Front. Two of the largest battles ever fought – Verdun and the Somme – were fought during that year. Each of these battles involved hundreds of thousands of men and guns and munitions in prodigious numbers. The fact that made such battles possible on the Western Front but not elsewhere is often forgotten. The complex rail networks of Western Europe were employed by both sides to bring men, food and fodder for the many horses that pulled the guns and munitions close to their respective fronts. Then light railways, laid with rapidity and skill, brought these necessary components of war to the front lines. This was a feat of considerable magnitude. The commanders might not yet be able to plan a battle efficiently but they ensured that their men were fed and supplied with sufficient munitions, if not to advance, then at least to beat off an attempt by the other side to advance.

Germany was the first to undertake an offensive in 1916. Their commander General von Falkenhayn had watched will ill-disguised impatience and jealousy while his rivals Hindenburg and Ludendorff scored mighty victories on the Eastern Front against the Russians. Falkenhayn thought – correctly as it happened – that the war would be decided in the West. In late 1915 he put a plan to the Kaiser for an attack against the French fortress city of Verdun. The aim of the plan was to capture what was thought to be a vital point in the French line, but Falkenhayn hedged his bets. The French would defend Verdun to the last, he argued. He was correct in this except that given the prevailing doctrine on the French side they would have defended any French objective to the last. Anyway, Falkenhayn reasoned that even if he failed to make ground against Verdun the concentration of artillery he planned to bring to bear would bleed the French army white. So if he advanced he would be successful but if he did not advance he would be just as successful. Such logic as there was in this won the Kaiser over – an additional factor being that his own son would command the German Fifth Army that would launch the attack.

The battle (which is dealt with in depth in Chapter 4 above) can be quickly summed up. Falkenhayn assembled an unprecedented number of guns – some 1,200. But he was asking of them an unprecedented task. They would be required to bombard the two rings of forts that protected Verdun, demolish the defended villages that also stood in the way and what trench defences the French had been able to construct when the German preparations for battle became obvious.

His one chance of success lay with the sloth of the French. After the Germans had demolished the Belgian forces defending Antwerp in 1914, the French had declared forts redundant and removed from Verdun many guns and the garrisons that went with them. The warnings of local commanders went unheeded, and when the Germans attacked in February 1916 many forts such as Douaumont and Vaux, thought to be the last word in fortification by the French public, were little more than empty shells.

Falkenhayn's plan could no more escape the lessons of trench warfare than any other. To establish the concentration of artillery needed to demolish the French defences of Verdun, he concentrated his guns against the bulk of them that were clustered on the right bank of the River Meuse. For a time this succeeded. French defenders were blasted out of their positions as the Germans slowly progressed. Then a new commander, General Pétain, a master of defensive warfare, was appointed to rectify the position. Pétain reorganised the French artillery on the left bank of the Meuse so that the further the Germans progressed the more they exposed their flank to the French guns. Fort Douaumont fell to the Germans but the French guns were exacting such a fearful price on the attackers that Falkenhayn had to rethink his tactics. He widened the attack to the left bank of the Meuse to deal with the French guns and used a new variety of poison gas (phosgene) as well. For a time the Germans once more gained ground, this time capturing Fort Vaux. But the fact was that the Germans were increasingly having difficulty in providing their troops with adequate fire support. The muddy ground proved a barrier to moving the heavy guns forward. The French, on the other hand, began to receive artillery reinforcements in numbers. And they were able to supply their men and guns through a masterpiece of improvisation. A continuous conveyer belt of trucks travelling along a single road for the first time in history was able to supply an entire army. The Voie Sacrée – as it was known after the war – kept the French in the battle. When the British offensive at the Somme drew German reserves away from Verdun, new commanders (Nivelle and Mangin) were able to return to the offensive. By November 1916 the Germans had been pushed back to within a few miles of their start point. The battle had cost each side over 300,000 casualties. The results were nil.

Meanwhile the British had been making plans that proved to be no better than Falkenhayn's. Their new Commander-in-Chief, General Haig, in consultation with Joffre determined on a joint attack astride the River Somme in Picardy. As planning proceeded, however, French troops earmarked for the battle were leached away to Verdun. By May 1916 it was clear that the offensive would mainly be a British affair.

Haig was confronted by three German trench systems some 2,000 yards apart, although the third was in the process of construction and not of the strength of the first two. In addition the Germans had fortified many villages in the area and built deep dugouts – impervious to all but the heaviest of shells – to protect their garrisons. Overall they had made the Somme one of the most strongly defended areas of the Western Front. Haig consulted his army commander General Rawlinson, of Neuve Chapelle fame, on the type of operation that should be conducted. Rawlinson, rather reverting to the Neuve Chapelle model, counselled that only the German first line should be attacked. Once captured, the guns could be brought forward and a similar attack made on the next German position. The object, he stated, was to kill Germans, rather than gain ground. There was much sense in this. What Rawlinson was advocating was true attrition. The British would overwhelm a small area of ground with their artillery, ensuring that their casualties would be fewer than the Germans'. If the dose was repeated often enough victory would eventually follow. Haig rejected the idea entirely. He thought not in terms of attrition but of gigantic Napoleonic cavalry sweeps that would roll up the entire German position in the West. To unleash the cavalry, therefore, all three German trench systems would have to be overwhelmed at one blow. Here Haig was making a similar error to Falkenhayn. He had at his disposal an unprecedented number of guns, but most of them were small calibre. The heavy guns needed to demolish trenches and the dugouts in which the German garrisons lurked were in short supply. In even shorter supply were counter-battery guns – that is, guns that could neutralise the German artillery. Haig counted the guns but he made no calculations regarding their tasks. This was to prove fatal.

The battle opened on 1 July 1916 and was one of the great disasters in British military history (Map 8.2). In attempting to demolish all the German defences

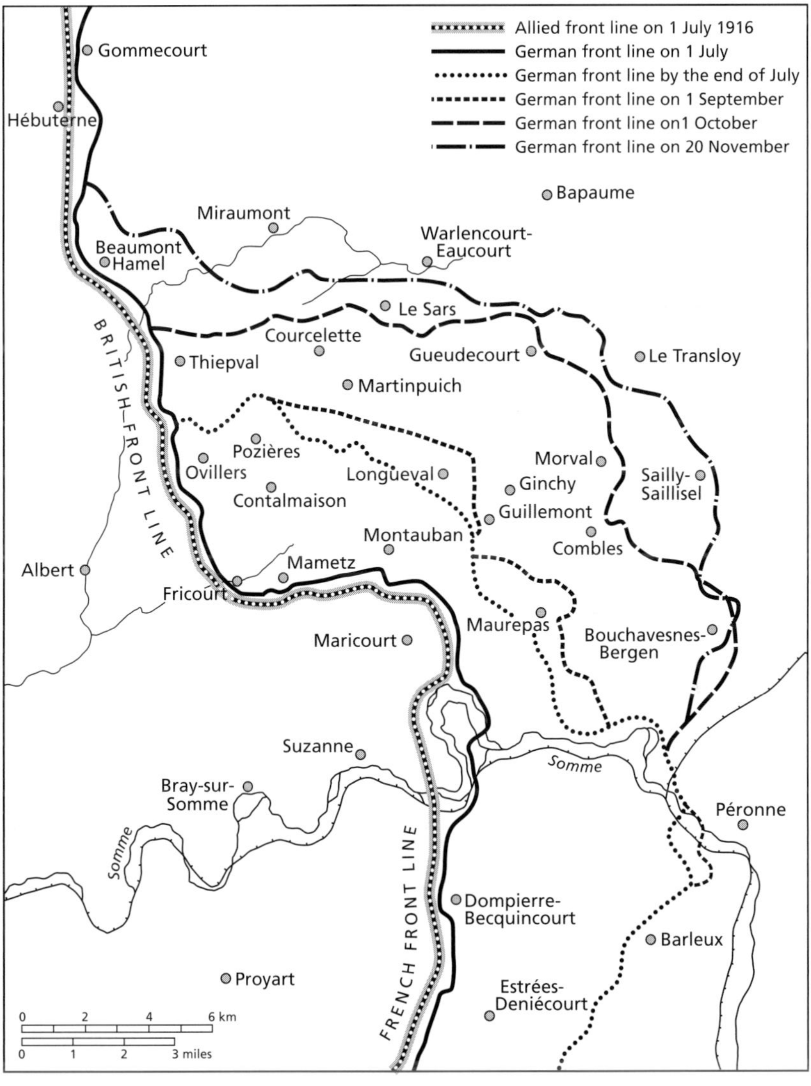

Map 8.2 The Battle of the Somme, 1916.

he managed to demolish very few of them. This left many German machine gunners unscathed, much wire uncut and the German guns almost entirely intact. The British infantry – who did not walk to their doom shoulder to shoulder at a slow pace but rather attempted all manner of innovatory tactics in attempting to traverse no-man's-land – stood no chance. Before lunch, at least 30,000 of the 120,000 committed had become casualties, many before they reached their own front line. At day's end the toll was 57,000 casualties of which 20,000 were dead. Only in the south, with the aid of a vast quantity of French artillery, did the British (and the French) make some ground.

Logic proclaimed that the battle be halted and a radical reappraisal conducted. Nothing of the kind happened. The French implored the British to continue in order to relieve pressure on Verdun. Haig needed no prompting. The battle would continue. This it did for almost five months. There were a few encouraging signs for the British. It so happened that on the first day some troops that captured the German front line did so behind a curtain of shells that at the same time fell just in front of them and onto the German front line. The 'creeping barrage', as it became known, then progressed at a predetermined pace so that the troops could arrive at the German line as the shells were still falling on it. The defenders were thus faced with the unpalatable choice of manning their weapons and risking the falling shells or remaining in their dugouts and being set upon by the attackers. Soon this type of infantry protection became standard in all British attacks. It had its defects however. The guns still lacked the accuracy to ensure that all shells fell just in front of their own infantry. So some casualties were caused by shells landing short and those that landed too far away provided no protection. Moreover, in the early days too few shells were fired in the barrages, allowing some defenders to remain unattacked. Worse still, the creeping barrage was not effective in bad weather. Muddy conditions meant that troops had great difficulty in keeping pace with the barrage, and low cloud and rain meant that the artillerymen and airmen had difficulty in gauging where the shells were landing in relation to the advancing infantry. Nevertheless, this was a significant breakthrough and would remain the most effective method of infantry protection for the remainder of the war.

A second British innovation was the tank – an armoured vehicle equipped with a small gun or machine gun, generally impervious to rifle or machine-gun fire and capable of smashing down barbed wire entanglements and shooting up trench defenders. These machines were first tried at the Somme at the Battle of Flers-Courcelette in September. They proved of variable utility. Half of the fifty used broke down before they reached the enemy front line. Conditions inside these primitive machines were appalling, with temperatures rising to 140 degrees Fahrenheit. Petrol fumes inside the tanks also reduced the endurance of the crews. They did cause panic on some parts of the front and allowed some villages such as Flers to be captured at modest cost. But they were not weapons of exploitation. They could only proceed at walking pace over good going and the churned up ground of most battlefields meant that the going was often anything but good. The Germans also adapted to the tank and in short order produced armour-piercing bullets that made life inside these vehicles more precarious.

The creeping barrage and the tank sum up British accomplishments at the Somme. For most of the battle small groups of troops struggled forward against strong trench defences. They came on in the same old way and were killed in the same old way. At one point in the battle Haig's forces were actually attempting to advance in three different directions. Only complete failure prevented the British front from splitting into three widely separated sections. The battle ground on into the autumn when rain had turned that battlefield into an inland lake. Haig remained optimistic. In his world German morale was about to collapse, although the evidence for this was not obvious to an outside observer. In London, the government, though provided with accurate statistics which demonstrated that it took three British soldiers to kill two Germans, did nothing. Or rather, they allowed the battle to continue and congratulated Haig on his achievements. What these achievements amounted to was the unprecedented wearing down of his own army. At the end of the battle British casualties amounted to over 400,000, the Germans to over 200,000. The amount of ground gained was derisory – about ten miles. The strategic gains amounted to nothing.

At the end of 1916 the Germans straightened their line on the Somme front by withdrawing to prepared defences some miles in the rear (Map 8.3). The British and French plodded forward over a countryside laid waste by the enemy. The communications problems this caused meant that there would be no resumption of the Somme offensive in 1917.

Indeed on the Allied side the end of the old year heralded changes at the top. Joffre was held to have shot his bolt. The lack of preparations at Verdun and the lack of achievement at the Somme saw him replaced by General Nivelle who, somewhat optimistically, was held to have done well in the final counter-attack stage at Verdun. In Britain the changes were political. Asquith was not thought to have the vigour to prosecute the war with determination. He was replaced by Lloyd George, who immediately promised to deliver to Germany the 'knock out blow'. Yet Lloyd George was no devotee of Haig. He

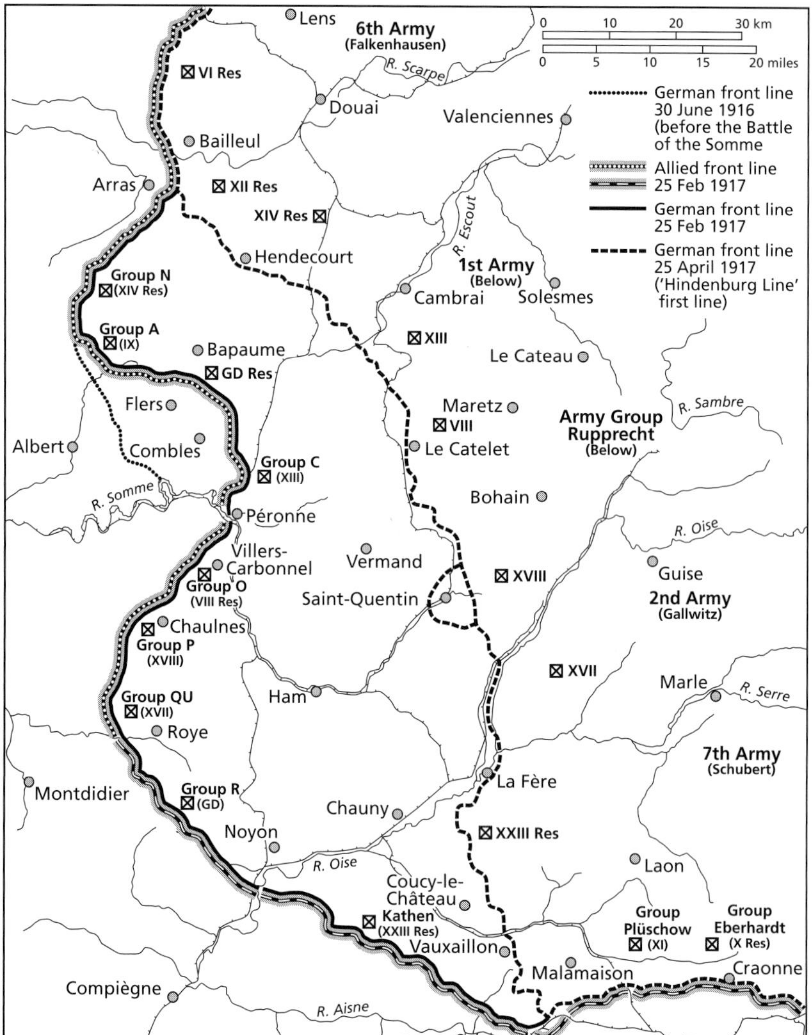

Map 8.3 German withdrawal, 1917, Operation Alberich.

regarded the Somme as a disaster for British arms and sought offensives elsewhere. This proved fruitless. The Italians, when approached, were not eager to see their men cast away in the prodigious numbers that had characterised the offensives on the Western Front in 1916. The Russians too were looking fragile. In the meantime General Nivelle had developed his own plan for the Western Front. Lloyd George, without studying the plan in any detail, immediately declared himself an enthusiast for it. Its main attraction for him was that it was not to be conducted by Haig. An attempt by the British Prime Minister to subordinate Haig to Nivelle failed, though it managed to poison relationships between the military and political leadership of Britain for the remainder of the war. In the event Haig would be 'guided' by Nivelle for the duration of the battle, a phrase so vague that in effect it meant nothing.

Haig would, however, kick off the offensive by attacking to the north of the French around Arras in April 1917. The main French offensive would follow on the Chemin des Dames in April. The planning for Haig's offensive indicated that some on the British side were still learning their jobs, but later events would show that Haig himself could be excluded from this list. The important phase of the attack would be made by the Canadian Corps on the heights of Vimy Ridge. This formidable position required the most careful artillery plan to reduce it. On this occasion such a plan, devised largely by Major General Alan Brooke (the Alanbrooke of Second World War fame), was provided. The combination of the creeping barrage, trench destruction and meticulous counter-battery work were the hallmarks of the preliminary bombardment. The Canadians, attacking on 9 April, captured the ridge. Haig seized on this limited but important achievement to unleash his cavalry. He had obviously learned nothing from the Somme, where for a brief moment a few horsed-soldiers had pushed through, only to be mowed down by German machine guns and artillery. A similar result occurred at Arras. The cavalry as a weapon of exploitation were useless on the Western Front. They were shot down in numbers without being able to hold a square foot of ground. Further attempts to push the infantry through ran up against fresh German reserves, held too far back initially but now arriving on the battlefield in strength. Haig kept hammering away but to no avail.

On 17 April Nivelle's offensive opened. Nivelle claimed to have the secret to success on the Western Front. His artillery preparations certainly showed an improvement on anything that the French had attempted on the Somme. And Nivelle had promised that there would be no more attritional warfare. If his method failed he would break off the offensive. This proved attractive to politicians who had lived through Verdun and the Somme. But Nivelle's preparations for battle were only too evident to the Germans. Indeed a raiding party had captured Nivelle's entire plan. So the Germans withdrew many of their divisions from the area to be bombarded and there constructed new defences of great depth. Nivelle's new artillery techniques therefore largely bombarded ground devoid of German defenders. But Nivelle gained sufficient ground to announce that victory was assured if his troops just pressed on. After some weeks this 'pressing on' took on the appearance of Joffre's failed operations in 1916. This occurred first to the troops who were conducting these increasingly futile attacks. Spontaneous acts of 'collective indiscipline' broke out among the rank and file. No fewer than sixty-eight of France's 112 divisions contained at least some troops who refused to attack. If this was mutiny, it was conditional. Most troops declared themselves ready to hold the front against an enemy attack – they would not, however, undertake any offensive operations of their own. The French government declared the whole affair the work of agitators and revolutionaries, but they acted quite differently. Some ringleaders were shot (the number varies between fifty and seventy depending on which sources are consulted). Notwithstanding these executions, the overall response was conciliatory. The troops were promised better leave conditions, improved food and more rest. Above all the offensive was called off. Nivelle was sidelined in favour of Pétain, the general most careful with the lives of the ordinary soldier. This ended the mutiny. But for the foreseeable future the French army would be in no position to conduct a large offensive. The main burden of the war on the Western Front now fell on the British.

This was despite the fact that a very large event had occurred in April 1917. The United States had entered the war on the Allied side. Provoked by the sinking of American ships by German U-boats and by preposterous German schemes to raise revolt in Mexico, Woodrow Wilson, the President too proud to fight in 1916, took a united country to war. But the American army was very small and would not appear in numbers on the Western Front until 1918. This fact seemed to indicate a careful policy on the part of the British until the Americans arrived. But that was not how Sir Douglas Haig viewed events. He came forward with a plan for a gigantic offensive out of the Ypres salient in Belgium. He would sweep through to the Belgian coast and then turn south and roll up the whole German line. If this sounded like the Somme with a sharp right turn instead of a left, it was. But Haig now pronounced that he had the men and above all the munitions to accomplish in 1917 what had eluded him the year before. Given his antipathy towards Haig, it was surprising that Lloyd George agreed to this plan. On the other hand, perhaps the Prime Minister thought that after all Haig might just deliver the knock-out blow that he promised when he replaced Asquith. The stage was set for the Third Battle of Ypres, or as it became known, Passchendaele.

The preliminaries of this battle were promising. The Messines Ridge to the north of the Ypres salient overlooked the ground to be crossed by the infantry and had to be captured before the main operation could start. As it happened, the British had been tunnelling under this ridge since 1915 and placing great stores of explosives or mines in the shafts. All told, 1 million pounds of TNT was in place by June 1917. General Plumer, in charge of the Second Army at Messines, exploded them on 7 June 1917. At the same time an enormous artillery bombardment was directed against the German artillery. This combination of mines and shells enabled the British to capture the ridge at moderate cost.

It might have been reasonably expected that the Fifth Army, which was going to conduct the main attack, would have moved immediately to take advantage of the rather shattered state of the Germans after Messines. Nothing of the sort happened. There was a seven-week pause during which Haig introduced a new commander for this army, General Gough, who had done nothing so far in the war to mark him out for high command. His main qualifications were that he was a cavalry general and a favourite of Haig's. Gough, Haig thought, would provide the drive to ensure that the cavalry swept forward to the Belgian coast.

The battle started well enough on 31 July. The opening bombardment showed some more sophistication than that of the opening day of the Somme. A creeping barrage was fired along the entire front and there were many more heavy guns to shell the German batteries. Gough made reasonable ground, securing much of the Pilckem Ridge on the left of the attack. However he made absolutely no progress against the Gheluvelt Plateau on the right, an area that contained the greatest concentration of German guns. On 1 August rain fell and continued to fall for the rest of the month. The advantages Gough had – newer tanks, increased artillery resources, the ability to fire an accurate creeping barrage – all went for nothing, as the battlefield quickly became a quagmire. Troops drowned in the mud. Low cloud meant that aircraft could not spot the fall of shell for the guns. The troops could hardly get out of their trenches, let alone follow a creeping barrage. Gough, however, remained optimistic, resorting when failure could not be concealed to blaming the troops for their lack of vigour. In a month the line hardly moved. This was too much even for Haig. Gough was sidelined to command only the northern section of the attack. Plumer was brought in to command the main event, which would be the capture of the Gheluvelt Plateau.

Plumer made several crucial demands before he proceeded. He insisted on time to ensure that his preparations were thorough and he insisted on a period of fine weather. Nor, he insisted, would he aim for distant objectives such as the Belgian coast or even the village of Passchendaele, some seven miles distant, that was meant to be captured on the first day of battle. Haig acquiesced. In three battles in late September and early October – Menin Road, Polygon Wood and Broodseinde – Plumer captured the plateau. The battles were perfect examples of the 'bite and hold' technique, where huge amounts of artillery were fired against the German defences. The creeping barrage was slowed and thickened so that troops could take the newest German form of defence, the concrete pillbox. Then, when the infantry had reached their objectives, which were usually no more than 3,000 yards away, a standing barrage was fired in front of them for some hours. This negated new German tactics, which involved thinning out their front lines to avoid casualties and massing most of their troops well behind the front to counter-attack before the British could establish themselves in their newly won positions. To launch an effective counter-attack the Germans first had to penetrate this barrage. They soon abandoned the attempt, the cost being too high and the number of troops arriving at the new British front line being insufficient to launch concerted attacks. Instead, during the last of the three Plumer battles (Broodseinde) the Germans once more packed troops in the front positions in an attempt to prevent the British from obtaining a hold. All these tactics meant, however, was heavier German casualties as Plumer's bombardment destroyed these positions. And these battles produced another hopeful sign. The six French divisions that were operating on the northern flank of the British attack advanced with their Allies with considerable élan. The trauma inflicted upon the French army by Nivelle was beginning to wear off. Under suitable conditions the French could fight with tenacity and resolve.

The German command had no answer to these tactics. The British artillery resources overwhelmed them in the attack and prevented any kind of counter-attack. The limited objectives ensured that the gains won could be held. A formula to grind down the German army had been discovered and successfully implemented. But the method required fine weather, and after Plumer's third stroke, that deserted the British. In October the rains returned and so did the quagmire. But by now the British command, including Plumer, had the bit between their teeth. The conditions that had ensured success in September and October had gone, but the battle was pushed forward on the usual grounds that German morale was on the verge of cracking. No such happy event ensued. Instead the conditions of August were repeated except that they were rather worse. The ground being fought over was low-lying and the continual shelling had destroyed what remained of the water table in this part of Flanders. The objective was now scaled down to the Passchendaele Ridge, a feature of no tactical importance whatever. The troops, in conditions which beggared the imagination, clawed or crawled or swam their way forward. On 17 November Haig announced that the Passchendaele Ridge had been secured. Actually it had not – all the British had managed was to establish a tenuous hold on part of it. This ground, gained at such cost (250,000 British casualties), had to be evacuated in three days when the Germans attacked it the following year. A battle that contained episodes of great promise, in the end proved as futile as those conducted in 1916.

Yet the year would finish on a hopeful if ambiguous note. Well to the south of Flanders laid an untouched area of ground around Cambrai. Quietly, Haig assembled troops, tanks and artillery. The ground was firm, tanks were to be used en masse and, of greater importance, new artillery techniques were to be tried. Sound ranging – a method that increased artillery accuracy and will be discussed in more detail later – was used. Other methods, also to be discussed, added to artillery accuracy. These new methods meant that there was no need to fire a preliminary bombardment, thus alerting the enemy to an impending attack. An element of surprise had been returned to the battlefield. These methods ensured that in the first instance the British caught the Germans by surprise and made good ground at modest cost. If Haig had halted he might have chalked up a notable success. But as always the idea was to get the cavalry through. So the British infantry kept fighting under more and more adverse conditions as the tanks broke down and the artillery support became less sure. In the end, the Germans counter-attacked these over-extended lines and recaptured almost all the ground initially lost. Church bells had been rung in England to mark the initial success. Hands were also soon wrung as failure rapidly followed. The British, however, had learned some valuable lessons in 1917. The question was: would they apply them in 1918 or would the Germans strike first?

The fact was that it was always likely that the Germans would strike the first blow in the West in 1918. Haig had worn down the British army at Passchendaele; the French were not yet ready to take the offensive after the mutinies; and the Americans were not yet trained to play a major role. Ludendorff, however, was very aware of the build up of American forces in France and determined to strike before they could be fully deployed. In addition Ludendorff was in a position to transfer troops from the Eastern Front. The Bolshevik Revolution saw the exit of Russia from the war and there were potentially millions of men available for redeployment to the West. Typically, however, Ludendorff only transferred some of them. The remainder was left to fulfil as yet unachieved German war aims in the East.

Where was he to strike? The south of the Western Front was quickly ruled out because it was too mountainous. The French front was tempting, but no great strategic objectives lay behind it. In any case Ludendorff had identified Britain as the major foe, so he determined to strike at their section of the line. There were two possible areas for an offensive. One was around Ypres and was attractive because of its proximity to the Channel ports. But as Passchendaele had demonstrated, the ground could be boggy. Between Arras and Saint-Quentin the ground was much firmer and would dry earlier in the year. This would allow an offensive in the early spring. Here is where the Germans would make their first strike.

Ludendorff had at his disposal about 6,600 guns deployed along the Western Front. To achieve a massive concentration of artillery he gathered three-quarters of them on the front of the attack. He also massed his infantry. No fewer than 750,000 men were also grouped opposite the British, and these men would be used in a new way. The elite of his force would be concentrated in storm troop divisions. They would not advance in coherent linear formations as of old. Instead they would penetrate as deeply as possible into the British defences, bypassing strongpoints and centres of resistance without pausing for flank protection. These bypassed areas would be captured by the ordinary infantry divisions that would follow the storm troopers. The plan was that once the breakthrough had been made the Germans would head for the Channel and then turn north, entrapping the BEF and a proportion of the French and Belgian armies as well. Victory must follow.

The number of guns available to the Germans allowed for a short bombardment of incredible ferocity. The British rear areas and headquarters would be deluged with shells in order to disrupt the functioning of command. Then the guns would be turned onto the front system in an attempt to stun the defenders just before the infantry support.

Historians have made much of the innovatory nature of these tactics, but in some ways they bear a desperately old-fashioned look. To achieve his objectives Ludendorff could not support his troops with artillery beyond the initial phase. The big guns in particular would soon be left far behind. All this meant that in short order the storm troops would be required to achieve their objectives by their own efforts. What Ludendorff was attempting was to win the battle (once the initial breach had been made) by infantry alone. It might be thought that the time was long gone when a commander on the Western Front would seek victory through his foot soldiers. Unless his foes collapsed Ludendorff was risking the annihilation of his armies.

Ludendorff's offensive opened on 21 March 1918 (Map 8.4). It fell on weak British defences recently taken over from the French. Behind them were few

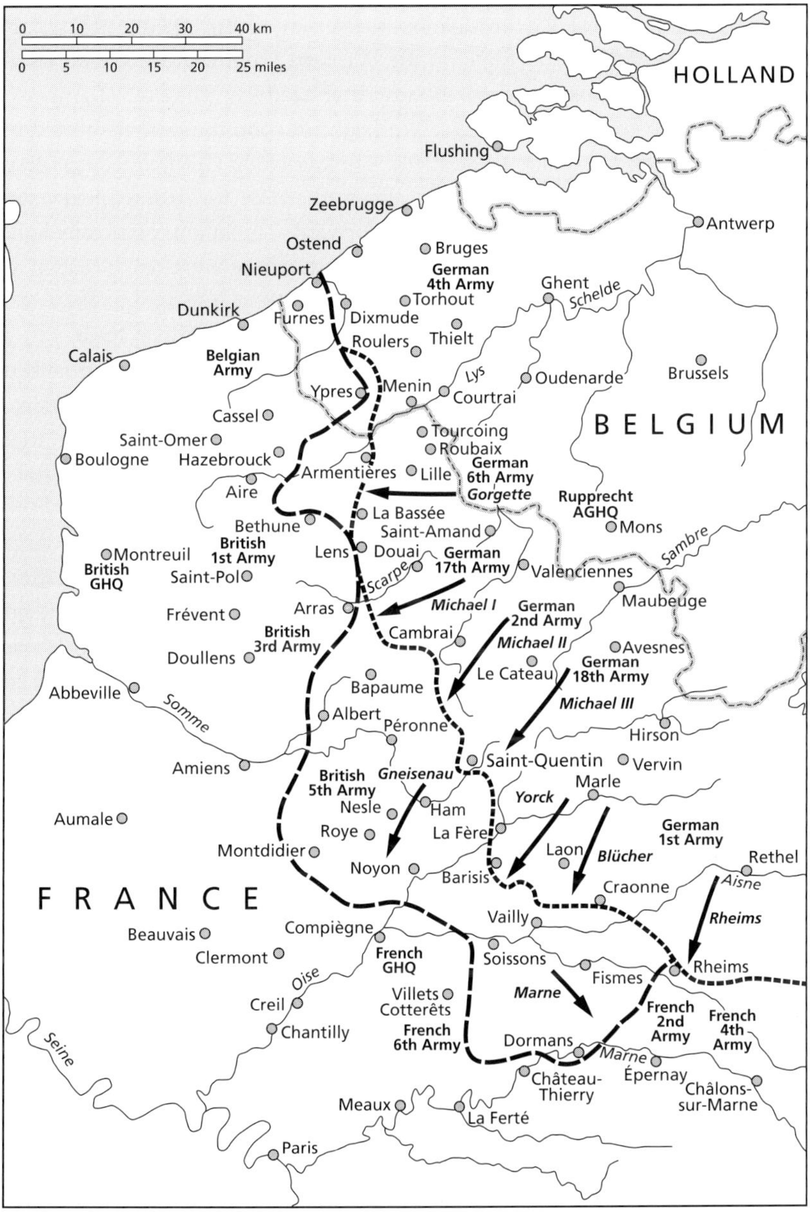

Map 8.4 The German offensive, 1918.

reserves because Haig had cast them away at Passchendaele. In the south the storm troops quickly broke through. In a week they advanced forty miles, thus bringing to an end the stalemate on the Western Front that had lasted from late 1914. Soon they approached the important railway junction of Amiens. Ludendorff's tactics seemed to have worked. But soon the crucial shortcomings in his method revealed themselves. The marching German troops were nearing exhaustion. Casualties, especially in the elite formations, had been heavy. The artillery was struggling to get forward. The infantry had only light weapons for fire support. On the other side fresh troops were being rushed to the battlefield by rail. These came mainly from the French sector but also from the unattacked section of the British front and even from Britain itself.

Thwarted in the south, Ludendorff turned north. On 9 April he attacked just south of the Ypres salient. Once more there were immediate gains, especially on the front of two bemused Portuguese divisions. But here too, however, and for the same reasons as noted, the offensive ground to a halt. The British army was battered but intact.

Nor were the Allies showing any inclination to give up the fight. At a meeting at Doullens on 26 March, the French and British put national differences aside and appointed General Foch as Supreme Commander of all Allied forces on the Western Front. The symbolism here was important. Foch was determined to see the war through to a successful conclusion. There would be no capitulation while he remained in charge.

Ludendorff was now in a quandary. He had attacked the British twice and failed. He now announced that as it was French reserves that had saved Britain he must now attack the French. He did on 27 May in the Chemin des Dames. His methods again won immediate gains, helped by the obtuseness of the French commander, who had packed his troops into the forward positions. Soon German troops were back on the Marne and in sight of Paris. Then French reserves began to arrive and Ludendorff's men ran out of steam. Further attacks, now directed against Paris, followed. These were partly thwarted by the intervention of the Americans at Chateau Thierry.

In all, Ludendorff launched five offensives in the West between March and June 1918. All gained ground but none of it was strategically significant. Indeed, the great bulges made in the Allied line meant that in July the Germans were required to hold a front twice the length they had held in March. And they were required to hold it with fewer men. These offensives bore out the slogan of the French General Mangin: 'Whatever you do you lose a lot of men.' Ludendorff had certainly done that. The offensives had cost the German army 800,000 men. The Allies had themselves lost about 900,000 but they had greater manpower resources and were able to bear the strain at least somewhat better. Nor had Ludendorff unlocked any key to victory in the West. The breakthrough must be achieved by the artillery. That much he knew. But as to what happened next he was as clueless as had been Joffre and Falkenhayn in 1916.

Events that soon followed Ludendorff's last offensive demonstrated that the Allies were far from being a spent force. The French army, now recovered from their nadir of the previous year, led the way. On 18 July two French armies accompanied by 750 tanks fell on the flank of the salient Ludendorff had created by his advances in May and June. The Germans were immediately overwhelmed and ordered a withdrawal. The French followed up by extending the front of battle. By August the Germans were back on the Aisne.

After these efforts the French stalled. But the task was now to be taken up by the British to the south of the Somme. In their forthcoming battle they were to demonstrate just how much they had learned in the previous year – at least at the intermediate levels of command. Concerning artillery accuracy, a method tried at Cambrai came into its own. Sound ranging consisted of a series of microphones placed across the front to be attacked. These microphones could detect the muffled sound of the firing of a distant gun. The sound waves were then plotted rather as a seismograph measures an earthquake. These readings could then be compared and the exact position of the gun established. By the time the battle began the sound rangers had established the position of almost all the German batteries with some precision. Other variations on already established techniques were also implemented. The creeping barrage was to be fired across the whole front using more shells than previously and proceeding at a rate that allowed for various aspects of the advance to be checked. Moreover, now each batch of shells was weighed before battle so that guns would not be rendered inaccurate by firing shells of differing weights. In addition at least six weather forecasts were being received per day by the batteries so that guns could be recalibrated in order to adapt to the new conditions. And before battle each gun was taken out of the line and tested for wear and adjusted accordingly. What all this meant is that for the first time the guns had a reasonable chance of hitting the targets for which they aimed.

The British infantry battalions now contained more firepower than ever. Portable machine guns (Lewis guns) introduced in 1915, were now available in number, as were grenades fired from rifles. Trench mortars accompanied the troops in unprecedented numbers. So while infantry battalions contained fewer men than in 1914 (such was the price of Haig's failed offensives) they contained more clout. Accompanying the troops would also be about 450 Mark V tanks, a weapon far more reliable than those used on the Somme and in the battles of 1917. What all this amounted to was a weapons system – the first in modern warfare – where each weapon supported the other and all would be required to be neutralised to bring an attack to a halt.

All this had come about by the impressive efforts of the Allied munitions industries. They had been able to replace all the equipment lost in the prodigious German advances earlier in the year, and in many cases replace it with better equipment. On the other side the situation was quite different. The German economy, under the supervision of the military since Hindenburg and Ludendorff had taken over in August 1916, had been run into the ground. The general rule was that absolute priority went to the military. In this fashion the German railway stock had been diverted to the needs of the army and worn out. Nor were the military capable of running a modern munitions industry, so the farcical situation arose where shell factories were constructed out of the very steel that was needed to make the shells. Some had then to be demolished to provide the shells that the Germans desperately needed.

On the battlefield the overall decline on the German side soon became apparent. Because of the casualties caused by Ludendorff and his insane obsession with obtaining his war aims on the Eastern Front, infantry divisions in the West had to be reduced in size. But, unlike the British and French, the

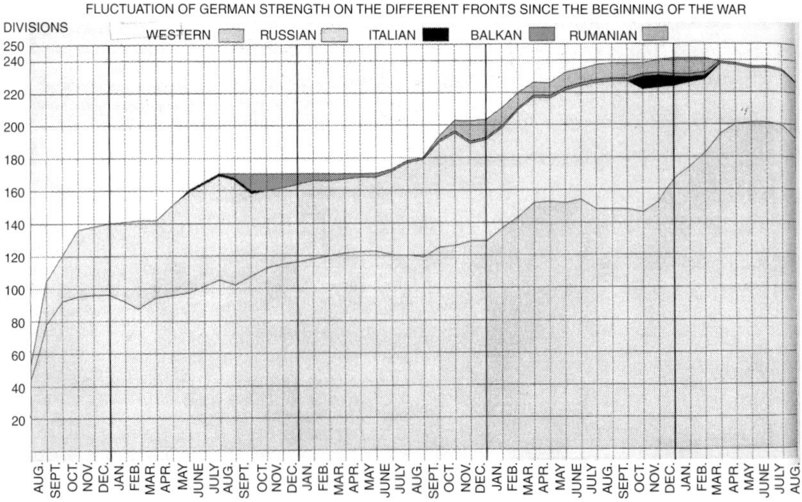

Fig. 8.1 Distribution of German forces 1914–18 by front.

Germans could expect no incremental increase in firepower from Germany's declining war industries. So when the Allies went over to the offensive, the equipment lost by the Germans would not be replaced.

The British Fourth Army began its offensive on 8 August 1918. A small-scale rehearsal for this larger battle (at Hamel) launched on 4 July, and appropriately including American as well as Australian troops, had demonstrated the efficacy of the new methods. Now they would be tried on a large scale. South of the Somme the Canadian and Australian Corps would attack. These were formidable fighting units. They had been out of the line during the major German attacks earlier in the year and were at full strength. To the north of the Somme, the British III Corps would provide flank guard as would the French to the south. At the end of the day the Germans had been driven back eight miles on a nine-mile front. The Allies captured 400 guns and inflicted 27,000 casualties on the Germans. Their losses were 9,000 men.

The key to this success lay in the new weapons system employed. Walking over the ground after the battle, it was found that most German guns had been accurately located by the sound rangers and blanketed when the bombardment came down at zero hour. So this method of artillery location obviated the necessity of firing a preliminary bombardment to locate the enemy guns. Surprise had returned to the battlefield.

The other instrument which had stopped infantry attacks, the machine gun, was neutralised by the creeping barrage which kept the heads down of the defenders until they could be set upon by the attackers advancing close behind the curtain of shells. Those missed by the barrage were cleaned up by the troops firing rifle grenades and trench mortars from a flank. Finally the tanks, unhampered by the hostile artillery, had also helped keep down enemy resistance and in some cases had forced German soldiers to flee from the battlefield. The tank was but one instrument of the weapons system, but there is no question that it helped push the advance further than it would otherwise have gone.

This battle marked a breakthrough in methods of waging war. If German artillery and machine guns could be dominated, the stalemate of the Western Front need never return. Whether the troops facing the Allies were of good morale or poor hardly mattered if they were to be deprived of their main weapons of resistance. Either the Germans had to discover a way of thwarting these new methods or the end of the war was inevitable.

The Germans, though downhearted, still considered that they could reintroduce the stalemate which might at least force a compromise peace on the Allies. At Amiens their defences were rudimentary. But behind the front stood the formidable Hindenburg Line, which after the Battle of the Somme, the

Germans had developed into a sophisticated defensive system. How would the Allies' new methods of attack stand up to this formidable obstacle?

This question did not arise immediately. The Fourth Army continued on its successful way in the days following Amiens. But after a few days its attacks became more and more uncoordinated. Command was now more difficult, many of the tanks had broken down, the system of sound ranging took time to move forward, so the new German guns that had been rushed to the area were more difficult to locate. Casualties rose as ground gained diminished. Were we about to witness a repeat of the successful phase at Passchendaele? Were Foch and Haig about to push their troops further than they could reasonably go? The answer was no. Haig and Foch wished to press on but they encountered stiff resistance from their lower order commanders. General Currie, who led the Canadian Corps, indicated that he might appeal to his own government if he was forced to continue. Rawlinson backed him up. Haig, despite objections from Foch, backed down. He would attack on another part of the front where preparations were well advanced, but he would not push on at Amiens. With this Foch had to be satisfied.

So Amiens was closed down and a new front opened just to the north of it involving the British Third Army. Using similar tactics it too made ground. When that attack stalled, the First British Army was set in motion. By these means the whole front moved forward one step at a time. The Germans were being comprehensively outfought, as the seizure of the tactically important Mont Saint-Quentin north of Amiens demonstrated, or they were forced to withdraw to maintain a coherent front, as in Flanders. By the middle of the month the outskirts of the mighty Hindenburg Line were reached.

The next series of battles saw the climax of the war on the Western Front. The Americans and the French moved first. On 26 September they attacked in the Meuse-Argonne region. So far the Americans had played only a small role in the fighting. Even now they found the going difficult, as their inexperienced armies came up against war-hardened German veterans. Nevertheless, the attack made some progress, though at high cost.

But by then their efforts had been overshadowed by operations to the north that commenced on 27 September and involved five British and two French armies, the Belgian army and two American divisions of troops fighting with the British. The Hindenburg defences were formidable. In places they were three miles deep, with protecting wire and concrete machine gun posts. In some sectors they were protected by steep-banked canals. Against these obstacles there was no question of employing surprise as had been used at Amiens and at other battles. A long bombardment was necessary to destroy enough wire and machine gun posts to allow the passage of the infantry. Also, because the Saint-Quentin Canal lay across the main area of operations, tanks could only play a limited role.

But the Fourth Army (which once again was to play the major role) had several advantages. It had captured the German defensive plans, it had the same methods of artillery accuracy as at Amiens and the British munitions industry had provided it with shells in unprecedented numbers.

The battle which started on 29 September revealed the potency of these factors (Map 8.5). Counter-battery fire was as effective as it had been on

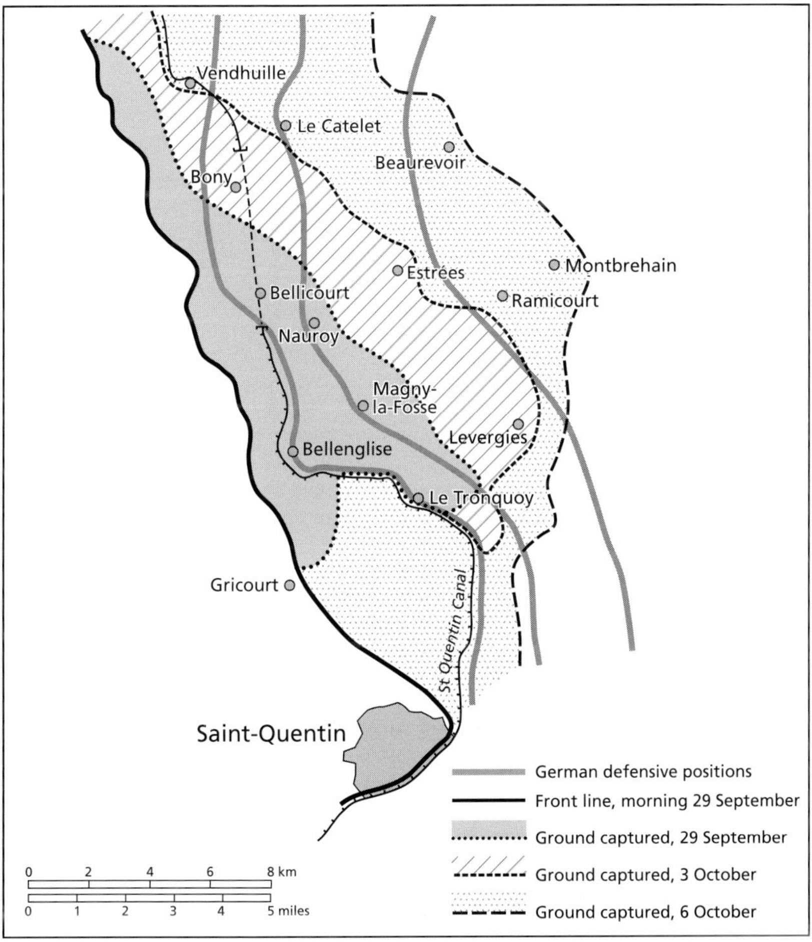

Map 8.5 Breaking the Hindenburg Line, autumn 1918.

8 August, so most German guns had been neutralised at zero hour. Not all the attack went well. In the northern sector, the powerful defences held up the American and Australian attackers and thus deprived them of a supporting barrage. Little progress was made. Events further south redeemed this lack of progress. A British division supported by an unprecedented number of artillery shells crossed the Saint-Quentin Canal and outflanked the German defenders holding up the Australians and Americans. For each minute of this attack, 126 shells from the field guns alone fell on every 500 yards of German trench. And this intensity was maintained for the eight hours of the attack. No defence could withstand this. The Germans fell back. The Australian and American attack regained momentum and by 5 October the Hindenburg Line – the last major German defensive line in the West – had been breached.

The Allied armies had now developed methods that could overcome the Germans whether they lurked behind strong defences or were in the open. There were limitations to the method. No attack could be pushed beyond the point where it could be protected by the guns. So, between October and early November, the Allies made a series of successful, if unspectacular, advances along their entire front. By the beginning of November all the German armies could do was to accelerate the speed of their retreat.

In a rare lucid moment, Ludendorff realised that the game was up. On 28 September he recommended making peace. He then changed his mind but the newly appointed civilian government was not listening. They sought an armistice, which was really a surrender on terms, the terms being Woodrow Wilson's Fourteen Points as modified by the British and French. The Armistice was granted on 11 November 1918. Finally, all was quiet on the Western Front.

It had taken the Allies an unconscionable time to learn the lessons of the Western Front; that is, troops could not be pushed beyond the point where the artillery could protect them. For far too long Haig and Joffre and Nivelle and Foch thought that Napoleonic principles of war applied, that the war would be won by gigantic offensives culminating in cavalry sweeps. For this they had some excuse. In the past all armies had available to them weapons of exploitation – usually the cavalry. In this war there was no weapon to exploit a break-in. The tanks were too unreliable, the cavalry too good a target for the machine gunners. Gaining ground was not as important as wearing down the opposition. No Allied commander set out to do this. All their battles were meant to win the war – or to go a long way towards it – on their own account. Attrition was what occurred when these plans failed. But at least in the end some on the Allied side did grasp the new realities. No one on the German side had these insights. The main factor in wearing down the German army was the Ludendorff offensives of 1918. These desperately old-fashioned affairs wreaked havoc on Germany's dwindling supplies of manpower. No sense of what was possible ever seems to have occurred to the German High Command. They would later complain about being stabbed in the back by the collapse of the home front. In fact they were the victims of their own folly. Their armies were out-manoeuvred and out-thought by those of the Allies. That the military leadership of Germany refused to recognise this truth would have dire consequences in future years.

9
The Eastern Front

HOLGER AFFLERBACH

'Russia is not a country that can be formally conquered – that is to say occupied – certainly not with the present strength of the European States . . . Such a country can only be subdued by its own weakness, and by the effects of internal dissension.'[1] Carl von Clausewitz had drawn this conclusion from Napoleon's march on Moscow in 1812. He concluded that Napoleon, if he wanted to make war against Russia, had done everything right, but 'the 1812 campaign failed because the Russian government kept its nerve and the people remained loyal and steadfast'.[2] It is also of some importance that Clausewitz wrote about Napoleon's Russian campaign in his chapter on 'The plan of a war designed to lead to the total defeat of the enemy.'[3]

Clausewitz's analysis proved to be right in the First World War too. However, he was not the only one to believe that Russia could not be subdued. As a result of the Napoleonic experience, this was a general belief in Europe before 1914. There had been wars against Russia and the Tsarist Empire had lost some of them, even major ones like the Crimean War or the Russo-Japanese War, but it had fought them at its very periphery. Napoleon was the last man who had tried to subdue the country and 'his example did not invite imitation'.[4]

One of the most important developments which the First World War brought in its wake was that the notion that Russia could not be subdued started to change – with enormous consequences for the history of the twentieth century. No less important was the fact that the Russian government, on the other side, relied for too long on the experience of victory against

1 Carl von Clausewitz, *On War*, edited and translated by Michael Howard and Peter Paret (Princeton University Press, 1976), *Vom Kriege* (Bonn: Ferd Dümmlers Verlag, 1980), p. 627. Translation changed by author for greater precision.

2 *Ibid.*, pp. 627ff. 3 *Ibid.*, p. 617.

4 Erich von Falkenhayn, *Die Oberste Heeresleitung 1914–1916 in ihren wichtigsten Entschliessungen* (Berlin: E. S. Mittler, 1920), p. 48.

Napoleon and other invaders, and disregarded any warning that it could be brought down by inner weakness when there was still time to leave the conflict with no, or only moderate, harm.

The Eastern Front is an enormous topic which deserves much more research than it has received.[5] This front stretched from 1914 to 1916 from the Baltic Sea to the Romanian border (Map 9.1). After Romania entered the war in late August 1916, it stretched even further, reaching as far as the Black Sea. A huge number of battles and encounters took place in this vast theatre of war, among them important events like the battles of Lemberg and Augustow in 1914, the battle in the Carpathian Mountains in early 1915, Vilna in 1915, Hermannstadt and Bucharest in 1916, Riga in 1917 and the Kerensky offensive 1917, to mention only some of many encounters. Most of these battles were closely linked with military operations or political events in other parts of Europe, in other theatres of war like the Balkans, the Dardanelles, Italy or the Western Front. Obviously there is also an ocean of other questions which could be asked in this context.

Instead of trying to cover this vast ground, I will focus on only three events which I hope will serve as examples to demonstrate some of the larger military developments on the Eastern Front. First, I offer a short description of three important battles on the Eastern Front – a battle narrative; then, I want to show why they were turning points of this war and how they influenced its duration and outcome. The encounters I have chosen are the Battle of Tannenberg in 1914; the fall of Przemyśl in March 1915 and the Battle of Gorlice-Tarnów in May 1915; and the Brusilov offensive in June 1916. Together they changed the history not only of the Eastern Front and of the First World War, but also of twentieth-century Europe.

Tannenberg

The first month of the war started with an important and impressive German victory over the Russians – the Battle of Tannenberg, which was fought from 26 to 30 August 1914 in Eastern Prussia. The victory happened on a front where nobody had expected it. During the first weeks of the war the largest part of the German army moved through Belgium and northern France to encircle the French army. Seven German armies fought in the West, while only one

5 This chapter on the Eastern Front 1914–18 will not try to cover all important aspects of the events – there are far too many. For the essential historiography, see the bibliographical essay to this chapter below.

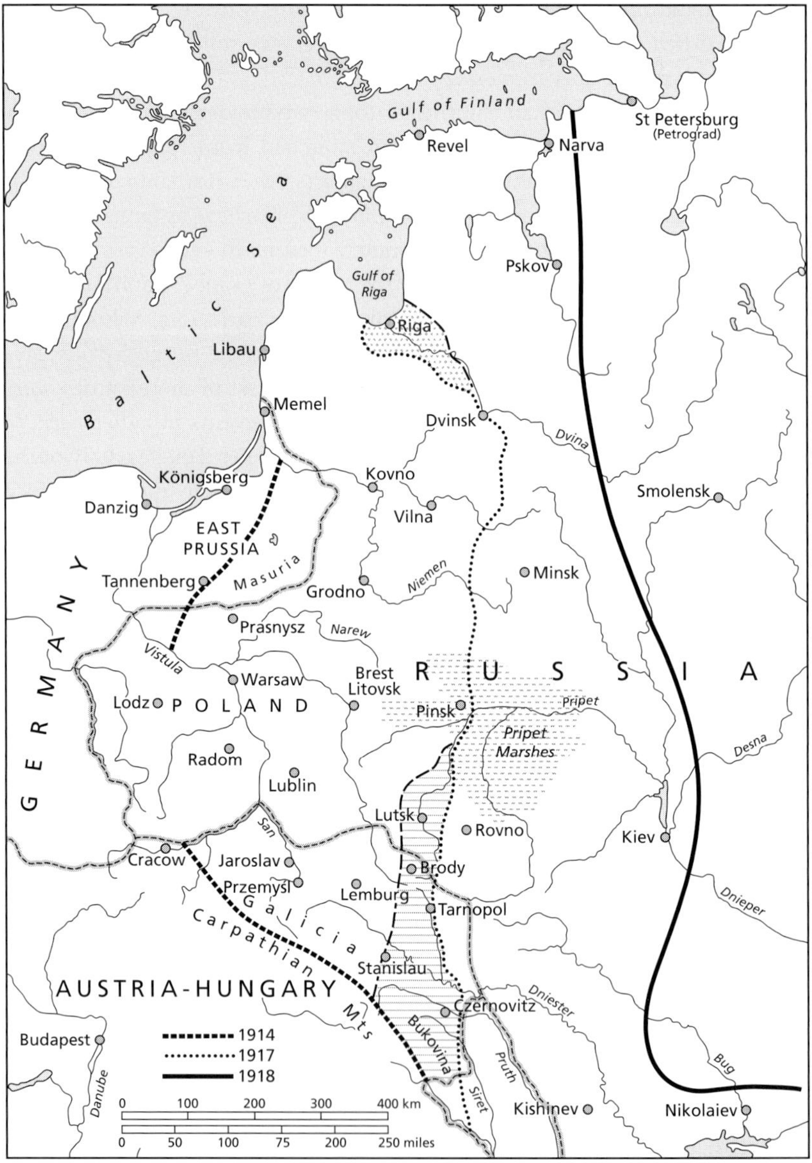

Map 9.1 The Eastern Front, 1914–18.

army in the East defended Eastern Prussia. The Russians could not focus on Germany alone, but had to take care of Austria-Hungary too. The Russian High Command (Stavka) at Baranovichi, whose strongest figure was General Danilov, the Quartermaster General, was relatively powerless, blocked by intrigues – as Norman Stone has shown – and could not agree on a main objective. The Russian army was split into two halves (fronts) which operated with a very large degree of independence. Important decisions were made by the commanders of these fronts.[6] The north-western front was commanded by Jakow Zhilinski; his three armies faced the German army. The south-western front, with four armies, was commanded by Nikolai Ivanov and faced the Austro-Hungarian army.[7] The question of where to start the main offensive caused great concern and a number of poor decisions followed.[8] Despite its being the smaller part of the Russian army, Russian superiority on the German front was still substantial. The German Eighth Army in Eastern Prussia seemed far too weak to offer effective resistance; but this was, from the point of view of German Headquarters, not regarded as necessary. The German war plan – commonly called the Schlieffen Plan, though recently its authorship and even its existence has been a matter of considerable controversy[9] – required the defenders in the East only to delay the Russian

6 Norman Stone, *The Eastern Front, 1914–1917* (London: Penguin, 1998), p. 51. 7 *Ibid.*

8 Bruce W. Menning, 'War planning and initial operations in the Russian context', in Richard F. Hamilton and Holger Herwig (eds.), *War Planning 1914* (Cambridge University Press, 2010), pp. 80–142.

9 Gerhard Ritter, *The Schlieffen Plan: Critique of a Myth* (London: Oswald Wolff, 1958). In 2002 the American historian, Terence Zuber, surprised the world with the statement that there was no Schlieffen Plan: Terence Zuber, *Inventing the Schlieffen Plan: German War Planning, 1871–1914* (Oxford University Press, 2002). The controversy can be found mainly in *War in History*, and has not yet come to its end: T. Zuber, 'The Schlieffen Plan reconsidered', *War in History*, 3 (1999), pp. 262–305; T. Holmes, 'A reluctant march on Paris', *War in History*, 2 (2001), pp. 208–32; T. Zuber, 'Terence Holmes reinvents the Schlieffen Plan', *War in History*, 4 (2001), pp. 468–76; T. Holmes, 'The real thing', *War in History*, 1 (2002), pp. 111–20; T. Zuber, 'Terence Holmes reinvents the Schlieffen Plan – again', *War in History*, 1 (2003), pp. 92–101; R. Foley, 'The origins of the Schlieffen Plan', *War in History*, 2 (2003), pp. 222–32; T. Holmes, 'Asking Schlieffen: a further reply to Terence Zuber', *War in History*, 4 (2003), pp. 464–79; T. Zuber, 'The Schlieffen Plan was an orphan', *War in History*, 2 (2004), pp. 220–5; Schlieffen Plan: R. Foley, 'The real Schlieffen Plan', *War in History*, 1 (2006), pp. 91–115; T. Zuber, 'The "Schlieffen Plan" and German war guilt', *War in History*, 1 (2007), pp. 96–108; A. Mombauer, 'Of war plans and war guilt: the debate surrounding the Schlieffen Plan', *Journal of Strategic Studies*, 27 (2005), pp. 857–85; T. Zuber, 'Everybody knows there was a "Schlieffen Plan": a reply to Annika Mombauer', *War in History*, 1 (2008), pp. 92–101; G. Gross, 'There was a Schlieffen Plan: new sources on the history of German war planning', *War in History*, 4 (2008), pp. 389–431; T. Holmes, 'All present and correct: the verifiable army of the Schlieffen Plan', *War in History*, 16:1 (2009), pp. 98–115; T. Zuber, 'There never was a "Schlieffen Plan": a reply to Gerhard Gross', *War in History*, 17:2 (2010), pp. 231–49; and T. Zuber, 'The Schlieffen Plan's "ghost divisions" march again: a reply to Terence Holmes', *War in History*, 17:4 (2010), pp. 512–21. In 2006 a major volume was

advance, until the victorious armies arrived from the West and changed the strategic balance in the East. This was also what Moltke and his Austro-Hungarian colleague, Conrad von Hötzendorf, had discussed before the war; not only the Eighth Army, but also the Austrians expected speedy German relief. It is remarkable and also characteristic of German pre-1914 military thinking about Russia, that there was no plan as to how this war in the East could be fought and won after the supposed victory in the West. All plans ended with the completion of operations in the West. We can suppose that staff officers imagined being able to force Russia to conclude peace after winning some decisive victories on the soil of the very western border of the Empire, in cooperation with Austria-Hungary. No large-scale invasion plans against Russia were extant, and all previous war plans against Russia focused either on defence or on limited operations against Russian Poland.

Already in August 1914 things were not moving according to the German plan. The Western Front looked fine and until early September victory in the West seemed possible and imminent; but the Russian army mobilised much faster than expected, and following urgent French demands it began advancing towards Eastern Prussia. This created panic among the civilian population. The fear seemed justified, especially from a military point of view: ten-and-a-half German divisions fought against nineteen Russian divisions, which were also superior in artillery.[10] Only 173,000 German soldiers were fighting on this front against 485,000 Russians – which meant that the Russians had a superiority of 2.8:1.[11] The first firefights brought mixed results and the engagements were broken off by the German commander Prittwitz von Gaffron. The German troops retreated and the Russian 'steamroller' started to move westward into Eastern Prussia, occupying German territory. The behaviour of Russian troops during the occupation is at this moment the object of promising historical research, comparing it to the atrocities committed by German troops in the West.[12] Afraid of Russian cruelties, more than 800,000 Germans

published in which Schlieffen and Zuber's arguments were torn apart: Hans Ehlert, Michael Epkenhans and Gerhard Gross (eds.), *Der Schlieffenplan: Analysen und Dokumente* (Paderborn: Schöningh, 2006).

10 Fritz Klein *et al.* (eds.), *Deutschland im ersten Weltkrieg*, 3 vols. (Berlin: Akademie Verlag, 1968), vol. I, p. 322.

11 *Der Weltkrieg 1914–1918: die militärischen Operationen zu Lande. Bearbeitet im Reichsarchiv*, 14 vols. (Berlin: E. S. Mittler, 1925–44), vol. II, p. 238.

12 Alexander Watson, '"Unheard of brutality": Russian atrocities against civilians in East Prussia, 1914–15', *Journal of Modern History*, forthcoming. See John Horne and Alan Kramer, *German Atrocities, 1914: A History of Denial* (New Haven, CT: Yale University Press, 2001).

fled their homes and moved westward.[13] Long lines of refugees filled the roads, with carts full of hastily collected luggage and household goods, sometimes even followed by livestock. Occasionally this human traffic hindered the operations of the German defenders. Cossacks sacked and destroyed 34,000 houses. Civilians as well as the general staff wondered if the Russians could be stopped before they overran the whole of Eastern Prussia and perhaps even Silesia. Prittwitz, in a moment of panic, wanted to retreat to the Vistula.

The younger Moltke was terrified and decided to change the command in Eastern Prussia immediately. He sent his ablest strategist, Ludendorff, to the East; Ludendorff was too junior to become an army commander. Paul von Hindenburg took that roll, though he was ordered not to interfere with his Chief of Staff.[14] Prittwitz and his Chief of Staff Waldersee were sacked. When Hindenburg and Ludendorff arrived by train in Eastern Prussia, they found that the staff of the Eighth Army, among them Max Hoffmann,[15] had already sketched out an operation against the Russians which made good use of weaknesses that were the consequence of the hasty Russian advance.[16]

Leaving aside the stories of Russian troops and staff stopped by well-stocked wine cellars, there were several strategic weak points in the Russian advance. Russian wireless messages were not encoded, but neither was some of the German traffic; wireless operation was in its infancy. The Russian plans were therefore accessible to the Germans.[17]

Of even greater significance was the way the terrain of Eastern Prussia crippled the Russian offensive. The two advancing Russian armies, the First (Njemen) Army commanded by General Rennenkampf and the Second (Narev) Army commanded by General Samsonov, were divided by the Masurian Lakes. If one of them was attacked at the right moment, the other one would be unable to help straightaway. Of further help were the north–south rail lines which worked entirely in German favour and helped to deploy German troops with the necessary speed. The attack against the Narev Army was led by Hindenburg, a figurehead who, thanks to his phlegmatic nature,

13 Walter Elze, *Tannenberg. Das deutsche Heer von 1914: Seine Grundzüge und deren Auswirkungen im Sieg an der Ostfront* (Breslau: Ferdinand Hirt, 1928), p. 112; Peter Jahn, '"Zarendreck, Barbarendreck – Peitscht sie weg!" Die russische Besetzung Ostpreussens 1914 in der deutschen Oeffentlichkeit', in *August 1914: Ein Volk zieht in den Krieg* (Berlin: Herausgegeben von der Berliner Geschichtswerkstatt, 1989), pp. 147–55.

14 Wolfram Pyta, *Hindenburg* (Munich: Siedler, 2007); and Manfred Nebelin, *Ludendorff Diktator im Ersten Weltkrieg* (Munich: Siedler, 2010).

15 Max Hoffmann, *Der Krieg der versäumten Gelegenheiten*, 2 vols. (Munich: Verlag für Kulturpolitik, 1923).

16 Max Hoffmann, *Tannenberg wie es wirklich war* (Berlin: Verlag für Kulturpolitik, 1926).

17 Stone, *Eastern Front*, p. 51.

was a good match for his nervous Chief of Staff. According to Hoffmann, Hindenburg was a military nullity ('The guy is a really sad fellow; this great commander and hero of the people . . . Never did a man become famous with so little physical and mental effort').[18] The recent research by Pyta and Nebelin on Hindenburg and Ludendorff has confirmed this polemical assessment. Hindenburg was a mere figurehead,[19] and the battle design was mainly the work of Ludendorff, Hoffmann and other staff officers.

The success of German tactics exceeded all expectations, but was, as Norman Stone rightly emphasises, the result not only of good German soldiering, but also of sheer luck.[20] On the one hand Samsonov's army pushed forward into the German trap and therefore played into German hands, on the other the insubordination and uncoordinated manoeuvres of German commanders like General François led to results which were not planned, but successful nonetheless.[21] The 153,000 German troops attacking the Narev Army were numerically inferior against this Russian army of 191,000 men. But they could envelop large parts of the enemy's army in the Masurian swamps and lakes near Ortelsburg-Neidenburg-Hohenstein. The Russian commander General Samsonov shot himself in despair, and his staff fled by foot. Here was a battle which produced a 'Cannae-style' victory of annihilation by encirclement.[22] Over 100,000 Russians were captured;[23] the army destroyed; several hundred heavy guns and machine guns taken. The result was not that Eastern Prussia was free of the enemy – Russian occupation lasted until 1915 – but that the threat of a Russian offensive was stopped for the moment. In addition, the other Russian army was attacked in the Battle of the Masurian Lakes. This did not lead to the complete annihilation of the Njemen Army, but to its retreat, with high losses.

For the German population of East Prussia, the initial Russian advance into German territory had been a traumatic experience. Hundreds of reports were

18 'Der Kerl ist ein zu trauriger Genosse, dieser große Feldherr und Abgott des Volkes . . . Mit so wenig eigener geistiger und körperlicher Anstrengung ist noch nie ein Mann berühmt geworden.' Quoted in Karl-Heinz Janssen, *Der Kanzler und der General: Die Führungskrise um Bethmann Hollweg und Falkenhayn (1914–1916)* (Göttingen: Musterschmidt, 1967), p. 245.

19 Pyta, *Hindenburg* and Nebelin, *Ludendorff*.

20 Stone, *Eastern Front*, pp. 44–69.

21 *Ibid.*

22 See *Der Weltkrieg 1914–1918*, vol. II, pp. 242ff.: 'Nach Leipzig, Metz und Sedan steht Tannenberg als die größte Einkreisungsschlacht da, die die Weltgeschichte kennt. Sie wurde im Gegensatz zu diesen gegen einen an Zahl überlegenen Feind geschlagen, während gleichzeitig beide Flanken von weiterer Übermacht bedroht waren. Die Kriegsgeschichte hat kein Beispiel einer ähnlichen Leistung aufzuweisen, – bei Kannae fehlte die Rückenbedrohung.'

23 *Ibid.*, p. 243.

written by local authorities and sent to the civilian Cabinet of the Kaiser describing the huge devastation and expressing the gratitude of the province for having been saved.

Given the numerical odds on the German side, contemporaries talked at first about the 'miracle' of Tannenberg. Simultaneously a new story began to be told, another interpretation of this victory which was responsible for an important shift in German approaches to the war against Russia. Hindenburg and Ludendorff had a great talent for self-promotion; indeed, Hindenburg especially, despite being slow as a military leader and as an individual, was a real master in so doing.[24] The battle was given a highly symbolic name: Hindenburg and Ludendorff suggested to Wilhelm II that it should be called 'The Battle of Tannenberg' after the defeat suffered by German knights at the hands of a Polish Lithuanian army in 1410.[25] In the immediate pre-1914 period the battle of 1410 was misinterpreted by nationalists as a symbol of the eternal fight of Slavs against Germans. This was the Polish as well as the German view. The Polish national painter Matejko had produced an enormous painting of the battle, and four years before the outbreak of the First World War the Polish population of Krakow had celebrated the fifth centenary of the 'Battle of Grunwald' (as they called it), and it is said that 150,000 people attended. In August 1914, the Russian commander Grand Duke Nicolai tried to create a 'Slavic bond' between Russians and Poles with his 'Grunwald Manifesto' in an attempt to win the Polish people's support for the Tsar. Hindenburg showed that he was a child of his time when he wrote: 'The misfortune of 1410 is avenged, on the old battleground.'

The victory of Tannenberg was of major significance. It gave Germany time to organise its defence in the East, and indeed during the rest of the war Russian forces were unable to defeat German troops in a major battle. But the psychological consequences of this victory were even more important than the practical ones. One aspect was the Hindenburg myth, the myth of German invincibility, with its disastrous consequences for subsequent German history.

In October 1914 Hindenburg and Ludendorff became commanders of the German troops on the Eastern Front, as 'Oberkommando der Deutschen Streitkräfte im Osten' (Ober Ost). They used their prestige and command in sharp opposition to the Imperial German general staff. They started to intrigue immediately, in the conviction that they knew the recipe for German victory,

24 See Pyta, *Hindenburg*, *passim*, for the main idea of seeing Hindenburg as an active manipulator of opinions and as a creator of his own image.

25 *Der Weltkrieg 1914–1918*, vol. II, p. 238.

but the others did not. They took over the leadership of the whole of the German army in late August 1916. The defeat in 1918 and the 'stab-in-the-back legend' were their responsibility. Despite the defeat, Hindenburg became President of the Weimar Republic – and made Hitler Chancellor in 1933. The fruits of Tannenberg ripened disastrously in later years.[26]

The success of Tannenberg was important for another reason too. It was the result of good German leadership, but also of luck and of huge mistakes by an enemy who remained strong and would probably not commit the same errors again. Indeed, Tannenberg was and remained the only successful encirclement of a Russian army during the war. But a growing group of German strategists, especially Ludendorff and his followers, interpreted Tannenberg not as a victory which they had won under very favourable circumstances, but as the result of their strategic genius. They believed they now had a recipe for victory which could and should be repeated on a larger scale. More than fifty years ago Jehuda Wallach called this notion 'belief in the battle of annihilation', '*Das Dogma der Vernichtungsschlacht*'.[27] Karl-Heinz Frieser used similar terms in his book on 1940, entitled *The Blitzkrieg Legend*,[28] showing how a surprising and extremely lucky operational success could be transmuted into proof of the validity of a belief in the battle of annihilation, which could be repeated on the next occasion.

This position can be traced as early as late 1914 when, fuelled by Hindenburg and Ludendorff, Ober Ost and its followers advocated the idea of an 'Über-Tannenberg', that is to say, a huge encircling operation against the Russian army. The significance of the Battle of Tannenberg lies here: in the gradual abandonment of the idea that it was impossible to subdue Russia; a change which had monumental consequences. And yet even Hindenburg, Ludendorff and Hoffmann did not believe, from one moment to the next, that it was easy to defeat Russia. This would be a terrible oversimplification. Their arguments have also to be seen in the context of a reckless power struggle within the upper echelons of the German army.[29] 'Ober Ost' saw the

26 Anna von der Goltz, *Hindenburg: Power, Myth, and the Rise of the Nazis* (Oxford University Press, 2009), as the most recent book on the Hindenburg myth.

27 Jehuda Wallach, *Das Dogma der Vernichtungsschlacht: Die Lehren von Clausewitz und Schlieffen und ihre Wirkungen in zwei Weltkriegen* (Frankfurt am Main: Bernard und Graefe, 1967).

28 Karl-Heinz Frieser, *Blitzkrieg Legende: Der Westfeldzug 1940* (Munich: R. Oldenbourg Verlag, 1995).

29 Ekkehard P. Guth, 'Der Gegensatz zwischen dem Oberbefehlshaber Ost und dem Chef des generalstabes des feldheers 1914/15: Die Rolle des Majors v. Haeften im Spannungsfeld zwischen Hindenburg, Ludendorff und Falkenhayn', *Militärgeschichtliche Mitteilungen*, 35 (1984), pp. 75–111.

difficulties and sometimes even the impossibility of defeating the Russians, due to insurmountable problems of time and space. Hoffmann said in spring 1915: 'It is impossible to annihiliate the Russians completely.'[30] Nevertheless, after Tannenberg the impossible started to turn into the thinkable.

To some extent, this bolder German attitude towards defeating Russia was more surprising than a hesitant and cautious one. Respect, even fear, of Russia's enormous power was a part of the Prussian military heritage. Frederick the Great, who owed his survival in the Seven Years' War only to the timely death of the Russian empress and the new Tsar's abandonment of the enemy coalition, was afraid of Russia's growing might. Bismarck was also always aware of Russian power and saw the secret of good politics 'in a good treaty with Russia'. Imperial Russia had started a huge rearmament programme after the Bosnian annexation crisis which began the last round of the pre-1914 armaments race[31] and which created growing anxiety in Germany. Chancellor von Bethmann Hollweg said that in Russia 'an amazing economic development started in this huge empire, so well equipped with inexhaustible resources, and at the same moment the Russian army was reorganised in a manner never before seen.'[32] He concluded on 7 July 1914, more than a week after the Sarajevo assassination, that 'The future belongs to Russia, which is growing and growing and is becoming an increasingly burdensome nightmare for us.'[33] The fear of this Russian rearmament was also Moltke's main argument for promoting a war 'the sooner the better'.[34] Time, German strategists believed, was working in favour of the Russians and the Entente, not of Germany. The growing fear of the Russian 'steamroller' played an important part in the pre-1914 official German mindset.[35]

30 As cited in Karl-Heinz Janssen, *Der Kanzler und der General: Die Führungskrise um Bethmann Hollweg und Falkenhayn, 1914–1916* (Göttingen: Musterschmidt, 1967), p. 90.

31 David Stevenson, *Armaments and the Coming of War: Europe, 1904–1914* (Oxford University Press, 1996).

32 Andreas Hillgruber, 'Deutsche Russland-Politik 1871–1918: Grundlagen – Grundmuster – Grundprobleme', *Saeculum*, 27 (1976), pp. 94–108, 103.

33 Kurt Riezler, *Tagebücher, Aufsätze, Dokumente*, ed. Karl Dietrich Erdmann (Deutsche Geschichtsquellen des 19. und 20. Jahrhunderts, Band 48) (Göttingen: Vandenhoeck & Ruprecht, 2008), p. 183.

34 Holger Afflerbach, *Falkenhayn: Politisches Denken und Handeln im Kaiserreich* (Munich: R. Oldenbourg Verlag, 1994), p. 147.

35 Wolfgang J. Mommsen, 'Der Topos vom unvermeidlichen Krieg: Außenpolitik und öffentliche Meinung im Deutschen Reich im letzten Jahrzehnt vor 1914', in Mommsen, *Der autoritäre Nationalstaat: Verfassung, Gesellschaft und Kultur des deutschen Kaiserreiches* (Frankfurt am Main: Fischer Taschenbuch Verlag, 1990), pp. 380–406. See also Holger Afflerbach, 'The topos of improbable war in Europe before 1914', in Afflerbach and David Stevenson (eds.), *An Improbable War? The Outbreak of World War I and European Political Culture before 1914* (New York and Oxford: Berghahn Books, 2007), pp. 161–82.

Therefore it is remarkable that a single battle, a battle which did not change Russia's numerical superiority and which did not eliminate the big Russian advantage of space, and which was furthermore outweighed by huge Russian successes on the Austrian Front, could change these long-lasting assumptions and begin to replace them with a growing feeling of German superiority. Andreas Hillgruber has argued persuasively that German attitudes towards Russia were marked by sudden swings between contradictory perceptions of Russia as a 'steamroller' or as a 'colossus with feet of clay'.[36] The year 1914 was one such moment when attitudes turned.

Symptomatic of German wartime attitudes towards Russians, Poles and other peoples in the East,[37] was a feeling of alienation from them mixed with a sense of German superiority. A good example for this was the report by the war correspondent of the *Frankfurter Zeitung*, Theodor Behrmann, who described the 100,000 or so Russian prisoners of war captured in late August 1914 in Eastern Prussia:

> The endless lines of Russian prisoners who passed my position offered a monotonous picture of stupid suffering so that I started to feel pity for this living cannon fodder. God knows, these here in front of me were no captured lions or wolves. Tolstoy's 'Cholstomjer' came to my mind, the worn down horse, so thin that you can see its ribs, which looks around with dreary eyes on its way to the slaughter house. . . . The Russian farmer . . . is, in his real self, neither a hero nor a knight; he is not fighting, he is only killing, murdering; hence his failure on the battlefield, therefore also his cattiness, his senseless cruelties.[38]

Russia, so Behrmann believed, had not learned anything from the Russo-Japanese War: the entire organism of the Russian army was rotten, the officers gutless and scheming rear-echelon cowards. Behrmann claimed that this had always been his opinion. Maybe; but the upper echelons of German politics and the army had seen the Russian army very differently only a few weeks before. But now, after Tannenberg, and close to the supposedly final victory in the West, Bethmann Hollweg's secretary compiled the 'September programme'. Its importance should not be overrated;[39] but it shows that the idea of creating buffer states in the west of the Russian Empire now became a

36 Hillgruber, *Deutsche Russland-Politik 1871–1918*, pp. 98ff.

37 Vejas Gabriel Liulevicius, *War Land on the Eastern Front: Culture, National Identity and German Occupation in World War I* (Cambridge University Press, 2000).

38 Theodor Behrmann, *Frankfurter Zeitung*, August 1914.

39 Fritz Fischer, *Griff nach der Weltmacht: Die Kriegszielpolitik des kaiserlichen Deutschland 1914–1918* (Düsseldorf: Droste, 1961).

German war aim. Initially the demands were comparatively moderate, but they tended to grow over the duration of the war.

Some believed it was possible to get rid of Russian military pressure on Germany once and for all. This started with relatively limited plans for a 'Polish border strip'[40] and escalated during the war, thus mirroring military developments. Tannenberg and the September Programme were the beginning; the idea of being able to beat Russia came later, and the Peace of Brest-Litovsk came at the end. But this was in the future. After Tannenberg the idea was to beat the Russians in a second Tannenberg and to force them to conclude a peace. Bethmann Hollweg formed an alliance with Ober Ost, especially with Hindenburg. Ober Ost promoted the idea of a battle of annihilation: the Russian army was obviously so bad that it could not resist the German army. Ideas first raised in autumn 1914 of focusing now on the Eastern Front, given the fact that the Western offensive had failed, and starting a decisive operation there, culminated in summer 1915 in the plan to destroy the Russian army in a gigantic encircling manoeuvre and to kick Russia out of the war.[41]

But these plans, advocated by Hindenburg and Ludendorff, met the resistance of officers trained in the Prussian tradition that Russia was too big to be subdued. They thought and said that a battle like Tannenberg was not easily repeatable, and saw also no solution for the geostrategic challenge of the enormity of Russian space, especially while having to wage war on the Western Front. Russian military doctrine since Kutuzov's time was that only the conquest of the entirety of Russia could force the country to conclude peace, and this was an impossible task. Chief of Staff Erich von Falkenhayn thought that it was possible to have successes against the Russians, but that Russia itself could not be subdued. He claimed that Napoleon's example did not invite imitation.[42] He also thought that the Russians knew by now the dangers of encirclement and would retreat, if necessary, into the vastness of their territories.

But Hindenburg and Ludendorff, as well as Conrad von Hötzendorf, were in favour of large encircling manoeuvres against the Russians, and for Conrad, as well as for Ober Ost, the Polish salient was too big a temptation not to try a large encircling manoeuvre. In general terms, since autumn 1914 the plans followed one basic idea. Conrad wanted to push north-eastwards, Hindenburg

40 Immanuel Geiss, *Der polnische Grenzstreifen 1914–1918: Ein Beitrag zur deutschen Kriegszielpolitik im Ersten Weltkrieg* (Hamburg and Lubeck: Matthiesen, 1960).

41 Afflerbach, *Falkenhayn*, pp. 259–65, 286–315.

42 Falkenhayn, *Die Oberste Heeresleitung*, p. 48.

and Ludendorff south-eastwards, then both armies would unite east of Warsaw, cut off large parts of the Russian army and destroy them. Falkenhayn thought this to be impossible: the Russians would escape the encirclement, and he did not have the forces necessary for such a big manoeuvre. He predicted that the Russians would retreat, if necessary, and therefore escape any encirclement. Here we may note that Conrad was out of touch with reality, even according to one of his defenders. Colonel Bauer said of him, 'His operational ideas were always broad in scope, but unfortunately he overlooked the fact that the Austrian troops were unable to realise them.'[43]

Falkenhayn was a sober strategist and followed another line: limited successes against Russia followed by generous political offers. After November 1914 he advocated a separate peace with Russia, and perhaps also with France. Endless debates followed with Hindenburg and Ludendorff, who thought that Falkenhayn was incompetent, jealous and a defeatist. In one of their discussions, Falkenhayn repeated his belief that it was impossible to defeat the Russian army: 'We do not have the preconditions for that, because it is impossible to try to annihilate an enemy who is numerically far superior, who has excellent railway connections, unlimited time and unlimited space to retreat, if necessary.' When Hindenburg insisted, repeating his opinion that the Russian army could be 'annihilated', Falkenhayn replied sarcastically on 31 August 1915 that he doubted 'that it was possible, in any conceivable way, to annihilate an enemy who was inclined to retreat, regardless of land and people, when attacked seriously, and who has the vastness of Russia at his disposal'.[44] Ludendorff called Falkenhayn a criminal who was sacrificing the chance for a final victory, and thought that he had to be fired; otherwise the war would be lost. Falkenhayn favoured a political solution to the war; Ludendorff wanted to achieve a victory in the East, then in the West. He did not favour compromises with the Russians, 'because we are strong'.[45]

Przemyśl: a Stalingrad of the First World War?

We have gone ahead of events. Now it is time to turn towards the southern part of the Eastern Front where things took a very different turn. In August 1914 Austria-Hungary had begun an offensive against the Russians which

43 Quoted by Günther Kronenbitter, 'Von "Schweinehunden" und "Waffenbrüdern": Der Koalitionskrieg der Mittelmächte 1914/15 zwischen Sachzwang und ressentiment', in Gerhard Gross (ed.), *Die Vergessene Front: Der Osten 1914/15: Ereignis, Wirkung, Nachwirkung* (Paderborn: Schöningh, 2006), p. 135.

44 Afflerbach, *Falkenhayn*, p. 309. 45 *Ibid.*

collapsed after some successes with great losses.[46] German operations against Russia in autumn 1914 were only partially successful. In the winter of 1914/15, German and Austrian troops tried to complete a big encircling manoeuvre, planned and advocated by Hindenburg and Ludendorff and also by the Austro-Hungarian Chief of Staff, Conrad von Hötzendorf, but it failed too. One of the consequences of not succeeding was that the Austrian fortress of Przemyśl, with a garrison of more than 130,000 men, remained encircled by the Russians.[47] The strategic dilemma posed by this fortress was older than January 1915; it had started with Austrian defeats in early September 1914 which were followed by the Austro-Hungarian retreat into the Carpathians.

Przemyśl, commanded by General Kusmanec, was a huge fortress and the decision was made to hold it instead of giving it up to save the troops. The fortress was relieved once, but the Russians quickly began a second attempt to envelop it, which they completed by 11 November 1914. The fortress was so strong that the Russians did not try to assault it; they encircled it and waited for it to run out of food and ammunition. They were helped by the oversized garrison of Przemyśl: according to contemporary testimonies, half of them would have sufficed to hold the fortress. Relief and breakout attempts were poorly coordinated. The Austrian column sent to help got stuck in high snow; the closest they came to it was about thirty miles. In February 1915 the Habsburg High Command informed the fortress commander that no further relief efforts would be attempted. The commandant ordered his men to destroy equipment and surrendered to the Russians on 22 March 1915. Nearly 130,000 men fell into Russian hands.[48]

The American war correspondent Stanley Washburn described long columns of Austro-Hungarian prisoners, barely guarded by Russian soldiers, marching in the direction of Lemberg.[49] He voiced the same type of stereotypes of the character of the defeated as Behrmann had advanced the year

46 Stone, *Eastern Front*, pp. 70–121; Lothar Höbelt '"So wie wir haben nicht einmal die Japaner angegriffen": Österreich-Ungarns Nordfront 1914/15', in Gross (ed.), *Die Vergessene Front*, pp. 87–120; Günther Kronenbitter, 'Von "Schweinehunden" und "Waffenbrüdern": Der Koalitionskrieg der Mittelmächte 1914/15 zwischen Sachzwang und ressentiment', in Gross (ed.), *Die Vergessene Front*, pp. 121–45.

47 Graydon A. Tunstall, *Blood on the Snow: The Carpathian Winter War of 1915* (Lawrence, KS: University Press of Kansas, 2010); Franz Forstner, *Przemyśl: Oesterreich-Ungarns bedeutendste Festung* (Vienna: Österreichischer Bundesverlag, 1987).

48 Dennis Showalter, 'By the book? Commanders surrendering in World War I', in Holger Afflerbach and Hew Strachan (eds.), *How Fighting Ends: A History of Surrender* (Oxford University Press, 2012), pp. 279–97.

49 Stanley Washburn, *On the Russian Front in World War I: Memoirs of an American War Correspondent* (New York: Robert Speller, 1982).

before with reference to Russian prisoners. The uniforms of the defeated were different, but the arrogance of the victors was identical.

The surrender of Przemyśl could easily have been a Stalingrad of the First World War. It looked, initially, as if it were the beginning of the end of Austria-Hungary and of the Central Powers. The Austrians were understandably deeply depressed and felt the first pangs of the agony of inevitable defeat. The neutrals too, especially Italy, started to believe that Austria-Hungary was finished; the government in Rome made its fateful decision to intervene in the weeks around Przemyśl's surrender.[50]

The Battle of Gorlice-Tarnów

The reason that Przemyśl did not become the *coup de grâce* for Austria or the Stalingrad of the First World War lay in the Battle of Gorlice-Tarnów – which was, perhaps, the most decisive military event on the Eastern Front between 1914 and 1917 (Map 9.2). This battle is probably less known – at least outside the camp of military historians – than Tannenberg or the Brusilov offensive, but is perhaps even more important. It was one of the most decisive battles of the entire First World War. It did not have the consequence that the victors – Germany and Austria-Hungary – also then won the war, but it enabled them to escape defeat and to be able to fight on for more than three years. For Russia it was the beginning of the end – Tsarist Russia never fully recovered from this blow.

The logic of this offensive was closely connected with the Austrian defeat at Przemyśl. Falkenhayn originally had no intention of becoming heavily engaged on the Austrian part of the Eastern Front. He considered the Western Front as the decisive theatre of war and there Germany was under constant pressure from numerically far superior Allied troops. German diplomats had other urgent agendas too; they wanted to force the general staff to

50 See Holger Afflerbach, *Der Dreibund: Europäische Großmacht – und Allianzpolitik vor dem Ersten Weltkrieg* (Veröffentlichungen der Kommission für die Neuere Geschichte Österreichs, Band 92) (Vienna: Böhlau Verlag, 2002), epilogue; Holger Afflerbach, 'Vom Bündnispartner zum Kriegsgegne: Ursachen und Folgen des italienischen Kriegseintritts im Mai 1915', in Johannes Hürter and Gian Enrico Rusconi (eds.), *Der Kriegseintritt Italiens im Mai 1915* (Schriftenreihe der Vierteljahrshefte für Zeitgeschichte) (Munich: R. Oldenbourg Verlag, 2007), pp. 53–69; Holger Afflerbach: '"... vani e terribili olocausti di vite umane ...": Luigi Bongiovannis Warnungen vor dem Kriegseintritt Italiens im Jahre 1915', in Hürter and Rusconi (eds.), *Der Kriegseintritt Italiens*, pp. 85–98.

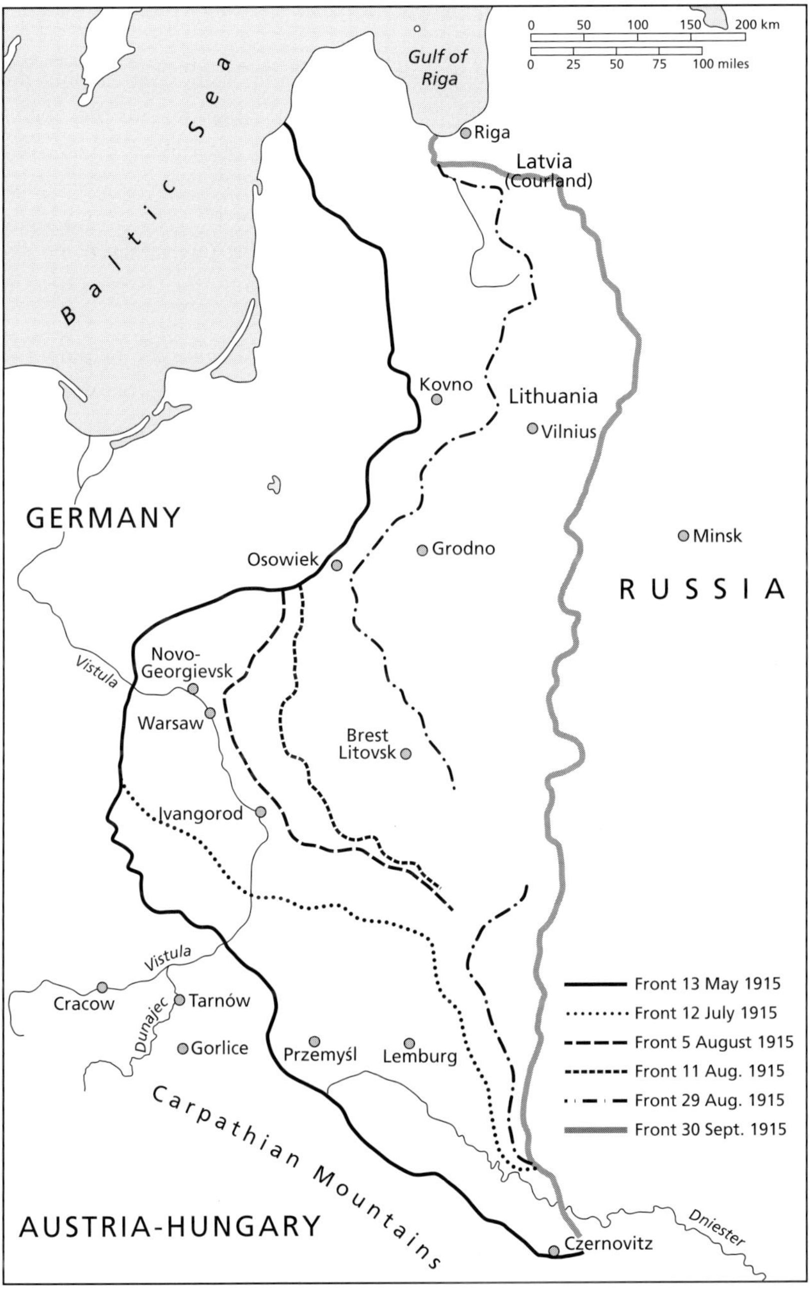

Map 9.2 The conquest of Poland and the Battle of Gorlice-Tarnów.

conquer Serbia so as to be able to get German supplies to the Dardanelles where the Ottoman Turks were under heavy Allied pressure.[51]

But the surrender of Przemyśl seemed more important than helping the Austrians. There were two main reasons: first, to avoid the collapse of this essential ally and secondly, to deter the Italians and Romanians from intervening on the Allied side. Falkenhayn thought that if Italy joined the Entente that would mean losing the war, and Conrad (for once) agreed.[52] After conquering Przemyśl, the Russian army tried to break through the Carpathian front and invade Hungary. Conrad von Hötzendorf asked urgently for German help to assist his weakening lines.

From a German perspective, there were several ways of helping the Austrians. One was to assist with a comparatively small force, between one and four divisions strong. This could have helped to stabilise the Austrian lines and strengthen the most endangered parts of the front. This was what Conrad suggested. Falkenhayn disagreed. He thought that this would not be sufficient; he was also afraid that his precious reserves would disappear piecemeal in the Austrian front lines and he would never get them back.

Falkenhayn favoured a different approach. He wanted to start a limited German offensive, attacking frontally. The task would be to relieve Russian pressure on the Austrians. After reaching well-defined and limited objectives, he would be able to pull his troops out and use them elsewhere. The units would return to his reserves and not be permanently bound to the Austrian front. Falkenhayn was notoriously miserly with his reserves – with very good reason. Reserves were the precondition for any sort of operational planning, and reserves, or the building up of reserves, were the key problem of the German general staff. All the reserves created in late 1914 by using hastily trained volunteers had been used by February and March 1915 in ultimately unsuccessful attacks on the Eastern Front. The German reserves were now minimal and this severely limited the possibilities open to the general staff. The Prussian War Ministry, however, had an idea how to create new reserves. They suggested restructuring the divisions on the Western Front, reducing the number of regiments per division from four to three, reinforcing the remaining units with new soldiers and artillery and using the freed regiments to form new divisions. By doing so, they were able to create a new army reserve of fourteen divisions without dangerously weakening the existing

51 Volker Ullrich, 'Entscheidung im Osten oder Sicherung der Dardanellen: Das Ringen um den Serbienfeldzug 1915', *Militärgeschichtliche Mitteilungen*, 32 (1982), pp. 45–63.

52 Afflerbach, *Falkenhayn*, pp. 266–85.

units. This number was not sufficient for any decisive operation in the West, for which a minimum of thirty divisions was considered necessary, but it was enough for a limited operation elsewhere. This new army reserve was both the beginning and the precondition for an impressive series of successes of the Central Powers on the Eastern Front and in the Balkans.[53]

Falkenhayn began planning where to use his new reserves in late March 1915. He wanted to free 'the front of the Austrian allies from Russian pressure'; his additional aim was to destroy the Russian capability for further offensives. But where to attack? Colonel Hans von Seeckt, who would have a prominent role in the battle, later explained the reasons for Falkenhayn's choice of Gorlice. He argued that an attack on the German part of the Eastern Front would not bring the Austrians the necessary relief. The eastern part of the Austrian front – Bukovina and Galicia – was excluded because of poor lines of communication. An attack in the Carpathians did not promise a quick result. Therefore he decided on a frontal attack in the centre of the Russian front, to fold back the entire Russian front in the Carpathians by breaking through north of it; this was the War Minister Wild von Hohenborn's summary of the matter. Seeckt said afterwards that looking at the map of the Eastern Front and bearing in mind the military and political constraints, the place to attack had been an obvious choice.[54]

Everyone in the German general staff was broadly in agreement about the operation; the only debate was over whether the attack should be launched more to the north between Pilica and the Vistula, or to the south between the Vistula and the Carpathian Mountains. Falkenhayn first favoured the northern solution, but was convinced by his advisers that the southern solution was more promising. The advantage of attacking in the area of Gorlice-Tarnów in the direction of Lemburg was that if the breakthrough was successful, the Russians would be unable to attack the flanks of the German advance because it was protected by the Carpathians in the south and the Vistula in the north. Advancing this way would mean placing the Russian army in the Carpathians in a precarious situation by threatening their flanks and their rear. They would be forced to retreat. The Russian lines of communication in the Carpathians were poor and the terrain would hinder any rapid Russian reorganisation. In a word: this was the 'Archimedian point' of the entire Russian front. A

53 *Ibid.*, p. 286.
54 'Seeckt an das Reichsarchiv, 13.11.1927', in *Der Weltkrieg 1914–1918*, vol. VII, p. 439.

successful attack would force the Russians into a hasty retreat, if they were to avoid being enveloped from the rear.

As always in military history, we have to ask what the defenders were doing at this moment. If the danger was obvious, why did the Russians not react before it was too late? This question was even more urgent because the Russian army was already severely weakened by hard fighting in the Carpathians. Nevertheless the Russian High Command did not abandon its own attack there, underestimating both the danger and the Austrians (despite being informed by Austrian deserters about the upcoming offensive[55]) and hoping that Italy – which had in the meantime promised to enter the war at the latest in mid May 1915 – would help out, so that both armies could crush Austria, the Russians from the east and the Italians from the south-west. The Russian High Command was ready and willing to give Austria the *coup de grâce*. To be able to exert pressure in the Carpathians, they had even transferred troops there from Galicia.

Therefore everything worked in favour of Falkenhayn's plan. The Russian front in Galicia was an obvious weak point and nothing was done to strengthen it. The commander of the Russian Third Army, General Dmitriev, knew that his army was going to be attacked. But the Russian High Command, used to being victorious on this front, felt safe – too safe.

What happened in the meantime on the German and Austro-Hungarian side? In mid March 1915 Falkenhayn asked Colonel von Lossberg, a member of the *Operationsabteilung*, to check the possibilities for a breakthrough in the region of Gorlice, and he asked the railway section of the general staff to prepare the transport of four German army corps to Gorlice.[56] He also asked the German Liaison Officer to the Austro-Hungarian general staff (the '*Deutscher Militärbevollmächtigte*'), General von Cramon, to collect information in the greatest secrecy about road conditions in the area and about the condition of the Russian army. Cramon told him on 8 April 1915 that 'the Russian Army . . . will not be able to withstand an attack by superior forces'.[57] Cramon thought that four army corps were probably sufficient for the task. Falkenhayn kept Conrad von Hötzendorf in the dark about his intentions until 13 April 1915. At this moment German troops were already at the railheads preparing to be shipped to Gorlice.

55 Manfried Rauchensteiner, *Der Tod des Doppeladlers: Österreich-Ungarn und der Erste Weltkrieg* (Graz: Styria Verlag, 1993), p. 212.

56 Oskar Tile von Kalm, *Gorlice* (Schlachten des Weltkriegs in Einzeldarstellungen, vol. xxx) (Berlin: Gerhard Stalling Verlag, 1930), p. 13.

57 Afflerbach, *Falkenhayn*, p. 289.

Lengthy debates about who was the 'father' of the success are therefore futile; Seeckt claimed that it was Falkenhayn and he had very good reasons for this judgement. Conrad was pleased to learn that he was getting German assistance to help bolster his difficult military situation, but this did not stop him haggling about questions of supreme command. After enervating debates, Falkenhayn and Conrad agreed that a new German army, the Eleventh, would be commanded by Generaloberst von Mackensen and his Chief of Staff, Colonel von Seeckt, but would receive its orders nominally from Conrad because they were fighting on the Austrian front. The Austro-Hungarian Fourth Army would be under Mackensen's command, too.

Falkenhayn had limited the aims of the operation: he wanted to free western Galicia from the Russians and to advance to the Lupkow Pass. These objectives seem very limited, especially if they are compared with the final success of the operation, which exceeded them by far. But he had a pressing feeling about the risks of this offensive, not only because of the unclear attitude of Italy, but also and especially because of German inferiority on the Western Front. In May 1915 1.9 million German soldiers had to fight against 2.45 million British and French in this theatre of war.[58] Understandably, Falkenhayn felt uneasy and was perpetually worried about the Western Front.

The Central Powers were able to create substantial numerical superiority in the area of attack. On the entire Eastern Front around 1.8 million Russians were fighting against 1.3 million soldiers of the Central Powers. Nevertheless, in the area of attack Falkenhayn and Conrad had created a local superiority: seventeen infantry and three-and-a-half cavalry divisions fought against fifteen-and-a-half infantry and two cavalry divisions of the Russian Third Army. In numerical terms, 357,400 German and Austrian soldiers attacked 219,000 Russians. The Central Powers also had substantially more guns, a superiority that proved to be decisive: 334 pieces of heavy artillery against the Russians' 4, and 96 trench mortars where the Russians had none.[59] The Russians were also short of shells (more because of disorganisation in Russian logistics than because of real shortages of supply, in Norman Stone's opinion).

On the morning of 2 May 1915, German and Austrian artillery fired for four hours and the Russians could not reply. The Russian troops in the first line and the reserves were annihilated before they could take part in any fighting. Then the infantry attacked and achieved a breakthrough against sometimes stiff Russian resistance. In three days three Russian lines of defence were seized.

58 Falkenhayn, *Die Oberste Heeresleitung*, pp. 247ff.
59 These figures are from *Deutschland im ersten Weltkrieg*, vol. II, p. 75.

The Russian defence was hindered by Stavka's order not to retreat because the Headquarters believed that this was a defeat of purely local importance. This belief was shared throughout large parts of the Russian army, where recognition of the magnitude of the defeat came slowly.[60] The commander of the Russian Third Army, General Dmitriev, had suggested retreating to the River San. Not following this suggestion was a huge mistake: the 11th Army was able to advance some 180 kilometres by mid May, and the Russians lost some 210,000 men in a few days around Gorlice, among them 140,000 prisoners of war.[61]

Kaiser Wilhelm II called the victory of Gorlice 'a Napoleonic concept', and Falkenhayn received the Order of the Black Eagle. The battle was undoubtedly a huge success. The material consequences were substantial and the psychological ones even greater, especially for the Austrians. One observer wrote: 'Only someone who had experienced the deep depression after the Carpathian battle can really understand what Gorlice meant [for the Austrians]: relief from unsustainable pressure, relief from most serious worry, the regaining of hope and new hopes for victory.'[62]

The breakthrough came too late to influence the Italian decision for intervention, because the government in Rome had signed the Treaty of London on 26 April 1915, only six days before Gorlice, and had already promised to enter the war on the Allied side. But the victory of Gorlice gave the Central Powers the chance to shoulder this additional burden, in the short as well as in the longer run.[63] Gorlice gave the Habsburg armies the forces and, even more importantly, the self-confidence to face the new enemy and to stop him close to the border.

The Gorlice attack reached its objective, the Lupkow Pass, on 10 May. Things were going so well that Falkenhayn and Conrad decided to let it continue and to abandon all other plans. Therefore Gorlice, originally a

60 Washburn, *On the Russian Front, passim.*

61 Holger Afflerbach, 'Najwieksze Zwysciestwo Panstw Centralnych Wi Wojnie 'Swiatowej – Bitwa Pod Gorlicami', in Andrzej Welc (ed.), *Militarne I Polityczne Znaczenie Operacji Gorlickiej W Dzialaniach Wojennych I Wojny 'Swiatowei* (Gorlice: Tow. Opieki nad Zabytkami d. Powiatu Gorlickiego i Upiekszania Miasta Gorlic z Okolica, 1995), pp. 85–95, 92.

62 August von Cramon, *Unser Oesterreichisch-Ungarischer Bundesgenosse im Weltkriege: Erinnerungen aus meiner vierjährigen Tätigkeit als bevollmächtigter deutscher General beim k.u.k. Armeeoberkommando* (Berlin: E. S. Mittler, 1922), p. 15.

63 Höbelt, 'Österreich-Ungarns Nordfront 1914/15', claims the Italians were inefficient and the danger overrated; this is true only to a certain extent. My arguments why Italy's intervention had very important consequences for the outcome of the First World War can be found in Holger Afflerbach, 'Entschied Italien den Ersten Weltkrieg?', in Rainer F. Schmidt (ed.), *Deutschland und Europa: Außenpolitische Grundlinien zwischen Reichsgründung und Erstem Weltkrieg* (Stuttgart: Franz Steiner, 2004), pp. 135–43.

limited operation, became a strategic one. The German Headquarters moved to Pless in Silesia on 8 May, a decision which shows that the general staff expected more decisive action in the East in the coming months. Indeed Gorlice was the first of a series of victories on the Eastern Front arising from the continuous progress of Mackensen's army, forcing the Russians to retreat in the Carpathians and later also in Russian Poland. The Russians started the 'Great Retreat' and saved their army, but had to give up Warsaw and Poland, Lithuania and Courland. They left behind them 'scorched earth' and millions of refugees (3.3 million followed the Russian army eastwards at the end of 1915).[64] From May to September 1915 the Russian army lost 1.41 million men; from the outbreak of war until the end of 1915, they had lost 2.2 million men.[65]

The losses were one important aspect of these events. Another equally important element arose from their political consequences. Falkenhayn and Conrad both suggested to their political leaders in late spring 1915 that the military successes enabled them to offer Russia a generous separate peace. Despite the favourable situation on the Eastern Front, they advised not insisting on territorial concessions or war indemnities and wanted to offer Russia an alliance and even free transit through the Dardanelles.[66] But the Russian government remained stubborn. The Tsar's answer to German overtures was that Russia was bound to its Allies and could not conclude a separate peace: 'My reply can only be a negative one.' Diplomatic observers reported that Russia did not feel beaten because the Russians did not consider Courland or Poland as Russia, and felt able to continue the struggle because of their vast territory.

This points to a very important argument. The Russians had a particular interpretation of past military events. Looking back to the defeat of invaders like Napoleon or Charles XII, they felt invincible and thought that the vastness of space at their disposal made it impossible for them to lose a war of invasion and impossible for their enemies to win. As has been said, Clausewitz had considered two conditions necessary for a Russian success: a firm government (the government in 1915 was firm, probably too firm) and 'loyal and steadfast' people. Here was the weak point. The Russian government had grown out of touch with its own people and disregarded the influence of growing internal difficulties and unrest and also its loss of prestige and faith. There was also a

64 Vejas Gabriel Liulevicius, 'Von "Oberost" nach "Ostland"?', in Gross (ed.), *Die Vergessene Front*, pp. 295–311, 298.

65 *Deutschland im ersten Weltkrieg*, vol. II, p. 81.

66 Afflerbach, *Falkenhayn*, p. 301.

growing feeling that for a multi-national empire like the Russian one, time was running out.

The year 1915 was a crucial moment in which the Tsarist government missed several excellent opportunities to quit the war under favourable, or at least acceptable, conditions and thereby save the country from its monstrous misfortunes later in the twentieth century. The reasons for this refusal were the fear of being diplomatically isolated from the Western Allies and of then being at the mercy of an arrogant and dominating Germany.[67]

This ill-fated Russian stubbornness also changed German attitudes. Plans to move the German frontier further to the East – the 'Polnische Grenzstreifen' – became more pronounced. Ludendorff started to conquer the Baltic territories – he called them 'his kingdom' – and Bethmann Hollweg was tempted to play the 'Polish card'. The political context of military events was now very different from what it had been before Gorlice.

In addition, the German advance brought their soldiers into close contact with Eastern territories and their populations. As almost all the sources show, they experienced feelings of estrangement, unfamiliarity and also of disgust towards the 'filthy' or 'dirty' Eastern territories.[68] Nevertheless recent research on this topic rightly warns us not to overstretch the continuities between the First and Second World Wars. German soldiers of the First World War were generally friendly and accommodating towards the Jewish population, with whom they shared a common language.[69]

The Brusilov offensive

During the Great Retreat, the Russians had lost a territory of the size of France. Up to 7.5 million refugees were moving eastwards; these huge numbers of refugees destabilised Russian society.[70] The country was experiencing deep economic problems: rolling stock was not being properly maintained, food and ammunition were not where they were needed and inflation was rising rapidly.[71] The prestige of the government and the army was severely damaged,

67 Examples for this attitude can be found in the following: Alexander Kerensky, *The Kerensky Memoirs* (London: Cassell, 1966); and Alexander Isvolski, *Recollections of a Foreign Minister* (New York and Toronto: Doubleday, Page & Co., 1921).

68 Liulevicius, *War Land*, *passim*.

69 Peter Hoeres, 'Die Slawen: Perzeptionen des Kriegsgegners bei den Mittelmächten. Selbst- und Feindbild', in Gross (ed.), *Die Vergessene Front*, pp. 179–200.

70 Peter Gatrell, *A Whole Empire Walking: Refugees in Russia during World War I* (Bloomington, IN: Indiana University Press, 2005).

71 Stone, *Eastern Front*, pp. 194–231.

but the leadership was still hanging on to the example of Kutusov and did not lose hope of finishing the war victoriously.

Despite growing internal difficulties, the Great Retreat was for the moment a military success.[72] The Russian Commander-in-Chief, General Alexejev, had shortened the long Russian front by giving up the Polish salient, and as a result of their advance the Central Powers had serious problems with their supply lines. This gave Russia the breathing space needed to survive for another year and even to prepare new offensives. Russia stayed in the war out of fear of isolation, because she was afraid of being dominated by the Central Powers and because she felt bound to her Allies. Therefore it is not very surprising that the last big success of the Russians in this war was linked to a military campaign promised to their alliance partners.

From 6 to 8 December 1915 the Allied military leadership met at Chantilly to coordinate their strategy for 1916. The Allied Powers saw the reason for the military successes of the Central Powers in 1915 – the defence of the Dardanelles and of their front in France, the successes in Russia and the conquest of Serbia – as the result of the ability of the Central Powers to use interior lines to deploy troops rapidly, to build local superiorities and to have reserves always where they were needed. To counterbalance this advantage, the Allied Powers decided to attack on all fronts at the same time. This would prevent the Central Powers from pulling out reserves at one place to send them somewhere else; the pressure deriving from the large numerical superiority of the Entente powers would be enormous and at some point the Central Powers' front would break. This was the hope behind a collective endeavour which became more famous for its distinctive parts – the Battle of the Somme starting in July 1916, the Isonzo battles on the Italian Front, and the Brusilov offensive in the East (Map 9.3).

This attack, named after Alexei Brusilov, one of the ablest Russian generals, was launched against the Austrians on the south-western front. Originally the Russian main effort was to be directed against the Germans, but a large attack in the north at Lake Naroch in March 1916 had failed miserably. General Evert and his peers followed the example of the Western Front and started the attack after heavy bombardments. As with all attacks in the West, they failed. As a consequence, many Russian generals developed an outspoken defeatist attitude and did not believe in success, perhaps rightly so.

Brusilov, previously commander of the Russian Eighth Army and, since March 1916, commander of the entire south-western front, had offered to

72 *Ibid.*, pp. 165–93.

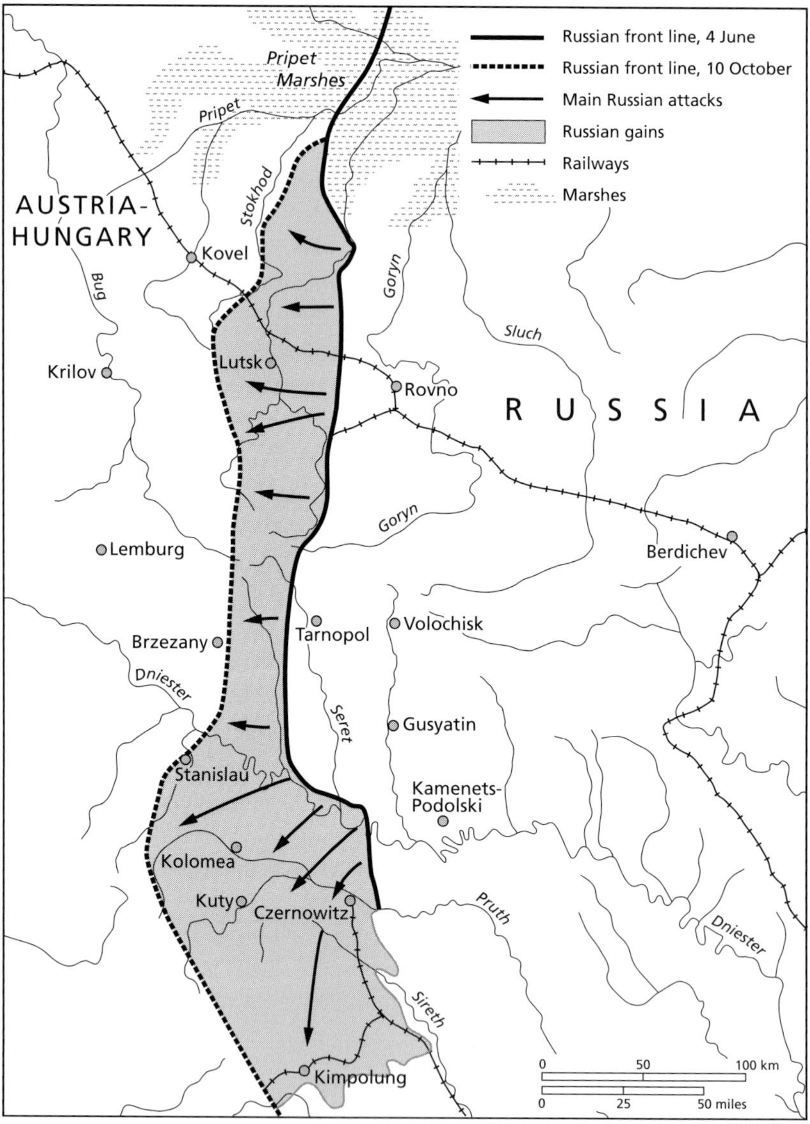

Map 9.3 The Brusilov offensive.

attack with his own reserves and finally got permission to do so. He decided to use the element of surprise. He trained his troops very carefully – even using models of Austrian trenches to train his soldiers – let them dig attack trenches, but did not prepare for a long preliminary artillery bombardment. He also decided to attack on an unusually large sector of the front, so making it impossible for the Austrians to close down a local breakthrough with troops from another sector of the front. His attack also started earlier than the others, to relieve the Italians who were suffering an Austrian attack in the Tyrol (the so-called punitive or '*Strafexpedition*').

The most prominent feature of Brusilov's attack was that it was conducted without a significant numerical superiority. In the sector of attack some 600,000 Russians were fighting around 500,000 Austrians who were entrenched and had an advantage in medium and heavy artillery.[73] The attack hit the Austrian lines on a large sector of the front, and very quickly became a major success. The reasons for this are the subject of debate. The impression contemporaries had of Russian superiority in artillery was ill-founded. But there are two major explanations which do not exclude one another. The first one is that Brusilov's decision to use the element of surprise instead of trying to amass an overwhelming superiority had worked. Instead of concentrating all his forces on a small sector, carrying out lengthy and heavy bombardments of the enemy lines before attacking them, and therefore indicating his intentions long beforehand, Brusilov ordered his troops to attack after a very short bombardment, on a very large sector of the front, out of attack trenches which were dug in preparation beforehand. The surprise worked perfectly; the Austrian Fourth Army (commanded by Erzherzog Joseph Ferdinand) disintegrated and fled backwards; this led to a similar fate for the Austrian Seventh Army (under General Pflanzer Baltin). The Austro-Hungarian army lost around 200,000 men in a few days; many of them surrendered.

Therefore one could argue, as Norman Stone does, that this success was the consequence of revolutionary new tactics and able and imaginative leadership. On the other side, the argument of Austrian weakness and mistakes must be discussed. The Austrian trenches in this sector of the front were excellent; they were inspected shortly before the attack began and were considered to be of high standard.[74] A German general, Stolzmann, had visitied the Austrian trenches in March 1916 and concluded that a major Russian success was out of the question, as long as the Russians did not bring in huge reinforcements.[75] But, as the in-depth analysis of the Austrian troops and their commanders shows, there was a great deal of carelessness and an atmosphere of a 'holiday-camp' on the Austrian side.[76] Here we may propose a hypothesis: on this part of the Austrian front, there was established a well-developed version of the

73 Stone, *Eastern Front*, p. 239. 74 *Ibid.*, p. 242.
75 *Der Weltkrieg 1914–1918*, vol. x, pp. 442f. 76 Stone, *Eastern Front*, p. 241.

'live-and-let-live' system Tony Ashworth described as operating on the Western Front.[77] The Austrian soldiers – from the soldiers in the trenches up to the army commander – had made themselves comfortable in the trench system.[78] Brusilov's new tactic did not include a warning that preparations for a heavy attack were under way in the weeks and months beforehand, so the attack came out of the blue. The officers had not ordered attacks on the Russian entrenching parties, 'no doubt for fear they would be driven into troublesome minor action'[79] – reflecting an Austrian reluctance to engage in costly activism which was another typical element of the 'live-and-let-live' system. The Austrian troops had obviously thought that the war would end without seeing any major activity on this front.

The Austrian High Command bore a large share of the responsibility. Conrad von Hötzendorf was obsessed with punishing the Italians and had pulled some of his best troops out of the Eastern Front to start an offensive in the Tyrol. Therefore he had, as he admitted himself, 'critically weakened' the strength of the Eastern Front.[80] The attack against the Italians (the *Strafexpedition*) started promisingly, but ran aground quite quickly. Brusilov could exploit Conrad's mistake.

Therefore at least two factors were responsible for the Russian success: the Austrian Front was vulnerable, and the Russians had a new tactic which worked well. Brusilov was extremely successful in causing the Austrians enormous losses. Falkenhayn did not want to help out with German reserves – he was still fighting his ill-fated Battle of Verdun at the time – and first forced Conrad to stop his offensive in Italy. Only when a real and complete breakdown of the Austro-Hungarian army seemed to be both possible and imminent did he start to help out with German troops. This help began with German divisions that were supposed to give the Austro-Hungarian Front a more rigid structure of resistance; these troops were called in the vernacular, military 'corsets', or '*Korsettstangen*' for the Austrians.

77 Tony Ashworth, *Trench Warfare 1914–1918: The Live and Let Live System* (London: Macmillan, 1980). A similar analysis for the Eastern Front seems urgent to me, for the single fact that, for example, all three Great Powers had drafted around 1.5 million Polish soldiers and therefore the question of unofficial 'arrangements' between Poles in the front lines is an interesting one. Piotr Szlanta mentions that during Christmas 1914 Polish troops on both sides of the trenches were singing Polish Christmas songs. See Piotr Szlanta, 'Der Erste Weltkrieg von 1914 bis 1915 als identitätsstiftender Faktor für die moderne polnische Nation', in Gross (ed.), *Die Vergessene Front*, pp. 153–64.

78 Rudolf Jerabek, 'Die Brussilowoffensive 1916: Ein Wendepunkt der Koalitionskriegführung der Mittelmächte', 2 vols. (PhD thesis, University of Vienna, 1982). It is an excellent study which unfortunately was never published as a proper book.

79 Stone, *Eastern Front*, p. 241.

80 Afflerbach, *Falkenhayn*, p. 412.

The next step was to establish a German High Command on the Eastern Front. Conrad and Falkenhayn opposed this idea when it became clear that Hindenburg would be the obvious choice. Falkenhayn knew that his opponents from Ober Ost would make it impossible for him to dispose of any reserves under their command, and therefore that such a command structure would be an enormous obstacle to any further strategic planning. In the end, with the Central Powers under enormous strain as a result of the Brusilov and the Somme offensives, he and Conrad had to give way. Hindenburg became commander of the largest part of the Eastern Front – and shortly afterwards German Chief of Staff, replacing Falkenhayn himself.

The reason for Falkenhayn's dismissal was the Romanian declaration of war on 27 August 1916. The Romanian government long hesitated over this step, but now the success of the Brusilov offensive seemed to be the death knell for Austria, and therefore the Romanians wanted to get their share of the spoils. The news of Romania's declaration of war seemed to be the end for the Central Powers. Falkenhayn had to go and Hindenburg und Ludendorff were appointed to command the army in his place.

It became clear very quickly, though, that the Romanian danger was completely overrated. German, Austrian and Bulgarian troops, invading from the south under the command of Mackensen and from the west under the command of Falkenhayn, conquered the largest part of Romania in a few months. The poorly equipped Romanian army could not focus on one front only but had to shift its troops back and forth, and was overwhelmed from both sides. Bucharest was taken on 6 December 1916. Shortly afterwards the Central Powers made a peace offer.

Norman Stone considered the entry of Romania into the war a major liability for the Entente. Instead of deciding the war at a moment when things seemed to be on the very edge, the country was overrun by the Central Powers which afterwards squeezed raw materials out of the country – raw materials which helped them, according to Stone, to continue the war until 1918. For Russia, Romania was indeed a strain on its already over-extended front lines and resources.

If Romania's intervention was a consequence of Brusilov's success, his offensive must be considered a disaster and not praised, as it is by Stone, as the 'most brilliant victory of the war'.[81] This is true in all other aspects except one: Brusilov was indeed able to do much harm to the Austro-Hungarian army. He damaged its fighting power in what may have been a decisive way.

81 Stone, *Eastern Front*, p. 235.

In all other respects, his attack was a disaster in military as well as political terms. In military terms, the Brusilov offensive and the attack at the Somme failed to achieve their purpose and their strategic objective – victory over the Central Powers. Germany and Austria-Hungary won a defensive success of enormous magnitude. The events in the summer of 1916 had proved that the entire forces of the Entente did not suffice to overrun them.

And yet on the other hand, the success cost the Central Powers dearly, with the feelings of deep exhaustion and material inequality overshadowing any feeling of triumph, and seducing them to radicalise the seemingly endless war. One step in this direction was to slam the door on a separate peace with Russia. Here is another decisive feature of the Eastern Front: the Central Powers offered Russia golden bridges to get out of the war. A political settlement that ended the war on the Eastern Front years earlier might have saved Russia from the consequences of total defeat, civil war and the rest of the communist period of rule. But this was not to be; the moment in which a compromise peace in the East was still in the air ended in October 1916.

Even before then, in August 1915, the Central Powers had occupied Warsaw and Russian Poland. The question was what to do with them. On 19 August, Bethmann Hollweg produced his Polish proclamation and promised the Poles their liberation from the 'Russian yoke'.[82] Despite this proclamation, as long as there was hope of reaching a political settlement with Russia, the fate of Poland was a question left open. After all, restoring Polish independence would mean reopening the question of Polish territories controlled by Germany and Austria-Hungary. The Central Powers' plans were not very imaginative and dealt only with the Russian share of Poland; moreover, both Germany and Austria-Hungary started to haggle over who should control Russian Poland in the future.[83] The more stubborn the Russians were, the more determined the Germans became to move forward and try to use the Poles for their own future political designs in Eastern Europe.

Plans for Poland were closely linked with the hope of creating a Polish army against the Russians. Already in autumn 1915 the German general staff had had this idea; it was realised in November 1916 when the Central Powers proclaimed the foundation of a 'Kingdom of Poland', of course without being able to promise something substantial to the Poles. The Austrians fancied the

82 Afflerbach, *Falkenhayn*, p. 314.

83 Still excellent, Werner Conze, *Polnische Nation und Deutsche Politik im Ersten Weltkrieg* (Cologne and Graz: Böhlau Verlag, 1958); see also Heinz Lemke, *Allianz und Rivalität: Die Mittelmächte und Polen im ersten Weltkrieg (bis zur Februarrevolution)* (Berlin: Akademie Verlag, 1977).

so-called 'Austro-Polish solution', a unification of Galicia and Russian Poland under Habsburg rule, which at least had the logical advantage of answering the question of what would happen next with Galicia. It had the disadvantage that Austria-Hungary was the weaker partner in the alliance and yet asked for the bigger part of the spoils. The question of Poland was a major conflict between Germany and Austria-Hungary for the rest of the war. The story of the German and Austro-Hungarian military government in Poland and in the Baltic is extremely interesting *per se*, but cannot be dealt with here in any detail.[84] But it is worth mentioning that the *Polenproklamation* was a disaster in terms of recruiting large numbers of Polish volunteers.

The Polish perspective on the First World War is somewhat different. From the Polish point of view, the disastrous fight among the three empires was a blessing because it led to the defeat of all three partitioning powers and the resurrection of a united and independent Poland. From the perspective of the Central Powers and of Russia, the likelihood of finding a compromise peace was becoming more and more remote, though hopes of realising it were still alive.

Here is the context in which to judge the effect of the Brusilov offensive on the outcome of the war. Some give Brusilov praise. Norman Stone writes that he was 'the best type of commander – striking the fear of God into his subordinates, but never to the point where they became terrified of responsibility',[85] but his success can be compared with that of Ludendorff's offensive on the Western Front in 1918: a successful attack which did much damage to the enemy, but which failed to achieve its objective. The Russian government had for too long put its trust in the seeming certainty that the history of the Napoleonic experience would repeat itself: that the vastness of Russia would make it impossible for the Central Powers to win; that the Russian army could always retreat; and that time and space were working entirely in Russia's favour. This was not true because Russia's internal situation took a turn for the worse and ended in catastrophe. It is undeniable that Russia experienced economic growth during the war, but her war effort was hindered by a transport crisis; rolling stock was in a poor condition, grain and ammunition were available but not where they were needed, the big cities were without

84 See Liulevicius, *War Land*, *passim*; Conze, *Polnische Nation*; and Stephan Lehnstaedt, 'Das Militärgeneralgouvernement Lublin: Die "Nutzbarmachung" Polens durch Österreich-Ungarn im Ersten Weltkrieg', *Zeitschrift für Ostmitteleuropa-Forschung*, 61:1 (2012), pp. 1–26. Lehnstaedt demolishes the idea of a more 'benign' Austrian attitude towards the Poles (in comparison with German views and policies).

85 Stone, *Eastern Front*, p. 238.

supplies and the growing disorganisation and hunger led to revolution in March 1917. The Tsar abdicated but the new government, especially Kerensky, decided to fight on. In summer 1917 Kerensky started a new offensive against the Austrians, again led by Brusilov, which had early successes – but they faded away rapidly. Kerensky's insistence on staying in the war threw the country into the abyss of the second revolution, towards the Bolshevik take-over and finally to the peace negotiations at Brest-Litovsk, which, poorly handled by the Russians, completed the disaster on the Eastern Front.

Conclusion

The Eastern Front during the First World War is called 'the forgotten front'.[86] The events are of a daunting level of complexity, in part because of the multi-ethnicity of this theatre of war, and the numerous languages necessary to understand the full implications and viewpoints and vicissitudes of different nationalities.

The immediate as well as the lasting consequences of the fighting on the Eastern Front are stark and fundamental. On the Eastern Front we find the origins of the complete defeat of Russia and the collapse of its government which had overstretched the military capacity of the country. The loss of the war, connected with the revolution and regime change, was a result of the relentness stubbornness of both the Tsarist regime and of the Kerensky government. What Ludendorff did in Germany, the Tsarist government did to a greater extent in Russia: both pushed the war effort beyond the capacity of the army to win it. Germany, unlike Russia, never had an offer on the table from its enemies to leave the war on the basis of the status quo. Russia's government had several of them and refused to save itself for reasons which were, from an historical perspective, secondary compared with the necessities of bailing out of a disastrous war. Therefore the first reason for the catastrophic defeat of Russia on the Eastern Front was less the inability to organise transport and logistics properly – one of Norman Stone's main points – but rather the blind determination to continue this war while ignoring all signs of the coming catastrophe, in the hope that the story of Napoleon and Kutusov would repeat itself. It didn't, and the descent of Russia into civil war and the communist period was the outcome.

The Austro-Hungarian Empire won the war in the East, but disintegrated less because of the – comparatively minor – pressure exerted by the Italians,

86 See the title of the quoted volume of Gross (ed.), *Die Vergessene Front*.

but more because of the centrifugal powers of its nationalities. By early 1918, the Austrian army was the shell of an empire in the process of dissolution.

On the German side, the outcome was equally disastrous, and for a reason which led to further catastrophes a mere twenty-three years later. The notion that Russia was 'a house of cards' and that it was possible to defeat her decisively and completely was a precondition for the disastrous Operation Barbarossa in 1941. Generals always plan the last war. In 1914–17, the Russians thought about Kutuzov; in 1941 Hitler and his generals thought about the Eastern Front in the First World War – and both showed that history can be a very dangerous guide, if you trust too much in the value of past success.

10

The Italian Front

NICOLA LABANCA

A neglected front

In the best general and international histories, references to the Italian-Austrian Front in the First World War are rare, and often inaccurate.[1] The responsibility for this neglect lies not only on the shoulders of international historians, nor can it be explained only by the language barrier. The roots of the problem are not only global but also local.

One reason was that, from very early on, there was both in Italy and in the Austro-Hungarian Empire, little of the institutional support the war effort enjoyed elsewhere. This was not a popular war, as it was initially elsewhere, and thus was easily forgotten. The Empire dissolved in 1918 and 1919, and in Italy the rise of the fascist regime in the long run obscured rather than deepened the memory of Italian participation in the Great War. For twenty years the Italian dictatorship permitted the erection of imposing war memorials and helped construct myths about the war, but the public and private memories of war did not coincide. Later, during the Cold War, when Italy and Austria become democracies, nationalist prejudices and language barriers between Italians and Austrians for a long time prevented a dialogue either among historians or in the general public. After the end of the Cold War, two decades of national revival in former Eastern bloc countries did not help, nor did the Yugoslav civil wars. All these factors made it difficult to study and interpret the war effort of the Habsburg Empire. In a word, national

The author wishes to thank Dr Oswald Überegger (Hildsheim University) and Matthias Egger (Innsbruck University): without their competent help, the necessary bibliography of German-speaking literature would have been more incomplete.

1 Exceptions to the rule are Gerhard Hirschfeld, Gerd Krumeich and Irina Renz (eds.), *Enzyklopädie Erster Weltkrieg* (Paderborn: Schöningh, 2003); and John Horne (ed.), *A Companion to World War I* (Chichester: Wiley-Blackwell, 2010). The latter contains Giorgio Rochat, 'The Italian Front, 1915–18', pp. 82–96, and Mark Cornwall, 'Austria-Hungary and "Yugoslavia"', pp. 369–85.

particularities – Italian and Austrian – obscured our understanding of the Italian-Austrian Front in the Great War.

Another reason was the imbalance between the two sides. An ancient empire faced a young nation-state, which defeated it. Vienna fought on at least three fronts (Eastern/Russian, south-western/Italian and southern/Balkan) while Rome, the last of the Great Powers, focused almost entirely on its Alpine-Karst front; their war efforts were clearly very different. Nonetheless they faced common challenges and sometimes found similar solutions. It is clearly time to go beyond old national hostilities in our understanding of a war whose hardships both populations shared.

A history of the Italian fronts is essential in creating a more comprehensive and global interpretation of the history of the First World War. The Western Front has dominated discussion long enough, though its decisive position in the outcome of the war is not in doubt. Much about the Great War becomes clearer once we shift our attention south and east to the Italian-Austrian frontier.[2]

A battlefield different from the other fronts

The first distinctive element in this story is the terrain on which Italy and Austria-Hungary fought. It was in many ways different from both the Western and the Eastern Fronts. The line was not straight but described a great double curve (a large S) about 600 kilometres long, with two major highlights: the Austrian Tyrol-Trentino, penetrating up to the Po Valley, and the Italian Friuli, framed by the Alps to the north and north-east and by the Karst in the south-east. Looking at the theatre of war from west to east, there were areas – such as Cadore – where passes and valleys were almost all above 2,000 metres. The border was in the mountains 80 per cent of the time, and often in the high mountains – sometimes, indeed, the mountainous character of the terrain made the border impassable. This was the realm of the 'white war', fought between snow and glaciers, between the Stelvio Pass and the Adamello range of the Alps. Farther east, in the Carnic Alps, the conflict took on the most celebrated form of mountain warfare, that of small Alpine units.

Further east, in the valley from Bovec/Plezzo to Tolmino, dominated by Monte Nero, and then to the plateau of Bainsizza and Gorizia, it began to be possible for larger units to operate, even if their movements were hampered

2 Jay Winter (ed.), *The Legacy of the Great War: Ninety Years On* (Columbia, MO: University of Missouri Press, 2009).

by the River Soca / Isonzo, which runs through the valley. From the Austrian side these positions could be seen as ideal positions to defend against superior forces: in front of them, a great stream of water; at their back, a ridge from where they could shoot Italians as if from a ten-storey house. In some sense, Austrian positions were a land fortified by nature, with the mountains a natural strength.

Finally, the last stretch was the realm of the Karst, or 'Carso' in Italian, a barren terrain, with its characteristic erosion and sinkholes. It was a land difficult to turn into a trench system, one in which artillery shelling produced dangerous rock splinters. Here was a terrain controlled by the Italians on the lower areas, but from which it was difficult to climb under the fire of Austrian higher positions.

In a word, the Italian side was obviously and naturally disadvantaged, made worse by the fact that the Empire had fortified strategic points in the Trentino salient. In contrast, Italian fortifications were recent and poorly constructed. On this front, lines of communications also favoured the Austrians. There were only a few lines running from the Italian side, with a single-track railway, which at the beginning of the war made it difficult to move Italian troops up the line. In contrast, there were multiple lines and railways on the easier Austrian side.[3]

From the very beginning, this terrain and these logistical constraints made everything more rudimentary and more difficult on the Italian-Austrian Front compared to the Western Front. The trenches system here was not the same as the one in France and Flanders, and the contrasts were sharper on the Italian than on the Austrian side. Later, when new tactics were put into practice in 1916–17, or when battles of materiel (from big guns to tanks) replaced at least partially human effort as in 1917–18, differences between the Italian-Austrian Front and the Western Front grew sharper. Posing the question of how to use tanks on the Karst, and how to make them cross the Piave or the Isonzo rivers was not the same as posing the same question in France or Belgium. The sheer diversity in topography made it more difficult for international observers (and for later historians) to understand the peculiarities of the Italian-Austrian Front: hence their relative undervaluation of its special difficulties.

3 *Österreich-Ungarns letzter Krieg, 1914–1918*, Hrsg. vom österreichischen Bundesministerium für Heereswesen und vom Kriegsarchiv, 8 vols. (Vienna: Verlag der Militärwissenschaftlichen Mitteilungen, 1930–8), vol. II, p. 352, vol. V, p. 632; and Ministero della guerra, Comando del corpo di stato maggiore, Ufficio storico, *L'esercito Italiano nella Grande Guerra (1915–1918)* (Rome, 1927–88).

Different strategies and war aims

However, if topography drew Italy and Austria together on this mountainous terrain, the war aims of the two sides were nevertheless worlds apart. Vienna entered the war in July 1914[4] in order to preserve its own role in the Balkans and Central Europe, under the illusion that it could win a short and local war – a general belief at that time. But by 1916 Austria realised that it was in a war of survival. Given this depressing general picture, Austria's aim was to come to terms with its former ally and now despised enemy, Italy.

On the other hand, Liberal Italy would rather not have entered the war, for which the Liberal ruling elite knew it was quite unprepared.[5] Therefore their first line in 1914 was one of benevolent neutrality. Once in the war in 1915, however, Sidney Sonnino and his allies saw the opportunity to use the war to regain the Trentino, South Tyrol, Trieste, Istria and Dalmatia (in addition to various colonial territories too). Because of these large ambitions the defeat of the enemy, the Habsburg Empire, became its primary objective. Winning the war, for the Italian ruling elite, was a matter of national identity, a way to reconfirm Italian prestige as a Great Power. Austria could live without defeating Italy, but Italy – the strictly conservative Italy of Sidney Sonnino and of his nationalist supporters – would not survive a war without victory. A political debate soon arose in Rome about whether they wanted to defeat Austria or to dismember it, but overcoming Austria was the objective. Given divergent war aims, which moved further apart after 1917, military strategy in the two countries could not have been more different.

There was one aspect of the war they did share: both conducted the war along lines different from the plans they had envisaged before summer 1914. On the one side, in July 1914 General Luigi Cadorna, Chief of the Italian general staff, had inherited a '*piano di guerra*' from Alberto Pollio, who was a strong supporter of the Triple Alliance including Austria: but it was a plan for a defensive war. Between August and September Cadorna began to prepare a new, offensive plan. On the other side, General Franz Conrad von Hötzendorf had thought for years that Austria should have punished its faithless ally: his plan was to take the offensive quickly and decisively against Italy, with a combined attack from the Trentino and from the Isonzo, even before that against Russia or Serbia. But, like the Italians, he too had to change his mind,

4 Manfried Rauchensteiner, *Der Tod des Doppeladlers: Österreich-Ungarn und der Erste Weltkrieg* (Graz: Styria Verlag, 1993).

5 Mario Isnenghi and Giorgio Rochat, *La grande guerra 1914–1918* (Florence: La nuova Italia, 2000).

since by 1914 Serbia and Russia came first. Conrad was therefore forced to fight Italy defensively.

The strategies of the two sides diverged immediately. The Habsburg Empire was committed both on the Eastern Front against Russia, and on the Balkan front against Serbia. There was also the risk of being asked to help on the Western Front too, when the Italian Front settled into a defensive stalemate in 1914–15. While occasionally taking on the offensive, including the 'punitive' or *Strafexpedition*, on the Asiago front in 1917, Vienna maintained a holding position until the preparation for Caporetto in late 1917. This was a strategy of maintaining the status quo, typical of a great empire bent on holding its position of advantage.

For the smaller power, Liberal Italy, on the other side, war meant offensive operations. Many in command of other European armies believed in the 'spirit of the offensive'. It did not matter if it was put in terms of the 'sacred egoism' of the nationalist Sonnino or the 'Delenda Austria' of democratic interventionists: Italy had to attack. To 'liberate' Trent and Trieste, the most democratic leaders among the irredentists called for offensives. To be sure, after Caporetto in late 1917, Italy was momentarily forced on the defensive: but soon another offensive became even more necessary, to regain the lost territories – and to expand the nation to its rightful boundaries.

The end of the conflict pushed Austria and Italy even further apart. The old Empire was destroyed and its territory divided. Italy, the last of the Great Powers, came to Versailles – along with much more powerful Britain, France and the United States – finally a decision-maker in Europe. For Italy, the outcome of the peace was not as rosy as expectations at its outset.

Two (even if not entirely) different armies

Let us return to the matter of different strategies suiting different war aims. The Austro-Hungarian Empire and the Kingdom of Italy had two very different military structures at their disposal. It was not so much the size of the population of both countries respectively – about 50 million in Austria-Hungary and 34 million in Italy – which made the key difference. Indeed, the recruitment system of the two armies was based on a *national* and non-local territorial conscription, which enabled Vienna to keep different nationalities under control, and which in Rome helped reduce fears of past regional divisions interfering with current military plans.

Even the size of the two armed forces facing each other was similar. Austria before the war had a standing army of about 440,000, which expanded to

2 million after the outbreak of the war. Italy had 275,000 men under arms in peacetime, but by December 1914 its army had expanded to over 1.1 million men. This apparent Austrian advantage paled though, since Italy fought on one front, whereas Austria fought on three. The Austrian problem in fighting the war is illustrated too by the fact that both Italy and Austria spent the same proportion of their national income on military expenditure before the war – 10.6 per cent.

Separating the armies too were different traditions, political roles and professional cultures. In terms of traditions, for centuries the Austrian army had been the bulwark of the throne and the Empire. In Italy the army was a new creation from the period of Unification, and it embodied the strength of the nation-state. Furthermore, the pre-war record of the Italian army was not particularly glorious, not to mention its frequent use against labour unrest and protest, from the state of domestic siege in 1898 to the 'Red Week' in 1914.

For these reasons, the political weight of the military within the state was entirely different in the two countries. In Austria, as in Germany, the army was very close to the emperor.[6] In Liberal Italy, in peacetime Parliament and in particular the minister of war played a more significant role in Italy than in Austria. While there was resentment against the militarisation of politics, Liberal Italy had some political resources to use against the creation of a 'garrison state' in the Prussian (and partly Austrian) model.[7] Even while weakened, Parliament continued to function in Italy while it was suspended in Austria from 1914 to 1917. The political power of Franz Conrad von Hötzendorf was hardly surprising in Austria; and neither was the less powerful position in Italy of Luigi Cadorna.[8]

The social structure of the officer corps was also different. In Austria, as everywhere, the aristocracy played a diminishing role, but one-quarter of all

6 Gunther E. Rothenberg, *The Army of Francis Joseph* (West Lafayette, IN: Purdue University Press, 1976), pp. 177, 180, 218, 198, 202.

7 John Gooch, *Army, State, and Society in Italy, 1870–1915* (Houndmills: Macmillan, 1989); Giovanna Procacci, *Soldati e prigionieri italiani nella Grande Guerra, con una raccolta di lettere inedite* (Rome: Editori Riuniti, 1993); Giovanna Procacci, 'La Prima Guerra Mondiale', in Giuseppe Sabbatucci and Vittorio Vidotto (eds.), *Storia d'Italia*, vol. IV: *Guerre e Fascismo* (Rome and Bari: Laterza, 1997); and Nicola Labanca, 'Zona di Guerra', in Mario Isnenghi and Daniele Ceschin (eds.), *Gli italiani in guerra: conflitti, identità, memorie dal Risorgimento ai nostri giorni*, vol. III: *La Grande Guerra: dall'Intervento alla 'Vittoria Mutilata'* (Turin: Utet, 2008), pp. 606–19.

8 Hermann J. W. Kuprian, 'Warfare – welfare: Gesellschaft, Politik und Militarisierung Österreich während des Ersten Weltkrieges', in Brigitte Mazohl-Wallnig, Hermann J. W. Kuprian and Gunda Barth-Scalmani (eds.), *Ein Krieg, zwei Schützengräben: Österreich-Italien und der Erste Weltkrieg in den Dolomiten 1915–1918* (Bolzano: Athesia, 2005); and Hermann J. W. Kuprian, 'Militari politica e società in Austria durante la Prima Guerra Mondiale', *Memoria e Ricerca: Rivista di Storia Contemporanea*, 28 (2008), pp. 55–72.

officers who served during the war were still of noble descent. In contrast, the Italian officer corps was much more bourgeois in character. But, more important still, the national problem plaguing Austria did not exist in Italy. The Austrian Emperor commanded not one but three armies: the united-federal-permanent army (*k.u.k. Heer*), the two national militias (*Landwehren*) – on the Austrian side '*k. k. Landwehr*', on the Hungarian one the '*k. u. Honved*' – and the reserve army (*Landsturm*). These three different identities never faded during the war, and at its end, this division helps account for the dissolution of the Empire. Nevertheless, the officer corps was mainly German-speaking Austrian, and the same was true in the personnel running the Ministry of War.[9]

Nothing like this happened in Italy. There were still complaints about the high percentage of posts Piedmontese officers occupied compared to officers from other regions: but the Italian army did not have the national problem that plagued the Austrian army.[10]

However, social and national homogeneity did not guarantee efficiency and professional culture. The more middle-class nature of the Italian army's officialdom did not prevent Giovanni Giolitti from observing that the military in Italy was a venue for the 'naughty and deficient' sons of the best families. This was not without consequences: a strong conservative, bureaucratic style circulated in Italian forces, slowing the pace of reform and further imbedding traditional professional cultures in their old ways. In Italy, for instance, it would have been very difficult to give junior officers wide initiative in training, and then in combat itself, something Conrad had believed in for years. Rather, much – perhaps too much – in Italy remained in the hands of higher officers, with the aggravating consequence that in Italy, non-commissioned officers were scarce.

In conclusion, the Italian Front was a theatre very different from that of the other major sectors: the armies were different, their war aims and strategies were different, the topography was completely different from the Eastern and Western Fronts. To a number of foreign military observers (and later to

9 Holger Herwig, *The First World War: Germany and Austria-Hungary 1914–1918* (London: Edward Arnold, 1997); Richard Georg Plaschka, Horst Haselsteiner and Arnold Suppan, *Innere Front: Militärassistenz, Widerstand und Umsturz in der Donaumonarchie 1918* (Vienna: Verlag für Geschichte und Politik, 1974), p. 35; and Ernst Zehetbauer, *Die 'E.F.' und das Ende der alten Armee: der Krieg der Reserveoffiziere Österreich-Ungarns 1914–1918* (Vienna: Staatprüfungsarbeit, Ist. f. öst. Gesch., 2000), pp. 7, 19, 24, 28, 64, 70, 77, 100, 133, 163.

10 G. Caforio and P. Del Negro (eds.), *Ufficiali e società: interpretazioni e modelli* (Milan: Angeli, 1988); and Piero Del Negro, 'Ufficiali di carriera e ufficiali di complemento nell'esercito italiano della grande guerra', in Gerard Canini (ed.), *Les fronts invisibles: nourrir fournir soigner* (Nancy: PUN, 1984).

military historians) this created a peculiar situation, sometimes difficult to understand. Stereotypes or prejudices about national character stood in for considered analysis, or some concluded the Italian Front was simply insignificant. This was a major error, since developments on this front directly contributed to decide the outcome of the war.

Building a front, 1914

In July 1914 the Italian Front did not exist;[11] it had to be created. While politicians deliberated, the military were preparing. In Vienna, Conrad, assuming that Italy had abandoned the Triple Alliance, planned an attack on the 'traitor' by a pincer movement from the Isonzo and the Trentino. But in Rome, Chief of general staff Alberto Pollio was in favour of staying in the alliance, for which he was prepared to send three army corps to the Rhine to fight against France. This plan dated from an 1888 secret agreement, but it was suspended in 1911 because of Italian commitments in Libya.[12] Only at the end of August, when neutrality was on the line, did Pollio's successor, Cadorna, begin to prepare for war against the Habsburg Empire, while telling his government the Italian army was not ready for it.

For Austria the war began with full military commitments on the Russian and the eastern Balkan fronts. There was little to boast about in early actions either in Serbia or in Galicia. In Italy, too, the war had started indirectly: trade and exports had to change course; German investments had gone; the military, as we saw, concretely prepared for war; the general political atmosphere of internal politics was inflamed by a struggle between neutralists (a majority in the country and in Parliament) and interventionists (nationalist-imperialist or democratic). For these reasons, although there was no fighting, an Italian-Austrian front began to exist: at least hypothetically. War plans were unfolding: the Italian government spent about 2 billion lira to enhance military preparedness between summer 1914 and spring 1915.[13]

11 Holger Afflerbach, *Der Dreibund: europäische Grossmacht- und Allianzpolitik vor dem Ersten Weltkrieg* (Vienna: Böhlau Verlag, 2002).

12 Massimo Mazzetti, *L'esercito italiano nella Triplice Alleanza* (Naples: Esi, 1974); Maurizio Ruffo, *L'Italia nella Triplice Alleanza: i piani operativi dello SM verso l'Austria Ungheria dal 1985 al 1915* (Rome: Ufficio storico, Stato maggiore dell'esercito, 1998); and Nicola Labanca, 'Welches Interventionstrauma für welche Militärs? Der Kriegseintritt von 1915 und das italienische Heer', in Johannes Hürter and Gian Enrico Rusconi (eds.), *Der Kriegseintritt Italiens im mai 1915* (Munich: R. Oldenbourg Verlag, 2007), pp. 73–84.

13 Mario Montanari, *Politica e strategia in cento anni di guerre italiane*, vol. II: *Il periodo liberale*, t. II, *La grande guerra* (Rome: Ufficio storico, Stato maggiore dell'esercito, 2000).

In some sense, on both sides of the border these preparations were inadequate. First let us consider the Italian side, preparing a future attack. Having chosen to remain neutral, in July–August 1914 the Italian government did not declare mobilisation, as the general staff had asked. The Prime Minister, Antonio Salandra, feared that a military mobilisation without a formal declaration of war could offer Vienna an excuse to attack Italy while she was still unprepared. Politically correct it may have been, but this choice made everything more difficult for Cadorna. For example, gathering soldiers and mobilising the army, based on national and not regional-territorial conscription, was difficult in a short time. Moreover, Italy was still suffering from the large military expenditures for the war in Libya, while its industry was much less developed and less specialised in the production of weapons compared to Austria, both before and during the first phase of the war.

But it was not just a matter of political decisions and industrial backwardness: even military professional culture was part of the problem. For example, Cadorna had received reports on how the war had been fought on the Western Front between the summer of 1914 and the spring of 1915.[14] But in February 1915 he still sent out a circular repeating old-fashioned ideas of frontal attack, not considering that the novelty of trench warfare required another approach. In one way this is not surprising. The Western generals persisted with this approach (with varying degrees of sophistication) until the end of the war. So when war was declared in May 1915, the Italian army had not updated its preparation for a war already nine months old.

Across the border, 1915

On 26 April 1915, the Italian ambassador in London, Guglielmo Imperiali, signed a secret pact with the Entente that in less than thirty days it would deliver Italy to the Entente. Formally, with this act the Austrian front (for Italy), or southern-western front (for Austria), was born.

For the Central Powers, the entrance of Italy into the war was a diplomatic failure, threatening a military setback. In May 1915 the Habsburg Empire was already busy on two fronts, while Italy represented a third. Austria still had some demographic resources to mobilise, but its industrial–economic resources were not unlimited, and it had to consider the dangers of internal

14 Giorgio Rochat, 'La preparazione dell'esercito italiano nell'inverno 1914–15', *Il Risorgimento*, 1 (1961), pp. 10–32; and Giorgio Rochat, 'La convenzione militare di Parigi, 2 maggio 1915', *Il Risorgimento*, 3 (1961), pp. 128–56.

nationalistic turmoil. In addition, Italian intervention helped consolidate the naval blockade of the Central Powers, and particularly of Austria, with Rome dominating the Adriatic Sea.

Italy's entry into the war rapidly led to strategic disagreements between the two Central Powers. In Vienna, Conrad's intention remained a pincer attack on Italy from the Trentino-Tyrol and from the Isonzo; Berlin seemed more concerned by the Eastern and Western Fronts, rather than the Italian one, which irritated Vienna. Then, in the first phases of the war, the only concrete military help Germany gave to Austria was the Bavarian *Alpenkorps*. Without German support, Austrian forces were capable of holding the line, though not without worries due to their poor military quality and their ethnic composition. But they were certainly unable numerically to conduct the offensive which Conrad had in mind.

In the very first days of the war on the Italian Front, there were about 28 divisions (7 more in reserve) on the Italian side and up to 25 on the Austrian side, which meant for Italy (all the army included) 560 battalions, while Austria – on that front – had 125 battalions in May 1915, and 275 in July 1915.

The Italian army's task was apparently less daunting than the one the Austrians faced. The Isonzo and Karst were the only front the Italian army had to secure (apart from minor commitments in Albania, Libya and Thessaloniki). Moreover, the war Salandra and Sonnino wanted to wage was strictly national and – apart from some support in weapons, raw materials and finances – Liberal Italy seemed reluctant to ask for additional troops from its Allies.

In Rome too the High Command thought about a pincer attack, even if smaller than Conrad's one, but no less ambitious: from Villach to Trieste's Karst, thereafter, leaving the road open to Vienna and Ljubljana. Though Italian political propaganda spoke of aiming at Trent and Trieste, in order to win the war the military aimed, with some exaggeration, at Ljubljana and Vienna.

It is apparent that on the Italian Front both sides' aims were difficult to realise and both sides lacked the strength to achieve them. Berlin did not give troops to Vienna, and the latter never had enough to crush the Italian army. On the other side, Italy was not able to achieve any initial advantage of '*sbalzo iniziale*'. In the very first days of the war the Habsburg forces generally retreated from the frontier – something that Rome claimed as a first victory (which it was not). In fact Austrian battalions did so only to move to a 'military border', that is, a line easier to defend. Italian propaganda pretended that Austrian fortifications made it very difficult for anyone to take the Austrian positions. Austrian propaganda justified inaction itself by saying that Italian troops were quantitatively overwhelming. But in fact, particularly in the earliest phase, Austrian fortifications were weak and Italian troop levels were never adequate for a decisive attack, in part because of the complication of mobilising an army based on national and not regional conscription. Moreover, Italian troops were not supported by heavy artillery, absent in the first years of the war, while the Austrian army was better supplied. In this context, it is hardly surprising that dreams of a war of rapid advances, strategic movements and invasions gave way to stalemate and trenches.

Military operations

From 1915 onwards, Italian offensives can be subdivided into several phases (Map 10.1). The front was too small to distinguish most battles by place names, as in the Western and Eastern Fronts. Italians and Austrians then began to number them. Four battles were launched on the Isonzo. Fighting went on also on Trentino and in Carnia, but certainly the Isonzo took the brunt of the

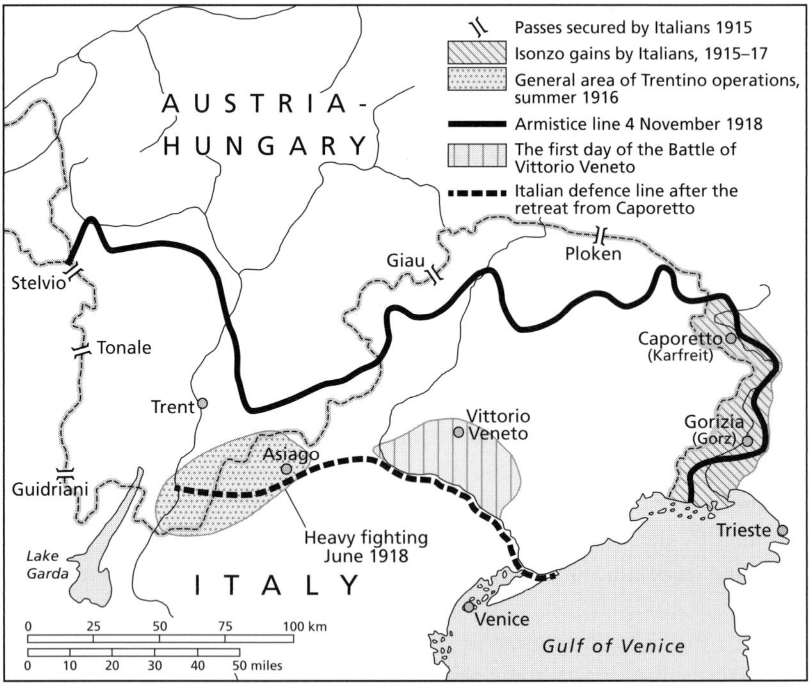

Map 10.1 The war in Italy, 1915–18.

fighting. The first battle took place between 23 June and 7 July, the second between 18 July and 3 August, the third between 18 October and 4 November and the fourth between 10 November and 2 December, when the weather was already freezing. These four battles of the Isonzo suited the two commanders perfectly: Cadorna firmly believed tactically in frontal attack, and Svetozar Boroević von Bojna was unwilling to yield even metres of land. With minor gains to show for this effort, the Italian army suffered 200,000 casualties. Austrian losses were about 130,000.

Some lessons had been learned, though, on the tactical level. For example, in Austria's judgement, already in the Second Battle of the Isonzo Italian troops aimed at more realistic tactical objectives than in the first battle; at least in some areas the infantry attack did not follow a heavy artillery bombardment, disorienting the opponent; in the third battle, some low-level military units avoided completely destroying all enemy positions and tried just to pierce opposing lines of trenches; the third and fourth battles were shorter than the first two, with fewer casualties in their wake. In the meantime, the Austrians had improved their trench system, and the same commander Boroević decided in some cases to save his troops by limiting counter-attacks and concentrating on defence. But what was learned in one sector was not shared in others. For Austria this was still a secondary front, with many less than outstanding units, and Italy went on in not fully understanding the novelty of the war, and not gaining knowledge about this new kind of war from reports coming from the Western Front.

Manpower soon became a problem for the Austrians. In contrast, less-industrialised Italy initially suffered a basic problem of a shortage of armaments rather than a shortage of men. We will see that by the end of the war these problems would have changed places: Italy would have sufficient supplies of weapons and men, while Austria would have neither. But in 1915 the Italian army entered the war with only two machine guns per regiment, while the Austrians had already two per battalion. Italy had plenty of light artillery, useful in a war of movement, but very few pieces of heavy artillery capable of breaking barbed-wired and articulated trench systems.[15] This also explains the high losses of Italian troops. They did not lack determination, as the heavy Austrian losses on the defensive show. In fact, these casualties weighed more on Boroević than on Cadorna, as a percentage, because of the

15 Filippo Cappellano and Basilio Di Martino, *Un esercito forgiato nelle trincee: l'evoluzione tattica dell'esercito italiano nella Grande Guerra*, con un saggio di Alessandro Gionfrida (Udine: Gaspari, 2008).

greater number of soldiers and units Italy could throw into the battle, and the multiple engagements Austria faced.

At the general level, 1915 ended with the Central Powers having the upper hand in Bulgaria and Serbia. But for different reasons, on the Italian Front the two sides seemed unable to overwhelm each other, while problems of a different order (industrial for Italy, demographic for Austria) loomed ahead.

Partial successes, 1916

With the new year the Italian Front had become much more challenging: From the 35 infantry divisions, with 560 battalions and 515 artillery batteries of 1915, the Italian army now fielded 43 divisions with 693 battalions and 1,122 batteries. It was also a year of clarification, because it was not until 27 August 1916 that Italy declared war on Germany. Formally, the front was no longer only between Austria and Italy, but it was now fully integrated into the European war.

In both official histories and national historiographies, the year 1916 is often presented as a time of success, albeit partial. Indeed, Austria inflicted a severe blow on Italy with its spring offensive from Trentino; and after that the Italians conquered the important site of Gorizia, on the Karst front. And yet both episodes proved to be very costly to the two armies. The fighting in 1916 highlighted the mutual deficiencies of Austrian and Italian forces, and showed how different this front was from the Western and Eastern Fronts.

The stark difference between the Italian Front and the rest of the European war was soon clear to Italian and Austrian officers and soldiers who fought around the Adamello. This was a war in the mountains, where only small units – and no large regiments and divisions – could operate. Digging a trench in the snow and the ice was completely different than doing the same thing in the hills of the Chemin des Dames or the plains of Verdun. Just feeding and equipping combat units at those heights was a massive problem. Modern technology was essential in this war. Assuring artillery supplies, communications and food through baggage-trains made this 'white war' a logistical nightmare. The accuracy of sniper fire, the cunning of the mine war and especially the endurance of mountain troops deployed in ice caves opened by explosives, gave this war its grim character.[16]

16 Luciano Viazzi, *La guerra bianca in Adamello* (Trent: Arti Grafiche Saturnia, 1965); Luciano Viazzi, *La guerra bianca sull'Adamello* (Trent: G. B. Monauni, 1968); Gunda Barth-Scalmani, 'Kranke Krieger im Hochgebirge: Einige Uberlegungen zur Mikrogeschichte des

But if the 'white war' in the mountains was a *basso continuo* in the war on the Italian Front from 1915 to 1918, the two most relevant episodes in 1916 were certainly the spring offensive and the Italian capture of Gorizia. Historians now agree that the spring offensive was the last successful Austrian battle of the war.[17] However, it was not without its headaches. After few positive results in 1915, Conrad was able to convince his Emperor that crushing Italy would strengthen the prestige of Austria. He was not successful alike in convincing his German ally that winning the battle with Italy would create a strategic advantage for the Central Powers; for this reason German engagement in the spring offensive remained restricted. Then, when Conrad ordered the attack (15 May 1916) he had to amend his previous strategic plan: he launched not a simultaneous move from east and west, but only one attack from the Trentino; this was not a great Austro-German joint attack, but only an Austrian assault with some German support. In addition, he was wrong in not concentrating all his forces on one point, and instead he dissipated them on a rather broad front. For all this, the Austrian offensive did not break the Italian defences, and Conrad's dreams of arriving in Venice in six days faded rapidly. The punitive or *Strafexpedition* (as it is known in Italy) stalled no later than 27 June for two reasons: first, the strength of Italian positions and the ability of Cadorna to inject reserves into the battle, and secondly, the Austrian difficulty in transforming a trench war into a war of movement. Advancing infantry was no longer protected by artillery, which was unable to move in sequence; supplies did not arrive for the advancing troops and there was a shortage of reserves. For all these reasons the offensive ran out of steam. Nevertheless, Conrad gained the strategic surprise, and thereby presented a serious danger to Italy: Austria threatened to descend to the plain and cut off supply lines coming to the Italian Front of the Karst from the Po Valley, from its industries and its agriculture – in a word, from the Italian hinterland.

The half-success of the spring offensive was further reduced by the Italian counter-moves. After a few weeks Cadorna managed to take control of Gorizia. By this, he threatened Trieste and complicated the defence of the Austrian Karst. This Italian victory over the Austrians, in the sixth Italian

Sanitatswesens an der Dolomitenfront' and Luciana Palla, 'Kampf um die Dolomitentiler: Der Große Krieg im Grenzgebiet', both in Mazohl-Wallnig, Kuprian and Barth-Scalmani (eds.), *Ein Krieg, zwei Schützengräben*, pp. 341–60 and 361–76 respectively; and Mark Thompson, *The White War: Life and Death on the Italian Front, 1915–1919* (London: Basic Books, 2008).

17 Vittorio Corà and Paolo Pozzato (eds.), *1916, la Strafexpedition: gli altipiani vicentini nella tragedia della grande guerra*, preface by Mario Rigoni Stern, introduction by Mario Isnenghi (Udine: Gaspari, 2003).

Isonzo battle, was due to the enormous investment of personnel and resources ordered by Cadorna. Stocks of Italian artillery, after the shortages of 1915, were now growing. Furthermore, after the humiliation of the spring of 1916, which forced the government to fall, Liberal Italy needed a successful summer. The fight was fierce, as seen from the number of losses which, for the first time, were quite similar (51,000 Italian casualties, 40,000 Austrian). However, as in the case of the Austrian spring offensive, the Italians were unable to move beyond Gorizia, bringing the offensive to an end.

In both the *Strafexpedition* and in taking Gorizia, tactical gains did not lead to a change in the strategic balance. The war on the Italian Front continued more or less in late 1916 as it had eight months earlier. Italy, still on the offensive, launched five other battles on the Isonzo: the Fifth from 11 to 29 March, the Sixth (the one for Gorizia) from 6 to 17 August, the Seventh from 14 to 17 September, the Eighth from 10 to 12 October and the Ninth from 1 to 4 November. The Italians gained some advantage but suffered heavier losses, more than 280,000 men, while the Austrians lost about 230,000. Again Cadorna, instead of concentrating his attack, had chosen to keep repeating attacks at different points – straining enemy units but also dissipating his own ration strength. The Italian command looked less to take territory and more towards wearing down the Austrian lines. This *grignotage* was costly on both sides.

National efforts and alliances

While in 1916, the year of Verdun and the Somme, the war was becoming increasingly difficult to win, especially on the Western Front, the Italian Front had become increasingly important for its two main contenders. For Rome, after the fall of the centre-right government of Salandra and his replacement by Paolo Boselli, with a broader political base (though never a 'sacred union'), the prestige of the Liberal state was at stake in the war. The effort required by the nation was increasingly heavy: about 5.9 million Italians were mobilised throughout the conflict; 1 million were not assigned to the army, for medical or other reasons. At the end of 1916, 2 million Italian men were on the fighting front. If we consider that at the beginning of the war the standing army numbered 900,000, and at the end of the conflict the army's ration strength was about 2.3 million, one can easily understand the dimensions of the Italian war effort even before 1917.

For Vienna, after the *Strafexpedition* and after Gorizia, but especially after the setbacks suffered on the Russian and Romanian fronts (inflicted by

Brusilov), a defeat on the Italian Front would have had very serious consequences. Conrad had never forgotten Austria's defeat either at Königgrätz (Sadowa) in 1866, or at Solferino in 1859. In the context of the First World War, losing again to the Italians would have been an unbearable blow.

Moreover, the Italian Front was not isolated from the other fronts. Italy and Austria were part of international alliances whose fate depended, to varying degrees, on the Italian Front. They were both an integral part of a wartime alliance. Italy depended heavily on economic and financial alliance, but called for little (and nothing was given) at the military level. Austria's posture was rather different. The initial imbalance in military power with Germany was severely aggravated by the defeats of 1916, to the point that between September and December, it was said with regret in Vienna that Austria had lost its military independence. The military command of the alliance was passed to Kaiser Wilhelm II, that is to Ludendorff and Hindenburg, and German staff officers were sent to advise Austrian units: this subordination was not total but it was evident.[18]

Vienna also gained from this unequal partnership with its most powerful ally: Austrian officers were trained in German units able to apply, from winter 1916–17 onwards, lessons learned by the Germans on the Western Front at the tactical level about attack and defence. The techniques of infiltration, attack in small units and defence in depth, that together would change war in the trenches of the Western Front in 1918, arrived on the Italian Front a year earlier. The Austrians took these lessons to heart, helping to explain the outcome of the Battle of Caporetto in late 1917.

The geographical peculiarities of the Italian Front remained decisive. In the 'white war' and the stalemate in the high mountains, there was not so much to learn from other fronts. That said, the Karst began to see some changes in the efficiency of the Italian army facing the Austrians. The doyen of Italian military historical studies, Giorgio Rochat, noted that in 1915 Italy was at a tactical disadvantage vis-à-vis Austria, but that in 1916, the Italians made up for it. As Rochat put it, the taking of Gorizia and in general the battles of 1916

18 Manfried Rauchensteiner, 'Österreich-Ungarn', in Hirschfeld, Krumeich and Renz (eds.), *Enzyklopädie Erster Weltkrieg*, pp. 68, 76; Graydon A. Tunstall, *Blood on the Snow: The Carpathian Winter War of 1915* (Lawrence KS: University Press of Kansas, 2010), pp. 12, 209; Günther Kronenbitter, 'The limits of cooperation: Germany and Austria-Hungary in the First World War', in Peter Dennis and Jeffrey Grey (eds.), *Entangling Alliances: Coalition Warfare in the Twentieth Century* (Canberra: A.C.T., 2005), pp. 74–85; Günther Kronenbitter, 'Austria-Hungary', in Hamilton and Herwig (eds.), *War Planning 1914*; and Wolfgang Etschmann, 'Die Südfront 1915–1918', in Klaus Eisterer and Rolf Steinenger (eds.), *Tirol und der Erste Weltkrieg* (Innsbruck: Studienverlag, 2011).

caused heavy casualties on both sides; and 'the fact that the losses were almost equal is a demonstration of the efficiency of Italian artillery and of . . . the determined defence of Austrian trenches'.

What saved the Italians and the Entente was the fact that the war was a total war, and that it could not be won solely on the battlefield. Mobilisation of men and materials was not less decisive than military efficiency. However, until 1918 and despite the defeat of Caporetto, Italy managed to put armies in the field and equip them in a way Austria became increasingly incapable of doing.

Morale

Manpower mattered, but so did troop morale. Especially after the great effort of 1916, resignation rather than a belief in victory was widespread. After the carnage of 1914 to 1916, securing the consent of soldiers was only possible now through showing that the war was for something, that war aims were real. But both armies on the Italian Front were slow in organising a systematic propaganda effort directed at their own soldiers. In Italy this kind of propaganda would appear only after Caporetto.[19]

And even if an effort at persuading men of the justice of their cause had been made, would it have worked? Even in Cadorna's army many soldiers did not know what the war was for. In Conrad's army – where higher literacy rates would have made propaganda easier – different nationalities had always remained unconvinced of the war aims of the Habsburg Empire.[20]

As everywhere else in the war, soldiers' morale depended on many variables: the layout of the trenches, the quality and quantity of armaments and food, the efficiency of the military post: in a word, the degree of concern from commanders about soldiers' 'welfare' and of course the stiffness (or slackness) of military discipline and courts-martial. Considering these issues, it is clear that the Austrian army[21] provided better conditions than did the Italian,[22] but not always. In 1917, when conditions got worse for Italian soldiers, the space

19 Mario Isnenghi, *Giornali di Trincea 1915–1918* (Turin: Einaudi, 1977).

20 Mark Cornwall, *The Undermining of Austria-Hungary: The Battle for Hearts and Minds* (New York: St Martin's Press, 2000).

21 Plaschka, Haselsteiner and Suppan, *Innere Front*, pp. 148, 90; Lawrence Sondhaus, *In the Service of the Emperor: Italians in the Austrian Armed Forces, 1814–1918* (Boulder, CO: East European Monographs and New York: Columbia University Press, 1990), p. 104; and Mark Cornwall, 'Morale and patriotism in the Austro-Hungarian army, 1914–1918', in John Horne (ed.), *State, Society and Mobilization in Europe during the First World War* (Cambridge University Press, 1997), p. 175.

22 Giorgio Rochat, 'Il soldato italiano dal Carso a Redipuglia', in Diego Leoni and Camillo Zadra (eds.), *La Grande Guerra: esperienza, memoria, immagini* (Bologna: Il

opened for 'defeatist' propaganda.[23] Bad conditions helped explain an increase in cases of self-mutilation and even of war neuroses.

Military justice was active on the Italian Front. The Italian army opened 262,000 court cases and issued 170,000 condemnations. A total of 1,061 men were convicted of capital charges out of 4,280 accused, and 750 were executed. To these deaths, at least 290 summary executions must also be added.[24] The total number of Austrian troops sentenced to death was at least 1,913 after a regular trial, and many more in the end.[25] Taking the two sides together, on the Italian Front, military courts executed more of their own soldiers than did courts on other fronts, with the possible exception of Russia. Perhaps executions served as a form of intimidation, but they certainly did not improve the morale of the soldiers.

Above all, the strength and solidity of the Austrian army were undermined by its own composition – three armies (permanent, Hungarian, reserve) where orders could be given in three languages to soldiers of many nationalities. Eventually, this factor proved decisive. There were deserters who went home or who left the line (rather than surrendering to the enemy) on every front: but towards the end of the war Austrian deserters were exceptionally numerous, hundreds of thousands of men, who roamed the country in bands. The ethnic divisions in the Austrian army provided an easy target for Italian propaganda, especially after the 'Congress of the peoples oppressed by Austria-Hungary' in Rome (8–10 April 1918), which ended in the publication of a Pact of Rome. By this period of the war, it was clear that morale mattered at least as much, if not more, than numbers. Setbacks in the German offensive in France helped undermine Austrian troop morale even further.

Fatigue, exhaustion and the big blow, 1917

The year 1917 was one of fatigue, if not exhaustion. French mutinies made it evident that enough was enough for their armies on the Western Front at the

Mulino, 1986), pp. 613–30; Enzo Forcella and Alberto Monticone, *Plotone di esecuzione: i processi della prima guerra mondiale* (Bari: Laterza, 1968); Lucio Fabi, *Gente di trincea: la Grande Guerra sul Carso e sull'Isonzo* (Milan: Mursia, 1994); and Vanda Wilcox, 'Generalship and mass surrender during the Italian defeat at Caporetto', in Ian F. W. Beckett (ed.), *1917: Beyond the Western Front* (Leiden: Brill, 2009).

23 Bruna Bianchi, 'La grande guerra nella storiografia italiana dell'ultimo decennio', *Ricerche Storiche*, 3 (1991), pp. 698–745.

24 Procacci, *Soldati e prigionieri italiani nella Grande Guerra*; and Marco Pluviano and Irene Guerrini, *Le fucilazioni sommarie nella prima Guerra Mondiale*, preface by Giorgio Rochat (Udine: Gaspari, 2004).

25 Karl Platzer, *Standrechtliche Todesurteile im Ersten Weltkrieg* (Berlin and Stuttgart: WiKu-Verlag, 2004).

time of the Nivelle offensive: but the Italian Front was not so far away from a similar outbreak of indiscipline. The year opened with an exceptionally hard winter, which certainly did not contribute to letting the troops rest, from the mountains to the Karst. Then it saw two more Italian Isonzo battles, exceptionally hard-fought ones. Then came Caporetto.

This end of the year must not lead us to conclude that 1917 was full of Austrian successes. First, the Austrian regime – unlike the Italian one – had undergone significant changes between the end of 1916 and March 1917. There was the death of Franz-Joseph, the accession of Karl I, the replacement of Conrad by Arthur Arz von Straussenburg. More generally, for the Central Powers, Austro-German hopes to exploit the Russian Revolution and to liquidate the Eastern Front were undermined by the entry of the United States into the war. The Entente would have fresh and substantial armies at its disposal as well as the backing of American finance and industry.

Meanwhile, on the military level, a decisive point had arrived on the Italian Front. Cadorna could not be satisfied with the results achieved in 1916. Now he called his offensives '*spallate*' (shoves), clearly aiming at undermining – rather than destroying – the opponent, wearing him out, while wearing out his own troops a bit less. Italian soldiers, in the meantime, could make use of enhanced and abundant supplies of weapons. For these reasons the Isonzo battles became shorter, even if more deadly – for the Austrians as much as for the Italians. The Tenth (from 12 May to 8 June) launched 430 Italian battalions against an Austrian force half the size, and cost 160,000 casualties. The Eleventh battle (from 18 to 31 August) was even more impressive, perhaps involving 600 Italian battalions, compared with about 250 on the Austrian side: but the cost for Italy was 160,000 men lost. On the Austrian side, estimates of losses range from between 150,000 and 250,000 casualties.

The Eleventh battle earned the Italians the control of Bainsizza. But, despite an exceptional new commitment of artillery, the casualties the Italian side suffered were unprecedented – and once again inconclusive. Under these conditions, speaking about lassitude, or the profound fatigue of the troops, is just a euphemism. The mute rebellion of Italians soldiers against the war and their commanders was growing, although it was not expressed openly in a mutiny as in France.

On the other side, if possible, the weight of the losses was even heavier. The Austrian Emperor was told by the civil and military authorities that the army could not endure similar losses. In Vienna, the gnawing sense of a possible defeat was evident.

It was for this reason that Berlin eventually agreed to help Austria in a significant military way, to bolster her ally, now in serious trouble. In great secrecy thousands of German troops were moved towards the Italian Front. On its own part, Austria made available additional units for use on the Italian Front, so that the joint offensive could form a strong invading force of about 350,000 men.[26]

In addition to the manpower and the artillery, new tactics proved decisive. Following the lessons learned on the Eastern and Western Fronts, military commanders from Berlin and Vienna agreed to start with a heavy but short artillery barrage, supplemented by a large discharge of gas. New tactics of infiltration were set, giving less control to senior officers and more autonomy to junior officers and troops. A green light was given to small units, operating in the bottom of valleys and not on the peaks of the mountains, to act rapidly and to break opponents' tactics and resistance. The aim of this penetration in depth was to disrupt the enemy's rear and then – here was the masterstroke – to attack from the rear, and not to assault it with a frontal and linear offensive. Infiltration was the exact opposite of Cadorna's approach to the Isonzo battles and his repeated and futile 'shoves', and infiltration had a stunning effect on Italian troops massed in the front line in the offensive posture forced on them by their Supreme Commander.

The attack started on 24 October.[27] The Italian command, without a true system of trenches and a flexible defence in depth, and devoid of significant reserves in the rear, soon found itself obliged to order a retreat. Although infiltration and disruption had occurred on only a small portion of the front between Bovec and Tolmino, at Caporetto, the penetration of Austro-German troops threatened to cut all the way to the Italian first line. Units from 'Area Carnia', the Lower Isonzo Karst and even the Trentino were put in danger.

To be true, the objective of the attacking generals – the Austrian Boroević and the German Otto von Below, with staff officers such as Krafft von Dellmensingen – was limited to the Tagliamento, just to force Italian troops back to the political border from which they had started the war on 24 May 1915. What they could not imagine was that the Italian Front, in particular the

26 Oskar Regele, *Gericht über Habsburgs Wehrmacht: Letzte Siege und Untergang unter dem Armee-Oberkommando Kaiser Karls I. Generaloberst Arz von Straussenburg* (Vienna and Munich: Herold, 1968), p. 68.

27 Nicola Labanca, *Caporetto: storia di una disfatta* (Florence: Giunti, 1997); and Manfred Rauchensteiner (ed.), *Waffentreue – Die 12: Isonzoschlacht 1917* (Vienna: Fassbänder, 2007).

Second Army, would collapse so quickly, dragging with it the other armies, back to the Piave. Infiltration completely bewildered Italian commanders, cut communication lines and separated troops from their chains of command, leaving them lost, without any idea how to fight and against whom. Soldiers realised that the battle was lost and many cultivated the illusion that maybe the war was over. Beaten or isolated, many threw down their weapons and left the front. Some units fought, led by their junior officers, but they could do nothing but retreat. Seeing the military wreckage, local civilian populations in the area tried to escape the advancing enemy forces. The roads then became very congested, with women and men en route, in uniform or not, flocking to the bridges, from the mountains towards the plain and the Po Valley. It was possible to stop them only once they had passed the Piave, where Cadorna in the meantime had established a new line of resistance. The battle was a catastrophe: 40,000 killed and wounded, 300,000 prisoners, 350,000 soldiers lost or wandering around as stragglers and more than 3,000 pieces of artillery lost – fully two-thirds of the entire Italian stock of heavy artillery and half of all middle-range guns in the Italian arsenal (Map 10.2).

In a word, Caporetto nullified the extraordinary effort and expense of two years of war. The front was shortened by almost 200 kilometres, the Italian front line moved 140 kilometres to the west, about 38,850 square kilometres of national territory were seized by the enemy and 2 million people were left at the mercy of enemy occupation. The whole Italian war effort, on the offensive since 1915, within two weeks became entirely defensive in order to prevent the enemy passing the Piave to the Po river valley. If possible, Cadorna eventually managed to worsen all this: in his statement on 28 October, instead of taking responsibility for the defeat, he accused soldiers of not having fought for their country. Taken together, this was Caporetto (Map 10.3).

Immediately the view spread that Caporetto was a 'military strike' against the war.[28] In reality, the root causes of Caporetto were military. However, they were intertwined with the general exhaustion of the troops, forced to fight a war of attrition with very meagre results (apart from Gorizia, the Bainsizza and some minor border changes). Against this thesis of the military strike, more or less immediately another, second interpretation arose: Italian soldiers did indeed fight at Caporetto.[29] It is no surprise that it was well received and corroborated retrospectively by the fascist regime, and also very

28 Mario Isnenghi, *I vinti di Caporetto nella letteratura di guerra* (Padua: Marsilio, 1967).
29 Paolo Gaspari, *Le bugie di Caporetto: la fine della memoria dannata*, preface by Giorgio Rochat (Udine: Gaspari, 2011).

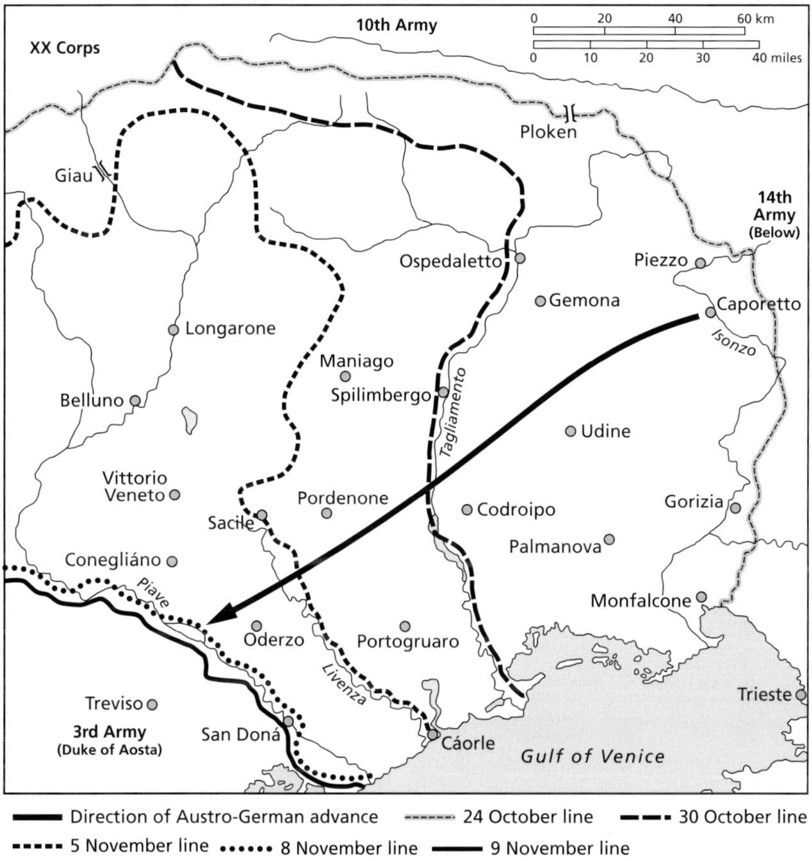

Map 10.2 Caporetto and after.

recently has returned to the scene. Intended to save the honour of the Italian military, this second interpretation is, however, as partial as the one it wants to counter. In fact it is at least as obvious that some units fought and some officers commanded them, as it is that other units and officers were able to retire without being overwhelmed and without breaks in the chain of command. But it is hard to deny that the defeat of Caporetto led Italian soldiers from the mountains and from the Karst to the plain, and that many guns and uniforms were cast away in the general flight.

After the great victories on the Eastern Front, the German victory on the Masurian Lakes (September 1914) and the Russian victory led by Brusilov in south-western Russia and Galicia (September 1914), Caporetto was the biggest and most unexpected victory of movement in the war to date.

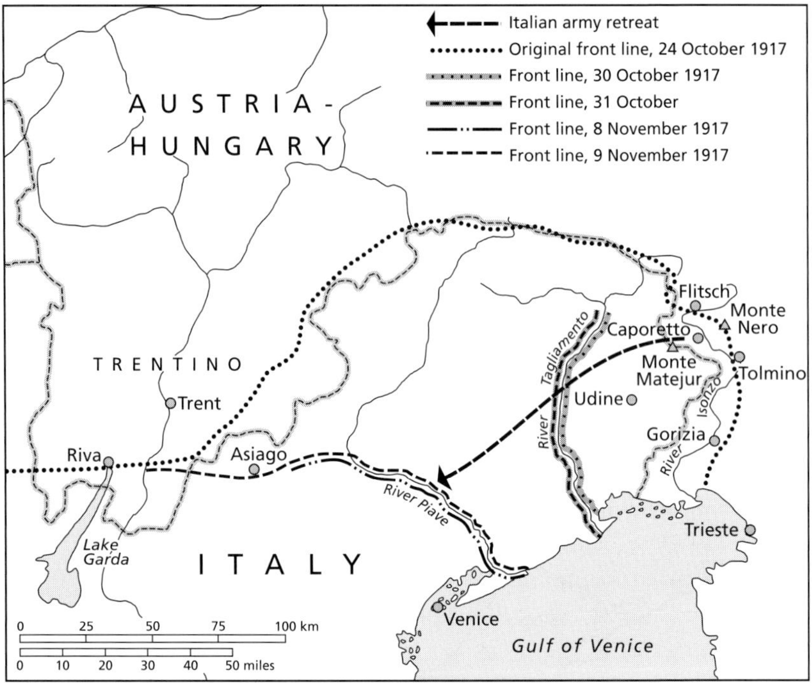

Map 10.3 Retreat of the Italian army after Caporetto.

Winner and loser, 1918

Tactically, Austria-Hungary and Germany had won. But let us pause for a moment and consider what Italy had lost. Because of its dimensions, under-estimating Caporetto is truly difficult in the context of the history of the Italian Front and of the Italian war. Yet a renowned scholar like Holger Herwig called it a 'cosmetic victory' for Vienna.[30] Why?

In Paris and London it was feared that an Italian defeat could lead to disaster. That is why the Entente sent substantial military and economic aid to Italy. The Italian government dismissed Cadorna, the Supreme Commander who had lasted longer than any other in the entire war, and replaced him with the more malleable Armando Diaz. The most important support to Italy from the Entente, however, was not military but economic and moral-political.

30 Herwig, *The First World War*, p. 336.

The Prime Minister, Vittorio Emanuele Orlando, asked for fifteen divisions from his Allies; Diaz asked for twenty. In the end six French and five English divisions arrived. Their commanders, fearful that the virus of the '*caporettisti*' and defeatists could infect their own men, deployed these units away from the front line. Meanwhile, however, before and during their arrival, between November and December 1917 Italian soldiers held the line on the Piave, against a final Austro-Hungarian attempt to cross the river – an encounter in which Allied troops were not directly involved. Behind the Piave, the new Italian High Command had to reorganise the whole army, while the country was polarised between hardened supporters of a defence to the bitter end and those who preferred a return of peace, many former neutralists, and all who in various ways had opposed the intervention in the war.

On the other side, Caporetto was a cosmetic victory for Vienna because it allowed Austria to hide for a while the growing structural weaknesses of its Empire. Undoubtedly, the Central Powers had won a major victory on 24 October; but thereafter, they did not make any progress on the Italian Front. The fighting in the first half of 1918 produced no effect, the great attack on the Piave from 15 to 22 June revisited the previous situation in the Karst, but with reversed roles: the Austrian attackers lost 150,000 men, the Italian defenders, 90,000. Above all, Austria was not able to break through. Like the great German attack on the Western Front in March (the *Kaiserschlacht*), what the Italians called the 'Battle of the Solstice' (15–22 June 1918) was the last Austrian attempt at breaking through. After that, for Vienna, defeat was certain: the date was not yet defined, but the outcome was sure. Austrian failure confirmed on the Italian Front what the great German offensive meant on the Western Front.

From 1915 to the end of 1917 Italy and Austria had shared many things, perhaps more than the two national historiographies have acknowledged. But after the reaction to Caporetto, Italian and Austrian destinies began to diverge notably and irreversibly.

In fact, Austria then found itself in greater need of men, more men than it had available, more weapons and more resources than its overstretched domestic economy could supply. Italy, on the other hand, thanks to the internal reaction of its ruling class and to the renewal of its war effort and resistance, and thanks too to Allied support, was able to keep its men fed and armed through an extraordinary effort of its industrial economy. On the eve of the end of hostilities the Italian army had 2.2 million men in the field, 6,970 guns and 5,190 machine guns, with 650 airplanes (290 fighters, 74 bombers, 286 reconnaissance): a very large force, one that Austria could neither afford nor sustain.

Life on the Italian home front in 1918 had not been easy, but in war the comparisons that matter most are relative, not absolute, and life on the home front in Austria was much worse. Since January, and even more since July, after the failure in the 'Battle of the Solstice', the ethnic and national mix of the Austro-Hungarian Empire began to fall apart. Nationalities rebelled, workers went on strike, soldiers deserted or lost much of their military efficiency. Between September and October, the Poles of Galicia, the Czechs, Slovaks, Slavs, Croats and Hungarians began to distance themselves from 'German' Austria. While the home front was collapsing, the fighting front was in ruins. To stop total disaster, Emperor Karl issued his manifesto of 16 October 1918 granting independence or autonomy to subject populations. This was too little and too late.

If the Austrian situation was now desperate, Italy's went from strength to strength. The new Italian High Command successfully reconstituted and shrewdly administered its forces. Already in the summer of 1918 the Allies urged Italy to attack. But, fearing that his army was still weak, and that it needed to avoid defeat at all costs, Diaz wanted to attack only with complete assurance of victory. Thus he waited a substantial period of time. Between September and October, while Austria was coming apart, Diaz remained inert. He promised an attack on 15 October, but he postponed it. He moved only on 24 October, a year after Caporetto: then he attacked decisively, without accepting any request for an armistice coming from Berlin or Vienna. This was the Battle of Vittorio Veneto. Even when Austria surrendered on 3 November, he wanted to prove Italian strength and humiliated the opponent, continuing to move forward to regain lands lost a year earlier, stopping only in the afternoon of 4 November 1918 (Map 10.4).

Most critics have refused to see Vittorio Veneto as a real battle, given the state of dissolution of the Austrian army. The Austrians have always refused, even in name, preferring to speak of a 'third *Piaveschlacht*'. After June 1918, Austria was considered (and probably considered itself) beaten, and this may have had a bearing on the Western Front and German moves there. Vittorio Veneto has been frequently misinterpreted. A serious scholar, in a serious study, wrote of this offensive as a joint Italian-Anglo-French move[31] – one of the many cases in historical writing where international and national stereotypes, and some lack of precise knowledge, completely betray the author. For better or for worse, Vittorio Veneto

31 Tim Travers, 'The Allied victories, 1918', in Hew Strachan (ed.), *The Oxford Illustrated History of the First World War* (Oxford University Press, 1998), p. 288.

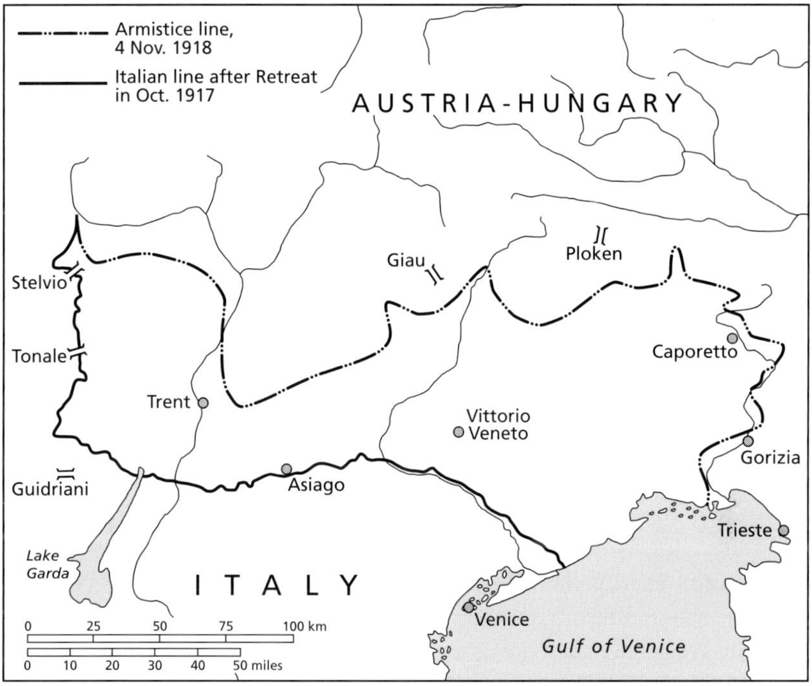

Map 10.4 Lines reached by the Italian army in late 1918.

was an Italian battle. Exaggerating its size, a frequent feature of old nationalistic Italian historiography, is also an error. This battle was a unique episode at the end of the Great War.

The total cost of the conflict, however, was heavy for all. In the war as a whole, Austria had mobilised 8 million men: 1.4 million had died, about 2 million had been injured, 1.7 million had been made prisoners of war, not counting the nearly 4 million afflicted by illness or other conditions. Italy had conscripted 5.9 million men, dismissing as unfit or leaving in the factories about 1 million men. The country lost 600,000 men; 1 million had been injured and the war left 280,000 orphans, not to mention widows. Yes, Italy had won and Austria had lost, but war had devastated both countries.

Farewell to arms? Demobilisation, 1919

Formally, the war ended in November 1918. But for societies the effects of the war ended much later. The demobilisation of armies took time. In Italy it was completed in 1920; at the end of 1919 there were still 500,000 men in the Italian army.[32] In the former Habsburg Empire the war ended effectively before the Armistice, at a time when the Imperial Army and political institutions were dissolving.[33]

The end of fighting gave way to the two diverging post-wars. The Habsburg Empire was not only defeated but destroyed. In the Balkan territories, a new kingdom of Serbs, Croats and Slovenes emerged. It became the Kingdom of Yugoslavia in 1929. Czechoslovakia, Galicia and Bukovina split off too.

Italy's post-war fate might appear more stable – but it was not. Italy had won, in spite of Caporetto, but the Liberal ruling class would not have time for celebrations. The war had greatly weakened the Italian political system. The conflict had led to an authoritarian transformation, reflected in the limitation, if not silencing, of Parliament. Moreover, the brutalisation of men and norms caused by the war would inspire a small movement, which chose to militarise its party: the Fascist Party of Benito Mussolini.

In short, for domestic reasons Liberal Italy won the war but lost the peace. Here again, even if the collapse of Liberalism had domestic origins, as in Austria, external factors played a role. The decisions of the Conference of Versailles rejected Italian claims for territory on the Adriatic, territory given to the new Yugoslavia. Fascists claimed that Italy had been 'victimised' and that the victory had been 'mutilated'. A world war was over, but the groundwork for another war had been laid.

Memory

In the minds of people, war took a much longer time to fade away. One novelty of the Great War was its staggering human costs, which went beyond the slaughter in the front lines, and was measured as well by the number of soldiers and civilians who went mad on account of the war.[34] For many the war never ended.

32 Giorgio Rochat, *L'esercito italiano da Vittorio Veneto a Mussolini (1919–1925)* (Bari: Laterza, 1967).

33 Reinhard Nachtigal, 'The repatriation and reception of returning prisoners of war 1918–22', *Immigrants & Minorities*, 26:1–2 (2008), pp. 157–84.

34 Antonio Gibelli, *L'officina della guerra: La Grande Guerra e le trasformazioni del mondo mentale* (Turin: Bollati-Boringhieri, 1991); and Bruna Bianchi, *La follia e la fuga: nevrosi di guerra, diserzione e disobbedienza nell'esercito Italiano, 1915–1918* (Rome: Bulzoni, 2001).

Then there was an accounting to give. An event so grand had to be explained. This gave origin to an exceptional tide of books and publications. Both in Italy and Austria, generals were among the first to publish their memoirs and to debate their own merits and responsibilities, perhaps more in Italy than in Austria. But it was not the high command but officers and reserve officers who were to establish national versions of the victory (in Rome) and defeat (in Vienna).

Unlike in Germany, it was very difficult for Austrians to construct a stab-in-the-back legend. The debacle of the last weeks, and especially days, of the war made it impossible for soldiers to conjure up an image of an army that fought until the bitter end.[35] More marketable, and perhaps peculiarly Austrian, was the creation of a mood of imperial nostalgia: a perfectly understandable sentiment among the Austro-Germans, but to which the new states and nations, equally understandably, were immune. All this made more difficult a common understanding, after 1918, of the war fought by the Austro-Hungarian Empire.[36]

In Italy it was the ghost of Caporetto that agitated the minds of the military. Without explaining that defeat, it was difficult to explain the Italian victory. In general, however, the prevailing narrative was set by reserve and recalled officers (*'ufficiali di complemento'*). It recounted the great national effort made by civil society wearing the uniform of the nation in arms. In short, this public narrative imposed the version of democratic interventionism, a version that fascism was able to quickly adopt and adapt. All the alternative memories of the war – the ones by isolated pacifists, socialists and militant communists – were drastically limited in appeal. In time, political developments further occluded the war on the Italian Front: in Italy after 1922,[37] in Austria, at the latest, by 1932.

35 Oswald Überegger, 'Tabuisirung, Instrumentalisierung, verspätete Historisierung: die Tiroler Historiographie und der Erste Weltkriege', *Geschichte und region/Storia e regione*, 11:1 (2002), pp. 129, 133; Christa Hammerle, '"Es ist immer der Mann der den Kampf entscheidet und nicht die Waffe": Die Männlichkeit des k.u.k. Gebirgskriegers in der soldatischen Erinnerungskultur', in Hermann J. W. Kuprian and Oswald Überegger (eds.), *Der Erste Weltkrieg in Alpenraum* (Innsbruck: Wagner, 2011), p. 36; and Oswald Überegger, *Erinnerungskriege: der Erste Weltkrieg, Österreich und die Tiroler Kriegserinnerung in der Zwischenkriegszeit* (Innsbruck: Wagner, 2011), p. 84.

36 Rudolf Jerabeck, 'Die österreichische Weltkriegsforschung', in Wolfgang Michalka (ed.), *Der Erste Weltkrieg: Wirkung, Wahrnehmung, Analyse* (Munich: Piper, 1994), p. 955; and Oswald Überegger, 'Vom militärischen Paradigma zur "Kulturgeschichte des Krieges"? Entwicklungslinien der österreichischen Weltkriegsgeschichtsschreibung zwischen politisch-militärischer Instrumentalisierung und universitärer Verwissenschaftlichung', in Überegger (ed.), *Zwischen Nation und Region: Weltkriegsforschung im interregionalen Vergleich. Ergebnisse und Perspektiven* (Innsbruck: Wagner, 2004), pp. 63–122.

37 Gianni Isola, *Guerra al regno della guerra! Storia della Lega proletaria mutilati invalidi reduci orfani e vedove di guerra (1918–1924)* (Florence: Le Lettere, 1990).

This silencing of memories was another difference in the way the Italian Front receded from view, compared to the war on the Western Front.

It is still difficult to say whether or up to which point the mass of soldiers recognised themselves in the books written by their former generals or officers, permanent or reserve. Maybe their memories of the war were different. Maybe they took refuge in literature. But who told them or anyone else about the Italian Front and its unique features? Henri Barbusse, Erich Maria Remarque and Ernest Hemingway were neither Italian nor Austrian.

Studying history

A small section of publications on the war was by historians, and in particular military historians. The sophistication of Austrian and Italian historiography cannot be analysed in detail here, but something can be said once again about shared and peculiar features on the two sides of the Italian Front.

Obviously, Italian and Austrian military historians worked in two very different contexts and had perhaps opposite tasks. In Austria they had to explain the reasons for the defeat of an old empire; in Italy, the reasons for a young nation's problematic victory. In Austria, the official military report on the war, published in 1930–9, could be seen at the same time as the last act of the Empire and an effort to build a new nation (as its authors were deprived of access to papers found outside the new Austrian government), because of its taking an Austrian-national much more than imperial perspective. In Italy, the exaltation of the national effort became, after 1922, part of the political religion. This did not make it easier for the officers of the post-war Historical Office of the general staff to explain realistically Italian problems and defeats, as well as victories. Mussolini reportedly said in 1925 that the time of myths had come, not of history. Then the official report on the Italian war stopped at the volume on 1917 in the mid 1930s, and it would be resumed only in 1968, to be completed in 1988.

Only a few scholars tried to build bridges between these two nationalist military histories, different but parallel. In the years between the two World Wars, Luigi Cadorna (and afterwards Piero Pieri) and Krafft von Dellmesingen wrote to each other, and their exchanges were published in learned journals or newsletters.[38] Apart from these initiatives, Austrian and Italian military

38 Piero Pieri, *La prima guerra mondiale 1914–1918: problemi di storia militare*, new edn, ed. Giorgio Rochat (Rome: Ufficio storico, Stato maggiore dell'esercito, 1986 [1947]).

histories grew in mutual splendid isolation. This separate set of trajectories – more than the language barrier – made it more difficult to deepen our knowledge of the Italian Front, to spread it internationally to countries other than Austria and Italy and to integrate it into the general histories of the First World War.

Moreover, at the national level, both in Austria and in Italy, studying military history remained unfashionable. After the Second World War, when military history grew all over Europe, it took forty years for a major book to emerge – Manfried Rauchensteiner's publication of 1993.[39] In Italy, things were only slightly better. Piero Pieri published a short history of the war between 1958 and 1965,[40] and Piero Melograni a more comprehensive and widely researched one in 1969.[41] But to have histories of the Great War other than the old myths, here and there still echoed by Melograni, it was necessary to wait longer in Italy than it took in Austria: it took until the late 1990s, with the works of Giovanna Procacci (1997), Antonio Gibelli (1998) and especially Giorgio Rochat and Mario Isnenghi (2000),[42] whose synthesis, twelve years after its publication, remains unsurpassed.

Conclusions

The Italian Front mattered in the final unfolding of victory and defeat in the First World War. One scholar claimed that 'Germany might indeed have surrendered if it had not been able to count on Austria-Hungary.' And yet the same author claimed that 'Italy brought less in benefits than a burden to its great power Allies.'[43] Both claims require revision. The progressive weakening of Austria, in fact, had a direct effect on the central front in the war, the Anglo-Franco-German Western Front. Let us not forget that out of fifty months of war, the Italian army spent thirty-nine months reducing, wearing out and degrading the Austrian army. No explanation of the dissolution of the Dual Monarchy can ignore this fact, and that progressive erosion helped doom the Central Powers in 1918.

39 Rauchensteiner, *Der Tod des Doppeladlers*.
40 Piero Pieri, *L'Italia nella prima guerra mondiale* (Turin: Einaudi, 1965).
41 Piero Melograni, *Storia politica della grande guerra 1915–1918* (Bari: Laterza, 1969).
42 Antonio Gibelli, *La grande guerra degli italiani 1915–1918* (Milan: Sansoni, 1998); Procacci, 'La prima guerra mondiale'; and Isnenghi and Rochat, *La grande guerra 1914–1918*.
43 L. L. Farrar, 'The strategy of the Central Powers, 1914–1917', in Strachan (ed.), *The Oxford Illustrated History of the First World War*, pp. 28, 32.

On the other hand, it is true that a former multi-national empire and a young nationalist kingdom were very different. But they had many more common features than the two national historiographies – generally ignoring each other – have long been willing to admit. In a transnational and global history of the Great War, perhaps it is now time to reintegrate fully the story of the Italian Front in the military and human chronicle of the conflict.

11

The Ottoman Front

ROBIN PRIOR

There is some irony in the fact that Britain, the country that mainly prosecuted the war against Ottoman Turkey, had spent the last 100 years attempting to prop up the 'sick man of Europe' against its foes. By the early years of the twentieth century the position had changed. The Young Turk Revolution in 1908 promised much but delivered little in the way of reform. The Balkan wars of 1912 and 1913 saw Turkey lose most of its European possessions. In Europe it was now reduced to a small amount of territory around Adrianople. Britain and France had been aware for some time of the alienation of the tribes in the Arabian Peninsula from Turkish rule. Was the Ottoman Empire finally on the brink of collapse? And if it did collapse would the British in particular face a series of hostile states on the flank of its communications with the East through the Suez Canal? Clearly, the British would have an interest in events in the Ottoman provinces, and France had a long declared interest in the fate of what are now the states of Lebanon and Syria. Vultures seemed to be gathering before there was a carcass to consume.

The Young Turk government was not unaware of British and French interest in their fate. In an attempt to shore up their position they staged a coup in Constantinople in 1913, centralising affairs under the triumvirate of Enver Pasha (Minister of War), Jemal (Cemal in modern Turkish spelling) Pasha (Minister of the Navy) and Talat Pasha (Minister of the Interior). Enver, in particular, was pro-German. He had been Military Attaché in Berlin and was a great admirer of German military efficiency. On the other hand Jemal leaned towards the French and Talat towards the Russians. It soon became clear however, that the Entente powers were not prepared to accept Turkish conditions, which included the return of the Aegean islands lost to Greece in the Balkan wars and the abolition of the Capitulations – the series of tax concessions forced upon Ottoman Turkey by the powers. All the Entente was willing to offer was a guarantee of Ottoman Turkish sovereignty in the event of war.

The Central Powers could offer more. Liman von Sanders was head of the German military mission in Turkey, and more assistance in retraining and equipping the army was offered. This suited Enver, who as early as July 1914 had asked the Germans for an alliance which was signed on 2 August.

The outbreak of war in August put all these moves on hold. Turkey for the moment put the German alliance in abeyance and declared its neutrality. The Triumvirate were concerned that on the one hand Turkey's great enemy, Russia, had sided with the Entente, and on the other that this, added to the strength of Britain and France, might mean that the Entente would win. The Young Turks bided their time. By October they had definitely decided to trigger the German alliance. The German ships *Goeben* and *Breslau* had arrived in Constantinople after evading the British Mediterranean Squadron. They made useful replacements for the two dreadnoughts being built for Turkey by Britain, but withheld for its own use after the declaration of war on Germany. The Germans now promised the Turks that they would abolish the Capitulations and, if Greece intervened, restore the lost islands.

The incident which caused the outbreak of war is shrouded in mystery. On 29 October, Admiral Souchon, with the *Goeben* and *Breslau* (now with Turkish names) bombarded Odessa and attacked Russian shipping in the Black Sea. The Triumvirate had almost certainly agreed in secret to this operation, and after it occurred dissidents within the government were convinced to stay as a sign of national unity. On 2 November Russia declared war, followed by Britain and France on the 5th. Indeed the British fleet off the Dardanelles had bombarded its outer forts even before the declaration of war.

It seems reasonable to conclude that neither Britain nor France wanted war with Ottoman Turkey but they were prepared to do very little to avoid it. Possibly they saw the break up of the Ottoman Empire as inevitable and wished to safeguard their interests when it occurred. On the other side, Enver, in particular, became convinced that the Central Powers would win the war and that Ottoman Turkey's long-term interests lay with them. This was a fearful miscalculation that took little note of British sea power and its determination to protect its communications with India. But all this lay a long way in the future. Given that Britain and France were having a great deal of difficulty even containing the Germans on the Western Front and that the Russians had received an early thrashing at Tannenberg, exactly what forces did the Entente have to spare to deal with Turkey and how were they to be deployed?

In fact the war against Ottoman Turkey evolved piecemeal and over disparate areas. In the initial phase (1914–15), with the exception of Gallipoli, only relatively small forces were involved and many of these did not originate in Britain. By the end of the war, however, 500,000 troops had been committed against Ottoman Turkey and Egypt had become the greatest base for British troops outside the homeland. There were four main areas of British involvement against the Turks and although the operations in all four areas overlapped at one time or another, they will be dealt with roughly in chronological order – Mesopotamia, Gallipoli, Sinai and the Arabian Peninsula. The considerable conflict between the Turks and Russians has been considered in Chapter 9 on the Eastern Front.

British involvement in Mesopotamia (now modern-day Iraq and to a lesser extent Iran), although eventually successful, was a farrago of divided counsel and indeterminate aims from the beginning. The usual reason given for the British invasion of Mesopotamia was the protection of the oil refineries around Abadan at the head of the Persian Gulf. No doubt this played a part. But the principal reasons for intervention given at the time were: a demonstration to the Turks that the British could strike them in any part of their Empire; an encouragement to the Arab populations to rally to Britain; and to safeguard British interests in the Persian Gulf, which was seen as an outlier in the defence of India and without Arab support would remain attached to Britain. Oil was mentioned, but the fact that the main supplies were in the hands of a friendly sheik and that oil could also be obtained easily from the United States, made this a lesser matter.

The initiative for intervention came from London – which in the light of subsequent events had more than a touch of irony. Two divisions of the British Indian Army (a composite force largely consisting of Indian troops but with British officers and a 'stiffening' of a few British battalions) were being transported across the Arabian Gulf to Europe for service on the Western Front. On the insistence of the Cabinet (but to the annoyance of the Viceroy, Lord Hardinge), a brigade of the 6th (Poona) Division was diverted to the Gulf. It anchored off Bahrain on 23 October awaiting further instructions. On the outbreak of the war with Turkey these instructions soon followed – they were to be convoyed to the Shatt-al-Arab and proceed to occupy Abadan.

Facing the British were two divisions of the Ottoman army, the 35th and 38th. They were not of the highest quality; the best troops being grouped much closer to Constantinople. Each division contained about 5,000 men and had thirty-two pieces of light artillery. Few of these troops, however, were at the head of the Gulf, so the British were able to land without difficulty. They then advanced several miles up river until they were two miles northward of the oil installations. Abadan was safe.

However, by then the remainder of the 6th Division had arrived, and its commander General Barratt had fresh orders. The better to protect Bahrain, he was to occupy Basra. As it happened, this was not difficult. Intelligence arrived that the Ottoman Turks were evacuating Basra. He immediately dispatched several battalions of his force and on 21 November 1914, Basra was in British hands.

At this point the factor that plagued British policy in Mesopotamia began to reveal itself. Basra had been captured to protect Abadan; Querna, thirty miles up river at the junction of the Tigris and Euphrates, was now deemed essential for the protection of Basra. A British expedition was sent north. Querna, due more to the incompetence of the local Ottoman Turkish commanders than the enterprise of the British, capitulated with its garrison of 1,000 men on 9 December.

Another perennial factor that was to hamper the British was also revealed at Querna. The floods that would turn the whole area of the two rivers into a gigantic flood plain were imminent. Yet the British had little water transport. They had a few small gunboats capable of carrying small garrisons and two 18-pounder guns, but that was all. Also, the waters were ubiquitous but shallow. The only answer seemed to be to employ hundreds of local canoes called bellums. These could hold around eight men who were required to row them as well as fight. The weird addition of canoe-borne infantry thus made its first (and surely last) appearance in the British army.

While the British were pondering their next move, the Ottoman Turks were preparing to recapture Basra. They gathered a motley force at Nasiriyah and began to march (or wade) towards their objective. The result was a fiasco. The British had good intelligence about the approach of the Turks and, reinforced with another division of troops from India, sallied forth to attack them. Three days' fighting in March saw the end of the Turkish thrust. The Turks lost heavily and retreated towards Nasiriyeh. The lack of transport meant that the British were unable to follow. The Turks would survive to fight another day.

A more threatening Turkish move had already taken place – but at the Suez Canal rather than Mesopotamia. The Canal Zone of course ran through Egypt, which was still legally part of the Ottoman Empire but actually semi-autonomous under a Khedive and actually (since 1883) controlled by the British. The defence of the Canal Zone therefore fell to the Commander-in-Chief of Egypt, General Sir John Maxwell. At his disposal were about 30,000 troops from the Indian Army and, from December 1914, a contingent of Anzacs, supposedly on their way to Britain but due to crowded facilities there, training in Egypt. A Turkish invasion force to attack the canal had long been in preparation. By January 1915, 20,000 men and 10,000 camels and a few pontoons had been assembled in the Beersheba area, under the nominal command of Jemal Pasha but operationally controlled by the wonderfully named General Friederich Kress von Kressenstein. The organisation of this force was a far cry from the rabble around Basra. Careful preparations in the form of adequate water and food supplies had been made to cross the desert. Marches were made by night to avoid detection and the heat. As a result of this efficient organisation the force arrived at the canal in good shape.

When the Turks arrived at the canal, they soon found that organisation was not enough. The defenders were well dug in along the banks of the canal, which was on average 150 feet wide. The canal was interspersed with some wider lakes but these were controlled by small British gunboats. The Turks were therefore forced to scramble down the steep banks of the canal and attempt to launch the small amount of small boats that they possessed. There was never any prospect of success. Most pontoons were holed by rifle and machine-gun fire before they reached the water. By 4 February it was all over. The British awoke to find that the Turks had withdrawn in good order back to Beersheba. The hoped-for rising of the Egyptian population against the British had failed to materialise. By June 1915 Kress's force had been withdrawn from Sinai to reinforce Gallipoli. The canal was safe.

There was no attempt to pursue the Turks. The British forces lacked mobility and supplies of food and water to traverse 100 miles of desert. They were even short of camels. For the moment stalemate reigned in Sinai.

While the early operations in Mesopotamia had been proceeding and the Turkish attack on the canal was being fought off, Winston Churchill, the First Lord of the Admiralty, had been casting about to find a way to use the navy to influence the war on land. A number of schemes put forward by him all came to grief on two grounds. The first was that all Churchill's naval advisers thought the proposals risked ships from the Grand Fleet in mine- and torpedo-infested waters. The second was that the War Office and its formidable head, Lord Kitchener, insisted that there were no troops to land anywhere.[1]

In January 1915, Churchill cast his eyes on Ottoman Turkey. A squadron of British warships was guarding the entrance to the Dardanelles Straits and Churchill put enough pressure on the Admiral in command, Carden, to get him to reluctantly agree to attempt to force the Dardanelles. Churchill now had an operation, and it would use only old battleships that could not stand in a line of battle against the modern German types faced by Britain in the North

1 For this period see Robin Prior, *Gallipoli: The End of the Myth* (New Haven, CT and London: Yale University Press, 2009), chapter 1.

Sea. This factor would overcome much naval disapproval. And it would not use soldiers – which would please the military. So on 13 January he took the scheme to the War Council, a committee of the Cabinet which oversaw the running of the war in Britain. The War Council was enthusiastic. The ships would demolish the forts, proceed to Constantinople, overawe the Turks and force them out of the war.

As it happened the attack by ships alone was a fiasco. Churchill has been blamed for its failure, but the fact is that the quality of naval advice offered to him by the experts at the Admiralty was lamentably low. These men could have calculated, but did not, that the guns of the old ships were so worn and inaccurate that they could not hit the forts (and the guns they contained) with any accuracy.[2] Moreover, even had the guns been demolished, little thought had been given by the Admiralty to the problem of sweeping the minefields that also protected the Straits. The sweeping force provided to Admiral Carden consisted of nothing more than North Sea fishing trawlers, manned with civilian crews. They were so slow that they could hardly reach the minefield against the strong current flowing down the Dardanelles. The result was that after two weeks some guns at the entrance of the Straits had been demolished, not by the ships, but by landing parties of marines, and no mines had been swept.

This indifferent progress led Churchill to prod Carden into making a major assault with all his battleships on 18 March. Carden's response was to collapse and leave the task to his second in command, Admiral de Robeck. No forts were demolished in this major effort and no mines swept, but one-third of the Anglo-French force was sunk or disabled by a combination of mines and gunfire. This failure marked the end of Churchill's naval venture. Already there had been voices inside the Admiralty and the War Council calling for the commitment of troops to convert the affair into a true combined operation. Now de Robeck added his voice with the statement that the navy could not succeed alone.

Although one of the appeals of the naval attack initially had been that no soldiers would be involved, there was no question that the decision-makers in London would now call the whole thing off. An immediate search for troops began, led by those such as the Secretary of State for War, Lord Kitchener, who had claimed just a few weeks before that there were no troops to be had for operations against Turkey. Within days, however, a motley force was,

2 For this point see 'Report of the committee appointed to investigate the attacks delivered on the enemy defences of the Dardanelles' Straits' (London: Naval Staff Gunnery Division, 1921), p.78. The report is popularly known as the Mitchell Committee Report.

after all, deemed to be available. It consisted of one-and-a-half divisions of Anzac troops training in Egypt; the British 29th Division; the last of the pre-war regular army, the so-called Royal Naval Division (RND), raised from sailors surplus to the requirements of the Grand Fleet; and a French division offered in the spirit of sharing the spoils if the operation succeeded. This force totalled some 80,000 men, which was deemed sufficient to overthrow the Ottoman Empire. So, in late March 1915, preparations for turning Gallipoli into a combined operation commenced. Some four weeks later the first landings took place (Map 11.1).

The commander of the operation was to be General Sir Ian Hamilton, who had been Kitchener's staff officer in the South African War and had held the unimposing post of Commander, Eastern Command, in Britain since the outbreak of the war.

Hamilton had been dispatched to the Dardanelles just in time to witness the failure of the naval attack. He soon developed a plan for landing his troops. This plan was to some extent dictated by the topography of the peninsula. There were few beaches along the rugged coast of the Aegean side and the most obvious ones for effecting a landing – Brighton Beach near Gaba Tepe and the beaches at Bulair at the neck of the peninsula – were heavily defended. This left a number of small beaches at the toe of the peninsula around Cape Helles and a narrow strip to the north of Gaba Tepe. It soon became obvious that these beaches were too confined to land the whole force at any one of them, so Hamilton decided to split his landings. The Anzac force would land to the north of Gaba Tepe and the 29th Division would land at five beaches near Cape Helles. That force, aided by the guns of the fleet, would work northwards up the peninsula, while the Anzacs advanced across the peninsula to prevent Turkish reinforcements reaching their compatriots at Helles. To confuse the Turkish defenders, feint attacks would be made by the Royal Naval Division at Bulair and by the French at Kum Kale on the Asiatic coast.

This plan showed some imagination. By landing at six beaches Hamilton hoped to confuse the Turkish defence and institute a rapid advance while the Turks were off balance. But it also had some defects. At Helles, two substantial forces were to be landed at Y and S beaches on the flanks of the main landing at X, W and V. Short advances by these troops could have in fact cut off all Turkish troops opposing the major landings. But this promising scenario was vetoed by Hamilton and his staff. The force at Y and S were given no orders but to await the arrival of the main force from the south. They were to land, therefore, and remain in situ until the southern landings succeeded. That they might contribute to this result more

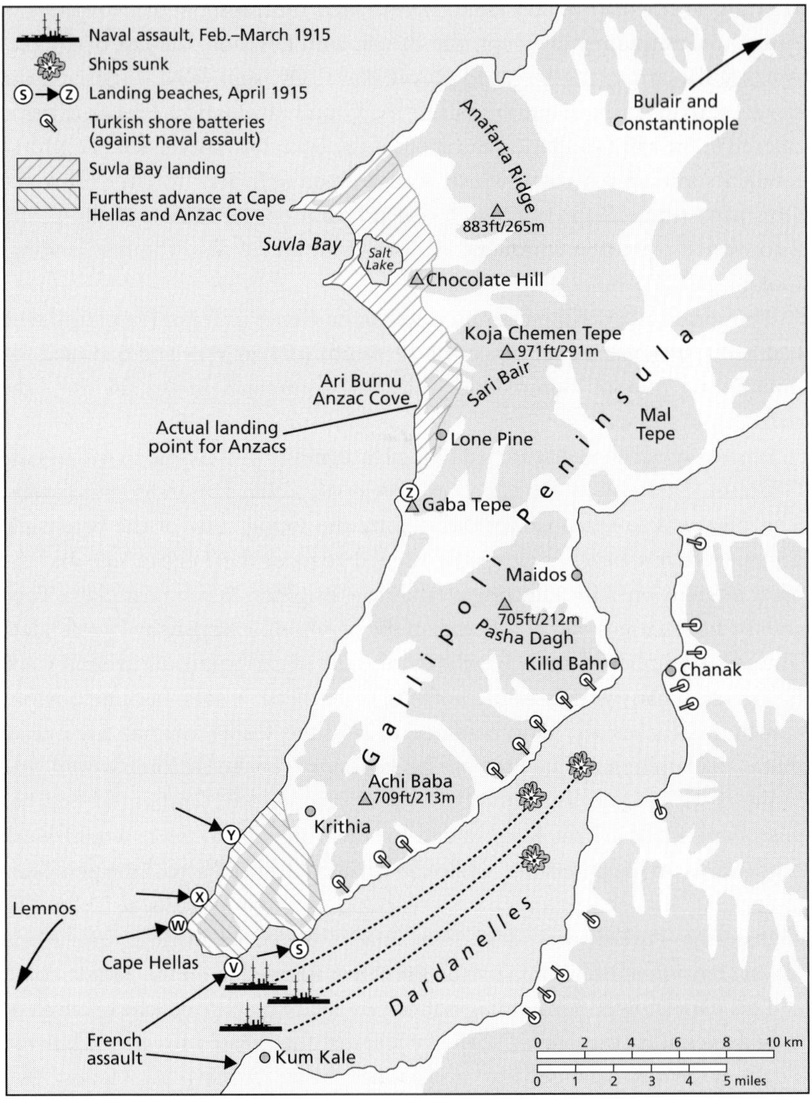

Map 11.1 The Gallipoli campaign.

directly apparently occurred to no one. This oversight was to have doleful effects on the day of landing (Map 11.2).

In the north, the Anzac objective was clear enough – the troops were to push across the peninsula, occupy the significant height of Mal Tepe and

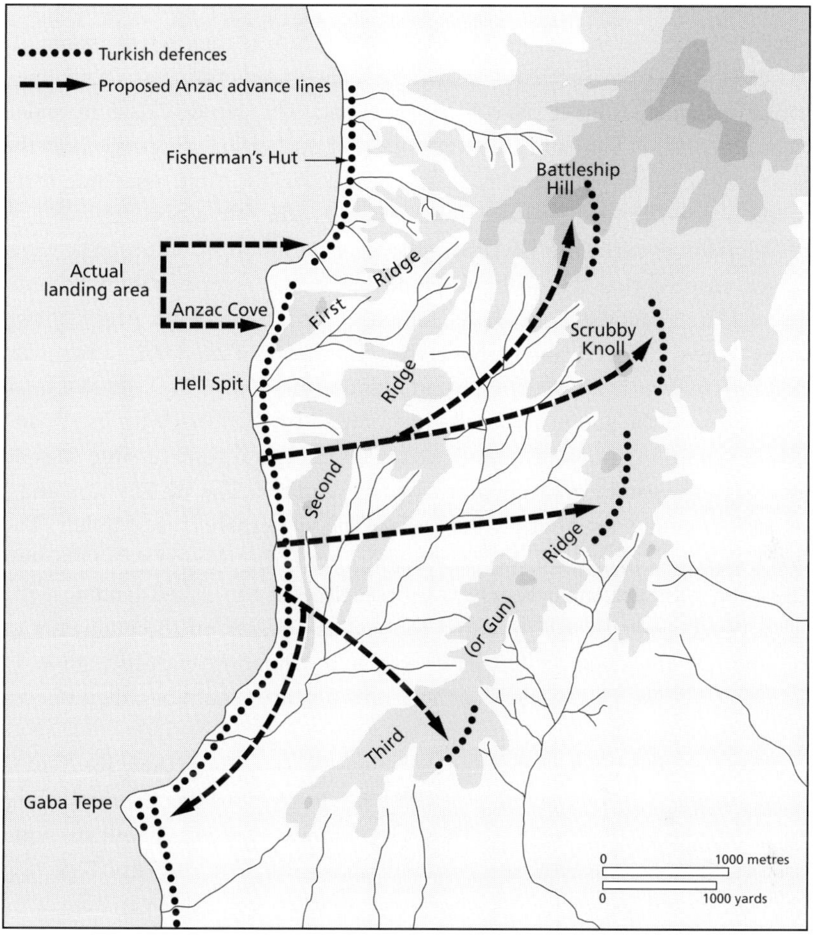

Map 11.2 Anzac landing area.

intercept Turkish reserves heading south. The problem here was that no order actually specified the exact position where the Anzac force was to land. All that was said was that the force was to land north of Gaba Tepe but south of Fisherman's Hut. This was a distance of some one-and-a-half miles. Yet Hamilton's staff was not prepared to be more specific. Nor did Birdwood's staff seek clarification. It was as though the Normandy force had been told to land somewhere between the Cotentin Peninsula and Caen.

Various expedients were adopted to transfer men from ship to shore. At some beaches troops would be transferred from warships or cargo vessels to lifeboats, which would be towed by trawlers until the water became too shallow for the larger craft. The men would then row themselves ashore. At V beach, where the main landing at Cape Helles would take place, 2,000 men would be landed from an old collier, *River Clyde*. The ship would be grounded near Fort Sedd-el-Bahr and the men would debouch from sally ports cut in the sides of the vessel. In this way it was hoped that the large assaulting force could overwhelm the garrison before it could come into action.

What forces could the Turks bring against Hamilton's landings? The naval attack ensured that the Gallipoli peninsula would receive reinforcements. By 18 March 1915 the Turks had decided to form a new Fifth Army of two army corps (six divisions) under the command of General Liman von Sanders, former head of the German military mission to Turkey. The landing places on the peninsula would be guarded by III Corps with its 7th and 9th Divisions. The 19th Division would be in central reserve, able to send troops to the southern or northern area as required. The 5th Division and a cavalry brigade were kept further back in the vulnerable area of Bulair. The XV Corps was placed on the Asiatic shore with the 3rd and 11th Divisions disposed near the main beaches. By the time of the Allied landings, the Turks had about 40,000 men and 100 artillery pieces on the peninsula or nearby. On the Asiatic side there were 20,000 infantry with fifty guns. In addition, the mobile batteries of the Straits defences could be called upon – about sixty guns in all.

The Turkish garrisons defending the peninsula were placed along the coast in small outpost screens, well dug in with wire, in positions that overlooked the most obvious landing beaches. These dispositions represented both strengths and weaknesses. Most of the coastline from Morto Bay to Gaba Tepe was covered by a thin screen of troops. However, these screening garrisons were small in number and there was every chance that if they were overwhelmed by the landing forces, counter-attacks would not be mounted in time or in sufficient strength to force the invaders back into the sea.

On 25 April 1915, British and Anzac forces landed on the Gallipoli peninsula (Map 11.3). Despite much muddle and incompetence on the British side, the Turks did not manage to dislodge them. The feint attacks were of dubious advantage; the landing of the French on the Asiatic shore did not deflect the Turks. The French were eventually withdrawn and landed at Helles alongside the British on 28 April. At Bulair, the appearance of British ships off the coast caught the attention of Liman von Sanders. He kept the Turkish 5th Division in the area at a time when it could have been directed against the Anzac landing. This has often been portrayed as a success for the feint. However,

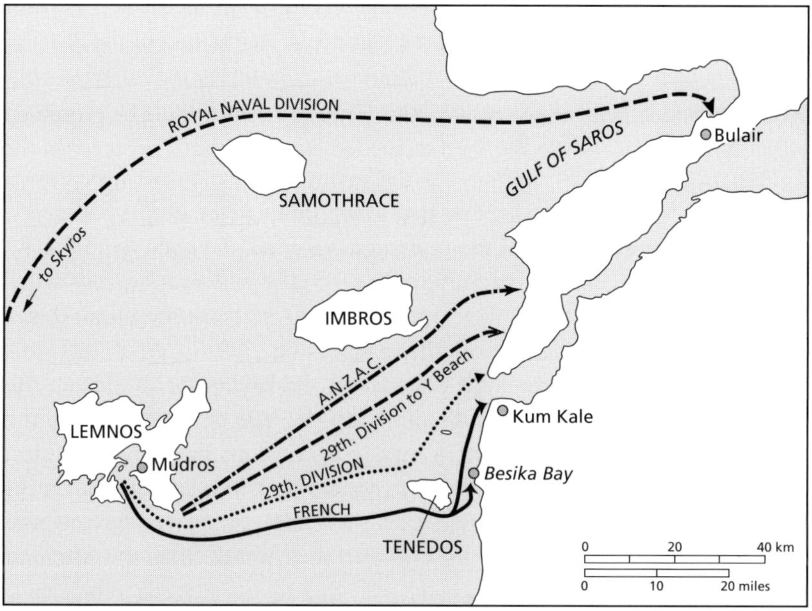

Map 11.3 Deployment of Allied forces landing at Gallipoli, 23–25 April 1915.

Sanders was so obsessed by the Bulair position that he would have probably kept troops in the area even had there been no feint.

At Helles the troops got ashore but at a fearful price. The main British force was landed at W and V beaches at the very toe of the peninsula. Here were the strongest Turkish garrisons (some concealed in the fort at Sedd-el-Bahr) and strong offshore defences in the form of barbed wire and iron stakes. All this was known to Hamilton, but in the prevailing doctrine of the day it was thought best to hit the Turks where they were strongest rather than try a more indirect approach. So, throughout the day, despite the mounting casualties, reinforcements were directed towards W and V beaches. *River Clyde* at V proved a doubtful expedient. Troops issuing from the sally ports proved excellent targets for Turkish machine gunners and riflemen on shore and by nightfall only some 200 men remained ashore unwounded. In the end, it was weight of numbers that told. By the 26th the British had some 12,000 men ashore, with the Turks only several hundred in that area to oppose them.

At what became known as Anzac Cove, contrary to legend, the troops were landed within the vague parameters specified in the orders. The tortuous country and some stubborn defence provided by the few hundred Turkish troops who opposed the landing put paid to any rapid advance. Then Turkish reinforcements began to appear on the battlefield. At the end of the day the Turks were firmly ensconced on such dominating positions as Battleship Hill, Baby 600 and Chunuk Bair on the left. They would not be removed from some of these lodgements for most of the battle

This problem of fire support for the infantry would prove a perennial difficulty at Gallipoli. The troops had very rudimentary artillery support, especially in the early days of the campaign. After all, the main British army on the Western Front was chronically short of guns and ammunition at this time, and the Gallipoli forces were only provided with those munitions that it was thought could be spared from the major battle.

Pushing on from the toeholds obtained at the landing or dislodging the Allied troops from them would be difficult. This was demonstrated by the Turks at Anzac on 19 May. There, under instructions from their political masters in Constantinople to push the invaders back into the sea, the Turks mounted one of the largest attacks of the entire campaign. Somewhere between 30,000 and 42,000 infantry took part in an attack along the whole of the Anzac perimeter. The Anzacs had hardly dug any continuous trench lines, had little artillery support, and were outnumbered by at least two to one. However, during the course of the attack they fired no less than 948,000 rounds of small arms ammunition, most of it from machine guns. It was enough. The Turks suffered 10,000 casualties and gained no ground. It was an omen of how devastating even small arms fire could be against troops in the open, insufficiently supported by heavy guns.

By the end of May the campaign at Gallipoli had developed into a slogging infantry battle. So, at Anzac, the small perimeter held by the Australian and New Zealand troops remained virtually as it was on 19 May. In the south, Hunter-Weston conducted the three poorly thought out battles of Krithia that gained some unimportant ground at high cost. At the end of June and in early July, there were more hopeful signs at Helles. Hunter-Weston and the French commander General Giraud found that by pooling their artillery resources and limiting their objectives to just a few lines of Turkish trench, they could take small amounts of ground at reasonable cost. 'Bite and hold' operations had arrived on the peninsula but their exponents were soon to return home – Hunter-Weston due to exhaustion and Giraud because he had been seriously wounded. At the very moment of their departure a new plan was called for by Hamilton to employ new troops that London had decided to dispatch to Gallipoli.

The debate to send reinforcements to Gallipoli was hard-fought and encompassed the fall of the Liberal government and its replacement by a coalition, which left Asquith as Prime Minister but included members of the Conservative Party. This might easily have become the death-knell of the Gallipoli campaign, as many leading Conservatives such as Bonar Law had opposed the operation from the outset. But office had a sobering, or perhaps paralysing, effect on the decision-makers. However badly the campaign was proceeding, a decision to 'cut and run' was beyond the courage of the new government. Not for the last time in military affairs, it was considered that one more push (or 'surge', in contemporary terms) might do the trick. Three divisions were to be sent to Hamilton, with a promise of two more should they be required.

Hamilton now had to decide how to use this substantial reinforcement. He had received a plan from the Anzac commander Birdwood that won his favour. Birdwood conceived a left hook around the Anzac perimeter across the difficult but undefended country to the north. A rapid swing to the left would then seize the heights of the Sari Bair Ridge from Hill 971 to Chunuk Bair. An attack would then be mounted down the ridge in concert with the troops already at Anzac. The Turkish positions would thus be rolled up and one of the reinforcing divisions would dash for the Narrows and seize the forts. With these defences in Allied hands, the fleet could sail up to Constantinople, the Turks would surrender and perhaps a gigantic Balkan coalition could be formed against the Central Powers. As a coda to the plan, Birdwood suggested that a force be landed at Suvla Bay and convert that relatively flat area into a base of supply for all the forces in the north.

Birdwood's plan held the day and during July it was developed and fine-tuned by both the Anzac Corps Commander and by Hamilton's staff at GHQ. During this process, however, something peculiar happened. The Suvla Bay aspect of the plan increased from a small landing to one that was to absorb almost two of the three reinforcing divisions. This left Birdwood with just his existing force and one new brigade to carry out the left hook, and the more this movement was studied, the more troops it was thought to need. Finally, all Birdwood's forces would be absorbed in capturing the Sari Bair Ridge. No one at Corps Headquarters or at GHQ seemed to notice that there would now be no force available to cross the peninsula and seize the Narrows. In other words, the entire objective of the new attack was the ridge. Now there were many more ridges between Sari Bair and the Narrows, so Birdwood's plan had shrunk from a campaign-winner to one that promised just a tactical success. And no one noticed.

The new campaign was slated to begin in early August when the troops had arrived and had time to acclimatise. In any event, the Suvla landings took place on 6 August 1915 as Anzac columns were winding their way up the ravines to the Sari Bair heights.

The Suvla operation was carried out by the newly formed IX Corps commanded by General Stopford, formerly the commander of the Tower of London. It consisted of the 11th and 10th (Irish) Divisions of the New Armies, formed by Kitchener on the outbreak of war. This operation has been much misunderstood. Its purpose was to establish a base for the troops in the north. It was to take out a few guns on the flank of the Anzac advance and any spare troops were to advance along the heights, which overlooked Suvla Bay, and attempt to aid the Australians in capturing Hill 971. However, when Stopford looked at the plan he soon realised that his force would be fully absorbed in driving the Turks back from the base, capturing the guns and occupying the heights. Any thought of assisting the Anzacs was dropped as impractical.

In some ways the landing at Suvla Bay showed an increase in sophistication from those on 25 April. Purpose-built landing craft called 'beetles', with light armour and shallow draught, were used to bring the troops from the larger ships to shore. In other ways, however, lessons were not learned. The charts of the Suvla Bay area were not checked by an offshore reconnaissance as the original landing places had been. As a result many of the landing craft came to grief on uncharted reefs and it took some hours to free them. Water supplies also met the same fate, and the lack of water played a major role in slowing the advance inland on the first and second days of the landing. Nor were the Turkish defences known in any detail. One of the first battalions ashore spent some time in attacking an undefended sand dune, only to be cut down by the defenders of their real objective a little further inland. Moreover, the guns, which were a major target for the first day, were found after much elaborate manoeuvring to be non-existent. Then the boats bringing the 10th Division in lost their way and deposited the troops right across the bay from the assigned area and thus separated them from their commander.

Once ashore, matters did not proceed much more smoothly. Most of the brigadiers showed a lack of initiative that almost amounted to paralysis. Stopford, offshore on the HMS *Jonquil*, showed a similar lack of initiative. Hamilton was too preoccupied with events at Anzac to notice that no advance was taking place at Suvla. When he finally intervened, nine hours after the landing, he managed to disrupt the advance that Stopford had finally got around to organising. The result was that no advance at all was made until late on the 8th. As it happened, none of this mattered. The Turks had been taken by surprise and were as slow in organising a counter-attack as the British were in advancing on the ridge overlooking the beach. By the time the Turks arrived in strength on the 9th, the British were well-enough established to beat them back with great slaughter. In the event, the Turks could not drive the British back into the sea and the British could not capture the high ground that seemed essential to make the base safe. In the end this proved not to matter either. The Turks never possessed the artillery resources to make the base area untenable. Although continuously under fire, the base was established and remained established until the evacuation. Despite the supine efforts of the British command and the muddle at the landing, Suvla proved the one successful amphibious operation carried out by the Allies at Gallipoli.

The attempted left hook at Anzac failed, but in circumstances where it could be portrayed as 'almost a success'. Failure in fact set in early. The three columns making their way over unmapped territory in the dark soon got lost. Only a small contingent of Ghurkhas and a party of New Zealand troops got within hailing distance of the ridge. On the next day, due to confusion on the Turkish side, some men from both groups briefly gained two important heights on the ridge (Hill Q and Chunuk Bair). However, they were soon counter-attacked off by the considerable reinforcements that the Turks had rushed to the area. On Hill Q the navy – whose fire had been quite ineffectual in support of the troops – was accused of shelling off the Ghurkhas and, indeed, these troops did take some friendly fire as they were being counter-attacked. However, the fire almost certainly came from some Anzac howitzer batteries, and in any case the grip of the Ghurkhas on the ridge could not have been maintained in the face of the large number of Turks that were brought against them.

It is these two incidents that have led some historians to claim that the Anzacs 'almost' secured the ridge. This is not the case. The two points on the ridge were open to enfilade fire from other points on the ridge. This fire must, sooner or later, have driven the Anzacs back. If the ridge was to be secured, it needed to be captured entire. Whether the Anzacs had sufficient troops to accomplish this or whether the troops could have been supplied with food, water and ammunition had they done so is extremely dubious. The fact is the ridge was never held. The August offensive was no close run thing, but a failure pure and simple.

This August 1915 attack was in fact the last hurrah at Gallipoli. Despite two more divisions of reinforcements and some desultory efforts to capture part of Sari Bair, the military effort was at an end.

Evacuation was discussed in London but there was a Cabinet rebellion. British prestige, it was said, could not withstand such a humiliation. The fact was that British prestige would hinge on whether Britain won the war, and it was obvious to many that this issue would not be decided at Gallipoli. The rebels were finally crushed by a visit by Kitchener to the peninsula where he too recommended evacuation.

It only remained to extricate the troops. This was done in December 1915 at Anzac and in January 1916 at Helles. No troops were lost and this became an occasion to boast of the resourcefulness of the Allies in fooling the Turks. This had to stand in the place of victory. It was little enough to show for an operation of eight months. Gallipoli had failed. Whether Turkey could now be knocked out of the war depended on existing operations in Sinai and Mesopotamia.

In Mesopotamia the situation seemed quite promising. With the arrival of the new troops a general had been put in charge, a 'thruster' by the name of General Sir John Nixon. Under him were grouped the 6th Poona Division under General Townshend and the 12th Division under General Gorringe. That Nixon would need all the troops he could get was soon apparent. In April 1915 he received instructions from the Indian government that his main task was now the occupation of the entire province (*vilayet*) of Basra. This extended well beyond the territory so far captured and extended to Nasiriyah in the north. In all it encompassed approximately 16,602 square miles of territory. Even more alarming, their next instruction was to prepare a plan for the capture of Baghdad. Only incidentally was the protection of the oil pipeline mentioned. What all this portended, but was not clear to either Nixon or London, was that the Indian government and particularly the Viceroy Lord Hardinge had great plans for Mesopotamia. Indeed, they intended to annex it once the war had ended in order to develop the country and make it suitable to absorb the surplus populations of India. In short, it would become an Indian colony. The sub-imperialists of Simla had the bit firmly between their teeth.

To carry out these tasks Nixon reported that he would need more animal transport, a light railway, armoured cars, aircraft and a huge increase in river transport. But he sent these requests to London, which was unaware of the growing ambitions of their colleagues in India. To make matters worse he sent the requests through the ordinary post. When they eventually arrived, no one in London realised that the demands, which they regarded as extraordinary, were designed to fulfil the ambitions of the government in India. Most were turned down.

Meanwhile, despite the priorities of India, Nixon had to delay all thought of an advance until he had secured the oil pipelines which were threatened by various Arabian tribes. Once Gorringe had achieved this he was ready to advance. His first destination was Amara, some sixty miles from Basra.

Townshend's canoe-borne troops, accompanied by three shallow draft gunboats, set off in May and by 3 June Amara had surrendered. Nixon then set off to Nasiriyah, with an ominous coda to his orders that this town would be more secure if Kut-al-Amara, some 120 miles beyond and which lay outside the Basra *vilayet*, was also captured.

Nasiriyah fell as easily as Basra and Amara. There was no doubt that these easy victories emboldened Nixon to attempt to capture Kut-al-Amara which he now regarded as a matter of 'strategic necessity'. Reluctantly, the Secretary of State (Austen Chamberlain) gave his approval for the next advance. But he was unaware that the Indian government saw Kut-al-Amara as merely a staging post for the ultimate prize of Baghdad.

One matter soon became clear: the commander who was to advance on Kut-al-Amara was against the whole idea. While Gallipoli remained in the balance Townshend thought gains made in Mesopotamia should be consolidated. He knew that his force was chronically short of water transport and that this might endanger his hold on Nasiriyah, let alone anything further up river. Nevertheless, he had his orders. On 28 August his troops set off, this time not by canoe – because the dry season had arrived – but by foot in temperatures of 116 degrees Fahrenheit.

Moreover, the Turkish army was recovering. Two new divisions had arrived and their overall commander Nureddin Pasha had dug formidable defences on the left and right banks of the river seven miles from Kut-al-Amara.

Townshend took a typically gloomy view of his chances to force these defences. But a clever deception plan, which caused the Turks to concentrate their men and guns on one side of the river while Townshend sent his main force against the other, won the day. After hard fighting, on 28 September the British found that the Turks had decamped. They had lost 4,000 men as against Townshend's 94 killed. A slow pursuit up river ensued to a point where the British were within sixty miles of Baghdad. But the fact still remained that the pursuit was too slow. The main Turkish army had once again escaped.

The question now was Baghdad. Townshend and the War Office opposed it. But soon the prospect of the evacuation of Gallipoli changed the minds of the London decision-makers. By October the Foreign Secretary (Grey) was speaking of a success in Mesopotamia as a suitable antidote. Typically the Cabinet could not come to a definite decision, so they sanctioned a 'raid' on Baghdad, whatever that meant.

Meanwhile Nixon blithely continued up river. This fact on the ground won the Viceroy around. He sanctioned the capture of Baghdad if Nixon's forces were strong enough and promised two additional divisons at a time not specified. Townshend therefore began the advance on 14 November. At Ctesiphon (the ancient Assyrian capital) he defeated a Turkish force, but the victory meant little. His troops had outrun their tenuous supply chain. So, having arrived at the gates of Baghdad, Townshend promptly ordered a retreat. And the retreat would continue until he could be assured of sufficient supplies – that is, he would return from whence he had come, Kut-al-Amara. He reached the town on 4 December and declared – not without reason – that his force was exhausted. They would stand at Kut-al-Amara and if besieged (which soon followed) await a relief column. The siege would last until May 1916. It was characterised by three lame efforts by Nixon to break through, Townshend's propaganda barrage blamed the siege on his superiors. The eventual depletion of food supplies meant that capitulation was the only option. In the end 13,000 men from the 6th (Poona) Division went into captivity. Townshend, through no fault of his own, was treated well and lived in relative luxury on an island in the Marmara. His men were less fortunate. Decades before the German 'death marches' of the inmates of concentration camps, the Turks used a similar policy on British prisoners taken at Kut-al-Amara. About 10,000 men set out from Kut-al-Amara. Marching across the desert in blazing heat with what seems wilful neglect, most of these men died. Indeed the marches seemed so purposeless that this appeared to be their only end. This episode gives the Turks the dubious distinction of carrying out the first genocide of the twentieth century and inventing the death marches as well.

The government in London quickly responded to the fall of Kut-al-Amara. Nixon was sacked and a new man, General Maude, was put in charge. He was to have four full-strength divisions – an accretion of 50,000 men to his force. Also the port of Basra, sunk into a mire of inefficiency and ruin, was reorganised. River transport capacity increased from 450 to 700 tons per day. With this new force, Maude set off for Kut-al-Amara in December. The well-equipped troops advanced in good heart, but the real success belonged to the gunboats. Their fire reduced a Turkish retreat to a shambles. In January 1917 the British were back in Kut-al-Amara.

What followed was the inevitable pause as the British, even with improved logistics, had outrun their supplies. But when his resupplied force set out in March, it was not to be denied. The force was far too strong for anything the Turks could spare in this area. On 9 March Baghdad was in British hands.

The remainder of the Mesopotamia campaign was anti-climactic. Maude sent columns beyond Baghdad but the Turks had recovered and offered stiff resistance. Then, in mid November, Maude died of cholera. But his job was virtually over. Allenby's campaign in Palestine was now the main event, and in 1918 the Mesopotamia campaign ground to a halt. There was a flurry of activity in November when a British force raced ahead to secure Mosul before the Armistice was concluded. But that was all. Attention had long since shifted elsewhere.

It was the situation in Palestine which made Mesopotamia irrelevant, but it has to be said that it was a long time coming. After the defeat of the Turkish attack on the canal the British had cautiously moved into Sinai. An attempt to dislodge them by Kress failed disastrously at Romani in August 1915. The question now was: what was British policy in this area to be – attack or consolidation? In fact it was to be a combination of both. Maxwell had been despatched back to Britain and a new commander – Sir Archibald Murray, former Chief of the general staff – took his place. Murray was a cautious man and with some reason. He had no desire to fling a force across the wastes of the Sinai Desert only to see it retreat through lack of supplies. In this respect he was the opposite of his fellow generals in Mesopotamia. So he would advance across the Sinai but only at the pace of the water pipeline, a railway and an improvised wire-based road across the sand that accompanied him. The pace of all this was glacial. By December 1916 British forces were still in Sinai near El Arish. They were now accompanied by a formidable cavalry component in the form of the Desert Column and the Anzac Mounted Division. Indeed, these forces played a major role in the action at El Arish which saw Turkish forces expelled from Egypt.

The next prize was Gaza, the position which anchored the Turkish defence of southern Palestine. Murray's plan for the First Battle of Gaza was imaginative. He would attack the city frontally while at the same time outflanking it with his mounted troops. It started promisingly on 24 March 1917. The mounted troops carried out their role to perfection and were well to the north of Gaza. But an intelligence failure led them to believe that the frontal attack had gone disastrously wrong, which it had not. As a result the mounted troops withdrew and the Turks were left in full possession of Gaza.

In London, the Cabinet was not pleased with this outcome and urged Murray to try again. Murray pleaded lack of reinforcements and guns as a reason to delay. But political pressure won out. The Second Battle of Gaza commenced on 17 April with weapons such as a handful of tanks and poison gas – the first time this weapon had been deployed outside Europe. (So ineffective was the gas that it dispersed quickly in the warm desert air and the Turks were unaware that it had even been used.) The plan was, however, unimaginative. Three divisions were to assault Gaza frontally. This they did to no effect whatsoever. British losses amounted to 6,500 men. Turkish losses were only a third as much. That was the end of Murray. He had proved an excellent administrator and a disastrous general. Lloyd George wished to replace him with Jan Smuts, but when the South African turned down the command, General Allenby, then commanding the Third Army on the Western Front, got the job. It was to prove a fortunate circumstance.

Allenby was to discover that he had an energetic and sometimes troublesome ally at the base of the Sinai Peninsula at Aqaba. This was T. E. Lawrence and his Arabian Army, nominally commanded by Sharif Hussein of the Hejaz. Hussein had been induced to join the war against Turkey in 1916. There had been an exchange of letters between Hussein and the British High Commissioner in Cairo, Sir Henry McMahon. These letters have a certain desperate opaqueness about them but on the surface anyway they promised Hussein certain territories around modern Syria and the Arabian Peninsula in return for support. Hussein, with the encouragement of Lawrence, then a member of the Arab Bureau in Cairo, was happy to oblige. Arabian nationalism had grown in the nineteenth century and disillusionment with Turkish rule had grown with it.

The Arab uprising against the Turks began in the Hejaz on 5 June 1916. The Turks had just a single division in this area and Hussein and his four sons – the most notable of whom was Feisal – were able to capture Mecca within a few days. Feisal, who increasingly took the lead on the Arab side, then besieged Medina, but his forces, though large in number, were short on discipline and firepower and failed to take it.

The return of Lawrence to act as a kind of Chief of Staff to Feisal changed the way operations were conducted. Lawrence developed a double strategy. He would allow just enough material to pass down the Hejaz railway to sustain the Turks but not enough to increase their strength. This would confine most Turkish troops to the Hejaz while Lawrence with Feisal's Arab army advanced along the coast northward to Aqaba. Lawrence knew that it was necessary to link up with British forces in Palestine as quickly as possible if the Arabs were to have the territory seemingly promised them by McMahon. And Lawrence knew this because he was privy to another division of the Middle East decided by Britain and France under the Sykes-Picot Agreement of May 1916. Under this plan France would be pre-eminent in Syria and Lebanon, while the British would be the dominant power in Palestine, Jordan, Mesopotamia and the Persian Gulf. Clearly, if this agreement was put into practice there would be little room for the Arab states already agreed to by the British. The best way, Lawrence considered, to make certain that the Arabs got their due was for them to occupy such key points as Damascus, Aleppo and Homs.

Lawrence accomplished his first purpose. With the aid of the Royal Navy, Arab forces with British supplies advanced along the Red Sea coast and by 6 July 1917 were occupying Aqaba. The next question for Lawrence was how the newly appointed Allenby would deal with the situation.

Allenby's arrival saw an immediate lift in British morale. He stayed in close touch with his troops and ensured that time was taken to prepare the third assault on the Gaza–Beersheba position. This time the plan showed some imagination. Gaza would be attacked frontally but only as a feint attack. Meanwhile the mounted troops would seize Beersheba and its precious water wells by coup de main. The main attack would then be launched by British infantry on the centre right of the position. The Turkish line would then be rolled up from Beersheba to Gaza while mounted forces cut off any Turks attempting to flee. In all Allenby would have seven infantry divisions, three mounted divisions and 300 guns. He would also have air superiority due to new types arriving in the Middle East from Britain.

The operation began on 31 October 1917. The Australian Light Horse took the wells of Beersheba in a spirited charge, thus ensuring water supplies for the centre-right force, which also captured its objectives without undue difficulty. The attack on Gaza itself began on 1 November. It was an unexpected success. Indeed, although designed as a feint, it turned the flank of the whole Turkish line and forced a general retreat. On the right, Turkish counter-attacks were beaten off, but lack of good supplies of water prevented the mounted troops from cutting off the Turks. Nevertheless, the advance continued but at a slower pace. Yet by 16 November the British had advanced an average of fifty miles and were within striking distance of Jerusalem.

Jerusalem presented a problem to Allenby. A city regarded as Holy by three major religions could hardly be stormed. Allenby planned an encircling movement to the east of the city but the Turkish defence was too strong and it was beaten back. A second attempt to the west met with more success. The Turkish Seventh Army with 16,000 defenders had to be overcome, but the series of defeats already inflicted by the British had sapped its morale. So on 8 December, this potentially formidable fighting force withdrew from Jerusalem and Allenby famously entered it bare-headed on foot on the 11th. Lloyd George's self-serving wish to present the capture of Jerusalem to the British people by Christmas had been fulfilled.

Winter now settled over the area and the British army needed rest and recuperation as well as resupply. Conventional operations were therefore temporarily suspended. Lawrence meanwhile was continuing to launch nuisance raids on the Turks. The most spectacular of these – the attack on the Yarmuk railway bridge – failed. Nevertheless, Lawrence's operations did tie down a number of Turkish troops to the east of the River Jordan while Allenby got on with the main business in Palestine. While Lawrence's contribution has been wildly overblown (mainly by himself) there is no doubt that he played a role in the Turkish retreat.

In Jerusalem, Allenby began to plan his campaign for 1918. Several factors delayed it. The first was the failure of the British to capture the important junction of Amman to the east of the Jordan, but at least the failure convinced the Turks to concentrate more forces in the area, taking them away from the coastal strip along which Allenby always intended to make his final thrust. The other factor was the situation in France. Ludendorff launched the first of his great offensives on 21 March and Allenby was soon required to free British units to stop the German advance. On 23 March two divisions were despatched to the Western Front, followed by artillery batteries and more battalions of troops as shipping became available. Apart from small-scale raiding operations of dubious value, this saw an end to major British activity in Palestine for four months.

In fact the next major British battle in Palestine did not take place until 19 September 1918. Allenby, having coaxed most of the Turkish forces to the east of the Jordan, struck along the coast. The force at his disposal was formidable. The British had 35,000 infantry, 9,000 cavalry and 383 guns on a front of only fifteen miles. The Turks who faced them had just 10,000 men and 130 guns. Before the battle the RAF had played a significant role. By repeated bombing it had cut all railway traffic from the north to Palestine, thus making reinforcement of the Turkish army virtually impossible. The outcome of the battle was never in doubt. The preliminary bombardment dropped 1,000 shells per minute on the Turkish defenders. The infantry broke through near Megiddo (the ancient Armageddon) and this time the cavalry did manage to encircle the retreating Turks. By 21 September the Turkish Seventh and Eighth Armies had ceased to exist. Allenby, sensing that victory was within his grasp, pressed on. The Third Australian Light Horse entered Damascus on 1 October, closely followed by Lawrence's Arab forces, eager to stake their territorial claims. What followed was a diminuendo. British troops followed the increasingly disintegrating Turkish army to Aleppo, which was taken on 26 October without a shot. Armistice negotiations commenced on the same day and were concluded on 31 October. The war against Turkey had been won.

The general consensus about this war is that it should not have been fought; that in future years and decades the West lost more because of the instability in the Middle East than if it had left the Ottoman Empire alone. Despite its wide acceptance, doubt must be thrown on this argument. It is certainly true that the Western powers acted with great duplicity against those who would control the successor states to the Ottoman Empire. They promised Lawrence's Arabs one territorial settlement (the McMahon–Hussein letters which promised Syria, Lebanon and perhaps Palestine to the Arabs), while they acted quite otherwise in their own interests. Sykes-Picot, as Lawrence and Feisal were to discover, trumped all this. It was to be the French who ruled in Syria and in Lebanon, while the British took over Palestine and effectively Iraq, although Feisal was to be the nominal ruler. Yet another new state (Transjordan) was created to meet Arab aspirations, but also placed under the effective control of the British. The Hejaz was actually given to Hussein, but his tenure even there was to be short. In a protracted war between 1919 and 1925, Ibn Saud drove him out and created the new kingdom of Saudi Arabia. Meanwhile, the Balfour Declaration in 1917 muddied the waters further by promising Jews a national home in the area, while at the same time guaranteeing the Arabs their existing territorial rights, an act of sophistry that has not yet played out.

What, it may be asked, could have created a greater shambles than these acts? The answer is many things. The Ottoman Empire was in terminal decline in 1914. There is little doubt that it would have collapsed in short order even without the First World War. The result would have been perhaps a different constellation of successor states than those created by the Western powers. But it is hardly credible that these states would have been stable, democratic or capable of living in harmony with one another. The result would no doubt have been a different kind of shambles to that which we have today in the Middle East, but that it would have been a shambles of one kind or another cannot be doubted. Moreover, the discovery of large oil reserves in the area in the post-war world would sooner or later have drawn in the Western powers as their economies grew increasingly dependent on those supplies.

Finally, it is difficult to feel pangs of nostalgia for the Ottoman Empire. This was the first state, bar the Kaiser's in Africa, which indulged in genocide in the twentieth century, the first state that marched prisoners around the desert for the sole purpose of killing them. Moreover, even under the enlightened Atatürk, over 1 million Greeks were expelled from Turkey shortly after the war. In short, this is not a regime over which people should grow misty-eyed. The continued existence of the Ottoman Empire, in light of a putative German victory or a compromise peace, or its transformation into a militant Republic tied to a victorious Imperial Germany, after 1918, is a counter-factual we can all live without.

12

The war at sea

PAUL KENNEDY

In the late 1920s a debate that had long been simmering broke out openly, and to public bewilderment, as retired British admirals, naval historians and newspaper editors quarrelled over the thing that obsessed them most. The issue was this: why was the role of sea power in the Great War not given higher renown; and, much more specifically, why had the 1916 Battle of Jutland not resulted in as crushing a defeat of the Kaiser's navy as Nelson's brilliant 1805 Trafalgar battle had done to the combined French and Spanish fleets? To the protagonists in this debate, all convinced of A. T. Mahan's argument about 'the influence of sea power upon History', nothing else mattered. This was existential, not least because it raised the awkward question of the future of large battle fleets in modern, technology driven warfare. If they hadn't won at Jutland, what was the point?

The problem was, and is, that all the participants in those angry debates, and almost all later naval historians, fail to ask (and therefore address) the really big question, which is: why did sea power itself play such a relatively limited role in the Great War, as compared to its magnificent and undoubted importance in both the French Revolutionary/Napoleonic Wars and the Second World War? Viewed from the broad sweep of History, humankind has witnessed three massive, global and increasingly total wars since 1789, and in the first and the third of those mighty contests maritime force was critical. So, why do navies occupy only a secondary position in the unfolding of the First World War? It is the purpose of this chapter to attempt an answer to that conundrum.

As to the epic fighting between 1793 and 1815, perhaps Napoleon put it best when he said, bitterly: 'Everywhere I go, I find the English Navy in the way.' Of course he was finally defeated on land, at Moscow, in the Spanish peninsula, at Leipzig and at Waterloo. But everyone at the time came to appreciate the influence of sea power upon history, long before Mahan popularised the phrase.[1] The French navy was given an early mauling at the Glorious First of June (1794), and never again contested the vital Western Approaches or the English Channel. At Cape St Vincent (1797), British tactical superiority over the Franco-Spanish fleets was manifest, as was Nelson's burgeoning genius. His accomplishment at the Nile (1798) – in sending six of his heaviest ships to attack the anchored French fleet from the shallow, landward side, while he attacked simultaneously from the seaward – has no equal. In the previous year, Duncan had clobbered a much tougher opponent, the Dutch navy, at the Battle of Camperdown (1797). The Royal Navy then moved to control the Baltic and, helped by Nelson's blind-eye disregard of instructions, destroyed the Danish fleet at Copenhagen (1801). The greatest moment came in October 1805 at Trafalgar, where Franco-Spanish sea power was destroyed, and British naval mastery could be advanced, in the Mediterranean, in the West Indies, off Finisterre and in the Eastern Seas. Small wonder that the magnetic centre of London today is still Trafalgar Square, with the one-armed admiral's column and statue loftily above it. Small wonder that his fighting genius intimidated a century of latter-day admirals.

The importance of sea power in the Second World War was even more striking. For how could one think of the eventual defeat of the Japanese, Italian and German aggressor-states without the Grand Alliance (Churchill's phrase) wresting control of the Atlantic, Mediterranean and Pacific? Stalin's mass peasant armies could resist invasion under extraordinary conditions, but there was no way that they alone could bring down the Axis powers. This could only come when that purely land struggle was joined by the exertion of massive maritime force. Of critical importance was the (chiefly) Royal Navy's victory in the Battle of the Atlantic, the longest-lasting fight of all, and one upon which success in North Africa and the Mediterranean, and the eventual Normandy landings, ultimately depended. And the gigantic 1941–45 campaign in the Pacific and East Asia was, by the very nature of its geography, determined by combined air-sea power: when dozens of American and British aircraft carriers stood off Okinawa in June 1945, the message was clear. Symbolically, the Japanese High Command surrendered on the poop-deck of the battleship USS *Missouri*, just as Napoleon had delivered himself to the British in 1815 by boarding the battle-scarred HMS *Bellerophon*.[2]

1 A. T. Mahan, *The Influence of Sea Power upon History, 1660–1783* (Boston: Little, Brown, 1890).

2 The author has tried to capture the monumental nature of this struggle for control of the Atlantic, Mediterranean and Pacific seas in his recent book, Paul Kennedy, *Engineers of*

No comparable record is to be found in the story of the naval aspects of the First World War. Was sea power worthless, then? No. It remained vital for the survival of the island-nation, so dependent upon the inflow of overseas supplies; by extension, it must have been vital for France, Belgium and Italy, which relied upon the inflow of British-dug and British-convoyed coal. It was also clearly vital for the extension of Japanese maritime influence across the waterways of Asia and the Indian Ocean; eventually, a Japanese destroyer squadron was to operate out of the Grand Harbour, Malta.

But in the ways in which we usually measure the displays of offensive sea power, the First World War offers a dismal record. Each aspect will be discussed in more detail below, but a summary can easily be made now. Of great fleet actions, there were hardly any, and the most promising, at Jutland, was inconclusive. Of amphibious operations, that is, not mere coastal raids but the large-scale and permanent emplacement of a full army onto enemy territory, there was only the sad story of the Dardanelles expedition of 1915–16, perhaps the most humiliating setback since the ill-fated Sicilian Expedition by the Athenians. Of the struggle to either protect or disrupt shipping lanes, the Allies had a mixed record, almost losing that campaign to U-boat attacks in 1917 before surmounting the challenge in the year following. The economic blockade of the Central Powers was, well, a subject much misunderstood at the time, and still badly misunderstood today. If there is one, single noticeable aspect to the history of sea power in the 1914–18 conflict, it must be the increasing restriction upon any fleet's freedom to operate off an enemy's shoreline: the fast torpedo-boat, the submarine and (perhaps especially) the naval mine had put paid to that. Although battleships had to be retained if other Powers kept up their own, less and less could such vessels be called collectively 'mistress of the seas'.

The naval balance

The overall naval balance in August 1914 between the fleets of the Great Powers helps to explain a lot, though by no means all, of this conundrum. America was, obviously, not a player, and only British naval intelligence kept an eye upon events in the New World. Given Italy's early neutrality, the Austro-Hungarian navy (3 dreadnoughts, 3 semi-dreadnoughts, 6 pre-

Victory: The Problem Solvers who Turned the Tide in the Second World War (New York: Random House and London: Penguin, 2013), in chapters 1 (the Battle of the Atlantic), 4 (amphibious warfare) and 5 (the war in the Pacific).

dreadnoughts, 7 cruisers, 18 destroyers, 61–70 torpedo boats, 10 submarines, 3 coast-defence vessels) found itself without an enemy, unless Anglo-French warships were reckless enough to attack ports along the rocky, difficult Adriatic shore; far better for the Allies simply to close the mouth of those waters and establish the Otranto Blockade, which was to last throughout the war.[3] The Imperial Russian Navy (10 pre-dreadnoughts, 1 coast-defence vessel, 12 cruisers, 25 destroyers, 72 torpedo boats, 22 submarines, 12 gunboats) was hopelessly divided between its Baltic, Black Sea and Far Eastern fleets – 'strong nowhere, and weak everywhere', to use Frederick the Great's term. Since the Japanese navy (2 dreadnoughts, 1 battlecruiser, 10 pre-dreadnoughts, 4 coast-defence ships, 33 cruisers, 50 destroyers, 12 submarines) dominated the eastern seas, and since in any case Japan swiftly entered the war in August 1914 as Britain's ally, there was nothing for the Russian ships to do on that maritime front.

The French navy, once representing the world's second maritime power since the late seventeenth century, was now strategically eclipsed.[4] Apart from having a fleet to secure its imperial possessions, Paris had invested in sea power to oppose the Germans (which the British could do on their own), keep Italy in its place (no longer necessary after the new alliance restructuring) and assist Russia (geographically impossible after Turkey entered the war in November 1914). It could participate in certain eastern Mediterranean campaigns (Gallipoli, Salonica) and join, in a limited way, anti-submarine patrols. But it was a navy without an enemy – the exact opposite of its far more dominant partner, the French army.This brought things down to where they were always going to be: the Royal Navy versus the German High Seas Fleet, that is, surface warship encounters in the North Sea and then, after 1917, U-boat versus Allied convoys and their escorts that gradually extended across the Atlantic. In the first regard, the Royal Navy's material preponderance was impressive. The British fleet numbered 22 dreadnoughts, 13 dreadnoughts under construction, 9 battlecruisers in service, 1 battlecruiser under construction, 40 pre-dreadnoughts, 121 cruisers, 221 destroyers, 109 torpedo boats and 73 submarines. The Germans were fewer in nearly all of

3 Those interested in more detailed statistics on the size of the each navy in 1914 should consult Paul Halpern, *A Naval History of World War I* (Annapolis, MD: Naval Institute Press, 1994).

4 Its size in 1914, though, was still considerable: 2 dreadnoughts, 6 semi-dreadnoughts, 14 pre-dreadnoughts, 28 cruisers, 81 destroyers, 187 torpedo boats, 67–75 submarines and 1 coast-defence vessel.

the classes above: 15 dreadnoughts, 5 dreadnoughts under construction, 5 battlecruisers in service, 3 battlecruisers under construction, 22 pre-dreadnoughts, 8 coast-defence ships, 40 cruisers, 90 destroyers, 115 torpedo boats and 31 submarines.

Early actions, overseas and in European waters

Here, six vignettes will suffice to show the iron corset into which naval operations had been forced in 1914–15: early Allied captures and victories overseas; the ever-tightening grip of the blockades, from Dover, Scapa Flow and Rosyth, upon the exits from (and entrances into) the North Sea; a bold German fleet escape along the Mediterranean and into the safety of the Bosphorus; a German victory, then an even more stunning defeat at sea, in the waters of the South Atlantic; a harrowing British experience of the disasters that would befall close-in blockades in the new age of U-boats, plus the shock of German surface bombardments of towns along the Yorkshire coast. Taken together – for there are far too many single populist narratives with titles like 'The Flight of the Goeben' and 'Coronel and the Falklands' – the geopolitical and naval topography of the First World War established itself, and with only one exception (the Battle of the Atlantic after 1917) scarcely changed before the German High Command requested an armistice in November 1918.

The ruination and elimination of Germany's overseas positions came fast and total, and there were few surprises here, for the British 'new' imperialists, their self-governing Dominions and their allies in the French Ministry for Naval and Colonial Affairs, had been obsessed for three decades about German colonialism. The year 1884 was Bismarck's 'first bid for colonies'; thirty years later came that youthful empire's liquidation, which had no chance at all once London and Paris had settled their own imperial quarrels and formed a united front against Wilhelmine ambitions. It is rarely recognised how much Grand Admiral Tirpitz played a part in the creation of this geopolitical prison, but it was he who had fought with grim determination against the deployment of greater German naval forces overseas, arguing always, as he had done in his famous Memorandum of 1897, that the North Sea was the 'lever' by which a growing High Seas Fleet would one day compel the British to concede equal world status to the Second Reich. The result, as detailed below, was that the far-flung German warships, however competently handled, were in 1914 at the mercy of a vast imperial coalition which held all the cards in the renewed struggle for the mastery of the Middle East, South Asia, the Southwest Pacific and all of Africa.[5]

If German warships overseas were out-powered, so also were the spatchcocked, thinly held German colonies. When London and Paris announced they were at war, rough plans to seize those German overseas territories were already developed. With great delight New Zealand moved in on German Samoa, while Australian forces took German New Guinea: both Dominions had held an exaggerated fear of Prussians in the South Seas, and now welcomed the chance to eliminate those alien presences. In West Africa, superior French and British forces quickly moved into Togoland and the Kamerun. The South Africans were equally keen to crush what they saw as the threatening German hold over South West Africa (present-day Namibia), though it took Smuts and Botha's forces until 1915 to do so. Only in German East Africa did that remarkable General Paul von Lettow-Vorbeck lead far larger numbers of South African, Indian and British troops a merry dance around Mount Kilimanjaro until the Armistice itself, after which he returned to a hero's welcome in a morale-depressed Berlin.[6]

When one pulls back from this bustle of military and naval actions, a basic strategic point emerges: there was not going to be a 'war in the Eastern Seas', or a bitter struggle for Caribbean sugar islands, or even surface actions off North Africa. The Germans were the great losers here, of course, but so also were French justifications for having a large navy; so, too, at least after the Falklands battle (below), were those Fisher-ite delusions about turning the Royal Navy into a force built around fast, long-range battlecruisers dominating the distant waters of the world. Scapa Flow, Dover, Gibraltar and Alexandria did that nicely.

In the Far East the Japanese marched, as ever, to their own drummer, seeing the European crisis as an opportunity further to expand their influence. Qingdao and the province of Shandong, precariously held by Germany, were invaded and possessed. Tokyo had used an expansive interpretation of the revised 1907 Anglo-Japanese Treaty to enter the war on the side of the Allies, and the British Foreign Office was somewhat surprised at Japan's boldness. To the cold, calculating, neutralist Americans, it was Japan's ready seizure of

5 'Renewed', because this global struggle among the European powers probably first began during the age of Louis XIV and William and Mary, continued through no less than seven major wars in the long eighteenth century, resumed in a less violent form in the post-1871 scramble for colonies and was only settled by the 'Entente Cordiale' agreements of 1904–06, deals that were heavily driven by a mutual concern at the perceived ambitions of Wilhelm's Germany.

6 Leonard Mosley, *The Duel for Kilimanjaro* (London: Weidenfeld & Nicolson, 1963). It is one of the very few *entertaining* accounts of fighting in 1914–18.

Germany's island possessions in the Central Pacific – the Marshalls, the Carolines, the Marianas – that caused strategic concern. Still, the larger point would surely be about the disposition of these German colonies when – or if – the war was won by the offshore Powers. It was highly unlikely that any would be returned to Berlin; in the future, the pan-Germans would head for the grain-fields of the Ukraine and the coal of the Donbas instead.

These overseas campaigns were decided so relatively swiftly because of course the German navy could not get out of the North Sea (and the Austro-Hungarian navy had nowhere to go even if it managed to exit the Adriatic). Once the British ultimatum expired on 3 August 1914, Royal Navy squadrons closed off the Straits of Dover and the waters between Scotland and Norway. At the same time, German submarine cables to the outer world were lifted and snipped by specialist cable ships, and the Second Reich was isolated, except to secondary strategic centres such as Scandanavia and the Balkans. Not only could German warships not get out to reinforce positions overseas, but German merchant ships could not get in, because of this throttling blockade. Nor could neutral merchant ships make up the 'gap', for they were escorted into British ports for inspection (and confiscation of goods intended for Germany) before being released to Amsterdam, or wherever. As is argued below, it is doubtful whether neutral sources could supply the massive German demand for foodstuffs and raw materials in any case, but the maritime blockade made that option moot.

Within the North Sea, however, the British naval policy still had flaws. It should have been clear to all senior naval commanders that a 'distant' blockade based on Dover and Scapa Flow was the sensible strategy, with one caveat. But the Admiralty had not given up on the folly of 'close' blockade, and on 22 September 1914 disaster occurred, when three large, but elderly, British cruisers (HMSs *Aboukir*, *Hogue* and *Crecy*) were sunk within an hour by a minuscule and obsolescent U-boat: a staggering 1,400 sailors were sunk. As Corbett put it in his official history, 'nothing so emphatically proclaimed the change that had come over naval warfare'.[7] Shortly afterwards, in October, the brand-new dreadnought, HMS *Audacious*, hit an enemy mine and sank quickly. From this time onwards, the thought of the damage that submarines, torpedoes and mines could do to giant dreadnoughts obsessed Commander-in-Chief Jellicoe's mind. If his Grand Fleet went to sea without minesweepers,

7 Julian S. Corbett, *History of the Great War Based on Official Documents by Direction of the Historical Section of the Committee of Imperial Defence: Naval Operations*, 2 vols. (London: Longmans, Green and Co., 1920–1), vol. II, p. 389.

it might crash into a newly laid enemy minefield. If it went out preceded by minesweepers, they were limited to a speed of ten knots, and thus very vulnerable to U-boats. And if the British battlecruisers and the fast (Queen Elizabeth-class) battleships steamed at full speed for safety's sake or to catch the enemy, the fleet destroyers that were supposed to be protecting them could not keep up, except in the smoothest of waters.

This difficulty was accompanied by two other ones. First, it was a shorter distance for the High Seas Fleet to steam over and bombard ports of the east coast of England than for the Grand Fleet to get to that area from Scapa Flow. Secondly, the year-long heavy mists and fog in the central North Sea made sightings and communication so very difficult – this was not Cape St Vincent or Aboukir Bay! The first problem was being gradually solved by the decryption team in the Admiralty's Room 40, for the German navy was notoriously prolix in its ship-to-ship radio traffic as it readied itself to go to sea. But that system was by no means perfect, and no one could solve the problem of the North Sea fogs. Thus it was that when, on 15–16 December 1914, both fleets came to sea, as usual with the fast battlecruiser squadrons ahead of the larger battlefleets, a comedy of errors took place. Admiral Hipper's battlecruisers shocked the British nation by bombarding Scarborough, Hartlepool and Whitby, then narrowly missed a British trap due to poor messaging by Beatty's flag captain to the cruisers scouting ahead. But the British forward squadrons had also perhaps narrowly missed encountering the entire High Seas Fleet, before its commander became worried at massed destroyer/torpedo attacks and returned to Wilhelmshaven. Both admiralties were furious at the lack of decisive action, but the fact is that fleet commanders were now worried stiff at operating in the central North Sea.

London ordered Beatty's battlecruisers to relocate southwards to be based at Rosyth in the Forth, and placed an enormous number of cruisers, destroyers and submarines at Harwich. Nonetheless, this still was a preventative action, for no one wanted to be out on the waters, except for each sides' submarines, which were getting ever bolder – the British ones now moving to operate in the Baltic itself. The dangerous shallows of the Dogger Bank, the threat of new minefields, the possibility of a destroyer attack out of the mists and the sheer scariness of the submarine – one British sub accidentally lost control, rose suddenly to the surface and caused a number of German heavy warships to scatter in fright! – were now intimidating. When war began, the proud signal went out that 'The King's Ships are at Sea', but they were less and less so. The contours of the disappointing outcome of Jutland were already emerging in the first few months of the surface war.

There was also disappointing news for the British in the Mediterranean, although a better result in the South Atlantic. There were two small, but significant, German flotillas abroad in 1914. The first consisted of the modern battlecruiser SMS *Goeben* and its accompanying cruiser SMS *Breslau*, under Admiral Souchon, and rather vainly called the 'Mittelmeerflotte'. Starting in the western Mediterranean, they made an intrepid voyage eastwards, pursued by a superior but cack-handed British force, ending up safe and sound in Constantinople, and thereby unfolding a much larger escalation of the war that would consume Turkey's own involvement on the side of the Central Powers, the isolation and slow strangulation of Russia's Black Sea as well as Baltic export trades and the invitation to the British and French to expand across the entire Ottoman Middle East. The British Admiral (Troubridge) was not shot like his eighteenth-century predecessors, because the Admiralty's own instructions had been so confusing; in fact, everybody's radio messages had been unclear. But all this confirmed the vast difficulties of conducting major naval warfare after a century of relative peace, plus revolutionary technological advances.

The second small, though modern and very powerful German battle squadron overseas in 1914 was its East Asian flotilla, commanded by Admiral Count von Spee and based at Qingdao, in North China. This was no place to be when the Japanese navy, already dominant in these waters, entered the conflict and took the German colony, while expeditionary forces also seized the Caroline, Mariana and Marshall islands. Spee was therefore already on his epic journey across the vast Pacific, always desperate for coal and feeling like a fox hemmed in by ever-more hunting groups; but he had two relatively fast armoured cruisers in the *Scharnhorst* and *Gneisenau*, plus some useful modern light cruisers – one of the advantages of Tirpitz's new navy was that it was, well, new. This was not the case with the many scattered Royal Navy units in overseas waters: desperately slow pre-dreadnought battleships, outdated heavy cruisers and lightweight smaller craft. When Fisher pushed through his many naval reforms between 1904 and 1906, he argued for scrapping older warships, partly because he wanted to get their seamen for the new North Sea squadrons, partly because those vessels might be annihilated by a fast enemy raiding squadron, gobbling them up as an armadillo gobbles up ants. There were still too many elderly ships left when war broke out.

This was exactly what happened at the Battle of Coronel off the coast of central Chile on 1 November 1914, when no less than five British warships were sunk, with enormous losses, when surprised by Spee's squadron. This time, and since the defeat was so shocking, the reaction from London was swift and massive, with the two fastest and most powerful battlecruisers, HMS

Invincible and HMS *Inflexible*, rushed from Scapa Flow to the South Atlantic. If they met up with the German flotilla, as they did so on 8 December, the latter hadn't a chance of surviving; now it was their turn to meet their Maker, and the defeat was even more crushing than that of Coronel. German light cruisers that escaped did so only for a while. The southern oceans were at this time, and even as late as the Second World War, a British-dominated world, with only an occasional German raider tiptoeing into it, though never for long. The legendary light cruiser SMS *Emden* lasted until she met up in the Indian Ocean with the Australian cruiser HMAS *Sydney*, but that was just a romantic episode. This was not the Seven Years' War, with its epic struggles for the West Indies, Canada and India.

What is the problem? Geography, geography, geography

However random these naval actions off the Falklands, off Heligoland, off Qingdao and in the Mediterranean might have seemed to readers of (say) *The Times* in those six months, they actually pointed to a single conclusion that would shape the maritime history of the First World War. That point was that in the never-ending 'Mahan versus Mackinder' debate over whether sea power could shape global history and Great-Power politics,[8] Mackinder had the best of the argument regarding the 1914–18 struggles. In the Napoleonic War, both views were right: the heady French expansionism could only be checked, then defeated, by a combination of massive maritime power and the deployment of geographically determined military force. And the same was true, as we have argued above, for the Second World War, especially in the struggle against Japanese expansionism. But in a mass-based industrial conflict triggered off by an assassination in Sarajevo, followed by a German invasion of Belgium and northern France, Russo-Habsburg clashes in Galicia, German-Russian struggles at Tannenberg and the Masurian Lakes; then joined by campaigns in Palestine and Iraq after Ottoman Turkey entered the war in November 1914, then seventeen bloody battles around the Isonzo river when Italy rashly came in the fray; the end-result was largely due to the multiple exertion of land power. Of course control of the sea was important for an insular, import-dependent Britain, and in turn for her seaborne supplies of coal

8 Paul Kennedy, 'Mahan versus Mackinder: two interpretations of British Sea Power', in Paul Kennedy, *Strategy and Diplomacy, 1870–1945: Eight Studies* (London: Allen & Unwin, 1983), pp. 41–85.

to both France and Italy by 1917 or so. But the powerful, well-organised Germanic coalition was eventually brought to its knees by what Foch and Joffre fondly referred to as *'un effort du Sang'*. Blood, indeed.

It was not just that the titanic struggles on the Western, Eastern, Italian and Balkan fronts overshadowed everything; it was also, painfully, that grand and expensive navies never had a chance to display their unprecedented armaments' power. Given the size of the various nations' fleets in 1914 (see above), it was clear that the maritime balance of power could not radically be changed as it was in, say, the Pacific War after, first, Pearl Harbor and then, secondly, Midway. The navies of 1914 were mired in their geopolitical destinies.

Germany was always in a geopolitical pickle, as anyone who had read Carlyle's classic biography of Frederick the Great would come to know: it had Russia (or Russia-Poland) to the East, and France to the West; sometimes it also had a hostile Sweden to the North, and a hostile Austria to the South. By 1914 the latter two threats were gone, but in its creation of a large North Sea fleet and its invasion of Belgium, Germany had bestirred an even greater, much less conquerable foe: Britain and its Empire. Hobbled by its ties to a fast-weakening Austro-Hungarian Empire, it now faced three undoubted Great Powers, so that even its industrial strength and superbly efficient internal lines of communication could not turn the balance. The geopolitical consequences, especially the naval ones, were enormous. In so many of his writings before 1914, perhaps especially in his now-neglected classic, *Britain and the British Seas*,[9] Sir Halford Mackinder had argued that the Kaiser's navy would be useless unless it obtained a preponderance of numbers: as noted above, it did not. The Habsburg Empire was even more hemmed in, and when Ottoman Turkey entered the war it was denied the Mediterranean. Russian and German warships tussled in the Baltic, Russian and Turkish warships tussled in the Black Sea and Italian and Austro-Hungarian navies tussled in the Adriatic. It meant very little. Essentially, the British and Japanese navies were sealing up the seas. That story would not really change until Midway, in June 1942.

Gallipoli – and Okinawa

In their classic study of the US Marines and amphibious warfare in the 1942–5 Pacific campaigns, Isley and Crowl[10] begin with a very blunt comparison:

9 Sir John Halford Mackinder, *Britain and the British Seas* (London: Heinemann, 1902).
10 Jeter A. Isley and Philip Crowl, *The U.S. Marines and Amphibious Warfare* (Princeton University Press, 1951).

'Success at Okinawa – Failure at Gallipoli'. Both were extremely bloody amphibious operations, but the second ended in catastrophe, and the former eventually yielded victory to the American forces. Their point is not to boast about their beloved Marines, but to stress, painstakingly, just how difficult an amphibious landing – any amphibious landing – was. Ideally, an invading army likes to arrive in a safe, well-organised port, as Pershing's troops were to arrive in Le Havre and Cherbourg, and Eisenhower's into Glasgow. But enemy-held port cities are usually very well protected, so the ships offshore are at a great disadvantage; Nelson himself, perhaps thinking of the ill-fated British efforts to take Cartagena (1741) with 20,000 men and 186 ships, believed that 'ships against forts' was nonsensical. Going against a place as massive as Constantinople in 1915 would be like going against London. If the Western Allies were to take the Ottoman Turkish capital and give relief to their increasingly weaker Russian partner, they would have to do it another way.

Moreover, the rashness of the Anglo-French campaign of 1915 had been compounded by both governments swallowing Churchill's argument that the Straits could be forced chiefly by warships, assisted by some naval landing battalions. Thus it was that on 18 March no fewer than eighteen British and French capital ships (many redundant and detached from superfluous North Sea duties) steamed into the narrows. Unfortunately for them, an aged Turkish mine-layer – originally German, sent slowly down the Danube – had laid ten lines of naval mines, upon which the unsuspecting Allied fleet crashed. At the end of the day, three battleships were sunk (two British, one French), another three knocked out of action and another four damaged. This was a heavier loss than at Jutland, and led to all sorts of political consequences. There was hereafter no prospect of giving direct support to a floundering Russia. Ottoman Turkey was now an energised foe. The failure of the naval attack caused the further stupidity of throwing British, French and Anzac divisions onto the miserable, ravine-filled, thorn-bush-clad hillside of Gallipoli, and then their eventual withdrawal in 1916. Why such an epic failure?: because there had been no systematic preparation, there were no specially equipped units, there was no command-and-control system, little intelligence or deception and no central command position. Army–navy control systems were awful. However one parses this, though, the Admiralty had taken another bad hit.

The whole Dardanelles/Gallipoli operation was a monumental failure. No wonder, then, that the US Marine Corps studied this campaign throughout the interwar years. From our viewpoint, however, it was just another example of the crimping of the influence of sea power in this new era of mines, torpedoes, entrenched coastal gunnery, motor tropedo boats and submarines. The German term for this type of warfare is *Kleinkrieg* (small war), but by 1914–15 it had already become big warfare. Surface warfare in the Mediterranean now became a sort of 'dead sea' for the first time in thousands of years, although submarine operations would increase. When the British and French made their next significant moves in this region, it would be on land: Gaza, Palestine, Mesopotamia, Lebanon, Syria. The future would belong to the Allenbys, the Lawrences, the Greenmantles; not to the Troubridges or the Beresfords.

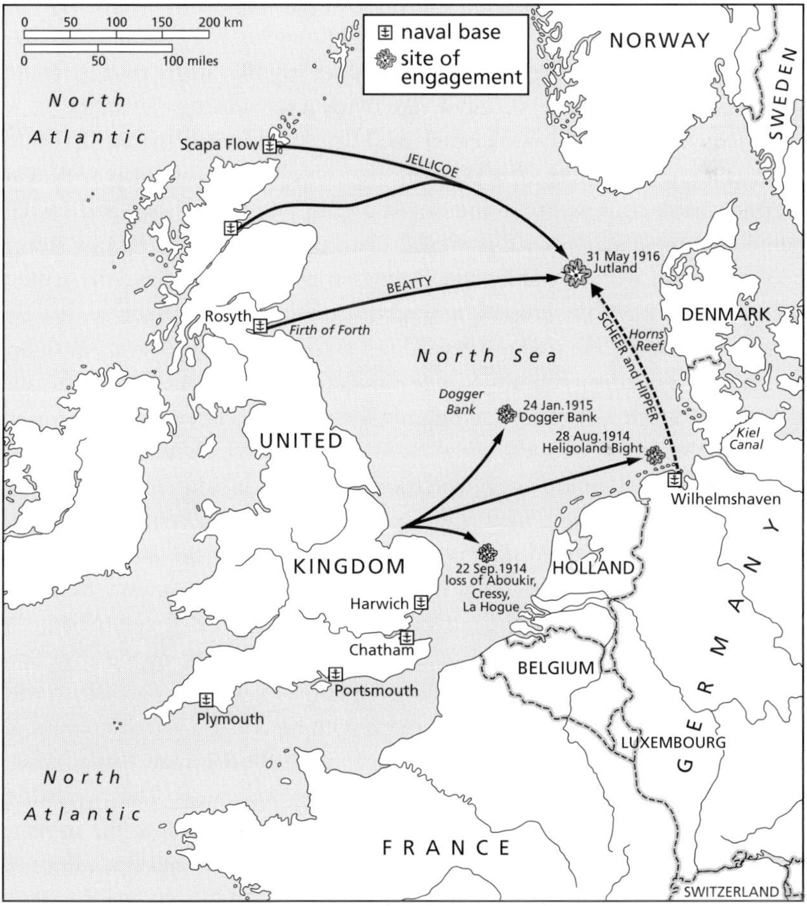

Map 12.1 Major naval engagements in the North Sea, 1914–16.

The North Sea and its constraints, 1915–18: Jutland understood

Neither the German nor the British navies understood the North Sea, and the French had no intention of going there. Flag signals were hopeless in the mists. Morse messages via a flashlight from the Commander-in-Chief were erratic. Radio messages had to be brief, and were therefore often ambiguous. Jellicoe had the worst of it here. He had to take in messages from the Admiralty that might no longer be up-to-date, assess from the Harwich cruisers what was going on in the southern North Sea, try to keep in touch with Beatty's wayward battlecruisers, decide whether to send the fast battleship squadron in advance of the Grand Fleet and pay attention to any sightings of U-boats. Many years after the war, that rising, cocky star, Lord Louis Mountbatten, began to appreciate how great had been Jellicoe's conflicting duties. By that stage, though, others regretted that he had not been shot, like Byng, *pour encourager les autres*.

In January 1915, the two fleets clashed at last, although the Battle of the Dogger Bank was more of a skirmish that an all-out fight (Map 12.1). The German battlecruisers had come out in a tempting sort of 'bait and switch' game, but their much more powerful British equivalents, alerted by Room 40's intercepts, were in waiting; the *Bluecher* was blown to bits and the *Seydlitz* was reduced to a slow, limping mound of iron. The British rejoiced, but the result was that the High Seas Fleet did not come out to the central North Sea for another seventeen months – understandable perhaps, but hugely frustrating when Europe's armies were fighting life-and-death struggles.

When the surface struggle in the North Sea resumed, the mutual desire for a great victory was mixed again with their commanders' mutual caution about untoward losses in these new and unpredictable fighting conditions. In one sense, the Battle of Jutland story is an easy one to tell, and it is amazing that so much ink has been spilled upon it. The Admiralty's now-famous Room 40 picked up a heavy amount of German naval radio traffic inside and outside the Jade anchoring base in late May 1916, concluded that a sortie by the High Seas Fleet was impending and ordered Jellicoe at Scapa Flow, Beatty at Rosyth with his battlecruisers and Tyrwhitt at Harwich with his cruisers and destroyers, all to get under way. Scheer had sent Hipper with the German battlecruisers ahead of the main High Seas Fleet, to scout out the waters. The two battlecruiser forces fought a sort of renewed Dogger Bank action in the mists as Scheer raced back to the main fleet, though inflicting very heavy damage on Beatty's lightly armoured and imprudently provisioned vessels (sinking HMSs *Queen Mary*, *Indefatigible* and *Invincible* – revenge for the Falklands!). No

Fig. 1 German colonial clock: Our future lies on the seas.
Germany's late-comer status as an imperial power was a source of irritation to her leaders and a call to action to create in Africa and Asia a presence appropriate to the leading industrial nation in Europe.

Fig. 2 Exhibition on German East-Africa, Leipzig, 1897.
Orientalism was imbedded in all imperial projects. The cross on the image at the top suggests that Germany was engaged in both a 'civilising mission' and one which would provide raw materials and markets for German industry.

Fig. 3 Sir Edward Grey's juggling act: dangerous diplomacy.
A French critique of the smugness of the British Foreign Secretary, Sir Edward Grey. He stands like a bell boy on the tip of the European balance of power, juggling explosive international problems, without the slightest concern or idea as to what he is doing. Secret treaties protrude from his pocket.

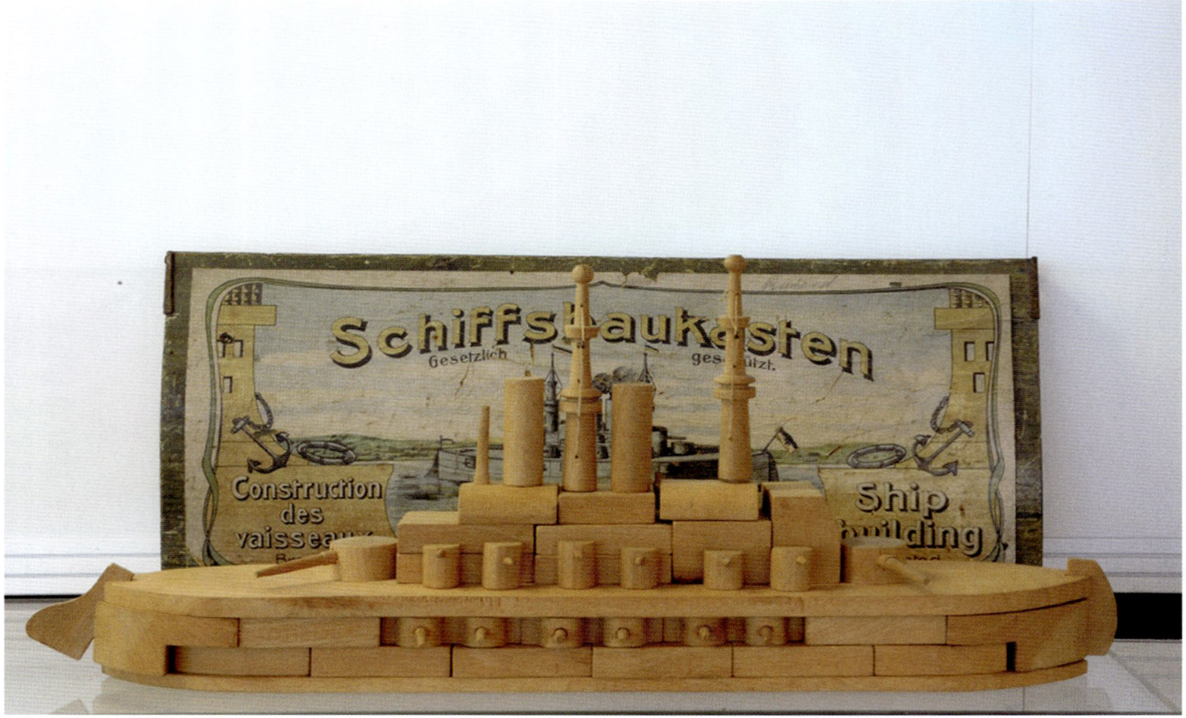

Fig. 4 German toy model warship.
Naval power had extraordinary popular appeal in the pre-war years. This model ship was a kind of advertisement to generate wide support for the finance of this effort, which ultimately failed. Germany antagonised Britain while never coming close to matching British naval power.

ONZIÈME ANNÉE

6 Pages — 5c

l'Humanité

JOURNAL SOCIALISTE

Directeur Politique : JEAN JAURÈS

SAMEDI 1er AOUT 1914

6 Pages — 5c

ABONNEMENTS

JAURÈS ASSASSINÉ

JEAN JAURÈS

LOUIS DUBREUILH

SA VIE

GROUPE SOCIALISTE AU PARLEMENT

LA FÉDÉRATION DE LA SEINE

A NOTRE DIRECTEUR

LA RÉDACTION

LETTRE du président de la République à Mme Jaurès

LE MANIFESTE DU GOUVERNEMENT

République Française

L'ASSASSINAT

LA MORT

Fig. 5 Jean Jaurès assassinated.
The newspaper Jaurès used to disseminate his message of peace and justice announces his death at the hands of a right-wing fanatic on 31 July 1914, removing thereby the one internationally respected socialist leader who could have led a campaign to stop the war. Jaurès's own views were not clear, but without him, the anti-war movement collapsed.

GREAT BRITAIN DECLARES WAR ON GERMANY.

The Daily Mirror

LATEST CERTIFIED CIRCULATION MORE THAN 1,000,000 COPIES PER DAY

No. 3,364. WEDNESDAY, AUGUST 5, 1914 One Halfpenny.

DECLARATION OF WAR BY GREAT BRITAIN AFTER UNSATISFACTORY REPLY TO YESTERDAY'S ULTIMATUM.

Neptune's imps. They are torpedo boats steaming in close order to enable them to send verbal messages one to another by means of a megaphone.

Field-Marshal Sir John French. Rear-Admiral C. E. Madden. Admiral Sir John Jellicoe. Field-Marshal Earl Kitchener.

Remarkable picture of a submarine rising to the surface. Are we soon to know what these unknown quantities are capable of?

There are four men—two sailors and two soldiers—to whom the Empire will turn in her hour of need. The sailors are Admiral Sir John Jellicoe (known as "the future Nelson"), who has assumed supreme command of the Home Fleets with the acting rank of Admiral, and Rear-Admiral Charles E. Madden, who has been appointed to be his Chief of Staff. The soldiers are Lord Kitchener, whose achievements are known to everyone, and Sir John French, probably the finest cavalry leader in the world, who performed brilliant feats in South Africa, "the grave of reputations."—(Bassano, Symonds, Russell and Gale and Polden.)

Fig. 6 Great Britain Declares War, *Daily Mirror*, 5 August 1914.
Britain's declaration of war is announced in this popular newspaper with reassuring images of naval power – called 'Neptune's imps' – and two admirals flanked by the new Secretary of War, Lord Kitchener, and the head of the British Expeditionary Force, Field Marshal Sir John French.

Fig. 7 Britain and France giving Germany a final rinse on the Marne, 1914.
A French caricature of the Kaiser being given a final washing by a French soldier with the aid of 75 mm cannons, and a British soldier about 'to put the kybosh on the Kaiser', as a popular song of the period had it.

Fig. 8 Allied military leaders 1914, painted ceramic plate.
(From left to right clockwise) General Paul Pau, Commander of the French Army in Alsace, Marshal Joffre, Grand Duke Nicholas, and Field Marshal French, in 1914.

Fig. 9 German military commanders 1914, painted ceramic plate.
All combatants took confidence in the brilliance of their military and naval commanders at the outbreak of the war. Here is Germany's military leadership in 1914, surrounding Kaiser Wilhelm II.

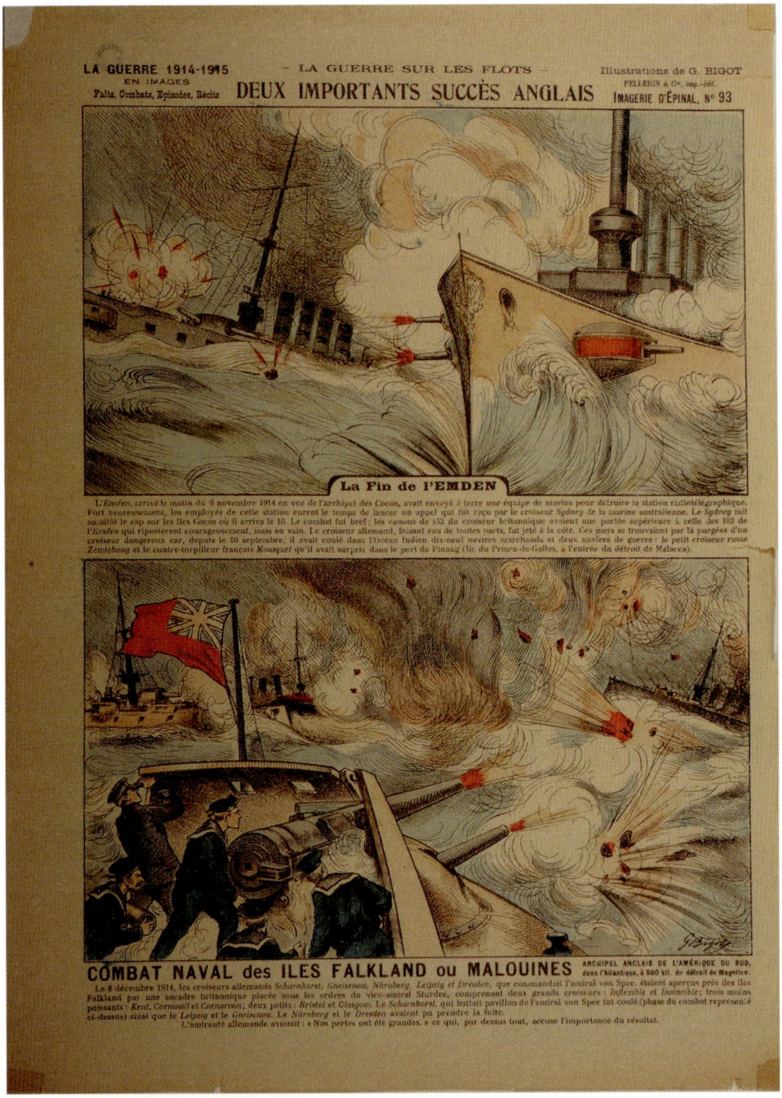

Fig. 10 Two British naval victories, 1914.
Global war at sea, from the Indian Ocean to the Atlantic. The top portrays the destruction of the marauding German light cruiser *Emden* by the Australian cruiser *Sydney*, south of Sumatra on 9 November 1914. The lower shows the destruction of the *Scharnhorst*, Admiral von Spee's flagship near the Falkland Islands, on 8 December 1914. These victories did little to alter the balance of power in the war, but served to bolster public morale nonetheless.

Fig. 11 Hindenburg and Ludendorff celebrating the victory at Tannenberg.
The German army's decisive victory in late August 1914 crushed the Russian invasion of East Prussia. A brilliant plan created by staff officer Max Hoffmann was executed by the newly appointed commanders, Hindenburg and Ludendorff, who thereby became national heroes. Tannenberg was chosen as the name of the battle, since it had been the site of a medieval defeat of Teutonic warriors, now symbolically reversed.

Fig. 12 Dardanelles defended, 1915, ceramic plate.
The German army and navy provided the Ottoman forces with the weaponry and training used to defeat the Anglo-French attempt in March 1915 to force the straits of the Dardanelles and thereby to knock the Ottoman Empire out of the war. Here is a celebratory German plate commemorating their victory.

Fig. 13 German sailors in Ottoman uniforms on horseback.
German soldiers and sailors served as advisers and trainers to the Ottoman army and navy throughout the war. This had positive outcomes initially. Nevertheless, the Ottoman army suffered staggering casualties in the war. Best estimates are over 700,000 who were either killed or died of disease, and 400,000 wounded. Nineteenth-century sanitary conditions and poor nutrition added to deaths inflicted by twentieth-century weapons.

Fig. 14 HMS *Chester* with damage from the Battle of Jutland.
The Battle of Jutland (31 May–1 June 1916) was technically a draw. The British Navy suffered severe damage to capital ships, but kept the blockade of the German Imperial Navy intact.

Fig. 15 Pitcher: Haig, the man of push and go.
A 'toby jug' or beer mug, with Field Marshal Sir Douglas Haig sitting on a tank with 'Somme' written on its gun. The title 'push and go' on the base of the toy is a partisan joke. Haig supporters stole the phrase coined by supporters of his arch-enemy, Lloyd George. Haig certainly pushed, but the front did not go.

CAPT. GUYNEMER IN FULL FLIGHT.

Fig. 16 Air war: Captain Guynemer in flight.
Having fifty-four 'kills' of enemy aircraft to his name, Guynemer was one of the great French aviators of the war. He was shot down and killed over Belgium on 11 September 1917.

Fig. 17 Air war: biplane over Compiègne.
Photographs from airplanes provided detailed images of enemy lines and troop movements. Here we can see the trench system near Compiègne, France, in stark relief. By 1918, the coordination of artillery by aerial reconnaissance and triangulation enabled the Allies to finally break the stalemate on the Western Front.

Fig. 18 German soldier near Fort Vaux at Verdun.
Verdun was a battle which pushed men beyond the limits of human endurance. Lasting ten months in 1916, it was the longest battle of the war. Here a German infantryman deployed near Fort Vaux takes aim next to a dismembered French soldier, identifiable only by his helmet.

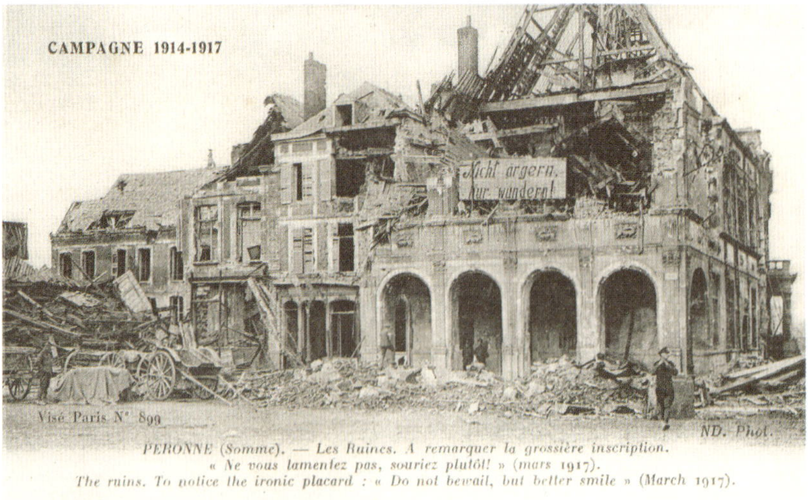

CAMPAGNE 1914-1917
Nicht ärgern,
nur wundern!
Visé Paris N° 899
ND. Phot.
PÉRONNE (Somme). — Les Ruines. A remarquer la grossière inscription.
« Ne vous lamentez pas, souriez plutôt! » (mars 1917).
The ruins. To notice the ironic placard : « Do not bewail, but better smile » (March 1917).

Fig. 19 Péronne town hall destroyed, 1917.
A postcard of the destroyed town hall of Péronne, on the Somme front. When German troops withdrew in 1917, they left nothing of use intact. It is possible that the building was hit by Allied shelling. On the demolished first floor is a placard, which says 'Don't be angry just be amazed.' The French postcard has an alternative, and lighter, translation.

Fig. 20 Panel left on destroyed town hall of Péronne by German soldiers, 1917: 'Don't be angry just be amazed'
The Australian troops who occupied Péronne after the German withdrawal of March 1917 kept this placard and donated it to the Imperial War Museum in London, which, much later, returned it to Péronne, where it now is displayed in the Historial de la Grande Guerre.

Ph. Ufficio Speciale della Marina. — Copyright 1917 by Alfieri e Lacroix, Milano.
VENISE. — SCUOLA DI SAN ROCCO.
PLAFOND DE LA SALLE SAINT-MARC DÉTRUIT EN PARTIE PAR UNE BOMBE ENNEMIE.

Fig. 21 The decorated ceiling of the Scuola di San Rocco in Venice destroyed by Austrian fire.
One of the glories of Venice, the Scuola di San Rocco was hit by Austrian fire from aircraft or artillery after the Italian retreat from Caporetto in late 1917. Its ornate ceiling suffered extensive damage, as did many other buildings in Venice.

Fig. 22 Statuette of Lenin.
Lenin marching into the future is the subject of this small sculpture. The motif of movement was essential to revolutionary art.

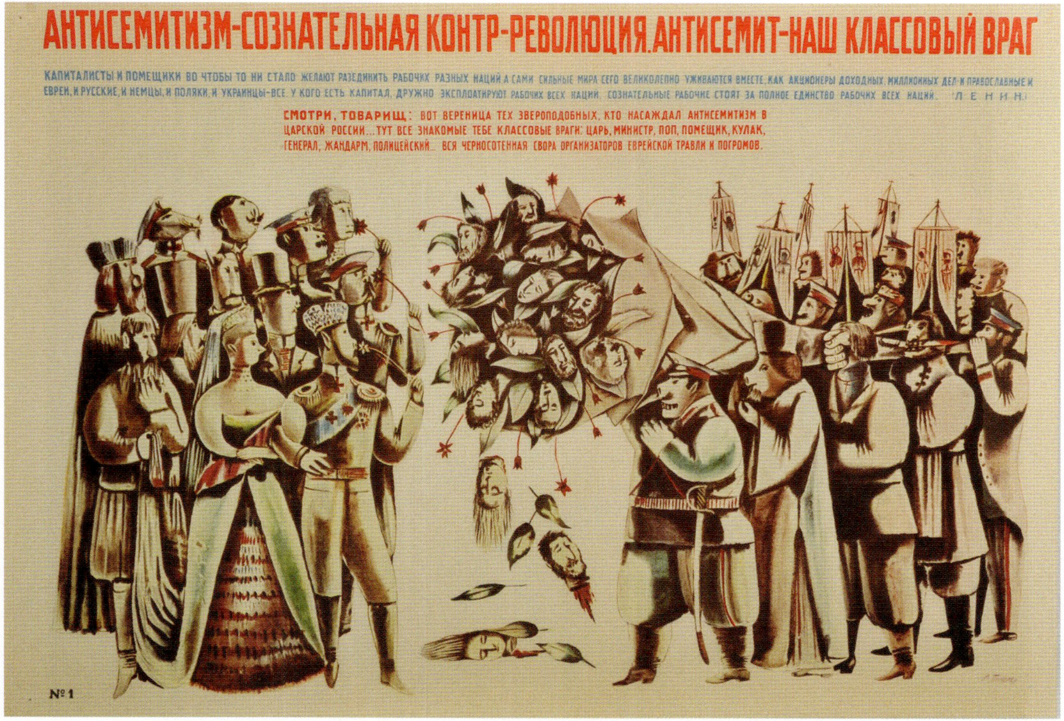

Fig. 23 'Anti-Semitism is the enemy': Russian revolutionary poster.
The portrayal of reactionary forces – aristocrats, priests, generals and the rich – as pigs and other animals drove home the point that the failure of the old regime would no longer be covered by anti-Semitic campaigns and pogroms. The Revolution took anti-Semitism to be its enemy.

Fig. 24 Black American troops in France.
Over 100,000 black Americans served in combat in France. They served in segregated units. Another 250,000 were drafted but were not deployed overseas. On demobilisation, these veterans returned to racial hatred and race riots at home no less severe than those they had known before the war.

Photographie prise le 11 Novembre 1918 à 7 h. 30, au moment où le Maréchal Foch part pour Paris remettre au gouvernement français le texte de l'Armistice qui vient d'être signé avec l'Allemagne.
1. Maréchal FOCH.
2. Amiral Sir R. WEMYSS.
3. Général WEYGAND.
4. Contre-amiral G. HOPE.
5. Captain MARRIOTT.
6. Général DESTICKER.
7. Capitaine de MIERRY.
8. Commandant RIEDINGER.
9. Officier-Interprète LAPERCHE

Fig. 25 Allied signatories of the Armistice at Compiègne, 11 November 1918.
The moment of victory. General Foch, second from the right (number 1), is carrying an attaché case with the document of capitulation just signed by the German delegation on 11 November at 7.30 a.m.

Fig. 26 Homecoming.
This embroidery shows the joy of the reunion of mother and child with the father, who had spent five years in a prisoner-of-war camp in Saxony. An imprisoned soldier, unable to fight, has used a traditionally female art to express his relief at liberation.

Fig. 27 Commemorative plate: U-boat 9.
The sailors who served in German U-boat 9 commemorated their years together in many ways, including commissioning this painted porcelain image of their ship at sea. Probably made in Meissen, this plate celebrated a submarine which sank three British cruisers on 21 September 1914.

Fig. 28 Model submarine made of bullets.
The ingenuity of artisans in uniform extended to the conversion of an infantryman's bullets and copper scraps into the hull of a small submarine.

Fig. 29 Figurine of an African soldier.
The dignity of African soldiers who served in French forces is evident in this carefully designed figurine, with weapon, cloth puttees and uniform.

Fig. 30 North African soldier's family war album.
A collage of photos of a North African Zouave and his family shows how ubiquitous were images recalling the military service of colonial troops.

Fig. 31 Model airplane.
Recycled wire and bits and scraps of metal enabled an anonymous artisan metalworker in uniform to create his own private airplane as a distraction from the terrestrial war.

pre-war designer appears to have realised that shells fired at extreme distances would be dropping almost vertically onto the opponent's thin decks, and the British had great stores of munitions in very exposed positions.

Eager to settle matters, Beatty pursued Hipper then soon found himself facing well over twenty German battleships. The hounds became the fox, and Beatty ran to the north. Scheer's pursuit itself was thrown into danger when it then encountered Jellicoe's far more powerful Grand Fleet. The British signals system was appalling, while Scheer's fleet carried out a well-practised 'main turn-around' manoeuvre and headed for Wilhelmshaven. But his destroyer flotillas rushed forward, intent upon a mass torpedo attack, and Jellicoe ordered his own fateful order to turn around. By this stage the Grand Fleet was in much confusion and it then returned home, its lookouts sighting possible U-boats on all flanks. There was no second Trafalgar. Nor would there be.

What should we make of this? First of all, the Royal Navy's control of the North Sea was not in question after Jutland. It lost more ships, especially those thinly armoured battlecruisers (the same would happen to HMS *Hood* against the Bismarck exactly forty years later), but *nothing* changed strategically. As the *New York Times* put it, 'The German Navy has assaulted its jailer, but is still in jail.' What else is to be said? If the High Seas Fleet had lost fifteen capital ships, what would have changed? Would Haig have pulled troops out of the Ypres salient to be tossed onto the insecure beaches of the Frisian Islands? Absolutely not. If Jellicoe had lost fifteen capital ships, would the German High Command pull divisions from the Western Front just a week or so before the Somme offensive (1 July 1916) began, to throw them at Yorkshire or Scotland? Absolutely not. All that Jutland did, on the German side, was to increase the steady fall of Grand Admiral Tirpitz, and push a desperate German High Command towards unrestricted U-boat warfare, a new form of commercial blockade, but probably the only thing that would bring America into the war. The British and German admirals of 1916 didn't think like that. Few later historians do.

Fisher's concept of very fast but lightly armoured battlecruisers was clearly in shreds; they were great for destroying German armoured cruisers in the South Atlantic, but not for a pounding battle fleet match in the North Sea. Yet there were still more even faster, even lighter such vessels on the stocks of British shipyards in 1916–18. Churchill, making his political comeback after his own disaster at the Dardanelles, jokingly called them HMS *Improbable*, HMS *Dubious* ... etc. Until naval air power properly came into its own, as late as summer 1944, powerfully armoured fast battleships, however expensive, were the way to go. For example, the *Warspite* took a terrible beating at Jutland, but survived; it would take another beating from a glider-bomb off Rome in 1943 and another off Walcheren in late 1944, part of its fourteen battle honours: a battlecruiser couldn't take that punishment. Still, the larger point was that all capital ships were now really vulnerable – to plunging fire, to mines, to torpedoes, to submarines, to destroyers and MTBs. And bomber aircraft were already in some designers' minds. The old tactical textbooks would have to be torn up.

Then there were serious questions to be asked about 'the rules of the game', as Andrew Gordon called his innovative study of how possible cultural inhibitions, together with clashing views over battle tactics, really hurt the Grand Fleet's enormous theoretical fighting power.[11] It is easy to be critical of Jellicoe's 'turn away' order, and there were armchair strategists in the 1920s who called for his court-martial. But how exactly did an admiral command all his warships if they were no longer steadily sailing in parallel lines at four knots and in fine weather (The Saints; Cape St Vincent), but steaming at twenty knots in the fogs of the North Sea, with cruiser squadrons scattered forwards for reconnaissance, destroyers trying to keep up and a battered battlecruiser squadron either advancing into trouble or returning? There seemed to be submarines all around, and the threat posed by the torpedoes of Scheer's destroyers was intimidating. How did one keep control of all of this, except by implementing those so-frequently-rehearsed 'turn around' and 'turn forward' manoeuvres? Drake, Hawke, Nelson and Cunningham would have gone forward, brushing aside the destroyers. Jellicoe deemed it wiser to back off for a while, and the battle was over.

It is not true, as the legend goes, that there were no further sorties by the High Seas Fleet into the North Sea after Jutland. Two were made in 1917, but they were hesitant and desultory, thus achieving nothing. A better raid was made by cruisers against the so-called 'Norwegian Ferry'. But the strategic stalemate continued to the end of the war. The Grand Fleet remained at Scapa Flow, with Beatty replacing Jellicoe as Commander-in-Chief, and gloomy at the lack of action. 'Grey Skies, Grey Seas, Grey Ships', says Beatty in a letter to his wife. As for the Germans, there was no way they could break out of this strategic box until they had seized, say, Brest and Bergen. That would come, but twenty-five years later.

11 Andrew Gordon, *The Rules of the Game: Jutland and the British Naval Command* (London: John Murray, 1996); there is nothing quite like it in naval literature.

The most significant act of war which happened in the North Sea in the post-Jutland years was not a naval event at all. It occurred on 25 May 1917, when twenty-one Gotha bombers made a successful daylight raid upon the seaside town of Folkestone in Kent, killing 165 people and seriously wounding another 432, all civilians. This, and the bombings of London that followed, produced panic and riots, galvanising Lloyd George's government into providing barrage balloons, high-level guns and other defensive equipment. When the French aviator, Louis Blériot, had flown across the Channel in 1909, landing, symbolically, next to the great fort of Dover Castle, the press had proclaimed that Britain was 'no longer an island'. Now it was really true, and there was nothing that the Royal Navy's superiority in capital ships could do about it.

Worse was to come, at least from the navalist perspective, for the Imperial War Cabinet swiftly commissioned what was to be known as the Smuts Report of August 1917 (named after its chief author, the former South African general who was now a key member of the Cabinet). The report's key conclusion lay in a single paragraph:

> unlike artillery an air fleet can conduct extensive operations far from, and independently of, both Army and Navy. And the day may not be far off when aerial operations . . . may become the principal operations of war, to which the older forms of military and naval operations may become secondary and subordinate.[12]

Thus was the scene set for the creation of a third and rival service, the Royal Air Force, in April 1918. Thus was the scene also set for those post-war claims by the advocates of air power (one thinks here of Billy Mitchell, Trenchard, Douhet) that battleships were things of the past, vulnerable and ineffective. Now the admirals of the world had another set of critics, against which the rigidity of their chiefly Mahanian upbringing gave them little force of reply.

The German switch to U-boat warfare

So, with surface naval action in the North Sea essentially closed down, what was left for the German High Command but to go for unrestricted U-boat warfare, and not just against the limited trades of the North Sea, but further afield, out into the Atlantic? If neutral citizens got in the way and died, did it matter? One European army had already suffered 500,000 casualties at Verdun, the other on the Somme. Why did neutral states matter? The

12 Quoted in Kennedy, *Engineers of Victory*, pp. 82–3.

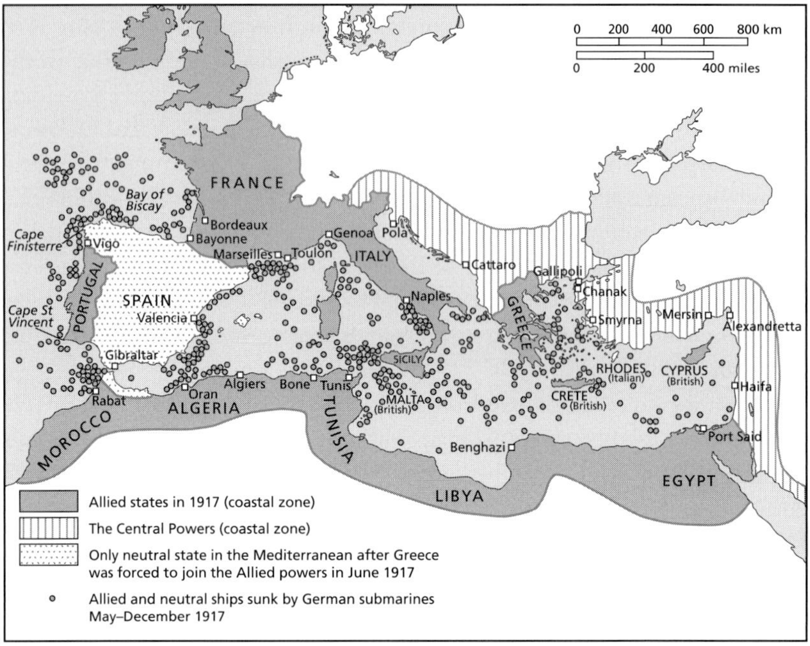

Map 12.2 Allied losses in the Mediterranean, 1917.

problem was that most of those neutral citizens were American, yet there was little time given to that consideration when deciding where and how the U-boat war was to evolve (Map 12.2). The *Kriegsmarine* had to cut the Atlantic sea lanes, or Germany would never win the war. Hitler had the same problem in 1941.

The other complex of problems, rarely addressed in the literature, concerned those changes which the coming of ironclad ships made to attitudes towards the capture or destruction of enemy vessels. In the age of fighting sail, the purpose of engaging the enemy's battle line was not to destroy those vessels but to capture them! You dismantled their masts, your boarding-parties ran across their desks and forced their crews to surrender; you then towed the warships back home and made them your own, often with roughly the same names – *La Gloire* became HMS *Glorious*. In the age of iron and steel and high-explosive shells, you didn't want to do this. What on earth would the Royal Navy have done with a battered-to-pieces *Bismarck* in June 1941? Even by the time of the Dogger Bank or Jutland, the purpose was to sink the enemy.

In the same way, the takeover of an enemy-flagged merchantman, with a cargo of value, would in ancient days have led to the captured crew being seized, and then a skeleton crew being put on board the captive vessel and sailing it to the nearest friendly port. Clandestine German commerce-raiders could still do this, a bit, after 1914, but since their own crew sizes were limited and there were few 'friendly' ports in the world, their actions made hardly a dent on the 10,000-plus British-flagged vessels on the seas each day. For U-boat commanders, this was a logistical and tactical nightmare. Did one actually rise to the surface, signal to an Allied merchantman to stop, require the crew to get into their lifeboats, sink the vessel and then bring the indignant Laskars and Filipinos into the U-boat? The Hague Conventions were utterly useless here. Obviously, one had to sink the merchant vessel, and leave the scene.

One other lesson came from those days of sail. The Dutch could not get their rich-laden East Indiamen through the Channel without protecting them with fighting warships; the British could not get merchantmen from the New World to Liverpool and Southampton without putting them in convoys. This lesson had to be learned again in the First World War.[13] So, here was another boxed-in situation: the Germans had to sink Allied merchantmen on sight, and the Allies had to return to the older operational concept of convoys. When the latter plan was implemented, the U-boat threat was eliminated. And America was now in the war, at huge cost to the Central Powers.

The return to convoys: the threat contained

Mahan and Corbett had made it very clear what the essence of sea power was: it was not, at heart, about warship design or fire control, but about 'command of the Great Commons'. This is fairly easy to explain, at least to anyone who has seen sheepdogs herding sheep down an Anatolian hillside into their pens, and turning to lunge at any predatory wolves. Corvettes, sloops and frigates were shepherds of the oceans, indeed, against U-boat groups which Doenitz (a First World War submariner) would later call 'wolf-packs'.

Protecting these flocks of merchantmen was vital to the supply of the UK. At first, Germany's aggressive policy seemed worth the risk of having alienated Wilson and the US Congress. A scary total of 520,000 tons of merchant shipping was sunk in February 1917, an amazing 860,000 tons in April (Maps 12.3 and 12.4). British naval strategists obliged the *Kriegsmarine* by having written studies which showed that grouping ships together would

13 Jay Winton, *Convoy: Defense of Sea Trade 1890–1990* (London: Michael Joseph, 1989).

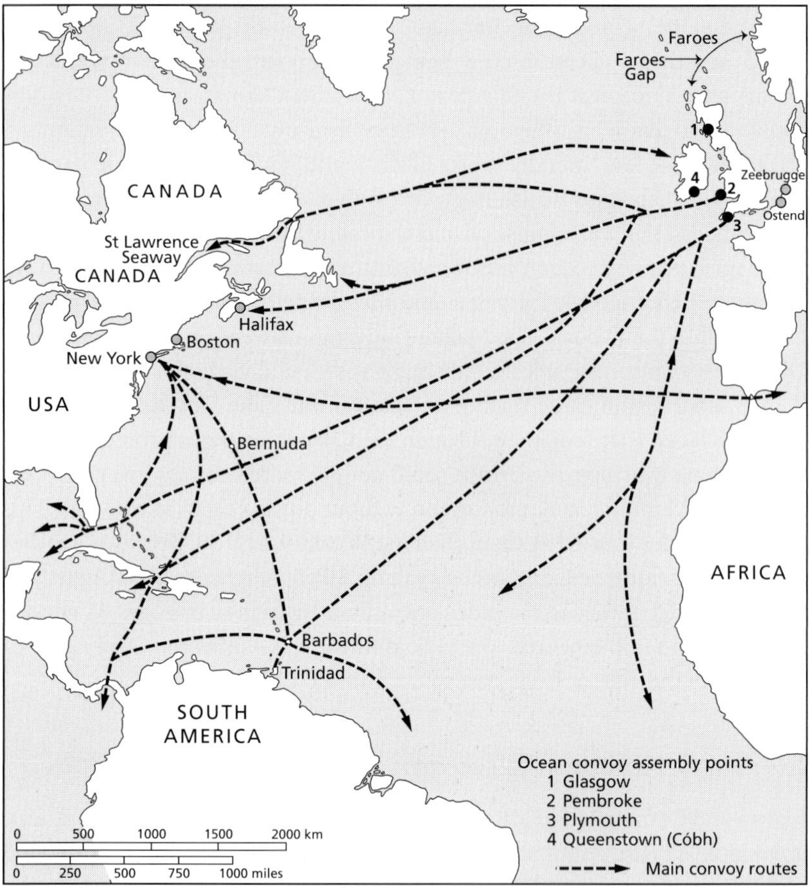

Map 12.3 Allied convoy routes in the Atlantic.

actually entice enemy submarines to find the targets! Far better to steam independently – and get sunk.

Slowly, slowly, under pressure from Lloyd George himself, under pressure from the new Ministry of Shipping, and under their own sensible reassessments, the Admiralty turned towards the idea of convoys; after all, if it worked for the vital French coal trades and the Norway routes, why not for the Atlantic and the Bay of Biscay? By December, losses were down to 400,000 tons; by the next spring, to less than 300,000 tons, a huge drop in the percentage of total shipping being sunk compared to eight months earlier. The shipping crisis was over, although the Royal Navy's record here was

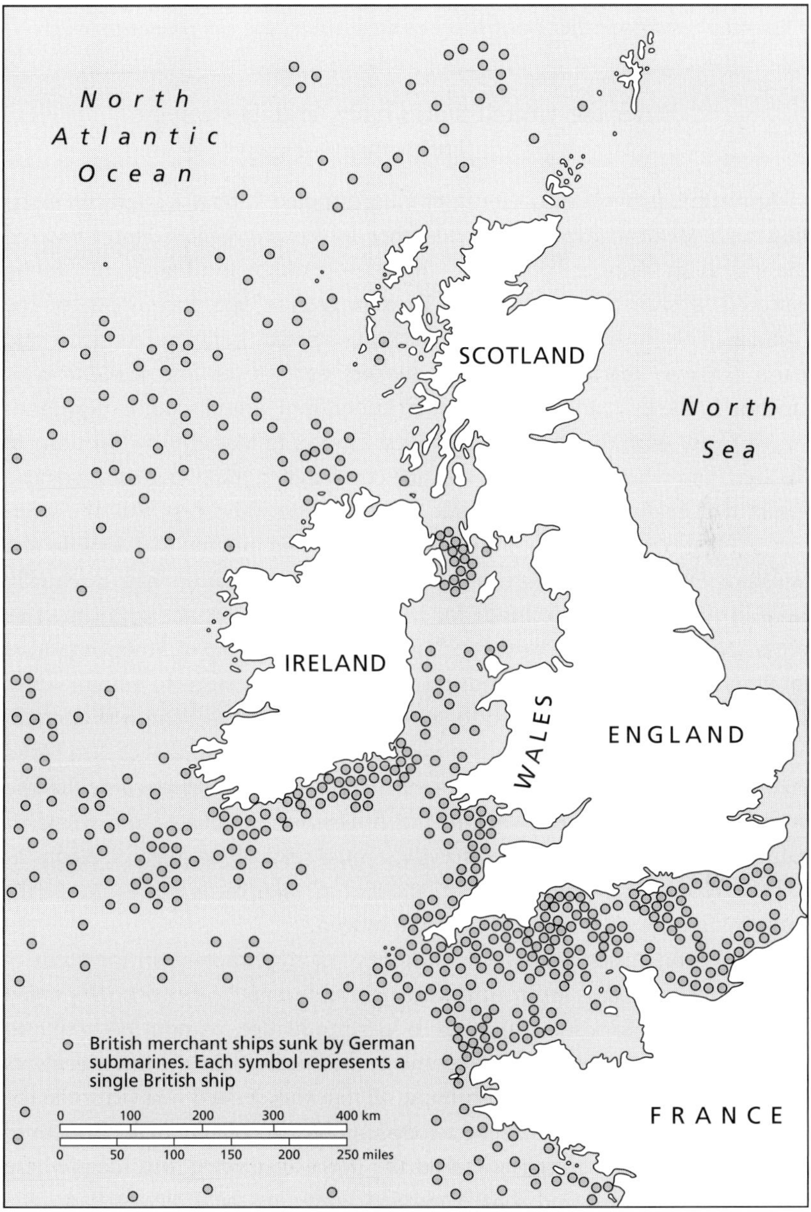

Map 12.4 British merchant shipping sunk, 1917.

much less impressive than in the heroic Battle of the Atlantic months of 1943. This simply was another poor story of a failure to use sea power properly.

Enter the United States navy, and its strategic irrelevance

In April 1917, provoked by Germany's unrestricted U-boat warfare, its flirtation with Mexican irredentists and other follies, the United States entered the war as an 'associate power' on the side of Britain and France, just as the battered, dysfunctional, absolutist Russian regime was forced out of the conflict. This turbulent switch of partners greatly benefited London and Paris, however fearful French policymakers were of the loss of their tsarist 'anchor' in the East, and however much Ludendorff would acquire more lands by his treaty with the Bolsheviks at Brest-Litovsk in March 1918. For none of the flattened wheat-lands of the Ukraine could match the two great American assets that really did turn the tide for the West. The first was the ever-increasing flow of the double-sized US army and marine divisions to the Western Front. This took time, of course, for the nation had essentially been in a Rip-van-Winkle mode for half a century despite the jingoism of its press and politicians. But by the spring of 1918 the build-up of American forces in France was remarkable, causing all the other powers to rethink their situation. It caused the French to see that they would win the war after all, and thus stiffened their demands regarding a peace settlement. It caused Lloyd George, Milner, Smuts and others in the British War Cabinet to realise that the war must be won in 1918, before the Americans dominated the world. It caused the Germans to realise that they must relocate as many divisions as possible from the East to the West, and cast all their cards into Ludendorff's 1918 spring offensive – a *Vabanque-Spiel*, indeed.

The second American asset was money, money, money, in the form of inter-Allied war loans. From now on, Belgium, Britain, France and Italy could devote all their domestic capacities to war production without bothering to pay for it. That reckoning would come in the heated debates over war debts and reparations in the 1920s. At present, all that was desired was victory in the field, which would come with the astonishingly swift collapse of the front lines of Germany, Austria-Hungary and Turkey in the autumn of 1918. Everywhere their armies buckled and started moving home, as the Russians had done before them.

The American navy (unlike in 1942–5) could add little to this, at least in terms of altering the battleship balance in the North Sea. Despite the massive anti-British prejudice in the service, a squadron of battleships was sent to Scapa Flow under the unusually Anglophile Rear-Admiral Hugh Rodman, backed up by the head of the US naval mission to Britain, Admiral William Sims. Although the US navy was probably the second largest in the world by this time (37 battleships, 7 coastal monitors, 33 cruisers, 66 destroyers, 17 frigates, 44 submarines, 42 patrol, 96 auxiliary and 160 surface warships) and certainly the most expensively built, ton for ton, it had atrophied as a fighting force. Its Atlantic-based vessels had not operated as a fleet for two years, and its target practice and training was pathetic – it was a good job all it had to do was to stay in Scapa and observe the surrender of the High Seas Fleet the next year. Its destroyer flotillas made more of a difference, operating out of Irish ports like Queenstown against the U-boats. Still, the ancillary actions of the American navy were important in two regards, usually neglected in maritime accounts: the laying of the gigantic minefields across the northern stretch of the North Sea (the mines were laid at various depths), to deter U-boats reaching the Atlantic; and the escorting of over 900,000 troops to France without losing a single one. There was nothing wrong with navies being in a support role, when it mattered.

The curious myth of the Allied naval blockade and the great German hunger

If there was one thing that navalists and the 'British way in warfare' protagonists like Liddell Hart had on the one hand, and Adolf Hitler and Nazi propaganda had on the other, it was that the Allied (chiefly Royal Navy) commercial blockade had throttled the life out of the German economic machine and therefore had won the war. To the navalists, it was a desperately clutched-at rationale that sea power worked, even without Nelsonic victories. To Hitler, it was the reason for going eastwards, to grab his needed '*Lebensraum*'. The Allies had imposed a naval blockade upon all ships going to and from the Second Reich. The people of the Second Reich were in a starving, desperate condition by mid 1919. Ergo, the Western navies won the war.

This argument is ridden with holes: it doesn't usually distinguish between the pre- and post-Armistice blockade, it jumps far too fast to conclusions and it has no economic sense to it. Perhaps the greatest cause of the German 'hunger' of 1918–19 was Ludendorff's decision in early 1918 to requisition all farm horses and other draught animals for logistical support of his last, desperate offensive of the war; without those animals, German agriculture was devastated. And the spring offensive was halted, after severe, bloody and grinding contestations, with the British and the Americans throwing in more and more reinforcements. But the Ludendorff autocratic regime – that was what it was becoming – also lost on the home front, for the German workers, sailors and soldiers could not take any more hardship. Without your own food supplies, how can you fight on? (The Russian soldiers and workers had given the answer a year earlier.) The stage was set for the uprisings of November 1918, including the revolt of the German sailors against Scheer's manic 'suicide operation'.[14] But what had this internally induced food catastrophe to do with the influence of the Allied navies upon the war?

Well, it is argued, without the throttles of the naval blockade, the German people could have imported all the food they needed from neutral sources (presumably this argument does not assume that Canada or Australia, losing tens of thousands of men to German action, would be shipping their foodstuffs?). But that is the greatest fallacy of all in this argument about the naval blockade, and for the following obvious reasons. First, where would the food come from? Ludendorff had completely destroyed the Ukrainian grain-basket, Poland was a wasteland and Hungary a disaster. The American, Canadian, New Zealand and Australian grain-baskets were on the other side, and Argentina's food stocks were tightly tied to Britain. There were NO external supplies. Secondly, even if there were, who would have carried them, who would have crewed them, how would they have been ordered, who would have insured them? The British, American, Italian, Greek and French merchant fleets probably comprised 85 per cent of the whole; and the German fleet was rusted up. Its seamen were long gone. All German undersea cable communications to the outside world were cut off by specialist Cable & Wireless ships on 3 August 1914, so how could one order a food shipment from, say, Montevideo? And Lloyds of London, which insured German ships and cargoes before the war, was now hostile. Even if the Americans, British and French had lifted their actual naval blockade, it wouldn't really have made a difference. There was nothing out there. The Germans had starved themselves, most stupidly.

From time to time, an enterprising 'blockade-runner' would try to get through, with its cargo of phosphate or copper ores. Most were seized at sea, but it didn't really matter whether they were caught or not. Their contribution to Ludendorff's grinding war demands would be really small.

14 Gerd Hardach, *The First World War 1914–1918* (Berkeley and Los Angeles: University of California Press, 1977), which is the best source here.

In sum, all assertions about the grand or cruel effects of the Allied maritime blockade are mythological. Nonetheless, it remains one of the greatest myths in naval historiography.

Scapa Flow and the rendering of accounts

It was the most extraordinary event in the 3,000-year sweep of naval history; more than Salamis, more than Lepanto, more than the Armada, in its way more than Trafalgar. In the late morning of 21 November 1919, the British light cruiser HMS *Cardiff*, having left the Firth of Forth several hours earlier, flashed a signal to the oncoming battle fleet, received an acknowledgement and turned to lead them in. She was leading in what was left (that is, what could steam) of the High Seas Fleet, a force covered in rust and salt, shaken by the recent mutinies: in all, nine dreadnoughts, five battlecruisers, seven light cruisers and forty-nine destroyers (the U-boats surrendered separately, chiefly into Harwich). American and British battleships then came out, glowering, fully armed, to take up position on each side, and make the German surrender more obvious than ever. It was all over. After the massive Allied breakthroughs on the Western Front from August 1918 onwards, Ludendorff realised that his bold springtime bid had fully lost its chance, and advised Berlin to surrender; the Kaiser fled into the neutral Netherlands, and the Second Reich was no more. The struggle had chiefly been won on land, not at sea, though the artists' renderings of Reuter's great ships coming across to the Scottish coast to surrender were inordinately impressive and Turneresque. Surely sea power had prevailed? That the German vessels were interred, with skeleton crew, in the massive base at Scapa Flow was testimony enough.

What to do with the surrendered German battle fleet – that is, which Ally got how many capital ships, how large a slice of the pie? – promised to be a massively contentious item in the complicated peace settlement, but the Germans settled that themselves. On the Sunday morning of 21 June 1919, a secretly coordinated mass self-sinking saw all the German warships gurgling to the bottom of the sea, with the British guard vessels rushing around and shooting haphazardly. The French and Italian admiralties suspected that the Royal Navy had connived at this act of maritime suicide, but that would be giving Whitehall too much credit. After a while, all the Allies agreed that this had been the best outcome possible. The only real beneficiary was a Glasgow-based scrap metal merchant, who steadily raised and cut up the German warships from Scapa's chilly waters for the next thirty years.

Thus was the scene set for almost two decades of maritime retrenchment, and for the rise of land-based dictators (Stalin, Hitler) who had little patience with the writings of Mahan, Corbett or any of that ilk.

Reflections on a most difficult naval war

It was and is not the intention of this chapter to belittle the importance of the First World War in the general history of sea power, broadly understood. On the contrary, this was the conflict where – much, much more than in the Crimean War, the American Civil War and the Italo-Austrian War, even more than that of the Russo-Japanese War – the history of naval war-fighting bumped into the varied impacts of the Industrial Revolution which, by their essence, shaped and modified the contours of the influence of sea power upon history. One could not expect those retired British and German admirals re-fighting Jutland among themselves all through the 1920s, or the amateur navalist historians of the 1960s,[15] to grasp this historic shift, because they did not have the training in world history and geopolitics to do so. But it is disappointing to this author that so many recent naval historians have never escaped from the arcana of matters such as fire-control, battlecruisers, signals and intelligence, naval finance, procurement and weapons design, as to distinguish the branches and trees from the larger forest. It is rather sad: imperial history flourishes again, in many new forms, while strictly naval history atrophies.

Still, if one stayed for a moment at the technological rather than the larger geopolitical level, simply consider what new and deadlier weapons-systems either had their birth pangs during this armed struggle, or were enormously enhanced in their striking power, a power that could be transferred to lesser as well as to more powerful navies. The naval mine came into its own, creating 'no-go zones' that even Nelson would have marvelled at. By the end of 1918 British advances in aircraft-carrier technology were reaching forward to the possibilities only truly fulfilled in the Pacific after 1943. The U-boat had moved from being a coastal defence craft – a sort of motor torpedo boat with underwater capacities – to being the greatest commerce-raider ever

15 Richard Hough's conclusion on p. 321 of *The Great War at Sea 1914–1918* (Oxford University Press, 1983) is perhaps the most egregious: 'It is no reflection on the prodigious and continuing effort and glorious courage of the armies in France and the numerous other theatres of war, or of the airmen who gave them such valiant assistance, to say that the Royal Navy provided the greatest contribution to victory . . .' This is asserted, but not proven, a dogma but not an established fact.

imaginable. The torpedo itself was stunning in its multiplicity of launch platforms – MTBs, destroyers, aircraft, submarines and cruisers (the dreadnought has come and gone; the torpedo lives afresh). And then there was the coming of air power. Was it any wonder that the negotiators at the Washington Naval Treaties of 1921–2 grappled desperately to understand all this? The maritime world was turned upside down. The point is that you cannot understand this particular revolution without going back to 1793–1815, when naval fighting was understandable, and then coming forward to 1939–45, when naval fighting (say, the American advances upon the Gilberts, Carolines, and so on) became understandable again. There was no such clarity to First World War navies.

And simply because this was such a brave and bewildering new world, not even the most thoughtful strategic critic drew all the correct lessons from the naval war of 1914–18. How could one? For instance, some conclusions were both half-right and half-wrong. Protecting merchant shipping in the Atlantic and the North Sea by returning to the Napoleonic War practice of convoys and escorts was absolutely the right thing to do, and the Second World War's grim battles for the sea lanes would only confirm such a decision. But supposing, as the 1918 British Admiralty did, that the introduction of asdic (sonar) had solved the challenge of detecting U-boats, missed the fact that, as Doenitz's wolf-pack tactics in 1939–45 showed, submarine attacks on the surface still had not found their counter-measure. Successful code-breaking by one side was going to lead to vastly improved encipherment by the other. Radio detection techniques led to radio silence. Aircraft attacking warships could be driven off by aircraft defending such fleets. Technology usually has no favourites, and 'lessons learned' in one conflict may have to be unlearned in the next. Which admiral of 1919 foresaw Taranto and Pearl Harbor? And, just for comparison, which generals of 1919 foresaw anything like the Fall of France?

What did it mean both to win and yet not feel a winner? To be sure, the Japanese navy gained, and hugely, but Eurocentric maritime historians scarcely think of that series of distant gains.[16] The United States navy gained, but it was building an enormous battle fleet in any case; to extreme American navalists, the meaning of the various peace settlements of 1919 to 1923 across the globe was to ruin their ambition to be the clear Number One naval power.

16 The exception here is A. J. Marder, *Old Friends, New Enemies: The Royal Navy and the Imperial Japanese Navy*, vol. I: *Strategic Illusions 1936–1941* (New York: Oxford University Press, 1981).

Germany lost. Russia lost. Austria-Hungary also lost navally, but hardly noticed that in the breakup of its own Empire. The French navy felt eclipsed, the Italian navy felt robbed. There remained the Royal Navy, both a winner and a loser. It had won because the island-nation had not been invaded, it had protected the sea lanes between itself and the far ends of the globe and it had been able to transport its troops to distant theatres of war. But it felt it had not really succeeded because it had not properly demonstrated its naval mastery. It had failed to crush the enemy's main fleet.

There is a symbolic ending to this rather disappointing tale and it occurred, properly enough, during that later, far more stirring and more epic war at sea. As the story goes, the last two boats in the brand-new King George V-class battleships were scheduled to be named HMS *Jellicoe* and HMS *Beatty*, but the Prime Minister, Churchill, sensibly realised that those titles might attract scorn in 1941–2, when the Home Fleet was flinging everything into the hunt for the *Bismarck* and Cunningham's Mediterranean Fleet was fighting for its life off Greece and Crete, regardless of its heavy losses. So the new battleships were named instead HMS *Anson* and HMS *Howe*, after safe, steady, brave and successful eighteenth-century admirals of the Royal Navy. One could now forget about the naval history of the First World War.

13

The air war

JOHN H. MORROW, JR.

Pre-war

Flight offered the prospect of a new arena of warfare from its very origins, and the adoption of captive observation balloons by European armies in the latter half of the nineteenth century paved the way for their later acceptance of powered flight, by leading to the formation of civilian aviation societies and small military aviation units. The invention and evolution of small, reliable and efficient high-speed gasoline engines in the 1880s and 1890s enabled the invention of the dirigible in France in 1884 and the airplane in the United States in 1903. In 1883, Albert Robida's book, *War in the Twentieth Century*, envisaged a sudden crushing air strike, while Ivan S. Bloch's 1898 treatise on warfare anticipated bombardment from airships in the near future.

European armies acquired their first airships – the French army bought the Lebaudy brothers' non-rigid dirigibles, and the German army, Count Ferdinand von Zeppelin's gigantic rigid dirigibles – in the years 1906–08. Noted Englishmen such as press magnate Alfred Harmsworth, Lord Northcliffe and the Honourable Sir Charles Rolls of Rolls-Royce, recognised, in the words of the former, that 'England was no longer an island', although his conception of the threat as 'aerial chariots of a foe descending upon England' indicated a classical, and unrealistic appraisal of its nature.[1] H. G. Wells's popular tome, *The War in the Air*, published in 1908, dramatically portrayed the destruction of cities and, ultimately, of civilisation by gigantic airships and airplanes in a future aerial conflict. Other European authors proclaimed that aviation would bind nations together and make war too terrible to endure. In any case, airships and airplanes were just emerging from the experimental stage by the end of 1907.

1 Alfred Gollin, *No Longer an Island: Britain and the Wright Brothers, 1902–1909* (Stanford University Press, 1989), p. 19.

In 1908, popular interest in aviation surged with a twelve-hour Zeppelin flight and the first cross-country flight and closed circuit flights of more than two hours by airplanes. In January 1908, Frenchman Henri Farman, flying a Voisin biplane, took off under the plane's own power to fly the first officially monitored closed-circuit kilometre. On 30 October he made the first cross-country flight, some twenty-seven to thirty kilometres, from Bouy to Reims. French and German military observers considered these two achievements signals of the birth of aviation sufficiently practical for military use. While they acknowledged the Wright brothers' astounding duration record of two hours and twenty minutes aloft, the Americans' airplane required a launching apparatus and had flown over a manoeuvre field, not overland.

Even during these early days of aviation, international jurists deemed its destructive potential significant enough to assess the ramifications of aerial warfare for international law. They disagreed on the legitimate uses of aviation for warfare – some were willing to allow aerial bombing but not fighting, while others would permit reconnaissance, communications and exploration but not bombing. Peace conferences at The Hague in 1899 and 1907 included discussions of air warfare. In 1899 the dirigible's potential as a bomber led to five-year prohibitions against the discharge of projectiles and explosives from balloons and against the bombing of undefended towns and cities. Yet in the absence of effective and proven bombers, the French, German and Russian representatives would not foreclose the use of new weapons in warfare. In 1907 the conferees agreed only not to bomb undefended towns and villages. The closer aircraft drew to being a useful weapon, the closer international jurists edged to acknowledging its legitimacy as a weapon. At the dawning of 1909, aeronautics stood on the verge of acceptance by military establishments; the years 1909 to 1914 would witness its transformation into an embryonic instrument of modern warfare.

In 1909 French achievements – Louis Blériot's crossing of the English Channel in July and the Reims aviation week in August – stimulated aviation development, public enthusiasm and military interest across Europe. Military aviation leagues and aero clubs became extra-parliamentary pressure groups for military aviation, with highly placed patrons such as Prince Heinrich of Prussia, Grand Duke Alexander Mikhailovich of Russia and First Lord of the Admiralty Winston Churchill in Britain. European crowds of hundreds of thousands of spectators thronged to see air shows, and aviators became the popular heroes of the day as aviation displaced automobile racing as the most popular sport.

The French army bought its first airplanes after Reims, and army manoeuvres in September 1910 demonstrated that airplanes served effectively for reconnaissance and liaison. In the French manoeuvres of 1911, airplanes located an enemy's exact location sixty kilometres away and prompted army officers to contemplate aerial fighting and bombing troops arrayed in dense formation. In the *Revue générale de l'aéronautique militaire* in 1911, Belgian officer Lieutenant Poutrin suggested that the aerial bombardment of urban centres and government capitals could disorganise a nation's life and weaken its morale.[2]

While the French concentrated on airplanes, the Germans divided their resources between airplanes and airships – the former for tactical reconnaissance and the latter for strategic reconnaissance and possibly bombing – although airships were unreliable, particularly in bad weather. The German War Ministry, which regarded the airship as a symbol of German aerial superiority and a political and military means of pressure on foreign countries, refused to acknowledge the repeated failures of airships. Ironically, across the English Channel, R. P. Hearne's book, *Aerial Warfare*, published in 1909, proclaimed that everything was at the mercy of the Zeppelin, whose raids would destroy morale and disable military forces. By 1911 all the European powers were engaged in the development of military aviation, while some observers predicted that the very fear of air war would lead to the dissolution of armies and navies, and aerial warfare would be so gruesome that war would die 'of its own excesses'.[3]

In fact, after the Moroccan crisis of 1911 prompted expectations of European war, armies began studying and testing aircraft armed with machine guns and cannon and equipped to drop shells and fléchettes, six-inch metal darts in canisters. The Michelin brothers launched an annual bombing competition in 1912, and published brochures that advocated bombing troops and supplies beyond the range of artillery. Despite such initiatives, the French army went to war in 1914 with 141 airplanes intended for reconnaissance, not combat.

In contrast, German Chief of the general staff, Helmuth von Moltke, desired to have as many airships as possible operational for a future war, and held exaggerated notions of the Zeppelin's 'first-strike capability'. On 24 December 1912, he informed the War Ministry that

2 Philippe Bernard, 'A propos de la stratégie aérienne pendant la Première Guerre Mondiale: mythes et réalités', *Revue d'Histoire Moderne et Contemporaine*, 16 (1969), pp. 354–55.

3 Felix P. Ingold, *Literatur und Aviatik: Europäische Flugdichtung* (Basel: Birkhäuser Verlag, 1978), pp. 96, 104, 116–17.

> in the newest Z-ships we possess a weapon that is far superior to all similar ones of our opponents and that cannot be imitated in the foreseeable future if we work energetically to perfect it. Its speediest development as a weapon is required to enable us at the beginning of a war to strike a first and telling blow whose practical and moral effect could be quite extraordinary.[4]

German aviation journals echoed Moltke's sentiments, anticipating pinpoint and unstoppable Zeppelin attacks on enemy targets in the dead of night.[5] German war plans in 1913 placed dirigibles directly under the High Command and army commands for strategic reconnaissance and bombing missions, although the dirigibles performed only one bombing trial before the war and the army had only seven of the monsters in the summer of 1914. The German army did have 245 airplanes for tactical reconnaissance, communications and artillery spotting.

Britain, lagging behind both France and Germany in its development of aerial machines, did have in Winston Churchill, First Lord of the Admiralty, a staunch supporter of aviation. The darling of the British aviation press, Churchill, dubbed the 'fairy godfather' of naval aviation in January 1914, proclaimed that aviation's 'great driving power is derived from its military aspect and utility' and that the 'Navy and the Army . . . must be the main propulsive force of aviation in this country'.[6] Both navy and army agreed that the airplane's primary mission would be reconnaissance, although the navy's aviators yearned for a fighting aircraft as well.

In Italy, the visionary army major, Giulio Douhet, predicted aviation would become the decisive element of modern warfare and supported aircraft designer Gianni Caproni's efforts to design and build a fleet of multi-engine bombers for tactical and strategic missions. Every European power facing the likelihood of war by 1914 had an army air service, with a smaller naval service if its navy was large enough to require reconnaissance craft. Yet four powers merit particular attention in the evolution of military aviation: France, Germany, Britain and Italy. Military procurement spurred the rapid development of aircraft and aero-engine manufacturers in France and Germany, and to a lesser extent in Britain and Italy. Other countries lagged behind. Russian

4 Kriegswissenschaftliche Abteilung der Luftwaffe (KAdL), *Die Militärluftfahrt bis zum Beginn des Weltkrieges 1914*, 3 vols., 2nd rev. edn, ed. Militärgeschichtliches Forschungsamt (Frankfurt am Main: E. S. Mittler, 1965–6), vol. II, p. 86.

5 Jürgen Eichler, 'Die Militärluftschiffahrt in Deutschland 1911–1914 und ihre Rolle in den Kriegsplänen des deutschen Imperialismus', *Zeitschrift für Militärgeschichte*, 24:4 (1985), pp. 407–10.

6 *Flight*, 5:10 (7 March 1914), pp. 248–9.

inventor, Igor Sikorsky, designed a giant four-engine biplane, the *Il'ia Muromets*, which flew 2,575 kilometres in six-and-a-half hours in 1913, but Russian industry would struggle to manufacture the giant. The United States, far away from an increasingly militaristic and bellicose Europe, lacked the impetus to develop military aviation, although aviator Glenn Curtiss excelled in the development of seaplanes and flying boats. Clearly, doctrine often did not necessarily accord with the technological and industrial state of aviation, as German expectations of the dirigible illustrated. On the whole, however, a limited doctrine restricting the aircraft's use to reconnaissance and communications accorded well with the state of aviation prior to the outbreak of war.

1914: An instrument of war

Starting with the Battle of the Marne in September 1914, French reconnaissance planes played a key role in detecting the German army's turn to the north-east of Paris, thus enabling the French and British to strike the Germans in the flank. At the tactical level, some artillery commanders used aerial observation planes to direct artillery bombardments of enemy targets, and the aircrews used the occasion to drop 90 mm shells and fléchettes on the enemy.

In November, French High Command (*Grand Quartier Général*, or GQG) began to consider the strategic bombardment of German industrial centres. As early as 2 August, War Minister Paul Painlevé and industrialists such as the Michelin brothers and aircraft builder Paul Schmitt, had expressed interest in bombing Essen, the centre of the Krupp works in the Ruhr Valley – a task beyond the capacity of the tiny air arm. On 23 November, however, GQG formed four squadrons of Voisin biplanes into the First Bombardment Group (GB1) of eighteen planes. This force struck the railway station at Freiburg on 4 December, and was drawing up a list of important and vulnerable targets by the end of the year.

The German High Command (*Oberste-Heeresleitung*, or OHL) used four Zeppelins in August and September for reconnaissance and bombing missions against cities such as Antwerp, Zeebrugge, Dunkirk, Calais and Lille. All four airships were destroyed by enemy action, the last during a British bombing attack on its shed in Düsseldorf on 8 October. By the end of the year the army had given up on the airship, but German naval airship commander Peter Strasser remained determined to strike at England, although he had no suitable ships.

German airplanes performed such critical reconnaissance on the Western and Eastern Fronts – particularly in the East at Tannenberg where Russian cavalry outnumbered German – that by the end of August the airplane had developed from 'a supplementary means of information relied upon principally for confirmation' to 'the principal means of operational reconnaissance – an important factor in forming army commanders' decisions'.[7] At the end of August, in two separate incidents, German pilots dropped small bombs on Paris and a note advising Parisians that 'The German army stands before the gates of Paris. You have no choice but to surrender.'[8] Perhaps these feats should count as early, if unsuccessful uses of the airplane for psychological warfare.

German parliamentary deputies reflected a sentiment in military, diplomatic and business circles that favoured 'breaking British resistance' through aerial bombing. In late August, the German minister in Stockholm, Franz von Reichenau, hoped 'with all his heart' that 'Germany would send airships and aircraft cruising regularly over England dropping bombs' until 'the vulgar huckster souls' of those 'cowardly assassins' would forget 'even how to do sums'. The industrialist Walther Rathenau also advocated 'systematically working on the nerves of the English towns through an overwhelming air force'.[9] The German High Command did form a bombing corps under the fanciful and intentionally deceptive name, the Carrier Pigeon Unit Ostende (*Brieftauben Abteilung Ostende*). However, as the Germans never captured Calais, their bombers could not reach England and contented themselves with raids on Dunkirk, French harbours and railroad junctions.

The British Royal Flying Corps (RFC) won the praise of BEF (British Expeditionary Force) commander Sir John French on 7 September for its 'admirable work' in providing him with 'the most complete and accurate information, which has been of incalculable value in the conduct of operations'.[10] The Royal Naval Air Service (RNAS), stuck with the unwelcome task of home defence, although the British navy's precedence over the army endowed the naval air service with nearly equal strength to its military counterpart, interpreted its home defence mission aggressively and struck Zeppelin sheds in Germany.

7 John R. Cuneo, *Winged Mars*, 2 vols. (Harrisburg, PA: Military Service Publishing Co., 1942–7), vol. II, pp. 92–4.

8 Charles Christienne *et al.*, *Histoire de l'aviation militaire française* (Paris: Charles Lavauzelle, 1980), p. 88.

9 John H. Morrow, Jr., *German Air Power in World War I* (Lincoln, NE: University of Nebraska Press, 1982), pp. 16–17.

10 Peter Mead, *The Eye in the Air: History of Air Observation and Reconnaissance for the Army 1785–1945* (London: HMSO, 1983), pp. 51–8.

Such offensive efforts notwithstanding, aerial reconnaissance constituted the airman's essential contribution to warfare in 1914, although the airplane would require further advances in photography and wireless telegraphy to make it a truly efficient instrument of observation. Yet even in its embryonic state, the airplane forced armies to conceal their activity more extensively. A French artilleryman, pointing to a German aircraft over the Péronne road near Albert early in October, commented to a British reporter, 'There is that wretched bird which haunts us.'[11] In 1914 the bird of war had spread its wings, casting its shadow over the battlefields of Europe. In 1915 it would grow fierce talons to become a bird of prey, and the skies, like the earth and seas below, would become an arena of mortal combat.

1915: The air weapon

In 1915, particularly in the latter half of the year, observation, pursuit and bombing became distinct specialties. Aviation arms concentrated on reconnaissance and artillery spotting, both of which improved markedly, while pursuit aviation and aerial combat, despite significant strides, remained less developed.

French GQG focused on aerial bombardment in an effort to carry the war to the enemy. In 1915 and again in 1918, GQG concentrated on the development of French bomber forces, emphasising bombers and more powerful aero-engines. Aware that the war was becoming a conflict of materiel, GQG selected industrial targets for a strategic bombing campaign intended to shorten the war. The sturdy Voisin pusher biplanes that the French employed in 1915 could carry 40-kilogram 155 mm artillery shells, and from May through to September the French bombed such west German cities as Ludwigshafen, Karlsruhe, Trier and Saarbrücken.

By July, German armed aircraft, including the new Fokker monoplane fighter, were taking higher tolls of the slow and vulnerable Voisin and Farman biplanes, although the French bombers now flew in groups in V formation for defence. GQG responded by using the bombers increasingly on night raids as extra long-range artillery against military targets right behind the front. Night operations sacrificed speed for heavier bomb loads, although they complicated navigation and decreased the precision and intensity of the raids.

In early June, GQG proposed an air arm of fifty squadrons (500 bombers) to attack Essen, the home of the Krupp works, but it required more powerful

11 *Flight*, 3:41 (9 October 1914), p. 1026.

bombers and thus more powerful engines. In July, and again in September, the French Parliament's aviation commissions demanded the bombardment of German industrial centres and the construction of large long-range bombers for the mission. Even a university professor wrote to the government advocating an aviation arm of 1,000 planes each capable of carrying a 300–400 kilogram bomb load to attack German communications, stations, supply and munitions depots in the Rhine region around the clock.[12] GQG, however, was renouncing its hopes for strategic aviation because of the cost, materiel deficiencies and its awareness that Paris would become Germany's prime target for reprisal raids in any strategic air war.

In the winter of 1914–15, the German army and navy jockeyed to undertake strategic attacks on England with dirigibles, the navy claiming that the material and moral (morale) results of bombing London could diminish British determination to prosecute the war. Two German dirigibles did bomb the British coast in January 1914, but the Kaiser initially forbade attacks on London out of concern for opinion in neutral countries, particularly the United States. Late in April, the Kaiser consented to raids to demoralise the population, damage war production and divert British airplanes to home defence. During the year the Zeppelins grew larger and more powerful, approaching 182 metres in length, with a volume of more than 28,000 cubic metres, speed of 80.4 kilometres per hour and a bomb load of over two tons (Map 13.1).

The loss of two army airships, one of which had staged the first bombing raid on London the night of 31 May–1 June, prompted the army to transfer its Zeppelins to the less heavily defended Eastern Front. The navy remained determined to use airships to scout for the fleet and bomb England, and its Zeppelins bombed London in August, September and October. In 1915 raiding Zeppelins dropped 1,900 bombs totalling just over 36 tons, killing 277 and wounding 645, and causing an estimated damage of £870,000. The onset of winter halted the raids, but the navy prepared to continue its campaign in 1916, as British airplanes were unable to intercept the fast-climbing airships.

In 1915 the BEF's Royal Flying Corps concentrated on tactical aviation, artillery spotting and reconnaissance and aerial fighting, while the RNAS continued its bombing raids on Belgian targets, particularly Zeppelin bases. Members of the government and parliament, increasingly dissatisfied with the

12 Bernard, 'Stratégie aérienne', pp. 359–60. Correspondence of Flandin to D'Aubigny, 21 Sept 1915, File A81, Service Historique de l'Armée de l'Air (SHAA, in service historique de la Défense (SHD)).

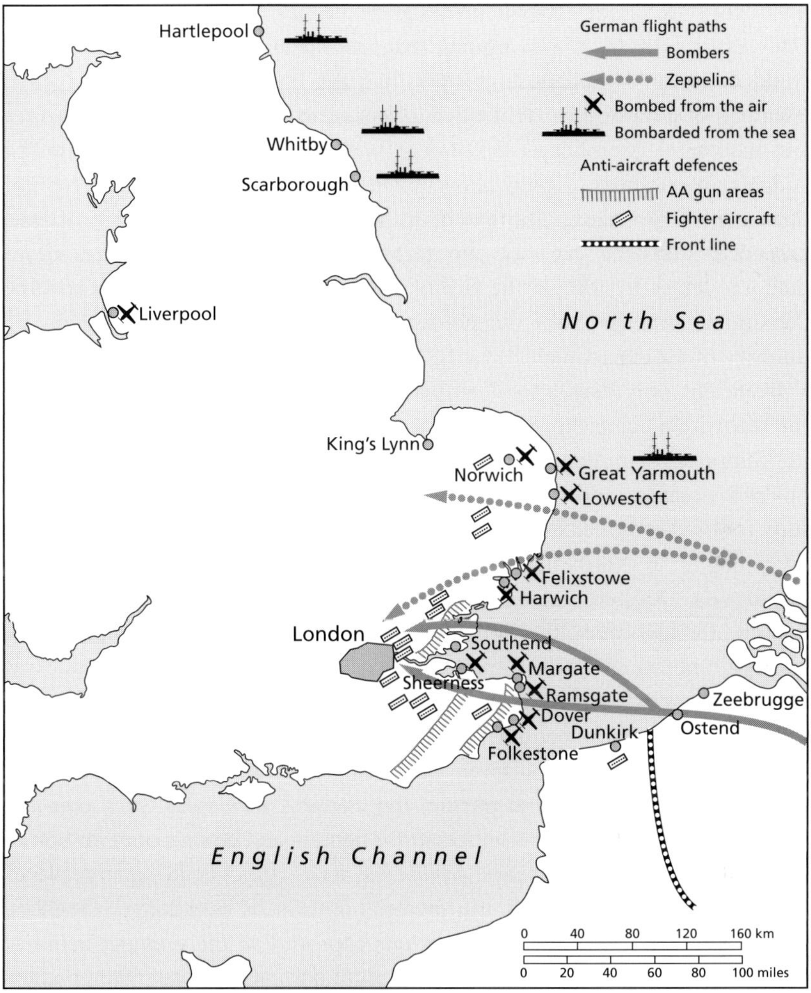

Map 13.1 Strategic bombing of Britain, 1914–18.

air war effort, contemplated devastating aerial attacks on Germany. At a meeting of the War Council on 24 February 1915, one member advocated an air attack to distribute a 'blight' on Germany's next grain crop, while another preferred to burn the crop using thousands of little discs of gun cotton. Winston Churchill preferred burning, while David Lloyd George, then Minister of Munitions, averred that the blight 'did not poison, but merely deteriorated the crop'. The Prime Minister, Asquith, resolved to resort to such measures only under extreme provocation.[13] In a manifesto published in the *Daily Express*, H. G. Wells, arguing that 2,000 planes, even if half were lost, could demolish Essen more cheaply than the cost of the Battle of Neuve Chapelle or a battleship, demanded a fleet of 10,000 airplanes with reserves and personnel. Member of Parliament William Joynson-Hicks took up the cudgels for a 10,000- or even 20,000-plane force to end the war with reprisal bombing of Germany. The extent to which such preposterous proposals exceeded industrial capacity and technological capability indicates more than a touch of hysteria in the face of Zeppelin raids, but a more reasonable demand to emerge from the debate focused on the formation of an air ministry or air department.[14]

Ironically, only Italy, a small air power in comparison to the others, began the war with a plane expressly designed as a bomber, the Caproni Ca1, which the Supreme Command used for long-range reconnaissance and bombing railroad junctions and stations. Behind the front, however, Giulio Douhet's superiors had removed him from command of the Italian aviation battalion for exceeding his authority in authorising the Caproni bombers in the first place. In July 1915, Douhet, undaunted, was sowing the seeds of strategic bombing doctrine by advocating the formation of a huge group of heavy airplanes for strategic operations against enemy military and industrial centres, railroad junctions, arsenals and ports.[15]

In 1915 air arms became more sophisticated, performing specialised functions at the front and adapting or developing new types to perform these missions. Bombardment and pursuit, the aircraft's new roles, prompted the adaptation of suitable types – light craft for fighting and heavier ones for bombing – but in general, the absence of powerful aero-engines enabling large planes to carry defensive armament and greater bomb loads over longer distances, limited bomber development. Yet in 1915 appeared all the eminent issues of strategic bombardment – daylight versus night bombing and attendant matters of accuracy and aircraft type, around-the-clock bombing, appropriate target selection – that would continue through the Second World War and even today.

Vocal demands on all sides for bombers captured the attention of civilians and military alike, but the most significant development in aviation in 1915 was the beginning of fighter, or pursuit aviation. The appearance during the

13 File AIR 1/2319/223/29/1–18, National Archives (NA), Kew.

14 *Flight*, 7:26 (25 June 1915), pp. 446–8, 455; *Flight*, 7:30 (23 July 1915), pp. 525–6, 539–42; and *Flight*, 7:43 (22 December 1915), pp. 798, 802.

15 Frank J. Cappelluti, 'The Life and Thought of Giulio Douhet' (PhD thesis, Rutgers University, NJ, 1967), pp. 67–110 *passim*.

summer of the Fokker *Eindecker*, a monoplane with a machine gun synchronised to fire forward through the propeller arc, signalled the beginning of the race for aerial mastery. By the end of 1915 an effective fighting machine required speed and manoeuvrability, as well as fixed forward-firing machine guns. The early pursuit pilots on all sides – Frenchmen Roland Garros and Georges Guynemer, Germans Max Immelmann and Oswald Boelcke and Englishman George Lanoe Hawker – evolved fighting tactics to maximise their chances of becoming aerial predators without falling prey to the enemy. They even recommended technical improvements for fighter aircraft. Their efforts would make the skies over Europe's battlefields far more dangerous in 1916.

1916: A watershed in military aviation

The great land battles of Verdun and the Somme on the Western Front in 1916 necessitated the first major struggles for aerial control over the battlefield, as fighter, or pursuit, aviation became necessary to prevent enemy aerial observation and protect one's own vulnerable observation planes over and behind the lines. Here again the fundamental choices of fighter escort of reconnaissance or bombing airplanes arose – close protection of one's own planes or constant sector patrols to sweep the skies clear of enemy planes. Verdun demonstrated that aerial mastery over and behind the battle lines was essential to the progress of the land battle and required a concentration of fighter forces to achieve it. On the other hand, aerial control remained transitory and incomplete depending upon the shifting concentration of force at points of penetration of airspace over the battlefield, and it was thus practically impossible for either side to attain absolute security.

By October 1916, French tactical bombing in daylight over enemy lines would practically cease because of the heavy casualties German fighters exacted. Until then, GQG had targeted German industrial centres – first chemical and powder plants and metallurgical shops, and then munitions and armaments plants – within a 300-kilometre radius of the French bombardment group's base at Malzéville near Nancy. Raids struck railway stations, blast furnaces and even airfields, but the losses on raids even escorted by French fighters became too prohibitive and forced a shift exclusively to night attacks. In December 1916, GQG's new bombardment programme limited targets to within 160 kilometres of Nancy, in particular the metallurgical shops of the Saar-Luxembourg-Lorraine region, as French bombers' performance in fact barely enabled them to reach those targets.

Behind the front, a triangular struggle over control of aviation production programmes among GQG, the War Ministry and parliamentary aviation subcommittees continued, as French aviation lurched from crisis to crisis and programme to programme in the political arena. At least in the procurement realm, French military administrators rationalised the research and procurement offices in their attempt to improve aircraft types and manufacture.

In 1916, French observation squadrons, like their bomber counterparts, suffered from the use of outmoded, outclassed and thus highly vulnerable airplanes. One Voisin squadron chose a snail as its emblem, while fragile Farman biplanes burned easily because of the gas tank's location directly above the hot engine.[16] These numerous army corps squadrons bore the brunt of the mounting losses the expanding French air service experienced in 1916.

French fighter aviation excelled in 1916, as pursuit groups formed, featuring such aces as Georges Guynemer and Charles Nungesser flying light, manoeuvrable Nieuport biplanes, armed with a Lewis machine gun attached to the top wing and thus firing over the propeller arc. Yet, as of the summer of 1916, the Nieuport could barely manage against new German fighters, and as 1916 drew to a close, the French air arm faced 1917 with a desperate need for modern airplanes. Fortunately, although it had taken a year, two French manufacturers had designed such planes – Louis Béchereau's SPAD fighter, powered by the revolutionary Hispano-Suiza 150-hp. V8 watercooled engine, and Louis Breguet's reconnaissance/tactical bomber framed of duralumin and steel tubes for lightness and strength. The former, in SPAD 7 and 13 versions with ever-higher horsepower Hispano-Suiza engines, would power French fighter aviation to the end of the war, while the Breguet 14s, powered by Renault 300-hp engines, would spearhead the resurgence of French tactical bombardment in 1918.

As French fighter aviation excelled, particularly in the first half of 1916, so its opponent, the German fighter arm, desperately needed a new fighter airplane to replace its obsolescent Fokker monoplanes, which the Nieuports easily outclassed. Max Immelmann fell to his death in combat, and Germany's remaining star pilot, Oswald Boelcke, was withdrawn from the front to preserve German morale. Boelcke took the occasion to draw up the 'Dicta Boelcke', guidelines for aerial fighting that still apply today: seek the advantage before attacking; attack from the rear, if possible with the sun at one's back (thus the Allied dictum of two world wars, 'Beware the Hun in the sun'); carry

16 Louis Thébault, *L'Escadrille 210* (Paris: Jouve, 1925), pp. 29, 49, 53, 59.

through an attack keeping the opponent in sight and firing only at close range; if attacked from above, turn and meet the adversary; and never forget the line of retreat over enemy territory.[17]

If Verdun had been difficult for the German air service, the opening of the Battle of the Somme brought disaster, as the British and French air services outnumbered the German by a three-to-one ratio. In mid September, however, Oswald Boelcke returned to the front with fighter units equipped with the new Albatros D1 twin-gun fighter, a sleek, sturdy and powerful killer that wrested aerial supremacy from the British and French. Although Boelcke, with forty kills to his credit, fell to his death on 28 October after a collision with a comrade, he bequeathed his dicta and his most adept pupil, Manfred Freiherr von Richthofen.

The Germans now concentrated their strength on the Somme front and reorganised the air service during the summer and fall to reflect the increased importance and specialisation of function of the aerial units. Fighter units (*Jastas*, short for *Jagdstaffeln*) became a new elite. Flight units (*Fliegerabteilungen*) divided into two types of armed two-seat single-engine biplanes (C-planes). The former were equipped with special cameras for long-range reconnaissance and the latter designated for artillery observation. Embryonic ground-support squadrons (*Schutzstaffeln*) of light, well-armed and highly manoeuvrable CL-planes flown by ground attack fliers (*Infanterieflieger*), protected observation planes and conducted ground attacks in offensive or defensive roles. Lastly, a few bomber units (*Kagohl*, or *Kampfgeschwadern der OHL*) under the OHL were now equipped with twin-engine Gotha bombers for longer-range striking power.

On 8 October 1916, the German High Commanders, Paul von Hindenburg and his Chief Quartermaster Erich Ludendorff, established a Commanding General of the Air Forces (*Kogenluft*, or *Kommandierer General der Luftstreitkräfte*) directly subordinate to them. The next month the aviation staff officers assigned to German army commands became Aviation Commanders with the authority to employ their units tactically. A cavalry general, Ernst von Hoeppner, became *Kogenluft*, but the key to the future of German aviation lay with his subordinates, his Chief of Staff Colonel Hermann von der Lieth-Thomsen and the procurement chief, Major Wilhelm Siegert, who had guided the rise of German aviation since early 1915 as chief and deputy chief of field aviation. The elevation of the air forces in the German

17 Johannes Werner, *Boelcke: Der Mensch, der Flieger, der Führer der deutsche Jagdfliegerei* (Leipzig: K. F. Köhler, 1932), pp. 158–68.

command hierarchy coincided with the proclamation of the Hindenburg Programme, which decreed total mobilisation in an all-out effort to win the war. Thomsen requested and received from Ludendorff special status for aviation procurement in Germany's total mobilisation, as the army prepared to face the increasing war of attrition over the Western Front. Army aviation had clearly assumed a position of major importance in the German military hierarchy, and Thomsen abandoned army Zeppelin operations because of their high costs and negligible results.

The German navy, on the other hand, increased its Zeppelin raids on England during 1916, now employing gargantuan airships nearly 198 metres long, with a gas volume of nearly 56,000 million cubic metres and capable of carrying a bomb load of some five tons at 96 kilometres per hour. The naval airship commander Captain Peter Strasser set out to destroy England, to deprive it 'of the means of existence through increasingly extensive destruction of cities, factory complexes, dockyards . . . railways, etc.'.[18] Yet by the late summer of 1916 the Zeppelin could no longer elude more powerful British fighters equipped with explosive and incendiary bullets, and the increasing losses of Zeppelins indicated that the time of the Zeppelin as a bomber had passed, although Strasser was determined to persevere. Now the Zeppelin's major duty became scouting for the High Seas Fleet, which also acquired capable armed floatplanes, built by designer Ernst Heinkel at the Hansa-Brandenburg works, that would give the British a rude shock over the Flanders coast in 1917.

As Britain prepared to take the offensive in 1916, RFC commander General Hugh Trenchard was initially concerned about inadequate aircraft and aircrew training. Nevertheless, the RFC quickly seized the initiative from the start of the Somme offensive on 1 July and dominated the skies over the battlefield, as Trenchard determined to fight the Germans over their own territory. RFC pilots flew constantly on 'contact' patrols to support infantry operations, on photographic observation missions to direct artillery fire and on tactical bombing missions. These missions cost unparalleled casualties because of the poor performance of the RFC's obsolescent two-seat biplanes. Confronted with resurgent German fighter forces in the fall, Trenchard did not relent, instead hardening his determination to conduct a 'relentless and incessant offensive' up to 30 kilometres over German lines regardless of losses.[19] British aircrews found themselves caught in a vicious circle: equipped

18 Douglas H. Robinson, *Giants in the Sky: A History of the Rigid Airship* (Seattle: University of Washington Press, 1973), p. 122.

19 Trenchard, 'Short notes on the Battle of the Somme 1 July–11 November 1916', File MFC 76/1/4, Trenchard Papers (TP), Royal Air Force Museum, Hendon (RAFM).

with inferior airplanes, they fell casualty to German fighters so quickly that their replacements arrived at the front with increasingly inadequate training, which rendered them in turn even easier cannon fodder for German fighter pilots.

The RNAS meanwhile pursued its bomber offensive against Zeppelin sheds and German airfields in spring 1916 using new Sopwith two-seat biplanes, and by the fall had placed one of its three wings of twenty-four aircraft at Luxeuil, near Nancy, where it joined the French in a first joint raid against the Mauser factory at Oberndorf. The fall's foul weather soon closed further operations. In England, the Admiralty and War Office grappled over control of wartime aviation, particularly strategic bombing and the production of powerful aero-engines for bombers, which the RNAS refused to relinquish to the RFC. Inadequate British aircraft and engine production forced reliance on a hard-pressed French aviation industry, but developments towards the end of the year boded well for the future. Rolls-Royce was starting to hit its stride in delivering its superlative, if highly complex combat engines, the 200-hp. (later 275-hp.) Falcon and the 275-hp. (later 360-hp.) Eagle for fighters and bombers respectively. Britain's three most famous fighters – the Sopwith Camel, the SE5 and the Bristol F2 two-seat reconnaissance fighter – appeared in the latter part of 1916 and would serve through to the end of the war. The first De Havilland DH-4 single-engine day bombers and Handley-Page 0/100 twin-engine night bombers also appeared at year's end.

In 1916, Italy had the most operational multi-engine bombers, as the Caproni factory delivered 136 tri-motored bombers powered by increasingly powerful Fiat engines during the year. Raids of up to fifty-eight bombers struck Austro-Hungarian railway stations and even the city of Trieste. While strategic bomber aviation formed the centrepiece of the Italian aerial effort, its staunchest advocate, Giulio Douhet, left a memorandum criticising the Italian war effort on a train, and found himself duly sentenced to one year in prison in October. There he would have time to write, and ultimately he would be exonerated in 1920.

The year 1916 became a watershed in the First World War, as Verdun and the Somme dashed both sides' hopes for imminent victory. These battles also marked the true beginning of aerial warfare, as the combatant powers committed to building and wielding larger air forces to attain aerial superiority. France took the lead in industrial mobilisation, as its aero-engine production far outdistanced Germany and England because of France's early mobilisation of its automotive industry to manufacture aviation engines. The aerial policies of the major powers reflected these industrial realities and their basic military strategies. British and French air policy and overall military strategies were offensive, the British more relentlessly than the French. The Germans, in danger of being overwhelmed numerically on the Western Front, reorganised and elevated their aviation forces in importance, husbanded their resources, fought defensively and planned to concentrate their aviation forces to seek occasional mastery limited in time and space. In 1916, with the pre-eminence of fighter aviation, the air services provided the European combatants with their most revered heroes – aces like Albert Ball, Oswald Boelcke and Georges Guynemer – youth who epitomised the national will to sacrifice in the monstrous struggle on the Western Front. The era of the individual ace would last into 1917, but individuals would soon find themselves submerged in the burgeoning aerial war of attrition, as the deployment of aviation forces en masse became indispensable to the conduct of war.

1917: An aerial war of attrition

In early April 1917, the French commander General Robert Nivelle launched an ill-fated assault on the River Aisne, at the Chemin des Dames, where the Germans had already withdrawn to their recently constructed Hindenburg Line. At GQG Nivelle exhorted, 'The aerial victory must precede the terrestrial victory of which it is both part and pawn. It is necessary to seek out the enemy over his own territory and destroy him.'[20] The offensive, in the air and on land, turned into an abysmal failure, with high casualties and few results, other than Nivelle's removal and the refusal to conduct any further suicidal attacks by French army units.

General Henri-Philippe Pétain succeeded Nivelle and promptly confined the army to limited offensives, husbanding his infantry while wearing down the German forces with superior artillery, aviation and assault tanks. Pétain informed the Minister of War, Paul Painlevé, on 28 May: 'Aviation has assumed a capital importance; it has become one of the indispensable factors of success . . . It is necessary to be master of the air. The obligation to seize aerial mastery will lead to veritable aerial battles.'[21] By December 1917, Pétain sought certain aerial mastery, first against the anticipated German offensive of 1918, by using the tactical bomber defensively: '[I]n great mass, systematically, with continuity, on the enemy's rear along the front of attack, it is perfectly

20 'L'aéronautique militaire française pendant la Guerre de 1914–1918', vol. II: '1917–1918', *Icare, revue de l'aviation française*, 88 (Spring 1979), p. 17.

21 Guy Pedroncini, *Pétain: général en chef 1917–1918* (Paris: PUF, 1974), pp. 41, 57.

capable of paralysing the offensive.'[22] Furthermore, in an Allied offensive, he anticipated that his bombers could attack enemy lines of communication and prevent the Germans massing their troops to block attacks.

French and German aviation commands concentrated their fighter forces in steadily larger formations, but the French fighter pilots, imbued with a sense of 'knightly' individualism and independence that such aces as Guynemer, Nungesser and René Fonck embodied, were reluctant to embrace the new massed tactics. Jean Villar's memoir, *Notes of a Lost Pilot*, lamented: '[T]he veterans want to hunt individually, through overconfidence and a desire to work on their own; the novices imitate them through vanity and ignorance. And both finish by being killed.'[23]

At least French fighter pilots had the SPAD as a mount. Observation and bomber crews flew planes that were cannon fodder. GQG concentrated on battlefield aviation in 1917, but some bomber commanders yearned to strike Germany and regretted the feeble state of French strategic aviation. In April, Captain Kérillis longed for reprisal raids to 'strike the morale of the enemy, to intimidate him'. Kérillis believed that a fifty-plane raid on Munich 'would have flung enough German entrails on the pavement of the city to give the torpedoers of the *Lusitania* and the arsonists of Reims pause for reflection'.[24] Pétain did not consider German morale susceptible to reprisal raids and feared their degeneration into a cycle of atrocities. The French air staff, which understood that Kérillis's sanguine fantasies were out of the question, in 1917 and 1918 planned to concentrate on accessible and vulnerable targets within 160 kilometres of Nancy, while acknowledging that destruction of such targets would be 'problematical'.[25]

In the French political arena at the beginning of 1917, parliamentary deputies were concerned about an increasingly debilitating schism between GQG at Chantilly and the War Ministry and politicians in Paris. Fortunately, in March, Minister of War Paul Painlevé appointed as Under-Secretary of Aeronautics Daniel Vincent, a radical socialist who had served as reporter of the aviation budget in parliament and earlier as an observer in a Voisin squadron. Radical socialist deputy, J. L. Dumesnil, who succeeded Vincent

22 *Ibid.*, pp. 41–2.
23 Lieutenant Marc [Jean Béraud Villars], *Notes d'un pilote disparu (1916–1917)* (Paris: Hachette, 1918), translated into English by S. J. Pincetl and Ernst Marchand as, *Notes of a Lost Pilot* (Hamden, CT: Archon, 1975), pp. 211–21.
24 Bernard, 'Stratégie aérienne', p. 363.
25 AEF account of the aviation plan of bombardment, 18 November 1917, AIR 1/1976/204/273/40, National Archives, Kew; and Pedroncini, *Pétain*, 58.

as reporter of the aviation budget, would again succeed Vincent as Under-Secretary five months later and serve to the end of the war. These two men did much to improve aviation, as they struggled to mesh GQG's ever-escalating demands for airplanes with the materiel and manpower resources of the rear. Finally, the appointment of Georges Clemenceau as Prime Minister in mid November meant that France had now acquired a civilian dictator in the person of 'The Tiger', who planned to control all such matters from above. Despite such political and bureaucratic instability during 1917, compounded by labour unrest in French industry, the French aircraft and engine factories increased production, aided by the procurement bureaucracy's decision to concentrate on the production of SPAD fighters and their Hispano-Suiza engines and Breguet bombers and their Renault engines. The results of their labour would become evident in 1918.

In 1917 the German air service, like the army, pursued a defensive strategy on the Western Front. Fending off the French attack at the Chemin des Dames and the British attack at Arras, German fighters fought only over their lines, while lone, high-performance two-seat biplanes flew high-altitude photographic reconnaissance missions over enemy lines. The fighters' toll of British aircraft in April 1917 caused the month to be known as 'Bloody April', as German fighter units led by Manfred von Richthofen and equipped with the superior Albatros D3 fighter, ripped into British two-seaters over German airspace. By the summer, however, SPADs, SE5As, Sopwith Camels and Triplanes and Bristol fighters easily outclassed the latest Albatros D5s, and not even the introduction of the first Fokker DR1 triplanes offset the Allied aerial superiority. Still, high above the front, expert long-range reconnaissance crews received superior airplanes, particularly Rumpler C-types, which could perform such missions at 6,096 metres with little loss of altitude. They thus evaded British and French interceptors or, if the Germans chose to fight, held their own against even the newest Allied fighter planes.

Far below these altitudes, at ground level the Battle of Arras also witnessed the debut of German aerial 'infantry', 'battle flyers', or, as these aviators preferred to be called, 'Storm fliers' (*Sturmflieger*). Filling the ranks of the *Schutzstaffeln* formed in late 1916, the Storm fliers, who were non-commissioned officers and soldiers, many of whom had served in the trenches, supported the infantry on offence and defence with machine guns, grenades and fragmentation bombs. Mounted in small, strong, light and highly manoeuvrable two-seat Halberstadt and Hannoverana biplanes, they ranged over the front at 600 metres altitude, then descended to strafe enemy troops, batteries, strongpoints and reserves from 100 metres above the trenches, in the dead zone between the artillery fire of both sides. On days when heavy rain and low cloud grounded other aviators, these determined crews of anonymous aviators from the ranks flew under the low ceiling below 100 metres over the '*rue de merde*', or 'shit street,' as they called the front, to support their kin on the ground, the anonymous front-line infantry.[26] As the war continued they also received AEG, Albatros and Junkers armoured infantry planes, the last of which was the first all-metal airplane. The Junkers J1 '*Möbelwagen*', or 'furniture van', was slow and ungainly, but impervious to machine-gun fire from the ground.

In Germany's strategic air war against Britain, *Kogenluft* launched a bomber campaign named 'Turk's Cross', with thirty-six Gotha twin-engine bombers and a few gigantic four- or five-engine R-planes (*Riesenflugzeuge*), in late spring 1917. By summer, losses over England or from crashes upon landing forced the bombers to strike at night, and *Kogenluft* decided to cut its losses and allocated precious materials to fighter, not bomber construction. Naval Airship Commander Peter Strasser, however, persevered fanatically, lightening the giant Zeppelins to fly up to 6,096 metres, where crews suffered from cold and oxygen deprivation, and unanticipated gale-force winds scattered the airships all over Western Europe. At the end of 1917, Strasser was ordering even larger Zeppelins, thus expending Germany's scarce resources to wage a separate strategic campaign, uncoordinated with the army. At least the navy seaplane fighter fleet, equipped with Hansa-Brandenburg two-seat twin-float monoplanes, regained command of the air from English flying boats over the Flanders coast from Zeebrugge to Ostende.

In the German rear, with the new year came the understanding that the Hindenburg Programme's total mobilisation had only partially succeeded, as material and labour shortages prevented the aviation industry from meeting production goals, while the lapse in German fighter development undid their razor-thin qualitative superiority. Ludendorff planned a great German offensive to win the war in 1918, before the might of a mobilised United States fell upon Germany. To this end, on 25 June 1917 *Kogenluft* declared the America Programme, primarily to double the number of fighter squadrons to eighty. Yet only a month later the OHL warned that Germany's economic situation made complete fulfilment of the programme doubtful. Shortages, strikes and transportation delays plagued a German economy strained to the breaking point.

26 Georg P. Neumann (ed.), *In der luft unbesiegt* (Munich: Lehmanns, 1923), pp. 79–91, 166–75.

British fortunes during 1917 began with RFC commander Trenchard's determination to stage an ever more vigorous offensive, thrusting patrols far behind enemy lines to raid supply depots and troop assembly points, which culminated in 'Bloody April'. At least if the RFC was taking a beating in the air, BEF commander General Douglas Haig acknowledged the efficiency of the RFC's artillery, photographic and contact patrols and their importance for the land battle.[27] After suffering disturbingly high casualties during the summer and early fall, which elicited much criticism of the offensive policies from the airmen who flew the patrols, the RFC's superior fighter aircraft enabled its pilots to gain the advantage over their German opponents. Day bomber crews received the speedy DH4 bomber, deficient only in the location of its main fuel tanks between pilot and observer, impairing communication.

Britain's position in the tactical air war thus improved in 1917, but it lacked a strategic riposte to the German air assault that began in May. The Admiralty redirected the naval wing from ineffective strategic raids to assist the RFC on the front, yet many British officials, including Haig and Trenchard, persisted in overestimating the damage strategic raids inflicted upon German materiel and morale even at night, when crews had difficulty hitting targets smaller than a large town.[28] If the navy was relinquishing strategic bombing over land, its acquisition and modification of American Glenn Curtiss's large twin-engine flying boats enabled systematic anti-submarine patrols from naval air stations that covered some 10,360 square kilometres of the North Sea.

In British political circles the German raids provoked an intense desire not merely for defence, but also for retaliation. The British War Cabinet assigned South African soldier-statesman, J. C. Smuts, to assess the situation in two reports, the second of which advocated in August an independent, unified air service to gain overwhelming aerial predominance in order to carry the war to Germany, strike its industrial centres and lines of communication and win the war.[29] The Ministry of Munition's aviation and aircraft supply chief, William Weir, firmly believed that British industry could supply sufficient planes to equip a greatly expanded air force, and everyone had tired of the wasteful RFC-RNAS rivalry over industrial output. Unfortunately, Weir's enthusiasm

27 Correspondence Haig GHQ no. O.B./1826 to Secretary, War Office, 18 May 1917, AIR 1/2267/209/70/34, NA.

28 George Kent Williams, 'Statistics and Strategic Bombardment: Operations and Records of the British Long-Range Bombing Force during World War I and their Implications for the Development of the Post-War Royal Air Force, 1917–1923' (PhD thesis, Oxford University, 1987), pp. 45–64, 186.

29 MFC 76/1/1, TP, RAFM.

outran his discretion, and no surplus of production materialised. In fact, British aero-engine production failed miserably, except for bright spots such as superlative Rolls-Royce engines. The year ended with the matter of a unified air service unresolved.

In Italian aviation the Caproni bombers continued to hold centre stage, carrying out wave attacks against enemy front and rear areas in support of infantry offensives during the battles along the Isonzo river. The collapse of the Italian Front at Caporetto and retreat to the Piave river during the disastrous Twelfth Battle of the Isonzo, forced the bombers to undertake repeated ground attacks in an effort to stem the enemy tide. The Caproni works at Taliedo was building one biplane and one triplane bomber daily with completely standardised wing construction, while Fiat steadily manufactured more and more powerful engines. Giulio Douhet and Gianni Caproni were advocating an Allied fleet of strategic bombers. Writing from prison in June, Douhet called for Allied production of 20,000 airplanes in order to bomb enemy cities.[30] He anticipated, incorrectly, that the United States, which had entered the war in April, would contribute 12,000 aircraft. The potential industrial giant across the Atlantic was totally unprepared to serve as an arsenal of democracy.

In 1917 the airplane rapidly evolved into a multi-faceted weapon of war, undertaking missions from close air support to strategic bombing. The differing nature of the major air forces emerged clearly during the year. The RFC, relentlessly aggressive, carried the fight to the Germans regardless of circumstances, denigrating the significance of high losses while touting them as proof of the service's contribution to the war effort. It replaced its losses with men from the Dominions, took delivery of new fighter aircraft, surmounted the mid-year crisis by the fall and soared into 1918 anticipating an enhanced ability to bomb strategic targets in Germany with a unified air force. The French air service pursued a more circumspect offensive policy to conserve dwindling manpower, as its army confined itself to limited offensives after the debacle at the Chemin des Dames. Pétain had taken a pragmatic approach to strategic bombing, prioritising targets and assessing bombing effectiveness based on military results, not calculations of the effect on morale like the British. Now the French army was concentrating on the combination of the SPAD 13 pursuit plane and the Breguet 14 tactical bomber to regain French aerial ascendancy over the front in 1918. The German air service, like its army, fought a defensive war over the Western Front, but the OHL also undertook a strategic air

30 Cappelluti, 'Douhet', pp. 138–45.

offensive against England, along with its unrestricted submarine warfare, in an attempt to drive England from the war.

By 1917 the British and German commands believed that ground attack aircraft proved a powerful weapon in battle. British fighter pilots assumed responsibility for ground attack, although they reviled the duty and engaged in random, uncoordinated and individual strafing missions. In contrast, the Germans developed suitable airplanes for ground attack and manned them with former infantry, who valued the task. The French did neither, and lagged far behind in ground attack operations. The airplane's heightened military importance and its expansion of military roles coincided with heightened aviation mobilisation by all powers in order to wage the bitter war of attrition. This rapid evolution of air power demonstrated the signal importance of aero-engines, the heart of the airplane, and France displayed best the ability to manufacture high-powered aviation engines in quantity.

In Britain and France aviation mobilisation occasioned much political strife. The British administration of aviation was as highly politicised and personalised as the French, but the former system was not wracked by ministerial instability as was the constantly shifting French government. Parliament played an important role in aviation in both countries, as representatives desired strategic air arms with which to bomb Germany. In France, where the army's control of aviation was a given, the deputies interpellated and intrigued to get their way, to no avail. In Britain the air lobby pressed for an independent air force, which the Lloyd George government established in order to resolve the army–navy conflict over aviation, and to give the Prime Minister an independent ally in his struggle for control against the army and BEF commander Douglas Haig.

Compared to these complex situations, the authoritarian German system made the German military aviation bureaucracy a paragon of stability, as the same officers presided over the air service and aviation production from the beginning to the end of the war. In light of serious shortages of materiel and manpower in a blockaded country, such stability and unity was more imperative for Germany than the Allied Powers. Furthermore, the lack of coordination on the Western Front between the English and French air forces enabled the German air service to survive, despite the Allies' increasing numerical superiority. Allied coordination would be necessary to bring American forces to bear against Germany as quickly as possible, and any joint strategic air offensive would necessitate inclusion of Italian planes and engines to attain as much aerial superiority over the Western Front as possible. French military and political leaders, however, were not prepared to wage strategic air warfare, while the British cared little for inter-Allied strategic coordination.

1918: To the bitter end

As the year 1918 opened, the French army commander Pétain, emphasising the importance of concentrating aerial forces, planned to destroy enemy aviation to gain definitive aerial mastery over the battlefield and directly behind the front in tactical offensive operations. During the defensive struggle against the German March offensive, bomber and fighter aviation supported French ground forces in constant operations over the battle zone. In April and May, when French fighter protection waned, GQG formed the Aerial Division of day bombers and fighters for tactical operations over enemy lines. Although the reluctance of French army commanders to liaise with the Aerial Division limited its effectiveness, it continued its offensives and formed the nucleus of American General 'Billy' Mitchell's 1,400-plane strike force in the American offensive at Saint-Mihiel in the fall. In fact, it was primarily the French, and to a lesser extent the British, who trained and equipped most of the squadrons of the US Air Service.

The Breguet 14 proved to be an outstanding tactical day bomber and high altitude photographic reconnaissance plane for distances up to ninety-six kilometres behind the lines, as well as being a sturdy artillery observation craft. The Breguet and Salmson 2A2 radial-engined biplane finally gave French army corps pilots a fighting chance against German fighters. Night bombers remained a weak link in French aviation throughout 1918, but the French had no further plans to conduct strategic bombing operations and instead struck at German railroad traffic in iron ore within seventy-two kilometres of the front. The French army, preoccupied with the war at the front, opposed both strategic aviation and an autonomous air force. In May, long-range heavy bombers appeared last on Pétain's list of priorities for aircraft types.

On the home front, the politics and administration of French aviation stabilised considerably in 1918, as the Prime Minister, Clemenceau, and Minister of Munitions Louis Loucheur supported GQG before the parliament. Up to the very end of the war, French parliamentary deputies harped on the absence of a strategic air arm, ignoring the fact that France possessed the world's largest air fleet on the Western Front, with 4,000 planes and 2,600 in reserve, and was in the process of producing more airplanes (52,000) than either Britain (43,000) or Germany (48,000), and more aero-engines (88,000) than the other two powers (Britain and Germany each had 41,000) combined.

The German air service began the March offensive effectively, but then found itself increasingly overwhelmed by Allied numerical superiority in 1918. The German fighter squadrons, grouped into larger formations of some sixty airplanes, labelled 'circuses', took delivery of the superlative Fokker D7, whose BMW 185-hp. high compression engine and thick wing granted it superiority over all Allied challengers to the end of the war. Manfred von Richthofen, with eighty kills to his credit making him the ace-of-aces of the First World War, fell in combat in April, thus meeting the fate that greeted practically all of the top 'aces', with the exception of Frenchman René Fonck. The German air arm, short of experienced pilots and fuel and severely outnumbered by the Western forces, spent the last days of the war retreating from airfield to airfield. The OHL relinquished its strategic bomber campaign in May to assign all bombers to tactical raids over the Western Front. The flaming death of Peter Strasser, after his Zeppelin was shot down over England, ended the navy's Zeppelin campaign. Aircraft and engine production flagged in the face of material and labour shortages, ensuring defeat in a war of attrition. Similarly to army fighter forces, German naval fighter forces possessed a superior craft in Heinkel's Hansa-Brandenburg floatplanes, but never enough to perform its various missions over the Channel and the North Sea. By the end of the war, German front line airplanes had declined from some 3,600 in January to 2,700, and the looming winter of 1918–19 would have brought all production to a crashing halt due to coal, material, fuel and food shortages.

The RFC confronted the German offensive initially at a disadvantage in March 1918, but despite heavy losses, which it could replace, the RFC had regained aerial ascendancy by the end of the month. With the British introduction of the tank in numbers in 1918, the army assigned aerial squadrons to the tank corps, to develop aircraft-armour liaison and to neutralise German anti-tank artillery. Starting with an offensive against Amiens in early August, the British army, coordinating its tank, artillery and airplane forces, advanced inexorably for the rest of the war. From the beginning of 1918 to the Armistice, British fliers carried the war to the Germans in constant offensives over enemy territory. They paid for this dominance with high casualties until the very end. As one fighter pilot calculated, a pilot's life in France during 1918 averaged under six weeks, to be terminated by nervous exhaustion, crashes, injury, capture or death.

The tactical air war consumed the bulk of the air arm's attention and resources to the end of the war, although the creation in April 1918 of the Air Ministry, the Royal Air Force (RAF) and an Independent Bombing Force under 'Boom' Trenchard often receive disproportionate attention from historians because of the controversial and political nature of the new aviation establishment. In fact, Secretary of State for Air, William Weir, planned to build the Independent Force to conduct a massive aerial offensive against German cities, and in September he wrote to Trenchard: 'I would very much like it if you could start up a really big fire in one of the German towns . . . The German is susceptible to bloodiness.'[31] Meanwhile, Trenchard considered the Independent Force under his command as a 'gigantic waste of effort and personnel', and proceeded to ignore directives from the Air Ministry to strike at chemical factories and iron and steel works in favour of striking at tactical targets such as airfields and railways.[32] The sole achievement of the Independent Force was to divest naval aviation of its focus on strategic bombing and force the navy to concentrate on fleet and anti-submarine patrol duty. The Ministry of Munitions did succeed in mobilising the aviation industry, which with nearly 350,000 workers was the world's largest at the end of the war. The RAF split its forces between the Western Front and far-flung imperial bases stretching to the Middle East, and its long logistical 'tail' meant that it was the world's largest air force in terms of personnel at the end of the war.

Finally, Italian military and naval aviation dominated its Austro-Hungarian enemy in 1918. Giulio Douhet returned to aviation to serve as Director of Aviation in a General Commissariat established in April 1918, but he retired from the army in June aged 49 in order to write. Caproni manufactured 330 bombers in 1918, the last 290 powered by three 200-hp. engines, double the power of the early Capronis. Both the English and French rejected Caproni bombers for use on the Western Front, and no Allied strategic bombing campaign ever occurred.

Conclusion

In August 1914 the European powers had gone to war with rudimentary air services and embryonic aviation industries. Once airplanes proved themselves as a means of reconnaissance and, most importantly, of artillery spotting, air commanders required more of them to conduct effective aerial operations and prevent enemy aerial reconnaissance. The second aim led to armed aircraft and then the development of specialised pursuit, or fighter, aircraft. The

31 Weir to Trenchard, 10 September 1918, MFC 76/1/94, TP, RAFM.
32 Williams, 'Statistics', pp. 233–51, 257, 260–2.

battles of Verdun and the Somme forced the codification of aerial combat tactics and brought home the importance of mass. The size of the air services and aviation industries consequently spiralled rapidly upwards. Airplanes became more specialised in function, although the basic wartime types remained the two-seat, single-engine, all-purpose biplane and the single-seat, single-engine pursuit biplane. All the aviation commands contemplated strategic bombing to damage enemy production and morale, but early aviation technology limited size, speed, load, range and accuracy of navigation and bombing that would not be overcome until the middle of the Second World War, twenty-five years later.

Military aviation did not determine the outcome of the First World War, but the airplane did establish its very real significance in support of the army and especially the artillery on the battlefield. Airplanes served on all the far-flung fronts of the war, although the heat and humidity of Africa and the Middle East made the life cycle of wood and fabric biplanes short indeed. Control of the airspace over the battlefield became essential to victory in the First World War, just as it would be in the next world war. Strategic aviation in fact played little role in the 1914–18 conflict, although it seemed to offer the key to victory in future wars. The fighter pilots and ground attack aircrews evolved the basic techniques employed for the rest of the twentieth century, and many of those young airmen became the aerial commanders of the Second World War. In both strategy and tactics the air war of 1914–18 portended the larger aerial struggle of 1939–45.

The war of the masses bequeathed to them a new individual hero, the aviator, in particular the fighter ace – honoured as a demigod, object of a secular holy cult – whose fame and heroism were quantifiable, measured in terms of his number of conquests, or 'kills', although the figures were usually inflated. This very circumstance prompted disproportionate attention to fighter aviation, when the lessons of the battlefields of 1914–18 proved the worth of the airplane as a tactical weapon for observation, artillery spotting, bombing and strafing in the land battle. The fighter was necessary primarily to protect these other airplanes in the performance of their duties, but aerial fighting took on a life of its own, above the fray.

Theory and wishful thinking after the Great War focused on strategic aviation and nearly drove the lessons of tactical aerial importance and success from the minds of post-war observers. The more post-war aviation theorists speculated on the ability of strategic bombardment to force enemy capitulation by bombing cities, wrecking war industry and civilian morale, the less they seemed to remember the contributions of battlefield aviation. Giulio

Douhet was the most eminent of these theorists. His work, *The Command of the Air*, encapsulated in 1921 the claims for strategic air power that striking directly at civilian centres with bombs or chemicals would bring states to their knees because civilians could not withstand such pounding. Such assertions sprang less from the limited and inconclusive experience of 1914–18 and more from inductive speculations and extrapolations. Sir William Weir's desire to 'start up a really big fire in one of the German towns' sowed the seed of RAF Bomber Command's devastating fire raids of 1943–5, which cost Bomber Command and German civilians horrendous casualties, without ending the war as the theorists had claimed. Victory in 1939–45, in fact would require tactical air power to support ground and naval forces and the more precise targeting of key strategic industrial and transportation sites, which confirmed the actual experience of the air war of 1914–18.

14

Strategic command

GARY SHEFFIELD AND STEPHEN BADSEY

Issues of command are at the centre of present academic discourse on the military history of the First World War. This chapter examines one aspect of this topic: command at the strategic level, concentrating on certain important themes rather than strategy *per se*, and on the major belligerents. It is impossible to examine strategic command in isolation, so where necessary reference has been made to operational and even tactical command issues.

Definitions

Modern definitions of what constitutes strategic command derive chiefly from nineteenth-century military thought and practice, but have only recently reached their present form as part of a wider taxonomy of conflict. While there are obvious risks in applying these definitions to an earlier age, it was the experience of the First World War that gave the greatest impetus to their development. As the war progressed, deficiencies were exposed in the thinking and institutions of both the Allies and the Central Powers, and how they responded to these deficiencies became an important part in determining victory, with innovations being made usually in response to specific crises.

From a wide range of similar definitions, strategic command in war may be defined as 'the management of command: the assessment and dissemination of information and orders needed to direct military force'.[1] Already in 1914, the image of a general on horseback personally commanding his forces had been something of a myth for some time. Too often the reality was of a man at the end of a telephone in an office behind the lines, struggling to make decisions based on scraps of information that were incomplete, out of date and, not

1 Quoted in G. D. Sheffield, 'Command, leadership, and the Anglo-American experience', in Sheffield (ed.), *Leadership and Command: The Anglo-American Military Experience Since 1861* (London: Brassey's, 2002 [1997]), p. 1.

infrequently, plain wrong. A well-known analogy sees a system of command and control in terms of the human body, with the commander and staff as the 'brain' making decisions conveyed by systems and procedures as the 'nervous system' to the 'muscles' or fighting formations.[2] For this reason, there is an increasing awareness among historians of the importance of studying staffs and the 'control' aspect of command alongside generals and admirals. Command in this sense, as it evolved in the course of the war, was as much a matter of the bureaucracy and technology of communication and staff procedures as personal military leadership, although many generals combined both functions in themselves.[3]

This is not to suggest that in the First World War personalities and matters of temperament, and even health, did not play a part in strategic command, given the enormous strains under which generals and admirals were often placed. Both Moltke in 1914 and Ludendorff in 1918 suffered from what would now be called nervous breakdowns under the pressures of command, while Joffre was renowned for his calm, phlegmatic fortitude. While personal command styles differed, from the desk-bound Moltke to Sir John French, who at Loos attempted to command on horseback away from his headquarters, the 'Mask of Command' – the ability to keep a calm exterior no matter what the military situation – was all-important to a general's credibility and authority. But with armies so large, it was difficult for commanders to impose their personalities on them, and charismatic strategic leadership was at a discount, with the arguable exception of figures such as Hindenburg and Kitchener who were elevated by the press to the status of national heroes.[4]

One definition of strategy is that it constitutes 'the use of armed force to achieve the military objectives and, by extension, the political purpose of the war'.[5] Conventionally it is subdivided into 'grand' and 'military' strategy. Grand strategy is concerned with the pursuit of national interests and overlaps with policy, involving not only a military dimension, but also much wider logistic, social and technological aspects. Military strategy includes the raising,

2 See, e.g., Spencer Wilkinson, *The Brain of an Army: A Popular Account of the German general staff* (London: Constable, 1895).

3 See John Keegan, *The Mask of Command* (New York: Viking, 1987); and Berndt Brehmer, 'Command and control as design', www.dodccrp.org/events/15th_iccrts_2010/papers/182.pdf, accessed 5 August 2012.

4 Richard Holmes, *The Little Field Marshal* (London: Jonathan Cape, 1981), pp. 303, 305; and Michael Howard, 'Leadership in the British Army in the Second World War: some personal observations', in Sheffield (ed.), *Leadership and Command*, pp. 119–20.

5 Peter Paret, 'Introduction', in Paret (ed.), *Makers of Modern Strategy from Machiavelli to the Nuclear* Age (Princeton University Press, 1986), p. 3.

developing, sustaining and use of military forces, to attain grand strategic – that is political – objectives.[6] This concept of a national grand strategy involving a military component, and the need for an awareness of military strategic issues being part of the business of government, was largely undeveloped before the First World War. Although naval and maritime strategic thinking included considerations of industry, commerce and trade as a matter of course, this was seen as a largely separate sphere of activity.[7] In the mid eighteenth century, a simple binary model of strategy and tactics was applicable: on campaign, strategy consisted of manoeuvring 'unitary' armies or fleets until they faced one another, and at this point tactics – the deployment for and fighting of battle – took over. Since then, military doctrines have come to recognise three 'levels' of war, with the operational level inserted between strategy and tactics. The First World War represents a point in this transition, and at the time the term 'strategy' had a meaning closer to military campaigning than to its much wider modern meaning.[8] These distinctions are far from trivial: demands by generals at the height of the war that they should be given the manpower and materiel to fight their battles without political interference derived ultimately from the view that authority over military operations, as distinct from grand strategy, lay with them.

In 1914, the German army had the clearest idea of the operational level of war, and its distinction between what would now be seen as military strategy and operations was unusually porous; strategic commanders frequently strayed into the operational level, and *vice versa*.[9] Both Moltke as Chief of

6 These definitions are informed by reading of various modern British, US and Australian doctrine publications, and Michael Howard, 'The forgotten dimensions of strategy', *Foreign Affairs*, 57:5 (1979), pp. 975–8.

7 For examples of this lack of understanding see Richard F. Hamilton, 'War planning: obvious needs, not so obvious solutions', in Richard F. Hamilton and Holger H. Herwig (eds.), *War Planning 1914* (Cambridge University Press, 2010), pp. 15–18. For naval and maritime strategic thinking see Jon Tetsuro Sumida, *Inventing Grand Strategy and Teaching Command: The Classic Works of Alfred Thayer Mahan Reconsidered* (Baltimore, MD: Johns Hopkins University Press, 1997). See also Nicholas Lambert, *Planning Armageddon: British Economic Warfare and the First World War* (Cambridge, MA: Harvard University Press, 2012).

8 Antulio J. Echevarria II, 'Clausewitz: toward a theory of applied strategy', *Defense Analysis*, 11:3 (1995), pp. 229–40, reproduced at www.clausewitz.com/readings/Echevarria/APSTRAT1.htm. The persuasive central argument of Claus Telp, *The Evolution of Operational Art 1740–1813* (London: Frank Cass & Co., 2005), pp. 1–2 places the emergence of operational art in the later eighteenth century; for older arguments placing the key developments in the 1860s–1870s see, for example, Michael D. Krause, 'Moltke and the origins of operational art', *Military Review*, 70:9 (1990), pp. 28–44; and Bruce W. Menning 'Operational art's origins', *Military Review*, 77:5 (1997), pp. 32–47.

9 David T. Zabecki, *The German 1918 Offensives: A Case Study in the Operational Level of War* (Abingdon: Routledge, 2006), p. 29.

the general staff, and Conrad von Hötzendorf in the same position in the Austro-Hungarian army, had grand strategic roles which crossed over into foreign policy (both had pressed for a pre-emptive war before 1914), but on the war's outbreak they assumed the role of essentially operational level commanders.[10] A phrase often used of German generals is that they took decisions for 'purely military reasons', meaning to gain an operational or tactical advantage in disregard or disdain of political, grand strategic or logistical considerations. The Russian army, which traditionally shared ideas with the Germans, also had the concept of an operational level, but this made minimal impact on its performance in the early campaigns of the war.[11] Only in the 1916 Brusilov offensive could Russian commanders be said to have demonstrated a grasp of operational art as well as military strategy.[12] The French, and occasionally the British, used 'grand tactics' to mean a transitional level between strategy and tactics, broadly equating to the operational level; but the French did not 'specify a function for the operational level and failed to distinguish clearly between operations and tactics'.[13] Joffre, Nivelle and Pétain, as successive Commanders-in-Chief of the French army at GQG (located just north of Paris at Chantilly after 1914), carried out functions from the high political level to the operational. The British did most to maintain the separation between strategy and operations: first Kitchener (who also held military rank as a field marshal but no active military command) as Secretary of State for War, and then from late 1915 Robertson and Wilson as successive Chiefs of the Imperial general staff (CIGS), acted primarily at the grand strategic level, but they also had influence over, and sometimes active involvement in, military strategy.[14] Sir John French, as Commander-in-Chief of the

10 Lawrence Sondhaus, *Franz Conrad von Hötzendorf: Architect of the Apocalypse* (Boston, MA: Humanities Press, 2000), pp. 82, 86, 88; Annika Mombauer, *Helmuth von Moltke and the Origins of the First World War* (Cambridge University Press, 2000), pp. 106–12; and Holger H. Herwig, *The First World War: Germany and Austria-Hungary 1914–18* (London: Edward Arnold, 1997), pp. 9–11, 20.

11 Jacob W. Kipp, 'The origins of Soviet operational art 1917–1936', in Michael D. Krause and R. Cody Phillips (eds.), *Historical Perspectives of the Operational Art* (Washington, DC: Center of Military History, 2005), pp. 215–16.

12 See Timothy C. Dowling, *The Brusilov Offensive* (Bloomington, IN: Indiana University Press, 2008), pp. 175–6.

13 Robert A. Doughty, 'French operational art: 1888–1940', in Krause and Phillips (eds.), *Historical Perspectives of the Operational Art*, p. 101; and Brian Holden Reid, *Studies in British Military Thought* (Lincoln, NE: University of Nebraska Press, 1998), p. 70.

14 George H. Cassar, *Kitchener's War: British Strategy from 1914 to 1916* (Dulles, VA: Brassey's, 2004), *passim*; David R. Woodward, *Field Marshal Sir William Robertson: Chief of the Imperial general staff in the Great War* (Westport, CT: Praeger, 1998); and Keith Jeffery, *Field Marshal Sir Henry Wilson: A Political Soldier* (Oxford University Press, 2006), pp. 219–28.

British Expeditionary Force (BEF) on the Western Front, functioned as an operational level commander with political responsibilities towards his own government and his French and Belgian allies. His successor, Sir Douglas Haig focused primarily on military strategy and sometimes on operations, but he also had influence at the grand strategic level, working closely with Robertson and Wilson, and being frequently consulted by the British War Cabinet.[15] Individuals such as Joffre and Haig held multiple political, strategic and operational responsibilities that in later wars would be routinely divided between two or three separate high-ranking posts.

On the Western Front on the outbreak of war in 1914, the Germans mobilised seven armies and the French mobilised five armies, each larger than, but broadly comparable to, an early nineteenth-century 'unitary' army; meaning that, in terms of scale alone, Moltke and Joffre faced unprecedented problems in strategic command. Each army typically contained between two and four corps, and modern theory regards the normal level of operational command as corps or army level. Partly to deal better with their Allies, the French rapidly improvised an intermediary level of command, placing Foch as Joffre's 'adjoint' in charge of an 'army group' including the BEF and the Belgians. The lack of this intermediate army group level of command was also identified by the Germans as one of the factors in the failure of their command structure leading to their defeat in the Battle of the Marne. Thereafter army groups became standard in the French and German armies, representing the upper level of operational command, shading into strategic command. The BEF under Haig had four or five armies, and could be regarded as an army group in itself.[16]

The nineteenth-century background

The major belligerent powers of the First World War were mass industrialised empires with powers, resources and a degree of organisation scarcely conceivable even a century beforehand. A critical part of this development was the impact of technology and industrialisation on all aspects of society, with an increased separation of human functions, both in the sense that industrial workers were no longer expected to produce their own food and clothing within the home, and in the rise of separate professions, managerial

15 For examples of Haig's involvement at the grand strategic level see Gary Sheffield, *The Chief: Douglas Haig and the British Army* (London: Aurum Press, 2011), pp. 265, 331.

16 See Andy Simpson, *Directing Operations: British Corps Command on the Western Front 1914–18* (Stroud: Spellmount, 2006).

classes and a structured bureaucracy. One consequence was a major increase in the size and destructive firepower of armies, as the military manifestation of the mass industrialised state. The first attempts to create military command and control structures for armies began in the later eighteenth century, and the armies of Napoleon I, which had staffs at army, corps and divisional level, had a distinct advantage over their enemies as long as they remained relatively small.[17] But as armies grew in size, from about 1809 onwards the possibility of achieving an Austerlitz, the annihilation of an enemy army in a single battle, became increasingly remote. In March 1905 the Japanese were victorious in the Battle of Mukden, the largest battle of the Russo-Japanese War, but their attempt to win a decisive battle of annihilation through a double envelopment of the ninety-mile-long Russian positions failed, not least because it proved too difficult to coordinate five widely dispersed armies consisting of more than 200,000 men.[18]

The introduction from the 1820s onwards of steam power in the form of rail transport and steamships revolutionised the mobilisation and transport of soldiers and materiel, but only at the expense of increasing difficulties in supply and movement that could only be addressed by bureaucratic systems.[19] The development of telegraph networks in the 1830s, followed by the telephone over shorter distances in the 1870s and radio telegraphy in the 1900s, also made it possible for political leaders in their capitals to communicate directly and rapidly with operational level commanders in the field, with major consequences for strategic command. Generals resented what they saw as interference by politicians, in the way that Lincoln and Stanton used the telegraph to issue orders directly from Washington in the American Civil War, although higher military headquarters also used the telegraph to communicate with separated armies, as Moltke the Elder did to some effect in the Austro-Prussian and Franco-Prussian Wars.[20] In the First World War, French and Haig were the first British army commanders in history to conduct their battles while still being within a day's travel of London and in constant

17 Robert M. Epstein, *Napoleon's Last Victory and the Emergence of Modern War* (Lawrence, KS: University Press of Kansas, 1994), p. 24.

18 Robert M. Citino, *Quest for Decisive Victory: From Stalemate to Blitzkrieg in Europe, 1899–1940* (Lawrence, KS: University Press of Kansas, 2002), pp. 71, 96–8; and Richard Connaughton, *Rising Sun and Tumbling Bear: Russia's War with Japan* (London: Cassell, 2003), p. 289.

19 Martin van Creveld, *Technology and War: From 2000 B.C. to the Present* (New York: Free Press, 1991), pp. 153–234.

20 Krause, 'Moltke and the origins of operational art', p. 113; and Martin van Creveld, *Command in War* (Cambridge, MA: Harvard University Press, 1985), pp. 107–9.

telegraph contact with their government. Radio telegraphy also brought about a fundamental change to naval strategic command; as Admiral Sir John Fisher declared in 1912, 'Wireless is the pith and marrow of war!'[21] Fleet commanders such as Jellicoe and Scheer at the Battle of Jutland in June 1916 were directed and provided with intelligence by radio signals from their respective Admiralty headquarters on the mainland that were critical in determining the battle's outcome.[22]

The belief that it was part of the function of a political head of state to lead its armies into battle declined after Napoleon I, in favour of the rival idea that political leaders and governments should make war and peace, and organise their country's wider war effort, but that they need have no great understanding of, or command over, the technicalities of military strategy and operations. As the nineteenth century progressed, Clausewitz's 'paradoxical trinity', separating the functions of a country at war into the spheres of the political leadership, the army and the people, became the philosophical expression of the claims made by an emerging institutionalised military leadership to its own sphere of professional rights and responsibilities. The last rulers of major powers to exercise even notional command of their troops on a battlefield were King Wilhelm I of Prussia and Emperor Napoleon III of the French in 1870 in the Franco-Prussian War, and the boundaries of where civil and military authority lay became an even greater issue later in the century. Military professionalism was largely interpreted as concerned with the mechanics of deploying and moving armies and navies, and as separate from wider issues of politics and government.[23] But as the impact of new technologies and of industrialisation on warfare increased, so the organisation, equipment and training of armies and navies in peacetime became only the most important of the many areas in which military professionalism interacted with civilian government and with the wider requirements of both state and society. Difficult civil–military relationships in the American Civil War and German Wars of Unification were early illustration of these emerging tensions; while Gambetta's organisation of the Third Republic for war *à*

21 Quoted in Brian N. Hall, 'The British Army and wireless communication 1896–1918', *War in History*, 19:3 (2012), p. 290.

22 See Hew Strachan, *The First World War: A New Illustrated History* (New York: Viking, 2003), pp. 199–200; and Paul G. Halpern, *A Naval History of World War I* (Annapolis, MD: Naval Institute Press, 1994).

23 Van Creveld, *Technology and War*, pp. 3, 161. See also Dennis E. Showalter, 'Mass warfare and the impact of technology', in Roger Chickering and Stig Förster (eds.), *Great War, Total War: Combat and Mobilization on the Western Front 1914–18* (Cambridge University Press, 2000), pp. 73–4.

l'outrance in the later stages of the Franco-Prussian War also gave early indications of the extent to which both state involvement in society and political involvement in military strategic command might be necessary in future wars.[24]

The strategic command relationships between civilian and military authorities in each of the major belligerents in the First World War were shaped first of all by the place of the armed forces within each country's nineteenth-century political traditions. In Germany, the ministers for war and for the navy were serving generals and admirals, while in France and Britain the equivalent posts were held by civilians, closely advised by the professional heads of the services. During the later nineteenth century, the armies of all major powers adopted some version of a centralised military staff organisation, based on the German general staff, to plan future strategy and wars. This was followed by equivalent naval staffs, although the German Imperial Navy did not form its SKL (*Seekriegsleitung*), the equivalent of Army Supreme Command (*Oberste-Heeresleitung*, or OHL), until August 1918.[25] But no major power developed the institutional mechanisms to resolve these civil–military issues; if anything, the separation between grand strategy as an aspect of government and diplomacy, and military strategy as a general staff prerogative, grew greater. Even mechanisms for coordination between each country's army and navy remained rudimentary. In France, Germany, Russia and Austria-Hungary, all of which had peacetime conscription for raising mass armies on mobilisation, the relationship between political and military needs, such as what percentage of the workforce and of industrial production should be allocated to the army and navy, were managed as issues of mainstream domestic politics.

In all major belligerents, the absence of grand strategic coordination between diplomacy and the war plans of armies and navies played a critical part in the crisis of 1914 leading to the outbreak of the war. In France, the appointment of Joffre as Commander-in-Chief in 1911 was accompanied by reforms giving him authority over the High Command and the general staff (*Grand Quartier Général*, or GQG) and the Supreme War Council (*Conseil Supérieur de la Guerre*); but although Joffre was required to present his plans to the Supreme Council of National Defence (*Conseil Supérieur de la Défence*

24 See James M. McPherson, *Tried By War: Abraham Lincoln as Commander in Chief* (New York: Penguin, 2008); and Michael Howard, *The Franco-Prussian War* (London: Rupert Hart Davis, 1961).

25 David Stevenson, *1914–1918: The History of the First World War* (London: Penguin, 2004), p. 491.

Nationale), which included prominent ministers, in practice his was the decisive voice in French military strategy before the war.[26] Britain, as a maritime imperial power without conscription, was unusual in the later nineteenth century in creating an embryo political–military institution for advising on grand strategy, which by 1904 had evolved into the Committee of Imperial Defence. In 1909 the professional head of the army was given the title Chief of the Imperial general staff (CIGS), although there was no actual *imperial* staff in the sense that positions for officers of the Dominions or the Indian Army were not included in its structure. Although some preliminary war planning took place in Britain, a nineteenth-century practice that continued until the First World War was that on deployment the Secretary of State for War gave broad 'instructions' to a Commander-in-Chief in the Field who was then responsible for his own plan of campaign, bypassing the CIGS.[27] This only changed when Robertson became CIGS in December 1915, insisting that he should be sole military adviser to the British government, and that orders to field commanders should come through and from him.[28] Even so, Robertson regarded Haig, who succeeded French as Commander-in-Chief of the BEF in the same month, as the senior member of their partnership, and rather than the general staff in London being clearly responsible for military strategic issues, its authority over both strategy and operations overlapped with that of BEF GHQ in France.[29]

France and Britain, as imperial powers, also established in the nineteenth century a tradition of senior officers acting as proconsuls, taking political and grand strategic decisions on their own authority or with minimal reference to any political leadership, as Kitchener did at Fashoda in 1898.[30] Something of this tradition was also visible in Pershing's actions during the Mexican Expedition of 1916–17. Away from the industrialised war of the Western

26 Holger H. Herwig, *The Marne 1914: The Opening of World War I and the Battle that Changed the World* (New York: Random House, 2009), pp. 55; and David Stevenson, 'French strategy on the Western Front, 1914–1918', in Chickering and Förster (eds.), *Great War, Total War*, pp. 299–300.

27 Shelford Bidwell and Dominick Graham, *Fire-Power: British Army Weapons and Theories of War 1904–1945* (London: Allen & Unwin, 1982), pp. 43–8; and Hew Strachan, *The Politics of the British Army* (Oxford: Clarendon Press, 1997), pp. 118–43.

28 John Gooch, *The Plans of War: The general staff and British Military Strategy c.1900–1916* (London: Routledge, 1974), pp. 323–30.

29 Dan Todman, 'The Grand Lamasery revisited: General Headquarters on the Western Front 1914–1918', in Gary Sheffield and Dan Todman (eds.), *Command and Control on the Western Front: The British Army's Experience 1914–18* (Staplehurst: Spellmount, 2004), pp. 39–70.

30 George H. Cassar, *Kitchener: Architect of Victory* (London: William Kimber, 1977), pp. 98–100.

Front, French and British campaigns in the Balkans and against the Ottoman Empire in the First World War had many characteristics of this colonial war tradition, and in all major belligerents, senior officers often distinguished between their own patriotism and the extent to which they recognised the authority of a particular government or minister. The appointment of Sarrail to command the Allied forces at Salonica in October 1915 had as much to do with his diplomatic as his military skills, while once in place his persistent disregard of his orders from Joffre and demands for more troops helped bring about a major change in the French strategic command structure, with Joffre being appointed 'Commander-in-Chief of the French Armies' on all fronts in December 1915.[31] Allenby's appointment to command the Egyptian Expeditionary Force in June 1917 was made in the absence of any agreed British military strategy towards the Ottoman Empire, and he exercised both military command over his multi-national force (which included British, Indian, Australian, New Zealand and French troops) and had dealings with his Arab nationalist and French allies through to the end of the war, very much in the British proconsular tradition.[32] In the German army, a rather different tradition existed of senior officers on campaign defying the orders of the general staff, despite the efforts of Moltke the Elder to eradicate it.[33] This form of high-level insubordination still continued in the First World War, notably in the behaviour of Hindenburg as commander of Higher Headquarters East (Ober Ost) on the Eastern Front in 1914–16.[34] An extreme case of a German officer defying orders, both in terms of geographical distance and the strategic consequences of the actions of a junior commander, was Lieutenant Colonel (later General) Paul von Lettow-Vorbeck, who, despite the civil government's plans to maintain neutrality for German East Africa, pursued a substantial military campaign chiefly against British imperial forces that lasted the duration of the war.[35]

31 Sarrail's appointment was also related to his domestic political views and rivalries with Joffre; see Robert A. Doughty, *Pyrrhic Victory: French Strategy and Operations in the Great War* (Cambridge, MA: Harvard University Press, 2005), pp. 220–33.

32 Matthew Hughes, *Allenby and British Strategy in the Middle East 1917–1919* (London: Frank Cass & Co., 1999), especially pp. 23–42, 158–63.

33 Citino, *The German Way of War*, pp. 174–82.

34 William J. Astore and Dennis E. Showalter, *Hindenburg: Icon of German Militarism* (Washington, DC: Potomac, 2005), pp. 23–36; and Robert B. Asprey, *The German High Command at War: Hindenburg and Ludendorff Conduct World War I* (New York: W. Morrow, 1991), pp. 151–60. See also Citino, *The German Way of War*, pp. 174–82.

35 Strachan, *The First World War*, pp. 80–4 argues that the conflict between Lettow-Vorbeck and the colonial governor Heinrich Schnee has been exaggerated, but that

Military strategic command

At the start of the war no belligerent had a clear national grand strategy, or war aims beyond a desire for the total defeat of its enemies. The main concerns of each country's civilian government were to maintain support for its actions as a continuation of peacetime domestic politics and diplomacy, together with the economics of how to fund the war and manage the massive disruption caused by mobilisation; or in the case of the British and their Empire, the creation of a new mass army initially through voluntary recruitment. Military strategy in 1914 was subsumed into operations, in the sense that the opening moves were largely pre-determined by implementing plans for mobilisation and deployment drawn up before the war. While the Austro-Hungarian and Russian war plans included options at the operational level depending on which opponents they would be fighting, all of the belligerents' plans were based on a strategic offensive.[36] The most successful of these war plans were also the most developed but also the most informal, those of the British Royal Navy and French navy, in rapidly limiting any naval threat from the Central Powers almost entirely to the North Sea and the Mediterranean, allowing the Allies almost complete freedom of the seas. Both the blockade of Germany and the free flow of materiel and men into Britain and France which followed, were constant and critical factors in the war. The Germans, in particular, hoped for a short and decisive war, but although the predominating elite and professional views in most countries were that the war would be long and hard, no institutional mechanisms were in place for the management of economic, societal and technological mobilisation, all of which became increasingly necessary after 1914.[37]

Consequently, the progress of the war saw the emergence of several 'civilian warlords', who were not primarily military men but had a major input into strategy, most obviously Winston Churchill as First Lord of the Admiralty in 1914–15, David Lloyd George as British Prime Minister from late 1916 and Georges Clemenceau, who became his French counterpart a year later. Clemenceau specialised in visiting the front to see conditions at first hand, to inspire troops and to engage with generals, not least to manage the

Lettow-Vorbeck's 'purely military' considerations won Schnee over; see also Lawrence Sondhaus, *World War One: The Global Revolution* (Cambridge University Press, 2011), pp. 114–20.

36 See Norman Stone, *The Eastern Front 1914–1917* (London: Hodder & Stoughton, 1975), pp. 37–91.

37 For the importance of these factors see Howard, 'Forgotten dimensions', pp. 975–8.

difficult triangular relationship between himself, Foch and Pétain.[38] By contrast, US President Woodrow Wilson did not wield the authority of Commander-in-Chief with any relish or success, either in preparing for war or in contributing to strategic command.[39] Equally unsuccessful in combining supreme political and military authority was Tsar Nicholas II, who took personal command of the Russian army in August 1915, based at general staff (Stavka) Headquarters at the town of Mogiliev, rather than in the field.[40] Only monarchs of the smaller belligerents, such as Albert I of Belgium or Peter I of Serbia, exercised direct battlefield command through their staffs.

Kaiser Wilhelm II as Commander-in-Chief of the German army also deployed some distance from the fighting front in 1914, with his Imperial Headquarters (*Grosses Hauptquartier*) described as a combination of a supreme military council and an imperial court. But although Army Supreme Command (OHL) was part of Imperial Headquarters, in reality it was Moltke as Chief of the general staff at OHL who exercised power over military strategy. Prior to the war, in strict constitutional terms there was no German army or German general staff, since the armies of the individual German states, including Prussia, retained their distinctive identities; but in practice the Prussian general staff in Berlin both functioned and was described as the German general staff, and after the first months of the war any distinction between individual states' armies was largely lost.[41] Although Wilhelm's role in operational planning was almost entirely a constitutional fiction, his contribution to strategy was still significant. He had an umpiring role when German military, naval and political authorities disagreed, and he was influential both in appointing individuals to senior posts and removing them. Both Moltke and Falkenhayn were Wilhelm's appointees, and he sustained Falkenhayn in his position in the face of much criticism, until the collapse of German strategy in August 1916 forced him reluctantly to withdraw his support. Wilhelm's personal and institutional military authority declined after Hindenburg became Chief of the general staff in succession to Falkenhayn, dealing directly on military strategic matters with his opposite

38 Eliot A. Cohen, *Supreme Command* (New York: Free Press, 2002), pp. 66–79.

39 Robert H. Ferrell, 'Woodrow Wilson: a misfit in office?', in Joseph G. Dawson III, *Commanders in Chief: Presidential Leadership in Modern Wars* (Lawrence, KS: University Press of Kansas, 1993), pp. 65–86. For an alternative view that is much more favourable to Wilson, see Arthur S. Link and John Whiteclay Chambers, II, 'Woodrow Wilson as Commander-in-Chief', in Richard H. Kohn (ed.), *The United States Military Under the Constitution of the United States, 1789–1989* (New York University Press, 1991), pp. 319–24.

40 For Nicholas II's Stavka see Stone, *The Eastern Front 1914–1917*, pp. 187–93.

41 Herwig, *The Marne 1914*, pp. xiv, 120, 313.

numbers in the other Central Powers, Austria-Hungary, Bulgaria and Ottoman Turkey, and taking grand strategic decisions on military strategic or operational grounds. But even so, Wilhelm retained a power of veto by which he could halt, or at least retard, a course of action of which he disapproved.[42]

After the failure of all the initial war plans to win decisively in 1914, no country on either side had complete control of either its own grand strategy or military strategy. But Germany's domination of the Central Powers meant that both Austria-Hungary and the Ottoman Empire, which entered the war in November 1914, rapidly adopted a strategy based on the expectation of sharing in an eventual German victory. In theory Germany and Austria-Hungary, the core Central Powers, should have been well prepared for fighting in alliance, having been allies since 1879, but mutual political suspicions and German concerns about the military effectiveness and reliability of Austria-Hungary had prevented them from formulating an integrated combined war plan. Although in the years immediately prior to the outbreak of war matters had improved superficially, with Moltke and Conrad holding annual meetings, neither pushed for unity of command in the event of war, and they failed to maximise the military strategic advantages available to longstanding alliance partners.[43] Conrad also failed to adjust his strategy in the light of Moltke's plain warnings that the main German effort would be made against France, and thus only limited support could be offered to Austrian offensives in the East. In 1914 the two allies fought 'parallel war(s)' against Russia 'without a common plan or in concert'; but with mutual suspicion and recriminations, and belated recognition of the consequences of the failure to coordinate their war plans.[44] During 1915 a creeping form of *de facto* unity of command emerged by default on the Eastern Front, the product of a series of Austro-Hungarian military disasters which reduced the Habsburg

42 Holger Afflerbach, 'Wilhelm II as Supreme Warlord in the First World War', in Annika Mombauer and Wilhelm Diest (eds.), *The Kaiser: New Research on Wilhelm II's Role in Imperial Germany* (Cambridge University Press, 2004), pp. 201–3, 206–16; and Robert T. Foley, *German Strategy and the Path to Verdun* (Cambridge University Press, 2005), pp. 122–3, 257–8.

43 Holger H. Herwig, 'Asymmetrical alliance: Austria-Hungary and Germany, 1891–1918', in Peter Dennis and Jeffrey Grey (eds.), *Entangling Alliances: Coalition Warfare in the Twentieth Century* (Canberra: Australian Military History Publications, 2005), pp. 57–61; Günther Kronenbitter, 'The limits of cooperation: Germany and Austria-Hungary in the First World War', in Dennis and Grey (eds.), *Entangling Alliances*, pp. 79–80; Dennis E. Showalter, *Tannenberg: Clash of Empires, 1914* (Washington, DC: Brassey's, 2004 [1991]), pp. 67–8.

44 Richard DiNardo, *Breakthrough: The Gorlice-Tarnow Campaign, 1915* (Santa Barbara, CA: Praeger, 2010), p. 8.

army to a very weak state and led to the Germans colonising their allies' formations with commanders, staff officers, regimental officers and even NCOs. The Germans also asserted dominance at high command level: although initial proposals for unity of command foundered in November 1914, German generals commanded in practice for the Gorlice-Tarnów offensive in May 1915; Mackensen's German Eleventh Army, which included Austrian formations, was technically subordinated to both OHL and its Austrian-Hungarian equivalent, but Conrad was unable to give orders to Mackensen unless they were approved by Falkenhayn. The catastrophic defeat of Austro-Hungarian forces in the Brusilov offensive next year consolidated German dominance, and in September 1916 a United Supreme Command (*Oberste-Kriegsleitung*) under Hindenburg and Ludendorff was created for the Eastern Front. Although one Army Group remained nominally under Austro-Hungarian command, its real command was exercised by a relatively junior German officer, Colonel Hans von Seeckt.[45]

German officers also played a major role in command and staff positions in the Ottoman army. However, the traditional Western view, that Turkish military success at Gallipoli in 1915–16 owed much to German command, is overly simplistic. Important preparatory work and training had already been carried out by Ottoman officers before the arrival of the German commander General Liman von Sanders to take over the Ottoman Fifth Army on 26 March 1915. Considerable credit for the initial Ottoman containment of the Allied landings on 25 April belongs to Brigadier-General Esat Pasha, the commander of III Corps, and his capable Turkish subordinates. This is not to deny that Liman and other German officers (who included technical advisers sent to pass on to the Turks lessons and techniques from the Western Front) were important. Rather, Ottoman success was founded on a partnership between Turks and Germans. The fact that Ottoman orders processes, logistics and doctrine were closely based on German originals greatly aided the integration of the two sides.[46] Indeed, in the last stage of the campaign, 'Ottoman and German commanders seemed to be essentially interchangeable parts in an effective machine.'[47]

After Gallipoli, German commanders and staff officers continued to take critical roles in Ottoman forces. In late 1915, the Ottoman general staff,

45 Herwig, 'Asymmetrical alliance', pp. 65–9; and DiNardo, *Breakthrough*, pp. 37, 41–3.

46 These two paragraphs are based heavily on the pioneering work of Edward J. Erickson. See his *Gallipoli: The Ottoman Campaign* (Barnsley: Pen & Sword, 2010), pp. 35–40, 42, 178–9, 185–7.

47 *Ibid.*, p. 182.

responding to setbacks in the Mesopotamian theatre, asked Field Marshal Colmar von der Goltz to take command there. Von der Goltz had served with the Ottomans in the 1890s, and his behaviour on arriving in theatre is suggestive of a continuing Ottoman/German partnership. He left his Ottoman subordinate Nurettin to continue to besiege the British/Indian force in Kut-al-Amara instead of taking command himself, giving Nurettin considerable latitude in his operations.[48] A command partnership also developed in Palestine, where by 1917 the strongest and most effective Ottoman formation was Army Group F or 'Yildirim', a German-Austrian-Turkish formation commanded by Falkenhayn.[49]

On the Western Front, the first clashes of 1914 confirmed pre-war expectations that the vast armies of millions, deployed along the length of the common frontier, could only be commanded with the most extreme difficulty. Although the telegraph and telephone, and even wireless telegraphy, worked well for communication between fixed points, they were of limited effectiveness in commanding marching troops, and military strategic commanders relied mostly on gallopers, carrier pigeons, or existing staff training and procedures. The German war plan in the West (best described as the 'Schlieffen–Moltke Plan'), was hugely ambitious, deploying seventy-three divisions.[50] Moltke bore a share of the responsibility for its failure; he was too remote from his subordinates, both physically at OHL in Koblenz (later moving forward to Luxembourg), but also in deciding against even attempting to maintain close supervision of his army commanders, one of whom, Kluck of the First Army, flagrantly disobeyed OHL's orders. The contrast with Joffre at GQG was stark. The French Commander-in-Chief kept up a stream of messages and orders, demanding information, keeping abreast of the situation by telephone and using his motorcar to carry out personal visits. He actively intervened to sack subordinates in large numbers, and perhaps most importantly, never lost sight of the bigger picture. It is indicative of French and German methods that in September 1914, while Joffre personally made the strategically critical decision to counter-attack on the

48 *Ibid.*, p. 177; and Edward J. Erickson, *Ottoman Army Effectiveness in World War I: A Comparative Study* (London: Routledge, 2007), p. 86.

49 For the formation and composition of Yildirim (or Jilderim) see General [Otto] Liman von Sanders, *Five Years in Turkey* (Nashville, TN: Battery Press, 1990 [1928]), pp. 173–84; and Erickson, *Ottoman Army Effectiveness*, pp. 115–16. Erickson argues that Ottoman–German tensions in Palestine had become evident by late 1918 for a variety of reasons, including resentment at apparent German downgrading of the importance of the Palestine theatre (p. 144).

50 Mombauer, *Moltke*, pp. 51, 65.

Marne, the equally critical German decision to withdraw was taken by Bülow as commander of the Second Army, on the recommendation of Lieutenant Colonel Richard Hentsch, a general staff officer acting as Moltke's representative; neither Bülow nor Kluck attempted to contact Moltke directly on the decision.[51] The contrasting roles of Joffre and Moltke offer evidence that Clausewitz's concept of a contest of wills between individual commanders remained valid under the circumstances of the First World War.

Once trench warfare began on the Western Front, the problems of strategic command changed considerably. With subordinate headquarters and formations static rather than mobile, communications were more straightforward, with headquarters being connected by elaborate telephone networks. But this produced further problems: by 1916, a subordinate army of the BEF required an average daily load of 10,000 telegrams, 20,000 telephone calls and 5,000 messages to function at all. Moreover this wire-based system ended in the front-line trench, and lacking effective portable radios, command on the battlefield was difficult in the extreme.[52] The issues involved in military strategy also multiplied under the strain of the war. When planning the Somme offensive in 1916, Joffre and Haig each had to take account of not only agreement with their own government and detailed military coordinated planning, but also what reserves of trained soldiers would be available against the demands of other fronts and the civilian workforce, whether Britain or France could produce and import the required military materiel, and what technological innovations might be available. There was also a host of other factors including logistics, the state of training of the troops, and their morale and discipline, the latter factors being closely linked to the provision of food, recreation facilities, the postal service and leave. The nature of war thus demanded that as an integral part of strategic command, senior generals became 'war managers', a previously almost unknown function in military thought.[53] Perhaps Pétain's greatest achievement as Commander-in-Chief in 1917–18 was to nurse the French army back to health after the mutinies following the Nivelle offensive.[54] By contrast, Conrad was a failure as a war manager; in launching a series of offensives in the Carpathians in early 1915, he

51 Herwig, *The Marne 1914*, pp. 267–86, 294, 311–14; and Annika Mombauer, 'German war plans', in Hamilton and Herwig, *War Planning*, pp. 72–5.

52 Van Creveld, *Command in War*, p. 158.

53 A sense of the breadth of Haig's work can be gained from his wartime diaries and correspondence. For a selection, see Gary Sheffield and John Bourne (eds.), *Douglas Haig: War Diaries and Letters* (London: Weidenfeld & Nicolson, 2005).

54 Doughty, *Pyrrhic Victory*, pp. 363–8.

failed (or refused) to see that the tasks he had set his armies were beyond their capabilities. Factors such as the weakness of units, the fragile morale of troops who lacked equipment and even uniforms, logistic challenges, problems of campaigning in mountainous areas in winter and lack of artillery were ignored during planning, and the resulting defeats proved highly damaging to the Austro-Hungarian army.[55]

Pershing, as Commander-in-Chief of the American Expeditionary Forces (AEF), offers another example of a failure of war management. He was convinced that his French and British allies' approach to war fighting, which from painful experience was, by the second half of 1918, underpinned by the heavy use of artillery firepower, was flawed, and that attacks by infantry should continue to dominate the battle. This was a reversion to the tactics that had proved disastrous in the early years of the war, and Pershing's insistence caused unnecessarily high casualties among US troops in the last weeks of the war. His imposition of this doctrine, in the face of plentiful evidence that it was unsuitable, is a sobering reminder of the importance and breadth of a strategic commander's purview.[56]

Increasing reliance on artillery, and so on industrial production and logistics, was central to the strategies of attrition – the wearing down of enemy strength and morale – that prevailed on the Western Front after 1914. For some commanders such as Joffre and Haig, attrition was the means to an end, the restoration of mobile warfare in which traditional methods could be applied to achieve victory. But the greatly increased lethality of firepower and size of armies, when compared to all previous experience, led some generals by about 1916 to a belief that traditional views on the importance of strategy and even operations had become irrelevant; that what mattered was inflicting massive casualties on the enemy forces, in the expectation of weakening them so that they could no longer adequately defend their positions, bringing about a collapse in morale, and a dislocation of the 'nervous system' of control. Although this view was held by some commanders and staff officers in all armies, it became most widely accepted within the German army. As early as 1914 Falkenhayn had discarded the idea of decisive battle, and at Verdun in 1916 his strategy was based on the principle that attrition was an end in itself, and that the French army was to be bled to death, principally by

55 Graydon A. Tunstall, *Blood on the Snow: The Carpathian Winter War of* 1915 (Lawrence, KS: University Press of Kansas, 2010), pp. 51, 68–9, 212.
56 Mark E. Grotelueschen, *The AEF Way of War: The American Army and Combat in World War I* (New York: Cambridge University Press, 2007), pp. 31–9, 48–50.

artillery fire.[57] Falkenhayn's vision of controlled attrition delivering military strategic victory proved impossible to achieve, and the Battle of Verdun cost both sides dearly. His replacement by the duumvirate of Hindenburg and Ludendorff in August 1916 marked the rejection of this approach. But as *de facto* military strategic commander on the Western Front thereafter, Ludendorff demonstrated that he too rejected the Napoleonic paradigm, and privileged attrition. He gave orders prior to the March 1918 *Kaiserschlacht* offensive that 'we talk too much about operations and too little about tactics . . . all measures have to concentrate on how to defeat the enemy, how to penetrate his front positions. Follow-on measures are in many cases a matter of *ad hoc* decisions', adding in his memoirs that 'tactics had to be considered over pure strategy'.[58] Ludendorff's failure in 1918 to think in strategic terms and his neglect of the issue of logistics, in particular the critical importance of Amiens as a rail communications and supply hub for the Allies, was an important contribution to his failure to convert tactical success into strategic victory.

Grand strategy and coalition command

The year 1914 came to an end with the absence of strategic victory on either side, or any immediate prospect of one. At the level of grand strategy, the famous remark attributed to Clemenceau in 1919 that 'war is too serious a business to be left to generals'[59] went to the heart of the new civil–military relationships that then evolved, as domestic political, industrial and manpower considerations interacted with the unprecedented demands of military strategy and operations. In France and Britain the civilian political leadership kept control throughout the war, but increasingly military strategy became an issue for protracted negotiation between politicians and generals. The most testing episode came for the British in January 1917 at the Calais planning conference, at which the Prime Minister, Lloyd George, despairing of British strategy, attempted to place the BEF under the command of Nivelle as the new French Commander-in-Chief, relegating Haig to an administrative role

57 Robert T. Foley, '"What's in a name?"': the development of strategies of attrition on the Western Front, 1914–1918', *The Historian*, 68:4 (2006), pp. 730–8, 772; and Foley, *German Strategy*, pp. 180–258.

58 Both passages quoted in Zabecki, *The German 1918 Offensives*, p. 29; see also Foley, *German Strategy*, pp. 82–126.

59 This remark, or variations on it, is also attributed to Talleyrand and to others; its exact provenance is uncertain.

and bypassing Robertson as CIGS. The British generals promptly threatened to resign, which would have collapsed Lloyd George's coalition government. A compromise was patched up whereby the BEF remained an independent force under Nivelle's strategic direction for his next planned offensive only.[60] Such compromises on both sides, however reluctant, were the key to both French and British civil–military strategic direction of the war, in which Clemenceau's skilful handling of his own generals contrasted with Lloyd George's maladroit and counterproductive manoeuvring against Robertson and Haig.

Two particularly blatant challenges to civilian political strategic authority on the Allied side are worthy of note. The *de facto* Italian Commander-in-Chief from 1914–17, Luigi Cadorna, pursued his favoured strategy safe in the knowledge that he had near-total independence from the government in Rome, beating off attempts to make him change course. It was only following the military disaster of Caporetto in 1917 that the government felt strong enough to dismiss Cadorna.[61] Similarly, at the end of October 1918, Pershing defied his own government by calling for the Allies to abandon plans to offer Germany an armistice in favour of the complete and total defeat of the German army, behaviour which highlights the influence of German military traditions on US army thinking even at this date.[62]

These problems only arose in countries with strong traditions of democracy and civilian primacy over military affairs.

In Germany, military imperatives continued to prevail over the concerns of the civilian leadership, and from August 1916 onwards under Hindenburg, the general staff increasingly assumed control of domestic government in the name of military necessity.[63] Germany, more than any other belligerent, had a tradition of the first loyalty of senior officers being the preservation of the

60 David R. Woodward, *Lloyd George and the Generals* (Newark, NJ: University of Delaware Press, 1983), pp. 116–59.

61 Brian R. Sullivan, 'The strategy of decisive weight: Italy 1882–1922', in Williamson Murray *et al.*, *The Making of Strategy* (Cambridge University Press, 1994), pp. 36–9; and Mark Thompson, *The White War: Life and Death on the Italian Front 1915–1919* (London: Basic Books, 2008), pp. 154–6, 245. For Cadorna's strategy and possible alternatives, see John Gooch, 'Italy during the First World War', in Allan R. Millett and Williamson Murray, *Military Effectiveness*, vol. I: *The First World* War (London: Allen & Unwin, 1988), pp. 165–7.

62 Russell F. Weigley, 'Strategy and total war in the United States: Pershing and the American military tradition', in Chickering and Förster (eds.), *Great War, Total War*, pp. 343–5.

63 For examples of civil–military relations in the major belligerents, see, e.g., David French, *British Strategy and War Aims 1914–16* (London: Allen & Unwin, 1986) and *The Strategy of the Lloyd George Coalition 1916–1918* (Oxford University Press, 1998); Doughty, *Pyrrhic Victory*; Jean-Jacques Becker, *The Great War and the French People* (Oxford: Berg, 1985); and Roger Chickering, *Imperial Germany and the Great War 1914–1918* (Cambridge University Press, 2004).

armed forces and their values as a way of life, rather than seeing the army (or navy) and military strategy as instruments of state policy. This was reinforced by strong strains of German militarism and romanticism; on the outbreak of war in 1914, Falkenhayn as war minister recorded that, 'Even if we go under as a result of this, still it was beautiful.'[64] The crisis of the defeat of Germany and the collapse of its armed forces in autumn 1918 resulted in two very dramatic acts of usurpation of governmental authority by senior officers. At the end of September, convinced that the German army on the Western Front was defeated and in danger of imminent collapse, Ludendorff demanded from Kaiser Wilhelm that negotiations for an armistice should begin, and that a new government consisting of the political opponents of the general staff should be appointed. The armistice negotiations themselves were conducted by civilians and by generals who were not members of the general staff hierarchy. The 'stab in the back myth' (*Dolchstosslegende*), that the German army had been undefeated but betrayed, was not a post-war rationalisation: it was the essential mechanism for ending the war by transferring blame for German defeat away from the military leadership of Hindenburg and Ludendorff, and the general staff.[65] The most charitable interpretation of Ludendorff's actions is that he believed that a proud and intact army was needed to keep order as Germany was threatened with revolution. More prosaically, the general staff cared more about preserving itself, in order to fight the next war, than it did about its country.

The High Command of the German Imperial Navy exhibited very similar behaviour at the end of October 1918. Rather than accepting the fact of defeat, Scheer as chief of SKL drew up plans for a final 'death battle' in which the High Seas Fleet would break out of harbour and head for the English Channel (the *Flottenvorstoss*). While the military rationale for this plan was that a naval victory would improve the German negotiating position with the Allies over the armistice, the political intention was that the Imperial Navy would both preserve its honour and improve the chances of its continued existence in a defeated post-war Germany. Neither Kaiser Wilhelm nor the new German government was informed of Scheer's intentions, and the plan backfired disastrously when the High Seas Fleet mutinied instead, contributing to Germany's collapse.[66]

64 Quoted in Herwig, *The Marne 1914*, p. 29.

65 Herwig, *The First World War*, pp. 425–8, 440–2; Sondhaus, *World War One*, pp. 433–4; and David Welch, *Germany, Propaganda and Total War 1914–18* (New Brunswick, NJ: Rutgers University Press, 2000), pp. 243–9.

66 Halpern, *A Naval History of World War I*, pp. 444–6; Stevenson, *1914–1918*, pp. 491–3.

To the French and British, following their almost complete success at sea in 1914, the Western Front was their greatest priority, and they needed to coordinate their military strategies there to an extent that (like much else about the First World War) was unprecedented in alliance warfare; but this was an evolutionary and tortuous process. The grand strategies of both countries were also transformed by the entry of the Ottoman Empire into the war in November 1914, severing strategic communications with Russia and opening up a large secondary campaign theatre. The confused strategic decision-making process and subsequent failures of strategic command in the 1915–16 Dardanelles campaign painfully exposed the weaknesses of both the existing British approach and of Anglo-French cooperation, which compared unfavourably to the relatively effective Ottoman strategic response.[67] The Allied failure in the Dardanelles also showed that the long-recognised difficulties and complexities of opposed amphibious operations – landing and sustaining ground forces from the sea – had grown vastly greater under the new conditions of industrialised warfare, and that a very high level of combined strategic and operational planning between armies and navies would be needed in future. Despite repeated British plans to exploit their naval superiority to outflank the Germans on the Western Front with an amphibious landing, this was never attempted other than a brief raid on Zeebrugge in April 1918.

With multiple fronts, and both large naval and land campaigns to manage, the development of British institutions for grand strategic command began with two improvised civil–military councils of war held by the Prime Minister, H. H. Asquith, on the war's outbreak, followed in November 1914 by the creation of a small War Council; the Committee of Imperial Defence also continued in its advisory role. In June 1915 the change to the new Asquith coalition government led to the War Council being renamed the Dardanelles Committee, and then the War Committee after January 1916 with Robertson as CIGS as its military adviser; it reached its final form as the War Cabinet with the new coalition government under Lloyd George in December 1916. It was to the War Committee and War Cabinet that Haig presented his plans for military strategy in 1916–18.[68] For France, although the political–military Supreme Council of National Defence remained the ultimate authority, military strategy continued to be made at GQG. As well as

67 Robin Prior, *Gallipoli: The End of the Myth* (New Haven, CT: Yale University Press, 2010 [2009]), *passim*; Erickson, *Ottoman Army Effectiveness*, p. 20; and Erickson, *Gallipoli*, p. xv.
68 For details of the final form of the War Cabinet see French, *Strategy*, pp. 17–26.

being made Commander-in-Chief of all French forces in December 1915, Joffre also pressed unsuccessfully for strategic command over the forces of all the Western Allies, including Italy, which had entered the war in May.[69]

The need for Britain and France to balance the priorities of the Western Front with the Dardanelles led to their first joint political–military strategy conferences of the war, held in Calais and Chantilly in July 1915. Results were inconclusive, but the foundations for unified command between them had at least been laid. The high point in Allied military strategic coordination came in December 1915, with a grand strategy conference at Calais followed by a military strategy conference at Chantilly, where it was agreed that all the Allies should launch major offensives in early summer 1916 on the Western, Eastern and Italian Fronts, with the intention of preventing the Central Powers from moving their reserves by rail from one front to another to meet the attacks. Although dislocated by the German pre-emptive attack at Verdun in February 1916, this decision produced the Brusilov offensive, the Somme offensive and the Sixth Battle of the Isonzo, as the only occasions in the war in which Allied military strategy was coordinated in this way. Strategic coordination on the Western Front was achieved between the British and the French, attacking side by side on the Somme, involving some forty-one meetings at army level or higher between March and the start of the offensive in July. But the actual result, in the French assessment, was that rather than acting in unison they had 'react[ed] constantly the one on the other, but are not sufficiently homogeneous'.[70]

Uniquely among the Allies, British military strategic command also had to deal with the national contingents of their Empire: the Dominions of Australia, Canada, Newfoundland, New Zealand and South Africa, and the Indian Army. In military affairs, the British relationship with their Empire had many of the characteristics of alliance warfare, as Dominion-contingent commanders had the right of appeal to their home governments, and the British were sensitive to both Dominion and Indian political issues. While the organisation of British armies and corps on the Western Front changed according to circumstances, by late 1917 the Australian Corps and the

69 Stevenson, 'French strategy on the Western Front, 1914–1918', pp. 302–25; and Elizabeth Greenhalgh, *Victory Through Coalition: Britain and France during the First World War* (Cambridge University Press, 2005), pp. 23–41.

70 Quoted in Greenhalgh, *Victory Through Coalition*, p. 71; a table of the Anglo-French planning meetings is in the same book, pp. 57–9. See also William Philpott, *Bloody Victory: The Sacrifice on the Somme and the Making of the Twentieth Century* (London: Little, Brown, 2009).

Canadian Corps had become permanent formations under their own national commanders. This increasing importance of the Dominions was reflected in the Imperial War Conference in March 1917, leading to the creation of an Imperial War Cabinet of the heads of government of Britain and the Dominions.[71]

The French saw Allied unity of military strategic command as an aim in itself, with the self-evident proviso that the commander should be a French general, and that France's voice should dominate. For the British, the issue of unity of command was almost entirely subsumed in their own national civil–military struggle. Much of the impetus for greater strategic coordination also came from the impact of the German unrestricted submarine campaign on British and French strategy on the Western Front, and the pattern of Allied failures and defeats throughout 1917. Having been so successful in 1914, the Royal Navy saw no reason to change a command structure that was both separate from that of the British army, and largely independent of political control. This changed markedly in 1917, when the German submarine campaign posed a threat not only to Allied naval dominance but also to the civilian war effort through losses to merchant shipping, and to strategy on the Western Front, playing an important part in the decision to launch the Third Ypres offensive.[72] The Royal Navy's protracted objections to introducing protected convoys for merchant ships were overcome by civilian political pressure and the entry of the United States into the war in April, providing an early opportunity for Allied cooperation. Generally, alliance warfare at sea proved much easier to manage than on land, with broad agreements being reached on strategy and on a division of responsibilities, while individual ships and squadrons could be placed under the overall command of an ally without losing their autonomy. One illustrative case is the Imperial Japanese Navy, which largely acted independently of the other Allies in the Pacific, but took part in convoy escort duties, and from May 1917 onwards stationed a squadron of destroyers and cruisers at the British naval base of Malta in the Mediterranean. Although nominally independent, in practice this squadron took part in anti-submarine operations under the British Commander-in-Chief Malta, Admiral George A. Ballard.[73] Air power, as the new third element in

71 French, *Strategy*, pp. 62–4, 255–7.

72 See Andrew W. Wiest, *Passchendaele and the Royal Navy* (Westport, CT: Greenwood Press, 1995).

73 Tomoyuki Ishizu, 'Japan and the First World War', paper delivered to the conference 'Asia, the Great War, and the Continuum of Violence', University College Dublin, May 2012; with gratitude to Professor Ishizu for this information.

warfare, evolved from almost nothing in 1914 to become an important, often essential, part of both land and sea warfare, and was gradually integrated into armies and fleets. Changes in the British governmental and military command structures over winter 1917–18, culminating in the creation of the Royal Air Force in April 1918 as the world's first independent air force, were made partly in response to the crisis caused by German bombing of British cities and the need to provide a new organisation for defence and retaliation, but were also very much part of continuing civil–military tensions.

In response to the crises of 1917, the Anglo-French-Italian Rapallo conference in November created the Supreme War Council, a political organisation with permanent military advisers, based at Versailles with a mandate to oversee and advise on national grand strategies including finance, food, munitions, transportation and naval – principally anti-submarine – warfare, and to review national military strategic plans.[74] This was far from true Allied unity of command: Russia was excluded from the Rapallo conference as it was on the verge of collapse into revolution; the United States was initially excluded as an 'Associated' rather than Allied Power, and the smaller Allied nations, Belgium, Romania, Serbia and Portugal, were also not represented. The almost immediate change in the French government, with Clemenceau becoming Prime Minister, also meant a greater assertion of civilian control over grand strategy and over GQG.[75] Lloyd George expected to use the Supreme War Council's authority over both British and French reserves on the Western Front as a way of controlling Haig, and his insistence that the CIGS should not also be the Supreme War Council's permanent military adviser led to Robertson's resignation in February 1918 and replacement by Wilson with reduced authority. The impact of these civil–military struggles on military strategy became apparent with the initial British defeat in the March 1918 *Kaiserschlacht* offensive, and the need for coordinating the British, French and also the American response. Pershing temporarily disregarded his political instructions, which were to use his troops in battle only as a unified national army, and instead allowed them to fight as part of larger French and British formations. At two Anglo-French political–military meetings, at Doullens in March and Beauvais in April, the latter including the Americans, Foch as French army Chief of Staff and permanent adviser to the Supreme War Council was placed in charge of coordinating military strategy on the

74 Michael S. Neiberg, *Fighting the Great War: A Global History* (Cambridge, MA: Harvard University Press, 2005), pp. 285–8; Greenhalgh, *Victory Through Coalition*, pp. 163–85.

75 John V. F. Keiger, 'Poincaré, Clemenceau, and the quest for total victory', in Chickering and Förster (eds.), *Great War, Total War*, pp. 247–79.

Western Front with the title of 'General-in-Chief of the Allied Armies', a politically sensitive position that was similar to Joffre's in 1914 in the extent of its official authority, which was extended to the Italian Front in May.[76] This arrangement continued up to the Armistice, and Foch's firm but tactful approach as Generalissimo, which recognised the practical limitations of his authority and national sensitivities, was a great asset to the Allies in 1918.[77]

Conclusion

The diversity of military strategic command problems of the First World War, among land, sea and air warfare, between differing fighting fronts and between countries and alliances, means that no single generalisation may be easily made regarding their nature, or their solution. The considerable attention paid by present military historical discourse on the First World War to issues of command reflects both these diversities and a recognition of the vital need to understand strategic command issues in the war. The difficulties faced by generals and admirals in reconciling their military strategies with larger national and alliance grand strategies, and in coping with the complexities of civil–military relations, had precedents in many previous wars. But the sheer scale of mass-industrialised warfare in 1914–18, including both the potential of newly developed technologies and – particularly in the sphere of communications – their limitations, was indeed without precedent. Moreover, the complexities faced in strategic command in the First World War would never be faced again in the same way, as political and military methods and structures were developed in the war's aftermath that, if they could not resolve the critical issues faced by industrialised states at war for their survival in the Second World War, did at least reduce the frictions which these issues caused, and the burdens placed on any one individual. The institutions and systems of strategic command that emerged in response to various crises of the First World War, together with the necessity for both political and military leaders to become war managers, both chiefly on the Allied side, provide an important part of the explanation for the war's wider nature and conduct, and for its eventual outcome.

76 Greenhalgh, *Victory Through Coalition*, pp. 192–203.

77 Michael S. Neiberg. 'The evolution of strategic thinking in World War I: a case study of the Second Battle of the Marne', *Journal of Military and Strategic Studies*, 13:4 (2011), pp. 9–11, 16–18. More generally, see Elizabeth Greenhalgh, *Foch in Command* (Cambridge University Press, 2011).

PART III

*

WORLD WAR

Introduction to Part III

JAY WINTER AND JOHN HORNE

The huge advantage the Allied Powers had from the very outset of the war arose from the stock of capital, human and material, which they had accumulated in imperial expansion throughout the nineteenth and early twentieth centuries. Both the German and Austro-Hungarian Empires mobilised resources within Europe, but the Allied empires and dependencies spanned the globe. In particular the British Empire operated on both formal and informal levels, with powerful friends and holdings in independent countries like Argentina and the United States. The French Empire drew substantial numbers of soldiers and labourers from Africa and Asia, but the British Empire and Dominions provided even more black, brown and yellow men for military service or for support in auxiliary units behind the lines.

The only equivalent in the Central Powers to a multi-ethnic and multinational mobilisation was that of the Ottoman Empire. But such efforts, while important, cut across the process of Turkification which was the objective of the triumvirate which ruled Ottoman Turkey, and which was responsible for the Armenian genocide, an event demonstrating the destruction of human capital of a kind which the Nazis repeated two decades later.

Imperial mobilisation meant cultural transfer on a global scale. Those who had out-migrated from Britain to the New World and the Antipodes returned 'home', as it were, and brought with them their skills and their determination to see the conflict through to victory. Some saw this movement towards Europe as one of the largest waves of 'tourism' in history. Too many of the 'tourists' died to accept this formulation, but there is little doubt that the experience and knowledge derived from imperial participation in the war had long-term consequences of the first magnitude. Hô Chi Minh in Paris during and after the war was but one of the major leaders of the twentieth century whose presence in Europe as young men marked their lives thereafter.

The 1914–18 conflict was both the apogee and the beginning of the end of imperial power. First went the German, Austro-Hungarian and Ottoman

Empires, but thereafter the other imperial powers – Britain, France and Russia recast as the Soviet Union – became slowly, but surely, incapable of maintaining their imperial holdings. Economic constraints mattered, but so did the determination, evident after 1918, of the subalterns to break their ties with the 'mother country'. Decolonisation after the Second World War was an extension of trends in motion after the First. The last empire to go was the Soviet Empire, in 1991, an outcome revealing the long shadow of the Great War on the twentieth century.

15

The imperial framework

JOHN H. MORROW, JR.

The First World War had its origins in the era of imperialism. It was fought by imperial powers to determine who would dominate Europe and the wider world, and concluded with the preservation of European imperialism for another generation.

Origins

In the 1880s a new era of imperial history began, the era of the 'New Imperialism', in which primarily European powers, and the United States and Japan, further expanded their dominion over the globe. A 'new navalism' arose, as American Captain Alfred Thayer Mahan's classic, *The Influence of Sea Power upon History, 1660–1783* (1890), which was based on the British experience, extolled to a receptive international audience the importance of capital ships – battleships and battlecruisers – and great sea battles of annihilation to achieve global hegemony. The reasons and justifications for imperial expansion varied: the pursuit of raw materials and markets, geopolitical advantage from the conquest of strategic territories and increased national prestige. European states, led by Britain and France, and the United States and Japan, endowed with superior technology, naval and military power and, most fundamentally, 'surplus' population, conquered much of Africa and Asia.

The 'New Imperialism' sprouted from, and in turn exacerbated, the racist nationalism prevalent in Europe and the rest of the Western world in the last quarter of the nineteenth century. In an era of the ascendancy of doctrines purported to be 'realist' or 'scientific', devotion to the nation-state acquired 'scientific' rationalisations, exemplified by social Darwinism and scientific racism. Humans were warlike and competitive; war, an alleged response to evolutionary pressures, was a biological necessity. Metaphors of 'a relentless struggle for existence', the 'survival of the fittest' and the 'law of the jungle' now applied to human conflict. The so-called 'white' races defined Jews and the 'coloured' peoples of the world such as Africans and Asians as inferior and dangerous, to be banished, barred, subordinated, subjugated or exterminated. The military victories, conquests of great territories and the subject peoples themselves became evidence of the racial and moral superiority of the conquerors. The irony, of course, lay in the fact that the imperial conquests resulted not from superior courage or virtue, but from superior technology, which the imperialists accepted as proof of their God-given greatness. Europeans transmogrified technological superiority into biological and even theological necessity; it was God's will that Europeans conquer and civilise, or exploit, the 'lesser' peoples of Africa and Asia and, if necessary, 'sacrifice' or exterminate them in the name of progress. Imperialists believed that extinction awaited the 'inferior races'; consequently, they were merely hastening the course of civilisation by weeding out, or deliberately annihilating, these 'inferiors'. Colonial or 'little' wars against 'uncivilised', 'barbarian' and 'savage' peoples were necessary, as Theodore Roosevelt, staunch racist, militarist and imperialist, explained in 1899, because 'In the long run civilized man finds he can keep the peace only by subduing his barbarian neighbor; for the barbarian will yield only to force.' The duty of superior civilised races was consequently to expand in 'just wars against primitive races'.[1] Charles Darwin contemplated 'what an endless number of the lower races will have been eliminated by the higher civilized race' in the not too distant future.[2]

Inventions, especially those in the military realm, found immediate application in the conquest of native populations. Cannon-armed gunboats, rapid firing artillery, the Maxim gun, the repeating rifle, smokeless powder – such weapons gave European intruders a crushing superiority. Lead-cored dum-dum bullets, patented in 1897 and manufactured initially in Dum Dum outside Calcutta, exploded on contact, causing large, painful wounds that dropped charging warriors in their tracks. Europeans used them in big game hunting and in colonial wars; conventions prohibited their use in conflicts between civilised states.[3] Even the airplane, though just in its infancy, offered prospects for future use in colonial ventures. By 1910 the British government clearly recognised the implications of the airplane for colonial domination and white

1 Manfred Boemeke, Roger Chickering and Stig Förster (eds.), *Anticipating Total War: The German and American Experiences, 1871–1914* (Washington: German Historical Institute, and Cambridge University Press, 1999), pp. 246, 392.

2 D. P. Crook, *Darwinism, War and History: The Debate over the Biology of War from the 'Origin of Species' to the First World War* (Cambridge University Press, 1994), p. 25.

3 Sven Lindqvist, *'Exterminate All the Brutes': One Man's Odyssey into the Heart of Darkness and the Origins of European Genocide* (New York: New Press, 1996), pp. 2–3.

imperial supremacy. The Committee of Imperial Defence directed the War Office to consider the use of the airplane 'in war against uncivilized countries such as the Sudan, Somaliland, and the Northwest Frontier of India'. In 1913, Charles Grey, editor of *The Aeroplane*, suggested the use of the airplane 'for impressing European superiority on the enormous native population'. In March 1914, Winston Churchill endorsed a possible joint project of the Colonial Office and the Royal Navy whereby the white population would employ aircraft to control and threaten the Empire's native populations to confront the 'distinct possibility' of black uprisings.[4]

Yet what barrier or boundary would ensure that imperialist states would not one day employ these weapons against one another? European expansion entailed the disappearance of entire peoples and the appropriation of their land, securing '*Lebensraum*', or living space, but Hitler's usage of the term was applied to Europe itself. Struggle between races was essential to progress and to avoid decay, as the superior would necessarily win. Within races, inferior types needed to disappear, as the increasing popularity of eugenics in the Western world during this epoch demonstrated. Europeans would not necessarily be immune from attempts at conquest on their own continent.

As the conquered territories became part of the power bloc of European empire, the integral nature of empire linked mother country to imperial possession in a complex, varied and yet seamless web. The importance of India, the 'Jewel in the Crown', to Britain, explained Lord Curzon in 1901, was critical: 'As long as we rule India we are the greatest power in the world. If we lose it we shall drop straightaway to a third rate power.'[5] Indian markets bolstered the British economy, and the 220,000-man-strong Indian Army led by British officers policed the Empire and enabled the British to avoid conscription at home, until the British refusal to use Indian soldiers against a white opponent, the Boers in South Africa, forced the mother country to use British, Irish and Australian soldiers during the Boer War of 1899–1901.

John A. Hobson's work, *Imperialism*, first published in 1902, warned of the deleterious effects of empire on the imperialists. The wars fostered an 'excess of national self-consciousness' among the imperial powers; the process of imposing 'superior civilization on the coloured races' would '[I]ntensify the struggle of the white races'. Finally, the 'parasitism' of the white rulers' relationship to the 'lower races' gave rise to the most 'perilous device' of 'vast native

4 Thomas A. Keaney, 'Aircraft and Air Doctrinal Development in Great Britain, 1912–1914' (PhD thesis, University of Michigan, 1975), pp. 147–8.

5 Aaron L. Friedberg, *The Weary Titan: Britain and the Experience of Relative Decline, 1895–1905* (Princeton University Press, 1986), p. 220.

forces' commanded by white officers and the possible 'dangerous' precedent of using these forces against another white race.[6]

Eight years later, in 1910, a book appeared in France that bore out Hobson's concerns and indicated the permeability of the boundaries between Europe and empire in plans for future war – General Charles Mangin's study, *La force noire*. France's declining birth rate required it to find other sources of men. Mangin proposed sub-Saharan Africa, whose valorous warriors had achieved significant feats of arms in the past and stood ready to repeat them for France. The objections of others notwithstanding, Mangin, a swashbuckling colonial officer who had fought in Africa and Indochina during his career, had no hesitation about sending his African soldiers to fight in France. The French defeat in the Franco-Prussian War of 1870–1 had driven Mangin's family from its ancestral home in Lorraine to migrate to Algeria, but, like other colonial officers, he never lost sight of Europe. In their minds, imperial and European battlefields were intertwined – a French African army would counter the Teutonic threat on the Rhine and gain revenge against Germany. Already the French army planned to bring North African soldiers – Algerians and Moroccans – to France in case of war. The war itself would make the *Force noire* a reality.[7]

The very culture of the imperialist age created an atmosphere in which European upper- and middle-class youth quite literally yearned for war, the ultimate violent sport. Sir Robert Baden-Powell, hero of the Boer War, founded the Boy Scouts to transform the puny offspring of industrial society, who had failed in large numbers to qualify for service in the Boer War, into sturdy potential warriors.[8] Garnet Wolseley, Britain's most admired soldier, considered war 'the greatest purifier' of an 'overrefined . . . race or nation'. The British Empire required an 'Imperial Race', purged of 'effeminate' and 'degenerate' traits. Sir Arthur Conan Doyle, creator of Sherlock Holmes, mused in August 1914, 'a bloody purging would be good for the country'.[9] The founders of the German boy scouts (*Pfadfinder*) were veterans of the vicious Herero War in South West Africa. The Germans, like the British, feared that urban life weakened young men, so the German youth movement,

6 John A. Hobson, *Imperialism* (Ann Arbor: University of Michigan Press, 1965 [1938]), pp. 11, 154–7, 174–5, 159, 282, 211, 222, 227, 136–7, 311–12.

7 Charles J. Balesi, *From Adversaries to Comrades-in-Arms: West Africans and the French Military, 1885–1918* (Waltham, MA: African Studies Association, 1979), *passim*.

8 Hobson, *Imperialism*, p. 214.

9 Michael C. C. Adams, *The Great Adventure: Male Desire and the Coming of World War I* (Bloomington: Indiana University Press, 1990), pp. 6–8, 59–61. See also Susan Kingsley Kent, *Gender and Power in Britain, 1640–1990* (London: Routledge, 1999), pp. 236–7.

the *Wandervogel*, sponsored escape into the purity of nature, while the *Jungdeutschlandbund* (Young Germany League) militarised youth work. Historian Derek Linton concludes that these organisations were 'very much products of the age of imperialism', which made war seem 'a heroic and glorious game, a test of a generation, and an escape from . . . urban life'.[10]

Imperial conquest and interaction affected Europeans' perceptions of themselves and other Europeans. They not only divided the world into races, but also conflated nationality with race as they warily eyed one another. Constant references to the Anglo-Saxon, Gallic, Teutonic or Slavic 'races' dotted the literature of the time. Continental imperialists, pan-Germans and pan-Slavs, in their respective determination to unite all ethnic Germans in one German state and all Slavs under Russian leadership, would upset the status quo in Central and Eastern Europe to achieve their goals. Once the Europeans divided themselves into separate and unequal 'races', what was to prevent the extension of the brutal attitudes towards 'coloured peoples' to other Europeans for the sake of progress and survival? After all, the future of one's inherently superior races and culture, and thus of civilisation, was at stake. The intertwined sentiments of nationalism, racism and imperialism thus rendered Europe and the world a more volatile place at the turn of the twentieth century. As historian John Whiteclay Chambers II observed, 'The ruthlessness of colonial warfare, with its lack of restraints, would return to haunt Europe in the slaughter of World War I.'[11]

Between 1905 and 1914, with the background of arms races on land and sea between Germany and Austria-Hungary on the one hand and Britain, France and Russia on the other, two flashpoints gave rise to intermittent crises that heightened the tensions among the powers: Morocco and the Balkans. Both regions had once belonged to the Ottoman Empire, now considered the 'Sick Man of Europe' as its power receded. Both were the sites of imperial contests: Morocco, primarily between the French and Germans; the Balkans, between the Austro-Hungarian and Russian Empires. In the Moroccan crises in 1905 and 1911, French and Spanish initiatives in their spheres of influence prompted German demands, reinforced in 1911 by a display of gunboat diplomacy, for equal access or compensation. Both times Britain responded to German bullying by standing firmly with the French, resulting in the German paranoia of 'encirclement', a French nationalist revival and the very rapprochement among Britain, France and Russia that Germany feared. After the Second

10 Boemeke *et al.* (eds.), *Anticipating Total War*, p. 187. 11 *Ibid.*, p. 247.

Moroccan Crisis, some Europeans began to believe that war was inevitable and launched further extensive preparations for it.

The First Moroccan Crisis of 1905 gave rise to deliberations in the British Admiralty about countering the German threat. Historians have generally focused on the naval construction race, naval plans to land a force on the continent, or plans for an economic blockade of Germany. Captain C. L. Ottley, Director of Naval Intelligence and then Secretary to the Committee of Imperial Defence, informed First Lord Reginald McKenna in 1908 that a blockade offered a 'certain and simple means of strangling Germany at sea', and that in a protracted war 'grass would sooner or later grow in the streets of Hamburg and widespread dearth and ruin would be inflicted'.[12] In fact, as historian Nicholas Lambert demonstrates, the ideas of Ottley and others in the Admiralty went far beyond naval blockade to economic warfare, which would entail 'unprecedented state intervention in the workings of the national and international economies' to 'harness not only Britain's naval power but also her monopolistic control over world shipping, finance, and communications'.[13] Although such ideas ultimately proved too radical and disruptive to the world economy in general and the United States in particular, their very existence shows how far some naval planners were prepared to go to defeat Germany.

A critical offshoot of the Second Moroccan Crisis was that the Italian government, stimulated by French success in Morocco, determined to conquer its own slice of North Africa from the Ottoman Turks, in Libya. The campaign would constitute a direct attack on the Ottoman Empire. In April 1911, the Italian Prime Minister, Giovanni Giolitti, who recognised that the integrity of the Ottoman Empire was integral to European peace, observed:

> And what if after we have attacked Turkey the Balkans begin to stir? And what if a Balkan clash provokes a clash between the two power blocs and a European war? Can it be that we could shoulder the responsibility of putting a match to the powder?[14]

Such musings did not prevent Italian aggression in September and a victorious war that lasted a year. Yet Giolitti's queries proved prescient. The Ottoman Empire was a critical factor in European peace, and the trail of the origins of

12 Avner Offer, *The First World War: An Agrarian Interpretation* (Oxford: Clarendon Press, 1989), p. 232.

13 Nicholas A. Lambert, *Planning Armageddon: British Economic Warfare and the First World War* (Cambridge, MA: Harvard University Press, 2012), pp. 124, 130.

14 James Joll, *The Origins of the First World War* (London: Longman, 1984), p. 164.

war would lead, as he had foreseen, from North Africa via the Ottoman Empire into the Balkan wars of 1912 and 1913, and ultimately the confrontation between Serbia and Austria-Hungary that did put the match to the powder. Giolitti, furthermore, was not alone in his willingness to run the risk of a major war; virtually all of his peers in the governments of Europe were willing to gamble with Armageddon.

Successive Balkan crises leading to war began in 1908–9, when Austria-Hungary annexed Bosnia-Herzegovina and agreed to compensate the Russian government by approaching Britain to achieve an enduring aim of Russian foreign policy – access to the Straits of Constantinople connecting the Black Sea to the Aegean and ultimately the Mediterranean Sea. Austria-Hungary reneged on its commitment, and only German intervention on behalf of Austria-Hungary forced the enraged Russians to back down. The Russians, however, then launched a military reform and expansion that would make the Russian army the most powerful in Europe by 1917. In October 1912, the Balkan League – Serbia, Bulgaria, Greece and Montenegro – prodded by the Russians, declared war on the Ottoman Turks, and quickly defeated them, practically driving them from Europe. The peace satisfied no one, and a second Balkan war ensued, in 1913, from which the Serbs emerged strengthened to confront the Austro-Hungarian Empire, and with future assurances of support from the Russian Empire.

The stage was now set for the assassination of Austro-Hungarian Archduke Franz-Ferdinand and the July crisis that precipitated Europe into war, a crisis that can only be understood in the context of imperialism. All the imperial powers eyed one another predatorily and warily, intent on expanding or defending their empires. Captain Ottley's plans indicated the likelihood that a future war with Germany would become a war to destroy a rising competitor on the continent. Nearly every power – Britain, France, Germany, Russia, Austria-Hungary, even Italy and Serbia – covetously eyed the Ottoman Empire and its far-flung territories. Historian Mustafa Aksakal's study, *The Ottoman Road to War in 1914*, points out that the Ottoman government viewed the events from the Balkan wars in 1912 through to the crisis of July 1914, 'in the context of Russian intentions to seize control over Istanbul and the Ottoman Straits'. The Young Turks, Aksakal explains, reeling in the aftermath of the disastrous Balkan wars, 'feared Russia' and thus sided with Germany.[15]

15 Mustafa Aksakal, *The Ottoman Road to War in 1914: The Ottoman Empire and the First World War* (Cambridge University Press, 2008), pp. 3, 190.

The Russian Empire's role in the origins of the war has recently drawn particular attention from historian Sean McMeekin, who pointedly suggests that after the Italian and Balkan wars from 1911 through 1913, the First World War was plausibly 'The War of Ottoman Succession', and that consequently, 'it was Russia's war even more than it was Germany's'. Russia also directly challenged Ottoman Turkey with its Armenian reform campaign of 1913–14, which McMeekin labels 'a scarcely disguised Trojan horse for the expansion of Russian influence in Turkish Anatolia', as preliminary to its plans to seize Constantinople and the Straits. Russian imperialists, he asserts, were 'dead serious' about dismembering Turkey and Austria-Hungary, whose army Russian generals considered a 'paper tiger'.[16] In fact, McMeekin labels the assumption that Russia went to war on behalf of Serbia 'naïve'. All the powers assumed that Ottoman Turkey was doomed, and Russia sought to fulfil its national interest of controlling Constantinople and the Straits and was willing to contemplate provoking a war to gain the Straits.[17] McMeekin's study demonstrates clearly that an interpretation of the origins of the Great War through the lens of imperialism prevents a simplistic attempt to blame any single power for the origins of the war. Even the Young Turks, who had seized control of the Ottoman Empire in 1908, planned to restore its imperial glory and harboured grandiose designs – at Russia's expense. Russian generals were not the only observers who considered Austria-Hungary vulnerable. Both friend and foe alike deemed the Dual Monarchy, with its volatile mix of nationalities and ethnic groups, the next empire likely to disintegrate. Even Britain and France, the leading imperialist powers, were determined to expand their empires.

Furthermore, the British plans for economic warfare, when viewed along with the extremist proclamations of pan-Germans and pan-Slavs that the other had to disappear, offer ample indication that a coming war might destroy the traditional order of the Great Powers. In an era of rampant imperialism, challenges to the existing international order elicited extreme responses that entailed the subjugation or destruction of one's opponents and the conquest of their peoples and empires. The European powers went to war in 1914 to determine who would control not only Europe, but also the world, and civilian and military leaders of all the powers were culpable and complicit in causing the war. The war's major fronts would lie in Europe, but its imperial

16 Sean McMeekin, *The Russian Origins of the First World War* (Cambridge, MA: Harvard University Press, 2011), pp. 4–5, 12, 21.

17 *Ibid.*, pp. 28, 31–2, 34–5.

aspects were factors on all fronts: Europe, the Ottoman Empire, Africa and East Asia. In order to impose some semblance of order on global events that were sometimes related, this chapter will proceed one continent at a time in the above order.

Europe

On the Western Front, Britain and France in particular had access to their colonial empires for manpower and materials. Both factors were important, but manpower posed the more volatile difficulty because of the issue of race. In 1914 the British and French both deployed colonial troops on the Western Front: the British, Indian infantry and cavalry; the French, North African infantry. The danger of employing colonial soldiers in Europe lay in the threat that their encounters with Europeans might pose to the colonial order. The Indian Army comprised mainly illiterate peasants from the north and north-west frontiers, whom the British deemed the most 'martial' races. The deliberate recruitment of the least-educated Indians was intended to minimise the penetration of 'dangerous' Western ideas into their minds. The arrival of Indian soldiers in England prompted the army and government to control their access to white society, in particular white working-class women, as stereotypes portrayed both the Indians and the women as highly sexual. Yet all the regulations in the world could not ensure absolute separation, so British censors concentrated on suppressing accounts of sex with white women and slighting references to whites in order to preserve white prestige in India.[18] In contrast, white Dominion soldiers never faced such restrictions in any theatre. Canadian and Anzac soldiers ran amok in London, the former achieving the highest levels of venereal disease of any Entente troops on the Western Front.

Indian combat service with the British on the Western Front culminated in 1915. The British had dispatched Indian Army expeditionary forces in the fall of 1914 to Basra, Egypt and East Africa, but primarily to France, where they entered combat in October 1914. They suffered heavy losses and the brutal cold of the European winter undermined morale, but in 1915 some 16,000 British and 28,500 Indian soldiers of the two Indian cavalry and two infantry divisions of the Indian Corps participated in British attacks at Neuve Chapelle in March, Festubert in May and Loos in late September. The Indian Corps

18 Philippa Levine, 'Battle colors: race, sex, and colonial soldiery in World War I', *Journal of Women's History*, 9:4 (1998), p. 110. See also David Omissi (ed.), *Indian Voices of the Great War: Soldiers' Letters, 1914–18* (London: Macmillan, 1999), pp. 27–8, 104, 114, 119, 123.

figured prominently at Neuve Chapelle, where their attack resulted in the loss of 12,500 men, and further debilitating losses at Loos undermined their effectiveness as assault infantry or shock troops, the favourite use of colonial troops on the Western Front. The prospect of another winter led the British to send the remnants of the infantry divisions to Mesopotamia, although the cavalry divisions remained until spring 1918.

As the Indian infantry departed, the British turned to forces from the white Dominions to fulfil their manpower needs. After serving at Gallipoli in 1915, the Australian and New Zealand forces, or Anzacs, formed into the five divisions of the Australian Imperial Force (AIF) and would demonstrate their superb fighting qualities on the Western Front from 1916 through to 1918. In fact, in 1917 and 1918 Britain's freshest and most aggressive soldiers came primarily from Canada, Australia and New Zealand. These soldiers performed particularly well in the offensives of 1918, as they became Great Britain's manpower reserves and shock troops on the Western Front. The Canadian Corps, in particular, could justifiably claim to be the best large unit on the Western Front during the campaign that ended the war.[19]

The British absolutely refused to use African, or 'aboriginal', soldiers in Europe or outside Africa, although they did send numbers of African and Asian labour battalions directly from the colonies to the continent. The presence of Indian soldiers in England posed sufficient concerns; the presence of Africans would have been insufferable. In France, however, notwithstanding the objections of the colonial governor of West Africa about the debilitating loss of manpower, Mangin wanted more shock troops, and Senegalese Deputy Blaise Diagne, who had been elected to Parliament in May 1914, regarded the service of African soldiers as an avenue to gain more rights in the colonies. He consequently argued that *originaires*, black inhabitants of the four urban communities in Senegal who already possessed greater legal rights and privileges than other Senegalese, should be integrated into metropolitan units (units from the French *Métropole*, or mother country) with white Frenchmen. The law of 19 October 1915 conscripted *originaires* and incorporated them into French units, and by the law of 29 September 1916 these Senegalese would become French citizens. Senegalese *originaires* in predominantly French units were treated as Frenchmen, but the army attempted to prevent contact between the greater number of Senegalese *tirailleurs* and French women. Nevertheless, *tirailleur* non-commissioned officers or

19 Shane B. Schreiber, *Shock Army of the British Empire: The Canadian Corps in the Last 100 Days of the Great War* (Westport, CT: Praeger, 1997), pp. 133, 139.

decorated soldiers often developed the same relationship with French women and families as the *originaires*.[20]

In the bloody battles of attrition at Verdun and on the Somme in 1916, the French deployed increasing numbers of black African troops. Mangin employed his African soldiers for the repeated attacks the French army launched at Verdun in the spring of 1916. Ultimately, on 24 October, Moroccan and Senegalese assault troops of the French Colonial Army retook the key fortress of Douaumont, the loss of which, at the start of the Verdun battle in late February, had signified the great success of the German offensive. In the British and French attack on the Somme on 1 July 1916, the First Corps of the French Colonial Army included twenty-one Senegalese battalions. French officers encouraged the Africans to close with the Germans with knives and French soldiers with the bayonet, which incurred needless casualties. General Pierre Berdoulat, commander of the Colonial Army Corps, believed that the Africans' 'limited intellectual abilities' made them useful 'for sparing a certain number of European lives at the moment of assaults'.[21]

The word 'sparing' appears frequently in commanders' references to the expenditure of Senegalese instead of French lives. In April 1917, Mangin's colonial soldiers – Algerians, Moroccans, Senegalese – served as one spearhead for the major attack planned at the Chemin des Dames by new French Commander-in-Chief Robert Nivelle. Nivelle demanded as many Senegalese soldiers as possible, to 'permit the sparing – to the extent possible – of French blood'. The French commander of a Senegalese regiment declared that his soldiers were 'finally and above all superb attack troops permitting the sparing of the lives of whites, who exploit their success *behind them* and organise the positions they conquer'. A battalion commander voiced similar sentiments, advocating the use of the *Force noire* 'to save, in future offensive actions, the blood – more and precious – of our [French] soldiers'.[22] On 16 April some 25,000 Senegalese, the core of Mangin's assault force, attacked the German lines. Among the few troops to penetrate the German lines, the first wave suffered grave casualties – 6,000 out of 10,000 soldiers. Nivelle's attack ended in failure and provoked French soldiers to refuse to attack, and French morale in general reached its lowest point of the war in mid 1917.

The French also deployed Madagascan and Annamite (Indochinese) troops as labourers and truck drivers behind the Western Front and as combat

20 Joe Lunn, *Memoirs of the Maelstrom: A Senegalese Oral History of the First World War* (Portsmouth, NH: Heinemann, 1999), pp. 66, 106–86 *passim*.
21 *Ibid.*, p. 139. 22 *Ibid.*

soldiers in the Near East. By 1916, 10 per cent of France's rapidly expanding labour force was foreign or colonial labourers. That year the government began to import large numbers of non-white workers, and race became an issue in the factories and farms on the French home front in 1917. Some 78,500 Algerians, 49,000 Indochinese, 35,500 Moroccans, 18,000 Tunisians and 4,500 Malagasy worked in France. Historian Guoqi Xu points out that 140,000 Chinese labourers formed the largest and longest-serving group on the Western Front from 1917 to 1920. The Chinese government had sent them as part of a grander plan to establish a link between China and the West in hopes of regaining Shandong from the Japanese and forestalling future Japanese incursions – in vain, as it turned out.[23]

The French War Ministry's Colonial Labour Organisation Service regimented the urban workers, forming them into labour battalions and housing them in isolation like prisoners of war. The government tried to separate the colonials from French women to prevent sexual contact, but marriages between French women and colonial workers increased.[24] The Service feared the workers would gain a 'taste for strong drink and white women', as well as experience with strikes and unions, all of which would upset established hierarchies in the Empire by returning a seasoned body of radicals to the colonies.[25] In fact, by importing no women of colour, the French government created exactly what it feared by concentrating large numbers of French women and colonial workers in the absence of white men and non-white women. The circumstances did lead to outbreaks of racial violence in the spring and summer of 1917.

France's 600,000 colonial soldiers did not face the resentment that the workers incurred. After all, as their officers constantly reiterated, they were sparing the lives of Frenchmen, who regarded foreigners as replacements to release them for military service and to break strikes. In December 1917 the French Prime Minister, Georges Clemenceau, who vowed unrelenting war against the Germans, sent a recruiting mission of 300 decorated West African officers and men to draft more African soldiers to fight in France.[26] In 1918 Blaise Diagne, appointed Commissioner of the Republic in West Africa, took

23 Guoqi Xu, *Strangers on the Western Front: Chinese Workers in the Great War* (Cambridge, MA: Harvard University Press, 2011), pp. 1–6.

24 Laura Lee Downs, *Manufacturing Inequality: Gender Division in the French and British Metalworking Industries, 1914–1939* (Ithaca, NY: Cornell University Press, 1995), p. 60.

25 Tyler Stovall, 'The color line behind the lines: racial violence in France during the Great War', *American Historical Review*, 103:3 (1998), p. 746.

26 Balesi, *Adversaries*, p. 90.

charge of recruitment. Diagne considered the 'blood tax' (*impôt du sang*) a means for Africans to achieve equal rights, while French officials still focused on saving French lives. Colonel Eugene Petitdemange, commander of the Senegalese training camp at Fréjus in the south of France, planned to use his 'brave Senegalese . . . to replace the French, to be used as cannon fodder to spare the whites'. Even Clemenceau, convinced of the debt that Africans owed France for its 'civilisation' and of the necessity to avoid further French sacrifice, told French senators on 18 February 1918, 'Although I have infinite respect for these brave blacks, I would much prefer to have ten blacks killed than a single Frenchman.'[27]

Diagne, however, extracted concessions from the French government for improved conditions in Africa and higher status for soldiers, including French citizenship upon request for distinguished *tirailleurs*. To Diagne, 'those who fall under fire, fall neither as whites nor as blacks; they fall as Frenchmen and for the same flag'.[28] In ten months Diagne recruited more than 60,000 soldiers, and on 14 October Clemenceau commissioned him to prepare to have 1 million Senegalese troops by spring 1919 in order for Mangin to form a shock army which would amalgamate French and Senegalese soldiers. Only Germany's surrender forestalled the total realisation of Mangin's *Force noire*, although much to Germany's chagrin and the outrage of Britain and the United States, the French stationed West African soldiers in the post-war occupation of Germany as a reward for their service and a demonstration of French power to them which might dissuade them from radicalism when they returned to Africa.

Concentration on the British and French should not preclude notice of events on the Eastern Front starting in 1915, when the German army, having overrun Poland, now began to enter the Baltic states, an area of some 65,000 square miles that dwarfed Prussia. Death's Head Hussars, wrapped in their grey cloaks, came to bring order, culture and civilisation to the primitive peoples of its newly acquired feudal fiefdom, Ober Ost. German soldiers conjured up images of themselves as *Landsknechte* in this 'war land'. German commanders Paul von Hindenburg and Erich Ludendorff ruled their new colony with an iron hand, using press-gangs of prisoners of war and native inhabitants to exploit the region's gigantic reserves of lumber, and sealing it off from the Eastern Front. The army mapped the region, re-established transport routes, registered everyone for a system of passes, generated propaganda and took control of education in order to produce a

27 Lunn, *Memoirs of the Maelstrom*, pp. 139–40. 28 *Ibid.*

population respectful of German authority and might.[29] Here was a foreshadowing, if far less murderous and rabidly racist – the army regarded the Jews as useful liaisons to the more 'primitive' peoples – of Hitler's drive to the East in the Second World War. In the tumult of the post-war era, German *Freikorps* units, composed mainly of former soldiers, would remain in the Baltic region to fight the Bolsheviks.

The Ottoman Empire

Next to Europe, the Ottoman Empire provided the focal point of imperial conflicts whose outcomes still directly affect our world today. The Turks secretly allied with the Germans in early August 1914. Two German cruisers, hotly pursued by the British in the Mediterranean, escaped through the Straits to Constantinople, then under the Turkish flag bombarded Russian Black Sea forts in October, thus announcing Ottoman entry into the war. The Entente powers seized the strategic initiative against the Ottoman Empire by attacking it in the Caucasus, at Gallipoli and in Mesopotamia, but the Caucasus front against the Russians would be the Ottomans' main front through 1916.

The Ottoman Turks lost an army in the winter of 1914–15 in the Caucasus Mountains, and then anticipated a Russian offensive. A division of Christian Armenians fought with the Russian army against the Turks and then declared a provisional Armenian government on Russian territory in April 1915. Russia's willingness to use Ottoman Armenians as a 'fifth column' rendered them 'pawns in a ruthless game of empire' that led to the Ottomans' Armenian genocide beginning in 1915.[30] The Ottomans, who had massacred some 200,000 Armenians in 1894–6 and another 25,000 in 1909, believed that the Armenians and the Russians were actively conspiring to raise a revolt of the Armenian population in eastern Anatolia. The Ottoman army and the ruling party formed a 'Special Organisation' to control any separatist movement, and then it deployed officers to lead units of brigands and convicts, an 'army of murderers', to 'destroy the Armenians and thereby do away with the Armenian question'.[31] When the anticipated Russian offensives and sporadic armed resistance by Armenians began in spring 1915, the Ottomans crushed the rebels brutally and in June deported Armenians en masse away from the

29 Vejas Gabriel Liulevicius, *War Land on the Eastern Front: Culture, National Identity and German Occupation in World War I* (Cambridge University Press, 2000), pp. 1–125.

30 McMeekin, *Russian Origins*, p. 242.

31 Panikos Panayi, *Minorities in Wartime: National and Racial Groupings in Europe, North America, and Australia during the Two World Wars* (Oxford: Berg, 1993), pp. 57–8.

Russian border and permanently to Mesopotamia and Syria. In the process, the Turks massacred, raped and brutalised Armenians and marched them into the desert to die.[32] Despite warnings from the Entente powers about punishment for 'crimes ... against humanity and civilization',[33] the Special Organisation continued its slaughter of the Armenians for another two years, ultimately killing some 800,000 Armenians, as the Russo-Ottoman war continued until the collapse of the Russian Empire in 1917.

Long before then the Turks had to turn their attention to confront the British, and ensuing events in the Middle East occurred, the consequences of which resonate to this very day. Britain's declaration of war reversed its traditional policy of protecting the Ottoman Empire as a barrier against Russia. The British government in London now determined to destroy the Ottoman Empire and use parts of it to lure Italy and the Balkan states into the war on the Entente side. They even contemplated allowing the Russians access to the Straits. British Secretary of State for War Lord H. H. Kitchener presumed that after the war the British would have to control most of the former Ottoman Empire, specifically the Arab part. Kitchener's men in the Arab Bureau in Cairo were already proposing to install a puppet Caliph, likely the Sharif and Emir of Mecca, Hussein Ibn Ali, and his two sons Abdullah and Feisal, through whom the British would reign.

The British government, with First Lord of the Admiralty Winston Churchill playing a leading role, decided to attack the Dardanelles with a substantial naval force to eliminate the Ottoman Empire and open a supply route to Russia. The Turks were waiting, having mined the straits and reinforced the forts there with mobile artillery. In mid March, when the naval force attempted to 'force the Narrows', it lost three battleships sunk by mines and six other capital ships were damaged. With British prestige at stake, Kitchener ordered Australian and New Zealand (Anzac), British and Indian troops under the command of General Sir Ian Hamilton to assault the Gallipoli peninsula, with the support of French forces. All gained a foothold, but that was all. Lieutenant Colonel Mustapha Kemal, the 34-year-old commander of the Turkish 19th Division, led a regiment of his men in a counter-attack with fixed bayonets against the Anzacs that beat the invaders off the high ground. For the next eight months, both sides launched ferocious and suicidal attacks and counter-attacks against the other. Men who survived

32 Edward J. Erickson, *Ordered to Die: A History of the Ottoman Army in the First World War* (Westport, CT: Greenwood Press), pp. 95–104.

33 Robert Melson, *Revolution and Genocide: On the Origins of the Armenian Genocide and the Holocaust* (University of Chicago Press, 1992), p. 148.

the shells, machine-gun fire and frenzied hand-to-hand combat died of diseases such as malaria, dysentery and enteric fever in the summer's oppressive heat. In the winter, as raging winter storms drowned soldiers in their trenches, a new commander, General Sir Charles Monro, recommended withdrawal which, when it ended in early January 1916, proved to be the Entente's greatest success of the campaign. The Entente had suffered some 265,000 casualties; the outnumbered Turks, 218,000.

The Australian media interpreted the heroic performance of the Anzacs at Gallipoli as a seminal event in the birth of Australian and New Zealand nationalism, and starting in 1916, Australians celebrated 25 April as Anzac Day, 'the natal day of Australia's entrance into the world's politics and history'.[34] After the war, Gallipoli would become the symbol of Australian national identity as it became a sovereign Dominion. Gallipoli proved equally important in the evolution of modern Turkish nationalism, as it heralded the rise to fame and leadership of Mustapha Kemal, who would become the symbol and the leader of post-war Turkey.

The disaster at Gallipoli gave new impetus to a British invasion of Mesopotamia that had begun in 1914. Unlike the British government in London, the British government in India, long accustomed to regarding the Russians as the greatest threat to Indian security, would tolerate neither Russian access to the Straits nor a unified Arabia in any form. Instead, it focused on protecting British interests, particularly the pipeline, refinery and terminal of the Anglo-Persian Oil Company in Mesopotamia and the Persian Gulf, as the Royal Navy had begun its transition from coal to oil in 1911. British imperial forces consequently took the offensive, and then, lured by the prospect of seizing Baghdad, advanced 115 miles up the Shatt-al-Arab channel to the junction of the Tigris and Euphrates rivers, and took the city of Kurnah in early December.

In early 1915, Indian Army forces moved further inland up the river system to eliminate Turkish threats to oilfields across the border in Persia. The British imperial forces used a variety of shallow-draught boats to navigate the marshy, three-foot-deep waterways of the interior in their hunt for Arab sailing vessels, or *dhows*, engaged in supplying the growing Turkish forces. A Turkish counter-attack in April ended in a disastrous rout, and prompted the 6th Indian Division under Major General Charles Townshend to attack further up the River Tigris to seize Kut-al-Amara, and then up the River Euphrates in

34 John F. Williams, *ANZACs, the Media, and the Great War* (Sydney: University of New South Wales Press, 1999), p. 110.

the west to seize Nasiriyah. Summer heat and disease notwithstanding, British imperial forces had advanced 140 miles inland on the waterways, and now Baghdad beckoned irresistibly. The Indian Army sailed another 180 miles to seize Kut-al-Amara, as the Turks retreated to fortified positions at Ctesiphon, thirty miles below Baghdad.

Late in October, the War Committee in London, in accord with the Raj, the British government in India, determined to strike for Baghdad to sever German communications with, and thus intrigues in Persia and Afghanistan, and to salvage prestige in the Muslim world lost at Gallipoli. In late November Townshend's division assaulted Ctesiphon, only to encounter Turkish artillery that drove the division back down the river, where Townshend and his troops found themselves under siege in Kut-al-Amara by Ottoman forces in December. The British imperial forces surrendered on 29 April 1916 and were marched off into captivity. They had overreached, and turned victory into defeat in the 'Bastard War'.

In February the British War Office assumed 'paternity' of the Mesopotamian campaign from the British government of India, and sent new officers and massed supplies. A new commander, Lieutenant General Sir Stanley Maude, began a methodical and steady advance towards Kut-al-Amara in September, then attacked up the River Tigris in December and entered Baghdad in March 1917. In the fall he resumed his offensive to capture as much of Mesopotamia as possible, although he himself died of cholera in November 1917. In 1918 the British imperial forces continued their advance through Mesopotamia and ended a war that had started so badly by occupying the oil-rich city of Mosul on 1 November.

As the Gallipoli and Mesopotamian disasters unfolded in 1915, Kitchener's advisers in the Arab Bureau in Cairo devised an 'Egyptian Empire' scheme, in which High Commissioner Kitchener would rule a single Arab state through two figureheads, the Sharif of Mecca as spiritual leader and the monarch of Egypt as political front. The Arab Bureau convinced itself and then the Cabinet in London that the Arabs in the Ottoman Empire might fight with the British if they could enlist Hussein, who was proposing himself as ruler of the Arab world. The British army would have to invade Syria and Palestine, since Hussein had no forces or unified political following, but such a move would threaten French interests in the Middle East. Mark Sykes, the staunchest proponent of this imperial plan, consequently met with François Picot, French colonial expert, in late 1915, and hammered out the secret Sykes-Picot Agreement in May 1916. In essence, Britain and France partitioned the Ottoman Empire. France would rule or control Lebanon and Syria, while

Britain would control Mesopotamia and the part of Palestine with ports connected to Mesopotamia.

In June 1916 Hussein, who was receiving funds from the Turks and the British, declared an Arab Revolt against the Ottoman Empire with only a few thousand tribesmen and no army. While Sykes began popularising the concept of the 'Middle East', the British funded the revolt and sent missions, one of which included a small, quiet, junior intelligence officer named T. E. Lawrence, who would become British liaison to Hussein's son Feisal, who commanded the tribesmen in the revolt.[35]

Lord Kitchener, who had not valued the Middle East, died when the cruiser *Hampshire*, taking him to Russia, sank from a German mine in June 1916. In the Prime Minister, David Lloyd George, who had replaced Herbert Asquith in December 1916, Britain gained a leader who valued the Middle East for its own sake and as a route to Egypt. Determined to establish British hegemony there, he ignored the Sykes-Picot Agreement and ordered British imperial forces in Egypt to attack in order to establish British power in Mesopotamia and Palestine. In March the Imperial War Cabinet in London plotted the post-war reconfiguration of the British Empire. Not only did it entail the independence of the white Dominions of South Africa, Canada, Australia and New Zealand, it also sought to connect the Empire in Africa and Asia. Palestine and Mesopotamia would provide Britain with the land bridge connecting the two continents and creating a continuous empire from the Atlantic to the mid Pacific Oceans. Lloyd George also sought Palestine for a Jewish homeland, and a Jewish Palestine would become the 'bridge between Africa, Asia, and Europe'. On 2 November, as British forces attacked towards Jerusalem, British Foreign Secretary Arthur Balfour conveyed to Lord Rothschild the government's intention to facilitate the establishment of a Jewish homeland in Palestine, a declaration that the United States and France later approved. What had begun in 1915 as a sideshow, namely the war against the Ottoman Empire, had now become the main theatre of Lloyd George's imperial policy.[36]

The Ottomans repulsed the first two British offensives in the spring, but in June 1917 General Sir Edmund Allenby, commissioned by Lloyd George to deliver Jerusalem as a Christmas present for the people at home, arrived from the Western Front to command the British forces. Allenby attacked in late

35 David Fromkin, *A Peace to End All Peace: The Fall of the Ottoman Empire and the Creation of the Modern Middle East* (New York: Henry Holt, 1989), pp. 168–98.

36 *Ibid.*, pp. 267–301.

October and entered Jerusalem on 9 December. The Arab Revolt under Feisal's leadership emerged full-blown in 1917, in the process transforming little Lawrence into the legendary 'Lawrence of Arabia'. Although its military significance paled before Allenby's brute force, its political implications proved significant. When Allenby launched his offensive in October, Feisal's Arab forces protected Allenby's right flank. Later in 1918 Allenby waited to take the offensive to conquer the rest of Palestine and advance towards Damascus, Syria until September, while Feisal's tribesmen continued to harass the Turks and seize their transport lines. Allenby entered Damascus on 2 October and swept on 200 miles to Aleppo by 26 October, bringing the Syrian campaign to a victorious close.

Africa

The global war of the empires in their African colonial possessions began simultaneously with the war in Europe in 1914. Entente colonies promptly invaded their German neighbours, although German colonial governors had pleaded, in vain, for neutrality. The Germans had also argued against the use of African troops in colonial warfare to forestall black men killing white men, but ultimately all the imperial powers mobilised their African subjects either as soldiers or labourers to such an extent that the war actually depopulated some regions.

The British government planned to seize German colonies as spoils of war. In the opinion of the Prime Minister, Herbert Asquith, the British Cabinet 'behaved more like a gang of Elizabethan buccaneers than a meek collection of black-coated Liberal Ministers'.[37] In August 1914 the German colonies in West and East Africa, which possessed key ports and powerful wireless stations, were attacked by colonial forces from surrounding French and British colonies, Indian forces and white South African and Rhodesian forces. These forces crushed the German colonies of Togoland, Cameroon and South West Africa rather handily between 1914 and 1916.

German East Africa was larger in area than France and Germany combined, and surrounded by British, Belgian and Portuguese colonies. Initial neutrality between the British and German governors yielded to small offensives by both sides in September. In November, a British Imperial Expeditionary Force of 8,000 British and Indian troops landed at the port of Tanga, its commander,

37 Paul G. Halpern, *A Naval History of World War I* (Annapolis, MD: Naval Institute Press, 1994), p. 83.

Major General A. E. Aitken, vowing to make 'short work of a lot of niggers' and to 'thrash the Germans before Christmas'.[38] Aitken was the first, but not the last, to underestimate his opponent, Lieutenant Colonel Paul von Lettow-Vorbeck and his *Schutztruppe* of a total of 260 European officers and non-commissioned officers, 184 African non-commissioned officers and 2,472 African soldiers, or *askaris*. Aitken lost the ensuing clash and his command, as Lettow-Vorbeck, outnumbered eight to one, counter-attacked and routed the Indian troops with minimal loss to his own men. The war in East Africa was just beginning. Lettow-Vorbeck acknowledged that defeat was inevitable, but wanted to prolong the struggle as long as possible to deflect Entente forces from the Western Front. He restricted his forces to guerrilla warfare, and by the end of 1915 his little army had grown to 3,000 white and 11,000 black soldiers. The British, in contrast, refused to arm black men on a large scale in East Africa, and formed no new King's African Rifle battalions in the west in 1915.

In February 1916, South African Jan Smuts assumed command of British imperial forces in East Africa, right after a German force of 1,300 had routed a 6,000 man force of Indians, Africans, English, Rhodesians and white South Africans, the last of whom, new to war, had turned and run in the face of a bayonet charge by yelling German *askaris*. Smuts launched 40,000 men against Lettow-Vorbeck's 16,000, but capture as much land as he might, Smuts could not run his German opponent to ground and destroy the German colonial army. Lettow-Vorbeck's *askaris*, or 'damned kaffirs' (niggers) as Smuts called them,[39] proved to be better soldiers in the bush than Smuts's white or Indian troops. Disease and parasitic infestations, from chiggers to guinea worm, plagued all the soldiers, regardless of rank or colour, while the steadily moving struggle consumed tens of thousands of porters who carried the soldiers' equipment. The war depopulated the region, created social instability, destroyed already primitive communications and transportation and often led to famine. As 1916 continued, Smuts acquired more black soldiers from West Africa, whose effectiveness he grudgingly acknowledged by replacing white South Africans with a Nigerian Brigade. By fall 1916, British imperial forces numbered 80,000 men against Lettow-Vorbeck's 10,000, but the German force continued to elude its pursuers.

38 Byron Farwell, *The Great War in Africa, 1914–1918* (New York: W. W. Norton, 1986), pp. 163, 165.

39 *Ibid.*, p. 266.

In January 1917 Smuts relinquished his command, proclaimed the defeat of the German resistance, and in March joined the Imperial War Cabinet conference in London at Lloyd George's invitation. Yet the fighting in East Africa continued, as Smuts's successors substantially increased the number of African soldiers. After a pitched battle in mid October 1917, Lettow-Vorbeck withdrew and invaded Portuguese territory; the British Empire had finally driven him from German East Africa. As 1918 began, the British imperial forces were now more than 90 per cent black, either African or West Indian. With the British in hot pursuit, the dwindling German forces plundered Portuguese supply depots, re-entered German East Africa in the fall of 1918, and then marched north-west into Northern Rhodesia. Lettow-Vorbeck learned of the German surrender on 13 November, and on 25 November he surrendered his tiny army of 1,300 men, the last German force to do so.

While the imperial forces waged war against one another, African rebellions against the imperial powers remained isolated. The British easily crushed a small uprising in Nyasaland in East Africa in January, and beat back an invasion of Egypt by the Senussi brotherhood from Libya. French soldiers suppressed another revolt in southern Tunisia. The colonial powers suppressed information on the scope of these conflicts and the brutal suppression of the rebels, which would have demonstrated the hypocrisy of their condemnation of German pre-war atrocities in Africa.[40]

Yet one struggle, the Volta-Bani War in French West Africa from late 1915 through to 1917, demonstrated the potential extent and savagery of these struggles. The onset of the war in Europe drained French and native forces from the region, and the violent and impulsive French colonial administration attempted first to repress the Muslims and then to conscript local men. The villages of the region declared war on the French colonial administration, and in a series of escalating battles in which the well-armed colonial forces killed thousands of tribesmen, the warriors, who were determined to persevere despite their losses, repelled the French, shattering the myth of their invincibility.[41]

The French, wretchedly frustrated by their failure to crush the tribes, amassed more soldiers and artillery and proceeded to wipe entire villages off the map, transforming the region into a 'desert' and destroying the tribes and their food sources throughout 1916. After a final sortie early in 1917

40 Mahir Şaul and Patrick Royer, *West African Challenge to Empire: Culture and History in the Volta-Bani Anticolonial War* (Athens, OH: Ohio University Press, 2001), pp. 1, 14, 24–5.

41 *Ibid.*, pp. 127–72.

essentially finished the war, the French continued to execute captured rebel leaders throughout 1917. The French had mobilised the largest force in their colonial history – some 2,500 West African *tirailleurs* and 2,500 auxiliaries with cannon and machine guns – to subdue villages with a total population of some 8–900,000 inhabitants. They slaughtered an estimated 30,000 villagers in a 'total war' in their successful 'pacification' of the Volta-Bani region.[42]

East Asia

As the British focused on their German opponent in Europe, they needed support in East Asia and in the Pacific and Indian Oceans; they turned to their Japanese ally for assistance. The Royal Navy needed assistance protecting the global sea lanes and British merchant ships from German raiders, supporting overseas expeditions against the German colonies and transporting Dominion and colonial troops to wartime theatres. When the British government requested Japanese naval assistance, the Japanese, recognising the war in Europe as an opportunity for expansion in China and the Pacific, responded enthusiastically. The Japanese army coveted further territory and influence in China, while the navy eyed Germany's Pacific possessions – the Marshall, Mariana and Caroline islands. Japan ordered Germany to clear eastern waters and surrender its leasehold of Kiaochou in China's Shandong province. On 23 August, Japanese forces, wasting no time in case of a short war in Europe, landed on the Shandong Peninsula and captured the port of Qingdao. When the President of the Chinese Republic, Yuan Shikai, declared the German territory in Shandong a war zone, the Japanese army seized this cloak of legitimacy to occupy the entire province, which in turn prompted Yuan to demand their total withdrawal. Clearly, Japanese assurances to Western powers that they merely intended to drive the Germans out of China and seek no territorial aggrandisement were moot.

In January 1915 the Japanese government presented the Chinese with Twenty-One Demands, which included recognition of its rights in Shandong and the extension of its lease on Manchuria for ninety-nine years. The most extreme demands would compromise Chinese sovereignty, grant the Japanese economic supremacy in China and make the Chinese government dependent on Japanese advisers and police officials. The Japanese government ultimately withdrew the

42 *Ibid.*, pp. 212, 230, 4–5.

extreme demands and agreed to relinquish some of their territorial acquisitions, and the Chinese government agreed to the ultimatum in May 1915.[43]

Yuan persisted in challenging Japanese privileges and authority in Manchuria, Mongolia and Korea, and the Japanese government decided in March 1916 to aid Chinese opposition movements. The Japanese government was now supporting Yuan symbolically while inciting opposition against him as it tried to increase Chinese dependence on Japan and secure Great Power recognition of Japan's pre-eminence in Asia. Behind the scenes, an increasingly impatient Japanese army command contemplated provoking a civil war as an excuse to subdue China. In fall 1916 a new Japanese Cabinet under General Terauchi Masatake used loans to the Chinese government to increase its influence, and successfully encouraged the Chinese government to sever ties with and declare war on Germany, all with the aim of gaining European recognition of its dominion over former German territories at a future peace conference. With the virtual elimination of the European powers from Asia, both the Japanese army and navy were also increasingly concerned during 1917 about an eventual conflict with the United States over the Pacific and East Asia.[44]

The Japanese force that deployed to Siberia in July 1918 in the Entente intervention to contain the newly formed Bolshevik government in Russia – some 80,000 soldiers in comparison to the 10,000-man forces that the British, French and United States sent – indicated the intent to strengthen Japan's presence on the Asian continent. Japanese governmental officials had already contemplated a major incursion into North Manchuria and Siberia in order to extend the Japanese Empire into northern Asia and reduce Siberia to a client state. The Japanese clearly planned to fill the vacuum in East Asia caused by the collapse of the Russian Empire in order to become a great imperial master like Great Britain and the United States. The army also pursued continental expansion with the domestic goal of securing primacy over the navy, which was facing an expanding American fleet in the Pacific that justified a greatly increased budget.

Ultimately Japan gained Shandong province and control of former German possessions in the South Pacific, but its wartime intrigue and self-aggrandisement in East Asia aroused the concerns of Great Britain and the United States. On the other hand, the Western powers' tendency to ignore the

43 Chris Wrigley (ed.), *The First World War and the International Economy* (Cheltenham: Edward Elgar, 2000), p. 115.

44 Frederick R. Dickinson, *War and National Reinvention: Japan in the Great War, 1914–1919* (Cambridge, MA: Harvard University Press, 1999), pp. 119–53, 157–80.

Japanese delegation at Versailles and their rejection of Japan's proposed non-discrimination covenant in the post-war treaties, indicated the West's continued perception of the Japanese as a second-rank power and people, and infuriated the Japanese.

Conclusion

The Great War of 1914–18 began and ended as a global conflict that imperial powers waged in Europe, the Middle East, Africa and Asia. Great Britain and France, with overseas colonies and control of the seas, relied on their possessions for men and materials to fight the war in Europe. The German government had stridently protested its encirclement by the Entente after 1905. By the end of 1914 that potential encirclement was not merely continental, but global, and Germany ultimately lost all of its overseas possessions; its thirty-year effort to gain a 'place in the sun' was in a shambles. The sheer complexity of the global conflict meant that its issues would elude simple solutions.

European and native soldiers of the empires had fought in Europe and around the globe. As the war eroded the traditional prohibition against using coloured troops from the colonies to fight against Europeans, it heightened the fear of white people towards peoples of colour. The monstrous slaughter of Europeans and their use of colonial soldiers to fight even along the Western Front, aroused the spectre of the demise of European supremacy. This very fear further exposed the true nature of imperialism in its insidious exploitation of coloured peoples through division, conquest and continuing repressive violence. The participation of African and Asian troops in the slaughter of white men, their access to white women in ways theretofore unimaginable and, finally, the French use of Senegalese soldiers in the post-war occupation of western Germany – all threatened the traditional imperial order of racial supremacy.

The war and the Russian Revolution, the latter the work of egalitarian Jewish Bolshevism, or 'Judeo-Bolshevism', as conservatives in the Western world labelled this new threat, exacerbated racial fears in the Western world. Anti-Semitism was rife, as fears that Bolshevism would penetrate the colonial world, undermine European power and destroy a racist, capitalist and imperialist world prompted racist theorists to propose the annihilation of the threatening 'inferior' races. The war thus heightened the imperialist racism already evident in the pre-war Western world. American Lothrop Stoddard's book, *The Rising Tide of Color against White World Supremacy*, published in 1920, lamented the irreparable losses of genetically superior white men in the Great

War. Other races would view the divisions of the European war as a sign of weakness, and Asians – Japanese, Chinese and Indians – might unite and assert themselves. The French use of African troops in Europe compromised and posed the worst danger to European superiority.

In light of these pervasive fears, it is not surprising that only the white Dominions – Australia and New Zealand, Canada and South Africa – became sovereign states and achieved autonomy within the British Empire. The Entente did not consider offering national self-determination to the coloured peoples of their empires. The war had drawn some 1.5 million Indians into military service for the British Empire and brought heavy taxes, war loans, requisitions of grain and raw materials and inflation, but it did not bring independence or even autonomy. Instead, the British resorted to repression and violence during and after the war to maintain their power in India, culminating in the Amritsar massacre of 1919. Such acts propelled the rise of Mahatma Gandhi, who launched a non-violent Non-Cooperation Movement. The British responded to any outbreaks of violence by crushing the movement and imprisoning Gandhi for six years in 1922.

Jan Smuts designed the mandate system of the League of Nations as a substitute for annexation of Germany's former colonies to appease Woodrow Wilson.[45] Europeans deemed Class A mandates the Arab regions of Mesopotamia (Iraq), Palestine, Syria and Lebanon eligible for independence at some indeterminate future time, but with no say in the matter. Class B and C Mandates in Africa and the Pacific faced no prospect of independence, although Blaise Diagne convened a Pan-African Congress in Paris that proclaimed the right of self-determination for African peoples.[46] Hô Chi Minh, a waiter in Paris during the Peace Conference, petitioned for the freedom of Indochina as his countrymen had served on the Salonica front and laboured in France, but to no avail.

African-American intellectual, W. E. B. DuBois, was an organiser and participant in the Pan-African Congress of 1919, and although he pleaded eloquently for the right of self-determination for African peoples, the American colonial expert at the Paris Peace Conference, historian George Louis Beer, declared, 'The negro [sic] race has hitherto shown no capacity for progressive development except under the tutelage of other peoples.'[47] The United States, which

45 Manfred F. Boemeke *et al.* (eds.), *The Treaty of Versailles: A Reassessment after 75 Years* (Cambridge University Press, 1998), pp. 572, 578, 584.
46 David Levering Lewis, *W. E. B. DuBois: Biography of a Race, 1868–1918* (New York: Henry Holt, 1993), pp. 574–8.
47 Boemeke *et al.*, *Treaty of Versailles*, pp. 494–5.

supported the mandate system and even acquired some Pacific islands in the bargain, never joined the League of Nations and assured itself of the immunity of the Monroe Doctrine of 1823, which asserted America's claim to dominate the Western Hemisphere, from any general agreements.

More critically, as Lothrop Stoddard's book on the concern over the demise of the white race suggested, white Americans viewed African Americans with the same prejudiced attitudes with which their European counterparts viewed the coloured peoples of the world. African-American soldiers had served primarily as labour troops, because of the fears of white Southerners in particular that arming black soldiers would enable them to challenge Jim Crow upon their return. If Amritsar symbolised the British repression of Indians, the race riots and lynchings of black Americans, including soldiers in uniform, that dotted the United States during the war and into the post-war years, were intended to disabuse African Americans of any ideas of improved, not to mention, equal rights that they hoped to attain through loyally serving their country. A popular American song jovially intoned, 'How're you gonna keep 'em down on the farm, after they've seen Paree?' With murderous violence; answered white mobs lynching black soldiers throughout the South and burning black residential and commercial neighbourhoods to the ground in Tulsa, Oklahoma.

In January 1919 the British Empire reached its zenith, with more than a million additional square miles, primarily in former Ottoman domains, as Lloyd George laid claim to dominance in the Middle East. In April 1920 the British and French agreed secretly to monopolise the oil supplies of the Middle East, and in July the French took control of Syria and would later rule in Syria and Lebanon. After riots in Egypt and Egyptian demands for complete independence in 1919 and revolt in Iraq in 1920, an over-extended British government granted both limited autonomy in 1922. That same year, Britain assumed the League mandate over Palestine, west of the River Jordan, while Eastern Palestine became Jordan.

More than a million African soldiers had fought on various fronts, and even more Africans served as porters or bearers. Most West and East African soldiers, though they no longer feared Europeans and had often lost respect for imperial power and prestige, essentially sought to resume their lives.[48] The war in Africa had led to famine, disease, destruction and depopulation, and

48 Lunn, *Memoirs of the Maelstsrom*, pp. 187–205, 215, 229–35; M. E. Page, *The Chiwaya War: Malawians and the First World War* (Boulder, CO: Westview Press, 2000), pp. 135–8, 164–6, 203–6, 229–35; and James J. Mathews, 'World War I and the rise of African nationalism: Nigerian veterans as catalysts of political change', *Journal of Modern African Studies*, 20:3 (1982), pp. 493–502.

had redrawn the imperial map of Africa, but it also imparted a new sense of black African nationalism and sowed ideas about 'self-determination of peoples and the accountability of colonial powers', which would influence events later in the twentieth century.[49] West Indian soldiers' service in their regiments in Africa and the Middle East stimulated the rise of black nationalism, as they began the struggle for national liberation in the British West Indies.[50]

Thus did the war of 1914–18, far from fulfilling Wilson's adage that it would make the world safe for democracy, end by protecting and enhancing the global rule of whites over other races. Still, violence in Egypt, India, Korea and China in 1919 and after exposed the fissures in the imperial world. The costs of the war weakened the imperial powers to an extent not clear at the Armistice, but the war both strengthened and weakened the imperial framework as a transnational system of white domination. Indeed, the beginning of the end of empire can be dated from 1919. The achievement of the aspirations for freedom and independence of the coloured peoples of the world would require another global war of an even greater magnitude in 1939–45.

With the end of the war and demobilisation of the armed forces, advocates of the new air arm confronted the challenge to justify and preserve air forces amid economic pressures and challenges from the older services. In Great Britain, the Royal Air Force, under the leadership of Chief of Air Staff Sir Hugh Trenchard, survived the post-war reductions through a policy of 'air control', policing the far corners of the British Empire more cheaply and effectively than the army. The successful use of a few RAF bombers to locate, then bomb and strafe, the camp of the 'Mad Mullah' in Somaliland in 1919 and 1920, and ultimately drive him into Ethiopia where he died, convinced the British government to enlarge the RAF's role in policing the Middle East. The RAF further stationed two squadrons in Ireland for population control, 'to fly low over the small villages and inspire considerable fear among the ignorant peasantry'.[51] Such events in Ireland, Africa and the Middle East demonstrated that the wartime progress of military aviation enabled the realisation of British pre-war visions of imperial domination through airplanes.

49 M. Crowder, 'The First World War and its consequences', in A. Adu Boahen (ed.), *General History of Africa*, vol. VII: *Africa under Colonial Domination: 1880–1935* (London: Heinemann Educational for UNESCO, 1985), pp. 283–311.

50 W. F. Elkins, 'A source of black nationalism in the Caribbean: the revolt of the British West Indies regiment at Taranto, Italy', *Science and Society*, 34 (1970), pp. 99–103.

51 *United States Military Intelligence, 1917–1927*, 20 vols. (New York: Garland, 1978), vol. XI, Part 2, p. 626.

The other colonial powers followed suit. The French, Italian and Spanish governments all employed airplanes to bomb, strafe and even drop poison gas on rebellious native populations in North Africa during the colonial wars of the 1920s. This practice culminated in fascist Italy's invasion of Ethiopia in 1935, during which Italian warplanes did all three to Ethiopian soldiers and civilians. The great war for empire had perfected more effective weapons – aircraft and poison gas – for European powers to use to control and annihilate native populations during the 1920s and 1930s. Thus what is now termed 'asymmetrical war', juxtaposing high-tech white armies against low-tech non-white populations, was born in the aftermath of the Great War. Its ravages have marked the century which has passed in ways which ought to make us pause. The long shadow of the 1914–18 war can still be seen today.

16
Africa

BILL NASSON

It is fairly commonplace for historians of modern Africa to see the two world wars, although European in origin, as watersheds in the history of the continent in the twentieth century. In one crucial – and general – respect, the significance of the First World War in African history was its place in the chronology of European colonisation. The war broke out at a pivotal moment when the leading colonial states were seeking to consolidate their territorial grip and to entrench their authority after the immense upheavals and sprawling violence of the previous two to three decades, linked to the imperial 'Scramble for Africa'. That great incursion into, and conquest of, the continent had been achieved virtually without warring between competing European interests. In the sense of their ordering of colonial arenas, the conflagration which erupted in 1914 can be considered as marking the culmination of the Scramble, and as finally tidying up and sealing the phase of European partition of the continent.

The war was, in the words of one authoritative recent history, 'the end of the beginning'.[1] Or, in other earlier words, those of another notable historian of Africa, the First World War may well be viewed as marking the final 'high point of the reign of crude force', lowering the curtain on the turbulent era of conquest and confirming colonial 'consolidation'.[2] If Europe's *own* settlement of 1919 was fated not to last for long, overseas, the partitioning settlement of a pacified Africa by its colonial powers would go on to endure for rather longer, setting the confines within which Africans would have to live.

Inextricably bound up with the experience of the First World War itself, and intrinsic to its outcome in the region, was the attainment of the fundamental objectives of colonial administrations, whose reach had at times

1 R. J. Reid, *A History of Modern Africa: 1800 to the Present* (Oxford: Wiley-Blackwell, 2009), p. 191.
2 B. Freund, *The Making of Contemporary Africa: The Development of African Society since 1800* (Basingstoke: Macmillan, 1998), p. 112.

been exceeding their grasp. During the conflict, or in its early aftermath, remaining pockets of African resistance or armed opposition to European encroachments were conclusively subdued, and the stabilising of colonial regimes and the formation of uncontested military power and general security was attained.

While not matching this in overall magnitude, there are, perhaps, at least four other striking features of Africa's entanglement with the 1914–18 war. First, and perhaps most self-evident, is that it was the second of two great imperial exceptions. The first essentially European war 'fought amongst and profoundly affecting African populations' had been the major war waged by Britain to subdue Boer republicanism, the Anglo-Boer War, or South African War, of 1899–1902.[3] A second feature, inescapably quixotic in nature, is that the first and last shots of a war which was won and lost in Europe were discharged on opposite sides of the African continent. Thirdly, for many regions and numerous inhabitants, the absorption into a global war was virtually imperceptible, and its impact on life barely felt. Indeed, for some remote and unconnected rural communities, the war simply passed over their heads. If some shortages came after 1914, such hardships were no more than customary, given the instabilities of local ecological systems. Moreover, the nature of colonial control that these people experienced in 1918 was more or less unchanged from what it had been in 1913, for instance. In that respect, not only were the battlegrounds of the First World War here 'less murderous' than on Europe's Western Front or Eastern Front.[4] For millions of people, the war would probably not have registered in their consciousness, let alone run across their faces.

Equally, at the same time, some of those large tracts of Africa that were locked most directly into the war were not without their share of its more harrowing circumstances of acute civilian suffering and loss of life, as fallen soldiers and labouring carriers and porters dropped into the soil of their native bush as well as into the fields of Europe. Lapping down, here the war triggered a series of what might be termed 'knock-on' events, processes and implications for colonial societies and economies across stretches of the continent. That larger tremor is the fourth and deepest inroad made by the European war, as respective imperial powers set about trying to extract the maximum

3 T. Ranger, 'Africa', in M. Howard and Wm. Roger Louis (eds.), *The Oxford History of the Twentieth Century* (Oxford University Press, 2002), p. 266.

4 P. Murphy, 'Britain as a global power in the twentieth century', in A. Thompson (ed.), *Britain's Experience of Empire in the Twentieth Century* (Oxford University Press, 2012), p. 38.

manpower and material resources from their colonial dependencies, and, in the case of British South Africa, a compliant Dominion ally yet also a satellite with its own sub-imperial national ambitions.

The declaration of European hostilities had immediate African consequences, as Britain and France lost no time early in August in turning upon Germany's lightly held West African colonial territories of Togoland and Kamerun. British entry into the war had ended any prospect of the conflict being confined to a European theatre. In effect the opening round of the First World War, this minor West African campaign was undertaken by British forces from the Gold Coast and French forces from Dahomey. Striking from the west and the east, these swift invasions terminated an early flurry of tortuous but stagey transactions between Allied and German colonial officials about sparing West Africa through the possibility of some regional armistice. Although almost all of the killing and dying would end up being borne by colonial African soldiers, European administrators were nervous about gambling with their inviolate position of dominance – who knew how Africans might react to the unsavoury spectacle of white men bloodying one another?

Little more than a sandy coastal sliver, Togoland was pocketed easily by the Allies. Kamerun, however, proved a harder nut to crack. Its mountainous interior with its densely forested approaches provided its 1,000 German and over 3,000 African troops under General Karl Zimmermann with stiff defensive prospects, and the swaying contest for the colony dragged on until February 1916, when the last of the last-ditch German defenders surrendered. It 'stuttered' to an end.[5] The French film director, Jean-Jacques Annaud, satirised this spurting little West African war in his 1976 anti-militarist black war comedy, *Noirs et blancs en couleur* ('Black and white in colour'), a story of dozy French and German colonists who eventually discover from the arrival of newspapers, several months old, that their countries are at war. Dutifully, they cease trading and other cross-border transactions to become adversaries in an ineptly conducted skirmishing war. Mindful of conserving their own valuable lives, they conscript cheap local Africans to do the fighting.[6]

5 G. Graichen and H. Grunder, *Deutsche Kolonien: Traum und Trauma* (Hamburg: Ullstein Verlag, 2007), p. 323.

6 B. Nasson, 'Cheap if not always cheerful: French West Africa in the world wars in *Black and White in Colour* and *Le Camp de Thiaroye*', in V. Bickford-Smith and R. Mendelsohn (eds.), *Black and White in Colour: African History on Film* (Oxford: James Currey, 2006), pp. 148–56.

Berlin's colony further south, German South West Africa, also occasioned early mobilisation and invasion by enemy forces. At the beginning of August, Britain's newest Dominion, the post-1910 Union of South Africa, was requested by its Colonial Secretary, Lewis Harcourt, to render London what he termed, memorably, 'a great and pressing imperial service'.[7] This was to mount a snap expedition to seize the harbours and to snuff out the wireless stations of neighbouring German South West Africa, in order to counter Berlin's naval threat in the South Atlantic Ocean. Again, with a minuscule mounted infantry garrison, backed by a handful of paramilitary police and a scratch contingent of reservists, this enormous colony (virtually twice the size of the German Empire in mainland Europe) was poorly defended. Its vulnerability was due not only to its massively exposed frontiers that were impossible to plug. Such defence preparedness as there was focused almost entirely on the spectre of possible internal African unrest in the light of the Herero rising of the early 1900s, rather than on the meeting of any external attack, let alone a combined land and amphibious assault by a strong and well-armed invader.

For German South West Africa's governor, Theodor Seitz, and his handful of senior officers, there was not much more to pin hope on than South Africa's domestic war-related troubles rumbling on and delaying an invasion of the territory until Germany could prevail in Europe, and then divert military resources to shore up its south-western position. Granted, the German colony had been given a little breathing space by the war not getting off to a good start within the Union's divided white Afrikaner-Anglo minority. A strategic pin on the board of British imperial defence, with the Ottomans an ally of the Germans and the Suez Canal route to India and Australia thus at risk, South Africa's sea lane around the Cape of Good Hope 'resumed its former importance'.[8] The country's Dominion status bound it constitutionally to follow the Crown on international decisions on war or peace. Its government was also, in any event, pro-war.

But, unlike the white settler dominions of the Pacific, in 1914 it lacked an emphatic popular mandate for war. Before an invasion could be got underway, there was a surge of anti-war Afrikaner nationalist opposition to be faced down and an insurrectionary 1914–15 Afrikaner Rebellion to be suppressed. That accomplished, with its assembly of vastly stronger forces,

7 See G. l'Ange, *Urgent Imperial Service: South African Forces in German South West Africa, 1914–1915* (Johannesburg: Ashanti, 1991).

8 A. Lentin, *Jan Smuts: Man of Courage and Vision* (Johannesburg: Jonathan Ball, 2010), pp. 30–1.

superior transport, supplies and equipment, South Africa overwhelmed its German opponents in a few short months, forcing surrender in July 1915. Following the first armistice of the First World War, German South West Africa passed effectively into South African hands and military rule under martial law until the early 1920s. Part of an ambitious African expansionist strategy fuelled by wartime opportunity, for the Union government conquest implied 'entering the prestigious adult world of colonial power'.[9]

With its combined death toll of just over 200, this engagement in South West Africa was, like the campaigning in West Africa, a relative sideshow compared to the spread and depth of armed hostilities in eastern and eastern-central zones, where the local violence of the war was felt at its most devastating. It was there that the conduct of fighting was most bitter and unrelenting, where the regional consequences of economic and social disintegration were most extreme, and where agonisingly drawn-out campaigning easily equalled the duration of the war in Europe and provided a version of its attritional aspects. The enormous dislocation, waste and brutality of a campaign which snaked across the region between British East Africa and Portuguese East Africa, thrusting across into north-eastern Rhodesia and Nyasaland, are a far cry from the romanticised or mythologised representations of the conflict in this part of the continent, which remain a staple of the war as imagined in more popular visual and literary culture. The quintessential film reflection has long been the inland gunboat bravado of John Huston's 1951 *The African Queen*, set in German East Africa in September 1914, while Peter Yates's 1971 *Murphy's War*, with its skulking German raider and river battle, reprised the Second World War as *The African Queen* had the first. A measure of recent literary reflections would include William Boyd's 1982 *An Ice-Cream War*, dealing with what the novel's dustjacket calls 'a ridiculous and little-reported campaign being waged in East Africa', although this picaresque satire is not short on mordant irony and grubbiness. To it could be added the overlapping evocation of Giles Foden's 2004 *Mimi and Toutou Go Forth: The Bizarre Battle of Lake Tanganyika*, in which a band of predictably intrepid and eccentric British misfits set out to wrest control of Lake Tanganyika from prowling German warships. In effect, the grim East African conflict becomes a watery war of white men, its toll that of those individual patriotic adventurers who had pushed their luck too far.

In reality, for the Allied forces which were engaged in criss-crossing combat with German forces manoeuvring down from East Africa into south-eastern

9 M. Wallace, *A History of Namibia* (London: Hurst & Co., 2011), p. 216.

Africa and across into central areas, there was precious little experience of a freshwater war of the waves. If it was a sideshow to Flanders, it was still a large sideshow, a deadly contest of 'tip and run' in which the overall death count 'exceeded the total of American dead in the Great War'.[10] Even after Tanganyika was eventually overrun and firmly occupied by his enemy, the German commander Colonel Paul Emil von Lettow-Vorbeck led a rump of tenaciously loyal troops on a gruelling campaign of attrition, darting through the coastal Portuguese East African colony of Mozambique, Nyasaland and the deep north-east of Northern Rhodesia. Rarely letting up in its winding movements, Lettow-Vorbeck's force of German *schutztruppen* and African *askaris* kept British, British African, South African, southern Rhodesian, Belgian and even Portuguese forces engaged for months and then years, entangling as well as tiring out his adversaries through adroit tactical improvisation, sometimes inviting minor set-piece confrontations, at other times carrying on bush fighting, turning to glancing blows and headlong flight to save the day (Map 16.1).

Although massively outnumbered by the combined Allied forces, this rag-tag assembly of experienced regular *askaris*, foxy turncoats who had swopped sides by decamping from the British King's African Rifles and clutch of steady and proficient *schutztruppen* infantrymen and officers, was always able to remain ahead of a pursuing enemy through bush experience and exertion. Although ground down by 1918 to around 150 Germans and about 4,400 African *askaris*, carriers and other labouring camp followers, including women, Lettow-Vorbeck's force retained its core cohesion, due in part to its Swahili-speaking commander's iron command. His obsessive immersion in long and hard campaigning had as its fanciful objective the tying down of substantial Allied forces which might otherwise have been turned against Germany on the Western Front.

Although the ruthless Lettow-Vorbeck is now no longer seen as an audacious exponent in Africa of classic guerrilla warfare, the fact that his loyal *askaris* remained in the field with him was, perhaps, due not only to the shooting or hanging of any deserters. For he adapted shrewdly to the traditional African mode of warfare to which many of his troops would have been accustomed: incorporated in the marching columns of his command was a throng of spouses, children and personal domestic porters, who provided aid, sustained an orderly social network as part of existence in the field and propped up morale, as homesickness was eased by coupling the home front to the front

10 E. Paice, *Tip and Run: The Untold Story of the Great War in Africa* (London: Weidenfeld & Nicolson, 2007), p. 3.

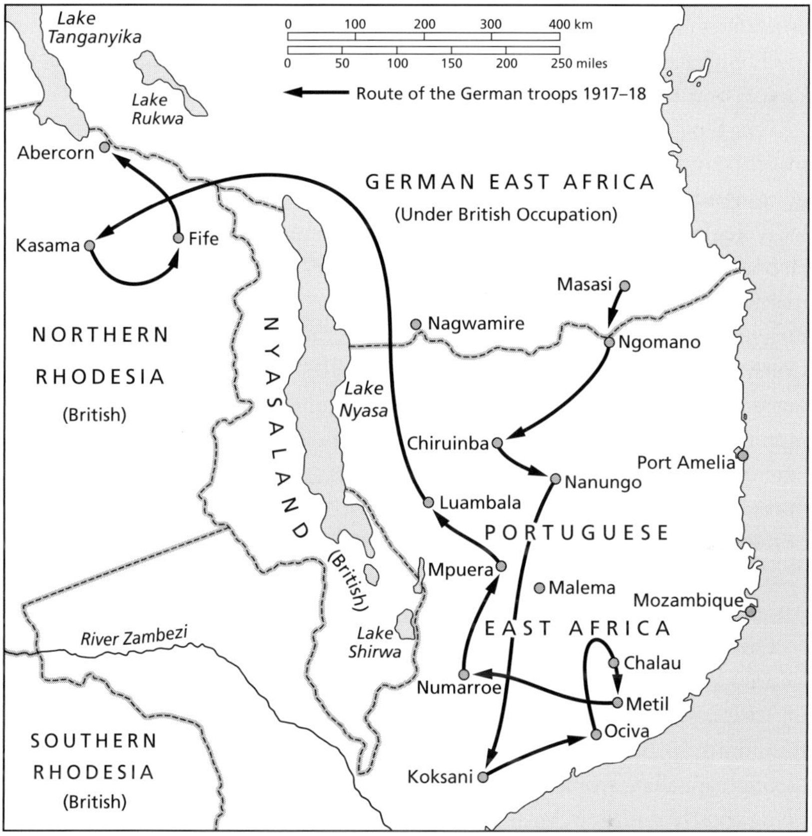

Map 16.1 The war in East Africa, 1917–18.

line. It meant that German worries were not so much over rates of desertion by their *askaris*, as these were relatively low due to a combination of fear and cultivated loyalty, but more about some of the less welcome aspects of conducting operations as a family mission. As a grumbling Lettow-Vorbeck recorded in his glowing 1920 reminiscences, it had been frustrating trying to get female followers to stick to 'a regular marching order', and impossible to cure many of his loyal *askaris* of the habit of going 'into battle with their children on their shoulders'.[11] That, though, was evidently not too great a hindrance, as in

11 P. von Lettow-Vorbeck, *My Reminiscences of East Africa: The Campaign for German East Africa in World War I* (Nashville, TN: Battle Press, 1996), pp. 233–4.

Africa Germany was never formally defeated. Lettow-Vorbeck only laid down arms on 25 November, having to overcome his disbelief that the war had ceased in a French forest a fortnight earlier. So ended the final recorded hostilities of the First World War.

The East African campaign was an enormous and costly slog through mostly unmapped fetid swamplands, dense bush, thickly wooded forests, gouging scrub and imposing hills and mountains. In an operational theatre, individual soldiers had always to be on their guard against collisions with elephants, hippos, giraffes, lions, leopards or venomous black and green mamba snakes. The deadly enemy beyond the flap of your bush tent could turn out to be a feline carnivore, and crossing the Rufiji river in south-western German East Africa entailed dodging crocodiles. Africa's river systems were not those of the Somme. A forbidding environment was rendered even more sapping by belts of tsetse fly and, for humans, debilitating parasitic illnesses like malaria, typhoid and dysentery. The rainy season served up its own version of Passchendaele mud, leaving men, even higher up in the foothills of Kilimanjaro, slithering about in an impassable morass. In their geographical scale and environmental extremities, fighting and logistical conditions in Africa had no equivalent elsewhere.

The sinews of war in protracted East African campaigning came from impressment, with both sides conscripting many hundreds of thousands of Africans into labouring service as heavy porters and carriers, hauling munitions, stores, food supplies and other army equipment on short rations through appalling tropical weather. With draught animals and motor vehicles being mostly useless in bush terrain, Britain alone employed at least 1 million porters. Riddled with respiratory and intestinal diseases, perilously exposed and malnourished transport conscripts suffered 'appalling deathrates'.[12] On the German side, the death rate among African carriers and their family camp followers has been estimated at around 350,000, with the British fatality count not too far behind.[13]

12 J. Iliffe, *Africans: The History of a Continent*, 2nd edn (Cambridge University Press, 2007), p. 215.

13 See, for instance, M. E. Page, *The Chiwaya War: Malawians and the First World War* (Boulder, CO: Westview Press, 2000); R. Anderson, *The Forgotten Front: The East African Campaign, 1914–1918* (Stroud: Tempus, 2004); Paice, *Tip and Run*; and B. Vandervort, 'New light on the East African theater of the Great War: a review essay of English-language sources', in S. M. Miller (ed.), *Soldiers and Settlers in Africa, 1850–1918* (Amsterdam: Brill, 2009), pp. 287–305.

As ranging hostilities assumed cycles of rippling intensity, the transformative and destructive violence of the war flooded into local pastoral and arable economies, uprooting the homesteads of smallholder farmers and choking commercial trade routes which usually conveyed grain and other cash-crops. With Germany's forces in Africa conducting war particularly on the cheap, its small army, never more than about 15,000–strong, settled into wholesale plunder. Rampaging forces requisitioned cattle, grain and other edible crops at will, and conscripted young and sometimes even older men, provided they seemed able-bodied. To deny succour to one or other approaching side, many villages were also torched, their crops burned and cattle run off when they could not be seized. The inevitable consequence of such wholesale wrecking was an acute food shortage after 1916 which verged on famine, in the view of some scholars.[14] With virtually anything that could be consumed being picked off, populations were left to subsist on roots and, on horrifically extreme occasions, to turn to cannibalism. In addition to labouring conscripts, some 300,000 civilians in German-occupied territories are estimated to have perished.

Dire food shortages gnawed away until 1918 and beyond in areas burdened – either directly or indirectly – by combat operations, with the highlands of German East Africa especially severely affected. In their common resort to scorched-earth tactics, both sides had recent thorough colonial experience upon which to draw. In the same East African region, the Germans had cut their teeth just a few years earlier suppressing the 1905–7 Maji-Maji rebellion, while, in South West Africa, the suppression of a mild revolt had produced the punitive and genocidal Herero War of 1904–7, conspicuous for laying waste and for the grisliness of concentration camps.[15] For their part, the British knew well how effective their recent scouring of the Boer farmlands of the Orange Free State and the Transvaal had been in ensuring that they would prevail over a guerrilla enemy in the South African War of 1899–1902. If anything, as a kind of colonial preamble to the First World War, Africa in the 1900s witnessed 'the introduction into state practice and political discourse of extreme forms of militarised brutalism against civilians'.[16]

14 Reid, *Modern Africa*, p. 192.

15 D. Olusoga and C. W. Erichsen, *The Kaiser's Holocaust: Germany's Forgotten Genocide and the Colonial Roots of Nazism* (London: Faber & Faber, 2010); Wallace, *Namibia*, pp. 155–82; and R. Gerwarth and S. Malinowski, 'Hannah Arendt's ghosts: reflections on the disputed path from Windhoek to Auschwitz', *Central European History*, 42:2 (2009), pp. 279–300.

16 J. Hyslop, 'The invention of the concentration camp: Cuba, southern Africa and the Philippines, 1896–1907', *South African Historical Journal*, 63:2 (2011), p. 263.

The diseases which felled transport auxiliaries and swept through battered villages were, inevitably, dwarfed by the scale of the Spanish influenza epidemic which coursed through large tracts of eastern, western, central and southern Africa in 1918 and 1919. Its virulent bacteria carried down to African coastal areas from Europe, and the influenza spread inland rapidly, inserting its feverish presence into the numerous arteries of transport and communication that had been laid down to ferry supplies, soldiers and communications from the imperial metropole. The lines – both short and long – implanted by the war provided ready rural channels through which the deadly influenza could be carried across the entire continent, to every port, urban location, mining compound and rural village. There are, unsurprisingly, no precise figures for African mortality, although there is a reasonable estimate of 2.38 million deaths, representing between 3 and 5 per cent of the population of every African colonial territory.[17]

When it came to fighting, in one fundamental way there was no great difference between opposing sides in their running of armed hostilities. Save for a light dusting of European officers, comparatively tiny numbers of regular white troops and Britain's deployment of Indian Expeditionary Force units, the soldiers who faced each other were all African. Indeed, Britain, unlike France, restricted its cheap and plentiful African troops to 'campaigns within Africa', where warfare always boiled down to 'upholding the colonial order'.[18] The insertion of Indian Army regiments into the African arena remains overlooked in accounts which stress how 'the experience of the Great War radically altered' sepoys' perceptions of Europe, and that the 'First World War can hardly be said to represent typical colonial warfare as it existed in India in the late nineteenth and earlier twentieth centuries.'[19] In Africa, though, it was, arguably, quite the contrary. The distances, blistering heat, incessant movement and almost total absence of large set-piece battles endowed campaigns there with a colonial ambience that would have been far from unfamiliar to soldiering Indians.

When it came to soldiering, though, it was almost always Africans whom colonial states had in mind. In neither Paris nor London was their ever much

17 N. P. Johnson and J. Mueller, 'Updating the accounts: global mortality of the 1918–1920 Spanish influenza epidemic', *Bulletin of the History of Medicine*, 76:1 (2002), p. 110. I am indebted to Howard Phillips for drawing my attention to this reference.

18 D. Killingray, *Fighting for Britain: African Soldiers in the Second World War* (Woodbridge: James Currey, 2010), p. 5.

19 H. Streets, *Martial Races: The Military, Race and Masculinity in British Imperial Culture, 1875–1914* (Manchester University Press, 2004), p. 200.

sense that metropolitan troops might be required to sacrifice in defence of empire. From the outset, in their search for local combatants, European administrations resorted to an almost enslaving form of conscription across large swathes of the continent, a practice which became systematic, harsh and often brutal. From their West African territories, the British recruited infantry to serve on the opposite side, in East Africa. Recruiters in French West Africa and North Africa scoured coastal forest and savannah regions, plucking younger men from virtually every accessible peasant village for army service. For most, theirs would not even be an African war, to be comprehended and made sense of within familiar horizons, for wartime would collapse the boundary between imperial France and its colonial dependencies.

Even before hostilities, pushy French colonial army officers like General Charles Mangin had been advocating the despatch to Europe of a *Force noire* as a contingency for a shortage of fighting men because of France's falling birth rate. The 'valorous warriors' of sub-Saharan Africa who 'had achieved significant feats of arms in the past' would 'stand ready to repeat them for France'.[20] The notion of colonies rallying to save the mother country became a potent symbol of the binding loyalties of empire. Ultimately, over 150,000 West Africans were extracted to be transported to the Western Front in both France and Belgium, there to be jammed in as compensatory belligerents for the increasingly horrendous losses of the home French army. In addition to this, French colonial authorities also recruited tens of thousands of other fighting *tirailleurs* from Morocco and Algeria. Europe took the lives of over 30,000 of these, killed in action, while immersion in combat and exposure to the intensities of a war-torn France stirred the political consciousness of others.

Conscription for an incomprehensible foreign war did not turn out to be all plain sailing, as those who were targeted did not necessarily all stand up straight to be measured. There were, to be sure, compliant conscripts. For unskilled young men, itching to escape the suffocating patriarchal authority of village elders, the army presented comparatively well-rewarded employment. For others who enlisted, war service offered the chance to retrieve a warrior identity which had shrivelled away after colonial conquest. The war was also a wily business in Africa, employment in it at times involving a rich tapestry of personal fabrication. British ethnic recruitment preferences in Nyasaland for the Yao, soldiers of 'the martial spirit', encouraged volunteers for the local battalions of the King's African Rifles to cultivate a strutting military aesthetic, claiming the character of a Yao masculinity known to be

20 J. H. Morrow, Jr., *The Great War: An Imperial History* (New York: Routledge, 2004), p. 17.

sought after. Once in the ranks, loyalties could turn out to be gossamer thin, and there were, as already noted, soldiers who served both British and German sides during the lengthy East African struggle. Regional migrant labour channels in British West Africa and in southern Africa also became enmeshed in military enlistment. In their sweeps for volunteers, recruiters had to make their way within them, with the result that many in the Gold Coast Regiment were not from British Africa but from the French territory of Upper Volta, while '60 to 70 percent' of Rhodesia Native Regiment soldiers in the First World War 'originated from other territories'.[21]

More prominent than joining up, however, were the various kinds of resistance which met increasingly forceful efforts to raise recruits, especially with growing recognition 'that the French system of *commandant* administration had entirely coopted local chiefs, making them enforcers of French demands'.[22] At their most extreme, these included acts of self-mutilation by recruits to render them incapable of service. Increasingly common was mass flight by young men, who often fled over colonial borders or hid out in remote refuges until ravenous French recruiting sergeants had turned their gaze elsewhere. Between 1915 and 1917, tens of thousands of potential conscripts from territories like the Cote d'Ivoire and French Sudan flocked to the Gold Coast and other neighbouring British colonies, secure in the knowledge that the British did not conscript their African subjects for trench service in Western Europe.

The instinctual resort to short-term migrations of non-compliance, the turning of backs in protest was, of course, an old habit in ducking burdensome peacetime colonial demands for taxes and labour levies. Once again, a harried peasantry turned less to overt resistance and more to slippery avoidance of the colonial grip and the subversion of its claims, the quintessential 'weapons of the weak'.[23] In that sense, for many ordinary Africans the experience of being squeezed by recurring army recruitment drives after 1914 was part of a familiar picture, the newest resented round in a cycle of onerous tribute impositions.

Aside from the tactic of trying to outrun the grasp of the war, there were also scattered peasant revolts or insurrections as predatory recruiters pushed

21 R. Marjomaa, 'The martial spirit: Yao soldiers in British Service in Nyasaland (Malawi), 1895–1939', *Journal of African History*, 44:3 (2003), pp. 413–32; and T. Stapleton, 'Extra-territorial African police and soldiers in Southern Rhodesia (Zimbabwe), 1897–1965', *Scientia Militaria*, 38:1 (2010), pp. 101, 106.

22 M. Thomas, *The French Empire at War, 1940–45* (Manchester University Press, 1998), p. 11.

23 J. Scott, *Weapons of the Weak: Everyday Forms of Peasant Resistance* (New Haven, CT: Yale University Press, 1985).

too hard against recalcitrant communities. For many French West Africans, conscription rapidly acquired a notorious meaning, the metaphorical menace of the *impôt du sang*, a bodily 'blood tax'. Sullen restiveness spilled over into an inevitable routine incidence of desertion and petty insubordination among men once in uniform, especially marked among French North African soldiers. Most African troops might have put up with brutality, callousness, bungling and shortages on their side, as did their metropolitan counterparts, but for some the deteriorating terms of survival on the European front broke the limits of personal endurance.

While the African war was associated with risings and rebellions against its demands, chiefly conscription, in some ways the depth of disaffection also represented the dragging out of older and more entrenched animosities, simmering away since the period of the Scramble. In that sense, again, in some of its consequences the First World War was not simply a sudden rupture, tearing at a colonially pacified continent. For there was always a duality to post-1914 grievances about treatment: some of these had been lurking there since the last years of the nineteenth century. The war was, among a myriad of other things, the architect of their intensification.

Militant, fire-eating brands of African-inflected Christianity stamped their apocalyptic imprint on a patchwork of rural societies, capturing and cultivating a popular millenarian temper. In volatile British Nyasaland, where wholesale conscription had come early and where losses in the early campaigns against the Germans had been high, the distinctively dignified figure of John Chilembwe, a towering evangelical preacher, whipped up a fleeting utopian uprising against colonial authority in 1915. Two years later, discontented chiefs in the south-east, egged on by clamouring spirit mediums, ignited the Makombe rising in central Mozambique. These and other war-related eruptions did much to dash contemporary missionary hopes of Africans settling themselves within the paternalism of an imperial civilising mission.

To the south, the Union of South Africa's declaration of an unprovoked offensive against German South West Africa helped to tip a body of more wild-eyed Afrikaner nationalist republicans into an armed insurrection. There, the dutiful Dominion government of Louis Botha and Jan Smuts was far from having won over a largely isolationist Afrikaner society, much of it coursing with anti-British imperialist, pro-German, anti-Anglicised Union or straightforward anti-war sentiment. Hit by landlessness and poverty, inflamed by the incandescent Old Testament prophecies of British imperial implosion by a famed religious visionary, Niklaas 'Siener' van Rensburg, and led by a knot of disaffected and disloyal generals who had swiftly shed their khaki, around

11,000 mostly poorer rural Afrikaners renovated their Anglo-Boer War commando heritage and rode out to topple the government, in a despairing lunge by the socially marginal and the politically estranged. Not for nothing has a recent authoritative account characterised it as a 'desperate rebellion'.[24] Seditious Afrikaner Christian fundamentalists, who thought that the war would open the way to a reclaiming of a lost republican independence, went the same way as yearning Africans who succumbed too readily to wartime ecstasies of anti-colonial redemption. Their spurts of rebellion were speedily extinguished.

Being less outwardly combative in nature, other religiously inflected wartime blossomings were able to endure on the margins. Thus, British and French West Africa also witnessed the emergence of independent Christian movements which brought out their disaffected followers against the intruding European war. While peaceable by inclination and inclined more towards defensive withdrawal, a kind of spiritual secession from wartime and its hated exactions, these local religious formations still took on a powerful millenarian tone, their growling dissidence looking towards a coming apocalyptic moment. From Northern Rhodesia in central Africa across to the Gold Coast and the Cote d'Ivoire, African religious leaders who not only expressed, but defined themselves in the language and imagery of the Bible, stood up to ram home the cataclysmic meaning of the times. Theirs was a moral imperative to repudiate or even to disobey the colonial order. And, on that basis, the need was for readiness as the plague of European rule receded, to embrace the imminent end of the sinful world and to welcome the second coming of Christ. On the more sober end of that scale, in South Africa there was the ironic gaze of the Xhosa Christian educationist, D. D. T. Jabavu. Early in September 1914, he declared wryly that African people 'were taken by surprise' to find 'that the European nations who led in education and Christianity should find no other means than the sword and accumulated destructive weapons to settle their diplomatic differences'.[25]

Alongside, and occasionally interpenetrated with these ripples of dissent, was a molecular range of other risings, some of them highly organised. Between 1915 and 1917 these included armed resistance against British and French colonial authorities in the British Niger protectorates and in Dahomey. And to the south-east, the Barwe along the Portuguese East African border

24 A. Grundlingh and S. Swart, *Radelose Rebellie? Dinamika van die 1914–1915 Afrikanerebellie* (Pretoria: Protea Boekehuis, 2009).
25 *Imvo Zabantsundu*, 8 September 1914.

with Southern Rhodesia rebelled against the flailing Portuguese in 1917 and 1918, by then haemorrhaging food provisions and stores through Lettow-Vorbeck's easy plundering of their garrison depots.

Never fully subterranean, but always drifting along and ignitable, were the throbbing Islamic militancies of French North Africa, which also criss-crossed the French-controlled West African savannah region. Militant Islam, which had long coloured political life across these areas in the modern era, served as the incubus of a string of localised rebellions in colonies to the west and to the north, including the unleashing in 1916 and 1917 of the Kaocen revolt, a series of repeated attacks against the French by Muslim Tuareg warriors, for whom wartime instabilities provided a chance to try to settle earlier pre-war scores.

On a score of another scale, there was also the Ottoman Empire, with Turkey having of course entered the war on the German side late in 1914. This had immediate implications for Africa. There, it can and has been argued that once 'holy war' was declared by the Sultan-Caliph, the Germans 'had had high hopes that all Islam would rise against the British'.[26] On the other hand, it could be suggested equally that the Germans themselves may well have been rather relieved that a crusade of that sort never got started – after all, what the Ottoman zealots had envisaged was an indiscriminately universal anti-colonial jihad, with the whole European colonial world in its sights. If that failed to materialise, the outbreak of European war certainly still brought the probing Ottomans an opportunity to try to regain territory lost across North Africa to France and Britain. Troublesome anti-conscription outbursts peppered Algeria, while in the French protectorate of Morocco there were anti-colonial revolts orchestrated by Abd al-Malik, reputedly fanned by the Germans.

Also embroiled with the Germans – as well as the Ottomans – by whom they were funded and equipped, were the Sanusiyya or Senussi Muslim formation, which had earlier resisted French expansion in the Sahara between 1902 and 1913, and had also fought vigorously against the Italian colonisation of Libya, starting in 1911. Resilient and effective exponents of guerrilla warfare, the concerted Sanusiyya intervention proved to be more than a handful for the jumpy Italians, whose hold on Libyan territory at this stage was still far from firm. Sure enough, early in 1915 Italian forces in the northern Libyan province of Misurata were defeated by Sanusiyya insurgents. Several months later, emboldened and fast-moving fighters extended their field of offensive operations across the Libyan frontier and launched themselves at the British in Egypt.

26 N. Stone, *World War One: A Short History* (London: Penguin, 2007), p. 57.

For the frustrated Allies, something serious was required to bring a worsening diversionary conflict to a halt. It appeared in 1916, with the accession as Libyan monarch of Sidi Muhammad Idris al-Sanusi, a pliable pro-British figure who sought to come to terms with a developing crisis of meandering hostilities on two fronts. In 1917, a ceasefire and then armistice were negotiated with Libya's Italian colonisers on the basis of an acceptance of their existing local ascendancy, a power which was anyway confined largely to coastal regions. Similarly, in Egypt, Sayyid Idris pulled up the disrupting Sanusiyya incursion and sealed more peaceful relations with the British. This cessation of hostilities did not, however, extend to more vulnerable parts further to the south. There, commencing in 1916, the Sanusiyya assaulted remote bases in the French Sahara and also lunged at colonial strongposts in Niger. Caught on the back foot there, the French had to enlist supporting British West African forces to assist in repelling these daring incursions.

While the war brought European powers in North Africa a fluctuating contestation of their position, disputed zones and, at times, a seemingly endless swirl of rebellion and raiding, it also handed London and Paris the spur of necessity to tighten the hold of their colonial presence. In the Sudan, with an eye on rocky wartime circumstances north of the Sahara, the infidel British flexed some muscle to push their control westwards. There, Ali Dinar, the ruler of the sultanate of Darfur, had been flirting alarmingly with the Ottomans, the Libyan Sanusiyya and the Germans since 1915, a nerve that prompted the British governor of the Sudan, General Sir Reginald Wingate, to bring the wayward territory to heel. In March 1916 he despatched a punitive expedition, the British Western Frontier Force (soon dubbed the 'waterless fatigue force' by British troops in its ranks) which swiftly subdued the sultanate, killing Ali Dinar himself.[27]

At the same time, heedful of what was set to remain a potentially turbulent Muslim region, the Scottish-born Wingate was sufficiently canny to avoid any further showdowns, reaching out to restore stability by breaking bread with the dominant Sufi orders of the Sudan. France similarly managed to disperse the worst of the storm-clouds gathered in Morocco and Algeria by pursuing much the same kind of rapprochement with key local interests. The outcome, in terms both broad and brief, was some neutralisation of the threat of rampant Islamic forces through the attainment of a nervous stability, a delicate equilibrium which just about held.

27 J. Slight, 'British perceptions and responses to Sultan Ali Dinar of Darfur, 1915–16', *Journal of Imperial and Commonwealth History*, 38:2 (2010), p. 241.

Beyond all this was the wartime crisis which Africa experienced as the sector of an imperial economy. To varying degrees, most of the more fledgling colonial economies experienced multiple strains and an overall setback. Most obviously, the volume of internal continental trade fell off sharply, notably the previously buoyant commerce that had tied together the interests of German, French and British colonies in West Africa, and the Anglo-German exchanges in East Africa of sisal, coffee, rubber and other cash-crops. Hamburg ceased being a port for South African frozen beef, dried fruit and ostrich feathers. Furthermore, the prices of some export produce declined sharply as Africa felt the pinch of a more general global downturn. Another hardship at the same time was fast-rising wartime prices for basic European imports to which many African consumers had become habituated. These also became subject to severe supply shortages, as the diversion of European plant towards military production slashed the output of civilian industrial goods and mass household commodities for colonial markets. To compound a tight situation, attacks on merchant shipping by raiders disrupted the flow of overseas trade.

For their part, colonial administrations screwed down hard on produce prices and wages, controls which hit the living standards of producers and workers, as neither party was able to benefit much from the increasing demand for certain key raw materials after 1914, as Europe's industrial economies limbered up for war-making. Inevitably, economic hardship and social distress soon became widely felt, with intensifying want adding further fuel to outbreaks of social upheaval. Social misery combined with other lacerating forces that struck at the well-being of many Africans – army conscription, forced labour service, the pillaging of peasant homesteads and the incineration of arable and pastoral lands, the requisitioning of goods and even the compulsory cultivation of prescribed crops dictated by the war-effort demands of this or that colonial power. Where the war hit hardest – as in parts of East Africa – it ripped the heart out of agrarian livelihoods.

Yet the economic impact of the war and the costs of adjustment to it were not everywhere a case of countries running into very heavy weather. In the industrialising far south, while South Africa suffered inflationary increases in the cost of imports, soaring prices and chronic shortages of common British imports such as blankets and confectionery stimulated local manufacturing, as import substitution powered a brisk expansion of what had previously been a distinctly moribund local secondary industry. If the officers of the Union's expeditionary infantry brigades may still have sailed off for Marseilles or Mombasa with British Jaeger or Pringle apparel, their blankets, candles and processed foods were now being supplied by local factories. Elsewhere, there were handsome increases in the country's old export staples such as maize, wool and meat, accompanied by a meteoric rise in the volumes of brandy, rum and other spirits shipped to Britain. Brandy rocketed from a faint sniff of 42 gallons in 1913 to almost 40,000 gallons by 1917.[28] By any measure, this part of the African empire did its bit to keep up spirit rations for Britain's mass working-class armies.

Notwithstanding the bite of occasional patches of drought, more prosperous white commercial farmers were in clover, with their agricultural house magazines exulting in increased yields in response to calls to fill the stomachs of vast Allied armies. These gains from war-induced agricultural expansion, stretched further by an infusion of government finance to boost productive capacity, came partly at the expense of what was left of the country's struggling African peasant cultivators and sharecroppers. With diminished access to fertile land further choked off by the segregationist 1913 Land Act, against which the recently formed South African Native National Congress had shelved its protest campaign in 1914 as a gesture of wartime patriotism, the plight of marginal smallholders worsened. Coming on top of the gnawing hunger caused by harvest failures in drought conditions after 1914, immiseration funnelled Africans from the countryside into civilian wage labour or into non-combatant South African Native Labour Contingent military service overseas.

While many of the Union's rural Africans buckled, another marked effect of the war's dislocations was a sudden advance in the modernisation of the continent's major industrial infrastructure, as electrification, transport and supply were given urgent new impetus. With labour, there was something of a parallel movement. In the economic heartlands, such as the Witwatersrand, the number of male African industrial workers doubled between 1916 and 1919, while the employment of white female factory operatives increased at almost the same rate, as the departure of white soldiers on expeditionary service sucked in civilian women who, of course, laboured on lower pay.

The 1914 scramble by thousands of patriotic immigrant British miners and artisans for army service in white imperial labour legions, opened doors to more than one kind of wartime worker substitution. In Johannesburg mines, vacant semi-skilled jobs, usually reserved by the job colour bar for white

28 *Union of South Africa, Report of the Acting Trade Commissioner for the Year 1919, U.G. 60–020* (Cape Town, 1920), pp. 14–15.

labour aristocrats, were filled by experienced black mineworkers at much lower wages. A boon as it cheapened the cost of labour, this dilution of the industrial colour bar by the controlling Chamber of Mines was acclaimed as the industry's bold response to the patriotic need to sustain national economic strength in war.

A large difficulty, however, was that unionised white workers were not blind to the implications of wartime adaptation, and between 1916 and 1918 the gold mines were rocked by agitation over the security and privileged status of white mineworkers' jobs. Thousands of those involved were new Afrikaner mineworkers, landless poor whites who had taken up the slack created by the exodus of fighting volunteers to Europe and East Africa. Having acquired a workplace anchorage, in due course they held on against wholesale displacement by returning ex-soldiers after 1918. At the beginning of 1914, roughly a third of white mine employees had been 'colonial-born' rather than 'overseas-born', in the classic lexicon of white Dominion identity. By 1918, that largely Afrikaner proportion had risen to over half. As the war's distant campaigns carried off large numbers of home country immigrants and their descendants, it is possible to see it as having quickened the pace at which South Africa's minority white working class was turning increasingly indigenous or 'national' in its composition.

Inevitably, gold production – and how to deal with it in wartime – was accorded high priority by the British. A vital strategic commodity, bullion was the lynchpin of the entire imperial coupling between the world's largest gold producer and London, with the Witwatersrand mines stocking the Bank of England with over two-thirds of its precious metal reserves on the outbreak of war. Wasting no time, the Bank sealed an agreement with South Africa's mining houses for its mineral to be sold exclusively to Britain at a fixed 1914 rate, frozen for the duration of what was not expected to be a long war.

At the time, it seemed mutually opportune. The bedrock of the global sterling system, precious gold supplies would not have to run the shipping hazards of German raiders but would be stored in an impregnable South Africa, while London would provide financial cover for most of the purchase cost until safe transportation could resume. The Union would gain not only from a guaranteed war price for its prize export commodity, but from British credit to ease the funding of its African and European expeditionary war effort. Britain's share of its Dominion deal was no less – if not more – satisfactory. The war notwithstanding, it was assured of a steady wartime increase in its gold reserves, the key global financial position of the City of London would be preserved and the Bank of England would also be able to advance its handily priced surplus gold to neutral countries in wartime at a rising world price.

In fact, as would soon enough become clear, for the mineowners the freezing of the gold price was not a secure bet, for it backfired. As the value of sterling kept shrinking, by 1916 the costs of essential equipment and stores on which the gold industry was dependent had risen precipitously. In addition, militant unionised white labour was able to capitalise on a scarcity of skilled labour to force through hefty wage increases as well as reduced working hours, so that gold output in 1918 was actually lower than its 1914 level. Hammered by spiralling costs and unable to inflate the cost of their commodity in response, mining capitalists were saddled with a major slump in profits. With Britain unwilling to budge on the price terms of its gold agreement, by 1917 the grumbling industry was denouncing the crippling effect of an intolerable European war on normal economic life and on the industrial health of a Greater South Africa on the continent. The conflict not only strained relations between London and the owners of the Witwatersrand gold fields. Domestically, their burden of sliding profitability and declining production left them itching to free themselves of the millstone of costly white labour. Their attempt to cheapen that cost, an assault on the entrenched position of unionised workers that led to the traumatic Rand Revolt of 1922, was a direct legacy of wartime troubles. Even as deeply sheltered a region as the industrial Transvaal was unable to escape being buffeted by the war, experienced there as a financial stranglehold.

In some important respects, the shape which the First World War took in Africa was acquired in an atmosphere which gathered not only within the continent but also outside. In that sense, it amounted to being both an internal settling of accounts between enemy colonial powers and an extra-mural war over Africa, directed by Allies so beset by mutual political suspicion and disregard that coordination arrangements and understandings were scarcely worth their paper. Belgium suspected Britain of wanting to deprive it of any conquered territory from the East African conflict, if not of scheming to dispossess Brussels of its existing colonies at the end of hostilities. For the British, the Belgians were risky as they might use any captured enemy territory as a colonial bargain if it ever came to stealthy negotiations with Germany for a separate peace. Then there was Portugal, undoubtedly the only European imperial state for whom the war in Africa counted for far more than in its heartland. But, financially shaky and with the war domestically unpopular, the Portuguese were too consumed by fear of the political repercussions of any colonial defeats to plunge in properly against the Germans.

Lisbon's tepid blustering about its part in campaign cooperation did nothing to dispel British scepticism, with its forces held in disdain as a liability in constant need of propping up. Unlike Portugal, South Africa fancied greater things but these came to nothing. The Portuguese declined to trade the colonial ports and colonial labour of Mozambique for South West Africa in a territorial swop proposed by the Union. And in the former German East Africa, its aspirations for a slice (along with those of Belgium and Portugal) were rebuffed by Britain, secure in its hold on Tanganyika.

At another imperial level across Africa, the war era witnessed the final consolidation of European-imposed colonial structures which, in the immediate post-war years, furnished systems of ruling authority that were positioned more strongly to administer political subjects, to exploit the potential of varied economic environments and to employ technologically and organisationally more efficient means to implant a secure and stable colonial order. As revealed by its early 1920s aftermath and onwards, the conflict heralded a major realignment of post-conquest conditions, ones which demonstrated the high-water mark of a maturing colonial rule.

The lurching, violent decades of the post-1880s Scramble were, in effect, swallowed by the First World War.[29] Its early legacy was that of an imposing *pax colonia*, as the imperial work of pacification was almost entirely completed by the time that Paul Emil von Lettow-Vorbeck and his die-hard *askaris* grudgingly consented to surrender to the South African General Jaap van Deventer at the southern edge of Lake Tanganyika on 25 November 1918. By and large, the flaring up of rebellion and insurrection had been extinguished, and with it the final flickerings of tactics of armed resistance in the hope of regaining an aboriginally independent identity. Beyond that, levels of rural banditry, smuggling and urban crime had also been severely diminished. With the screwing in of a colonial peace, in most of Africa the economic improvisations and social changes associated with a market economy and merchant capitalism could roll on. With that road secured and fully open by the beginning of the 1920s, 'soldiers repaired to their barracks, and market forces became more important than – or at least as important as – rapid-firing machine guns'. As the show of flourishing militarism receded, 'the commercial economy was now to define colonial society'.[30]

29 For that transition, see 'Africa and the First World War', special issue of *Journal of African History*, 19:1 (1978); M. E. Page, *Africa and the First World War* (New York: St Martin's Press, 1987); and H. Strachan, *The First World War in Africa* (Oxford University Press, 2004).

30 Reid, *Modern Africa*, p. 195.

Equally, the preceding shock of the world war left an ineradicable impression on many societies and communities. Naturally, it cut deepest into those who felt the extremities of its impact, be they the calamitous loss of a grain harvest to rampaging German *askaris* in Portuguese East Africa, or the strong-arm diversion of Senegalese *tirailleurs* towards the sea, to be wrenched away from home soil and shipped off to France; an alarming crossing of the water which saw some of them gripped by a claustrophobic crisis of inherited memories of the transatlantic slave trade's Middle Passage. Indeed, 'the war caused the largest movement of Africans from their home continent since the Trans-Atlantic Slave Trade'.[31] For men taken from land-bound peasant societies which had never developed a long-distance seafaring tradition of their own, the first taste of the war was that of an engulfing transgression, having been committed mostly against their will to the intimidating unknowns of the Atlantic Ocean.

No doubt, too, colonised Africans who had witnessed, sometimes at close quarters, Europeans slaughtering one another, would not easily forget so shocking a spectacle, nor the hardships and degradation wrought upon European life by the conflict. By shattering the imaginative boundaries 'between colony and metropole', the scale of the war 'undermined the privilege of the colonial authority to singly determine the portrait of the colonial power offered for consumption' by its subjects.[32] Nor would some soldiers and auxiliaries labouring in the depots forget their European encounter with Europeans. French West African troops felt the racist force of German hostilities which depicted them as sub-human. And the embattled host metropolitan society for which they were sacrificing themselves had its own currents of racist thinking and behaviour. In army service, there was the routine exposure to a predictable dribble of petty inequalities, discriminatory treatment and racial contempt. Even in positive propaganda imagery, embracing them as overseas colonial patriots who had hastened across the Mediterranean to save French home soil, Moroccan and Algerian troops were depicted as brutish and bloodthirsty cut-throats, straining at a leash.

Yet, for all that, for some there was a wartime realisation that Europeans in Europe were not necessarily always the same as Europeans in Africa: at times, there was, also, always a certain duality to how they were perceived and

31 T. Stapleton, 'The impact of the First World War on African people', in J. Laband (ed.), *Daily Lives of Civilians in Wartime Africa: From Slavery Days to Rwandan Genocide* (Pietermaritzburg: University of Kwazulu-Natal Press, 2007), p. 130.

32 J. E. Genova, *Colonial Ambivalence, Cultural Authenticity and the Limitations of Mimicry in French-Ruled West Africa, 1914–56* (New York: Peter Lang, 2006), pp. 41–2.

treated in the hub of the empire that had claimed them. While not many, there were bars, women and local homes with open doors which lubricated fraternisation and social familiarities between African soldiers and European civilians. That was not always allowed to remain a matter of live and let live. In the case of the South African Native Labour Contingent, the arrangement between the Union government and Britain's War Office was that its African service corps would be barred from becoming familiar with local civilians lest it expose them to the contagion of social equality, subverting the habitual discipline of segregation. To ensure subordination and control, members of the Contingent found that their European living circumstances had been made less unfamiliar – they were, quite simply, just Africanised. In rear depots such as Dieppe and Rouen, men officered by white superiors from the Union's Native Labour Bureau were cooped up in closed workers' compounds, modelled on those used to house migrant labourers on the diamond mines of Kimberley and the Johannesburg gold mines. Still, in wartime Europe the strongholds of segregation were never able to replicate the peacetime rigidities of colonial life, as racial boundaries were tested or crossed in myriad ways by the friction of weary black soldiers chafing for changed and improved circumstances.

On this front, part of the stock of Africans' more general war memories would have been those of having witnessed not merely the harsh ambivalence of colonial rule's 'civilising mission', but also the shortcomings and flaws of a weakened European population which was seemingly unable to resolve its war on an all-European basis. As the *Japan Times* observed on 3 December 1918, the war could not but have disrupted conventional perceptions of racial solidarity in an imperial world, for 'on the one hand, the white races were at war with each other. On the other, the British were bringing Indians to fight in Europe and the French were recruiting Africans, South East Asians and Pacific Islanders. Japan was allied to Britain, while Ottoman Turkey fought alongside Germany and Austria.'[33]

Nor was this all within the disturbed and manic European universe that was inimical to Africans' expectations. Not least was the foreign manner and ferocity of the waging of the war itself. Rural warriors versed in their own agrarian rhythms of highly personalised warfare – violently competitive nineteenth-century conflicts over control of the ivory trade, for the acquisition

33 Quoted in M. Lake and H. Reynolds, *Drawing the Global Colour Line: White Men's Countries and the International Challenge of Racial Equality* (Cambridge University Press, 2008), pp. 282–3.

of firearms or slaves, for pasture lands, or for prestigious booty and the gaining of symbolic tribute – were unlikely to forget quickly the protracted privations as well as the utter strangeness of their immersion in an industrial war. For many African combatants at the front, the cultural peculiarity of the conflict lay in it having been pre-eminently a war of excess, its deadliness rarely slackening and then only to be renewed. In that, it was beyond comprehension. Above all, perhaps, this was militarism without the insulation of familiar symbolism and ritual, such as the religious doctoring of bodies before battle. Nor did war-making hinge upon time or climate: armies did not break off because it was night-time, a rainy season or the harvest cycle into which their hands had to fit. After the wars of Africa's part-time militias, fought for commercial gain or direct personal benefit, the unrelenting momentum of the First World War was profoundly disconcerting.

Its unsettling experience also helped to fertilise the field of very early African proto-nationalist organisations and semi-political associations which were linked to the formation of distinctively modern identities of populist protest, wrapped in a mild creed of petitioning, deputations and declarations. For many of the discontented, those impulses of political protest against the confiscatory regimes of colonial rule had been rising in the wake of European invasion and conquest, some years before 1914. But the war buttressed anti-colonial politicisation, charging the political life of greater numbers of people with new dimensions of dissent. Although its overall scale ought not to be exaggerated, and historians now attach less weight than did earlier scholarship to the role of war veterans in protest politics, its social reach was still not inconsiderable.

In addition to mission-educated, westernised Africans who had been drawn in to occupy basic administrative and clerical jobs vacated by whites who had volunteered for military duties, the social and political sensibilities of urban workers and peasants were also touched. Having felt the effects of the war, Africa's principal remembrancers had their known worlds stirred and even subtly tilted by their experiences. After 1918, their disillusion with what they saw as conservative, archaic and compromised systems of African chiefly rule, working hand-in-glove with colonial power, began to search for a coherent shape as the expression of newly roused and newly educated African voices, wanting to register their worth and to challenge social and political exclusion.

In one sense, the 1919 Versailles Conference simply swept Africans into the margins of history as it resolved the fate of Germany's occupied colonies by handing them on as Mandate territories to the victorious Allies. These were to be held in paternalist trusteeship, with a humanitarian securing of African interests in lengthy preparation for eventual self-government. Thus, the First World War produced a concoction of European guardianship rather than a bluff imperialism, whatever the irony of the fact that the most powerful members of the new League of Nations were also the two greatest colonial states, Britain and France. From them there was now 'lip service, at least, to the ideal that colonies would be held in trust until the native peoples could stand on their own'.[34]

Pending that time, with neither precedent nor promise, some of a vanquished Germany's lost African territories were even sliced up before being handed out. Britain and France shared Togoland. While the French administered their share of the spoils separately, in due course the British incorporated their portion into the neighbouring Gold Coast. France acquired over three-quarters of Kamerun as Cameroon, with Britain picking up the remainder which bordered its Nigeria protectorate. With the closing of German East Africa, Tanganyika became a British Mandate. In that territory's hinterlands, the German possession of Rwanda-Urundi, situated on the north-eastern fringe of the Belgian Congo, became the responsibility of Belgium. Lastly, there was confirmation of some gain for the sub-imperial ambitions of the Union of South Africa and its wartime claims to having realised a steady and self-reliant white nationhood. In Southern Africa, the new conquistadors of colonial guardianship came not from London, Paris or Brussels but from Pretoria, as the former territory of German South West Africa was placed under South African administration.

Yet, in another quarter, something else was stirring in the shadow of European map-making and the devising of League of Nations Mandate classes for those pieces of Africa that had once been German. By making self-aware African elites more cognisant of their position in the world, and by clearing the ground for the formation of a new modern era of protest identities, the deliberations at Versailles, including US President Woodrow Wilson's Fourteen Points and the subsequent covenant of the League of Nations, caught the ear of politically connected groupings. For modernising clusters, wartime seemed to have clarified the basis of their general predicament, with the war having been akin to a 'national' experience well before the imaginative construction of any of their nations.

Thus, across parts of British West Africa there were mounting calls for greater representation of the skilled and the literate in local government.

34 Wm. Roger Louis, 'The European colonial empires', in Howard and Louis (eds.), *Oxford History of the Twentieth Century*, p. 94.

Much further south, the South African Native National Congress (forerunner of the African National Congress) went somewhat further in responding to global ideas about rights, democracy and nationalism as the terminus of peace-making. Petitioning the Crown in vain for the right to its own representation at Versailles, the movement underlined Africans' wartime contribution and sacrifice, reminding King George V, as their natural protector, that just as the subjects of the Habsburg Empire could now anticipate national freedom under the principles of the peace, Africans, too, had a just claim upon the right to self-determination and freedom from discrimination and oppression. Equally, that was not the only way in which the First World War registered a greater global awareness upon some of the continent's inhabitants. However disheartening the outcome of the war for the radical Afrikaner nationalist paper, *Het Volk*, all was not lost, its readers were reassured. For the conflict had still ended in 'a victory for republicanism, as in any case America was really responsible for the victory'.[35] Such were the dreams of not living by empire when it was exactly that into which a great war had just locked Africa more securely than before.

35 Quoted in Bill Nasson, *Springboks on the Somme: South Africa in the Great War, 1914–1918* (Johannesburg: Penguin, 2007), p. 243.

17

The Ottoman Empire

MUSTAFA AKSAKAL

War debris: with an axe and a bomb, İsmail dies in a cemetery

On Tuesday, 19 October 1920, around 3 o'clock in the afternoon, in the little village of Çay near Çanakkale (Gallipoli), 7-year-old Ferhad, a mute (*dilsiz*), came running to his friends, gesturing with great excitement about a shell he had found in the cemetery. A group of eight children followed Ferhad to examine the shell. Seventeen-year-old İsmail, the son of Ali of Limnos, who had brought along an axe, stood over the shell and struck it. The resulting explosion killed him in an instant, along with Hüseyin, son of Mehmed, and seriously injured their five friends. İsmail and Hüseyin had survived the Great War, but it killed them all the same.[1]

The First World War in the Middle East claimed at least 2.5 million other Ottoman lives, or about 12 per cent of the Empire's entire population, mostly civilians, and – though it is impossible to know for sure – probably many more, perhaps as many as 5 million.[2] The material and environmental devastation caused by the war has never been assessed, and the war's civilian experience has still not been studied in any detail. But even with all the questions still remaining, it is clear that the mayhem and suffering unleashed by the war incinerated the Empire's social fabric, assuring that it would take a long time, perhaps a century or more, before the region could recover from the destruction, and before an integrated history, one that takes the war for the human tragedy it was and without making it the exclusive story of a

1 Prime Ministry's Ottoman Archives (Başbakanlık Osmanlı Arşivi; hereafter BOA), DH. EUM. AYŞ 47/17, 25 October 1920.

2 James L. Gelvin, *The Israel-Palestine Conflict: One Hundred Years of War*, 2nd edn (New York: Oxford University Press, 2007), p. 77. Unfortunately for those desiring specific numbers of wartime casualties, Gelvin's 'approximately 5 million' war casualties covers the years 1914–23 and includes Egypt. The Ottoman population in 1914 stood at around 21 million, not including Egypt, and at around 25 million including Egypt.

particular national group, could be written. In many ways, the war's full history has remained covered up by war debris as well, and it continues to be no less explosive than the shell that killed the two curious boys in Çay.

Thus, while the main problem confronting most authors of new studies on the First World War is synthesising the mass of scholarship produced by nine decades of research, for the modern Middle East the problem looks rather different: the challenge here is to establish a coherent narrative and interpretation based on scholarly ground that remains relatively untrodden, not least because it is a political minefield, where the stakes are unusually high.

The study of the First World War has been impeded first of all by the politicisation of the late Ottoman period, especially scholarship on policies towards Christian minorities – of which the Armenian case is emblematic and one whose legacy continues to affect Turkey's domestic politics and foreign relations. Another impediment, not unconnected to the first, has been the limitations on the availability of primary sources. Access to the region's military archives has been restricted. As the literate segment of the Ottoman population remained in the single percentage points throughout the war, personal narratives of their experiences by soldiers and civilians in letters and diaries are not sufficient to make good the gaps in the official record. And if these obstacles were not enough, historians face the challenge of writing about a vast empire that was home to peoples speaking more languages than any one scholar can master: Arabic, Greek, Hebrew, Kurdish, Ladino, Western Armenian and, most important, Ottoman Turkish – a bureaucratese composed of a mixture of Turkish, Arabic and Farsi words and phrases, and dead now for more than eighty years. Finally, for many of the participating nations, other subjects have ranked higher on national historical agendas. In Arab historiography, for example, the war has been overshadowed by the subsequent mandate regime imposed by the League of Nations and the conflict over Palestine. Similarly, in Turkish historiography, assessments of the war have taken a backseat to the history of the Kemalist Revolution and attempts at secularisation and democratisation.

As a result, beyond a small group of specialists, nearly a century after it took place the war as experienced in the Middle East has remained largely unknown. Those who do remember the Ottomans typically think of them as the owners of a peripheral stage on which the main actors were outsiders: Germans declaring jihad; Australians and New Zealanders perishing on the Gallipoli peninsula; Sykes and Picot parcelling out the Arab lands (into future Western 'mandates'); T. E. Lawrence setting the spark for the so-called Arab Revolt; and Lord Balfour's letter, pledging British support for 'the establishment in Palestine of a national home for the Jewish people'.[3] In most Western histories, the one aspect of the war in which Ottomans themselves played an active role is the Armenian *Aghet* (Arm.: catastrophe). And yet, these events of the war, as significant as they are, are told in isolation from each other, and without the deeper Ottoman context they deserve.[4]

The historical oblivion into which the Ottoman war has been consigned seems all the more curious given that observers at the time often expressed their belief that the war was *all about* the region: 'The present war undoubtedly was largely a war for the control of Asia Minor', wrote one contributor to the British *The Nineteenth Century and After* in 1916.[5] In the Russian Duma, the delegates averred that the war was, after all, a war for Constantinople.[6] We need not take them entirely at their word – Russia entered the war, after all, for a variety of reasons – in order to note that the Ottoman Front was never just a sideshow. Bringing the Ottoman experience back into our understanding of the First World War, however, is not to reassert an importance clear to contemporaries, and even less, to offer an 'Ottoman' point of view (even assuming that there was such a thing), but to deepen existing histories of the war, and in such a way that the Near Eastern theatre, the Ottoman state and the millions of Ottoman peoples become subjects in their own right.

While European scholars have been writing from a Europe that has laid down its weapons, emphasising the tragic – and, increasingly, the unnecessary – nature of the war, in the Middle East, the war's memory is entangled with foundational stories of independence struggles and national liberation that both preceded 1914 and continued, in some cases, long after 1918.[7] In the Arab Middle East, the war is associated with Jemal Pasha's iron-fisted regime in Syria, where the Ottoman term for 'mobilisation' (*seferberlik*) continues to

3 British Foreign Secretary Arthur James Balfour to Lord [Walter] Rothschild, 2 November 1917.

4 For an exception see Donald Bloxham, *The Great Game of Genocide: Imperialism, Nationalism, and the Destruction of the Ottoman Armenians* (Oxford University Press, 2005), and his 'The First World War and the development of the Armenian genocide', in Ronald Grigor Suny, Fatma Müge Göçek and Norman M. Naimark (eds.), *A Question of Genocide: Armenians and Turks at the End of the Ottoman Empire* (Oxford University Press, 2011), pp. 260–75.

5 J. Ellis Barker, 'The future of Asiatic Turkey', *The Nineteenth Century and After: A Monthly Review*, 79 (January–June 1916), pp. 1221–47, for the quote see p. 1225.

6 9 February 1915. I am grateful to Professor Robert Geraci for his assistance with the Duma proceedings.

7 Michael Provence, 'Ottoman modernity, colonialism, and insurgency in the Arab Middle East', *International Journal of Middle East Studies*, 43 (2011), p. 206.

be remembered with a shudder today.[8] It is also, and perhaps especially, as Salim Tamari has shown, remembered for the Great Famine. No sooner had a plague of locusts descended in 1915, and seemed to eat up every green shoot, than the state requisitioned much of the remaining grain supplies, while an Anglo-French naval blockade prevented relief from arriving from outside. The result was widespread starvation by December 1915.[9] In Syria, one out of seven people had died by war's end. The famine's contribution to the Arab Revolt in 1916 cannot be underestimated. For even as the population starved, conscription continued, stretching not only Ottoman administrative capacity but also Ottoman legitimacy to the breaking point.[10] Every sign of Arab disaffection, however, brought down the wrath of the Ottoman state, which demanded unflinching loyalty from all its populations and meted out punishment where it could not obtain it. The potential for an Ottoman future with equal rights and citizenship for all ethnic and religious groups living inside the Empire had still existed, however faintly, before 1914.[11] But during the years of the war this potential was now snuffed out and locals embraced alternatives to Ottoman rule.[12]

On the Anatolian peninsula, the region that became the Turkish Republic in 1923, disloyalty among Christian and Kurdish populations was presumed from the outset, and punishment, in the regime's view, had to be pre-emptive, including the 'accidental' shooting of Armenian soldiers suspected of preparing to desert.[13] The Christian population plummeted from roughly 20 per cent to 2 per cent of the Anatolian population, in a programme implemented by the

8 Hanna Mina, *Fragments of Memory: A Story of a Syrian Family*, trans. Olive Kenny and Lorne Kenny (Northampton: Interlink Books, 2004), pp. 5–9, and Najwa al-Qattan, '*Safarbarlik*: Ottoman Syria and the Great War', in Thomas Philipp and Christoph Schumann (eds.), *From the Syrian Land to the States of Syria and Lebanon* (Beirut and Würzburg: Ergon, 2004), pp. 163–73, for a captivating discussion of the various derived meanings of the term in Greater Syria – including its use as synonym for death, starvation, forced exile and 'to go off and never come back again'.

9 Salim Tamari (ed.), *Year of the Locust: A Soldier's Diary and the Erasure of Palestine's Ottoman Past* (Berkeley: University of California Press, 2011), p. 142.

10 Elizabeth Thompson, *Colonial Citizens: Republican Rights, Paternal Privilege, and Gender in French Syria and Lebanon* (New York: Columbia University Press, 2000), pp. 15–70.

11 Michelle U. Campos, *Ottoman Brothers: Muslims, Christians, and Jews in Early Twentieth-Century Palestine* (Stanford University Press, 2011), pp. 1–19.

12 See, for example, the diary of Ihsan Turjman, in Tamari (ed.), *Year of the Locust*, p. 156.

13 Ali Rıza Eti, *Bir Onbaşının Doğu Cephesi Günlüğü*, ed. Gönül Eti (Istanbul: Türkiye İş Bankası Kültür Yayınları, 2009), p. 104; for the deportations of Armenians and Kurds from Diyar-ı Bekir province in eastern Anatolia, see Uğur Ümit Üngör, *The Making of Modern Turkey: Nation and State in Eastern Anatolia, 1913–1950* (Oxford University Press, 2011), pp. 55–169.

leaders of the Committee of Union and Progress (CUP), the government in power during the war years. The CUP justified this pre-emptive retaliation by referring to what they perceived to be the Great Powers' repeated assaults on the Ottoman Empire since the early nineteenth century. They became convinced that European diplomacy was a fixed game, yielding only military defeats, territorial losses and European support for the independence of the Empire's Christian minorities. From territories lost, moreover, came millions of Muslims, victims of ethnic cleansing from the Black Sea region, the Caucasus and the Balkans, now living as refugees in a shrinking empire. By July 1914, for the leaders of the CUP – many of whom themselves hailed from the Balkans – this history had produced a deep sense of violation, victimhood and humiliation that legitimised retaliation and self-defence against their remaining Christian minorities at any cost. Their view was not the only view, of course, as opposition parties, most notably the Liberal Union, had called for a programme of decentralisation and a greater level of regional self-rule within the Empire. But after 1913, these parties had been silenced or sent into exile.

Thus it should not surprise us that the Ottoman 'successor states' in the Middle East, not to mention the Greeks and the Armenians, have their own, competing stories about what took place. Nor should it come as a surprise that the Turkish Republic, founded in 1923 and conceiving of itself as much a 'successor state' to a defunct empire as Poland or Czechoslovakia, fostered its own memory of the war, a narrative that, while differing from the others, just as strongly delegitimised Ottoman rule – often using, in fact, the same orientalising, 'Sick Man of Europe' tropes as nineteenth- and twentieth-century European observers. And, as with the other narratives, the Turkish narrative too remains deeply tied to the state's own legitimacy today. It portrays the transition from empire to republic as a moment of monumental rupture – a clean break – despite what scholars have shown to be the many continuities in leadership and policies. Intervention in 1914 is presented as the deed of one man, Enver Pasha, the Minister of War. A 'war hawk in thrall to Germany' – and, in some versions, 'to hare-brained' dreams of Turkish expansion into Central Asia – Enver, the narrative claimed, had 'more or less single-handedly pushed the empire into a war' that no one else wanted.[14] But the Turkish narrative of the war takes a different turn from Kennan's 'seminal tragedy', one that engendered Europe's economic collapse, Bolshevism, fascism and another world war.[15] If getting into the war – as personified by Enver – is

14 Mustafa Aksakal, *The Ottoman Road to War in 1914: The Ottoman Empire and the First World War* (Cambridge University Press, 2008), p. 1.

15 George Kennan, *The Decline of Bismarck's European Order: Franco-Russian Relations, 1875–1890* (Princeton University Press, 1979), p. 3.

remembered as a disaster, surviving the war and getting out of it – as personified by Mustafa Kemal Atatürk – is remembered as the great national triumph, the Turks' 'finest hour'. In Turkey's collective memory today, the Ottomans lost the First World War; the Turks won it.

It is important to subject such memories to historical scrutiny. Regarding the first part of the traditional, monochromatic Turkish narrative, how the Ottomans got into the maelstrom when they were not part of the original quarrel: archival evidence and the occasional dissident memoir have put to rest the picture of 'Enver Did It!' The First World War itself is 'the era least explored' in the scholarship on Turkey, and yet, it was not only 'the most traumatic but also the most formative and important period in modern Turkish history'.[16] The Ottoman state's wartime policies and the profound social, political and especially demographic developments that occurred during the war, not only made the Turkish nation-state possible in the first place but also defined its character ever since.

These policies required the raising of a national army based on mass conscription, and they assured, until very recently, the army's unrivalled role in post-war Turkish politics. These policies also included the social and ideological mobilisation of the Muslim civilian population, a mobilisation that, to a very real extent, created the 'Turkish nation' – as did, by subtraction, the elimination by murder and forced expulsion of minority populations who were deemed to be liabilities – enemies within – and established the myth that this nation was homogeneous. It was the war that allowed Ottoman leaders, beginning in 1914, to create a National Economy (*milli iktisat*), one based on Muslim businesses, in explicit contrast to what was perceived as the previous dominance of trade and finance by Christians and Jews and their European protectors.[17] Yet even with the celebration of all these gains for the 'nation', the wartime suffering of the entire civilian population as a result of disease, famine and starvation imbued Turkish memory with its own narrative of anguish and victimhood.

Provincialising the First World War in the Middle East

In the case of the Ottoman Empire, there is good reason to speak of a 'ten-year-war', beginning in 1911 with Italy's grab for the Ottoman Dodecanese

16 Erik J. Zürcher, *The Young Turk Legacy and Nation-Building: From the Ottoman Empire to Atatürk's Turkey* (London: I. B. Tauris, 2010), p. 48.

17 Zafer Toprak, *İttihad-Terakki ve Cihan Harbi: Savaş Ekonomisi ve Türkiye'de Devletçilik, 1914–1918* (Istanbul: Homer Kitabevi, 2003), pp. 1–16.

Islands and Trablusgarp, today's Libya, and ending with the victory in 1922 of the Ottoman armed movement over the Greek army – that part of the Ottoman Empire on which the Turkish Republic would be established in 1923 under the presidency of Mustafa Kemal (Atatürk, after 1935).[18] But contextualising the First World War in the Middle East must go much further than acknowledging that the Ottoman state had been at war since 1911.

Any interpretation of the Ottoman First World War hinges on how we assess Ottoman–European interaction throughout the nineteenth century, and on where we place the Empire on a spectrum of two extremes: at one end, an example, in today's parlance, of a failed state, one that took out loans it could not repay, oppressed its subjects, violated non-Muslim minorities, remained hostile to international norms and thus precipitated Great Power intervention and paved its own road to destruction; at the other end, a 'Victim of Western Imperialism', always groaning under the predatory practices of the European Great Powers that sought its partition, in a game known as the 'Eastern Question', ever since Catherine the Great set her eyes on 'Tsargrad' and Napoleon Bonaparte declared that whoever possesses Constantinople could govern the world, but even so, 'a largely successful experiment in multinationalism that was destroyed by the great powers in World War I'.[19]

Few scholars today would embrace whole-heartedly either end of the spectrum, but most studies can be classified as gravitating towards one of these two poles. Those studies that cast the Ottoman Empire as a failed state – 'a landscape of oppressed nations'[20] – explain the growing European involvement in the region, which culminated in occupation during and after the First World War, as the result of a growing vacuum of power and authority that the Powers, as the custodians of global order, had no choice but to fill. On the other hand, studies that depict the Empire as the victim of imperialism ascribe Ottoman policies and ethnic violence too readily to external factors only,

18 See the Preface, for example, of Stanford J. Shaw, *Prelude to War*, vol. I: *The Ottoman Empire in World War I*, Turkish Historical Society, no. 109 (Ankara: Türk Tarih Kurumu, 2006), p. xxxiii; İsmet Görgülü and İzeddin Çalışlar (eds.), *On Yıllık Savaşın Günlüğü: Balkan, Birinci Dünya ve İstiklal Savaşları: Orgeneral İzzettin Çalışların Günlüğü* (Istanbul: Yapı Kredi Yayınları, 1997). Çalışlar's diary actually begins with the Balkan wars in 1912 rather than the Italian war.

19 Espoused by Donald Quataert and, in his words, 'many others,' review of Kemal H. Karpat, *The Politicization of Islam: Reconstructing Identity, State, Faith, and Community in the Late Ottoman Empire* (New York: Oxford University Press, 2001), in *American Historical Review*, 107:4 (2002), p. 1328.

20 James Renton, 'Changing languages of empire and the Orient: Britain and the invention of the Middle East, 1917–1918', *Historical Journal*, 50 (2007), p. 649.

while failing to acknowledge the suffering the Ottoman state itself inflicted. The difference lies partly in sources. Listening exclusively to European diplomats, travellers and expats could lead a historian to assume that the Empire was an obsolete entity whose shortcomings made intervention inevitable, just as listening exclusively to Ottoman voices encourages a picture of rapacious predators bent on destroying Ottoman rule.

The spectrum problem cannot be solved by locating a purportedly true, or correct point on the scale, but only by discarding the scale altogether, because it is a false one to begin with. Taking seriously *both* the effects of imperialism and the nature of the Ottoman state is crucial. In fact, the two sides were inseparable, the one constituting the other as they developed over time. The Ottoman state would not have treated its minority populations as ruthlessly as it did over the course of the nineteenth and into the twentieth century without the effects of European imperialism and the fear of being subjected to severe interference. Nor would European policies have taken the form they did without the repressive paths chosen by the Ottoman state. European imperialism and Ottoman response, together, produced the Empire's 'zones of genocide'.[21] Throughout this process European diplomacy fuelled within the Empire a new type of identity politics based on religion and ethnicity that proved explosive. Advocating minority and national rights could also mean advocating or sanctioning, if implicitly, population exchanges, ethnic cleansing and genocide.[22] Acknowledging this history as a shared process is not to excuse Ottoman actions, as Donald Bloxham has stressed,[23] but to see Europeans and Ottomans as 'all swimming in those waters . . . of the ocean of history'.[24]

21 Mark Levene, 'Creating a modern "zone of genocide": the impact of nation- and state-formation on eastern Anatolia, 1878–1923', *Holocaust and Genocide Studies*, 12 (1998), pp. 393–33.

22 Eric D. Weitz, 'From the Vienna to the Paris system: international politics and the entangled histories of human rights, forced deportations, and civilizing missions', *American Historical Review*, 113:5 (2008), p. 1316: 'It is not an accident, nor mere hypocrisy, that leading statesmen such as the Czechs Thomas Masaryk and Eduard Beneš and the Greek prime minister Eleutherios Venizelos (let alone Winston Churchill and Franklin Delano Roosevelt) could move without missing a beat from strong advocacy of democracy and human rights to active promotion of compulsory deportations of minority populations.'

23 Donald Bloxham, 'The First World War and the development of the Armenian genocide', in Ronald Grigor Suny, Fatma Müge Göçek and Norman M. Naimark (eds.), *A Question of Genocide* (Oxford University Press, 2011), pp. 260–84.

24 Edward W. Said, 'Clash of ignorance', *The Nation*, 22 October 2001.

Mobilisation

Surrounded by a crowd of weeping wives, mothers and children, Ali Rıza reported for duty near where he was born, in the vicinity of the north-eastern Anatolian city of Erzincan, answering the authorities' call for mobilisation issued on 3 August 1914. Twenty-seven at the time, within a few weeks, Ali Rıza found himself surrounded by snow and freezing cold, infected with dysentery and discharging blood 'in my urine and from my bottom', and, a few days later, secreting blood through his mouth. Within those same few weeks he had witnessed the first victims succumb to dysentery, before ever encountering the enemy. 'The poor wretches', he noted in his diary on 3 October 1914. The Empire had not yet entered the war. But they were on their way through the mountains to Sarıkamış, where in January up to 80 to 90 per cent of the Third Army would perish, in one of the worst military disasters in Ottoman history. Ali Rıza was a common soldier, even if the fact that his older brother was a doctor and officer meant that he was assigned to the medical corps, where he was assistant to the battalion doctor. His brother's position also meant that he had at his disposal some cash, enabling him to purchase food and additional clothing during these initial trying weeks of mobilisation. As Ali Rıza's unit marched east, bread was produced in the bakeries of villages they passed, in ovens fuelled with cow dung, which slowed down the process to an agonising speed. Four days into his unit's first engagement, on 11 November – the very day the Ottoman state issued its declaration of jihad – two of Ali Rıza's comrades froze to death in what would become a routine end to the lives of common soldiers.[25]

Too often their tragedy is glossed over with the Ottoman triumph of Gallipoli or rejected outright in the light of the brutal Ottoman policies towards Christian populations that culminated in the destruction of Anatolia's Assyrians and Armenians. Yet the extreme deprivation, poverty, exposure to disease and lawlessness enabled such policies of destruction. By this time, as Ali Rıza saw, many had already deserted – there would be at least half a million of them by the end of the war, or one out of every six

25 Ali Rıza Eti, *Bir Onbaşının Doğu Cephesi Günlüğü*, pp. 26 and 46. There is a significant range for the casualty numbers of the Third Army at Sarıkamış, as well as its original strength. See Hikmet Özdemir, *The Ottoman Army, 1914–1918: Disease and Death on the Battlefield*, trans. Saban Kardaş (Salt Lake City, UT: University of Utah Press, 2008), pp. 50–67; and Michael A. Reynolds, *Shattering Empires: The Clash and Collapse of the Russian and Ottoman Empires, 1908–1918* (Cambridge University Press, 2011), p. 125. Reynolds gives the strength of the Third Army as 95,000 men, Özdemir as 112,000.

conscripted.[26] Orders were given to have deserters shot on the spot, to oblige anyone else contemplating fleeing the colours to cease such thoughts immediately. Desertion, already significant and humanly understandable, would be in fact the first charge levied against the Armenians. And where would deserters go? By December 1914, Armenians in the ranks were being singled out as potential defectors to the Russian side and were already being shot preemptively – 'accidentally', as the saying went. Ali Rıza also had become filled with anger at Armenians, swearing, on 17 January, after the Sarıkamış campaign had already taken the lives of tens of thousands, although through horrific conditions as much as Russian action, to 'poison and kill 3 or 4 Armenians in the hospital'. He could not believe that Armenians and Turks would be 'brothers and fellow citizens' once again after the war; the campaign to invade Russian territory at Sarıkamış, waged in extreme winter conditions during December 1914 and January 1915, had been too much.[27] Ali Rıza's feeling that the war was severing irreversibly the ties that had held together the Empire's ethnic and religious groups for centuries proved devastatingly accurate.

The official figures released in 1921 by the Ministry of War, and self-admittedly incomplete, showed the total number of conscripts as 2.85 million. This estimate excludes, however, hundreds of thousands, both men and women, conscripted into labour battalions as well as those fighting with irregular formations, primarily in eastern Anatolia, consisting of Kurdish men under Kurdish leadership. Another reason to suspect that the 2.85 million number undercounts Ottoman conscripts is that in March 1917, the Ministry of War had given cumulative conscription as 2.855 million, with over eighteen months of fighting still ahead. The official casualty estimates of 325,000 dead and 400,000 wounded must be considered with equal scepticism.[28] A recent attempt at recalculating Ottoman casualties showed 771,844 dead, with over half succumbing to disease; a mortality rate of around 25 per cent.[29]

26 For a thorough treatment of the topic, based on research in the Archives of the Turkish general staff, see Mehmet Beşikçi, *The Ottoman Mobilization of Manpower in the First World War: between Voluntarism and Resistance* (Leiden: Brill, 2012), pp. 247–309. I thank Professor Beşikçi for allowing me to cite his manuscript.

27 Ali Rıza Eti, *Bir Onbaşının Doğu Cephesi Günlüğü*, pp. 104 and 135.

28 Beşikçi, *The Ottoman Mobilization of Manpower*, pp. 113–15.

29 Edward J. Erickson, *Ordered to Die: A History of the Ottoman Army in the First World War* (Westport, CT: Greenwood Press, 2001), pp. 237–43.

The state faced a constant shortage of manpower as it tried to fill its rank and file, a task made more difficult by the fact that military authorities questioned the loyalty of large segments of the populations on ethnic and religious grounds, even though the Ottoman Parliament, opened in 1908, had made military service mandatory for all men regardless of ethnic or religious background in 1909. The Empire's Christian and Jewish communities had responded to the law in a variety of ways. Some, such as the sons of Jewish middle-class families in Jerusalem, initially embraced military service in a spirit of civic Ottomanism following the Young Turk Revolution of July 1908, subsequent elections and the apparent arrival of representative government.[30] Others, especially Greek-Orthodox Ottomans, simply never presented themselves to the authorities.[31] The ethnic and religious composition of the Ottoman army has not been reconstructed with any precision. While the commonly used figure of Arab conscripts is 300,000, or 10 per cent of the total number of men mobilised, a recent study suggests that recruits from the Empire's Arabic-speaking provinces may have comprised over 26 per cent. Archival evidence shows that of the 49,238 men who had deserted in Aydın province between August 1914 and June 1916, about 59 per cent were Muslim, 41 per cent non-Muslim.[32]

Hagop Mıntzuri, like Ali Rıza, was born near the city of Erzincan, either in the same year or one year earlier. On 3 August 1914, the day the Ottoman state called up all men between the ages of 20 and 45, Hagop found himself on a visit to Istanbul, without his family. Immediately conscripted as a baker, a job he had done for many years, Hagop would not see his wife, Vogida, or any of his four children, Nurhan aged 6, Maranik aged 4, Anahit aged 2, or baby Haço, ever again. They, along with Hagop's 55-year-old mother, Nanik, and his 80-year-old grandfather, Melkon, and all the other Christians of the village, had been deported, never to be heard from again. The Mıntzuris were Armenians.[33]

30 Campos, *Ottoman Brothers*, p. 87.

31 Fikret Adanır, 'Non-Muslims in the Ottoman army and the Ottoman defeat in the Balkan war of 1912–1913', in Suny, Göçek and Naimark (eds.), *A Question of Genocide*, p. 117.

32 Beşikçi, *The Ottoman Mobilization of Manpower*, pp. 253–4.

33 Fatma Müge Göçek, *The Transformation of Turkey: Redefining State and Society from the Ottoman Empire to the Modern Era* (London: I. B. Tauris, 2011), pp. 198–205. For his memoirs, published posthumously in Turkish, see Hagop Mintzuri, *İstanbul Anıları, 1897–1940*, trans. Silva Kuyumcuyan, ed. Necdet Sakaoğlu (Istanbul: Tarih Vakfı, 1993; 2012), p. 133.

Battle

The men of state in charge of formulating high policy saw a potential collusion between the Empire's minority populations – Christians, but also Jews, Arabs, Kurds – and the Entente powers. And the Ottomans had their own version of their German ally's anxious obsession with *Einkreisung*, their putative encirclement. They feared Russia's desire for control over the Ottoman Straits and its designs on eastern Anatolia, a region stretching from the Russian Caucasus to the eastern Mediterranean and heavily populated by Armenian Christians and Muslim Kurds. Russia threatened the Empire north and east, while, since the late nineteenth century, Britain had ensconced itself in Egypt and the strategically vital Cyprus, a presence that could be expanded to the Empire's southern, Arabic-speaking regions, connecting British South Asia and Egypt. In the Empire's geographic centre, French influence over autonomous regions in Syria and British support of Zionism in Palestine posed further challenges to the deep sense of insecurity and imperial weakness that dominated the halls of power in Istanbul. Syria, moreover, was vulnerable from the Mediterranean and, further to the east, Iraq could be reached by the British from Basra and from Persia by both British and Russian forces, as those two powers had partitioned Persia, first, politically, in 1907 and then, militarily, in 1911, shaking the ground not only in Tehran but also in Istanbul.

In the face of this geo-strategic plight, the Ottoman leaders transformed the July crisis into an opportunity for a military alliance with a Great Power, Germany, which they hoped would provide the Empire with an umbrella of long-term protection, a period of imperial consolidation after the war, even if it meant that, in the shorter term, the Ottomans might have to do battle once again.

The Minister of War, Enver, who held the title of 'pasha', bestowed on the Empire's highest officials, had cut his teeth as a young officer fighting guerrilla-style warfare in Ottoman Macedonia against Bulgarian and Greek revolutionaries. When Italy occupied Libya in the fall of 1911, Enver again led regular and irregular troops against the Italians, who responded by showering the Arab population with propaganda:

> Let it not be hidden from you that Italy (may Allah strengthen her!), in determining to occupy this land, aims at serving your interests as well as ours, and at assuring our mutual welfare by driving out the Turks. . . . They have always despised you. We, on the other hand, have studied your customs and your history. . . . We respect your noble religion because we recognize its

> merits, and we respect also your women. . . . There is no doubt that with God's help, we shall drive the Turks out of this country.[34]

The Pope, moreover, 'blessed the Italian fighters and praised God for helping them to replace the Crescent with the Cross in Libya'.[35] Among the officer corps and the politicised classes these experiences, from the Balkans to North Africa, created a sense of crisis about the Empire's territorial security, which appeared attainable to many only through the display of military strength, and war if necessary.[36] As one paper put it: 'We must now fully realise that our honour and our people's integrity cannot be preserved by those old books of international law, but only by war.'[37]

On 28 July 1914, in a cipher classified 'very urgent', the governor of Edirne province, Adil, alerted the Ministry of the Interior to Bulgarian troop movements along the border and asked for news on the worsening international constellation. Interior Minister Talat, already one of Istanbul's most powerful men, replied immediately: 'Austria has declared war. We think the war will not remain local but spread. My brother, we are working day and night to protect ourselves from harm and to take advantage of the situation to the best of our abilities.'[38] On 2 August 1914, Talat sent out mobilisation orders to provincial governors:

> Because war has been declared between Germany and Russia our current political situation has become very delicate. It is probable that Russia will engage in hostile action and efforts against our borders in order to continue its policies and influence in the Caucasus and Persia. Therefore, as has already been instructed previously, all necessary measures for the completion of mobilisation are to be implemented immediately and without delay and with the greatest diligence and speed and whatever steps and measures are necessary for war and an attack on us must be undertaken right now and reports submitted regularly.[39]

For all their alarm, to the Ottoman leadership what would become the Great War appeared first as a great opportunity, an opportunity to secure a

34 G. F. Abbott, *The Holy War in Tripoli* (London: Longman's, Green, 1912), pp. 193–4.

35 Rachel Simon, *Libya Between Ottomanism and Nationalism* (Berlin: Klaus Schwarz, 1987), p. 87.

36 Aksakal, *The Ottoman Road to War*, pp. 19–41, 93–118.

37 *Ahenk*, 13 October 1912, quoted in Zeki Arıkan, 'Balkan Savaşı ve Kamuoyu', in *Bildiriler: Dördüncü Askeri Tarih Semineri* (Ankara: Genelkurmay Basımevi, 1989), p. 176.

38 BOA, DH. ŞFR 43/127, 28 and 29 July 1914.

39 BOA, DH. ŞFR 43/141, 2 August 1914, Talat to the governors of Erzurum, Adana, Aydın, Bitlis, Halep, Diyar-ı Bekir, Sivas, Trabzon, Kastamonu, Mamuret-ül-aziz, Mosul, Van, Bolu, Çanik, Kale-i Sultaniye and Antalya.

long-term military alliance with Germany that would survive the war and afford the Empire international cover. Their hope was to be able to sit on the alliance and to sit out the war. To obtain the alliance, Minister of War Enver had succeeded in convincing Berlin that his army would be able to contribute significantly to the German war effort, and that it would be able to do so immediately. By mid October 1914, however, the Ottomans had still not moved, despite having drawn on German gold, shells and guns, a German military and a naval mission of thousands of personnel and specialists and two German men-of-war, the battlecruiser SMS *Goeben* (renamed *Yavuz Sultan Selim*) and the light cruiser SMS *Breslau* (renamed *Midilli*), anchored in the Dardanelles since 10 August. With German assets came German pressure, however, to the point of threatening the rupture of the alliance by late October. At this point the Ottoman leaders resolved to open fire, in a spectacular night operation culminating in the sinking of Russian ships on the Black Sea and the bombardment, from the sea, of the Black Sea cities Sevastopol and (the once Ottoman) Novorossiysk on 29 October 1914.[40]

The Ottomans had launched this attack without a declaration of war, in the manner of Japan's strike against Russia in 1904 (and Greece's on the Ottoman Empire in 1897). The Black Sea raid was followed by two equally bold campaigns. The second of these campaigns, led by Jemal Pasha, the commander of the Fourth Army based in Syria, and the one more closely watched in the West, targeted the Suez Canal and British Egypt. The first, led by Enver Pasha himself, aimed at retaking the three Ottoman provinces lost to Russia in 1878 – Ardahan, Batumi and Kars – and had the advantage from the German perspective of diverting Russian troops away from the Habsburgs' eastern front. Ardahan and Kars would in fact be returned to the Empire before the war ended, to become part of the future Turkish Republic, but only after the Russian Revolutions of 1917, and only after the Ottomans' disastrous attempt to encircle Russian forces near Sarıkamış, located just across the border in territory ceded to Russia in 1878. Opening in December 1914, the operation by mid January 1915 had turned into a full-blown rout of the Ottoman Third Army.

Ottoman intelligence had followed closely the Russian troop concentrations, estimating, in August 1914, Russian strength on the Ottoman border in eastern Anatolia at about 100,000 men.[41] There was not only some hope that Russian Muslim populations of the Caucasus would support the Ottoman

40 Aksakal, *The Ottoman Road to War*, pp. 119–87.

41 BOA, DH. ŞFR 435/40, 3 August 1914; BOA, DH. EUM. VRK 12/60, 4 August 1914.

invasion, but also that both Afghanistan and Persia would come in on the Ottomans' side.[42] Moreover, Ottoman agents were sending reports in December 1914 of the feeble conditions that marked the Russian formations on the other side of the border. Agents estimated Russian strength at Sarıkamış to be around 50,000 and the men to be on half-rations and hungry, 'begging in the streets' and poorly equipped. The Tsar, it was said, had been in Tiflis and had to be evacuated.[43] Within a week, by 6 January 1915, this picture had shifted drastically, and it was clear that the Ottoman offensive had not only been beaten back but Enver's forces had been destroyed.[44]

Both campaigns, in the east into Russia and the south into British-held Egypt, aimed at territories with predominantly Muslim populations, and they attempted in both to employ Islam as a tool to mobilise those populations on the Ottomans' behalf. The territory on the Ottoman–Russian border, however, with large Christian populations on both sides, morphed into a 'bloodlands', as both empires deported and killed populations suspected of disloyalty. In January 1915, perhaps as many as 30 to 45,000 Muslims were killed inside the Russian border, and some 10,000 deported.[45] As staggering as these figures are, they would be dwarfed in 1915 and 1916 by Ottoman deportations and summary executions of, first, Christian and, later, Kurdish populations.

The proclamation of jihad against the Entente represented the Ottoman state's effort to mobilise both soldiers at the front and society at home. There had been no declaration of jihad during the Balkan wars, as such a policy would have alienated the Empire's non-Muslim peoples. By November 1914, however, this consideration was no longer valid for the decision-makers in the CUP, and they used the jihad declaration in an attempt to bind the Empire's Muslim populations closer to the state, especially in the Arabic-speaking parts of the Empire. That Berlin pushed the Ottoman government for such a declaration, because it hoped that Muslims all over – in British Egypt and India, in French North Africa, in the Russian Caucasus and Central Asia – would rise up in rebellion, has sometimes obscured the Ottomans' own purposes for instrumentalising Islam in general and jihad in particular. The forces sent to invade Egypt, for example, were presented on postage stamps as

42 BOA, DH. ŞFR 437/83, 17 August 1914.
43 BOA, DH. ŞFR 455/124, 28 and 29 December 1914.
44 BOA, DH. ŞFR 456/112, 6 January 1915.
45 Reynolds, *Shattering Empires*, p. 144; and, on the Second World War, Timothy Snyder, *Bloodlands: Europe between Hitler and Stalin* (New York: Basic Books, 2010).

'The Islamic Army of Egypt, Savior of Conquered Lands',[46] and those sent into Russian Baku in 1918 as 'The Caucasus Army of Islam'.[47]

Muslim populations sympathised with the Ottoman war effort when Ottoman victory promised to improve conditions or advance local agendas. The Nationalist Party in Egypt, for example, actively worked together with the Ottomans in their attempt to throw the British out of Cairo. Muhammad Farid, the Nationalist Party leader, hoped for a national revolution at home against British rule, and the formation of a regional alliance, backed by Germany, against the three powers of the Entente. While Farid objected to the Arab Revolt, he eventually also became deeply disappointed by Jemal Pasha's rule in Syria and growing expressions of Turkish nationalism.[48] Fraternity with the German-Ottoman cause persists to a degree in Egyptian memory. Yasin, a character in Naguib Mahfouz's *Palace Walk*, set in Cairo, 'wished the Germans would win and consequently the Turks too'. But then he shakes his head in utter frustration: 'Four years have passed and we keep saying this same thing.'[49] While resentment of British rule ran deep among 'ordinary Egyptians', as evident in popular folk songs and plays, for example, armed resistance would not erupt until 1919.[50]

Failures at the front were compounded by acute shortages of food in all parts of the Empire, but especially in Syria, whose inhabitants suffered from an Anglo-French naval blockade. In Syria, these dire conditions combined with an outbreak of locusts in 1915 that left over half a million dead – in part by famine-related disease – by the war's end. As the disaster was unfolding, the French consul in Cairo alerted his government to the fact that tens of thousands had starved to death and suggested providing relief through food shipments. The British response, however, was unequivocal: 'His Majesty's Secretary of State for Foreign Affairs expresses his earnest hope that the French Government will not encourage any such scheme.... The Entente Allies are simply being blackmailed to remedy the shortage of supplies which it is the very intention of the blockade to produce.' The French concluded that

46 Hasan Kayalı, *Arabs and Young Turks: Ottomanism, Arabism, and Islamism in the Ottoman Empire, 1908–1918* (Berkeley: University of California Press, 1997), p. 189. See the cover illustration for the stamp.

47 Reynolds, *Shattering Empires*, pp. 220–2.

48 Arthur Goldschmidt, Jr. (ed.), *The Memoirs and Diaries of Muhammad Farid, an Egyptian Nationalist Leader (1868–1919)* (San Francisco: Mellen University Research Press, 1992), pp. 6–7.

49 Naguib Mahfouz, *Palace Walk*, trans. William Maynard Hutchins and Olive E. Kenny (New York: Anchor Books, 1990), p. 56.

50 Ziad Fahmy, *Ordinary Egyptians: Creating the Modern Nation Through Popular Culture* (Stanford University Press, 2011), pp. 98, 117–33.

their British allies 'consider the famine as an agent that will lead the Arabs to revolt'.[51]

By the end of 1915, for some that breaking point appeared imminent. In Jerusalem, Private İhsan noted in his diary on 17 December 1915: 'If the government had any dignity, it would have saved wheat in its hangars for public distribution at a fixed price, or even have made it available from military supplies. If these conditions persist, the people will rebel and bring down this government.'[52] But the extreme impoverishment suffered by the people of Syria and Palestine pushed society to the brink of collapse rather than revolution. On 10 July 1916, İhsan's spirit of resistance had turned into resignation:

> I can hardly concentrate. We face both a general war and an internal war. The government is trying (with futility) to bring food supplies, and disease is everywhere. It's been over a month now since I have written anything in my diary. Jerusalem has not seen [worse] days. Bread and flour supplies have almost totally dried up. Every day I pass the bakeries on my way to work, and I see a large number of women going home empty-handed.[53]

The government in Istanbul proved poorly equipped to respond to the crisis and left its mitigation to Jemal Pasha, the regional boss and commander of the Fourth Army based in Damascus, who prioritised his soldiers in the allocation of supplies.

The food crisis gripped the Empire as a whole, however, and very early in the war. In fact, as early as October 1914, before the Ottomans had become a belligerent, reports started arriving in the capital complaining about the lack of food. Nor was there seed available to be planted for the next season. The governor of Edirne warned the government that he could not assume the responsibility for the 'famine and starvation' that would be certain to befall the people of his province. He therefore put the Interior Ministry on notice that if no seeds were provided it would become necessary to seize available seed supplies, and that he, the governor, would begin with collecting those supplies left behind by the Christians of Edirne who had now 'departed for Greece'.[54] Military authorities everywhere saw no alternative but to requisition available civilian food supplies. By the spring of 1916, military storage facilities had become depleted as well.[55] The War Ministry pressured the government to

51 Thompson, *Colonial Citizens*, pp. 19–23. For quotes see p. 22.
52 Ihsan Turjman, in Tamari (ed.), *Year of the Locust*, p. 143. 53 *Ibid.*, p. 154.
54 BOA, DH. SYS 123–9/21–3, 13 October 1914.
55 BOA, DH. İ. UM. 93–4/1–48, 13 March 1916.

resort to more extreme methods in securing the necessary collection of food for the army. 'We are unable to provide our soldiers even with a quarter of their meat ration. Their physical strength is withering away, as our doctors are reporting daily. The disastrous effects of these conditions on the war have already become apparent. Please take urgent measures for the securing of our meat supply.' The War Ministry demanded an annual supply of 67 million kilos of meat, 'requiring 4,666,000 [sic: 4,466,000] heads of sheep, at 15 kilos each. These sheep will be difficult to secure by purchasing them.'[56]

While the state's military machine ate up men by conscripting them, it left behind an insufficient number of capable workers to maintain agricultural production at levels that could sustain both an army and the civilian population at large. Feeding troops, moreover, clearly was the state's priority. The deportation of many men from eastern Anatolia left that area particularly vulnerable. In a cipher from July 1915, the commander of the Third Army requested the assignment of thousands of soldiers to agricultural work, as 'all Muslims have been conscripted and the Armenians in their entirety [*kâmilen*] have been deported'. Without such a labour force, Mahmud Kâmil went on, the region would descend into 'dearth and famine' and render his army without supplies, and possibly have 'catastrophic' consequences.[57] By 1917 the manpower problem had become so acute that the War Ministry requested information from the provinces as to the number of available 12- to 17-year-old boys.[58]

Private İhsan, the soldier serving in Jerusalem, did not live long enough to see the keys of his city handed over to the British. On 9 December 1917, Jerusalem surrendered, and two days later, General Edmund Allenby entered Jerusalem through Jaffa Gate, on foot, in a gesture of symbolic humility. The city's inhabitants cheered the apparent arrival of peace. But with the expulsion of Ottoman rule came necessarily the unpredictability of how and by whom the newly 'liberated' regions of the Empire would be governed. Initially, it seemed, a new order would be established through a deliberative process defined by Woodrow Wilson's call for self-determination and a new international body, the League of Nations. The reprieve, however, did not last long, and in Palestine the population understood quickly that the old Empire, swept away by the war, was being replaced by a new one, with its own imperial aims yet to unfold. The United States' special agent to the region, William Yale, who would serve on the King-Crane Commission charged with a fact-finding mission to Syria after the war, reported as early as April 1918:

56 BOA, DH. İ. UM. 93–4/1–48, 20 March 1916.

57 BOA, DH. İ. UM 59–1/1–38, 15 July 1915.

58 BOA, DH. UMVM 148/53, 9 June 1917.

> It is rather significant that Palestine, where there has been so much suffering and privation, and where the disaffection with the Turkish regime was so great in 1916 and 1917, that nearly every Arab talked open treason against the Ottoman government and longed for the deliverance of their country from the Turks, there should be in the spring of 1918, soon after the British occupation, a party, which, according to British political agents, wished to live in the future under the suzerainty of Turkey. The sentiments of this party cannot be altogether explained by an inherent dislike of Europeans and the very natural Muslim desire of wishing to be under a Muslim ruler. There undoubtedly enters into these sentiments of this party the belief that under Turkish rule the Zionists would not be allowed to gain a stronger foothold in Palestine than they now have.[59]

Indeed in 1914, after several waves of Jewish immigration, primarily from Europe, the Jewish population of Palestine stood at around 6 per cent. At this point an independent Jewish state in Palestine was on the agenda of only a minority of the Jewish population there. The majority urged the recent immigrants to take up Ottoman citizenship, to serve in the Ottoman military, to work together with the local Muslim and Christian population and thereby to build a Jewish community within the House of Osman, the Ottoman Empire. These views found expression in the widely circulated daily *ha-Herut*, which carried on the occasion of Istanbul's call for mobilisation the patriotic speech of a Jewish conscript: 'From this moment we are not separate people [individuals]. All the people of this country are as one man, and we all want to protect our country and respect our empire.'[60]

But with Ottoman collapse looming, even appearing imminent at such times as the Gallipoli campaign in 1915, this outlook disappeared, and for the first time Theodor Herzl's vision of a Jewish state appeared compellingly viable. The conditions of the war made this sea change possible. Institutions such as the Anglo-Palestine Bank together with the United States provided war relief directed for the Jewish population of Palestine. The British government promised 'a national home for the Jewish people' in the Balfour Declaration of 2 November 1917, even as they were actively encouraging Arab independence in their negotiations with Sharif Hussein of Mecca. The war had given rise to a radically new power relationship in Palestine.

59 Quoted in Abigail Jacobson, *From Empire to Empire: Jerusalem Between Ottoman and British Rule* (Syracuse University Press, 2011), p. 145, from 'The situation in Palestine', 1 April 1918, CM/241/33, Report no. 21, 11–13, Central Zionist Archives.

60 Quoted in Jacobson, *From Empire to Empire*, p. 27.

The end

The lack of adequate food both at home and at the front rendered soldiers and civilians highly susceptible to disease. About 14 per cent of all soldiers mobilised succumbed, with dysentery and typhus being the most lethal.[61] The great number of casualties, displaced people and forced migrations produced long-term socio-economic consequences: urban populations, for example, did not return to pre-war levels until the early 1950s.[62] In Anatolia/Turkey, living standards dropped dramatically, as GDP in the 1920s stood at about half that of pre-war figures.[63] The war's transformative effects on Syria were no less profound, as it left behind an equally devastated landscape and a 'shattered social order'.[64]

In the post-war limbs of the now-dismembered empire, the regimes quickly adapted to the new political realities and each appropriated its own, and often more than one, version of a usable Ottoman past. The military insecurity and national vagueness in which the new regimes were born gave rise to military dictatorships that presented themselves as safeguards of both territorial security and national unity. In Turkey, the military society that took root during the years of the First World War never returned to its former civilian self. The war shaped the Turkish Republic and the Kemalist period in fundamental ways. A basic textbook used in military high schools in 1926, for example, opened with the following lines: 'Wars have now become wars fought by the entire nation. Times have changed. Wars are no longer fought by the army alone. All women and men, each member of the nation, must take on a duty and a role according to his or her age and skills that will serve the war.'[65] Nearly identical lines could be found in European textbooks as well, of course. Unlike in most of Europe, however, in Turkey the sense of internal and external enemies has remained a central feature of the political culture, as in all the former lands of the Ottoman Empire for a century.

61 Erik J. Zürcher, 'The Ottoman soldier in World War I', in Zürcher, *The Young Turk Legacy and Nation Building: From the Ottoman Empire to Atatürk's Turkey* (London: I. B. Tauris, 2010), p. 187.

62 Istanbul's population in 1914 was about 1 million, of which 450,000 were Christian. See Çağlar Keyder (ed.), *Istanbul: Between the Global and the Local* (Lanham, MD: Rowman & Littlefield, 1999), pp. 10, 146, 175.

63 Michael Twomey, 'Economic change', in Camron Michael Amin, Benjamin C. Fortna and Elizabeth B. Frierson (eds.), *The Modern Middle East: A Sourcebook* (Oxford University Press, 2006), p. 528.

64 Thompson, *Colonial Citizens*, p. 19.

65 Cemil Tahir, *Askerliğe Hazırlık Dersleri* ([Istanbul:] Harbiye Mektebi Matbaası, 1926), p. 1.

18

Asia

GUOQI XU

The Great War has been studied from every possible perspective, from its wider significance to particular issues and incidents; yet knowledge about the important role Asia played in the conflict and the war's profound impact on Asian societies remains at best limited. If the world has not yet fully realised the deep connection between Asia and the Great War, Asians have not yet fully understood its legacy and impact on their history and the development of their nations. In this chapter I aim to fill this remarkable gap in the First World War literature by highlighting the multi-layered involvements and perspectives of various Asian nations on that 'great seminal catastrophe' of the twentieth century.

This chapter will weave together the diplomatic, social, political, cultural and military histories of China, Vietnam, India and Japan in a comparative way by focusing on the shared experiences, aspirations and frustrations of people from across the region. I will especially pay attention to questions such as how the various Asian involvements made the Great War not only a true 'world' war but also a 'great' war, and how that war generated the forces that would transform Asia both internally and externally. We might call the nineteenth century a 'long century' in Asia and the twentieth rather a short one, with the First World War serving as the dividing-line. In other words, from an Asian perspective, the twentieth century started in earnest at the outbreak of the

I am deeply grateful for Jay Winter and John Horne's comments and suggestions. John Horne also provided valuable help in granting me access to Trinity College Dublin's great library collections when I was writing this chapter. Robert Gerwarth deserves to be thanked for forcing me to sharpen my thinking on this topic when, as the editor in chief of the Oxford University Press's multi-volume studies of the war period, he convinced me to write a book on Asia and the Great War, and also for his generosity in inviting me to serve as a visiting professor at University College Dublin's Centre for War Studies, where I worked on this topic. I also have to express my gratitude to Santanu Das, Akeo Okada, Jan P. Schmidt and Radhika Singha, who were very kind in providing original and other sources and their own work (some even unpublished) for me to consult and use. As always, I am in deep debt to Terre Fisher for her crucial and great editing skills.

Great War. Due to concerns with thematic coherence and space limitations, this chapter will largely focus on the Western Front and on the four above-mentioned nations. Many other important areas and issues will have to be left untouched.

News of the European war reaches Asia

In 1914, the Year of the Tiger in the Chinese zodiac cycle, the 'guns of August' declared the coming of a Great War. Although the war began as an essentially European conflict, Asians grew both excited and worried when the news of its outbreak reached them. The seeds of what would become a deep interest in the European war had actually been planted in 1895 in the cases of China and Japan, while India and Vietnam – colonies of Britain and France, respectively – could only follow their colonial masters when they joined the fight.

The outbreak of a European war was a God-sent opportunity for the Japanese. Japan, like China, had been in almost a total isolation until Western powers forced it to open to the outside world in the mid nineteenth century. Unlike China, Japan soon decided to join the Western system and follow in Western footsteps with the launching of the Meiji Restoration in 1868. Some Japanese elites openly suggested that Japan leave its Asian identity behind, and emulating Western ways became both fashionable and national policy. Inoue Kaoru, an influential Japanese politician, declared, 'We must make our nation and people into a European nation and European people.'[1]

In less than a generation, Japan had become confident enough about turning itself into a Western-style empire that it took on China, formerly the economic and cultural giant of Asia. In 1894 war broke out between China and Japan, and by 1895 the Chinese had been soundly defeated. The war made Japan a major power in East Asia and an empire with its first colony Taiwan, which China was forced to cede. The war also laid the groundwork for Japan to acquire a second colony by forcing China to abandon Korea, traditionally a Chinese tributary state. Japan seemed to be bound for a major international military game.

The 1894–5 Sino-Japanese War further planted the seeds for Japan's direct entry into the Great War nearly twenty years later. Germany had played a leading role in the so-called triple intervention subsequent to the Sino-Japanese conflict, in which the Germans 'advised' the Japanese to return to

1 Akira Iriye, *Japan and the Wider World* (London: Longman, 1997), p. 5.

China the Liaodong Peninsula, which Japan had forced China to cede. This infuriated the Japanese, who became determined to find a way to take action against Germany. One Japanese newspaper's headline, 'Wait for another time' clearly conveyed this sentiment.[2] In 1902 Japan achieved a major diplomatic coup by signing an alliance treaty with Britain, which at that point was preparing for possible war with the Germans. On the basis of the relationship created with this treaty, when war broke out in 1914 Japan managed to insert itself into the war. With this background one might say that Japan had been preparing for this opportunity since its war with China in 1895. Japan became an imperial power in 1895 when antagonism between the Entente and the future Central Powers began to intensify.

As a rising power in Asia, Japan was determined to become a leading player in international politics. But Japan's efforts faced some resistance from the Western powers. It would have been difficult for Japan to fulfil its growing ambitions without external help, and so the outbreak in August 1914 was considered by many Japanese to be a great opportunity. The Japanese had been waiting for their chance, and now with the European war, the magic moment had arrived. No wonder elder statesman, Inoue Kaoru, hailed the news as 'divine aid of the new Taisho era for the development of the destiny of Japan'.[3] Four days after Britain's entry into the war, on 8 August 1914, Japan decided to declare war on Germany, though the official declaration of war was not announced for another week.

Getting revenge for being forced to give up the Liaodong Peninsula was of course a convenient excuse for the Japanese. As Baron Kato, the Japanese Foreign Minister, explained to one American journalist in 1915:

> Germany is an aggressive European Power that had secured a foothold on one corner of the province of Shan-tung. This is a great menace to Japan. Furthermore, Germany had forced Japan to return the peninsula of Liao-tung under the plausible pretense of friendly advice. Because of the pressure brought to bear on us, Japan had to part with the legitimate fruits of war, bought with the blood of our fellow countrymen. Revenge is not justifiable, either in the case of an individual or a nation; but when, by coincidence, one can attend to this duty and at the same time pay an old debt, the opportunity certainly should be seized.[4]

2 S. C. M. Paine, *The Sino-Japanese War of 1894–1895* (Cambridge University Press, 2003), p. 290.

3 Frederick Dickinson, *War and National Reinvention: Japan in the Great War, 1914–1919* (Cambridge, MA: Harvard University Press, 1999), p. 35.

4 Samuel G. Blythe, 'Banzai – and then what?', *Saturday Evening Post*, 187:47 (1915), p. 54.

Japan's real goal was to expand its interest in China while the major powers were occupied in Europe. The biggest payoff for Japan would be kicking German interests out of Asia and establishing itself as the dominant power in China. As I will explain in detail later, China was then in the process of becoming a republic, as a way to renew and strengthen itself in the face of modern threats. Japan was determined to make China a dependent before that transformation could be completed. The Okuma Cabinet declared, 'Japan must take the chance of a millennium' to 'establish its rights and interests in Asia'.[5]

The European war also served Japanese domestic politics because the war could be used as a national rallying point.[6] The death of the Meiji Emperor in 1912 meant the end of an era and the weakening of the existing political order. For some influential Japanese, Japan lost national purpose in the post-Meiji years, and its entry into the war would instil in the Japanese people some sense of higher purpose. Joining the Great War thus would help Japan to achieve three goals: revenging itself on Germany, expanding its interests in China and rejuvenating its domestic politics.

If the Sino-Japanese War of 1894–5 set the stage for Japan's involvement in the Great War, it also nearly sealed China's fate. The Chinese defeat in 1895 meant many things. It certainly subjected the country to much more extensive foreign control, but its psychological impact was even greater. The Sino-Japanese War compelled the Chinese leadership to think seriously about their destiny and the value of their civilisation; more importantly, it caused them to question their traditional identity. That war awakened the Chinese from what Liang Qichao, an influential author and thinker of the late Qing and early Republican period, called 'the great dream of four thousand years'.[7] The sense of frustration, humiliation and impotence in the face of Western incursions and a westernised Japan provided powerful motivation for change. The devastating loss to Japan thus served as both a turning point and shared point of reference for Chinese perceptions of themselves and the world. Chinese elites, no matter what their attitude to their tradition and civilisation, agreed that if China was to survive, it must change. And major change indeed arrived with the 1911 Revolution, when the venerable dynastic system was

5 Ikuhiko Hata, 'Continental expansion, 1905–1941', in John W. Hall *et al.* (eds.), *The Cambridge History of Japan*, vol. VI: *The Twentieth Century* (Cambridge University Press, 1988), p. 279.

6 For the best study on this issue, see Dickinson, *War and National Reinvention*.

7 Liang Qichao, 'Gai ge qi yuan' ('The origins of reform'), in *Yinbing Shi Heji* (Beijing: Zhong hua shu ju, 1989), p. 113.

overturned and a republic established, after the examples of the United States and France.

Under the powerful sweep of these changes and with a burning desire to become an equal member in the family of nations, China abandoned the institutions of Confucian civilisation and transformed itself from a cultural entity that had no official name, despite its long history, to become the first republic in Asia. Nationalism and social Darwinism replaced Confucianism as the defining ideologies in China. In the period between 1895 and 1914 profound changes took place politically, culturally and diplomatically.

Although during much of the First World War period the Chinese people suffered from political chaos, economic weakness and social misery, it was also a time of excitement, hope, high expectation, optimism and new dreams. This may be compared to the Warring States era in ancient Chinese history. The clash of ideas, political theories and the prescription of national identities provided high stimulation to China's ideological, social, cultural and intellectual creativity, and produced a strong determination for change.

These changes would motivate and push China to participate in the new world order and become an equal member in the family of the nations. Like the Japanese, the Chinese considered the outbreak of the European war to be an opportunity, or more precisely, a *weiji* (crisis). The term *weiji* combines two Chinese characters: danger (*wei*) and opportunity (*ji*). As Europe's 'generation of 1914', too young and innocent to suspect what bloody rites of passage awaited them, went off to war, the new generation in China experienced a sense of *weiji* at the challenge of dealing with new developments in the international system. China recognised the danger of becoming involved in the war involuntarily, given that the belligerents all controlled spheres of interest on Chinese territory. With the collapse of the old international system, China could easily be bullied by Japan, and its development thwarted. Yet despite the dangers, the European war also presented excellent opportunities. It could bring changes to the international system that would provide China with the chance to join the larger world. China might even inject its own ideas into shaping the new world order.[8] For contemporary Chinese like Liang Qichao, the war offered more opportunity than danger. Liang argued that the First World War presented China a once-in-a-thousand-years

8 For details on China and the Great War, see Guoqi Xu, *China and the Great War: China's Pursuit of a New National Identity and Internationalization* (Cambridge University Press, 2011).

opportunity. For Liang, the key reason for China's joining the war was to enhance its status in the new international situation; in this way China would not only survive in the short term, but would have an easier time being accepted into the international community in the long term.[9] The problem was how to take best advantage of this opportunity. Liang argued that if China exploited the situation properly, it could finish the process of becoming a 'completely qualified nation-state' and prepare for a quick rise in the world.[10]

To prevent the war from spreading to Chinese territory, China's Republican government on 6 August declared its neutrality. China would remain officially neutral until spring 1917. But this neutrality was only an expedient measure, a strategy intermediate to making a better move; China was prepared to give up its neutrality the moment a new opportunity arose. Modern-minded Chinese officials were especially enthusiastic about the prospects of China's active involvement in the war. As some have observed, these officials, 'with a knowledge of foreign diplomacy, took an immediate interest and combined to exhort the conservatives to action'.[11] Zhang Guogan, an influential government official, suggested to the then Prime Minister, Duan Qirui that the European war had such importance for China that it should take the initiative of declaring war on Germany. This might not only prevent Japan from taking the German concession on Qingdao in the short term, but would be a first step towards full participation in a future world system. Duan responded that he supported the idea of joining the war and was secretly preparing for this move.[12]

Liang Shiyi, who served in many powerful positions in the government and was Chinese President Yuan Shikai's confidant, also suggested in 1914 that China join the war on the Allied side.[13] Liang told the President that Germany was not strong enough to win in the long term, so China should seize the opportunity to declare war. By doing so, Liang reasoned, China could recover

9 Liang Qichao, 'Waijiao fangzhen zhiyan – can zhan pian' ('Critical talk about tendencies in [Chinese] foreign policy – the question of [China's] participation in the war'), in *Yinbing Shi Heji*, vol. IV, pp. 4–13.

10 Liang Qichao, 'Ouzhan zhongce' ('Some preliminary predictions about the European war'), *Yinbing Shi Heji*, vol. IV, pp. 11–26; see also Ding Wenjiang (ed.), *Liangrengong Xiansheng Nianpu* ('Life chronology of Mr Liang Qichao') (Taipei: Shi jie shu ju, 1959), p. 439.

11 'China's breach with Germany', *Manchester Guardian*, 23 May 1917.

12 Xu Tian (Zhang Guogan), 'Dui de-au canzhan' ('China's declaration of war on Germany and Austria'), *Jindaishi ziliao*, 2 (1954), p. 51.

13 Feng Gang *et al.* (eds.), *Minguo Liang Yansun Xiansheng Shiyi Nianpu* ('Life chronology of Mr Liang Shiyi') (Taipei: Commercial Press, 1978), pp. 194–6.

Qingdao, win a seat at the post-war Peace Conference and serve other long-term interests. Liang was famous for his foresight and shrewdness; indeed, some close observers called him 'the Machiavelli of China'.[14] In 1915 he argued again, 'The Allied Powers will win absolutely. [That is why] we want to help them.'[15] In one of his hand-written notes dated in November 1915, he insisted that the 'time is right [for China to join the war now]. We won't have a second chance.'[16]

If the main motivation for Japan joining the war was to expand its control in China, China's key reason to join the war effort was to counter Japan. Japan was China's most threatening and determined enemy. Only by joining the war might the Chinese gain leeway to resist and recover their national sovereignty. With the outbreak of war in 1914, the question of how to deal with German concessions became a concern for China and Great Britain, but especially for Germany and Japan. As a semi-colonised country, where powers like Germany and Britain had carved out spheres of interest, China was bound to be dragged into the war one way or another. Therefore, it would be better to take the initiative and join the war.

China's social transformation and cultural and political revolutions coincided with the First World War, and the war provided the momentum and opportunity for China to redefine its relations with the world by inserting itself into the war effort. Moreover, the era of the First World War represented, as James Joll has noted, 'the end of an age and beginning of the new one' in the international arena.[17] It signalled the collapse of the existing international system and the coming of a new world order, an obvious development that fed China's desire to change its international status. The young republic's weakness and domestic political chaos provided strong motivation to enter and alter the international system. The 1911 Revolution forced the Chinese to pay new attention to changes in the world system, and the Great War was the first major event to engage the imagination of Chinese social and political elites. Changes in the Chinese worldview and the destabilising forces loosed by the war set the stage for China to have a hand in world affairs, even though there seemed to be no immediate impact on China itself (Map 18.1).

14 Michael Summerskill, *China on the Western Front* (London: Michael Summerskill, 1982), p. 30.
15 Feng Gang *et al.* (eds.), *Minguo Liang Yansun Xiansheng Shiyi Nianpu*, pp. 271–2.
16 *Ibid.*, p. 289, Su Wenzhuo (ed.), *Liang Tanyu Yin Ju Shi Suo Cang Shu Hua Tu Zhao Yin Cun* (Hong Kong, 1986), p. 208.
17 James Joll, *The Origins of the First World War* (London: Longman, 1984), p. 1.

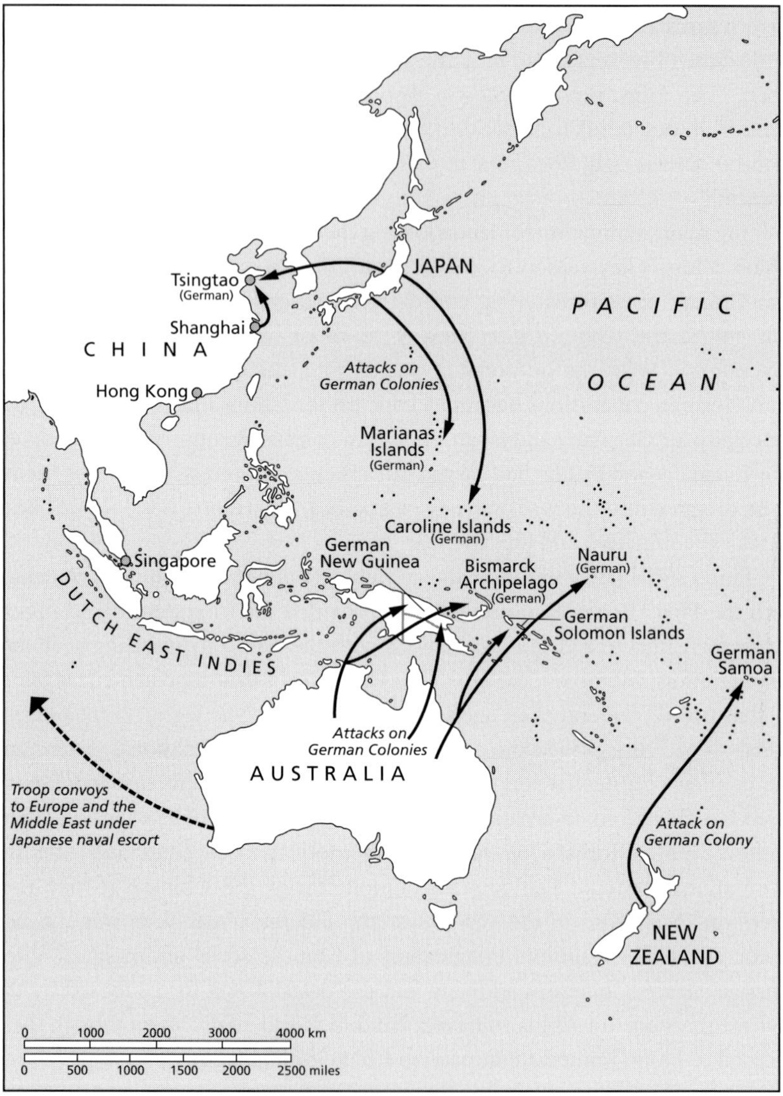

Map 18.1 The war in Asia.

The positions of Vietnam and India in 1914 differed from those of China and Japan due to their colonial status. Neither could make its own policies or pursue its own options. In the Vietnamese case, outbreak of the war in Europe did not command much attention, and the discussions and deliberations regarding the impact of the war on Vietnam were limited and inconsequential. But the Vietnamese, like the Chinese, had become deeply affected by the ideas of social Darwinism at the turn of the twentieth century, which spurred them to figure out a new direction for Vietnam. Although colonial control may explain the limited effect of Vietnamese efforts at political reform, 'events that occurred during and immediately after World War I wrought a real transformation of Vietnam's political elite and educational system, which in turn brought into the open further schisms in the Reform Movement'.[18] Hô Chi Minh, the future communist leader, wrote in 1914 to one of his friends and mentors:

> Gunfire rings out through the air and corpses cover the ground. The five Great Powers are engaged in battle. Nine countries are at war . . . I think that in the next three or four months the destiny of Asia will change dramatically. Too bad for those who are fighting and struggling. We just have to remain calm.

He soon realised that he needed to go to France to take the pulse of the larger world and to understand the role his country might play when the world was at war.[19]

Like Vietnam, India's involvement in the war was largely a by-product of its inclusion in the British Empire, not as a decision directly made in India's own interest. Indian nationalists were not in a position to make decisions on international relations. As a colonial master, Britain at first did not imagine it would need Indian help. The fighting, after all, was in Europe and between European peoples. But the British soon realised that they would have to mobilise Indian resources if they hoped to survive the conflict. Indian involvement in the war, even under British direction, was important to Indians for at least two reasons. First, it pushed to the fore Indian relations with the outside world. In their colonial past, the world had come to mean little, and Indian political elites rarely gave extensive thought to international and military affairs before the war. Their involvement in the war was 'the first time the people of Hindustan were brought to a realization of their relation to the rest of the Empire'.

Secondly, Indian involvement in the war sparked thinking about India as a nation and the rise of Indian nationalism. In 1914, India could not be

18 Hue-Tam Ho Tai, *Radicalism and the Origins of the Vietnamese Revolution* (Cambridge, MA: Harvard University Press, 1992), pp. 30–1.

19 Pierre Brocheux, *Ho Chi Minh: A Biography* (Cambridge University Press, 2007), p. 12.

considered a fully constituted nation, but seemed rather an agglomeration of many races, castes, and creeds 'who tolerate one another, but who have little in common'. But the war threw open a new world and helped the Indians 'realize their strength'. The British decision to seek Indian assistance seems to have 'furnished a common cause for which all could work, irrespective of racial distinctions or beliefs'. Thus the war gave the cause of nationalism and Indian identity 'a decided fillip'.[20] For Captain Amar Singh of the Indian Army, for example, his service in the Great War was an opportunity to fulfil his duty and 'express his sense of honor and nationhood'. He was gratified that Indian troops would have a chance to fight alongside European troops. He expected India to gain in stature as a result, a view of the war that was common among knowledgeable Indians.[21] Practically all prominent Indian politicians supported the British war recruitment effort. Mahatma Gandhi was one of them. Many of them linked support for the war to Indians' right to equality as citizens of the British Empire, and they hoped that Britain would reward India with a greater voice in its own governing once the war was over.

Even British authorities recognised the serious implications of the war. *The Times History of the War in 1914* explains:

> The more they [Indians] learned of the goodness of our Western civilization and the higher, especially, we raised the standard of our native Indian Army, the stronger became the pressure upon us from below, seeking some outlet for the high ambitions which we ourselves had awakened. Looking only at the military side of the question, no one conversant with the facts could fail to see that the time was at hand when we could no longer deny to a force of British subjects, with the glorious record and splendid efficiency of our native Indian troops, the right to stand shoulder to shoulder with their British comrades in defence of the Empire, wherever it might be assailed.[22]

The war thus opened some Indians' eyes to the outside world and allowed them to dream and set high expectations, as world politics were changing and their so-called mother country was engaged in a major war. When the 'king-emperor' asked for Indian help, India responded positively, especially so in the case of the educated class who saw in the war an opportunity. Ahmed Iqbal, the distinguished poet, reflected what was on the minds of elites when the war broke out:

20 DeWitt Mackenzie, *The Awakening of India* (London: Hodder & Stoughton, 1918), pp. 18–21.

21 DeWitt C. Ellinwood, *Between Two Worlds: A Rajput Officer in the Indian Army, 1905–1921, based on the Diary of Amar Singh* (Lanham, MD: Hamilton, 2005), p. 356.

22 *The Times History of the War in 1914* (London, 1914), p. 153.

The world will witness when from my heart
Springs the storm of expression;
My silence conceals
The seed of aspiration.[23]

China, India, Japan and Vietnam in the Great War

Japan and China, with their strong expectations of advantages, and India and Vietnam, out of both colonial duty and budding nationalism, all became deeply involved in the European war almost immediately. As pointed out earlier, Japan had inserted itself into the war the very month hostilities began. Japan's ultimatum demanded that Germany transfer its Chinese concessions to Japan, and when Germany refused, the Japanese launched an attack on Qingdao in Chinese territory. Japan contributed larger forces than Britain to fighting the Germans in China: 2,800 British and 29,000 Japanese troops engaged the Germans at Qingdao. Interestingly, Indian troops also joined the British and Japanese, so they got a taste of fighting even before they travelled to Europe to join the war effort. Even more interestingly, the Japanese military effort ended at Qingdao's fall, with about 2,000 Japanese casualties. On 11 November 1914, Qingdao was transferred from German to Japanese control.

In terms of actual fighting, only the Indians and Vietnamese took part by sending military forces. Although India held an unequal and inferior place under Great Britain, Indian soldiers contributed significantly to the British war effort. They 'served as an enormous reservoir of men in the Allied cause',[24] and India made the largest contribution of any British colony or Dominion in terms of sheer numbers. Both military and labour forces travelled to Europe to help the colonial motherland in the war. More than 130,000 Indians arrived in France over the course of the war to work side by side with their colonial masters. Casualties, declining morale and doubts about the wisdom of using non-white troops in Europe led to the permanent withdrawal of the India Corps from the Western Front at the end of 1915. But many Indian soldiers continued to serve in East Africa, Mesopotamia, Palestine and Egypt until the end of war, with Mesopotamia as India's main theatre of war, where the majority of Indian military forces and labour corps stayed, and heavy casualties took place. On the part of Vietnam, during the war about 49,000

23 Mackenzie, *The Awakening of India*, p. 159.
24 Ellinwood, *Between Two Worlds*, pp. 358–9.

Vietnamese soldiers and 48,000 workers were recruited for the French war effort, and the majority of them went to France, to serve predominantly on the Western Front.[25] By the end of the war, 1,797 Vietnamese had lost their lives, and the Indian forces in various theatres of the war had lost 53,486.[26]

Japan's meagre military support for its allies made sense since its true motive was expanding its interests in China. As the Europeans exhausted each other in battle, Japan would become more important to both sides, which would give Japan a free hand in Asia. So although Japan was technically at war with Germany, it treated Germans who lived and worked in the country well. As one American at the time observed, 'The Japanese have not disturbed any German residents in Japan – all are welcome to stay and continue their occupations as before – even the German editors are so very "continuing" in their way of writing, that they publish most outrageous and hostile editorials daily. We wait in amazement to see how much longer Japanese magnanimity will ignore such a breach of common sense and press laws.'[27] Because its true focus was China, the Japanese war effort immediately shifted with Qingdao's fall, to concentrate on its expansion in China.

On 18 January 1915, Japan presented China with the infamous 'Twenty-One Demands'. These reveal the Japanese ambition essentially to colonise China while the major powers were not in position to prevent it. The demands consisted of five sections with a total of twenty-one articles. The most serious and demanding section was the fifth, which demanded that China appoint Japanese advisers in political, financial and military affairs, and that the Japanese take control of Chinese police departments in important places across China. These demands were so severe that some called them 'worse than many presented by a victor to his vanquished enemy'.[28] Obviously, the Japanese meant to make China a vassal state.

Japan's demands presented the biggest challenge yet to China's survival and its desire to become a full-fledged nation-state. The Twenty-One Demands fully exposed Japanese ambitions in China and helped China to focus on the direction the country should head in terms of its war policy. If Japan provided China with a crisis of national identity by defeating it in 1895, the demands it

25 Richard Fogarty, *Race and War in France: Colonial Subjects in the French Army, 1914–1918* (Baltimore, MD: Johns Hopkins University Press, 2008), p. 27.

26 DeWitt C. Ellinwood and S. D. Pradhan (eds.), *India and World War I* (Columbia, MO: South Asia Books, 1978), p. 145.

27 Columbia University manuscript library: Carnegie Endowment for International Peace, correspondence 44, box 395: On 2 September 1914, letter to James Brown Scott of the Endowment.

28 Cyril Pearl, *Morrison of Peking* (Sydney: Angus & Robertson, 1967), p. 307.

presented in 1915 not only aroused Chinese national consciousness, they also helped the Chinese identify the first specific goal their response to the First World War should achieve: a place at the post-war Peace Conference. Although China had earlier expressed its intention to join the war, it was only after the Twenty-One Demands that sufficient momentum had gathered for the government to make concrete steps towards that goal. Among the many countries that participated in the war, China was perhaps the most unusual. No neutral country had linked its fate with the war so closely, had such high expectations and yet had been so humbled by the experience. The Chinese declaration of war on Germany and Austria-Hungary in August 1917 might not be considered significant in world affairs, but it was an extremely important event for China.

This was the first time in modern history that the Chinese government took the initiative to play an active role in affairs distant from Chinese shores. China's participation was also the first time in modern history that China came to the aid of the West on such a grand scale. Its strategy for participation in the European conflict indicated that China was ready to be part of the world and join the family of nations as an equal member. Its declaration of war on Germany and Austria-Hungary on 14 August coincided with the eighteenth anniversary of the Powers' entry into Beijing during the Boxer Rebellion. By entering the war, China did recover some degree of sovereignty, one of its major war aims. After breaking off relations with Germany and Austria, the Chinese government was able to finally assert itself against a European power: the navy confiscated German vessels in Chinese ports and Chinese police immediately took over German and Austrian concessions.

Perhaps no single foreign policy initiative had a stronger impact on China's domestic politics and society than its policy on the First World War. But instead of enjoying the fruits of its first major independent diplomatic programme, China tasted bitter social disorder, political chaos and national disintegration. Disputes over the war-participation policy exacerbated factionalism, encouraged warlordism and led to civil war. In the wake of China's declaration in 1917, a series of bizarre episodes – the dissolution of parliament, the restoration of the Qing Emperor, the frequent comings and goings of new governments, the dismissal and returns of Duan Qirui and the resignation of President Li Yuanhong – followed one after another. And the ironies go beyond the domestic realm. China's deadly enemy was Japan, but the Chinese joined the same side as Japan. Germany was China's declared enemy, but the 'declared' war between China and Germany was phoney because there had been no fighting and Germany was not the intended enemy. Germany became a victim – or vehicle – in China's grand strategy. Germany was in fact a friend in disguise since it helped China springboard into the world arena.

A key to understanding these seemingly contradictory developments is the Chinese obsession with their international status and the government's strategy to use its war policies to recover the sovereignty it had lost to Japan and other powers since the Opium War. Although China was eager to send military forces to Europe after its official entry into the war, only France was interested in having Chinese troops join the fighting. Japan strongly opposed this, while Britain was not very excited at the prospect. Due to lack of transportation and funding and lukewarm interest, China failed to land soldiers in Europe. Instead, its largest contribution was sending 140,000 Chinese workers to support the British and French war efforts.[29]

For the Chinese, sending labourers to Europe was key to their strategy of taking part in the post-war Peace Conference and so to joining the community of nations as a full member. As early as 1915, China worked out a labourers-as-soldiers scheme, designed to create a link with the Allied cause when its official entry into the war was uncertain. To strengthen its case for claiming a role in the war, the Chinese vigorously promoted the idea of sending labourers to help the Allies. This programme was the brainchild of Liang Shiyi, who called it the *yigong daibing* (literally, 'labourers in the place of soldiers') strategy.[30] When Liang Shiyi began thinking about his plan, his main target was Britain, with a suggestion that entailed use of military labourers, not hired workers. If Britain had accepted this proposal, China would have been fighting on the Allied side in 1915. But Britain rejected the idea immediately and so Liang had turned to France. One reason for the rejection was British domestic politics. For Britain, the issue of Chinese labour in South Africa had been a crucial one in the years before the war, and the protection of 'white labour' at home and in the Empire was crucial to understanding why the British trade unions were so determined to oppose using Chinese workers in the war, especially in Britain (Map 18.2).

As the Chinese reeled from the blow of Japan's Twenty-One Demands in 1915, the French faced a manpower crisis: how to continue the deadly war on the battlefield while maintaining the home front? When China offered help, the French immediately began planning how to get the Chinese into France. Eventually, about 40,000 Chinese workers were recruited and transported to

29 For details on China's labourers in Europe, see Guoqi Xu, *Strangers on the Western Front: Chinese Workers in the Great War* (Cambridge, MA: Harvard University Press, 2011).
30 Feng Gang *et al.* (eds.), *Minguo Liang Yansun Xiansheng Shiyi Nianpu*, p. 310.

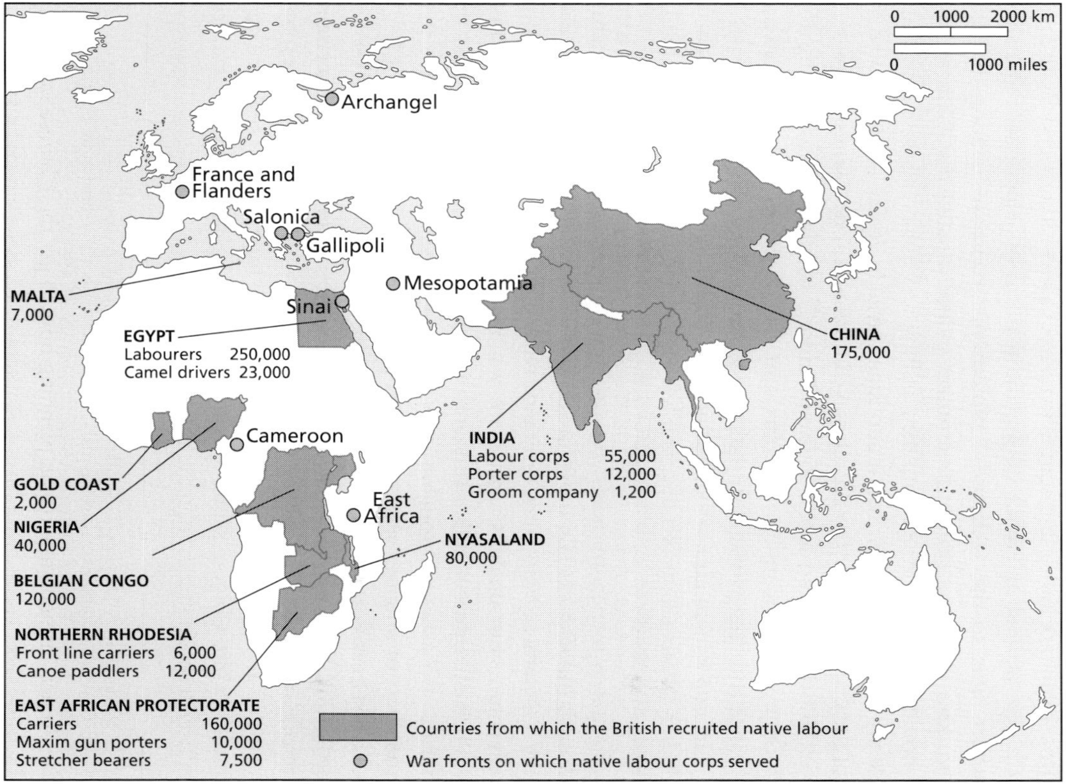
0 1000 2000 km
0 1000 miles
Archangel
France and Flanders
Salonica
Gallipoli
Mesopotamia
Sinai
Cameroon
East Africa
MALTA
7,000
EGYPT
Labourers 250,000
Camel drivers 23,000
CHINA
175,000
INDIA
Labour corps 55,000
Porter corps 12,000
Groom company 1,200
GOLD COAST
2,000
NIGERIA
40,000
NYASALAND
80,000
BELGIAN CONGO
120,000
NORTHERN RHODESIA
Front line carriers 6,000
Canoe paddlers 12,000
EAST AFRICAN PROTECTORATE
Carriers 160,000
Maxim gun porters 10,000
Stretcher bearers 7,500
Countries from which the British recruited native labour
War fronts on which native labour corps served

Map 18.2 Sources of manpower for British Labour Corps, 1914–18.

France. By 1916, when Britain's future was at stake, British arrogance had been replaced in part by desperation. In an address to the House of Commons on 24 July that year, Winston Churchill made the following speech: 'I would not even shrink from the word Chinese for the purpose of carrying on the War.'[31] British military authorities started to recruit Chinese in 1916 and about 100,000 Chinese arrived in France during the wartime to support the British war effort. Due to the widespread protectionist consensus among the British working class, the British government indeed insisted that Chinese labour should be treated in quasi-military fashion and not be allowed into Britain. Many Chinese under British supervision stayed in France until 1920, and most of the Chinese under the French stayed until 1922. The Chinese were the last of the British labour forces to leave France.[32] In other words, among all the foreign countries involved, China sent the largest number of workers to France and their workers stayed there longest.

In 1916 Britain also turned to India for civilian labour resources. The first Indian labour group of 2,000 men left for Europe in May 1917.[33] In June 1917, another group of 6,370 men arrived in France. They were soon joined by about 20,000 new men from India.[34] In 1915 France started to mobilise and recruited French Indochinese labourers for the war effort.[35] Like the Chinese, most of the Vietnamese who went to France went either to escape poverty or seek adventure. But unlike China, there was resistance among the Vietnamese. French recruitment of soldiers and workers was met with riots and other forms of resistance throughout Cochinchina; most such events were led by members of religious sects and secret societies.[36]

The Great War was a total war, fought on both the battlefield and the home front; on the Western Front it consumed fighting forces and other human resources on a vast scale. The Chinese, Indians and Vietnamese thus must be counted an important part of the war for their huge human resource contributions. The Chinese seemed to be experts at digging trenches. One British officer testified that among the 100,000 men under him – English, Indians and

31 Parliamentary Debates, *Commons* (84) (10–31 July 1916), p. 1379.

32 'General statement regarding the YMCA work for the Chinese in France', March 1919, Kautz Family YMCA Archives, University of Minnesota Libraries, Minneapolis (hereafter cited YMCA Archives) as box 204, folder: Chinese laborers in France reports, 1918–1919.

33 John Starling and Ivor Lee, *No Labour, No Battle* (Stroud: History Press, 2009), p. 258.

34 *Ibid.*, p. 25.

35 Kimloan Hill, 'Strangers in a foreign land: Vietnamese soldiers and workers in France during World War I', in Nhung Tuyet Tran and Anthony Reid (eds.), *Viet Nam: Borderless Histories* (University of Wisconsin Press, 2006), p. 259.

36 Ho Tai, *Radicalism and the Origins of the Vietnamese Revolution*, pp. 30–1.

Chinese – the Chinese dug on average 200 cubic feet per day, the Indians 160 and the Tommies 140. Another British officer supported that observation: 'In my company, I have found the Chinese labourers accomplish a greater amount of work per day in digging trenches than white labourers.'[37] Most workers' main duties were to maintain the munitions supply lines, clean out and dig the trenches and clear conquered territory. Besides digging trenches, three Chinese labour companies were involved exclusively in working with the most advanced weapons of the war, the tanks.[38] The employment of Chinese for highly skilled work in the tank corps was unprecedented, since such roles were normally reserved for white workers. Besides their skills, the Chinese were often praised for their efficiency and bravery. General Ferdinand Foch called the French-recruited Chinese 'first-class workers who could be made into excellent soldiers, capable of exemplary bearing under modern artillery fire'.[39]

The Indians and Vietnamese were also praised for their hard work and sacrifices. During the German offensive of March 1918, an Indian labour corps was commended for their work and behaviour when forced to leave camp at a moment's notice. The men's withdrawal was carried out with 'admirable steadiness'; there was no panic, though in some cases they had to endure shell-fire, attacks by aerial bombardment and machine-gun fire, both by day and by night. Whenever called upon, they halted and even turned back to work at the loading of stores on trains, lorries and wagons. 'One Company assisted the wounded with a hospital train and performed this work – for which they had no training – in such a manner as to win high praise from the Medical Officers.'[40] By the end of the war, at least 4,000 Indochinese had served as drivers, transporting men and supplies at and near the front. During the Battle of the Somme, Indochinese drivers remained at the wheel for thirty-six hours straight without displaying any more fatigue than did their French counterparts. There were suggestions that Indochinese drivers were easier on the machinery than their French colleagues, and the upkeep of trucks driven by the former cost less than a quarter of that for vehicles driven by French soldiers. They also drove safely, having successfully avoided any fatal

37 YMCA, *Young Men's Christian Association with the Chinese Labor Corps in France*, YMCA Archives, box 204, folder: Chinese laborers in France, p. 14.

38 Controller of Labour War Diary, July 1918, National Archives, Kew, WO 95/83.

39 General Foch's secret report to the Prime Minister, 11 August 1917, in Archives de la Guerre, service historique de la Défense, château de Vincennes, 16N 2450/GQG/6498.

40 Starling and Lee, *No Labour, No Battle*, p. 260.

accidents. One observer noted, 'intelligence, calmness, skill, aptitude for precise tasks seemed to be the chief qualities of the Indochinese'.[41]

Everyone suffered, but the Chinese were more used to the cold weather of the French winter than the Indians and Vietnamese, who had major difficulties. The Chinese rarely complained about the weather, but the Indians and Vietnamese frequently suffered terribly from the cold. On 27 December 1917, an Indian labourer wrote in a personal letter from France:

> You enquire about the cold? I will tell plainly what the cold in France is like when I meet you. At present I can only say that the earth is white, the sky is white, the trees are white, the stones are white, the mud is white, the water is white, one's spittle freezes into a solid white lump.[42]

Many Vietnamese were also startled at the cold: 'It was so cold', one Indochinese wrote, 'that my saliva immediately freezes after I spit it on the ground.' Another wrote, 'The chill of winter pierces my heart.'[43] Of the Chinese tolerance for the cold, Captain A. McCormick observed, 'One thing surprised me about them. I thought that they would have felt the cold more than we did, but seemingly not, for both when working and walking about, you would see them moving about stripped to the waist.'[44] Being more effective, skilled and much tougher, the Chinese were more widely sought after than their comrades from India and Vietnam.

For most Asians, the journey to France was largely a journey of hardships and suffering. Seasickness, disease, poor conditions and bad food were major complaints. Some Vietnamese had to sleep with livestock on their way to France. Many Asian workers were treated badly and had only tattered clothes to wear. Long hours and food shortages were common for the Indochinese workers. One Vietnamese complained, 'There has been no rest, not even a Sunday off.' Another Vietnamese labourer reported that the only food he had for two weeks was 'one loaf of bread'.[45] Most of these men served at the front or near front zones and thus sustained casualties and even lost their lives. About 3,000 Chinese died either on their way to Europe or in Europe. Almost

41 Fogarty, *Race and War in France*, pp. 65–6.

42 Letter 628, in David Omissi, *Indian Voices of the Great War* (Basingstoke: Palgrave Macmillan, 1999), p. 342.

43 Hill, 'Strangers in a foreign land', p. 261.

44 Captain A. McCormick files, 02/6/1, 207–208, Imperial War Museum, London.

45 Kimloan Hill, 'Sacrifice, sex, race: Vietnamese experiences in the First World War', in Santanu Das (ed.), *Race, Empire and First World War Writing* (Cambridge University Press, 2011), p. 58.

1,500 Indian workers died during their service in France, most of them from illness.[46] By the end of the war, 1,548 Vietnamese workers had died.

Despite the fact they came to support the British or French or both war efforts, Chinese, Indians and Vietnamese all suffered from European racism while in France. Among the British, the widespread assumption was, 'Asians and Africans were children, to be firmly dealt with for their own good.'[47] The official code 'forbade any hint of sentimental sympathy with colonial or subject peoples. Sternness in dealings with the heathen became a virtue never to be compromised; they were children to be judged, ruled, and directed. And yet mixed with this arrogant belief in racial domination one often finds elements of profound ignorance concerning, say, Oriental or African customs and cultures.'[48] They were even criticised for certain special habits or customs. Vietnamese sometimes blackened their teeth because they thought black teeth made them attractive. But this practice also made them a target of ridicule by the French and created confrontations. Indians were sometimes teased for not eating beef and other customs. British racist attitudes about 'Indian natural inferiority' to the white men were widespread. Due to racial stereotypes, some French thought the Vietnamese were not physically strong enough to do the solid kinds of work the white race could perform. General Joffre maintained that the Indochinese 'do not possess the physical qualities of vigor and endurance necessary to be employed usefully in European warfare'.[49]

Interestingly, despite French racism, it seems that both the Chinese and Vietnamese were popular with Frenchwomen. They often sought out Chinese or Vietnamese workers because they had money and were kind. Love and intimacy led to marriages. By the end of the war, 250 Vietnamese had married Frenchwomen and 1,363 couples lived together without the approval of the French authorities or parental consent. Although we do not have an exact figure, it is safe to say that many Chinese had sexual relations with Frenchwomen and some later married them. Frenchmen obviously disliked the fact their women were marrying Chinese or Vietnamese. A police report from Le Havre dated May 1917, noted that some local Frenchmen were

46 Starling and Lee, *No Labour, No Battle*, p. 260.

47 V. G. Kiernan, *The Lords of Human Kind: Black Man, Yellow Man, and White Man in an Age of Empire* (New York: Columbia University Press, 1986), p. 153.

48 Nicholas John Griffin, 'The Use of Chinese Labour by the British Army, 1916–1920: The "Raw Importation," its Scope and Problems' (PhD thesis, University of Oklahoma, 1973), p. 14.

49 Fogarty, *Race and War in France*, p. 45.

not happy to see Chinese workers there and even rioted against them. According to the report, the French were disappointed with the high war casualties their country had sustained:

> It is frequently said (in the munitions factories), that if this continues, there will not be any men left in France; so why are we fighting? So that Chinese, Arabs, or Spaniards can marry our wives and daughters and share out the France for which we'll all, sooner or later, get ourselves killed at the front.[50]

Although the war's positive impact and influence on Vietnamese national development was not as strong as on India or China, still we can discern some changes in peoples' thinking and expectations, especially with respect to Vietnamese who were in France during the war. As one scholar has suggested recently, the First World War marked a turning point in the history of French Indochina. For many Vietnamese, the journey to France meant more than answering the mother country's call; it was also an eye-opening learning experience. While in France, many of them were eager to learn, observe and study. Near Marseilles there was an Indochina club where Vietnamese could write letters home and socialise with fellow Vietnamese. The club provided magazines, newspapers and teas free of charge. The Alliance Française provided social services and organised cultural activities for Vietnamese workers and soldiers in France. The members of the Alliance offered free French lessons, and by the end of the war about 25,000 men had benefited from this programme.[51] The Indochinese were enthusiastic about opportunities to learn French while in Europe. One corporal in the cavalry, named Le Van Nghiep, was so proud of being placed second out of sixty candidates in the exam for the elementary certificate in French, that he wrote to a friend in Hanoi and asked him to publish an article about his success in a local paper along with his picture. The letter ended up in the desk of a French censor, who commented that this Vietnamese had carried his language studies 'rather far' and his 'modesty is fading'.[52]

Through learning, study and close observation, the Vietnamese who went to France 'were transformed, and in many cases radicalized, in varying degrees by their experiences'. Their experiences and observations in France and back home later, motivated many of them to fight to change the status quo. As one scholar suggested, 'By recruiting men from Indochina, France had inadvertently set in train events that would eventually contribute to the loss of its

50 John Horne, 'Immigrant workers in France during World War I', *French Historical Studies*, 14:1 (1985), pp. 57–88.

51 Hill, 'Strangers in a foreign land', p. 270. 52 Fogarty, *Race and War in France*, p. 153.

Indochinese colonies.' Hô Chi Minh even tried to join the French army at that time. Although it was not clear whether Hô Chi Minh fought in the war, he became a popular figure among his compatriots in France, and political tracts under his name were distributed among them advocating independence for Indochina.[53]

For Vietnamese men, even sex and marriage with Frenchwomen symbolised their coming of age and national awakening. Some, despite their status as colonial subjects living in France, believed they were no different from Frenchmen living in Indochina, marrying local women and frequenting local brothels and cabarets.[54] After the war, about 2,900 Vietnamese soldiers and workers remained in France.[55] The widespread practice among Vietnamese of pursuing romantic relations with Frenchwomen made a deep impact on their psychological and national consciousness. It demonstrated that they could cross the old boundary between colonials and masters; they could challenge the colonial order and political taboos established by the French in Vietnam.[56] Some Indochinese men openly characterised their sexual relations with Frenchwomen as political activity. For these Indochinese, sex with Frenchwomen was 'like a revenge on the European, the Frenchman who down there causes old Indochina to blush and incites jealousy'. Such attitudes among the Indochinese, many of whom would eventually return home, presented a significant potential threat to the colonial order. According to one scholar, 'The likely effect of such inter-racial relationships on the status of Frenchwomen in the colonies was apparent. If these women were supposed to be pillars of the community there, embodying French ideas about civilization and domesticity and defining the boundaries that separated colonizers from colonized', these relationships would present 'a significant potential threat to the colonial order.'[57] The Vietnamese experience in France made them feel no longer inferior to the French, and they began to question and resent French dominance in Vietnam.[58]

Relations between Frenchwomen and Vietnamese men worried French authorities deeply, and they tried to put a stop to them. One Indochinese man was imprisoned for fifteen days for 'daring to fall in love with a French girl'.[59] The French authorities were also concerned about the photographs Indochinese sent home of themselves in the company of white women. As it turned out, besides dating Frenchwomen, Vietnamese frequently sent home

53 Hill, 'Sacrifice, sex, race', pp. 62–5. 54 Fogarty, *Race and War in France*, p. 208.
55 Hill, 'Strangers in a foreign land', p. 281. 56 Hill, 'Sacrifice, sex, race', p. 60.
57 Fogarty, *Race and War in France*, pp. 202–12.
58 Hill, 'Strangers in a foreign land', p. 281. 59 Fogarty, *Race and War in France*, p. 214.

images of them, sometimes nude ones. Sergeant Major Ho sent his brother in Indochina letters he received from Frenchwomen, telling him to save them as 'sacred things' that the sergeant could, upon his return, show to European colonial masters who did not believe his stories and who might mock him for his pretensions to relations with white women.[60] For the French, such proof of inter-racial contact was damaging to 'our prestige in the Far East', so French censors confiscated any such images as they could find. Censors were quite candid about the ultimate consequences for public order and French rule in the colonies: examples like Sergeant Ho's 'deplorable attitude' would lead the population of Indochina to think that the French lived in a 'shameful debauchery'. As Indochinese men gained the kind of experience, skills and, in some cases, education that would make them leaders in their societies in the post-war years, French authorities feared that these men would return to Indochina with new ideas and be less 'submissive' to 'their traditional discipline'. They instructed the colonial government in June 1918 to interrogate and maintain close surveillance on returning soldiers.[61]

Large numbers of Vietnamese went to France to support their colonial masters' war effort, and had the opportunity to observe and interact with Westerners directly. This opportunity allowed them to compare and contrast the French with others. Some Vietnamese had opportunities to interact with American soldiers when they came to each other's assistance during battles. The personal letters of Vietnamese soldiers reveal their impressions. One wrote that the American army was 'the strongest and the most powerful among the allies'. Another wrote that the Americans were 'fierce fighters'. The third one even made the shocking suggestion that the French were not tough fighters: 'The presence of the Americans on the battlefield restored the confidence of the Vietnamese.'[62] It is interesting to point out that many Chinese had daily contact with the Vietnamese. In spite of language difficulties, the Chinese and Vietnamese got along well and at times developed close bonds. Whenever the Chinese got into fights with Africans, with whom the Chinese seemed to have ongoing difficulties, the Vietnamese joined in against the Africans. The French government did not want the Vietnamese to be infected by Chinese ideas of patriotism and nationalism and tried hard to keep them separate.[63]

60 *Ibid.*, p. 222. 61 *Ibid.*, pp. 220–5. 62 Hill, 'Strangers in a foreign land', p. 263.
63 Chen Sanjing, Lu Fangshang and Yang Cuihua (eds.), *Ouzhan Huagong Shiliao* (Taipei: Zhongyang yanjiuyuan jindai shi yanjiushuo, 1997), pp. 380–1.

The Chinese were also strongly influenced by their European experiences. Since Chinese workers were part of China's grand strategy for renewal and for promoting its international status, many other agencies besides the government became involved in their journey and experiences. One of them was the Young Men's Christian Association. When Chinese labourers arrived in France, the YMCA took a hand in shaping and influencing their lives. The YMCA secretaries, most of them elite Chinese who had graduated from Western universities, helped their countrymen learn to read, become informed and devise cultural entertainments for themselves.

During the war, many of China's best and brightest went to France because they had fallen under the spell of Woodrow Wilson's call for a new world order and the promise of a better world system from which China could benefit. They wanted to devote their knowledge, energy and experience to help jumpstart that new world order. Yet their worldview and understanding of China were very different from that of the labourers. They helped the workers by writing letters, teaching them to read and giving them the means to understand the world and Chinese affairs. Perhaps most importantly, they were determined to make the labourers into better citizens of both China and the world. The experiences of these elite scholars and talented students helped them develop a new appreciation for the Chinese working class, spurred them to find solutions to Chinese problems and changed their perceptions about China and its future. While the labourers learned from their own experience and from the YMCA workers and other Chinese elites who worked with them, the Chinese labourers also taught a lot to the Chinese elites. They would eventually become new citizens of China and the world, and developed a new understanding and appreciation of their republic and its position in the world. The Chinese workers in France were mostly common villagers who knew little of China or the world when they were selected to go to Europe; still, these men directly and personally contributed to helping China transform its image at home and in the world. Their new transnational roles reshaped national identity and China's internationalisation, which in turn helped shape the emerging global system. From their experience of Europe in a time of war and their work with the American, British and French military, as well as fellow labourers from other countries, they developed a unique perception of China and of world affairs. Further, future leaders such as Yan Yangchu, Jiang Tingfu, Cai Yuanpei and Wang Jingwei, among others, through their work with the Chinese workers in Europe, became convinced that China could become a better nation through a new understanding of their fellow citizens.

Like the Chinese and Vietnamese, Indian experiences and direct contacts with Westerners in Europe also collectively gave rise to new perceptions about Eastern and Western civilisations. General James Willcocks, commander of the Indian Corps, wrote in a letter to the viceroy, Lord Hardinge: 'Our Indian soldiers serve for a very small remuneration; they were serving in a strange foreign land; they were the most patient soldiers in the world; they are doing what Asiatics have never been asked to do before.'[64] To a great extent, the war service for Indians was a way of salvaging national prestige.[65] The war experience gave Indians fresh confidence and political awareness. As one Indian veteran later pointed out, 'When we saw various peoples and got their views, we started protesting against the inequalities and disparities which the British had created between the white and the black.'[66] One Indian elite member pointed out, 'The war has changed us very much. It has changed the angle of vision in India as well [as] in England.'[67] One sepoy wrote home, 'You ought to educate your girls as well as your boys and our posterity will be better for it.'[68] Amar Singh told his Indian officers that 'this is the first time we Indians have had the honour to fight Europeans on their own soil and must play up to the Government that has brought us up to this level'. Reflecting in October 1915 on the Indian troops present in France, Singh wrote in his diary, 'They must see it through whatever happens. It is on them that the honour of India rests. India will get tremendous concessions after the war which she would not have gained otherwise – at least not for several years to come.' In November 1914, he wrote in his diary, 'Ever since my coming to France I have been admiring and studying the avenues these people have in their towns as well in the country seats.' By June 1915 he was planning ahead, 'Since coming to France I have been awfully impressed with the forests and avenues and often think what I could do in this line in my own place [back in India.]'[69] As Annie Besant, who founded the India Home Rule League in 1916 declared, 'When the war is over . . . we cannot doubt that the King-Emperor will, as reward for her glorious defence of the Empire, pin upon her [India's] breast the jeweled medal of Self-Government within the Empire.' Mahatma Gandhi also suggested that change should be more easily earned through the war effort: 'It was more becoming and far-sighted not to press our demands while the war lasted.'[70]

64 Ellinwood, *Between Two Worlds*, p. 365.

65 Santanu Das, 'Indians at home, Mesopotamia and France, 1914–1918: towards an intimate history', in Das (ed.), *Race, Empire and First World War Writing*, p. 74.

66 *Ibid.*, p. 84. 67 Ellinwood and Pradhan (eds.), *India and World War I*, p. 22.

68 Das, 'Indians at home', p. 83. 69 Ellinwood, *Between Two Worlds*, pp. 370–404.

70 Das, 'Indians at home', p. 73.

It seems that the Indian war experience clearly ignited their national consciousness. The new Indian national awakening forced the British colonial authority to make some concessions. The 1917 British Declaration for India was one of them. The declaration, publicised in August 1917 in the name of the Secretary of State for India, promised constitutional reforms in 1919 and to promote 'the increasing association of Indians in every branch of the administration and the gradual development of self-governing institutions'.[71] Critics might suggest this high-sounding declaration was an empty promise, and the war and Indian sacrifices only brought India high inflation, a devalued currency and increased taxation. Still, even symbolically, the declaration must be viewed as a positive development in the long term. It announced the beginning of a new relationship between India and Britain, and that change occurred largely due to the war and India's contributions. By promising and allowing India to enjoy a level of self-rule, the 1917 declaration can be argued to be a major step on India's long journey to independence, no matter how small that step was or however half-hearted the British concessions were. As Timothy C. Winegard recently wrote, 'The First Word War was, more so than its 1939–45 counterpart, the decisive chapter of the twentieth century for the Dominions. It forever altered the configuration of the empire and, through momentous Dominion participation hastened the realization of full nationhood, both legally and culturally.'[72]

Besides contributing human resources, Asian countries also provided other important forms of assistance. For instance, besides ejecting German forces from Qingdao and German Micronesia in the South Pacific, Japan provided naval support against German commerce raiders in the Pacific and protected convoys of Australian and New Zealand troops from the Pacific to Aden. The Japanese navy also hunted German submarines in the Mediterranean and Japan provided shipping, copper, munitions and almost 1 billion yen in loans to its allies. India sent 172,815 animals and 3,691,836 tons of stores and supplies largely for the British war effort. In addition, these Asian countries raised substantial sums of money by selling war bonds, and these were turned over to the British and French governments.[73] China even sent to Britain large numbers of rifles that were moved secretly through Hong Kong. Some Asian women even got involved in the war. A few Vietnamese women volunteered to work in the health services or at factories in France 'by the side of our

71 Ellinwood and Pradhan (eds.), *India and World War I*, pp. 21–2.
72 Timothy C. Winegard, *Indigenous Peoples of the British Dominions and the First World War* (Cambridge University Press, 2011), p. 11.
73 Ellinwood and Pradhan (eds.), *India and World War I*, p. 143.

French sisters'. There were even reports of female Indochinese workers in workers' camps in France.[74] Seventy-five Japanese nurses travelled to France to work during the war.[75]

Although it is difficult to say whether India and Vietnam benefited materially from the war due to their colonial status, both China and Japan did achieve certain economic advantages. Japan enjoyed substantial economic growth: its net income from freight had been less than 40 million yen in 1914. By 1918 it was over 450 million yen. As for the commodity trade, average annual exports over the four war years were some 330 million yen larger than imports, while between 1911 and 1914 imports had exceeded exports by an annual average of 65 million yen. Overall industrial investment during the war multiplied seventeen times as enhanced profits were ploughed back into new development. Total production output in Japan grew from 2,610 million yen to 10,212 million yen in 1918.[76] Employment in industry increased accordingly. In Japan the industrial population nearly doubled between 1914 and 1919. More importantly, during the war, for the first time since the end of the nineteenth century, Japan was able to record significant trade surpluses and helped created balance-of-payments surpluses for the first time since the opening of the country.[77] China similarly benefited. Although it did not see trade surpluses during the war, Chinese trade deficits declined visibly. One can argue that the war helped China enjoy a bit of a boom and provided a foundation for China's golden age of capitalism.[78]

In short, Asians both benefited from and contributed to the Great War in many important ways. Their participation had made the war truly great and worldwide in scope, but more importantly, it marked a major turning point in political development and identity of Asians across the region. The collective excitement among the war's participants for the prospects of the post-war Peace Conference further indicates the war's importance to Asia.

Asians at the post-war Peace Conference

American President Woodrow Wilson's blueprint for the post-Great War world order raised high hopes among the Chinese, Indians, Koreans and

74 Hill, 'Sacrifice, sex, race', p. 55.
75 Jan P. Schmidt, 'Japanese nurses in WWI', unpublished article.
76 Kenneth D. Brown, 'The impact of the First World War on Japan', in Chris Wrigley (ed.), *The First World War and the International Economy* (Cheltenham: Edward Elgar, 2000), pp. 102–7.
77 Iriye, *Japan and the Wider World*, pp. 22–3.
78 For details on this point, see Marie-Claire Bergère, *The Golden Age of the Chinese Bourgeoisie, 1911–1937* (Cambridge University Press, 2009).

Vietnamese. Even the Japanese looked forward to the discussions of the post-war Peace Conference and the resulting new world order. The Japanese hoped the Paris Peace Conference would seal their long-cherished aspirations to be recognised as the dominant Asian power, and they hoped the Great Powers would give Japan's recently gained interests in China an international stamp of approval. More importantly, the Japanese hoped that Western powers would now accept Japan as a full equal. On that point, they were bound to be disappointed.

True, Japan was treated as one of the top five powers at the Peace Conference and was awarded its spoils in China. But Japan's call for a racial equality clause, a proposal it put forward with Chinese support, was rejected. When Japan first raised the racial equality issue on 13 February 1919, Chinese diplomat Wellington Koo expressed his support for this proposal even though China did not want to be distracted from its main focus.[79] On 11 April, when Japan made another proposal on the issue, China again supported it, arguing that the proposal should be incorporated into the official peace treaty.[80] Ironically, it was Woodrow Wilson who, as chair of the League of Nations Commission, eventually blocked the inclusion of this clause in the final treaty. As one scholar has recently pointed out, 'Perhaps the most glaring contradiction to the universalist message of Wilson's wartime pronouncements on self-determination was his record on race relations in the domestic American context', which was rife with racial assumptions and racist attitudes.[81] The Japanese were disappointed with Wilson and some called him 'an angel in rhetoric and a devil in deed'.[82] Japanese disillusionment extended to three other fronts: the League of Nations, increasing Anglo-American solidarity in East Asia and the Pacific and the 1924 US Alien Immigration Act.[83] This disillusionment and sense of betrayal may help account for Japan's later go-alone policy and expansionist drive into China. Japan remained outside

79 David Miller, *My Diary at the Conference of Paris: With Documents*, 21 vols. (New York: Appeal Printing Company, 1924–6), vol. 1, p. 205, entry for 26 March 1919; see also David Miller, *The Drafting of the Covenant*, 2 vols. (New York: Putnam's Sons, 1928), vol. 1, p. 336.

80 For Koo's support, see 'Lu Zhengxiang telegram to Waijiaobu', 13 February 1919, 12 April 1919, in Zhongguo she hui ke xue yuan, Jin dai shi yan jiu suo, Jin dai shi zi liao bian ji shi, and Tianjin shi li shi bo wu guan, *Mi Ji Lu Cun* ('Collections of secret documents') (Peking: Zhong Guo she Hui ke xue chu ban she, 1984), pp. 82–3; 129.

81 Erez Manela, *The Wilsonian Moment: Self-Determination and the International Origins of Anticolonial Nationalism* (New York: Oxford University Press, 2007), p. 26.

82 *Ibid.*, p. 197.

83 Naoko Shimazu, *Japan, Race and Equality: The Racial Equality Proposal of 1919* (Abingdon: Routledge, 2009), p. 171.

the white power club and continued to share second-class status with fellow Asians.

To make the situation worse, Japan was going through its own version of a national identity crisis. While the Chinese found the nineteenth-century world order terribly wrong, Japan was praised as the 'pioneer of progress in the Orient' for the successful adoption of the trappings of Western civilisation with special determination to emulate Germany. But the war and new world order forced Japan to conclude that it might have followed the wrong model – after all, Germany was now a denounced and defeated nation.

Like the Japanese, the Chinese experienced both expectations and disappointment at the post-war Peace Conference, and theirs was much deeper since China had pinned so many hopes on the war and the post-war world. The Chinese had been preparing for their chance at the Peace Conference since 1915, because they knew their country was so weak it had little other means to force any adjustments from the Great Powers. With its official declaration of war against Germany and the large number of labourers sent to Europe to support the Allies, China had earned its seat at the conference, but only as a third-rank nation, having two seats for its delegation while Japan had five. In many respects, Japanese success at the conference automatically meant failure for China. Even so, the Chinese took full advantage of the opportunity and managed to inject substantially new content and perspectives into the Peace Conference discussions and the emerging new world order.

Although not all Chinese believed in Wilson, feelings ran high at the dramatic conclusion of the war. Chinese students in Beijing went to the American Legation where they chanted, 'Long live President Wilson!'. Some of them had memorised and could easily recite his speech on the Fourteen Points. Chen Duxiu, dean of the School of Letters at Peking University, a leading figure in the New Cultural Movement and later a co-founder of the Chinese Communist Party, was so convinced of Wilson's sincerity that he called Wilson 'the number one good man in the world'.[84] For Chen, the end of the First World War was a turning point in human history, 'Might is no longer reliable, justice and reason can no longer be denied', wrote Chen.[85] Reflecting the widespread expectations and feelings among the Chinese, the Chinese took every possible step they could to push for recovery of lost territories at the Peace Conference. This aim had been prominent in Chinese thinking even before the opening of the

84 Chen Duxiu, *Duxiu Wencun* ('Surviving writings of Chen Duxiu') (Hefei: Anhui renmin chu ban she, 1987), p. 388.

85 Chen Duxiu, 'Fa kan ci' ('Preface for a new magazine'), *Mei Zhou Ping Lun* (Weekly Review), 1:1 (1918).

conference. Of course, the direct return of Shandong was one of these grand goals and objectives. Unfortunately, China did not achieve its goals and even failed to regain Shandong. This led to an outburst of anger against the United States and Wilson. Some Chinese complained that Wilson's new world order had not come to China. Chen Duxiu wrote in disgust that Wilson had proved to be an 'empty cannon' whose principles were 'not worth one penny'.[86] Students across China openly expressed their disappointment at the failure of Wilsonianism. College students in Peking cynically joked that Wilson had discovered a jolting new formula for the idealistic Wilsonian world order: '14 = 0'.[87] Such was the outrage at home that China became the only country which refused to sign the Versailles Peace Treaty.

What happened at the Paris Peace Conference sparked the May Fourth Movement, a key turning point in modern China's national development. When news of China's failure to win back Shandong reached China on 4 May, a body of over 3,000 students from across Peking rallied and tried to meet with the Allied ministers in the capital to appeal to them on China's behalf.[88] The May Fourth Movement marked the end of any all-out efforts by China to join the liberal Western system, efforts that had begun by China's seeking to join the First World War. With the May Fourth Movement, the Chinese sense of trust in the West had been replaced by feelings of betrayal and disillusion, and by a determination among many Chinese to find their own way.[89] No matter how we judge China's war contribution and effort, by studying China in the Great War, we can at the very least add a new dimension to our collective memory of the war, its human tragedy and its significance. China took the opportunity the Great War provided to radically readjust its relations with the growing community of nation-states at the turn of the twentieth century.

For India, Korea and Vietnam, all colonies with no official representations at the Peace Conference, Wilson's national self-determination ideas sounded very attractive. They were understandably excited at the outset of the Peace Conference. In 1919, Nguyen Ai Quoc (literally 'Nguyen who loves his country') appeared in Paris. This stranger would later become famous as Hô Chi Minh. He was very active in Paris, and in September 1919 even had an

86 *Mei Zhou Ping Lun*, 20 (4 May 1919).

87 Zhong Guo She hui ko xue yuan Jing dai shi yan jiu so (ed.), *Wu Si Yun Dong Hui Yi Lu* ('Recollections of the May Fourth Movement'), 2 vols. (Beijing: Zhong guo she hui ko xue chu ban she, 1979), vol. 1, p. 222.

88 Liang Jingqun, 'Wo su zhidao de wusi yundun', *Zhuanji Wenxue*, 8:5 (1966).

89 For the broad impact of the May Fourth Movement in Chinese history, see Rana Mitter, *A Bitter Revolution: China's Struggle with the Modern World* (New York: Oxford University Press, 2004).

audience with Albert Sarraut, the recently returned Governor-General of Indochina. Hô used the opportunity the Peace Conference provided to lobby for Vietnam and distributed a petition entitled 'The Demands of the Vietnamese People' to delegations at the Paris Peace Conference. The petition was clearly influenced and motivated by Wilson's ideas, but it was not radical at all politically. It did not ask for independence but rather for autonomy, equal rights and political freedom for the Vietnamese. It called for the following: a general amnesty for all native political prisoners; reform of Indochinese justice by granting the natives the same judicial guarantees as Europeans; freedom of the press and opinion; freedom of association; freedom of emigration and foreign travel; freedom of instruction and the creation in all provinces of technical and professional schools for indigenous people; replacement of rule by decree with the rule of law; election of a permanent Vietnamese delegation to the French parliament, to keep it informed of the wishes of indigenous people.

This was not the last time Ho Chi Minh would follow the American lead. The Vietnamese Declaration of Independence, issued after the Second World War in 1945, was '[t]he most clearly patterned' on the American Declaration of Independence.[90] Unfortunately for Ho and Vietnam, his petition was ignored, although Colonel House, Wilson's close confidant at the Peace Conference, politely acknowledged its reception. The French, however, dismissed Ho's petition as a 'libel', prompting Ho to depart for Moscow and Bolshevism.

There are sources that suggest that many of Ho's ideas in 1919 came from his contacts with Korean nationalists in the United States and Paris; Ho is believed to have borrowed heavily from the Korean independence movement.[91] The Great War did not have a significant impact on Korea, nor did it cause Koreans significant economic hardship. But the war nonetheless served as a major turning point in Korean history, due to the high expectations generated over the post-war Peace Conference. Excited by Wilson's ideas, in the spring of 1919, prominent Korean religious and civic leaders signed a declaration for Korean independence. Over the following months, more than a million people in Korea participated in demonstrations for independence. This series of events was called the March First Movement. This movement may not be considered a success, since it did not achieve its goal of gaining international recognition for the cause of Korean independence, nor even the

90 David Armitage, *The Declaration of Independence: A Global History* (Cambridge, MA: Harvard University Press, 2008), p. 134.

91 Sophie Quinn-Judge, *Ho Chi Minh: The Missing Years* (University of California Press, 2003), pp. 11–18.

more modest goal of raising the question of Korea officially at the Paris Peace Conference. Still, it signalled the beginning of modern nationalism in Korea. In other words, as had happened with the Chinese May Fourth Movement, 'March First transformed the Korean national movement and helped to shape its subsequent identity and development.'[92]

The Indian nationalist movement experienced a sea change during the war. The Indian National Congress had been a pillar of the Empire until 1914, but once the war was over, it became its determined enemy. The spring of 1919 in India was also a 'crucial watershed, in which the national movement swung decisively towards the goal of terminating British rule in India'. Mahatma Gandhi 'shifted in 1919 from a position of firm if critical support for Indian membership in the British Empire to one of determined opposition to it'. When the war was over, Indians expected great things from the Peace Conference proceedings. They called Wilson an 'ancient Asian sage', a 'Christ or Buddha' returning to his ancestral home. One Indian wrote to Wilson: 'Honoured Sir, the aching heart of India cries out to you, whom we believe to be an instrument of God in the reconstruction of the world.' Nobel Laureate Rabindranath Tagore was a great admirer of Wilson and wanted to dedicate his 1917 book, *Nationalism*, to him. Lajpat Rai expressed the hope that an 'immediate grant of autonomy to India and other countries under the rule of the Allies' would follow the conference'. When the Indian National Congress convened in December 1918 for its annual session, it adopted a resolution that demanded that India be recognised by the Powers as 'one of the progressive nations to whom the principle of self-determination should be applied'.[93]

Although Indian voices were largely ignored and their dreams were dashed when the new world order was planned by major powers in 1919, one can argue that India's experience in the Great War and in the post-war Peace Conference indirectly prepared it for full independence after the Second World War.

Conclusion

The story of the First World War is one of tragedy, ironies and contradictions. This applies to Asia as well. The war had a lot to do with empires, but China, which had destroyed its own empire, struggled to realise a republic and a nation-state. Over the course of the war, the last Chinese emperor returned to

92 Manela, *The Wilsonian Moment*, pp. 213.

93 *Ibid.*, pp. 213, 175, 9, 77–8, 92–6.

the throne and another Chinese politician dreamed of becoming emperor; neither succeeded, though. Japan used the war to strengthen its imperial claims while emerging nationalist movements in Korea, India and Vietnam tried to escape their imperial masters' control and secure national independence. The war was about defeat and victory. China, a partisan on the side of the victors, was treated like one of the vanquished at the post-war Peace Conference. Japan was a victor and saw its status in the world improve substantially. But its gains actually carried the seeds of its eventual destruction.

The Great War brought about an abrupt end to the nineteenth-century world system and opened opportunities for a general reordering of world affairs. Having suffered a great deal under the existing world order, Chinese, Koreans, Indochinese and Indians pinned high hopes on the creation of a new system. For educated Asians, the Great War represented the moral decline of Europe; but they were all disappointed at the outcome of the war's aftermath and quickly became disillusioned with the post-war order. China, India and, to a certain extent, Vietnam, in 1919 were fundamentally different from the way they had been in 1914 – socially, intellectually, culturally and ideologically. The sea changes that had taken place occurred to a great extent because of war experiences and broad dissatisfaction with the Paris Peace Conference. The war also served as a turning point in Japanese history.

The First World War years coincided with a period of tremendous change within Asia as China struggled to become a nation and India started its long journey to independence. While China and Vietnam eventually followed a socialist path, in Japan, the Great War gave rise to a new sense of national pride that would eventually lead the Japanese to adopt military methods to challenge the West outright.

In the existing scholarship on Asia, the First World War has been appraised as a 'lost war', an 'ignored war' or a 'forgotten war'. In Asian countries few people understand the significance of Asian involvement. Though not as devastating as in the case of Europe, their involvement transformed the meaning and implications of the conflict both for Asia and for the rest of the increasingly connected world system. It also helped begin the long journey towards national independence followed by many Asian countries. In short, the Great War was a milestone in Asian history which remains seriously under-appreciated and under-researched, even today.

19

North America

JENNIFER D. KEENE

The war in Europe had an immediate and direct impact on North America. The United States and Canada acted on their strong cultural, economic and political ties to Britain by contributing men, money and material to the Allied side. Mexico, long the site of economic competition between the United States, Britain and Germany, found itself at the centre of diplomatic intrigues which climaxed with the Zimmermann Telegram. Relations with Europe, however, only tell one side of the North American story. Within North America, populations shifted northwards to compensate for labour shortages once the war curtailed European immigration. To meet the Allies' escalating demands for industrial and agricultural products, Canada openly recruited US-based farm and factory workers, promising high wages and cheap transport until the US entry into the war dried up this labour stream. US labour agents turned southwards as well, fuelling the movement of southern workers to northern industrial centres with similar enticements. The 500,000 African Americans who joined this migratory wave (known as the Great Migration) set in motion a political and cultural reordering that transformed the racial landscape within the United States. Hundreds of thousands of Mexicans also migrated to the United States, mostly to escape the political and economic turmoil caused by the ongoing Mexican Revolution.

These demographic shifts are just one example of how considering North America as an entity during the First World War offers the alluring possibility of breaking away from the strictures of the normal nation-state approach to studying the war, presenting an opportunity to consider the war's regional and global dimensions. Uncovering the full scope of 'North America's War' requires evaluating Britain's dominant position in the global political economy, North America's contribution to the fighting, international relations within North America and how North American-based events and initiatives affected the course of the war and the peace.

Great Britain in North America

Britain's stature as the world's largest imperial power, centre of the financial world and dominant naval force, meant that its entry into the war affected nearly every nation in some way. Indeed the cultural, political and economic ties that bound the United States and Canada to Great Britain distinctly shaped the war experience of these two North American nations. As citizens of a self-governing Dominion within the British Empire, 'Canadians had no choice about their involvement in the war, but they did have a voice when it came to deciding on the extent of their participation', notes David MacKenzie.[1] The United States declared itself a neutral nation in 1914, but its financial and political elite offered aid to Britain that affected the course of American neutrality almost immediately. Taking advantage of these bonds, Britain moved quickly to facilitate economic mobilisation in Canada and the United States by establishing a robust munitions industry where none had previously existed. By managing a coordinated network that secured contracts, purchased machinery, inspected factories and transported goods overseas, Britain successfully funnelled North American resources towards its own shores and away from Germany.

The strong US-British trading and financial wartime relationship evolved naturally from pre-existing bonds. 'Britain was by far America's largest pre-war trading partner', Robert H. Zieger points out.[2] Less than six months after the war began, the House of Morgan, the financial powerhouse run by the J. P. Morgan bank, signed on as the purchasing and contracting agent for the British government within the United States. Over the next two years, the House of Morgan worked closely with British officials to award more than 4,000 contracts worth over $3 billion to American businesses.[3] Between 1915 and 1917 US exports doubled, with 65 per cent going to Great Britain.[4] In 1916 the British Foreign Office evaluated Britain's dependency on the United States, reaching the alarming conclusion that for 'foodstuffs, for military necessities and for raw materials for industry, the United States was "an

1 David MacKenzie, 'Introduction: myth, memory, and the transformation of Canadian society', in Mackenzie (ed.), *Canada and the First World War: Essays in Honour of Robert Craig Brown* (University of Toronto Press, 2005), p. 3.

2 Robert H. Zieger, *America's Great War: World War I and the American Experience* (Oxford: Rowman & Littlefield, 2000), p. 12.

3 *Ibid.*, pp. 30–1.

4 Paul A. C. Koistinen, *Mobilizing for Modern War: The Political Economy of American Warfare, 1865–1919* (Lawrence, KS: University Press of Kansas, 1997), p. 121.

absolutely irreplaceable source of supply"'.[5] This booming trade in rifles, gunpowder, shells and machine guns also benefited the American economy by pulling it out of recession, and created the industrial infrastructure that would eventually support the US war effort.[6]

The Anglophile House of Morgan aided the British cause even further by lending the British government enormous sums and putting pressure on other American banks to deny loans to Germany.[7] The money flowing from American coffers to the British bolstered the entire Allied side, as the British in turn loaned money to other Entente nations like France and Russia, that could not secure American loans on their own. The $250 million per month that Britain spent in the United States by 1916 (mostly to bolster the sterling–dollar exchange rate to keep commodity prices in check), 'reflected a dependence on American industry and on the American stock market which in German minds both justified the submarine campaign and undermined the United States' claim to be neutral', writes Hew Strachan.[8]

In November 1916, this flow of US credit suddenly appeared in jeopardy of drying up. The Federal Reserve Board warned the House of Morgan to refrain from making unsecured loans to Britain, which by this point had nearly extinguished the gold reserves and securities used as collateral for US loans. 'Lack of credit was about to crimp and possibly cut off the Allies' stream of munitions and foodstuffs', John Milton Cooper, Jr. contends, a scenario only averted by America's April 1917 entry into the war.[9] Hew Strachan remains more sceptical about any potential rupture in this financial partnership. Cutting off war-related trade with Britain would have sent the American economy into a recessionary tailspin, he argues. Strachan goes so far as to suggest that in the long run, continued US neutrality might have

5 Kathleen Burk, *Britain, America and the Sinews of War, 1914–1918* (Boston, MA: Allen & Unwin, 1985), p. 81.

6 Both the United States and Canada expanded agricultural production to meet Allied demand. Low-interest loans encouraged farmers to increase their production through mechanisation or buying more land. The high prices negotiated for overseas wheat and cotton sales made the increased debt seem negligible, but in the 1920s declining crop prices depressed the American and Canadian farming industry. These 'sick' economic sectors intensified the severity of the economic depression that swept the world in 1929, revealing how long North America suffered the aftershocks of the global economic mobilisation during the First World War.

7 After the United States entered the war, the government took over financing the Allies and lent them nearly $11 billion during the period of active fighting and reconstruction. 'Less than $1 billion of the money lent by the American government was ever repaid, but all of the approximately $3 billion owed to private U.S. investors was', writes Paul A. C. Koistinen, *Mobilizing for Modern War*, p. 135.

8 Hew Strachan, *The First World War* (London: Penguin, 2003), p. 228.

9 John Milton Cooper, Jr., *Woodrow Wilson: A Biography* (New York: Knopf, 2009), p. 373.

benefited the Allied side more than American belligerency, since its 'financial commitment to the Entente' had already 'bound the United States to its survival and even victory'.[10] As a belligerent the United States now competed with Britain for American-produced munitions and foodstuffs to supply its own army.

Great Britain also called upon Canada to produce iron, steel, artillery shells and chemical weapons. In 1914 Canada boasted only one munitions factory. Over the course of the war, a British-run Imperial Munitions Board (IMB) oversaw the creation of nearly 600 factories to produce shells, fuses, propellants and casings. 'Close to a third of the shells fired by the British army in 1917 were Canadian-made', notes Desmond Morton.[11] Booming Canadian textile, farming and lumbering industries helped pull the Canadian economy out of a pre-war recession, profits that Canadians used to purchase the domestic war loans floated by the Canadian government. Unlike Britain, Canada did not require massive loans from the United States to finance its war effort. Britain's desire to spend American loans in Canada, to the benefit of the Canadian economy, required a demonstration of reciprocity. In 1917, for instance, Britain only secured approval for using US-government loans for Canadian wheat purchases by promising to send at least half of it to American flour mills for processing.[12]

The cultural ties between the United States, Canada and Great Britain were very much in evidence throughout the war. Within the United States, Great Britain unleashed a ferocious propaganda campaign which emphasised German atrocities in Belgium and the loss of civilian life during Germany's forays into unconditional submarine warfare. British blockade practices arguably killed more civilians than Germany's unconditional submarine warfare, but German propaganda never found an equally compelling way to arouse American ire.[13] The Germans increasingly gained a reputation as the enemies of civilised mores. A good case in point was the overwhelming success that Britain had framing how Americans viewed the *Lusitania* sinking.

10 Hew Strachan, *The First World War*, vol. 1: *To Arms* (Oxford University Press, 2001), p. 991.

11 Desmond Morton, *Marching to Armageddon: Canadians and the Great War, 1914–1919* (Toronto: Lester & Orpen Dennys, 1989), p. 82.

12 Burk, *Britain, America and the Sinews of War, 1914–1918*, pp. 172–4.

13 Alan Kramer estimates that 478,500–700,000 German civilians (depending on the source) died from blockade-related starvation and disease as compared to 14,722 British merchant seamen. Alan Kramer, 'Combatants and noncombatants: atrocities, massacres, and war crimes', in John Horne (ed.), *A Companion to World War I* (Oxford: Blackwell, 2012), pp. 195–6.

On 7 May 1915 a German U-boat fired a torpedo into the *Lusitania*, a British passenger ship that Germany claimed was carrying munitions. The ship sank in less than twenty minutes, and the 1,198 victims included 128 Americans.[14] Germany noted that official newspaper notices had warned Americans to stay off ships headed to the war zone, but British propaganda successfully presented the attack as another example of Germany's inhumanity. US-based British agents distributed thousands of commemorative coins, which, they claimed, the German government had manufactured. In reality a private German citizen had created the coin, which showed a skeleton, representing Death, selling tickets above the caption, 'Business above all', to satirise the Allied willingness to endanger civilian lives while conducting a profitable arms trade. The original coins were stamped 5 May, not 7 May, a mistake that the British seized upon to accuse Germany of premeditated murder in the propaganda pamphlet that accompanied the coin duplicates.

The war strengthened Canada's cultural ties to Great Britain, even as it gave rise to Canadian nationalism. Over the course of the war Canada began to see itself, 'if no longer as a British colony, then at least as a British North American nation', notes Paul Litt.[15] English-Canadians openly called themselves British, not to deny or dismiss their Canadian nationality, but rather to express their enthusiasm for British liberal democracy, membership in the British Empire and British cultural traditions. Canadians used phrases like 'British civilisation', 'British justice', 'British citizenship' and 'British fair play' to express a British-Canadian ethno-nationalism that 'was imbued with a handful of assumptions about what kind of country Canada should be', according to Nathan Smith, which meant, among other things, English-speaking and white.[16]

Not all North Americans supported aiding Great Britain's war effort, however. Dissenters in the United States and Canada emphasised North America's geographic distance from Europe, arguing that the Atlantic served as a natural barrier that protected the continent from the possibility of an

14 The *Lusitania* sinking set off a firestorm of debate within the United States over whether neutrality gave Americans the freedom to travel unmolested into the war zone. Wilson's decision during the *Lusitania* crisis to define neutrality as a status that guaranteed neutral nations unassailable rights (rather than a pledge to treat both sides equally) ultimately set the United States on a collision course with Germany.

15 Paul Litt, 'Canada invaded! The Great War, mass culture, and Canadian cultural nationalism', in Mackenzie (ed.), *Canada and the First World War*, p. 344.

16 Nathan Smith, 'Fighting the alien problem in a British country: returned soldiers and anti-alien activism in wartime Canada, 1916–19', in James E. Kitchen, Alisa Miller and Laura Rowe (eds.), *Other Combatants, Other Fronts: Competing Histories of the First World War* (Cambridge Scholars Publishing, 2011), p. 305.

amphibious German invasion. These isolationists stood ready to defend their territorial borders, but found the idea of sending armies outside the Western Hemisphere unsettling. Throughout North America, scepticism flourished in ethnic and economic communities that had strong political reasons for opposing or limiting participation in the war. Isolationist sentiment within the United States was particularly strong among German Americans and Scandinavians in the Midwest, Irish Americans and the rural South. These populations embraced isolationism for a variety of reasons: support for relatives in Germany, religious objections, hatred of Great Britain and distrust of the eastern financial elite making loans to the Allies. Appeals to protect the British Empire failed to sway many French Canadians, who worried that wartime mobilisation would accelerate Anglo-Canadian nation-building. French-Canadian elites pledged support to the war, but many others embraced an ethnic-based North American nationalism that prompted them to resist fighting an overseas war. Concerned that the wartime push towards Anglo-conformism threatened their cultural autonomy and civil liberties, French Canadians proved reluctant to enlist and openly opposed conscription.

Critics of isolationism countered that it was not the Atlantic Ocean that protected North America, but the British navy. Canada and the United States benefited tremendously from the blanket of protection that British control of the seas offered to its former and present colonies, they argued. Britain maintained this naval dominance (with only occasional challenges from German U-boats) throughout the war by controlling shipping lanes, blockading the North and Baltic Seas through patrols and mines and providing ships to transport goods to Europe. Early 1917 was one crucial period when Germany threatened to gain the upper hand at sea. In February 1917 Germany resumed unconditional submarine warfare, knowing that this decision was likely to bring the United States formally into the war. Germany gambled that a relentless U-boat assault on shipping would force Britain and France to capitulate before the United States could offer much help on the battlefields. The sharp increase in German submarine attacks once it resumed unconditional submarine warfare (reaching a wartime high of 2.2 million tons from April–June 1917) left British Admiral John Jellicoe pessimistic over Britain's future capacity to wage war. Canadian-born US Admiral William Sims offered the solution – instituting a convoy system that relied on US destroyers (rather than Britain's slower battleships) to accompany groups of ships crossing the Atlantic. The use of convoys meant that in 1918, for the first time since 1915, Allied shipbuilding exceeded losses at sea. 'Better than almost any other single factor, the convoy system reveals the truly global nature of World War I', writes Michael Neiberg.[17]

During the war the United States switched from being a debtor nation, dependent on British financing for its industrial development, to a creditor nation that did more than lend money to belligerents to fund purchases of American goods. When British financiers began liquidating their assets throughout the underdeveloped world to fund the war, American bankers and industrialists seized on the chance to finance and construct mines, railroads, factories and oil fields throughout the Western Hemisphere. America's geographical location vis-à-vis Mexico became a distinct advantage that aided its penetration into markets previously dominated by Britain. Accelerating a shift already underway, US imports to Mexico rose from 49.7 per cent of all imported goods to 66.7 per cent, while the British market share dropped from 13 per cent to 6.5 per cent from 1913 to 1927.[18] Canada underwent a similar shift from borrower to lender, the result of credits extended to Britain for purchases of wheat and munitions.

Yet the war also laid bare the American and Canadian dependence on British purchases of its crops and manufactured goods for sustained prosperity – allowing Britain, at least for the time being, to retain its position as the epicentre of the international political economy. The twin effects of 'Britain's multiple centrality to the world economy [which] gave her critical leverage in moving resources toward the Allies and away from the Central Powers' and 'the United States' awesome productive capacity', produced a combination that was difficult for Germany and her allies to match, Theo Balderston concludes.[19] The outcome of the war seemingly reinforced Britain's world supremacy, as evidenced by its ability to call upon a variety of resources (men, money and material) from North America to defeat its European enemies.

North America's military experience

Both the United States and Canada entered the war unprepared. In 1914, Canada possessed a regular army of just 3,000 with 70,000 in volunteer militias. The Canadian Corps would eventually total four divisions, with a

17 Michael S. Neiberg, *Fighting the Great War: A Global History* (Cambridge, MA: Harvard University Press, 2005), p. 292.

18 Rosemary Thorp, 'Latin America and the international economy from the First World War to the world depression', in Leslie Bethell (ed.), *The Cambridge History of Latin America*, vol. VI: *1870–1930* (Cambridge University Press, 1986), p. 66.

19 Theo Balderston, 'Industrial mobilization and war economies', in Horne (ed.), *A Companion to World War I*, p. 229.

fifth division broken up to provide replacements. Overall, 619,000 Canadians served during the war, with 424,589 serving overseas, out of a population of 7.5 million people.[20] The situation was not much better within the United States in 1917, when the nation declared war with approximately 300,000 troops (federal and state) available. Eventually the United States would raise a force of 4.4 million, with nearly half of these serving overseas, out of a population of 103 million people.[21] Overall, each nation suffered a comparable number of casualties, with 66,665 Canadians and 53,402 Americans killed in battle. The discrepancy was evident in the proportions that these numbers represented, nearly 11 per cent of the Canadian forces and 1.2 per cent of the US military.[22]

The United States and Canada raised their forces differently. The United States adopted conscription immediately and eventually drafted 72 per cent of the armed forces. With this decision the United States broke with its tradition of fighting first with volunteers and only using conscription to fill the ranks when enlistments lagged. Introducing conscription after the nation suffered heavy losses on the battlefield would increase the likelihood of mass protests against the draft, American officials reasoned, aware that the nation had been sharply divided over entering the war. Canada opted to wait until replacement needs became acute, only turning to conscription in 1917 to raise nearly 100,000 troops.[23] The ability to apply for exemptions helped make the draft more politically acceptable within the United States and Canada. The majority of draft-eligible Americans and Canadians publicly registered for the draft, and then retreated to the privacy of their homes to fill out a form requesting an exemption. The pockets of outright opposition to conscription reflected pre-existing ethnic and regional schisms. Draft resistance occurred primarily in American southern rural communities that had opposed entering the war, and within French-speaking Quebec, which resisted the government's attempts to use wartime military service to underscore Anglo-Canadian dominance. Some Québecois even evaded conscription by fleeing across the border to New

20 Robert K. Hanks, 'Canada: Army' and James Carroll, Robert K. Hanks and Spencer Tucker, 'Canada: Role in war', in Spencer C. Tucker (ed.), *World War I: A Student Encyclopedia* (Santa Barbara, CA: ABC-Clio, 2005), pp. 257–9.

21 Jennifer D. Keene, *World War I: The American Soldier Experience* (Lincoln, NE: University of Nebraska, 2011), pp. 33, 163.

22 Newfoundland was a separate colony during the war, so its disproportionately high casualty rate is not included in these figures. The 8,500 men who enlisted in Newfoundland represented nearly 10 per cent of the adult male population. Of these, 3,600 were either killed or wounded.

23 J. L. Granatstein, 'Conscription in the Great War', in Mackenzie (ed.), *Canada and the First World War*, p. 70.

England French-Canadian textile communities. This immigrant community saw no contradiction between sending its own sons off to fight in the US army while simultaneously offering refuge to French-Canadian draft-dodgers.[24]

The time it took to raise, transport and train troops from North America meant that these armies did not actually enter the front lines until months after their respective nations entered the war. Initially both the Americans and Canadians fought under the tutelage of the more experienced French and British armies. Canada and the United States faced similar pressure to raise troops that could be amalgamated into the British and French armies, but domestic nationalistic sentiment and concerns about how European generals were conducting the war caused each to develop an independent, national army instead.

Unhappiness with the British decision to launch a counter-attack using Canadian troops after Germany's first mass gas attack during the Second Battle of Ypres ensured 'that the 1st Division became the core of Canada's national army rather than an "imperial" formation drawn from a dominion', Terry Copp concludes.[25] In April 1917, all four Canadian battalions went into action for the first time at the Battle of Arras, when they took Vimy Ridge. General Arthur Currie was credited with the victory and in June 1917 given command of the Canadian Corps. The Canadians became convinced that they were an elite fighting force which could succeed where the British and French could not. 'In those few minutes I witnessed the birth of a nation', Brigadier-General A. E. Ross declared after the war, a notion that has provoked much debate ever since.

Canadians placed tremendous faith in Currie (the first Canadian to attain the rank of full general) to use Canadian soldiers effectively and prudently while maintaining a certain degree of autonomy on the battlefield. General John J. Pershing, the commander of the American Expeditionary Forces (AEF), faced similar expectations within the United States. Seeking to demonstrate his own leadership abilities on the battlefield, Pershing steadfastly resisted any formal amalgamation of the American army into the Allied forces. An independent US army met Wilson's larger political goals as well. Pershing sailed to France with clear instructions from the American Secretary of War, Newton Baker, 'to cooperate with the forces of the other countries employed against the enemy; but in so doing the underlying idea must be

24 Christopher Capazzola, *Uncle Sam Wants You: World War I and the Making of the Modern American Citizen* (New York: Oxford University Press, 2008), p. 41.

25 Terry Copp, 'The military effort, 1914–1918', in Mackenzie (ed.), *Canada and the First World War*, p. 43.

kept in view that the forces of the United States are a separate and distinct component of the combined forces, the identity of which must be preserved'.[26] Wilson depended on having a strong, visible and independent American presence on the battlefield when the Allies won the war. The United States needed to play a major role in the fighting, Wilson believed, to guarantee him a prominent voice in fashioning the peace, which, after all, was one of the primary reasons the President had led the nation into war. The Americans never gained complete independence (they were always dependent to some degree on Allied logistical assistance), but by the fall of 1918 the AEF did occupy its own sector of the Western Front.

Americans and Canadians claimed that their troops embodied a new brand of masculinity born on the frontier, which emphasised aggression, ingenuity and individualism. These traits supposedly separated North American soldiers from their class-bound, weary European counterparts. In 1917, the Canadian Prime Minister, Sir Robert Borden, unsuccessfully proposed that the Canadian army take the lead in training the American army, 'because Canadians, like Americans, did not have an aristocracy that placed birth over merit'.[27] American military training doctrine explicitly underscored the differences in temperament between American and European soldiers, identifying individual rifle marksmanship and 'open warfare' as the hallmarks of the American fighting man. 'Berlin cannot be taken by the French or the British Armies or by both of them. It can only be taken by a thoroughly trained, entirely homogeneous American Army', General H. B. Fiske, the head of the American Expeditionary Forces training programme, told his colleagues.[28] The preference for rifles over heavy artillery remained the bedrock principle of US army doctrine that in Pershing's mind defined the American 'way of war'.

Both the United States and Canada also felt that their military contributions and valour went underappreciated by Britain and France. The fear that Britain might not adequately document the Canadian war effort led to the creation of a Canadian War Records Office that collected materials and publicised Canadian military feats to Canadian and English audiences. Likewise an outpouring of nationally focused books, articles and films in the United States left

26 *United States Army in the World War, 1917–1919*, 17 vols. (Washington, DC: Center of Military History, 2001), vol. 1, p. 3.

27 John English, 'Political leadership in the First World War', in Mackenzie (ed.), *Canada and the First World War*, p. 80. Mitchell A. Yokelson, *Borrowed Soldiers: Americans under British Command, 1918* (Norman, OK: University of Oklahoma Press, 2008), pp. 76–7.

28 Jennifer D. Keene, *Doughboys, the Great War and the Remaking of America* (Baltimore, MD: Johns Hopkins University, 2001), p. 106.

Americans with the clear impression that the United States had practically won the war single-handedly. The feeling of being junior partners in a European-led coalition no doubt caused some of this chest-thumping. More importantly, the political desire of the United States and Canada to parlay their wartime participation into greater influence within the new world order also necessitated impressing Britain and France with the contribution each nation had made to the Allied victory. The exact contributions of American and Canadian troops to the overall Allied victory continue to excite debate on both sides of the Atlantic to this day.

The increased importance of the Dominions to the British war effort led to the Imperial War Conferences in 1917 and 1918 which gave Dominion Prime Ministers or representatives a chance to negotiate how their economies and armies contributed to the war effort. The Dominions also sent their own delegations to the Peace Conference, then signed and ratified the peace treaties individually.[29] The leading American negotiator, Colonel Edward House, welcomed this development, viewing any fracturing within the British Empire as positive for the United States. The Canadian Prime Minister, Borden, 'deliberately brought the point of view of North America to the councils of the empire, a point of view that reflected the growing identity of Canadian and American interests', notes Borden's biographer, Robert Brown.[30] At the Peace Conference Borden experimented with a new international role as mediator between the two most powerful English-speaking world powers. In a manner of speaking, Canada had a foot in both camps, and saw itself as uniquely positioned to explain North American concerns to Britain and its Dominions and British Empire worries to America. Borden intervened several times to fashion compromises when American and British delegations clashed on treaty details, arguing especially forcefully (if futilely) against hefty German reparations to avoid antagonising the United States. 'Part of this was self-interest: a reoccurring nightmare in Ottawa was that Canada might find itself fighting on the side of Britain and its ally Japan against the United States', Margaret MacMillan

29 Robert Aldrich and Christopher Hillard, 'The French and British Empires', in Horne (ed.), *A Companion to World War I*, p. 532.

30 Robert Craig Brown, 'Canada in North America', in John Braeman, Robert H. Brenner and David Brody (eds.), *Twentieth-Century American Foreign Policy* (Columbus: Ohio State University Press, 1971), p. 359. See also Robert Craig Brown, '"Whither are we being shoved?" Political leadership in Canada during World War I', in J. L. Granatstein and R. D. Cuff (eds.), *War and Society in North America* (Toronto: Thomas Nelson & Sons, 1971), pp. 104–19.

asserts.[31] The shared ancestry, language, literature, political institutions and beliefs made a potential alliance between the United States and Great Britain 'sufficient to ensure the peace of the world' if the League of Nations failed, Borden told Lloyd George.[32] This plan never came to pass, but Borden's sentiments revealed that at the level of high diplomacy, relations between Britain and Anglo-North America emerged intact from the war.

The US and Canada: comparisons and relations

Comparing the war experiences of the United States and Canada uncovers an array of parallels that helped define the North American experience of war. These comparable paths underscore similarities in settlement patterns, political ideals and economic development. The national identities of the United States and Canada traced their political and demographic origins to the white-settler Anglo communities that had originally colonised the continent. This vision of national identity ignored the other demographic realities that had peopled North America: slavery, Spanish and French colonisation and large-scale immigration by non-Anglo peoples in the early twentieth century.

Throughout the war, the United States and Canada grappled with organised protests by marginalised minorities. The ongoing struggle for racial equality within the United States sparked racial riots, lynching and wide-scale state surveillance of African-American political organisations and periodicals. Over 400,000 African Americans served in the military, with 89 per cent placed in non-combatant, labouring roles. 'The attempted exclusion of African Americans from a national memory of the war complemented larger attempts to marginalize African Americans as citizens from the polity', notes Chad Williams.[33] The Canadian government's campaign to suppress bilingual schools, begun in 1912, stoked fears within Quebec that wartime military service would turn into one more vehicle that eliminated French-Canadian culture and autonomy. The lagging French-Canadian enlistments (estimated by the British War Office as the lowest in the Empire), draft evasion and the anti-conscription 1918 Easter riot in Quebec City, all attested to the vibrancy of this ethnic conflict. 'A war that many thought could unite French and English Canadians had proved everything to the contrary', Patrice A. Dutil

31 Margaret MacMillan, *Paris 1919: Six Months that Changed the World* (New York: Random House, 2001), pp. 47–8.
32 Quoted in *ibid*., p. 48.
33 Chad L. Williams, *Torchbearers of Democracy: African American Soldiers in the World War I Era* (Chapel Hill, NC: University of North Carolina Press, 2010), p. 301.

concludes.[34] Rather than breaking down the physical, cultural and political separation between the majority and minority populations, the war reinforced the isolation of these minority communities. Native peoples served in both the American and Canadian armies, an experience that provoked a contradictory mix of pressure to assimilate while in uniform and then, once they returned home, opportunities to revive traditional warrior ceremonies and traditions. The longstanding view of Native Americans as a 'vanishing race' fuelled an array of home-front assaults on Native American communities, as government agents in the United States and Canada leased indigenous lands to non-Indians as part of the drive to maximise wartime crop, mineral and livestock production. These minority groups thus ended the war with new sets of grievances over their poor treatment by the majority culture, amid fresh evidence that the federal governments in each nation intended to maintain the status quo.

The transatlantic labour market that linked North America to Europe had funnelled nearly 3 million people to Canada from 1896–1914 and over 8 million Europeans to the United States from 1900–09. Only British subjects could enlist in the Canadian army, consequently recruits came predominantly from the Anglo-British community, both Canadian and British-born. The ethnic composition of the military thus reaffirmed the 'British' identity of Canada. Besides putting their own German immigrant population under surveillance, Canada took concrete steps to protect its borders from the large anti-British immigrant populations residing in a neutral United States. Canadian fantasies that German spies might somehow entice German-American or Irish-American communities to conduct guerrilla raids, caused Canadian authorities to keep 16,000 soldiers stationed along the border, part of a 50,000-man force that remained at home to repel any direct attack on Canadian soil.[35] Once the United States entered the war, the need for such a strong southern border defence evaporated, allowing Canada to send reinforcements to France at a critical moment in the fighting. Within the US army, foreign-born soldiers (who had declared their intent to become citizens) composed nearly one-fifth of the wartime force, contributions to

34 Patrice A. Dutil, 'Against isolationism: Napoléon Belcourt, French Canada, and "La grande guerre"', in Mackenzie (ed.), *Canada and the First World War*, p. 125.

35 Granatstein, 'Conscription', p. 66. According to John Herd Thompson and Stephen J. Randall, the US-based German military attaché considered such attacks, but the only actual case of German sabotage that originated on American soil damaged a railway bridge in New Brunswick; John Herd Thompson and Stephen J. Randall, *Canada and the United States: Ambivalent Allies*, 4th edn (Athens, GA: University of Georgia Press, 2008), p. 94.

the war cause that helped recent immigrants from Allied nations assimilate into the mainstream culture.

Throughout the early twentieth century, native-born and immigrant workers moved freely back and forth across the US-Canadian border, helping solidify transnational bonds between labour unions, socialist groups and the radical Industrial Workers of the World that caught the attention of intelligence services in both countries. In the post-war period, Canadians and Americans accused recently arrived immigrants from southern and central Europe of diluting North America's Anglo racial and cultural heritage. These immigrants were also charged with importing radical, Bolshevik ideologies that threatened capitalism and representative democracy. Protecting North America from Bolshevism became a joint US-Canadian endeavour, with the two governments sharing information about suspect labour groups throughout the war and during the post-war Red Scare.[36]

Culturally, economically and politically there was little reason for conflict between the United States and Canada. Diplomacy helped maintain tranquillity along the northern border of the United States. By 1914 an embryonic bilateral US-Canadian relationship allowed for direct negotiations (albeit with British oversight on the Canadian side). In the early twentieth century, several international commissions began tackling the traditional causes of conflict (settling formal boundaries, access to fisheries and agreed use of shared rivers and lakes) between the United States and Canada. These permanent commissions operated outside the formal diplomatic channels still controlled by Britain, and their founding coincided with the closure of the last remaining British garrisons in North America in 1906. Canada was now responsible for resolving disputes, diplomatic and military, with the United States. The temporary appointment of an independent wartime Canadian representative within the British Embassy in Washington, DC, made Canada the only British Dominion that had the ability to talk directly to the US government. These developments paved the way for wartime cooperation and the eventual establishment of formal diplomatic relations in 1927.[37]

Cultural connections reinforced these growing diplomatic ties. A steady stream of US-produced movies, magazines, newspapers, books, advertisements and music poured into Canada. The sheer number of products created for the much larger American audience and the efficient railroad distribution

36 Donald Avery, 'Ethnic and class relations in Western Canada during the First World War: a case study of European immigrants and Anglo-Canadian nativism', in Mackenzie (ed.), *Canada and the First World War*, pp. 286–7.

37 Thompson and Randall, *Canada and the United States*, pp. 71–9, 96–7.

networks that transported them throughout Anglo-North America, made it difficult for distinctly Canadian cultural offerings to thrive. American touring companies regularly included Canadian cities and towns on their itineraries, exposing Canadians to a full range of American circuses, vaudeville shows, minstrel acts and Wild West shows. These facts dismayed the Canadian cultural elite, but the general public avidly consumed American movies and music with little debate or reflection before the war. The influx of British imports also hampered the development of Canadian cultural traditions, as many middle- and upper-class Canadians actively sought to maintain and cultivate this cultural connection to mother England.

The war, however, temporarily disrupted this benign cultural relationship between Canada and the United States. The first fissures appeared when Canada entered the war and the United States remained neutral. Wartime Canada avidly consumed Canadian-authored books explaining the war, along with British films like the *Battle of the Somme* (1916). 'Had American mass culture been merely inadequate, perhaps such [British] import substitutes would have seen Canadians happily through the war years', notes Paul Litt. 'But in fact, American cultural products were not merely lacking – they were offensive.'[38] Heightened Canadian patriotism, along with pride in fighting as part of the British Empire, suddenly made Canadians aware of how much flag-waving and jingoism permeated US-produced films, songs, books and plays. Canadians chafed at the tone of moral superiority that America adopted as a neutral nation, well aware of the profits flowing into US coffers from the healthy munitions trade. French-Canadian Senator Napoléon Belcourt aptly summarised Canadian views towards US neutrality: 'mere money making is after all but a very poor, indeed a very miserable compensation for the loss of national prestige, national honor, caused by neglecting or ignoring modern solidarity, the solidarity of civilized mankind'.[39] America's entry into the war helped ease these cultural tensions, but 'during the 1920s and 1930s, no Canadian forgot that Canada, with one-tenth the population, had more killed and wounded than the United States', noted historians John Herd Thompson and Stephen J. Randall.[40]

Conflict between Mexico and the United States

In 1916 it appeared more likely that the United States would go to war with Mexico than enter the Great War. Mexican politics had been in upheaval since

38 Litt, 'Canada invaded!', p. 338. 39 Quoted in Dutil, 'Against isolationism', p. 122.
40 Thompson and Randall, *Canada and the United States*, p. 98.

the Mexican Revolution began in 1910. The United States played a direct role in the revolution, temporarily intervening in 1914 with a landing in Veracruz that helped bring a new leader, Venustiano Carranza, to power. As Carranza fell out of favour with the Americans, his supporters hatched the Plan of San Diego, which called for a series of raids into US border towns to kill all the Anglo-Americans living there and incite an uprising among the remaining Mexican-Americans and blacks.[41] A Mexican invasion was to follow to establish Texas, New Mexico, Arizona, Colorado and California as independent republics that could opt to join Mexico. The plan fell apart when the US government got wind of it. An increased troop presence along the border dealt effectively with the few guerrilla raids attempted in 1915. On 9 March 1916, however, the anti-Carranza Mexican revolutionary, General Francisco 'Pancho' Villa, attacked Columbus, New Mexico with a force of 500, killing eighteen Americans. Villa intended to provoke the United States into invading Mexico, hoping to weaken Carranza's constitutional government by exposing its inability to prevent a US violation of Mexican national sovereignty. German operatives in Mexico helped finance these rebel activities, expecting a border war to distract the United States from the European conflict.

As Villa (and Germany) anticipated, Wilson answered this first attack on American soil since the War of 1812 by sending a 14,000-man expeditionary force into Mexico without Carranza's permission or approval. Another 140,000 National Guardsmen (state-controlled militias mobilised into active federal service) and regular army troops patrolled the border.[42] 'The deeper the expedition penetrated, the more Mexicans suspected that the dreaded *Yanquis* were bent on conquest', John Milton Cooper, Jr. notes. These suspicions led to a series of clashes between US troops and governmental forces, including a firefight in Carrizal on 21 June 1916.[43] In the wake of this clash Wilson prepared a request for congressional authority to occupy northern Mexico, which he subsequently abandoned upon learning that American soldiers had fired first. This was the closest the two countries had come to war since the Mexican-American War of 1846–8.

In contrast to American reluctance to enter the European war, Wilson faced strong pressure from some cabinet officials and Congress to go to war with

41 James A. Sandos, *Rebellion in the Borderlands: Anarchism and the Plan of San Diego, 1904–1923* (Norman, OK: University of Oklahoma Press, 1992).

42 War Department, *Annual Reports 1916*, 3 vols. (US Government Printing Office, 1916), vol. 1, pp. 13, 23, 189–91.

43 Cooper, *Woodrow Wilson*, p. 320.

Mexico in 1916. Realising that formal hostilities would lead to a lengthy war, Wilson and Carranza agreed instead to appoint a mediation commission that paved the way for the withdrawal of US troops on 5 February 1917. In 1916, Wilson ran for re-election with the campaign slogan, 'He kept us out of war.' Most historians equate the phrase with Wilson's handling of the *Lusitania* crisis, but Democrats campaigning for Wilson gave equal weight to Mexico during their stump speeches.[44] Wilson offered many reasons for wanting to avoid a border war, including suspicions that those pushing for armed intervention really wanted improved access to Mexican oil, which British and American business interests had long vied to control. Wilson also knew that having half a million troops bogged down in Mexico would severely hamper the creation of an American expeditionary force if the United States went to war with Germany. 'Germany is anxious to have us at war with Mexico, so that our minds and our energies will be taken off the great war across the sea', Wilson told his personal secretary.[45]

The Mexican punitive expedition failed in its stated goal of capturing Villa, but 'its real purpose was a display of the power of the United States', Secretary of War Newton Baker asserted.[46] The US military, under-strength and under-equipped in comparison to the European armies fighting along the Western Front, gained important experience fighting its first sustained campaign since the 1898 Spanish-American War. The invasion's commander, Brigadier General John J. Pershing, would go on to lead the wartime army, carrying the lessons learned from Mexico to France. The incursion gave the army its first test mobilising National Guard troops and readying them for combat, along with practice mounting the surveillance and logistics needed to maintain an army on the move. None of this went particularly well or smoothly in Mexico, a harbinger of the challenges ahead. These problems helped preparedness advocates win some funding to enlarge, reorganise and modernise the nation's military in the days leading up to America's entry into the First World War. Those determined to avoid any involvement in the European war had steadfastly opposed preparedness as one step removed from intervention. The armed clash with Mexico, however, allowed the preparedness faction to argue that the nation needed a stronger military to protect its borders.[47]

44 *Ibid.*, p. 322.
45 N. G. Levin, *Woodrow Wilson and World Politics: America's Response to War and Revolution* (New York: Oxford University Press, 1968), p. 311.
46 War Department, *Annual Reports, 1917*, 3 vols. (US Government Printing Office, 1917), vol. I, p. 10.
47 Russell Weigley, *History of the United States Army* (New York: Macmillan, 1967), p. 348.

The National Defense Act of 1916 increased the size of the peacetime army and federal supervision of state troops, and laid the groundwork for federal mobilisation of the economy – measures designed with the European war in mind. Visions of men going into battle without enough machine guns or flying airplanes that routinely crashed (as in Mexico), prompted Congress to appropriate more money for both.

Viewing the Zimmermann Telegram within the context of Mexican rebel border raids, the San Diego plan and armed clashes between US and Mexican troops, helps illuminate Germany's decision to send the telegram, and the subsequent US outrage. The Zimmermann Telegram proposed that Mexico ally with Germany to recoup territory lost in the mid nineteenth century, if Germany and the United States went to war. 'Mexico's hatred for America is well-founded and old', German Foreign Minister, Arthur Zimmermann, assured his German colleagues, citing the American military's recent poor performance chasing Villa to predict a long, drawn-out war between Mexico and the United States that would keep American troops tied down in North America.[48] Zimmermann's enthusiastic endorsement of this proposed German-Mexican alliance represented a complete change of heart. Only a year earlier he had rejected Mexico's offer to house German U-boat bases to avoid a rupture in US–German relations. In January 1917, however, Zimmermann believed that the German decision to resume unconditional submarine warfare would be likely to bring the United States into the war. By sending the secret telegram, Zimmermann inadvertently played a major role in ensuring American belligerency once the British intercepted, decoded and then passed the telegram on to the American government. The telegram's publication in March 1917 unified a previously divided American public in favour of war with Germany. 'The note had its greatest impact in precisely those areas of the United States where isolationism and thus opposition to U.S. involvement in the war were particularly strong: the Southwest', writes Friedrich Katz; border states where the recent troubles with Mexico loomed the largest.[49]

The aftershocks of the Zimmermann Telegram went beyond prompting US entry into the war. Within North America the note threatened further damage to US–Mexican relations, as Carranza hedged on his response. Publicly denying that he had ever received the telegram, Carranza privately contemplated the likelihood of another American invasion, what kind of

48 Friedrich Katz, *The Secret War in Mexico: Europe, the United States and the Mexican Revolution* (University of Chicago Press, 1981), p. 351.

49 *Ibid.*, p. 361.

military aid Germany could reasonably give and his advisers' assessment that the proposal was unworkable. On 14 April 1917, eight days after the United States declared war on Germany, Carranza told the German ambassador to Mexico that he intended to remain neutral.

As Wilson wanted, Mexico adopted a new constitution in 1917 that allowed for universal suffrage and land reform. But Carranza also moved to reassert national control over Mexican natural resources, especially oil and minerals. His government imposed higher taxes, required landowners to get official approval before selling land to foreigners and added a constitution clause that conferred ownership of all underground resources to the nation rather than the landowner. These measures had little immediate effect. The Mexican government made no effort to enforce this constitutional clause, and foreign warships ensured that oil fields along the Gulf coast continued to produce record amounts of oil for the Allied war effort. Reports that the Americans were seriously considering a limited occupation of Mexican oil fields, the ban on American loans to Mexico and a US embargo on arms, food and gold, however, prompted Carranza to continue ongoing, if fruitless, conversations with German officials for the rest of the war about a possible alliance. In the spring of 1919, the possibility of war between the United States and Mexico loomed once again. American oil interests and some members of Wilson's administration began plotting a coup with Carranza's opponents, all the while pressuring Wilson to break diplomatic relations. Coinciding with the incapacitating stroke that rendered Wilson bed-ridden for months, these plans went nowhere. The drumbeat of criticism in the press and Congress nonetheless strained relations with Carranza until his eventual overthrow by the military in the spring of 1920.[50]

The North American origins of Wilsonianism

The United States had long seen the Monroe Doctrine (an 1823 pronouncement by President James Monroe that the Western Hemisphere was off-limits to future colonisation by other world powers) as a commitment to guarantee the sovereignty of newly independent nations throughout the Western Hemisphere. Wilson's predecessors had already enlarged the scope of the Monroe Doctrine to include the 1904 Roosevelt Corollary (which justified US regional policing to prevent 'wrongdoing') and strengthen the US regional economic presence through dollar diplomacy. Wilson now attempted to apply

50 Mark T. Gilderhus, *Pan American Visions: Woodrow Wilson in the Western Hemisphere, 1913–1921* (Tucson, AZ: University of Arizona Press, 1986), pp. 147–9, 152–3.

the principles of the Monroe Doctrine globally. The wording of Wilson's famous 'Peace without Victory' speech of 1917, which proposed a negotiated settlement to the world war, explicitly presented the American experience in the Western Hemisphere as a model for future international relations. 'I am proposing . . .', Wilson stated, 'that the nations should with one accord adopt the doctrine of President Monroe as the doctrine of the world: that no nation should seek to extend its polity over any other nation or people, but that every people should be left free to determine its own polity, its own way of development, unhindered, unthreatened, unafraid, the little along with the powerful.'

Wilson's willingness to intervene militarily to make Mexico and the Caribbean 'safe for democracy' served as a 'rehearsal for preparing the nation for the grand task of global reconstruction' that Wilson would attempt once the United States entered the world war, Akira Iriye argues.[51] Many of the ideals that Wilson would go on to trumpet through his 1918 Fourteen Points address and at the Versailles peace negotiations, he initially proposed to improve US relations with its southern neighbour. Hoping to teach Mexicans 'to elect good men', Wilson floated a proposal for a Pan-American Pact that would allow the United States to work in concert with Argentina, Chile and Brazil to promote democracy, settle disputes and guarantee borders within the Western Hemisphere. 'Although nothing came of the Pan-American pact, its provisions contained language and ideas that Wilson would use in the Covenant of the League of Nations', Cooper notes.[52] The limits that Wilson imposed on regional interventions and his attempt to devise a method of collective security to handle disputes within the Western Hemisphere revealed that, 'in the Wilsonian way of war, the limits of force were equal in importance to the power of force', asserts Frederick S. Calhoun.[53]

Wilson ultimately failed to convince isolationists within the United States (who clung to the Monroe Doctrine as a way to limit US involvement in world affairs) that the time had come for active participation in the League of Nations. His opponents argued that joining the League of Nations would threaten US regional dominance and embroil the nation in 'entangling alliances' that would lead to involvement in future European wars. The desire to

51 Akira Iriye, *The Cambridge History of American Foreign Relations*, vol. III: *The Globalizing of America, 1913–1945* (Cambridge University Press, 1993), pp. 37–8.

52 Cooper, *Woodrow Wilson*, p. 246.

53 Frederick S. Calhoun, *Power and Principle: Armed Intervention in Wilsonian Foreign Policy* (Ohio: Kent State University Press, 1986), p. 251.

define its own foreign policy unilaterally and to continue relying on North America's physical distance from Europe to maintain diplomatic and political independence, ultimately prevailed over Wilson's suggestion that the United States take on more formal responsibility as the world's guardian of democracy and humanity. Participation in the world war thus only reaffirmed America's view of itself as a North American nation.

Conclusion

The war noticeably amplified American influence within the Western Hemisphere and the increased integration of North American economies and politics. The trend towards regional integration under the leadership of the United States did not go unchallenged. In 1919, Mexican President Carranza vocally disputed Wilson's claim that the Monroe Doctrine benefited nations seeking to determine their own futures. Instead, he assailed the policy as extending the imperial reach of the United States within the Western Hemisphere by imposing 'upon independent nations a protectorate status which they do not ask for and which they do not require'.[54] Carranza instead proposed pan-Hispanic cooperation to curb US hegemony in the region, foreshadowing future ideological disputes over whether America was a 'good neighbour' or 'imperialist' in the Western Hemisphere. Carranza unsuccessfully urged smaller and weaker Central American nations to join together to prevent the United States from intervening unilaterally in their domestic affairs. He had better luck fostering a strong sense of Mexican nationalism built upon a legacy of wartime tension with the United States.

Canada's embrace of imperial nationhood revealed its commitment to evolve as a nation within, rather than in opposition to, the British Empire. The centrality of the memory of the First World War within Canada helped reinforce its sense of solidarity with other Dominions whose national identities became inextricably linked to their battlefield experiences. No sense of shared wartime sacrifice bound the United States and Canada together in the post-war period. Instead, the memory of the war took quite different trajectories on each side of the border. The decentralised way in which American communities commemorated the war prevented any unifying collective memory of the war from taking root. The absence of a national monument to the war in Washington, DC, stands in notable contrast to the dominating presence of the Peace Tower and

54 Gilderhus, *Pan American Visions*, p. 146.

the National War Memorial in Ottawa. These sites of memory strengthened Canada's cultural identification with the British Empire, a relationship which bestowed economic benefits as well. The 1932 Ottawa Conference, for instance, established a five-year privileged trading relationship among Britain and its Dominions at the height of the Great Depression (much to America's irritation).

Overall, however, the war accelerated the coordination of the American and Canadian diplomatic goals and domestic policies, strengthening bilateral relations between the two nations. To the south, the war unsettled US–Mexican relations, ultimately prompting the United States to use force to assert its economic, political and military dominance. Whether the process was rocky as in the case of US–Mexican relations or relatively smooth as between the United States and Canada, the economic and political integration of North America was one of the key global legacies of the First World War.

20

Latin America

OLIVIER COMPAGNON

The First World War has long been considered a non-event in the history of contemporary Latin America, far from the main theatres of military operations. The only exception came in the form of two naval battles off the southern coasts at the end of 1914: a German victory over the Royal Navy at Cape Coronel on 1 November and the British victory at the Falkland Islands on 8 December, which gave the British control of Cape Horn. The subcontinent was spared the blood-letting which afflicted the main belligerent nations, and the score of states south of the Rio Grande were seen as distant spectators of the first total conflict. This was unlike the African and Asiatic colonial regions which were involved in the great mobilisation of the imperial capitals, and would finally suffer only passing economic consequences or distant echoes of propaganda from the two coalitions. In no case did the 1914–18 war appear as a significant rupture in the long course of a Latin American century routinely seen through the prism of two great turning points: the economic crisis of 1919 and the Cuban Revolution of 1959.

On the basis of a view of the Great War which gave pride of place to military matters, and from a representation of Latin America as a peripheral world region, this generally accepted historiographic view at least partially accommodates some well-known facts about the relationships between former Spanish and Portuguese colonies and Europe in the early twentieth century. In fact, the density of migrational ties between the two sides of the Atlantic, and the integration of the subcontinent into the worldwide financial and commercial markets since around the 1870s – like the intellectual cult of the Old Continent among most elites since the time of their national independence – all indicate a need to re-evaluate the effects of the Great War in Latin America.[1] The

Helen McPhail translated this chapter from French into English.

1 For a general overview on the history of Latin America at the turn of the nineteenth and twentieth centuries, see Leslie Bethell (ed.), *The Cambridge History of Latin America*, vols. IV and V: *c.1870–1930* (Cambridge University Press, 1986).

historian's examination of the archives immediately reveals the war as an omnipresent element in the national and religious press in all countries, in the very prompt attention that it received from governments and chancelleries, the mobilisation of important social sectors and the scale of intellectual output devoted to it, not only from 1915 onwards but until the end of the 1930s. Although we must therefore take care not to consider the region as a single whole, and to take into account the specificities of each national experience of the war as part of a reasoned comparison, the First World War nonetheless must be appreciated as an important moment in the Latin American twentieth century. It needs to be reassessed in its multiple dimensions.[2]

Neutrality in 1914

In the first days of August 1914, as the flames spread across Europe, all the Latin American nations declared their neutrality towards the nations at war. Unusual, in view of the recurrent diplomatic cleavages which had been a feature of inter-regional relations since the winning of independence, this managed consensus survived until 1917 and arose from a number of causes.

Unanimously, the war was first perceived as an exclusively European matter – even though protectorates, colonies and Dominions automatically joined the war alongside their 'mother country'. The Latin American diplomats *en poste* in the European capitals, most of whom had viewed the assassination of Archduke Franz-Ferdinand at Sarajevo as a simple item of news, saw the growing flames as the logical end point in the old Franco-German rivalry, the clash between imperial ambitions and territorial matters intimately linked to the assertion of nationalities. All these were stakes related only to an 'Old World' rationale. According to the teachings of the Monroe Doctrine of 1823, the basis of non-interference by the young American states in European affairs in exchange for European non-interference in American matters, the American hemisphere should not become involved in this Old

2 The works devoted to a comparative history of the Great War on the scale of the whole of Latin American are rare: see Olivier Compagnon and Armelle Enders, 'L'Amérique latine et la guerre', in Stéphane Audoin-Rouzeau and Jean-Jacques Becker (eds.), *Encyclopédie de la Grande Guerre, 1914–1918* (Paris: Bayard, 2004), pp. 889–901; and Olivier Compagnon and María Inés Tato (eds.), *Toward a History of the First World War in Latin America* (Frankfurt am Main: Vervuert, and Madrid: Iberoamericana, 2014). Some old works supply precious information: see, for example, Gaston Gaillard, *Amérique latine et Europe occidentale: L'Amérique latine et la guerre* (Paris: Berger-Levrault, 1918); and Percy Alvin Martin, *Latin America and the War* (Baltimore, MD: Johns Hopkins University Press, 1925).

World struggle. In the press or in diplomatic exchanges, the bloody ventures that were the consequences of imperialism or the crystallisation of nationalisms were denounced without any thought of involvement in the conflict. Like the Franco-Prussian War of 1870–1, it seemed distant and certain to be short-lived. In fact, this reaction to the flare-up in August 1914 reflected the relative indifference of Latin Americans towards the concert of European nations that emerged from the Congress of Vienna. One of a few marginal voices to see clearly what was coming was the Argentinian writer Leopoldo Lugones (1874–1938), who at the end of 1912 had published a series of chronicles in the daily newspaper, *La Nación* (Buenos Aires), in which a European war was judged unavoidable in the short or medium term.[3]

To this first level of analysis of Latin American neutrality in 1914 were added economic considerations of prime importance for the profitable investing nations, mostly exporters of raw materials – agricultural or mining – and importers of manufactured products, structurally dependent on the outside world. Over the previous two decades, many of South America's northern states had seen the United States replace Europe's industrialised countries as prime partners in finance and commerce. They felt less directly threatened by the flames in Europe. In 1914, Mexico, Central America, Cuba, the Dominican Republic and Haiti thus held 74.5 per cent of the United States' direct investment in Latin America, while the remaining 25.5 per cent was divided among the ten independent countries of South America. At the same date, Mexico and Central America were dependent on the United States for 62.7 per cent of their exports and 53.5 per cent of their imports. The situation was, however, very different in South America, where the European nations – with Great Britain in the lead, but also Germany since the last years of the nineteenth century and France to a lesser degree – remained by far the leading investors and commercial partners. Uruguay and Argentina depended on the United States for only 4 per cent and 4.7 per cent respectively of their exports, and 12.7 per cent and 14.7 per cent of imported goods. On the eve of the war, 24.9 per cent of Argentinian exports went to Great Britain, 12 per cent to Germany and 7.8 per cent to France, while 31 per cent of the imports of these countries came from Great Britain, 16.9 per cent from Germany and 9 per cent from France. In this context, a declaration of war – whether against the Entente or the

3 These articles are collected in Leopoldo Lugones, *Mi beligerancia* (Buenos Aires: Otero y García Editores, 1917). On anticipations of war in Europe, see, in particular, Emilio Gentile, *L'apocalisse della modernità: la Grande Guerra per l'uomo nuovo* (Milan: Mondadori, 2008).

Alliance – would necessarily lead to alienating strategic economic partners and would weaken the strong growth that had been characteristic of the region for several decades.[4]

Finally, the fear of reopening the question of the nation's homogeneity if it were to intervene in the war was not without significance in a region which, since the second half of the nineteenth century, had seen a massive degree of immigration from Europe and where some foreign communities still only had a very relative sense of belonging to their new home country. The scope of this argument should of course be adjusted in the case of the Andean states (Venezuela, Colombia, Ecuador, Peru, Bolivia) or of Central America, where the influx of European migrants was infinitely smaller than in the south of the subcontinent. Of the 8–9 million Europeans who sailed for Latin America between the 1820s and 1914, nearly 50 per cent settled in Argentina and 36 per cent in Brazil, the remaining 14 per cent choosing above all Cuba, Uruguay, Mexico and Chile.[5] Depending on the scale of these migratory streams, the possibility of a break-up of these melting pots on the occasion of a European war was more present in the thinking of the political elites, because the early twentieth century was a time of widespread questionings of identity in these young migrant nations – notably at the time of the independence centenaries which were celebrated in 1910 throughout most of Hispanic America. Chile is an example, where the many German colonies watched jealously over their inheritance, while in Argentina the substantial Italian community mobilised massively after May 1915. Brazil had a community of around 400,000 people of Germanic origin, mainly settled in the southern states of São Paulo, Paraná, Santa Catalina and Rio Grande do Sul, who were considered to be very poorly integrated and, since the end of the nineteenth century, had been observed by the intellectual leaders with lively distrust. Since then, neutrality was seen at least as much a necessity of internal politics as a preference in external policy. This attitude was stronger when the national political context was particulary unstable, as in Mexico where the revolution sparked off in 1910 had generated a civil war that entailed strong tensions in relations with the United States.

4 For the ensemble of the figures given, see Victor Bulmer-Thomas, *La historia ecónomica de América Latina desde la Independencia* (Mexico: Fondo de Cultura Ecónomica, 1998), pp. 95, 189–92.

5 On this point, see Magnus Mörner, *Aventureros y proletarios: los emigrantes in Hispanoamérica* (Madrid: Mapfre, 1992).

The mobilisation of communities of foreign origins and of intellectuals

Governmental neutrality and the relative indifference of the press in the first weeks of the war did not prevent early mobilisation in certain sectors of society. Faced with orders for military mobilisation sent by the diplomatic representatives of the belligerent nations in Latin America, and widely distributed in the community press, European immigrants were undoubtedly the first to be touched by the war, providing a remarkable insight into their sense of integration into the host societies. Although the great majority of Germans (or of those with Germanic origins) of military age could not cross the Atlantic because of the offshore naval blockade which was rapidly established around Latin America, French and British immigrants responded as conscientiously as possible to the call. Yet the total figures drawn up by Paris and London at the end of the war showed the very limited results of this mobilisation. Only 32 per cent of the 20,925 men born in France and living in Argentina, of military age in the classes of 1890–1919, seem to have reached the front, 2,834 of them being exempted or rejected, and 12,290 unsatisfactory in some way. As for the sons of Frenchmen born in Argentina and enjoying dual nationality, probably numbering between 40,000 and 50,000, only 250 to 300 seem to have embarked for Europe – fewer than 1 per cent of the total. Although submitted to strong pressure within community associations, the Italians who went to join the war in Europe appear to have been proportionately still less numerous, although there is no reliable quantitative study available that deals with the whole of Latin America.[6]

From these facts, it would, however, be wrong to conclude that most immigrants of European origin were indifferent to the war. This would be to underestimate the immense mobilisation undertaken by their press, charitable organisations or other associations, which spent the years 1914–18 with their eyes fixed on their European mother countries. The press in all the communities portrayed the very deep emotions stirred by the conflict, despite the separation of thousands of kilometres. Among the score of German-language newspapers published in Brazil at the beginning of the war, from

6 Hernán Otero, *La guerra en la sangre: los franco-argentinos ante la Primera Guerre Mundial* (Buenos Aires: Sudamericana, 2009); and María Inés Tato, 'El llamado de la patria: Británicos e italianos residentes en la Argentina frente a la Primera Guerra Mundial', *Estudios Migratorios Latinoamericanos*, 71 (July–December 2011), pp. 273–92. On the topic of comparison with the British in Uruguay, see also Álvaro Cuenca, *La colonia británica de Montevideo y la Gran Guerra* (Montevideo: Torre del Vigia Editores, 2006).

the anticlerical *Germania* in São Paulo to the very Protestant *Deutsche Post* in São Leopoldo, via the *Kompass* in Curitiba, all honoured the moral purity of the war initiated by the Reich in the first days of August 1914. All followed the sequence of military operations through to 1918 with passion and attention – some of them launching editions in Portuguese in order to encourage Brazilian feeling in favour of the Reich's cause.[7] Although they did not contribute to the war effort physically as much as the European belligerents would have liked, the communities of foreign origin were also quick to establish sites of memory directly linked to the war. Having paraded noisily in the streets of Buenos Aires, São Paulo or Mexico to celebrate Rome's joining the war on 23 May 1915, the Italian communities took to the streets each year on the same date to sustain the war effort 'back home', and publicly commemorated each important military advance until the decisive Battle of Vittorio Veneto. Above all, the immigrants and descendants of immigrants contributed massively to charity ventures and charitable works throughout the war. Patriotic committees and other community associations could be counted in their hundreds, in existence before the war or created especially in wartime to organise fund-raising and displays of support for one or other of the nations at war. In Argentina, for example, the Comité Patriótico Francés was responsible for the many displays of charitable welfare which received almost daily publicity in the *Courrier de la Plata*. Shortly after Italy joined the war, the Italian community of Salvador de Bahi organised a Comitato Pro-Patria and collections and subscriptions, notably for men permanently handicapped by the war.[8] In Buenos Aires, it acted as the relay point for loans floated by the Italian government to finance the war effort, through bodies as varied as the Pompieri Volontari della Boca, the Primo Circulo Mandolinístico Italiano or the Associazione Italiana di Mutualitá ed Istruzione. More evident in the southern 'cone' of South America and Brazil than in the rest of Latin America, and fundamentally urban, this mobilisation of the communities of European origin during the Great War remained constant from the end of 1914 to the Armistice in November 1918 – even, in some cases, into the 1920s – and played a decisive role in the gradual involvement of the Latin American societies in the conflict.

Once the illusion of a short war had vanished, currents of opinion also emerged, beyond these more or less immigrant communities, which clearly

7 Frederick C. Luebke, *Germans in Brazil: A Comparative History of Cultural Conflict During World War I* (Baton Rouge and London: Louisiana State University Press, 1987).

8 See the commemorative volume published by the Italian colony in Bahia: *Per la guerra, per la vittoria, 1915–1919* (São Paulo: Fratelli Frioli, n.d.).

leant towards one side or the other, although without challenging governmental neutrality. By way of the press, through conferences or by means of specially created associations, the intellectual elites played a front-line role in the crystallisation and diffusion of representations of a war which was setting fire to what they saw as the heart of the civilised world. In effect, following their independence in the early nineteenth century, most Latin American elites had rejected the models represented by Spain and Portugal, imperial powers henceforward held up to the most severe contempt. They looked instead towards the enlightened world as represented by Northern Europe. Under various headings, France, Great Britain and Germany then became the incarnations of modernity, the beating heart of a civilisation whose values were the finest guarantees of a reasoned advance in the former Iberian colonies. In discourse and in practice, this Europe was now the pattern on which public policies were shaped, the matrix for all cultural effort, a guide in everything which illuminated the future of societies. Published in Chile in 1845 and very widely diffused through all the nations of the region during the following decades, the *Facundo* of the Argentinian writer Domingo Faustino Sarmiento (1811–88) – subtitled *Civilización y Barbarie* – had endowed this Euro-worship with its fictionalised manifesto and definitively set up the Old Continent as the modernising totem.[9]

In these circumstances, the early mobilisation of Latin American intellectuals is no surprise, and reflects the geography of the dominant points of intellectual reference. The vast majority of them, in fact, were outspoken advocates of the Allied cause, basing their feelings fundamentally on the blind cult of France which was considered as the source of every freedom, as well as the cradle of letters and the arts, and the supreme location for every form of modernity. As a legacy of the nineteenth century and the 'tropical Belle Epoque',[10] the *afrancesamiento* of the elites explains why their dominant image of the war represented the clash between eternal and glorious French civilisation on the one hand, and German barbarity and militarism on the other. On 3 September 1914 the Uruguayan writer and politician José Enrique Rodó (1871–1917), whose essay 'Ariel' (1900) had been immensely popular with Latin American intellectual youth, published a text in the daily newspaper *La*

9 On this point, see Annick Lempérière, Georges Lomné, Frédéric Martinez and Denis Rolland (eds.), *L'Amérique latine et les modèles européens* (Paris: L'Harmattan, 1998); and Eduardo Devés Valdés, 'América latina: civilización barbarie', *Revista de Filosofia Latinoamericana*, 7–8 (January–December 1987), pp. 27–52.

10 To follow the expression of Jeffrey Needle, *A Tropical Belle Epoque: Elite Culture and Society in Turn-of-the-Century Rio de Janeiro* (Cambridge University Press, 1987).

Razón (Montevideo), assimilating the cause of France to that of humanity. In March 1915 the Liga Brasileira pelos Aliados was created in Rio de Janeiro, and brought numerous writers and politicians together to raise Brazilian awareness of the Entente cause. Its President, the famous writer and diplomat, José Pereira da Graça Aranha (1868–1931), whose Germanophobic novel, *Canaã*, brought him great fame on its publication in 1902, transmitted this representation of the war in his inaugural speech, declaring that 'from the unleashing of the war, we have come to France, moved by the same instinct which in this war has shown the renewed battle of barbarity against civilisation'.[11] Throughout the war, several publications, from the revue *Nosotros* in Buenos Aires in 1915 to the daily paper *El Universal* in Mexico in 1917, published the results of enquiries among the nation's leading intellectual figures who confirmed the commonly shared wish to see the courage of the *poilus* rewarded. A good indicator of this pervading francophilia, strengthened by the massive distribution of more or less fantastic accounts of the atrocities committed by the Germans during the first weeks of the war, can also be seen in the flow of volunteers enlisting in the French army, which was without equivalent in the armies of the other belligerents: between 1,500 and 2,000 individuals for the whole of the year, most of them literate, from the urban oligarchies and sometimes living in Paris, who proved their readiness to spill their blood in defence of the ideal of civilisation as represented by France. This followed the examples of the Colombian, Hernando de Bengoechea, or the Peruvian, José García Calderón, killed in action in May 1915 and May 1916 respectively.

It is still important to deal carefully with a body of opinion of which the outline remains blurred and which is without doubt less homogeneous than has sometimes been accepted. The great majority of sympathisers with Germany were committed figures who openly supported the cause of the Central empires or who, at least, claimed a strict intellectual neutrality – nonetheless combined with a Germanophilia in the context of the majority support for the Allies. This applied particularly to jurists and philosophers, often trained in the spirit of German science, such as the Argentinians Alfredo Colmo (1878–1934) and Ernesto Quesada (1858–1934), military men persuaded by the concept of *Reichswehr* supremacy, or members of the Catholic hierarchy for whom a French defeat would be just punishment after the teaching interdict laid on religious congregations in 1901 and the separation of Church and State in 1905. Further, the sense of being, on balance, favourable to the

11 Quoted by Gaillard, *Amérique latine et Europe occidentale*, p. 41.

Allies, often forged through the press, also deserves to be set in context in terms of the monopoly held by the Havas and Reuters agencies in the transmission of news and the many pressures exercised on these agencies by the propaganda services of the Entente powers. Finally, the particular case of Mexico should be mentioned, where the hostility shown by many intellectuals in the case of the military interventions by the United States during the 1910 revolution, generally brought them closer to the German cause – as witnessed in the editorial line of a daily such as *El Demócrata* (Mexico) – even before Washington joined the war.[12] Nonetheless, it remains true that the cultural prestige enjoyed by France in Latin America at the dawn of the twentieth century, combined with the financial and commercial domination still exercised by Great Britain across the whole region, naturally encouraged a majority of the elites to wish for the triumph of Paris and London rather than of Berlin and Vienna – at least until 1917.

War, economy and societies

To the extent that the nineteenth century had been a time of accelerated integration of Latin America into world markets, and spectacular growth in its commercial and financial relations with Europe, the economic effects of the war were quickly felt. Suspension of the gold standard for currency by some belligerent nations in the first days of August 1914 immediately raised the spectre of monetary instability. In order to avoid a banking panic, many governments temporarily suspended the activities of exchange bureaux and banned the export of gold bullion. However, these emergency measures did not prevent an immediate inflationary trend which was to last until around 1920. In addition, many European banks – notably British – fell in with the injunctions of their government, demanding the prompt repayment of loans granted to Latin American countries and annulling those which were being negotiated. The long-term loans to Brazil, which represented a total of \$19.1 million in 1913, consequently fell to \$4.2 million in 1914 and zero in 1915. The war context was also responsible for a considerable reduction in the flow of direct investment from Europe, and affected a certain number of activities such as mining, railway construction and the modernisation of urban transport systems. United States capital funds could partially replace the traditional

12 See Friedrich Katz, *The Secret War in Mexico: Europe, the United States and the Mexican Revolution* (University of Chicago Press, 1981); and Esperanza Durán, *Guerra y revolución: las grandes potencias y México, 1914–1918* (Colegio de México, 1985).

financial partners of Latin American states from 1915, but it was not until the 1920s that a volume of foreign investment comparable to that of the Belle Epoque was recovered. Seen from the financial angle, the Great War thus corresponded to a phase of shrinking investments and shortage of capital.[13]

More generally, the place of the conflict in the economic history of contemporary Latin America has resulted in numerous polemics, in which the stake has been to determine whether the years 1914–18 represented a phase of take-off, characterised by an acceleration of industrialisation, or on the contrary a period of contracting activity interrupting development in the secondary sector, which had begun cautiously in the final years of the nineteenth century. In a book which was for long a classic of the theory of dependence, André Gunder Frank attributed the underdevelopment of the region to its historically unequal exchanges with the 'First World'. He observed that the two world wars, marked by a weakening in the financial and commercial relations between Latin America and its traditional partners, could be seen as periods of real economic take-off, in that this would have enabled a break from the prevailing *rentier* logics, and initiated a dynamic of import substitution.[14] Although mentioned in many texts, this interpretation has been convincingly refuted. In the case of São Paulo, for example, Warren Dean has shown that the reduction in coffee exports from August 1914 hobbled the process of the accumulation of capital – which had effectively been at the root of local industrial expansion since the 1890s – and that the war restricted expansion despite the continued growth in many industrial enterprises from the mid-war period until 1920.[15] In emphasising the case of Argentina, Roger Gravil has also vigorously challenged Frank's assertions, showing that the secondary sector did not stop shrinking throughout the war because of a contraction in trade with Europe which was balanced by investments and the North American market, a shortage of labour and of a lack of capital equipment and rising energy costs.[16]

The chief effect of the war concerned the circulation of goods and assumed that it was possible to distinguish short-term effects from the long-term. During an initial phase, which lasted until the beginning of 1915, the shortage

13 Bulmer-Thomas, *La historica ecónomica de América Latina*, pp. 186–7.

14 André Gunder Frank, *Latin America: Underdevelopment or Revolution* (New York: Monthly Review Press, 1969).

15 Warren Dean, *The Industrialization of São Paulo, 1880–1945* (Austin, TX: University of Texas Press, 1969).

16 Roger Gravil, 'Argentina and the First World War', *Revista de História*, 54 (1976), pp. 385–419.

of shipping and the sudden shortage of commercial credit handicapped the usual transatlantic patterns of trade; substantial stocks built up and the price of many raw materials collapsed. As the economies of the nations at war changed direction to meet the needs of the war, however, a balance became established which, despite cyclical variations, was maintained until the beginning of 1919. On the one hand, the European need for strategic war products and basic food supplies destined for soldiers as well as civilians, created a rapid rise in trade and stimulated the exports of certain Latin American countries: Mexico with its oil, Bolivia with tin, Peru with copper and wool, Chile with its nitrates, Cuba with sugar, or Argentina with its meat and grain, all saw substantial growth in income from exports. On the other hand, countries without resources that were considered strategic – for example the great coffee exporters like Brazil, Colombia or Venezuela – could not genuinely profit from the rise in markets because of the reduction in transatlantic traffic, and suffered a clear drop in their trading balance throughout the war. In return, the European nations which normally supplied everyday consumer goods and capital equipment to Latin America were unable to meet the demand because of changes in their own economies. Although certain products from the United States partially made up for the shortage in traditional suppliers, Latin American imports rose in price and fell away in volume to the extent that the whole subcontinent was in a position of commercial surplus in 1915. This entailed a brutal fall in national income in states which were broadly founded on import rights. Further difficulties in honouring the servicing of debt and strong inflation characterised the full period of the war.[17]

Elsewhere, the sustained demand for strategic products from European belligerent nations and the increase in the prices of raw materials, did not lead to all the financial surpluses expected, given the limits imposed on maritime trade.

The Allies did all they could to prevent the Central Powers from gaining access to Latin America's immense resources, trying to control European neutrals potentially capable of acting as intermediaries and, in March 1916, establishing the famous 'black lists', an index of Latin American businesses and

17 For this data in full, see particularly Bulmer-Thomas, *La historia ecónomica de América Latina*, pp. 185–95. See also Bill Albert and Paul Henderson, *South America and the First World War: The Impact of the War on Brazil, Argentina, Peru and Chile* (Cambridge University Press, 1988); and Frank Notten, *La influencia de la Primera Guerra Mundial sobre las economías centroamericanas, 1900–1929: Un enfoque desde el comercio exterior* (San José: Centro de Investigaciones Históricas de América Central and Universidad de Costa Rica, 2012).

trading companies either under German control or considered as such.[18] At the same time, the German declaration of all-out submarine warfare early in 1917 made the Atlantic crossing even more dangerous, resulted in serious shipping losses and discouraged a certain number of shipowners, who saw losses by torpedo increasing dramatically. Within the entire Latin American region, the sectors associated with the export of strategic products were thus great beneficiaries of the Great War, but for more than four years the nations had to deal with an extremely precarious financial situation. With the expansion of local artisan or industrial activity capable of making up for the drop in European imports limited to a few urban or harbour districts, the populations suffered from shortages and the growing cost of many everyday consumer goods. To this was added the abrupt halt in immigration, which crucially had contributed to the growth of internal markets and had fuelled economic growth with a cheap and plentiful labour force. In consequence, although the Great War undoubtedly ensured the elites' growing awareness of the structural dependence which threatened their economies, and consequent drawbacks, it cannot be considered a key moment in the industrialisation process in Latin America.

Finally, to the extent that they affected people at the very core of their daily lives from the end of 1914, and increasingly from the first quarter of 1915, the economic effects of the Great War were, of course, not without a role in the widespread growth of social agitation between 1915 and 1920. From the outbreak of the war, many states tried to calm the financial crisis with the creation of new taxes – for example, in Peru where the sale of tobacco and alcohol was heavily taxed in September 1914. In the large Brazilian cities the prices of basic food products (flour, rice and oil) rose by between 10 and 35 per cent in the second half of 1914. In Buenos Aires, inflation reached 50 per cent for food products, 300 per cent for textiles and 538 per cent for coal between 1914 and 1918. Shortages affecting a whole range of consumer goods normally supplied by Europe were felt everywhere, but urban circles and the emerging middle classes, the main consumers of this imported modernity, characteristic of the Latin American Belle Epoque, were more affected than most rural people. Nonetheless, the latter also felt the effects of the war, for example in Brazil or Venezuela, in Colombia and some countries in Central America where the crisis in the coffee economy, brutal and long-lasting, considerably limited the demands of the workforce in this sector and stimulated a first wave of rural

18 On the black lists, see in particular Philip A. Dehne, *On the Far Western Front: Britain's First World War in South America* (Manchester University Press, 2009).

exodus which the cities could not absorb. More generally, the restrictions on trade led to the disappearance of many jobs, the appearance of chronic unemployment and a general lowering of real wages, despite the negative migratory balance of the second half of the 1910s. In Buenos Aires, 16–20 per cent of the population of working age thus faced a shortage of jobs during the war years. In São Paulo, the wages of workers in the O Cotonofício Rodolfo Crespi textile factory fell by 50–70 per cent between 1913 and 1917. These facts taken together help to explain the great number of strikes and social protests, as thousands of people demonstrated against fiscal pressure in Arequipa in southern Peru in January 1915, up to the 196 work stoppages recorded in Argentina in 1918, via a general strike which paralysed São Paulo in July 1917. Often repressed with violence, most of these movements explicitly associated their claims with the war, and called for peace in Europe at the same time as increased wages or better conditions at work.[19]

Because it seriously endangered the economic growth of the preceding decades, but also because it contributed to the hardening of the social question and the renewed challenge to the established order, the Great War thus imposed its reality on the Latin American governments despite its distance from them and the initially proclaimed neutrality. From that point of view, it was not only the foreign communities and intellectuals who took a sustained interest in the war, as in the second half of 1914, but large sectors of Latin American societies which suffered directly from the worldwide upsets arising from the state of war.

Omnipresent in the press from 1915, the war was also visible everywhere in daily life and popular culture, as in certain compositions in the literature of Brazilian *cordel*, many stage plays in Argentina, some Germanophile slogans painted on ceramics of the Bolivian Altiplano by an Aymara Indian, or the production of childen's games based on the European war.[20] Although in the current state of research it is not possible to confirm the existence of a real war

19 For these, see Clodoaldo Bueno, *Política externa da Primeira República: os anos de apogeu – de 1902 a 1918* (São Paulo: Paz e Terra, 2003), p. 468; Juan Manuel Palacio, 'La antesala de lo peor: la economía argentina entre 1914 y 1930', in Ricardo Falcón (ed.), *Nueva historia argentina*, vol. VI: *Democracia, conflicto social y renovación de ideas, 1916–1930* (Buenos Aires: Sudamericana, 2000), pp. 101–50; Héctor A. Palacios, *Historia del movimiento obrero argentino*, 4 vols. (Buenos Aires: Ediciones Gráfica Mundo Color, 1992), vol. I, pp. 106–25; and Maria Luisa Marcilio, 'Industrialisation et mouvement ouvrier à São Paulo au début du XXe siècle', *Le Mouvement social*, 53 (October–December 1965), pp. 111–29.

20 See Idelette Muzart dos Santos, 'La représentation des conflits internationaux dans la littérature de cordel, 1935–1956', in Denis Rolland (ed.), *Le Brésil et le monde: pour une histoire des relations internationales des puissances émergentes* (Paris: L'Harmattan, 1998), pp. 148–78; Osvaldo Pelletieri (ed.), *Testimonios culturales argentinos: la década del 10*

culture in Latin America, there is no doubt that the European war sent its shock waves fully and quickly to the other side of the Atlantic Ocean.

The great turning point of 1917

Diplomatic archives, both European and Latin American, reveal the scale of involvement of the main European belligerents in Latin America from 1914 onwards. Through the closest possible control of information in the press, the massive distribution of propaganda in Spanish and Portuguese – through the traditional written media or cinema newsreels – or tempting promises about the new world which would emerge from the war, public opinion was informed about the relevance of the struggle under way. In addition, the goodwill had to be sought of governments which had already strongly asserted their refusal to join the war, but whose economic collaboration could in the end prove decisive.[21] In this general setting, 1917 brought spectacular activity in the Latin American chancelleries and marked an essential break in a whole series of developments.

Mexico was at the heart of the tensions between Germany and the United States which intensified after the Zimmermann Telegram was sent. On 16 January the German Foreign Minister addressed a secret telegram to his ambassador in Mexico, Heinrich von Eckardt, encouraging him to conclude a German–Mexican agreement against the United States in exchange for which Mexico would recover Texas, New Mexico and Arizona, lost after the war of 1846–8 and the Treaty of Guadalupe Hidalgo. Intercepted by the British, this document was decisive in the collapse of relations between Washington and Berlin.[22] Furthermore, the unrestricted submarine warfare decreed by Germany in January had an even greater effect on the trade activities of most Latin American states and led some governments to reconsider their position in relation to Berlin. Finally, the break in diplomatic relations between the United States and the Reich in February, then Washington's declaration of war two months later, overturned the situation on the scale of the entire hemisphere.

(Buenos Aires: Editorial del Belgrano, 1980); Rodrigo Zarate, *España y América: proyecciones y problemas derivados de la guerra* (Madrid: Casa Editorial Calleja, 1917), p. 375; and Manuel Buil, *Juego de la Guerra Europea* (Buenos Aires: s.e., 1917).

21 On the case of Mexico, see Ingrid Schulze Schneider, 'La propaganda alemana en México durante la Primera Guerra Mundial', *Anuario del Departamento de Historia*, Universidad Complutense de Madrid, 5 (1993), pp. 261–72.

22 On this point, see Barbara Tuchman, *The Zimmermann Telegram* (New York: Dell Publishing Co., 1965); also Katz, *The Secret War in Mexico*.

In fact, the neutralist consensus of Latin America observed in August 1914 did not survive the United States' declaration of war on 6 April 1917. In the same year, Panama and Cuba (April), then Brazil (October), also declared war on Germany, followed in 1918 by Guatemala (April), Costa Rica and Nicaragua (May) and Haiti and Honduras (July). Six other countries broke off diplomatic relations with Germany, although without declaring war: Bolivia, the Dominican Republic, Peru, Uruguay, El Salvador and Ecuador. At first, the positions adopted from April 1917 by the different states in the region made it possible to construct a map of the zones of North American influence. With the exception of Brazil, the nations at war were all located in Central America or the Caribbean, which in the space of a quarter of a century had become a private hunting ground of the United States.

Since its emancipation following the war between the United States and Spain in 1898, Cuba – which joined the war only a few hours after the United States, on 7 April, and from where several dozen drafted soldiers were to depart to the European battlefields – was a *de facto* protectorate, because of the Platt Amendment approved by the American Congress in March 1901 and introduced into the Cuban constitution on 22 May 1903. Cuba suffered three US military interventions between 1906 and 1917. Seized from Colombia in November 1903 in order to put an end to the rivalries between Europeans and Americans over the project for the transcontinental canal – officially inaugurated on 15 August 1914 – Panama emerged as a political creation of the United States, pure and simple, while Nicaragua and Haiti were occupied by the Marines from 1912 and 1915 respectively. All these elements proved that for these countries, joining the war could not be seen as a deliberate choice of foreign policy, but rather illustrates the political and diplomatic dependence to which US policy had reduced them since the external projection of the *manifest destiny* at the end of the 1880s and the beginning of the 1890s.[23]

The case of Brazil, on the other hand, was different. Shaken by the fall in its exports throughout the entire war and by the torpedoing of merchant ships like the *Paraná*, the *Tijuc* and the *Macaú* in April, May and October 1917 by German submarines, Brazil had objective reasons for joining the Allied camp. Joining the war also provided Brazil with the opportunity to assert itself as the favoured partner of Washington, in the line of the policy led by the Baron de Rio Branco – Minister for External Relations from 1902 to 1912 and a great

23 On the origins of the United States' Latin American policy, see John J. Johnson, *A Hemisphere Apart: The Foundations of United States Policy toward Latin America* (Baltimore, MD: Johns Hopkins University Press, 1990).

partisan of a lasting alliance between Rio and Washington – and as the natural leader of Latin America. In fact, while revolutionary Mexico could not claim to play a major role on the international scene, and Chile held back from declaring war on Germany in view of the substantial political influence and numerical size of the German-origin immigrant community, the First World War was a privileged moment for observing Rio's strategies towards hegemony over the subcontinent and, more generally, the relations of internal power in the Latin American region. A telegram to the presidency of the Republic in July 1917 from the Foreign Minister, Nilo Peçanha, thus enjoined the Brazilian government to join the war in the wake of the United States in order to meet the urgent expectations of London, Paris and Washington, but also to avoid being overtaken by another South American nation. Concerned to play a substantial role on the international scene – with an eye to the end of the war – Brazil was thus to prove itself a much more cooperative ally than its neighbour Argentina, determined in its neutrality. It was, therefore, in the light of these various arguments of a diplomatic nature, but also in the hope of increasing sales of its coffee, of which stocks were continuing to accumulate – in 1917, 6 million sacks were piled up in the Santos docks waiting for buyers and transport – that Rio's declaration of war on the side of the Allies on 26 October 1917 should be interpreted. Participation in the war effort was nonetheless very limited, as much due to the relatively late declaration of war as to the limitations of the Brazilian army. Apart from thirteen officer airmen who joined the Sixteenth Group of the Royal Air Force, Brazil sent a medical mission to France which operated in the rue de Vaugirard in Paris until February 1919. Above all, the Divisão Naval em Operações de Guerre (DNOG) was integrated into the British naval force. It consisted particularly of the cruisers *Bahia* and *Rio Grande do Sul* and the anti-submarine ships *Piauí*, *Rio Grande do Norte*, *Paraíba* and *Santa Catarina*, under the command of Rear-Admiral Pedro Max Fernando de Frontin, with a force some 1,500 strong. This force left the north-east in July 1918, and was decimated by the Spanish flu during its stopover at Dakar in September. Finally, the naval force entered Gibraltar on 10 November in an ever-diminishing state and was unable to take any part in the fighting. Nonetheless, Brazil thus found itself in the victors' camp and, as such, participated in the peace negotiations.

Of the twenty states in the region, only six – Argentina, Mexico, Chile, Venezuela, Colombia and Paraguay – did not finally break off relations with the Central Powers. The maintenance of this absolute neutrality did not prevent the majority of them from gradually turning towards the Allies for reasons above all of economic pragmatism, as in the case of Argentina. In power until 1915, President Victorina de la Plaza had been concerned to hold on to the European markets in all their diversity at any cost. Despite the shooting of the Argentinian vice-consul in Dinant without apparent motive by the Germans in the first weeks of the war, or that the *Presidente Mitre*, a merchant ship flying the blue-and-white flag, but owned by a branch of the Hamburg Sudamerikanische Dampfschiffahrtgesellschaft, was accepted in port by the British in November 1915, the flabbiness of protests as to their neutrality was evident. In 1916, the coming to power of the radical Hipólito Yrigoyen – the first President of the Republic elected by male universal suffrage after the Sáenz Peña law of 1912 – did not challenge the choice of neutrality, but changed the situation to the extent that Argentina now envisaged playing an active role in the diplomacy of war. In 1917, when the United States was piling on the pressure for the whole of Latin America to join the war, and Argentina ceased trading with the Central Powers through the intermediary of European neutrals, Yrigoyen envisaged a conference in Buenos Aires with the neutral states of Latin America, thereby provoking fury in Washington. The obstinate refusal of the President to declare war – despite urgings to the contrary from Congress – nonetheless turned into goodwill towards Paris and London from January 1918, when Argentina signed a commercial treaty with France and Great Britain, with a view to the export of 2.5 million tons of wheat before November. Henceforward in favour of supplying the Allies and concerned primarily with the health of her external trade, the position of Argentina could then barely be distinguished from the unarmed engagement with the Allies of countries in Central America and the Caribbean. The more or less tacit tipping of governmental sympathies towards the Allies – in Buenos Aires as elsewhere – did not prevent the years 1917 and 1918 from being marked by growing anxiety over a possible United States expansion into Latin America under cover of the war. Caught between the diplomatic intrigues of Germany, the wish to counterbalance the omnipresence of Washington since the beginning of the revolution and the need to sell its oil to Great Britain, the Mexico of President Venustiano Carranza – in power between 1915 and 1920 – chose to frame an equidistant position between the two coalitions in being until November 1918, despite the tensions existing at the very heart of its government between those who leaned towards the Allies in the name of the old *afrancesamiento* and those who would be ready to yield to the siren voices in Berlin, out of dislike of the United States.

Finally, even after Washington declared war, 1917 also marked a turning point in that the war became a major issue everywhere in domestic politics. In

Argentina, the gulf between supporters and opponents of President Yrigoyen was the object of a semantic slippage from the beginning of the year and gradually turned into a confrontation between *neutralistas* and *rupturistas*.[24] In Brazil, a French diplomat reported in May 1918 that the world crisis was even affecting local elections: two of the candidates for the position of Senator for the state of São Paulo took the nation's participation in the war as the central argument of their campaign. In Cuba, the state of war led the government of President Mario García Menocal to introduce a law in August 1918 to make military service obligatory, thereby arousing great anger in public opinion which was largely hostile to conscription. Directly or indirectly, the war became a fundamental matrix of policy in Latin America until the end of 1918.

World war and national identity

News of the Armistice of 11 November 1918 was greeted with relief and enthusiasm by the press, political leaders and public opinion throughout Latin America. On the one hand, it enabled a vision of a return to normality in international economic life in the short or medium term, a recovery of the growth characteristic of the Belle Epoque and, as a result, a calming of social conflict. Alternatively, the propositions formulated by Woodrow Wilson in January 1918, designed to establish lasting peace in the world, had aroused great hopes for the settling of latent conflicts in the Latin American region – such as that which set Chile and Peru and Bolivia at odds (the latter having lost its access to the sea at the end of the 1879–84 Pacific War) and the possibility of better-integrated international relations within the subcontinent. However, circumstance at the end of the war dispelled the optimism that reigned in the final weeks of 1918, and strengthened a series of identity crises which had emerged during the war.

In the first place, the turning point in the war decade and the 1920s was not matched by a corresponding return to the world economic order of pre-1914. All the nations of Latin America returned to growth, as the currency was gradually restored to gold convertibility. Maritime trade was normalised and the volume of exports and imports increased rapidly, but they also had to settle with the new role and status of the United States as a consequence of the Great War. In 1918, the US took 45.4 per cent of Latin American exports, up

24 On this point, see María Inés Tato, 'La disputa por la argentinidad: rupturistas y neutralistas durante la Primera Guerra mundial', *Temas de Historia Argentina y Americana*, 13 (July–December 2008), pp. 227–50.

from 29.7 per cent in 1913, and supplied 41.8 per cent of the region's imports, against 24.5 per cent on the eve of war. Although this stronger commercial tendency tended to decline through the 1920s, while remaining clearly greater than in 1913, this increased commercial presence brought a degree of financial hegemony. It rested on direct United States investment in the region between 1914 and 1929 – from $1,275.8 to $3,645.8 million – and the great increase in the largest Latin American cities of banks whose mother houses were in New York.[25] As observed by many intellectuals at the beginning of the 1920s, from the Peruvian Victor Haya de la Torre (1895–1979) to the Argentinian Manuel Ugarte (1875–1951), the war had not only failed to change the structural dependence of Latin American economies on the outside world, but it had additionally redistributed the cards in such a way that the United States now possessed powerful financial and commercial weapons on top of the military power that Washington had regularly exercised in the region since the 1890s. From this came numerous questions about the future of Latin American states, apparently condemned to live in the shadow of their northern neighbour after having lived under Europe's economic guardianship throughout the nineteenth century.

Elsewhere, the hopes in the coming of a new international order were swiftly dispelled in the 1920s. Present during the peace negotiations, the representatives of the Latin American states which had declared war on Germany were unanimous in their complaints at the lack of attention paid by Paris, London and Washington to the positions that they were defending, and the attempts at manipulation from which they frequently suffered.[26] After the first assembly of the League of Nations in Geneva in November 1920, the experience of the states admitted was very similar, and generated profound scepticism about the new international order. Through the voice of its delegate, Honório Puyrredón, Argentina argued that the victory did not benefit her, and turned its back on the Geneva organisation from December 1920, disappointed at the fate reserved for neutrals and defeated nations in an assembly supposed to promote an ideal of universal peace. Peru and Bolivia followed suit in 1921, failing to obtain a settlement of frontier disputes which had occupied most of their diplomatic activity since the 1880s. Brazil in turn left the League in 1926, weary at not being able to obtain the permanent seat on the Council which it coveted. As for revolutionary Mexico, considered a

25 Bulmer-Thomas, *La historia ecónomica de América Latina*, pp. 189, 192.

26 See, for example, Yannick Wehrli, 'Les délégations latino-américaines et les intérêts de la France à la Société des Nations', *Relations internationales*, 137:1 (2009), pp. 45–59.

pariah in international relations, it was not invited to take a seat in the organisation at the time of its constitution and was not able to participate in its work until 1931 – by which date the hopes of perpetual peace as envisaged at the end of the war were already no more than sweet and distant utopian dreams.[27]

From the ensemble of these economic and diplomatic facts, should it be concluded that the Great War did no more than reinforce the peripheral status of Latin America in the concert of nations, and signify the simple transition from the European wardship of the nineteenth century to that of the United States from the 1920s? The answer is probably no, if the question is considered from the angle of cultural history, and if one returns to representations of the war among the elites of the region. In effect, the initially dominant concept in which the European conflagration signified confrontation between an eternal French civilisation and German barbarity was gradually replaced by a sense of a general European failure. In an article published by the satirical revue *Caras y Caretas* (Buenos Aires) on 22 August 1914, the Argentinian philosopher José Ingenieros (1877–1925), of Italian origin, interpreted the recent failed expectations of the Old World as a 'suicide of the barbarians'. Two years later, the Mexican anthropologist Manuel Gamio (1883–1960) published his *Forjando Patria*, in which he commented ironically on the futile combat being played out between France and Germany – as would be repeated, in 1919, by the Brazilian writer José Bento Monteiro Lobato (1882–1948) in his chronicles published in the *Revista do Brasil*. Indeed, the examples of disenchantment about Europe after 1916 and 1917 could be counted in their hundreds and in every Latin America country, and more still in the 1920s and 1930s. How could a continent considered to be the incarnation of the values of civilisation and modernity have sacrificed 10 million of its sons in the mud of the trenches? What had happened to the ideals of human progress and the cult of rationality that it could have produced such mass violence? From that point, the suicide of Europe logically rendered null and void the concept so characteristic of the nineteenth century and the Belle Epoque – even if the latter had already been heavily challenged before 1914 – according to which any form of modernity could only come from the Old Continent. 'Europe has failed. It is no longer up to her to guide the world', asserted the Argentinian jurist and writer Saúl

27 On Latin America and the League, see particularly Thomas Fischer, *Die Souveränität der Schwachen: Lateinamerika und der Völk erbund 1920–1936* (Stuttgart: Franz Steiner, 2012). On the particular case of Brazil, see Eugênio Vargas Garcia, *O Brasil e a Liga das Nações (1919–1925): vencer ou não perder* (Porto Alegre: Universidade Federal do Rio Grande do Sul, 2000).

Taborda (1885–1944) in 1918.[28] Fed by the wide distribution in Latin America of the 'decadentist' European literature of the immediate post-war period – from *Der Untergang des Abendlandes* by Oswald Spengler to *La decadenza dell'Europa* by Francesco Nitti, via *La crise de l'esprit* by Paul Valéry – the rupture was essential in the mimetic reflexes which had naturally been current until then, and invited renewed reflection on the true identity of the young nations born at the dawn of the nineteenth century out of the ruins of Spanish and Portuguese colonialism.

In very concrete terms, disenchantment with Europe was reflected first in a hardening of the national paradigm directly linked to representations of the Great War. The political terrain thus acquired multiple parties and movements which exalted each nation's grandeur and purity, reinventing its mythic origins and defining the new conditions of a collective destiny in a radical alternative to Europe.[29] Heralds of 'Argentinianism' in the 1920s and 1930s, Leopoldo Lugones, Ricardo Rojas (1882–1957) and Carlos Ibarguren (1877–1956) – to cite only three of many – were attentive observers of the Great War, and each in his own way exercised himself to redefine the contours of the 'race' and the ideal political regime to guarantee its perpetuation.

The 1920s and 1930s were also marked by cultural nationalism, reflected in the work of the Mexican mural artists who stopped reproducing the dominant pictorial styles of Europe to paint their true national identity – native-born and mixed race as much as white and Iberian – right through to Brazilian modernism. The dominant figure of this aesthetic movement launched in São Paulo in February 1922, and claiming the entirely new creation of a national art, Mário de Andrade (1893–1945) dedicated his earliest poems to the war, in a collection published in 1917 entitled *Ha uma gota de sangue em cada poema*, and analysed the recent aesthetic turbulence in Brazil in a work of 1929:

> With the end of the war of 1914, all the arts took on a fresh force. Was this an influence of the war? Of course. The four years of carnage were bound to precipitate matters. New governments rose up, new scientific thinking and new arts.[30]

28 Saúl A. Taborda, *Reflexiones sobre el ideal político de América* (Buenos Aires: Grupo Editor Universitario, 2007 [1918]), p. 121.

29 As was very well shown by Patricia Funes, without necessarily taking the full measure of the role of the Great War in this dynamic, in *Salvar la nación: intelectuales, cultura y política en los años veinte latinoamericanos* (Buenos Aires: Prometeo Libros, 2006).

30 Mário de Andrade, *Pequena história da música*, 8th edn (São Paulo: Livraria Martins, 1977 [1929]), p. 194.

In the long period of the building of Latin American nations, the Great War was thus an essential stage. It was also paradoxical, in that it was precisely the great carnage resulting from the exacerbation of European nationalisms which became the catalyst for Latin American nationalisms. However, the interrogation of identities emerging from the war could equally transcend the nationalistic frame to promote other possible ways of creating a sense of belonging. In the trajectory of a Manuel Ugarte, convinced from the first years of the twentieth century that the future of Latin America must lie in solidarity between its different national elements in the face of the threat of the United States, the years 1914–18 marked both a change of direction and led them to assert ever more strongly the need for Latin American unity.[31]

Conclusion

Study of the years 1914–18 in Latin America remains a historical work in progress. Although national experiences of the war, such as those of Argentina and Brazil, are becoming better known, many unnoticed corners remain and await researchers to examine them. What about the mobilisation of societies in Colombia or Bolivia, countries of which we know nothing or nearly nothing of their relationship with the Great War? Their intellectuals were as strongly Francophile as elsewhere in Latin America, but their immigrants of European origin were infinitely less numerous than in the southern 'cone' of the subcontinent. What about attitudes to the distant conflagration in the eminently rural world of Central America, where the vast majority of the population was illiterate at the beginning of the twentieth century? How were the war years experienced in Haiti, so closely linked to France both historically and linguistically, but occupied militarily by the United States since 1915? What microanalysis was at work in the reception and representations of the conflict between the national framework – reduced to capital cities and major cities in most cases – and the various local levels? All these questions remain unanswered, though the stakes far exceed the simple documentary dimension. In effect, to build a true comparative history of the years 1914–18 in Latin America would enable us to avoid the hazards of a rise in over-hasty generalisation based on the mistaken view that the region was culturally uniform, and naturally homogeneous. Such an enterprise would confirm – if confirmation

31 For these facts on the war as a whole as a break in identity, see Olivier Compagnon, '1914–18: the death throes of civilization: the elites of Latin America face the Great War', in Jenny Macleod and Pierre Purseigle (eds.), *Uncovered Fields: Perspectives in First World War Studies* (Leiden: Brill, 2004), pp. 279–95.

were needed – that the first total war was truly a world event, in that no region of the planet, or nearly none, was spared, independently of the geography of military operations. Finally, to re-evaluate more precisely the place of the Great War at the heart of the Latin American twentieth century, would naturally invite a rethinking of the commonly accepted periodic definition based on the rupture points of 1929 and 1959 and, notably, redefine the 1920s and 1930s which were the matrix of so many later developments. With the coming of the centenary of the Great War, the challenge is certainly great – but it deserves to be examined collectively.

It would be right, moreover, to question the motives for the oblivion which hid the Great War in Latin America until very recently. Of course, the region did not pay the blood price and did not suffer the extreme losses and mourning which confronted the societies of the principal belligerent countries. The men who enlisted voluntarily, and other migrants of European origin summoned to serve under the flag of their mother country, who have sometimes left the mark of their experience of mass violence, were not enough, some eight or ten thousand kilometres from the slaughter-houses of the Somme, to perpetuate the memory of the Great War. Of course, the Second World War created a curtain in Latin America as well as in Europe, and helped to conceal the period of 1914–18 behind a veil, which can still be seen in the school textbooks of many countries.

Nonetheless, there are also genuine historiographic reasons for this oblivion. In Latin America even more than elsewhere, the discipline of history consisted in the nineteenth century of the strict framework of young states issuing from the struggles for independence. It virtually never looked beyond the national frontiers. Until very recently, comparative history and the writing of national history into a global history were extremely rare, leading to an inward-looking pattern of writing history which has made it possible to ignore, or almost ignore, seismic shocks such as the two world wars. From this point of view, the contemporary rediscovery of the Great War in Latin America is equally capable of encouraging new approaches to the history of a region far less peripheral than is often appreciated, and routinely part of the rest of the world since the end of the fifteenth century.

PART IV

*

RULES OF ENGAGEMENT, LAWS OF WAR AND WAR CRIMES

Introduction to Part IV

ANNETTE BECKER AND ANNIE DEPERCHIN

It is a paradox that at the very time when a concerted effort was made to outlaw war, its explosive character grew radically and led to destruction on an unprecedented scale. This is one of the fundamental contradictions raised by the First World War.

The resolution of this paradox, if it exists, must be sought in the acts of the victors who, at the end of the war, tried to apply recently formulated norms of the laws of war, themselves in the process of development. The Treaty of Versailles in 1919, for the first time in history, arrayed the defeated powers in a legal judgement of their responsibility for the outbreak of the war and for having violated the rules in international law for the limitation of violence in wartime. No one contests that this response on the part of the victors was inadequate, not only because the outcome of this indictment was not what they had expected, but also because international justice itself, and the precise concepts it needed to act with authority, were not yet in existence.

In effect, the impact of the Great War on international law, and on the violence the law was intended to circumscribe, must be placed in a wider time span. Atrocities and massacres long before the war had left their mark on public opinion, which found them more and more unacceptable in terms of a civilised ideal, and provided a basis for sanctions against the perpetrators. But in 1914 and after, atrocities and massacres became violations of human rights. After 1945, such acts were subject to legal definition of a specific kind, bearing in mind the crimes in question: crimes against the peace, war crimes, the crime of genocide and crimes against humanity. Ironically, the evolution of peoples' wars as opposed to dynastic wars made violence against the 'other' as a member of a minority group within a state more vicious and widespread. This was perfectly evident during the Great War. At the heart of conflicts between states there emerged the possibility of the physical elimination, through different measures, of those deemed incapable of sharing a national destiny. That possibility became reality with the Armenian genocide perpetrated by the Ottoman Turkish state in 1915. The term genocide, first used by Raphael Lemkin in 1944, must be used here, since the term arose from his long reflection in the interwar years on the massacre, deportation and extermination of Armenians during the Great War.

The transnational approach we have adopted to analyse different facets of wartime violence permits us to see more clearly the legal and the political stakes in the effort to identify war crimes. To do so enables us better to understand the phenomenon of the violation of rights, and of German atrocities, within the ensemble of diverse reprisals and other acts of violence committed on every front and by every combatant force.

21

Atrocities and war crimes

JOHN HORNE

War has always been subject to religious and moral prescriptions (the 'laws and customs of war') which seek to codify its conduct and limit its violence. Yet the changing nature of that violence, owing to the evolution of both technology and culture, means that such norms are breached in every new conflict. They also result in polemic as each side blames the other for committing excesses while excusing or justifying its own. Afterwards, coming to terms with the new types and thresholds of violence produced by the war entails redefining what is considered legitimate conduct, reinforcing but also modifying the underlying principles. Yet the polemic lingers, especially as the victors have the greater say in who is to blame for what.

The First World War is a good example of this dialectic of norm, conflict and revision and of the passions and polemics that accompany it. The conduct of war had been legally codified by international agreement to an unprecedented degree in the half-century before 1914. During the war, for the first time, the habitual charge that the enemy committed atrocities was translated into charges that could be tried under international law. This led to the attempt to create tribunals for war crimes following the war. Although a failure, this opened the way to Nuremberg and Tokyo after the Second World War. The conventions on the conduct of war were also revised during the interwar period. But rather than serving as a lesson, the atrocities of the Great War turned out to be a harbinger of even greater violence in the future.

Before the war

During the nineteenth century, several developments made the idea that warfare was subject to moral norms more prominent than ever before. Enlightenment thinkers such Emmerich de Vattel and Jean-Jacques Rousseau had first insisted that ordinary soldiers and sailors, as the subjects of the state which alone had the legal authority to make war, were not personally liable for the violence they committed in its name, and so were entitled to humane treatment once they ceased fighting. But the idea was honoured more in the breach than the observance during the Revolutionary and Napoleonic Wars. It was only in the conflicts of the mid nineteenth century that a growing humanitarian spirit urged that all wounded soldiers and prisoners of war (POWs) should be treated decently without regard to the side they had fought on. These principles were enunciated by the International Committee of the Red Cross (ICRC), founded in 1864, and enacted by successive Geneva Conventions. Reducing the suffering of soldiers was the hallmark of a 'civilised' era.

No less significant was the distinction between soldiers and civilians. This had also been the subject of religious and philosophical prescription for centuries, but campaigning armies routinely mistreated civilian populations. Nineteenth-century sensitivities to the status of women and children reinforced the idea that civilians were innocent bystanders who should be protected. However, French revolutionaries countered this aspiration when, with the *levée en masse* in 1793, they imagined a Nation in Arms mobilising the whole population and all its resources. It took well over a century (with an early version in the American Civil War) before something like this vision of total mobilisation was realised in the two world wars, but it worked to dissolve rather than reinforce the distinction between soldier and civilian. For once universal military service became the norm, the male citizen or subject, mobilised as a reservist in time of war, became the basis of the armies of millions that fought the two world wars. Moreover, in the face of invasion or occupation, he might also act as an irregular soldier. Guerrilla warfare had deep historical roots, but it re-emerged as a concomitant of political activism in the Napoleonic Wars, the American Civil War and the Franco-Prussian War, when French irregulars, or *francs-tireurs*, resisted the Germans. Potentially, all adult men were the enemy.

The mobilisation of human and material resources imagined by the *levée en masse* went further and made the entire population, since it participated in the war effort, a potential military target for the enemy. Naval blockade began as a maritime siege, but both Britain and France used it during the Napoleonic Wars as a form of economic warfare. Reconciling it with the freedom of the seas and the right of neutral powers to trade in wartime became an increasingly thorny issue given the growing economic interdependence of the world in the nineteenth century. Just as the distinction between combatants and noncombatants was strengthened in principle, these converse developments threatened to blur it.

One further feature of the nineteenth century, the industrialisation of military technology, also raised ethical issues. With high explosives, rapid-firing guns and dense rail networks feeding the front, the battlefield became ever more lethal for soldiers. Since destroying a legitimate enemy was the essence of combat, this did not necessarily infringe the norms of war even if casualty rates increased. However, chemical weapons broke a taboo – that of killing men like animals or pests – and so posed the question of whether some weapons were so inhumane that they should be banned on the battlefield. Developments in military technology also exposed civilians to new threats, such as more destructive bombardment of besieged cities and, with the birth of air power, attack from the skies.

The idea of codifying the conduct of war in all the above regards in the name of civilised values was advocated by an influential 'peace movement', which had emerged in the century following the Napoleonic Wars. It was favoured by liberals and the left, but also found support among conservatives who wished to limit the potentially radical effects of war on politics. While the principal aim of the movement was to prevent war, it also sought to instil humanitarian restraints on the conduct of war. A series of international meetings addressed both issues in the half-century before 1914, culminating in two peace conferences organised at the behest of Tsar Nicholas II in The Hague in 1899 and 1907. As Fyodor Fyodorovich Martens, the Tsar's international lawyer, put it in a declaration adopted by the 1899 conference:

> It is our unanimous desire that the armies of the civilized nations be not simply provided with the most murderous and perfected weapons, but that they shall also be imbued with a notion of right, justice and humanity, binding even in invaded territory and even in regard to the enemy.[1]

Generals and admirals, however, were hard to convince. The German army was especially reluctant because it saw land war in Europe as vital to the preservation and extension of German power. It also feared democratic and revolutionary warfare, such as the *franc-tireur* resistance it had met in 1870–1. Yet reconciling the right of patriotic subjects to participate in a *levée en masse*, including irregular warfare, with the obligation on the military to respect non-combatant civilians, proved one of the most contentious issues, and not least because small countries, such as Belgium and Switzerland, relied on citizen militias for their defence. The German military (like many others) saw war as

1 Quoted in Geoffrey Best, *Humanity in Warfare: The Modern History of the International Law of Armed Conflicts* (London: Weidenfeld & Nicolson, 1980), p. 165.

the preserve of professionals in command of regular forces. If a 'people's war' was the ultimate horror, repression was justified in order to secure victory without disorder.

The British responded similarly regarding the naval warfare that was the key to their military security. Blockade and the control of neutral trade with enemy belligerents was as live an issue as that of a 'people's war' at the Hague Conferences and at the London Naval Conference in 1909. While Britain made some concessions to the right of neutral states to trade with belligerent powers in non-essential goods, it retained the authority to decide what fell into the forbidden (contraband) category, and by virtue of its maritime supremacy to decide the level of blockade that ultimately affected civilian living standards in the targeted countries. British naval opinion was no less reluctant than German military opinion to limit its conduct of war.

Before 1914, then, the 'laws and customs' of war had been reformulated in the humanitarian spirit of the age, but with military and naval establishments showing a marked dislike at having their hands tied in wartime. Governments shared their reluctance but had to reckon with a strong current of public opinion that favoured the humane treatment of wounded soldiers, prisoners and civilians. International law played a crucial role. Hague Convention IV Respecting the Laws and Customs of War on Land (1907) (hereafter Hague Convention IV) summarised Geneva law on the neutrality of medical personnel, the obligation to care equally for all wounded combatants and the right of soldiers and sailors to surrender as POWs and to be accorded the same material care as their captors. Civilian involvement in combat proved deeply controversial, with the Germans opposing it outright. But after strong pressure from Belgium and Switzerland, supported by France, civilians were allowed to resist an invading army (but not an occupation) provided they did so in an open, orderly fashion and carried some mark of their combatant status. The primacy of national allegiance in the age of nation-states was recognised by the exemption of an occupied population from having to work for the enemy's military effort and thus against its compatriots. The same stricture applied to POWs. New weapons were addressed in several ways. The right to bombard towns under siege, irrespective of collateral civilian damage, remained. But firing on undefended cities was prohibited, as was targeting properly marked hospitals, religious buildings and monuments. Indiscriminate bombing from the air and the use of poisoned gas were also banned.[2]

2 James Brown Scott (ed.), *Texts of the Peace Conferences at The Hague, 1899 and 1907* (Boston and London: Ginn & Co., 1908), pp. 209–29.

All the major powers ratified the convention and incorporated it into their military manuals. While there was no international court to enforce it, the influence of the convention was apparent in the way that public opinion in much of Europe and North America accepted the new norms – although the colonies remained a different moral universe. The Balkan wars of 1912–13 reinforced the strictures against the unrestrained conduct of war. The humane treatment of wounded soldiers and POWs was a test of civilised conduct that both sides seemed to pass in the first war between the Balkan League and Ottoman Turkey. However, the ethnic bitterness of the brief second war between Bulgaria and its former allies in 1913 saw brutality towards enemy soldiers and 'atrocities' against civilians as villages were destroyed and their inhabitants massacred. European opinion was shocked. In June 1914, the Carnegie Endowment for International Peace concluded that in the second conflict: 'National jealousy and bitterness, greed for territorial expansion, and mutual distrust were sufficient to initiate and push forward the most uncalled for and brutal war of modern times.'[3] But it also assumed that public opinion and rule of law would make such conduct less likely in the 'civilized world'.[4]

In 1915, Freud (with two sons and a son-in-law at the front) wrote that the European war that had broken out the previous year had brought 'disillusionment':

> It disregards all the restrictions known as International Law which in peace-time the states had bound themselves to observe; ignores the prerogatives of the wounded and the medical service [and] the distinction between the civil and military sections of the population . . . The civilized nations know and understand one another so little that one can turn against the other with hate and loathing. Indeed, one of the great civilized nations is so universally unpopular that the attempt can actually be made to exclude it from the civilized community as 'barbaric'.[5]

Freud expressed the widespread shock at the indiscriminate violence and disregard for the 'laws of war' generated by the First World War, which called into question Europe's very claim to stand for 'civilized' values. He also noted that each side blamed the other, rather than war as such, for this state of affairs,

3 George F. Kennan (ed.), *The Other Balkan Wars: A 1913 Carnegie Endowment Inquiry in Retrospect with a New Introduction and Reflections on the Present Conflict* (Washington, DC: Carnegie Endowment for International Peace, 1993), p. 265.

4 Kennan (ed.), *The Other Balkan Wars*, p. 271.

5 Sigmund Freud, 'Thoughts for the times on war and death' (1915), in *The Penguin Freud Library*, vol. XII: *Civilization, Society and Religion* (Harmondsworth: Penguin, 1991), pp. 64–5.

with Germany being especially vilified. The norms of warfare in the pre-war period served to judge the escalating violence of the war but also to blame the enemy for the worst transgressions, which occurred in various contexts – war on land, invasions and occupations, the home front, war at sea and war in the air.

War on land

Land warfare immediately revealed that the protected status of the legitimate combatant – the soldier or sailor who was wounded or taken prisoner – was far from secure. The French accused the Germans of using the Red Cross flag as a ruse in battle and of executing an 'immense number' of wounded soldiers, perhaps due to the punishing advance required by the Schlieffen/Moltke Plan.[6] In one case, it is clear that the commander of the German 58th Brigade (Sixth Army), Major General Stenger, instructed his men not to take prisoners in Lorraine in late August 1914.[7] However, while the killing of wounded soldiers and surrendering prisoners occurred, it is hard to say on what scale. It was certainly not German policy.

Once the fronts had stabilised, the logistics of dealing with the enemy wounded and prisoners became easier, though big offensives and the more mobile warfare of the Eastern Front in 1915 opened the way for renewed violation of Geneva and Hague law in both regards. Yet accusations that the enemy flouted the laws of war and fought in a 'barbaric' manner favoured reciprocal transgressions. Solomon Ansky, the Russian Jewish war correspondent, noted that progressive-minded Russian officers who had begun the war observing their own army's commitment to the Hague Convention on land warfare reacted to supposed German 'atrocities' against soldiers and civilians alike by 'arguing that the Russians had to respond to the German cruelties with even greater ones – like shooting explosive bullets and taking no prisoners. And soon these convictions evolved into an overall theory: war is war, and if you want to win, you have to be merciless . . . [and] exterminate the enemy.'[8] In Britain, France and Germany, too, tales of the maltreatment of wounded soldiers and POWs provoked anger over enemy barbarity.

6 *Rapports et procès-verbaux d'enquête de la commission instituée en vue de constater les actes commis par l'ennemi en violation du droit des gens* (hereafter French Commission), third and fourth reports (Paris, 1915), pp. 10–23 (p. 14 for the quotation).

7 John Horne and Alan Kramer, *German Atrocities, 1914: A History of Denial* (New Haven, CT: Yale University Press, 2001), pp. 194–5.

8 Solomon Ansky, *The Enemy at his Pleasure: A Journey through the Jewish Pale of Settlement during World War I* (New York: Henry Holt, 2003), p. 116.

While the laws of war concerning prisoners and the wounded remained uncontested in principle (unlike in the Second World War, when they did not apply to the Nazi–Soviet or Japanese campaigns), their application amidst claim and counter-claim of illegal treatment fluctuated for several reasons. The first was reprisal. Among many examples, the Germans considered the French use of some POW labour in its North African colonies an infringement of international law, and retaliated by subjecting selected French POWs to a harsher work regime. This the French denounced in turn.[9] The second factor was economic and military need. Labour shortages afflicted both sides and the sheer number of POWs made them a valuable resource. While POW labour was used on work not directly connected to the war, it was also employed by both sides behind the lines, especially on the Western Front, and thus against the prisoners' compatriots, at risk to their own lives and in defiance of Geneva and Hague law. Prisoners of the Central Powers worked in harsh conditions in Russia, though neglect was as common as repressive discipline. Finally, deteriorating conditions in Russia and within the Central Powers from 1916 meant that POWs, who were low priority, faced neglect, which stood in growing contrast to their more equitable material treatment in Britain and France. In all these cases, POWs were symbols of enemy inhumanity. In 1915, for example, the failure of the German authorities to treat a serious outbreak of typhus in POW camps resulted in British and French protests against what were seen as deliberate 'atrocities', and in charges of war crimes once the war was over.

Yet the logic of reprisal may also have worked to limit brutality. In the German case, the mortality rate for prisoners of war was 3 per cent for the British and French, 5 per cent for Russians but nearly 30 per cent for Romanians. National stereotyping may have contributed to this differential outcome.[10] But it was also due to the threat of reciprocity. This was low in the case of Romania (defeated in autumn 1916) and of Russia (most of whose prisoners were Austro-Hungarian), but high with regard to Britain and France. Retaliation may thus have brought more restraint in the treatment of POWs than the principled application of international law or inspections by the ICRC, though these continued to embody the norms of civilised treatment.

9 Georges Cahen-Salvador, *Les prisonniers de guerre (1914–1919)* (Paris: Payot, 1929), pp. 56–62.

10 Alan Kramer, 'Combatants and noncombatants: atrocities, massacres and war crimes', in John Horne (ed.), *A Companion to World War I* (Chichester: Wiley-Blackwell, 2010), p. 193.

One particular asymmetry in combatant status between the two sides arose from the contested use of non-European soldiers. The British and French both deployed colonial troops in Europe with the French bringing half a million soldiers to the Western Front, mainly from North and West Africa. The Russians, in addition to the Cossacks, recruited men from Central Asia. In a quarrel that went back to 1870, when Bismarck and Moltke the Elder had condemned the French use of North African soldiers, the Germans objected to colonial troops fighting in Europe as barbaric. They alleged in particular that French West African soldiers mutilated Germans with knives and machetes and took body parts as trophies. While there was nothing in Geneva or Hague law to cover it, German military and political doctrine declared the use of such soldiers to be a prime example of an Allied atrocity.[11]

Yet for all the mistreatment of protected combatants, the overwhelming violence of land warfare in 1914–18 occurred within the norms of Hague law. The dominant mode of combat in Europe (with the partial exception of the Eastern Front in 1914–15) was improvised siege warfare in open country. The technical advances used to try and break the siege (artillery, flamethrowers, aircraft and eventually tanks) caused most of the military deaths but did not break international law. The exception was poisonous gas, first developed and used successfully by the Germans in the Ypres salient on 22 April 1915, but countered by increasingly effective gas masks and copied by the Allies from autumn 1915. The German military claimed on a technicality that it had not breached Hague Convention IV, since this forbade the 'diffusion of asphyxiating or deleterious gases' by 'projectiles', whereas the Germans at first used canisters. But the effect was the same, and both then and in August 1917, when the Germans deployed the more deadly mustard gas, the Allies condemned them for violating the laws of war, but invoked self-defence and legitimate reprisal to use the same measure. After the war they made no attempt to try the Germans for violating the Hague Convention by initiating the use of gas (Fritz Haber, its German inventor, received the Nobel Prize for Chemistry in 1918). Yet although gas caused fewer than 3 per cent of military deaths in the war, its ability to kill or incapacitate en masse, along with each side's silence about its own use of the weapon, meant that public opinion saw it as a major

11 *Völkerrechtswidrige Verwendung farbiger Truppen auf dem europäischen Kriegsschauplatz durch England und Frankreich* (Berlin, 1915), translated as *Employment, Contrary to International Law, of Colored Troops upon the European Arena of War, by England and France* (Berlin, n.d.).

transgression of how war should be conducted. It was banned anew by international law in 1925.[12]

Invasions and occupations

We have seen that the non-combatant civilian was just as important as the wounded or captured soldier or sailor in contemporary understanding of the 'laws of war'. In reality, the highly organised and largely static fronts that resulted from trench warfare meant there was less scope for soldiers and civilians to encounter each other in combat situations than was the case during the Second World War, with its mobile fronts, military resistance and guerrilla activity. It is thus all the more striking that the issue should have become so prominent in the contemporary imagination during the Great War as a primary signifier of enemy 'atrociousness'.

The immediate reason for this was the invasions with which the war began and which, though untypical of the conflict, posed the issue of civilian involvement in combat just as the moral agenda and predominant imagery of the war were being created. This initial phase supplied about a third of the war crimes with which the Allies charged enemy subjects once the conflict was over.

The most notorious case was that of the German armies invading Belgium and France in August–October 1914. Convinced that they faced a widespread 'people's war' led by the priests and civic leaders, they responded by attacking the inhabitants in many localities, killing some 6,500, mainly in Belgium and the French department of the Meurthe-et-Moselle. They also raped and pillaged, and destroyed over 20,000 buildings, mainly by arson, striking fear into the population. In a third of the 129 major incidents in which ten or more civilians perished, the Germans forced the locals to act as human shields when they advanced. In the worst cases (such as at Andenne, Tamines and Dinant in Belgium), towns and villages were laid waste and civilians were executed collectively.[13]

In fact, as some German sceptics and astute minds in the Allied countries soon came to realise, there was no 'people's war'. But the bulk of German

12 The 1925 Geneva Protocol for the Prohibition of the Use in War of Asphyxiating, Poisonous or other Gases, and of Bacteriological Warfare, in W. Michael Reisman and Chris T. Antoniou (eds.), *The Laws of War: A Comprehensive Collection of Primary Documents on International Laws Governing Armed Conflicts* (New York: Vintage, 1994), pp. 57–8.

13 For the above figures concerning the German invasion, see Horne and Kramer, *German Atrocities*, pp. 435–50.

soldiers believed the contrary in a collective delusion that began with the first incursion into Belgium and swiftly spread back to Germany itself, convincing even the Kaiser and the Supreme Command of its reality. Highly nervous German soldiers interpreted every unidentified shot and strange event as the work of Belgian and French *francs-tireurs*, in what the leading Belgian sociologist, Fernand van Langenhove, writing for the Belgian government-in-exile in 1916, came to understand was a myth-cycle.[14] The Germans had summoned up their own worst fears derived from the Franco-Prussian War, and since their military doctrine prescribed harsh reprisals against a spontaneous *levée en masse*, these became a matter of military orders and even preventive violence. Where the German army and government angrily accused the Belgians and French of waging the worst kind of illegitimate warfare, the latter rightly pointed out that even had there been resistance of the kind alleged by the Germans, much of this would have been legal under Hague Convention IV. They accused the Germans in turn of conducting war by terror in contravention of the laws of war and elementary morality. Few saw like van Langenhove that while German actions amounted to war crimes, they had been based on a genuine belief in *francs-tireurs*.

Along with the question of who started the war, the 'German atrocities' of 1914 did more than any other issue to articulate the conflict's significance. The Allied countries pilloried German military conduct in what has traditionally been seen as a campaign of manipulative 'propaganda'. Recent research has shown this to be more complex. The Belgian, British and French governments published multiple reports based on the interrogation of their own soldiers, civilian refugees and German prisoners, which conveyed much of the truth of what had happened. But they attributed the most stereotypical motives to the enemy. Myths demonising German behaviour – such as the Belgian babies whose hands had been sawn off by German bayonets – flourished in the press and popular imagery. But they often originated with terrified civilian refugees, and government censorship sought to restrain rather than encourage them. Under pressure from disapproval in neutral states, the German government tried to counteract the negative propaganda by conducting its own enquiry. But faced with growing doubts about civilian resistance in 1914, it doctored its official report so as to sustain the original charge.[15] The bitterly contested truth of the German atrocities shows how the laws and norms of war were used

14 Fernand van Langenhove, *The Growth of a Legend: A Study Based upon the Accounts of Francs-Tireurs and 'Atrocities' in Belgium* (1916; translated from the French, London: Putnam's Sons, 1916).

15 For the reports, see Horne and Kramer, *German Atrocities*, pp. 229–61.

both as a measure of real actions and also as a means of condemning the enemy in a conflict that abolished moral neutrality.

Charges of guerrilla resistance marked other invasions, too. As the Russians entered East Prussia in 1914, German refugees related tales of brutal Cossacks and collective reprisals. In fact, two of the worst cases for which clear documentation exists consisted of the reverse – German military depredations against Polish civilians in the towns of Kalisz and Czestochowa, just over the border in Russian Poland.[16] While brutality by Russian troops in East Prussia did occur and was sometimes prompted by accusations of civilian resistance, it was spasmodic and not driven by a Russian delusion of a German 'people's war'. Even the Prussian Interior Ministry concluded that panicky German civilians had exaggerated the brutality.[17] The Russian invasion of Austrian Galicia and Bukovina over the following winter and spring prompted widespread violence against the inhabitants, notably Jews, in a series of pogroms. Despite Austrian protests, the total number of civilians allegedly killed by Russian forces amounted to only sixty-nine, though in the absence of detailed research the figures, which may have been higher, must be treated cautiously.[18]

Altogether more systematic was the violent treatment of the population by the Austro-Hungarian army during its invasions of Serbia. Precisely because it aimed to punish the Serbs collectively for the 'terrorist' assassination of the Archduke Franz-Ferdinand and to destroy Serbia as a nation-state, the Austro-Hungarian military was predisposed to see the entire population as made up of terrorists and bandits who were liable to rise up in a treacherous *levée en masse*. Considering itself the pillar of law and civilisation in a barbaric region, the High Command was initially unwilling to engage in mass punishment and instructed the army to observe Hague Convention IV even though Serbia was not a signatory. But it insisted that atrocities, such as the poisoning and mutilation of Habsburg soldiers, would be met with the 'harshest reprisals'. Akin to the German army's conviction that it faced a 'people's war' in the West, the Austro-Hungarian forces imagined they faced unrestrained warfare

16 A. S. Rezanoff, *Les atrocités allemandes du côté russe* (Petrograd: W. Kirschbaoum, 1915), pp. 120–65; and Immanuel Geiss, 'Die Kosaken kommen! Ostpreussen im August 1914', in Geiss, *Das deutsche Reich und der Erste Weltkrieg*, 2nd edn (Munich: Carl Hanser, 1985 [1978]), pp. 60–1.

17 Geiss, 'Die Kosaken kommen!', pp. 62–3; and Denis Showalter, *Tannenberg: Clash of Empires* (Hamden, CT: Archon, 1991), p. 159. For more credence to widespread Cossack atrocities, see Holger Herwig, *The First World War: Germany and Austria-Hungary 1914–18* (London: Edward Arnold, 1997), p. 128.

18 Horne and Kramer, *German Atrocities*, pp. 82–3.

even on the part of Serb regular soldiers. While Balkan traditions of guerrilla warfare provided some substance for this belief (where in Belgium and France there was none), the Austro-Hungarian response was disproportionate, with hostage taking, arson and summary executions, including of women and children.

This prompted the Serb government in turn to accuse Austria-Hungary of treating its civilians with brutality. The Swiss lawyer and Serb sympathiser, R. A. Reiss, who investigated the matter on its behalf, calculated that over 3,000 Serbs had perished in the two invasions of 1914 (which ended in Austro-Hungarian defeat) and in the final, successful invasion of late 1915. However, in the absence of new research, this, too, remains an estimate.[19] The Bulgarian occupation of the southern portion of the country (which had been part of Ottoman Macedonia until 1913) renewed the tit-for-tat ethnic violence begun in the Second Balkan War as the Bulgarian army tried to extirpate Serb and Greek influence. Atrocities remained a burning issue for the Serb government-in-exile, and it charged both Austria-Hungary and Bulgaria with war crimes in 1919.

The common factor in all these cases (aside from the inter-ethnic violence of Bulgarians and Serbs) was the overturning of the distinction between soldiers and civilians in situations of combat. In reality, civilian resistance was marginal in 1914–15, with the partial exception of Serbia, because vast regular armies continued to seek a conventional outcome. Even in the Serb case, some of the misunderstanding arose from reservists who were short of uniforms in an army exhausted by the Balkan wars, and who thus appeared to be 'bandits.' More important than the reality, however, was the fantasy of a 'people's war' which was rampant in the German and Austro-Hungarian armies, and possibly present in the Russian army during the invasion of East Prussia. This expressed the deep fear of the military elite and ordinary soldiers that future warfare might degenerate into terror and revolution. It led to real violence against civilians by way of reprisal or pre-emption.

Although occupations had received less attention than invasions before 1914, owing to the widespread expectation of a short war, it was evident that they too caused tensions between soldier and civilian, as the French recalled

19 R. A. Reiss, *Report upon the Atrocities Committed by the Austro-Hungarian Army during the First Invasion of Serbia: Submitted to the Serb Government* (London: HMSO, 1916); and Reiss, *Réponses aux accusations austro-hongroises contre les Serbes* (Lausanne and Paris: Payot, 1918). For the most recent estimates, see Jonathan Gumz, *The Resurrection and Collapse of Empire in Habsburg Serbia, 1914–1918* (Cambridge University Press, 2009), pp. 44–61.

only too bitterly from 1870–3. The legal position remained grey. Hague Convention IV had tried to provide civilians with some protection. It restricted the occupying force's right of military requisition and financial imposition, forbade the use of civilian labour for the war effort and enjoined respect for the culture and religion of the occupied. In reality, the military and administrative law of the occupier prevailed.

Unexpectedly, the military stalemate in 1914–15 brought a sizeable part of Europe under the control of the Central Powers for an indefinite period. Germany held most of Belgium and northern France, Russian Poland, a zone covering eastern Poland and parts of modern-day Belorussia and Lithuania (known as Ober Ost) and, from late 1916, two-thirds of Romania. In 1918 Germany's military writ also ran in the Ukraine and the Baltic region. Austria-Hungary held Serbia and from late 1917 north-eastern Italy. Although not on the scale of the Second World War, 'occupied Europe' was a reality and it offered fertile terrain for charges of atrocity and war crimes. How international law applied to the occupations is taken up in Chapter 23 below. Suffice it to say here that for the first two years the Germans administered their territories with some reference to Hague law. But by 1916 the 'totalising logic' of the war led to more brutal forms of occupation, and galvanised Allied outrage at German 'barbarity' in several regards.

From the start, the Germans used the occupied regions for their war effort, especially in the zones behind the front (*Etappengebiet*), which were subject to the operational needs of the army, as was the case in northern France, part of Belgium and Ober Ost. Initially, the military tried persuasion to find the necessary labour. But by 1916 the clear material advantage of the Allies forced the Germans to gear up their economic effort. Where the British and French could draw on their empires, bringing hundreds of thousands of colonial and Chinese workers to France, the Germans made more systematic use of labour across the occupied regions, conscripting workers for agriculture, industry and, in the *Etappengebiet*, war work.

The principle of coercion did not necessarily run counter to Hague Convention IV, especially since all wartime states established varying degrees of control over 'manpower' (the term dated from 1915). But forcing labour to work directly for the occupier's war effort did infringe the rights of the occupied, and civilians in Belgium and France, at least, were acutely aware of this.[20] Two developments provoked particular outrage, however, both in the occupied regions and internationally. The first was the deportation of large

20 Archives Nationales (Paris), F23 14, evidence of repatriated French civilians.

numbers of men to work as militarised labour on a variety of tasks both in the *Etappengebiet* and elsewhere in the occupied regions. Conditions were severe, leading to high mortality. But sending 60,000 workers from Belgium, and perhaps twice that number from the Government General of Poland and from Ober Ost, to labour in Germany was another step again. In the Belgian case, international protest ended this experiment in 'slavery' by early 1917 (though men were still sent to work behind the lines in France), but it continued for the Poles, who had no national government to protest on their behalf.[21]

The second 'outrage' was the extension of coercion to women in the zones the German army controlled directly, something that no state during the First World War (including Germany) dared impose on its home population. While this happened incrementally in both Ober Ost and northern France, the Germans drew dramatic attention to their practice when, in April 1916, troops descended on the major industrial conurbation of Lille and rounded up unemployed women and girls at gun-point, transporting them to the countryside for agricultural labour. While the measure marked a new threshold of brutality, the Germans claimed they were simply trying to make the best use of a poorly employed workforce. But it provoked uproar in France (where the government usually remained reticent about conditions in the occupied territories) and resulted in protests to Germany because of the gender of those arrested. Women incarnated the civilian as victim in war. Especially in France, where universal military service meant that adult men had been mobilised before the invasion, the more than 2 million people left in the occupied region were disproportionately female, which is why tales of rape during the invasion assumed a symbolic power beyond their incidence. The violation of the nation was equated to violation of women. Enemy control over women's bodies as well as the conquered territories remained a powerful subtext of the occupation, which the events of Lille dramatised. French outrage was still palpable when Lille was liberated in 1918.[22]

Resistance to enemy occupation was diverse and extensive (it was estimated after the war that 1,135 members of Belgian escape and intelligence

21 Fernand Passelecq, *Déportation et travail forcé des ouvriers et de la population civile de la Belgique occupée (1916–1918)* (Paris: PUF, 1928); Sophie de Schaepdrijver, *La Belgique et la Première Guerre mondiale* (1997; translation from the Dutch, Brussels: Peter Lang, 2004), pp. 222–30; and Vejas Gabriel Liulevicius, *War Land on the Eastern Front: Culture, National Identity and German Occupation in World War I* (Cambridge University Press, 2000), pp. 72–4.

22 Georges Gromaire, *L'occupation allemande en France (1914–1918)* (Paris: Payot, 1925), pp. 247–93; Liulevicius, *War Land*, p. 73; and French Commission, tenth report, 31 October 1918.

networks were executed or died in captivity).[23] But it had no legal protection under Hague law, so that its repression was not a war crime even if sympathisers considered it an outrage. In one notorious case, the Germans were entitled to punish the British nurse Edith Cavell in 1915 for having run an escape network for Allied soldiers in Brussels, but what shocked contemporaries was the imposition of the death penalty on a woman. Heroism and victimhood combined to create a martyr.

Internment was different. The Germans and Austro-Hungarians took civilians from the occupied territories to camps in Germany and Austria on a large scale (including women and children) both in response to the 'people's war' during the invasions and also as a measure of security or punishment during the occupation. The Russians did likewise. Seventy thousand Serbs were interned by the end of 1916, 100,000 French and Belgians for the whole war, and as many Germans in Russia.[24] The civilian 'concentration camp' had become a veritable institution and, as in the case of mistreatment of prisoners of war, the logic was often that of reprisal as well as repression. The procedure as such was not illegal any more than was the internment of 'enemy aliens' (i.e., those who found themselves on enemy soil when war broke out). But the conditions in which it was carried out might well be, since the occupying power was responsible for the well-being of the occupied population. Hence civilian internees came within the ambit of the ICRC and other humanitarian agents (neutral states, the Vatican). Internment struck contemporaries as a new phenomenon, and the frequently harsh conditions of detention led to charges of maltreatment by the detainees' own governments.

Forced labour by both sexes, deportation and internment on a substantial scale, along with the complete subjection of the economy to the 'military necessity' of the occupier, seemed to Allied opinion a return to the barbarity associated with the Thirty Years' War, or even the fall of the Roman Empire. In March 1917 it culminated in Operation Alberich, the planned retreat by four German armies on a sector of the Western Front fifty miles long and twenty-five miles deep to the fortified Siegfried Line. This had been built using 26,000 POWs and 9,000 French and Belgian forced labourers. The Germans forcibly evacuated 160,000 civilians and totally destroyed buildings and infrastructure so that, according to the orders of the First Army, 'the enemy will arrive to

23 Schaepdrijver, *La Belgique et la Première Guerre Mondiale*, p. 242.

24 For the figures, see Gumz, *Resurrection and Collapse of Empire*; and Annette Becker, *Oubliés de la Grande Guerre: humanitaire et culture de guerre, 1914–1918: populations occupées, déportés civils, prisonniers de guerre* (Paris: Éditions Noêsis, 1998), pp. 232–3.

find a desert'.[25] The misgivings of many in the German military, including Crown Prince Rupprecht who commanded the operation, showed the sense of transgression of the accepted conduct of war, as did the anger of the French. Ordinary soldiers reoccupying the abandoned zone were appalled at the destruction, including the apparently wilful cutting-down of fruit trees, while politicians declared their intention to exact reparation for a major violation of the 'laws of war'. Overall, the logic of the German and Austro-Hungarian occupation regimes had, by the second half of the war, abolished the protected status of civilians and hinted at what Michael Geyer has called the 'elements of a totalitarian syndrome'.[26]

The home front

The logic of national identity that presided over the cultural and political mobilisation for the war, and which resulted in the internment of 'enemy aliens', also risked exposing home minorities to harsh treatment. The vulnerability of religious and national minorities had loomed large in humanitarian concern before the war, especially regarding the Ottoman and Russian Empires. The massacres of Christian Bulgarians and Armenians with the connivance of the regime had provided one of the main excuses for the Great Powers to intervene in Ottoman Turkey in order to protect minorities. Pogroms against Jews in the Pale of Russia in the early twentieth century provoked international condemnation. Yet while such cases contributed to the language of 'atrocity', they had not usually been associated with war. Hague law said nothing about how a belligerent state should treat its own people.

As the Ottoman Empire entered the war in late 1914 and suffered a series of military setbacks in spring 1915, the Young Turks who ran the war effort triggered the measures that led to the destruction of the Armenians, including pillage, murder and expulsion to the desert. By 1916, about a million of the 1.8 million Armenians had perished. Made vulnerable by Russia's mobilisation of its own Armenians, the Ottoman Armenians (along with other minorities) became the 'enemy within' which the regime purged in pursuit of a wartime community defined in terms of Turkish ethnicity and Islam.

Observers in Germany, the Allied states and the USA knew that the violence differed in kind and scale from pre-war massacres. As early as

25 Michael Geyer, 'Retreat and destruction', in Irina Renz, Gerd Krumeich and Gerhard Hirschfeld (eds.), *Scorched Earth: The Germans on the Somme 1914–1918* (2006; translation from German, Barnsley: Pen & Sword, 2009), pp. 141–56 (here p. 151).
26 *Ibid.*, p. 149.

24 May 1915, Britain, France and Russia accused the Ottoman government of committing a 'crime against humanity'. This was the first time that the formulation had been used as an accusation between states, and though it had no legal status (that would only come with the Second World War) it tried to convey the collective nature of the crime in which an entire ethnic or religious group was indiscriminately targeted because of its identity. Reasonably accurate casualty figures of 800,000 were retailed in the press, and two respected British academics, James Bryce and Arnold Toynbee, drew up a detailed report for the Foreign Office in 1916 stating that 'a gigantic crime [had] . . . devastated the Near East in 1915'. The French Minister of Education was in no doubt that the Young Turks had attempted to 'exterminate the Armenian race'.[27]

Yet despite being a quantitative leap in wartime violence towards civilians, the destruction of the Ottoman Armenians was subject to what Donald Bloxham has dubbed 'the great game of genocide' (the term genocide, publicly formulated only in 1944, has been retrospectively applied to the episode by historians and governments).[28] Germany remained silent for fear of embarrassing its Turkish ally, while the Allies subordinated their condemnation of Ottoman Turkey to that reserved for Germany. French and British politicians and intellectuals gave the issue less attention than more minor transgressions by the main enemy, and also argued without evidence that Germany was behind the destruction of the Armenians. Even the USA, which was still neutral when the genocide occurred and well informed of its true nature by Henry Morgenthau, its ambassador in Constantinople, combined moral denunciation with political inertia. The inertia was reinforced when it joined the war, since the fate of Ottoman Turkey became a vital diplomatic issue, not to be jeopardised by precipitate action.

A similar need to fit moral humanitarianism to the exigencies of wartime is apparent in Allied reaction to the maltreatment of civilians by the Russian army during its Great Retreat from Galicia and Bukovina in 1915, at the same moment as the genocide in Turkey. The Russian High Command forcibly

27 James Bryce and Arnold Toynbee, *The Treatment of Armenians in the Ottoman Empire, 1915–1916: Documents Presented to Viscount Grey of Falloden by Viscount Bryce* (London: HMSO, 1916; new edn, Reading: Taderon Press, 2000), p. 649; Paul Painlevé, Minister of Public Instruction, and the *Illustrated London News*, 16 October 1915 (800,000 victims), both quoted in Annette Becker and Jay Winter, 'Le génocide arménien et les réactions de l'opinion internationale', in John Horne (ed.), *Vers la guerre totale: le tournant de 1914–1915* (Paris: Tallandier, 2010), pp. 291–313 (pp. 300–1).

28 Donald Bloxham, *The Great Game of Genocide: Imperialism, Nationalism and the Destruction of the Ottoman Armenians* (Oxford University Press, 2005).

deported some 3 million inhabitants, both from the region it had occupied and also from the tsarist territories it had to abandon, targeting ethnic minorities, especially Jews, many of whom were Russian subjects, and raising fears of a resurgence of pre-war anti-Semitism. Liberal opinion in Russia and the need to resolve the chaos caused by the refugees prevented this turning into reality. Prompted by Jewish lobby groups, the British government applied discreet pressure behind the scenes. But there was no question of publicly denouncing 'Allied atrocities'.[29]

War at sea and in the air

Naval warfare during the First World War turned out to be as much of a surprise as land warfare. The absence of a modern Trafalgar to settle the issue between the costly capital ships that had driven the pre-war naval arms race, echoed the failure of land armies to achieve a modern-day Waterloo. Fields of high-explosive mines parcelled out the sea into a maritime no-man's-land, controlling access to the enemy's coast. While not a new weapon, the submarine became an effective long-range predator and an alternative instrument of attack to battleships, especially on merchant shipping. Yet it was less these developments in themselves than their application to the old issue of naval blockade that caused controversy. For the deadlock of the main battle fleets, none of which could risk defeat by taking on its opponent, turned blockade into the main form of naval warfare, especially in an extended war between modern states that relied on global commerce.

Blockade was a legitimate weapon of war but two issues had dominated the pre-war debate on it: the permissible level of confiscation of enemy trade and the right of neutral powers to conduct that trade. The British, as noted, were reluctant to admit any restraint on their freedom to blockade, although the potential diplomatic fallout from offending neutral countries led to caution. The Admiralty itself opted initially to maintain the distinction between war goods and non-war goods, the former being forbidden as contraband, and to let neutral ships carry non-war goods to enemy ports. Yet from the start the Royal Navy set up a broad blockade of the western approaches to Germany, whose legal status, by comparison with the traditional 'close blockade', was unclear. Abundantly clear, however, was its potential to become the maritime siege of an entire enemy nation.

29 Peter Holquist, 'Les violences de l'armée russe à l'encontre des Juifs en 1915: causes et limites', in Horne (ed.), *Vers la guerre totale*, pp. 191–219.

Matters came to a head rapidly. The German government condemned the British goal as an atrocity. 'England treats us as a besieged fortress', protested Chancellor Bethmann Hollweg on 4 February 1915. 'They want to starve a people 70 million strong. Is it possible to imagine a more barbaric way of waging war?'[30] By way of reprisal, Germany declared the waters around Britain and Ireland open to unrestricted submarine warfare, meaning that vessels carrying civilians could be sunk without warning. The British immediately declared such behaviour a violation of the rights of civilians under the laws of war, and riposted with the Reprisals Order, which imposed a total ban on all goods travelling to and from Germany. They also pressured neutral countries to observe the blockade. The British case seemed to be dramatically vindicated by the torpedoing of the *Lusitania* off the coast of Ireland on 6 May 1915, with the loss of 1,198 passengers, including a number of American citizens. Diplomatic prudence forced Germany to suspend unrestricted submarine warfare until the gathering pressure of Allied material superiority led the military leadership to renew it from February 1917. Yet submarines found it hard to conduct 'restricted' warfare in the intervening period, since they could not take on board the crews of the shipping they sank and they put themselves at risk (especially from armed merchant ships) if they surfaced to warn of an impending attack.

By a reciprocal but opposed logic both sides broke new ground in targeting civilians. But each did so in ways that had important implications for the charge of enemy 'atrociousness' and its impact on neutral opinion. Whether or not the Allied blockades of Germany or of Austria-Hungary and Turkey in the Mediterranean contributed largely or solely to the hunger that all those societies were experiencing by the end of the war, is discussed elsewhere in this history. Germany claimed that this was the case and also justified the increasingly harsh treatment of occupied Europe by the same argument ('The attitude of England makes the feeding of the population more and more difficult', proclaimed the German commander to the population of Lille during the round-ups in 1916).[31] In 1923 a Reichstag commission of enquiry concluded that the blockade had caused the death of some 750,000 vulnerable German civilians, to which submarine warfare was a legitimate response. The figures are inflated and the causes of German malnutrition involved much else, such as food distribution policies.[32] But the British government and

30 *Frankfurter Zeitung*, 6 February 1915, quoted in Gerd Krumeich, 'Le blocus maritime et la guerre sous-marine', in Horne (ed.), *Vers la guerre totale*, p. 177.
31 French Commission, tenth report, p. 62.
32 Cited by Krumeich, 'Le blocus maritime', p. 178.

Admiralty undoubtedly aimed to starve the societies of the Central Powers of everything they could in order to force their surrender, and they were able to do so in a way that went far beyond the impact of the Napoleonic blockade a century earlier.

Yet precisely because the method was slow and incremental and its result conditioned by other factors, the 'hunger blockade' grabbed the headlines far less effectively than the sinking of merchantmen and passenger ships with the direct and indiscriminate loss of civilian lives. As Woodrow Wilson, significantly failing to grasp the real point of the British blockade, remarked:

> It is interesting and significant how often the German Foreign Office goes over the same ground in different words and always misses the essential point involved, that England's violation of neutral rights is different from Germany's violation of the rights of humanity.[33]

Allied outrage at German behaviour in this regard was a potent litany of sunken vessels (*Lusitania*, *Sussex*, *Leinster* . . .) which all lost passengers and crews. Allegations of naval war crimes figured in the charges brought against Germany after the war.[34]

Aerial warfare raised a different set of issues, which it shared with long-range artillery bombardment, but the common thread with naval warfare was how war eroded the protected status of civilians. As we saw, Hague Convention IV did not ban the shelling of cities under siege (though it exempted certain categories of clearly marked building), but focused instead on outlawing the destruction of 'open', or undefended, cities. In effect, it distinguished between combatant and non-combatant centres, and accepted the traditional view that civilians in the former might be hit by enemy fire. Although a few cities underwent conventional siege during the war (Przemyśl in Austrian Galicia in 1914–15, Kut-al-Amara in Mesopotamia in 1916), the stabilisation of the fighting fronts in effect extended siege warfare to entire societies, as the Allies made clear with the naval blockade. Logically, the home front as a whole became a potential target. Yet indiscriminate bombardment of 'innocent' civilians remained a powerful taboo whether conducted by warships, long-range guns or aircraft.

The issue surfaced from the very start. In late 1914, German warships shelled undefended seaside towns on the east coast of England while the

33 Quoted in A. C. Bell, *A History of the Blockade of Germany* (London: HMSO, 1937), p. 446.

34 French Commission, seventh report, listing over 200 French vessels sunk.

German army also bombarded towns just behind the Western Front (such as Nancy), though whether the target in this case was military or civilian remained ambiguous. Later in the war, the heavy German gun 'Big Bertha' shelled Paris randomly, the worst incident occurring when it struck the church of Saint-Gervais on 29 March 1918 during a Good Friday service, killing seventy-five people, many of them women and children. The British and French considered such attacks (which they were not in a position to reciprocate) to be illegitimate: 'such a crime committed in such conditions and on such a day . . . arouses condemnation in consciences everywhere', declared the Archbishop of Paris in relation to Saint-Gervais.[35] Yet it was long-range bombing by aircraft that dramatised the issue and exposed most clearly the choices involved.

From the outset both sides bombed military installations well behind the Western Front, and by spring 1915 French and British aircraft attacked war industries in the Ruhr and the major cities of western Germany. Civilians were killed but this was inadvertent. Simultaneously, however, the German military used their technical lead in airships, which initially had a greater range than airplanes, to target London and south-eastern England in raids whose principal aim was to terrify civilians and disrupt the domestic war effort. Retaliation was rapid, and in June 1915 French aircraft killed thirty people and wounded sixty-eight when they attacked Karlsruhe, the peaceful capital of Baden. In a spiral of reprisal, German Zeppelins and later Gotha bombers continued to attack Paris, London and other civilian centres, while French and British aircraft mounted retaliatory raids on major German cities as far afield as Munich. Similar developments took place on the Austro-Italian front.

Technical limitations restricted the damage – some 740 people died and 1,900 were injured in Allied bombing raids on Germany.[36] But the logic was clear. In addition to striking industrial targets that could legitimately be considered part of the enemy's economic effort, air power was deployed against civilians as such. Two German aviators forced down over London in 1917 explained that while they could clearly identify targets such as the Admiralty and the War Office, their objective was also to demoralise ordinary Londoners, especially in the East End, so that it mattered little if

35 Jules Poirier, *Les bombardements de Paris (1914–1918): avions, gothas, zeppelins, berthas* (Paris: Payot, 1930), pp. 229–31.

36 Christian Geinitz, 'The first German air war against noncombatants: strategic bombing of German cities in World War I', in Roger Chickering and Stig Förster (eds.), *Great War, Total War: Combat and Mobilization on the Western Front, 1914–1918* (Cambridge University Press, 2000), pp. 207–25 (p. 207, overall figures, p. 212, Karlsruhe).

their bombs went astray.[37] The British War Cabinet, for its part, believed that indiscriminate bombing would help 'depress the morale of the German people'.[38] There was little evidence to support this assumption any more than there would be during the Second World War. On the contrary, civilians discovered a new form of siege experience in blacked-out towns and cities, finding their way to underground shelters and listening to enemy aircraft, bombs and anti-aircraft fire overhead until the 'all clear' sounded. They became communities under fire. If this paled by comparison with the experience of mass aerial bombing twenty-five years later, it struck the contemporary imagination forcibly as evidence that in this regard at least the distinction between combatant and non-combatant had been abolished.

After the war

After the war came the reckoning. Reflecting the hold of international law on definitions of 'atrociousness', the Allies were determined to charge the enemy legally for its transgressions. Reparations for physical and financial damage were based on the principle of compensation, and figured prominently. Just as significant in 1919–21, however, was the idea of criminal responsibility for the way in which the war had been prosecuted, as well as for causing it in the first place, which meant upholding the legal and moral norms that had been flouted. This was the goal pursued by the Allies in Articles 227–30 of the Treaty of Versailles, which provided for the extradition from Germany of all those accused of 'violating the laws and customs of war', and for an international tribunal if they were sought by more than one power.

Belgium, Britain and France, plus four other powers, eventually presented an extradition list relating to 1,059 war crimes. The different categories indicate the Allied sense of enemy 'atrociousness' at the war's end. Thirty-eight per cent of the accusations (405) concerned the invasion of Belgium and France in 1914, mainly related to civilians. Forty-five per cent (477) involved crimes of occupation – cruelty to civilians, deportation, forced labour and destruction during the retreats of 1917 and 1918. The other 17 per cent (177) dealt with combat, including naval crimes and mistreatment of POWs. In all,

37 *Second Interim Report of the Committee of Inquiry into Breaches of the Law of War*, 3 June 1919, quoted by Best, *Humanity in Warfare*, p. 269.

38 Quoted by Geinitz, 'Strategic bombing', p. 213.

the erosion of the distinction between combatants and non-combatants was far more important than the threat to POWs and wounded soldiers, which accounted for 14 per cent of the total (151), and the 'German atrocities' of 1914 remained emblematic of enemy barbarity.[39]

The German military bitterly resented what they perceived to be a slur on their honour. Resisting extradition, they extracted a compromise by which a small number of high-profile Allied charges would be brought by German prosecutors before the German Supreme Court in Leipzig. When held in a blaze of publicity in 1921, this first attempt at quasi-international war crimes proceedings turned into a display of nationalist support for the German officer corps. The most serious cases were dismissed and the Belgian and French delegations left in disgust. The proceedings suffered from the unavoidable animosities of the aftermath of war.

The Allies were genuinely outraged at what they continued to see as barbaric behaviour stemming from German militarism. This viewpoint was understandable insofar as the political role and military culture of the German army predisposed it to use war to resolve the difficulties of the Second Reich and to brook no obstacles in doing so. In a conflict that they had been instrumental in unleashing, the German military more than any other confronted some of the key issues that transformed the nature of war. In the process they discarded the norms of war embodied in Hague law by crushing what in fact was an imaginary civilian uprising in 1914, extracting with increasing harshness the labour and economic value from their occupied territories, and conducting scorched earth warfare of extreme severity.

The Allies blamed the Germans for such transgressions all the more easily in that (with the partial exception of the Russians) they never had to confront these situations themselves. In other regards – chemical weapons, naval warfare, aerial bombardment – the two camps transformed the face of war reciprocally. And while the economic difficulties and political strains experienced by the Central Powers and Russia explain in large part the worsening fate of the POWs under their control, both sides violated the Geneva and Hague Conventions in their use of prisoners. Yet the logic of total enmity led each side to see the other as solely responsible.

As during the war, there was also a hierarchy of culpability that turned on the importance of the enemy, not the atrocity. The British prevailed on the post-war government in Constantinople to prosecute some of those involved

39 Bundesarchiv, Berlin, R 3003 Generalia/56, as categorised in Horne and Kramer, *German Atrocities*, pp. 448–9.

in the Armenian genocide in 1919–20. Yet great power rivalries in the Ottoman Empire (which was on the point of disintegration) and stiffening resistance by the alternative nationalist regime in Ankara led to the early abandonment of this effort, though not before seventeen death sentences had been handed down, largely *in absentia*.

In the political circumstances of the post-war period, the Allies did not have the power to impose their retrospective moral and legal vision of the war on their former enemies. Germany remained too powerful and German opinion resented what it saw as 'victors' justice'. It was with the Leipzig trials in mind that the Allies determined during the Second World War that the international tribunal to judge Nazi war crimes would be held under their control in a totally defeated Germany. As it was, the 'German atrocities' of 1914 and the Allied 'hunger blockade' in particular, remained unresolved issues that kept wartime enmity alive in the early 1920s.

This did not prevent attempts being made to revise the provisions of Hague and Geneva law in order to take account of the transgressions of the Great War. But despite intense debates at the ICRC, the League of Nations and elsewhere, the results were mixed and ultimately limited by the reality that much of the violation of the 'laws of war' in 1914–18 resulted not only from enemy 'atrocity' but also from the changing nature of war itself. Consequently, self-interest and the fear of being at a military disadvantage qualified the desire to limit the violence of war.

Progress was greatest on the core issue of the wounded or captured combatant, with two new Geneva Conventions in 1928 that addressed some of the weaknesses revealed by the war. Even here, ideological antagonism threatened the idea of humanitarianism in war when the USSR declined to sign up to 'bourgeois' international law. On the issues which had generated most war crimes charges and the greatest moral outrage during the war, progress was small. Apart from the Geneva protocol banning gas, there were no agreements of importance on aerial bombing (which merged with the fear of gas in the public mind), naval warfare or invasions and occupations, despite a much greater international revulsion against war in the second half of the 1920s than before 1914. But that was the paradox. Once it was over, the war itself, not the enemy, became for many the real horror, and it was summed up by the suffering of the soldiers, not the civilians. The wartime language of atrocity, distorted though it was by the logic of enmity, had addressed the underlying trend towards a 'total war' that abolished the distinction between soldier and civilian. That is why it would re-emerge, transformed, in response to the even greater violence of the Second World War.

22

Genocide

HANS-LUKAS KIESER AND DONALD BLOXHAM

Introduction

In Europe the First World War marked a lethal culmination of the imperialism of the modern nation-states and the end of the great dynastic land empires that dated from the late Middle Ages. The characteristics of the conflict itself, including not just developing strategic, tactical and geopolitical considerations, but the psychological, material and socio-political consequences of total war, are vital in explaining the extremity of policies against a range of civilian populations on both sides. Nevertheless, it was the *conjunction* of war and pre-existing ethno-political 'problems' that produced genocide and other extensive crimes perpetrated against population groups. Accordingly, the main and final focus of this chapter, which is a study of the murder of the Ottoman Armenians and other Anatolian Christians during the First World War, incorporates an account of pre-war state–minority relations.

Our contention is that there were two, related cases of outright genocide in the 1914–18 conflict: the deportation and murder of the Armenians, or the *Aghet*, and the fate of the Ottoman Syriac Christian populations (sometimes called 'Assyro-Chaldeans'), which is known in the survivor communities as *Sayfo*. Use of the word 'genocide' is still inflammatory in relation to the First World War, because of a lack of clarity about the applicability of the term, deliberate obfuscation and a vitiating confusion of moral, legal and historical criteria. In order to elucidate key conceptual issues, we will begin in the following section by considering its applicability to the Armenian case.

Like any other concept, 'genocide' must have limits to its applicability in order to serve the analytical purpose of differentiation, but there is nothing in

The authors would like to thank Mark Levene, William Schabas and the volume and series editors for their comments on drafts of this chapter. They thank Ahmet Efiloğlu for the statistics on the expulsions and deportations of *Rûm*.

the idea of meaningful distinction that precludes the idea of borderline cases. Genocide is on a continuum of strategies of mass destruction about which historical scholarship has much to say without reaching a consensus on a number of important points, and there are often good intellectual (as well as moral) reasons for making connections as well as distinctions between different modalities and goals of destruction. We recognise the problems caused for historical scholarship by a preoccupation with the distinction between genocide and non-genocide, and so this chapter is more concerned with historical contextualisation than overt comparison and sharp contrast. Accordingly, once we have addressed the technical conceptual issues around 'genocide', and before we address the Ottoman cases that unequivocally qualify, we consider a range of cases of mass violence from the First World War records of a range of participants. We loosely dub these 'sub-genocidal' and 'pre-genocidal' episodes.

Genocide: a concept, its uses, abuses and limitations

The primary obstacle in identifying genocide in the First World War is political rather than scholarly, notwithstanding the fact that the term 'genocide' was only invented and enshrined in international law later on, in 1944 and 1946 respectively. First, 'genocide' is a social scientific term as well as a legal term, and if some legally positivistic principle of anachronism were applied to prevent its retrospective application, then that would also apply to other social scientific concepts that we routinely apply to times before the term was invented: concepts such as feudalism, for instance. This is patently silly. Secondly, even in strictly legal terms, the only thing that the principle of anachronism would complicate is the punishment under law of perpetrators of genocide whose crimes occurred *avant la lettre*. This issue is not pertinent in the case of the First World War.

If we take the 'in whole or in part' clause of the UN genocide convention,[1] as that clause refers to population groups that are targeted for destruction 'as such', *qua* groups, then, judged proportionately to the Armenian population in 1914 and most other instances of communal destruction before and since, the Armenian case is not some controversial borderline instance of genocide, but an absolutely clear-cut manifestation of genocide. It is of no matter that a few Armenian populations were left relatively unscathed by deportation and murder. After all, a strike against a large enough part of the victim group *is*

1 Where the 'in part' clearly means 'in substantial part'.

a strike against the entirety of the group, as soon as one imagines, as perpetrators of such crimes generally have done, that the target group is a coherent, monolithic entity with a critical mass and an agenda. Such perpetrators construct victim groups for themselves; by extension they make calculations about the level of destruction necessary at one and the same time (for they are thought of as the same thing when abstract entities are reified) to destroy the group as a significant entity now and in the future and to prevent it from carrying out its alleged agenda.[2] Since the alleged agenda of the Armenian population was the provision of a fifth column for the Entente armies pursuant to staking the claim for Armenian autonomy in eastern Anatolia, that purported agenda was fatally crippled along with the collective body by the comprehensive obliteration of Armenian population centres in eastern Anatolia. In this context it is perfectly explicable that, say, fractions of Armenian communities survived in western cities, given the proximate reasons of the attitude of local Ottoman and German representatives (in İzmir, where many Armenians were nevertheless deported) and the impossibility of deporting a whole community under the gaze of the outside world (in Istanbul, where those born outside the community were nevertheless deported).[3] Besides, whatever the claims of those writing under the influence of Turkish nationalism, deportations were indeed conducted throughout western Anatolia and from 'European' Thrace.

For Turkish nationalist propagandists, and for those fewer scholars who broadly accept the scale of the Armenian fate but reject the applicability of the epithet 'genocide', the issue of the Ottoman state's destructive *intent* is critical, and related to the issue of destructive intent is the question of motive. Both considerations are tied together over the question of the timing of the decision (s) for the measures of destruction. The desire of those seeking to exculpate the regime is to present it as purely reactive in the face of a perceived wartime security threat, as opposed to acting in an ideologically proactive capacity. The proposition that the anti-Armenian measures were entirely reactive in inception ignores the violent and discriminatory history of pre-war (peacetime) action towards the Armenians and the state's (or the Young Turk committee government's) new anti-Christian economic and demographic agenda that it had begun to implement by force before August 1914. But even if we were to

2 Frank Chalk and Kurt Jonassohn, *The History and Sociology of Genocide: Analyses and Case Studies* (New Haven, CT: Yale University Press, 1990); and Mark Levene, *Genocide in the Age of the Nation-State,* vol. 1: *The Meaning of Genocide* (London: I. B. Tauris, 2005).

3 Taner Akçam, *The Young Turks' Crime Against Humanity: The Armenian Genocide and Ethnic Cleansing in the Ottoman Empire* (Princeton University Press, 2012), pp. 399–410.

accept that dubious proposition of pure reactivity, this would not remove issues of (dis)proportionality and (in)discriminacy in the measures carried out. Many apologetic positions remain predicated on the idea of collective Armenian guilt, and as such reproduce the viewpoint of the perpetrators themselves, as they assimilate all bearers of Armenian identity to some political agenda – a move that is in fact an important precondition for genocide. 'Softer' mitigations of Young Turk policy will depict collective measures as unfortunate because indiscriminate, but at the same time as somehow realistic under emergency conditions in which discrimination was not possible, and as ameliorated by the government's measures of care for the deportees. The proposition here is that such mass murders as are admitted are attributed not to the governing regime and its agents, barring perhaps some 'loose cannons' in the ranks of the latter, but to uncontrollable elements of the eastern Anatolian Muslim population. But even if this position had solid basis in the evidence, which it does not, it would not account for the way the regime had foreseen and thus effectively intended what those measures entailed in practice.[4]

Jurisprudence has codified common-sense concepts like inferable intent and indirect (or oblique) intent precisely in recognition that while intent may not be pre-announced in specific terms, patterns of action speak to prevailing assumptions, and certain actions have predictable results irrespective of the intentions that the implementers claim to have. If, via a remarkable faith in the good offices of the Committee of Union and Progress, one continues to believe that the central government was not implicated in the repeated mass murder of the deportees, even though it continued to systematically deport in the knowledge of such murder, then the deportation destination – the deserts of Iraq and Syria – is sufficient indicator of lethal intent, as we shall hear directly from the prime orchestrator of the genocide. But that faith would anyway have to be accompanied by a disregard for or wilfully naive reading of a significant body of evidence bequeathed by the perpetrators, some of which is coded in euphemism or worded in the interests of plausible deniability, as well as a vast corpus of non-Ottoman witness sources (including those of the Ottoman allies Germany and Austria-Hungary, and the neutral USA).[5] Ultimately it is impossible for those denying inferable genocidal intent directed against the Armenian population in general, or relating it to a pragmatic agenda of wartime security in the provinces bordering Russia in the spring of

4 The incorrect notion of removal limited to the eastern provinces, of purely temporary security measures and purely temporary confiscation of property has made its way up to some contributions to a recent issue of *Middle East Critique*, 20:3 (Fall 2011).

5 See the bibliographical essay to this chapter below.

1915, to explain such atrocities as the mass burning alive of orphans in the deserts in 1916, and myriad other murderous assaults over a vast area and many months against people of all ages and both sexes.

Preoccupation with the applicability of 'genocide' has perhaps had its greatest impact on historical writing in this area of proving intent. In response to the agendas of those who want to deny that anything approaching genocide took place in 1915–16, some scholars of Armenian history have sought to find *the* moment, decision, blueprint – perhaps prior to the war, and certainly prior to spring 1915 – with which to prove Young Turk intent for everything that followed from that point. This pastiche of some facets of legal thought, using the inappropriate model of the lone criminal who puts his plan on paper prior to packing a gun and to shooting his victim, obscures the nature of genocides as political processes. Such processes develop incrementally as a result of multiple decisions and inputs over significant periods of time, out of reciprocal relations between metropolitan regime centres and policy implementers 'in the field', and via the interaction of ideological outlook and contingencies. To recognise this is to concede no ground to the deniers. Any claim that the destruction of the Armenians when it unfolded was not a genocide, simply because there might not be unequivocal evidence of genocidal intent prior to, say, the major deportation orders of May 1915, is as wrongheaded as the suggestion that the Nazi 'final solution' was not a genocide because it was not inscribed before the invasion of Poland in 1939 or even the USSR in 1941, that all Jews within German reach were to be murdered.

The unusually extensive character of the Armenian genocide is indeed sometimes masked by contrast with the even more extensive Nazi German assault against Jews in the Second World War. Using the Holocaust as a legal, historical or, come to that, normative, benchmark for qualification as genocide is one of the favoured tools of many of those who argue against the applicability of the word genocide to the Ottoman treatment of the Armenians in the First World War. But such an approach runs counter to the clear intentions of the progenitor of the neologism 'genocide' (Lemkin, for whom the Armenian case was vital in the conceptualisation of the crime), the very wording of the convention with its depiction of genocide as a repeated blight on humanity, the great majority of social scientific enquiries into the phenomenon and the conclusions of the most notable legal experts to have examined the Armenian case.[6] One of the

6 The legal concept of genocide is the focus of William Schabas's *Genocide in International Law: The Crime of Crimes*, 2nd edn (Cambridge University Press, 2009). Schabas deals with the Armenian case in, *inter alia*, *Unimaginable Atrocities: Justice, Politics, and Rights at the War Crimes Tribunals* (Oxford University Press, 2012).

unfortunate effects of promoting the Holocaust to benchmark is to further the idea that all perpetrators of genocide must be like the Nazis, all genocidal states must look like modern Germany. Another is to trade on a concept of the Holocaust as a firmly pre-planned, always centrally determined and absolutely all-encompassing crime in a way that recent specialist scholarship has drawn into question. It is to create a benchmark that does not in all respects even work for the benchmark case.[7] That said, it is often forgotten in the rush to point out differences between the Armenian genocide and the Holocaust that Nazi leaders prosecuted at Nuremberg for crimes including the murder of the Jews were charged with 'crimes against humanity', not 'genocide', which had yet to pass into international law – and 'crimes against humanity' was precisely the term that the Entente used in their official pronouncement of May 1915 to describe Ottoman policies towards Christians.

One legitimate area of scholarly disagreement about the nature of genocide concerns the concept of 'destruction' of a group. An influential strand, bolstered by the jurisprudence of the genocide convention, puts emphasis above all on *physical destruction*. Even here, emphases differ on the relative weight that should be given on the one hand to *existential destruction*, namely murder and acts detrimental to physical survival and reproduction, and on the other hand *spatial destruction* (forced removal, 'ethnic cleansing'), with the courts – and the present authors – tending to require a significant element of the former. Another area of disagreement concerns the weight that should be given to *cultural destruction* as opposed to physical destruction, where the former concerns attacks not on the physical bodies of members of the groups, but on the conditions of their communal existence and reproduction, such as language rights and cultural institutions.

These distinctions are ideal type; slippage may occur between (a) the two sorts of physical destruction and (b) either of those and manifestations of cultural destruction. To be sure, the relative scale, intensity and manifest aim of any given type of destruction remain important. To take the matter of

7 The clearest recent instance of contrasting the two cases is the book by the Turkish diplomat Yücel Güçlü, *The Holocaust and the Armenian Case in Comparative Perspective* (Lanham, MD: University Press of America, 2012). For observations that Guenter Lewy, in his *The Armenian Massacres in Ottoman Turkey: A Disputed Genocide* (Salt Lake City, UT: University of Utah Press, 2005), seems to make the Holocaust into the paradigm of genocide, see Hans-Lukas Kieser's review in *Vierteljahreshefte für Zeitgeschichte – Rezensionen in den sehepunkten*, 7 (2007), p. 29. For the limits of Lewy's approach as it might be applied to the Holocaust, see Mark Levene's review of another of Lewy's works – in this case arguing that the Nazi murder of Europe's Roma and Sinti did not constitute genocide, in *Journal of Contemporary History* 37:2 (2002), pp. 275–92.

'cultural genocide' (if there is such a thing), the importance of scale, intensity and manifest aim requires us to be cautious, in order not to expand the concept to a point where it loses utility, say, in the matter of considering consumer goods as agents of 'cultural genocide'. To take distinction (a), there is clearly an analytical difference between a massacre committed with the intention of encouraging a population to flee a certain space where there is indeed somewhere safer to flee or be deported to and a massacre conducted to eliminate a captive population, and the difference in death tolls between such situations is likely to be very great.[8] Blends of and slippages between different modalities of destruction are, however, more characteristic of messy reality, with its dynamic, evolving situations and multiplicity of actors and agendas. Different combinations and intensities of types of destruction may be witnessed in the war records of a number of participants, and they helped contour the landscape in which the Armenian genocide occurred.

A landscape of sub-genocidal and pre-genocidal violence

For every case of outright genocide, however defined, there are more instances of unrealised genocidal potential, as well as policies and actions with some 'family resemblances' to genocide. Moreover, it is common for *genocidaires* to target multiple groups, even if their policies of persecution or destruction are uneven in severity and varied in manifestation. For instance, in the Ottoman case, from spring 1916 onwards, hundreds of thousands of Kurds were deported from eastern areas near to the war front and dispersed by settlement in western Anatolia. The deportations were conducted by the same office within the Interior Ministry that had orchestrated the earlier, murderous Armenian deportations. The specific goals of the policies were distinct: in the Kurdish case the goal was forcible assimilation within the collective body of 'Turkic' Sunni Muslims at the point of relocation, so while the death toll was nevertheless high because of logistical issues, the Kurds were neither deported to areas where life was impossible nor attacked en route.[9]

8 Philipp Ther, *Die dunkle Seite der Nationalstaaten: 'Ethnische Säuberungen' im modernen Europa* (Göttingen: Vandenhoeck & Ruprecht, 2011).

9 Fuat Dündar, *İttihat ve Terakki'nin Müslümanları İskân Politikası, 1913–1918* (Istanbul: İletişim Yayınları, 2001), pp. 139–55; Jakob Künzler, *In the Land of Blood and Tears* (Arlington, MA: Armenian Cultural Foundation, 2007), pp. 67–9; and Uğur Ümit Üngör, *The Making of Modern Turkey: Nation and State in Eastern Anatolia, 1913–1950* (Oxford University Press, 2011), pp. 107–22.

Nevertheless, the fate of these Kurds was linked to that of the Armenians by the developing ideology of Turkish ethno-nationalism (Turkism) and the associated belief that some populations were inherently more reliable in the new Turkified order than others.

To take one further step, an essential component of the outlook of the Ottoman rulers by 1915–16 was that some of the 'reliable' peoples moved into areas vacated by Armenians and Kurds were themselves Muslim victims or descendants of victims. Victimhood had been imposed during expulsion from now Christian-, formerly Ottoman-ruled lands in the Balkans, especially since the 'Eastern Crisis' of 1875–8 and more recently in the Balkan wars of 1912–13, and from the Caucasus, especially since the Crimean War and again the 'Eastern Crisis'. These expulsions would almost all fit the description of what has latterly been called 'ethnic cleansing'. Some of the killers of the Armenian deportees sprang from the milieu of recent and previous refugees, as did some of the most murderous Ottoman officials, such as Dr Mehmed Reşid, governor of Diyarbekir province, while some of the highest-ranking members of the Committee of Union and Progress and its post-war nationalist successor movements were natives of recently lost territories, notably the top leaders Talat Pasha and Mustafa Kemal Atatürk. The very organisation that conducted the Armenian deportations, what became the IAMM, the Directorate for the Settlement of Tribes and Immigrants, had been set up during the Balkan wars to deal with the influx of hundreds of thousands of desperate people from what had been the core land of the Ottoman Empire since the fourteenth century. The tale of the *muhacir* (refugees) and the IAMM indicates some sort of transmission belt of anti-civilian, state-minority violence across boundaries, reminding us of the important international context of mass atrocity.

For all these reasons, our chapter is mindful not just of the broader population policies of the Ottoman state, but the violent political landscape of a very large part of 'greater Europe' from the Baltic to the Black Sea and the eastern Mediterranean. The most extensive anti-civilian violence occurred in the lands of the older dynastic land empires in the east, south-east and east-central parts of the continent, where battlefronts were least stable, 'population problems' most toxic and, ultimately, where state frameworks fell under greatest pressure to act for their survival.

Clearly the turmoil of the Romanov and Ottoman Empires in particular did not correspond neatly to the 1914–18 parameters of the Great War *stricto sensu*, the conflict which is the main subject of this volume and chapter. The wars of the late Ottoman Empire extend to the conclusion of the Greco-Turkish conflict in 1922, as did ethnic and religious killing. We would also have needed to go beyond 1918 in order to consider the Russian civil war, as well as the Polish-Ukrainian and Russo-Polish wars. Each of those conflicts witnessed extensive atrocities against civilian populations, including anti-Jewish pogroms committed by most parties, though genocide as such is not identifiable in any. The small but vicious wars for territory and population homogeneity in Transcaucasia from 1818–1920 reunite the Ottoman and Russian trajectories, because the condition for temporarily independent Armenian, Georgian and Azerbaijani state agendas was the inability of either of the traditional regional powers to command that space prior to the reconfiguration of the Romanov Empire as the USSR and the residual Ottoman Empire as the Republic of Turkey.

If the First World War in Western Europe was free of genocidal atrocities, we can detect some continuities outside Europe between wartime violence and pre-war violence towards non-white colonial populations. While the nation-state combatants provided little in the direction of genocide during the 1914–18 war, one episode may have had some of the requisite characteristics. In the Upper Volta region of France's African empire, French forces with significantly superior weaponry responded to a massive revolt mounted from late in 1915 against imperial impositions including conscription. The precise death toll of the 'Volta-Bani War' is unknown. At least 30,000 Africans from the resisting communities were killed on or immediately around the battlefield in engagements that were often very one-sided in bodycount, but there were smaller confrontations, beyond the major pitched battles, of which no records exist. Taking into account the nature of the known French measures, which included literal obliteration of villages, the use of women and children as hostages and the destruction of the agricultural and pastoral basis of life for entire communities, the total mortality figure was surely vastly greater.[10]

In the European theatre of operations, some of the most murderous dynamics in the period operated along ethno-religious cleavages, from the Ottoman murder and expulsion of Armenian Christians to the Russian assaults on Jews and Muslims. Fantasies linking betrayal by 'enemies' within borders with fear of downfall and defeat were as important as the real threats

10 Mahir Şaul and Patrick Yves Royer, *West African Challenge to Empire: Culture and History in the Volta-Bani Anticolonial War* (Athens, OH: Ohio University Press, 2001), including pp. 2–5, 24–5 on scale and some tentative comparative considerations. Thanks to Mark Levene for drawing attention to this episode: see his *The Crisis of Genocide*, vol. I: *Devastation: The European Rimlands, 1912–1938* (Oxford University Press, 2013) for additional contextualisation.

posed by war, and in both the Ottoman and Romanov war efforts, suspicions of subversive intent were inflated beyond all reason; some internal populations were easier to stigmatise than others, though, and this is where older religious stereotypes obtained most clearly.

One sphere in which newer and older preoccupations met is the economic. Friedrich List's old doctrine of national economy (in Turkish *milli iktisat*) appealed to a number of polities trying to move the levers of economic control into the hands of – as they saw it – ethnically 'trustworthy' middle classes. European Jewish and Ottoman Christian communities alike provided particular targets for state-sponsored expropriation as well as popular plundering under conditions of war, given the commercial and financial functions into which some of their number had been channelled by the traditional norms of the dominant populations.

A clear illustration of the power of fantasy is the continent-wide paranoia about Jewish influence and subversion that was given such a boost by the Bolshevik Revolution but was already present throughout the war and on both sides. From the outset of the war Jews were removed by Russian forces from areas near the front, and the conquest of Habsburg territory saw the Russian army and its Cossack regiments as well as elements of local populations engaged in pogroms against Galician and Bukovinan Jews in September 1914. The imaginary Jewish 'internationale' was scapegoated for early Russian military failures and targeted 'pre-emptively', as in the mass deportations of Russian Jews that occurred in the face of the Austro-German offensive of spring 1915.[11]

A combination of anti-Semitism, insurgency paranoia and licence to pursue economic and demographic reorganisation at a crisis moment in the spring of 1915 lay behind the deportation eastwards, not only of up to a million Jews, but hundreds of thousands of Volhynian and other ethnic Germans (who were dubbed 'colonists' on account of the circumstances of their earlier settlement). The conditions of deportation, at times by railway, could be deadly under wartime conditions, though much hinged on the destination. By the time that the major Armenian deportations began in spring 1915, the Russian authorities

11 Eric Lohr, *Nationalising the Russian Empire: The Campaign against Enemy Aliens during World War One* (Cambridge, MA: Harvard University Press, 2003); Peter Gatrell, *A Whole Empire Walking: Refugees in Russia during the First World War* (Bloomington, IN: Indiana University Press, 1999); Alexander V. Prusin, *Nationalizing a Borderland: War, Ethnicity, and Anti-Jewish Violence in East Galicia, 1914–1920* (Tuscaloosa, AL: University of Alabama Press, 2005); and Peter Holquist, 'Les violences de l'armée russe à l'encontre des Juifs en 1915: causes et limites', in John Horne (ed.), *Vers la guerre totale: le tournant de 1914–15* (Paris: Tallandier, 2010), pp. 191–219.

in the Caucasus had also considered mass deportation of Muslims from the provinces bordering the Ottoman Empire, against the backdrop both of massacres of Muslims in the area by Russian troops, including Cossacks, and the collaboration of at least a few thousand Caucasian Muslim fighters with Ottoman forces, and smaller, targeted deportations. Despite having about as much (and thus as little) proximate 'justification' for such expansive measures as their Ottoman counterparts, the deportations did not, however, occur.

Why not? Russian policy did not become totalising, according to Peter Holquist, because, despite the great wartime power of the military, Russia remained an authoritarian state run along bureaucratic and functional rather than radical political lines. Amongst other things, this framework enabled something like a realistic threat assessment of the political state of the Transcaucasian Muslim communities – something that was utterly lacking in Ottoman policy towards the Armenians.[12] A structural explanation based on disunity between military and civilian authorities is also provided by Alexander Prusin to account for the fact that tsarist anti-Jewish policy did not progress from spatial destruction to existential destruction in spring–summer 1915.[13]

Both Holquist's and Prusin's explanations offer important contrasts with the contemporary Ottoman regime, but they are not entirely uncontested, and can be qualified by consideration of additional explanatory factors and other wartime episodes. In the case of Russian Jewish policy, Mark Levene suggests that the same Judeophobia that stimulated Russian atrocities, deportation and dispossession also served to temper Russian policies once the Russian leadership felt that international – 'Jewish' – pressure was being brought to bear. Such 'strategic' thinking was of a piece with the British offer of a Jewish national home in the Ottoman Palestinian territory Britain had earmarked for post-war control. Here, as Levene has also shown, the idea was that the policy would attract 'international Jewish support' for the Allied war effort and away from that of the Central Powers.[14] (Of course the libellous German *Judenzählung*, or 'Jew-count' of serving soldiers of 1916, shows how little Berlin felt itself allied with world Jewry, as does the ease with which

12 Peter Holquist, 'The politics and practice of the Russian occupation of Armenia, 1915–February 1917', in Ronald Grigor Suny, Fatma Müge Göçek and Norman M. Naimark (eds.), *A Question of Genocide: Armenians and Turks at the End of the Ottoman Empire* (New York: Oxford University Press, 2011), pp. 151–74, especially pp. 158–63.

13 Prusin, *Nationalising a Borderland*, p. 56.

14 Mark Levene, 'The Balfour Declaration: a case of mistaken identity', *English Historical Review*, 107 (1992), pp. 54–77. On Russian Jewish policy, see Levene, *The Crisis of Genocide*, vol. I.

German and other Jews were made scapegoats for the final German defeat in the war.) As to actions against Muslims, it was only a year later that the bloodiest tsarist campaign of the war targeting civilians began, against Islamic populations in central Asia.

The extremity of the violence – even by Russian military standards – of the campaign of murder and dispersal against the Kyrgyz and Kazakh Dungan populations of the Semireche region is again only explicable conjuncturally. Harsh repression followed a revolt against conscription, including the slaughter of recently arrived Russian settlers; but the state response had a distinctly colonialist tinge, and as such was characterised by the same sorts of violence that other European states had hitherto tended to reserve for their extra-European colonies. For the native population, the imperatives of total war, expressed through conscription, reinforced the existing logic of increasing state penetration into a periphery, and both were rejected at the same time. The Russian response, whose impact is known in Kyrgyz collective memory as the *Urkun*, issued in perhaps 100,000 direct deaths and the departure of hundreds of thousands of refugees, some of whom escaped to Chinese Turkestan, while many others perished in the exodus. This repressive episode was aimed not just at ending the insurgency, but at securing the region under Russian control for the long term.[15]

A combination of long- and short-term factors was to prove even more comprehensively destructive in the Ottoman Empire from 1915–16. The course of Ottoman genocide during the First World War was certainly closely linked to developments in the conflict, especially in this case in the eastern Mediterranean and on the Caucasus–eastern Anatolian fronts. As regards Ottoman history, however, the violent ethnic polarisation by the First World War contrasts sharply with the earlier emergence of a unique set of reforms instituted in the quest to modernise the Empire by an ambitious synthesis of Western ideas and the previous history of the multi-religious and multi-ethnic character of Muslim rule. Of these reform programmes the most urgent and contentious on the eve of the Great War concerned the eastern provinces of Anatolia, areas largely populated by Kurds and Armenians and bordering the Russian Empire. Thus we move to the central case of this chapter.

15 Edward D. Sokol, *The Revolt of 1916 in Russian Central Asia* (Baltimore, MD: Johns Hopkins University Press, 1954); for the deeper colonial context, see also Richard Pierce, *Russian Central Asia, 1867–1917: A Study in Colonial Rule* (Berkeley, CA: University of California Press, 1960).

War and genocide in the Ottoman Empire

At the time of the Young Turk Revolution of 1908, reform-oriented groups as different as the 'Young Turks', the Armenian Revolutionary Federation (ARF), American missionaries and Zionists all hoped for a constitutional Ottoman Empire which would frame the future of the Middle East. Even in this pre-war period, however, the enthusiastic common departure of 1908 was followed by boycott movements and press campaigns against Ottoman Christians, as external and internal tensions increased. Among young and educated Turkish-speaking Muslims and in the cohort of Young Turk activists in the early 1910s, a new ideology of radical, though not yet violent, Turkism loomed large, and with this the belief that an apocalyptic moment in the history of Turkish survival had arrived. Deeply frustrated, and acquainted with war since the Italian usurpation of Ottoman Libya in 1911 and then the Balkan wars, Young Turk activists saw the outbreak of the world war as an opportunity to forge a 'new deal' internally and in their external relations.[16]

The central committee of the Young Turk Committee of Union and Progress (CUP) controlled the Ottoman government as the result of a putsch of January 1913. Its members were the first revolutionary *komitaji*s of the twentieth century to accede to the reins of an empire. Radical ideologists gained civilian power, foreshadowing future radical phenomena in Europe. Before the Bolshevik Revolution, no other regime in greater Europe exercised violence of a comparable kind, scale and scope against a group of its own citizens during war as did the Young Turk regime, which obliterated the distinction between civilian and military targets and systematically cultivated propaganda and hatred against domestic populations.

In terms of internal politics, the Ottoman reform programme of 1908 had depended on cooperation between the ARF and the CUP.[17] In particular, it depended on the establishment of security and the restitution of property in the eastern provinces, or, in contemporary terminology, it depended on the solution of the Armeno-Kurdish agrarian question.[18] Anti-Armenian pogroms in Cilician Adana in April 1909, after a counter-coup by Islamist elements in the capital, helped rend the new Young Turk–Armenian fabric. The pogroms

16 The CUP triumvir Jemal Pasha is outspoken on this point: Djemal [Jemal] Pasha, *Memories of a Turkish Statesman 1913–1919* (London: Hutchinson, 1922), pp. 353–54.

17 Dikran M. Kaligian, *Armenian Organization and Ideology under Ottoman Rule, 1908–1914* (New Brunswick, NJ: Transaction Publishers, 2011).

18 Hans-Lukas Kieser, 'Réformes ottomanes et cohabitation entre chrétiens et Kurdes (1839–1915)', *Etudes Rurales*, 186 (January 2011), pp. 43–60.

were reminiscent of the Anatolia-wide massacres of approximately 100,000 mostly male Armenians in 1895.

The 1895 massacres had been the culmination of complex social and political developments over about three generations. The uprisings in the Balkans from 1875 and the consequent Ottoman-Russian war of 1877–8 had led to dramatic territorial losses in the Balkans, the Caucasus and Cyprus, all sealed at the Berlin Congress in 1878. As a consequence, the new sultan Abdulhamid II (r. 1876–1909) considered the more inclusive political principles of the earlier Tanzimat reform period a failure, and set on policies no longer designed to increase the equality of Christians but to empower the Muslims in Asia Minor, which was increasingly the Empire's core land given the territorial losses of previous decades. Abdulhamid II obstructed reforms in the eastern provinces because he feared they would lead to more British or Russian influence or the territorial autonomy of the Christians, as had happened in the Balkans. The Armenians, on the contrary, insisted on the reforms promised in Article 61 of the Berlin Treaty. When those reforms failed to appear, educated young Armenians founded revolutionary parties which championed armed rural self-defence and an activism informed by socialist and nationalist revolutionary ideas and directed against Ottoman authorities and Armenian notables. The 1895 massacres of Armenians took place against this background, and as an immediate reaction to a first detailed reform plan finally initiated by European diplomacy. Armenian land and property was seized by Kurds and other Muslims, and reform plans were again adjourned.[19]

While the programme of the party then most involved in revolutionary action, the Hntchaks, advocated an independent socialist Armenia for all inhabitants in the predominantly Kurdo-Armenian eastern provinces, the ARF or Dashnak party, which prevailed after the 1890s, set on an Armenian future within a reformed Ottoman state. As restitution and reform in the eastern provinces did not transpire after 1908, the ARF announced the end of its alliance with the CUP in August 1912, two months before the first Balkan war began. At the end of the same year, Armenian representatives contacted foreign diplomats to press for reforms.[20]

19 Jelle Verheij, 'Diyarbekir and the Armenian crisis of 1895', in Joost Jongerden and Jelle Verheij, *Social Relations in Ottoman Diyarbekir 1870–1915* (Leiden: Brill, 2012), pp. 85–145; and Jelle Verheij, 'Die armenischen Massaker von 1894–1896: Anatomie und Hintergründe einer Krise', in Hans-Lukas Kieser (ed.), *Die armenische Frage und die Schweiz (1896–1923)* (Zurich: Chronos Verlag, 1999), pp. 69–129.

20 Rober Koptaş, 'Zohrab, Papazyan ve Pastırmacıyan'ın kalemlerinden 1914 Ermeni reformu ve İttihatçı-Taşnak müzakeleri', *Tarih ve Toplum Yeni Yaklaşımlar*, 5 (Spring 2007), pp. 159–78.

Like the Hamidian government two decades before, the CUP government finally signed the reform plan on 8 February 1914. It divided the eastern provinces into northern and southern parts; put them under the control of two European inspectors, to be selected from neutral countries; prescribed publication of laws and official pronouncements in local languages; provided for an adequate proportion of Muslims and Christians in councils and police; and transformed the *Hamidiye*, an irregular Kurdish cavalry that, since its creation in 1891, had threatened non-Sunni groups in the eastern provinces, into cavalry reserves.[21] The signed plan was not in itself a first step towards Armenian autonomy, nor towards Russian annexation.[22] Nevertheless, leading CUP members had already signalled to their former revolutionary brothers of the ARF, as they had called themselves mutually, and to other Armenian representatives that by broaching the issue of reform internationally, they had crossed a red line with regard to a common future.[23]

In spring 1914, after hesitant steps towards population exchanges with its Greek and Bulgarian neighbours in the Balkans, on the Ottoman western coast, the CUP began to implement an agenda of anti-Christian demographic engineering diametrically opposed to the spirit of the reform plan for the east. The paramilitaries of its newly founded 'Special Organisation' terrorised and expelled from the Aegean littoral some 200,000 *Rûm* (the Greek- or Turkish-speaking Ottoman Christians of the Greek Orthodox Faith). When on 6 July the Ottoman parliament discussed the expulsions, Talat, Minister of Interior, member of the CUP's central committee and the most influential politician in the Ottoman 1910s, emphasised the need to settle the Muslim refugees of the Balkans in those emptied villages. If they

21 Plan published in Turkish in Yusuf H. Bayur, *Türk inkılâbı tarihi*, 3 vols. (Ankara: Türk Tarih Kurumu basımevi, 1991), vol. II, part 3, pp. 169–72; in French, taken from the *Livre orange russe*, no. 147, in André N. Mandelstam, *Le sort de l'empire ottoman* (Lausanne: Payot, 1917), pp. 236–38; first draft and final plan in German in Djemal Pascha, *Erinnerungen eines türkischen Staatsmannes* (Munich: Drei Masken Verlag, 1922), pp. 340–51. See Zekeriya Türkmen, *Vilayât-ı Şarkiye Islahat Müffettişliği* (Ankara: Türk Tarih Kurumu, 2006).

22 In the eyes of the CUP and of nationalist Republican historiography, however, it was. See Bayur, *Türk inkılâbı tarihi*, vol. II: 3, pp. 172–7. Talat Pasha's, Halil Bey's and, in particular, Jemal Pasha's memoirs, which reproduce both the final plan and the first Russian draft, prove the critical importance of this point: see *Hatıraları ve mektuplarıyla Talât Paşa*, ed. Osman S. Kocahanoğlu (Istanbul: Temel, 2008), pp. 38–44; İsmail Arar (ed.), *Osmanlı mebusan meclisi reisi Halil Menteşe'nin anıları* (Istanbul: Hürriyet Vakfi, 1986), pp. 173–6; and Djemal, *Erinnerungen*, pp. 337–53.

23 Koptaş, 'Zohrab', pp. 170–5.

were sent to the vast deserts of Syria and Iraq, he added, they would all die of hunger. Those deserts were precisely the destinations of the Armenians deported the following year.[24]

The international crisis of July 1914 saved the regime from a diplomatic backlash against the expulsion, and gave it room for manoeuvre and the opportunity to finally win over a formal ally. In autumn 1914, however, the Empire's German ally, eager to win over neutral Greece, insisted that acts of violence against *Rûm* henceforth be avoided. Approximately 300,000 *Rûm* were removed from different coastal regions to the interior in the course of the First World War, beginning in February 1915, and while some of the deportees suffered very violent attacks, they were neither systematically massacred nor sent into the desert.[25]

The German attitude to an alliance with the Ottoman Empire changed from the negative in late July 1914, when War Minister Enver Pasha made a proposal to the German ambassador Hans Freiherr von Wangenheim. Fears of an Ottoman alignment with the Entente had arisen, and Kaiser Wilhelm stressed that they must seize the opportunity to gain Turkey as an ally.[26] The secret alliance was concluded on 2 August 1914. Under its shield, the Young Turk regime began to implement its own domestic agenda and, despite being the junior alliance partner, improved its bargaining position vis-à-vis a senior partner eagerly anticipating Ottoman action against Russia, when the German campaign in northern France turned into stalemate. For their part, the Germans, who had been involved in the reform negotiations, did not seriously anticipate the launching of a campaign of extermination, and certainly did little of substance to prevent it. Indeed, on 6 August, Wangenheim portentously accepted six new Ottoman proposals, among them the abolition of the hated capitulations and 'a small correction of her [Turkey's] eastern border which shall place Turkey into direct contact with the Moslems of Russia'.[27] In contrast to Germany, Russia insisted on the continuation of the Armenian reforms in negotiations about the eventuality of an alliance; Russian

24 Fuat Dündar, *Crime of Numbers: The Role of Statistics in the Armenian Question (1878–1918)* (New Brunswick, NJ: Transaction Publishers, 2010), pp. 78–9; figures from Ahmet Efiloğlu.

25 Akçam, *The Young Turks' Crime*, pp. 97–123; figures from Ahmet Efiloğlu.

26 For the alliance with Germany and its implementation, see Mustafa Aksakal, *The Ottoman Road to War in 1914: The Ottoman Empire and the First World War* (Cambridge University Press, 2008), pp. 93–118; and Ulrich Trumpener, *Germany and the Ottoman Empire 1914–1918* (Princeton University Press, 1968), pp. 21–61.

27 Trumpener, *Germany and the Ottoman Empire*, p. 28.

representatives detected a lack of German sincerity with regard to the Armenians.[28]

Strong pan-Turkist and pan-Islamist propaganda began to appear in the Ottoman press in early August 1914.[29] Together with the suspension of the reform plan, this discourse alienated and intimidated the Ottoman non-Muslims, in particular in the eastern provinces, from the outset of the conflict. At the same time the regime started to make plans for joint hostilities with Russia. Bahaeddin Şakir, a senior CUP member and chief of the Special Organisation, invited the leaders of the ARF to lead an anti-Russian guerrilla war in the Caucasus, aimed at preparing a future Ottoman conquest.[30] Dr Paul Schwarz, a German agent in Erzurum, proposed that the Armenians sabotage the oil field of Baku. The Russian-born German socialist and proponent of *milli iktisat* (and architect of Lenin's return to St Petersburg in 1917), Alexander Helphand, who used the name 'Parvus', propagated a comprehensive plan of anti-tsarist insurrection in Russia's peripheral populations.[31] However, the ARF balked at these plans and stated that all Armenians should remain loyal to the country in which they lived.

Attempts at insurrection in the Caucasus without the ARF began in August,[32] while in September the regime announced the abrogation of the Capitulations and obtained large sums of money from Germany to prepare for attack. Though the Empire only officially entered the war in November, in August the Ottoman army began to mobilise and requisition to an unprecedented degree – this was but one early illustration of how, while less industrial, the World War was more 'total' in the Ottoman world than in Europe, being fought with every means at the state's disposition both outwards *and* inwards. The requisitions particularly hit non-Muslims in the eastern

28 Aksakal, *Ottoman Road*, pp. 107–8 and 127–30. For Gulkevich's telegram of 27 January 1914 see *Sbornik diplomaticheskikh dokumentov: Reformy v Armenii, 26 noiab: 1912 goda–10 maia 1914 goda* (Petrograd: Gosudarstv. Tipografija, 1915), doc. 148, pp. 165–174; with thanks to Peter Holquist for the reference.

29 Erol Köroğlu, *Ottoman Propaganda and Turkish Identity: Literature in Turkey during World War I* (London: I. B. Tauris, 2007); and Tekin Alp, *Türkismus und Pantürkismus* (Weimar: Kiepenheuer & Witsch, 1915).

30 Raymond Kévorkian, *Le génocide des Arméniens* (Paris: Odile Jacob, 2006), p. 221.

31 Wolfdieter Bihl, *Die Kaukasus-Politik der Mittelmächte: Ihre Basis in der Orient-Politik und ihre Aktionen 1914–1917* (Vienna: Böhlau Verlag, 1975), p. 66; Hans-Lukas Kieser, 'World war and world revolution: Alexander Helphand-Parvus in Germany and Turkey', *Kritika: Explorations in Russian and Eurasian History*, 12:2 (2011), pp. 387–410; and Hans-Lukas Kieser, 'Matthias Erzberger und die osmanischen Armenier im Ersten Weltkrieg', in Christopher Dowe (ed.), *'Nun danket alle Gott für diesen braven Mord' – Matthias Erzberger: Ein Demokrat in Zeiten des Hasses* (Karlsruhe: G. Braun Buchverlag, forthcoming, 2013).

32 Kévorkian, *Le génocide*, pp. 274–82.

provinces. Units of the Special Organisation began early on to terrorise and loot Armenian villages on and beyond the eastern frontier.[33] Ottoman troops, together with Kurdish tribal forces, attacked Persian Urmia, 110 kilometres east of Hakkâri in the province of Van, spreading anti-Christian jihad propaganda. Christians on the Ottoman and the Persian sides of the frontier looked to Russia for protection. From August 1914, Russia built up a local Persian–Christian militia based on Christian Armeno-Syriac solidarity.[34]

German-led Ottoman vessels attacked installations on the northern side of the Black Sea at the end of October. In reaction, Russia declared war and its Caucasus army crossed the frontier at Erzurum, but stopped before Turkish defences. Unsatisfied by his generals' defensive attitude and accompanied by his German Chief of Staff, Bronsart von Schellendorf, but against the advice of Liman von Sanders, head of the German military mission, Enver Pasha himself took the command for an offensive towards the Caucasus against numerically inferior Russian forces. On the first days of 1915 this campaign failed catastrophically in the snowy mountains of Sarıkamış. Half or even more of the 120,000 soldiers perished, and epidemics began to spread among the survivors and in the whole region.[35]

In early 1915, the campaigns with irregular forces led by Enver's brother-in-law Jevdet and Enver's uncle General Halil in northern Persia spread violence against Armenian and Syriac villages, but again failed in their military objectives. The Ottoman forces were decisively defeated in the Battle of Dilman in mid April, near to a place where hundreds of non-combatant Christians had been executed in March. General Andranik Ozanian's Armenian volunteer brigade in the Russian army participated in the battle.[36]

As a consequence of these defeats at Sarıkamış and Dilman, the pan-Turkist dream, which had galvanised the mobilisation in August 1914, turned to trauma in winter and spring 1915. The long eastern front was brutalised and

33 Hans-Lukas Kieser, *Der verpasste Friede: Mission, Ethnie und Staat in den Ostprovinzen der Türkei 1839–1938* (Zurich: Chronos Verlag, 2000), pp. 331, 335–336, 445; and Taner Akçam, *A Shameful Act: The Armenian Genocide and the Question of Turkish Responsibility* (New York: Metropolitan Books, 2006), pp. 136–8.

34 David Gaunt, 'The Ottoman treatment of the Assyrians', in Suny *et al.* (eds.), *A Question of Genocide*, pp. 244–59, here p. 249.

35 Maurice Larcher, *La Guerre Turque dans la Guerre Mondiale* (Paris: Chiron & Berger-Levrault, 1926), pp. 367–436; Joseph Pomiankowski, *Der Zusammenbruch des Ottomanischen Reiches: Erinnerungen an die Türkei aus der Zeit des Weltkrieges* (Vienna: Amalthea-Verlag, 1928), pp. 98–105; and Edward J. Erickson, *Ordered to Die: A History of the Ottoman Army in the First World War* (Westport, CT: Greenwood Press, 2000), p. 57.

36 Kévorkian, *Le génocide*, p. 285.

religiously polarised. Irregulars and regulars, militias and forces of self-defence were engaged in low-intensity warfare that took a heavy toll on civilians. Many Armenians fled to Russian Armenia, among them several thousand young Armenians who became volunteers in the Russian army. Most Christians in the eastern provinces had lost any trust in the government. Armed Christian forces, where possible, tried to rely on Russian help. Best known is the Russian relief of the Armenians in Van in mid May 1915. Since 20 April, after massacres in Armenian villages and the murder of Armenian individuals from Van, Armenian activists had resisted Jevdet's repression. Once relieved, they acted vengefully against Van's Muslim civilians, massacring many and so contributing to the flight of much larger numbers.[37] The failed campaigns and the chaotic situation at the long eastern front infuriated CUP leaders and made the local Armenian and Syriac Christians an easy target for the Ottoman propaganda of jihad.[38]

In contrast to the east, the Ottoman army in the west commanded by Liman von Sanders won its first decisive victory against the Entente naval offensive at the Dardanelles on 18 March. The widely propagated news of the victory and thus the securing of Istanbul had, according to the Austrian military attaché in Istanbul, Joseph Pomiankowski, a tremendous psychological impact on both the Turkish populace and the Young Turk leaders, who henceforth displayed a mixture of self-reliance and brutal chauvinism.[39]

Committee policies radicalised in the context of a general brutalisation of war in spring 1915. Apart from the attack on the outer forts of the Dardanelles and then the Gallipoli landings in late April, let us mention the use of poison gas on the battlefields in Belgium in April; submarine warfare against civilian vessels, e.g., the *Lusitania* in May 1915; anti-German riots in Britain and Moscow; the Gorlice-Tarnów offensive; the intensification of tsarist policies against Jews and ethnic Germans on Russia's western front; and the Russian military presence in eastern Anatolia and northern Persia. Henceforth, as Jay Winter has emphasised, the General War was called the Great War, a more total war than ever before.[40]

37 Kieser, *Der verpasste Friede*, pp. 448–53; and Bihl, *Kaukasus-Politik*, p. 233. Muslim witness accounts in Justin McCarthy, Esat Arslan, Cemalettin Taşkıran and Ömer Turan, *The Armenian Rebellion at Van* (Salt Lake City, UT: University of Utah Press, 2006), pp. 247–51.

38 David Gaunt, *Massacres, Resistance, Protectors: Muslim-Christian Relations in Eastern Anatolia during World War I* (Piscataway, NJ: Gorgias Press, 2006), p. 63.

39 Pomiankowski, *Zusammenbruch*, p. 154.

40 Jay Winter, 'Under the cover of war: the Armenian genocide in the context of total war', in Jay Winter (ed.), *America and the Armenian Genocide of 1915* (Cambridge University Press, 2004), pp. 37–51, here p. 41.

In such a military and psychological setting, the Committee government began to converge on a comprehensive anti-Armenian policy, becoming more radical at almost exactly the time that the tsarist regime discounted the most radical measures against its Transcaucasian Muslim population. Minister of the Interior Talat coordinated the developing policy in three main phases: first, the arrest of Armenian political, religious and intellectual leaders in April and May 1915; secondly, from late spring to autumn, the removal of the Armenian population of Anatolia and European Turkey to camps in the Syrian desert east of Aleppo, excluding Armenian men in eastern Anatolia who were systematically massacred on the spot; thirdly, and finally, the starvation to death of most of those in the camps and the final massacre of those who still survived. New research in the Ottoman state archives and military archives proves the new language and measures applied to the Armenians in a number of dispatches sent in this period.[41] As in other genocides, however, including the 'final solution of the Jewish question', there is no ultimate single order, but a whole complex of meetings, orders and acts from February / March through May that, taken together, amounted finally to the destruction of the Armenian nation in Asia Minor (Map 22.1).

In two long, seminal ciphered telegrams of 24 April to the provincial governors and to the army, with reference to Van and a few other places, Talat defined the situation in Asia Minor as that of a general Armenian rebellion, of Armenians helping the enemy's war efforts and of revolutionary committees that had long since wished to establish Armenian self-determination and now believed they could achieve it as a result of the war.[42] Provincial and military authorities, and in particular special CUP commissaries sent to the provinces, henceforth spread propaganda throughout Anatolia of treacherous, infidel Armenian neighbours who stabbed Muslims in the back.[43] In the night of 24 to 25 April, at the precise time of the Allied landing on Gallipoli, security forces began to arrest Armenian elites throughout Anatolia, starting with Istanbul, and to question, torture and murder most of them. Various Ottoman army sources of spring 1915 from the provinces certainly *do not* support the claim of a general uprising, albeit

41 Akçam, *The Young Turks' Crime*, pp. 158–93.

42 For the telegram to Enver Pasha, see T. C. Genelkurmay Başkanlığı, *Arşiv belgeleriyle Ermeni faaliyetleri 1914–1918* ('Armenian activities in the archive documents 1914–1918), 2 vols. (Ankara: Genelkurmay Basım Evi, 2005), vol. 1, pp. 424–5; the analogous telegram to the provinces is translated in Akçam, *The Young Turks' Crime*, pp. 186–7.

43 For example, in Eskişehir in the west (see Ahmed Refik, *İki komite, iki kital* (Ankara: Kebikeç, 1994 [1919]), pp. 28–46) or in Urfa in the south-east (see Künzler, *Blood and Tears*, pp. 16 and 21).

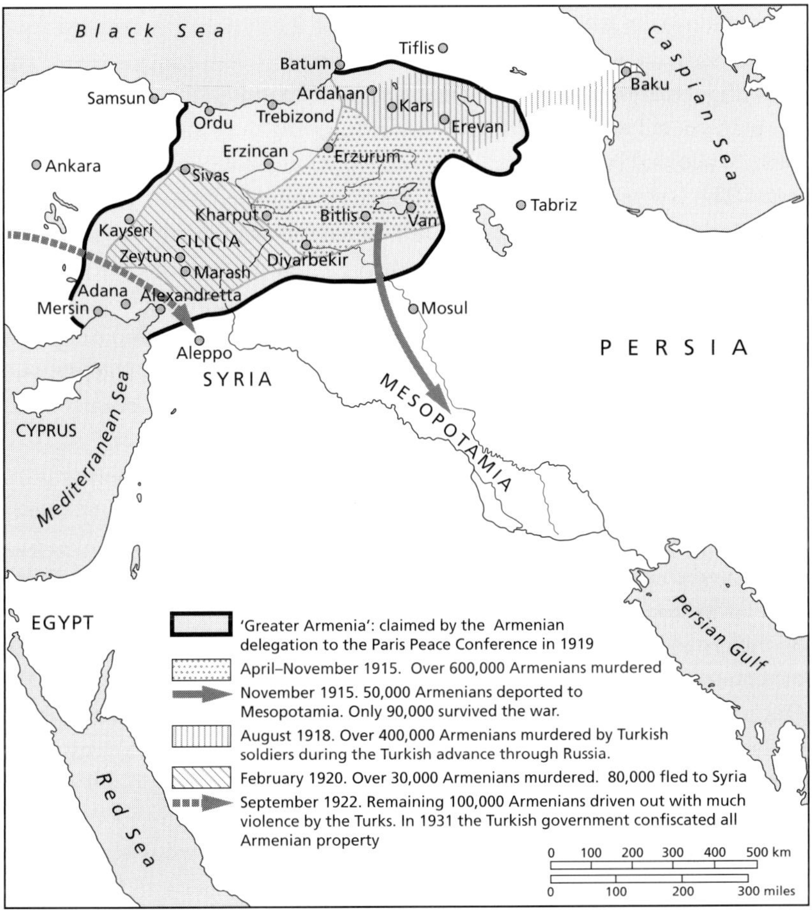

Map 22.1 The Armenian genocide.

that there were indeed instances of sabotage and some resistance to policies of oppression and massacre as well as the aforementioned desertions, while the Russian-Armenian volunteer battalions were clearly an incendiary element.[44] On the same day, 24 April, a telegram from Talat to Jemal Pasha, military

44 *Arşiv belgeleriyle Ermeni faaliyetleri 1914–1918*, vols. I and II reviewed by Hans-Lukas Kieser, 'Urkatastrophe am Bosporus: Der Armeniermord im Ersten Weltkrieg als Dauerthema internationaler (Zeit-)Geschichte', *Neue Politische Literatur*, 2 (2005), pp. 229–31; and Donald Bloxham, *The Great Game of Genocide: Imperialism, Nationalism, and the Destruction of the Ottoman Armenians* (Oxford University Press, 2005), chapter 2.

governor of Syria, announced that henceforth Armenians should be deported not to Konya, as had been the limited case of the Armenians expelled from Cilician Zeytun in March, but to northern Syria.[45]

Without mentioning the Armenians explicitly, a provisional law of 27 May – the parliament had been closed on 13 March, giving the CUP the freest of free hands – allowed repression and mass deportation if national security were at issue. The law served as legal cover for the comprehensive removal of Asia Minor's Armenians. Although it did not limit removal to clearly defined zones, and although the Entente publicly warned the Ottoman authorities of future punishment for crimes against humanity on 24 May, German officials still did not anticipate or counter the risk of an Empire-wide anti-Armenian campaign. On the contrary, they approved removals in the war zones, tried to appease German friends of the Armenians and regional experts and, in early June, backed a public Ottoman denial of what was unfolding in the east.[46]

The German approval of supposedly limited removal in the eastern provinces was a decisive breakthrough for a regime which a few months previously had found itself strictly bound to implement, under partly German pressure, a monitored co-existence of Christians and Muslims, Armenians, Syriacs, Kurds and Turks in eastern Asia Minor. Indeed, in a few instances German officers on the ground signed or approved removals. The best-documented case is that of Lieutenant Colonel Böttrich, head of the railway department of the Ottoman general staff. Against the will of the civil direction of the Baghdad Railway, he signed an order of deportation for Armenian employees of the railway, though he knew well in October 1915 that this would involve the death of most or all of them.[47] As early as mid June 1915, Enver's confidant, Hans Humann, the German naval attaché of the German embassy, stated that 'the Armenians are now more or less exterminated because they conspired with the Russians. This is hard, but useful.'[48] Ottoman propaganda succeeded

45 The Turkish Republic Prime Ministry General Directorate of the State Archives, Directorate of Ottoman Archives (ed.), *Armenians in Ottoman Documents (1915–1920)* (Ankara: Prime Ministry General Directorate of the State Archives, 1995), p. 26.

46 Political Archives of the German Foreign Office (Politisches Archiv des Auswärtiges Amts, Berlin, hereafter 'PA-AA'): Botschafter Wangenheim an PA-AA/R14086; Johannes Lepsius, *Der Todesgang des armenischen Volkes: Bericht über das Schicksal des armenischen Volkes in der Türkei während des Weltkrieges* (Potsdam: Tempelverlag, 1919), pp. v–vii; and Trumpener, *Germany and the Ottoman Empire*, pp. 209–10.

47 PA-AA/BoKon/171, 1915–11–18-DE-001.

48 Humann quoted in Hilmar Kaiser, 'Die deutsche Diplomatie und der armenische Völkermord', in Fikret Adanır and Bernd Bonwetsch (eds.), *Osmanismus, Nationalismus und der Kaukasus: Muslime und Christen, Türken und Armenier im 19. und 20. Jahrhundert* (Wiesbaden: Reichert, 2005), pp. 213–14.

in the provinces in creating the impression that the removal was German doctrine, though as the anti-Armenian measures progressed, German diplomats did mount limited and generally ineffectual protests. After his employee, Dr Mordtmann, had had a frank conversation with Talat, ambassador von Wangenheim began to understand in mid June 1915 that the supposedly limited removal from the war zones, for which the CUP government had secured German support, was part of a fully fledged programme of removal-cum-extinction throughout Asia Minor.[49] 'The expulsion and relocation of the Armenian people was limited until 14 days ago to the provinces nearest to the eastern theatre of war', Wangenheim finally wrote to Chancellor Bethmann Hollweg on 7 July, but 'since then the Porte has resolved to extend these measures also' to many other provinces, 'even though these parts of the country are not threatened by any enemy invasion for the time being. This situation and the way in which the relocation is being carried out shows that the government is indeed pursuing its purpose of eradicating the Armenian race from the Turkish Empire.'[50]

The removal of the Armenians from eastern Asia Minor mainly took place from May to September, and from western Anatolia and the province of Edirne in Thrace from July to October 1915. In eastern Anatolia, men and youngsters were mostly massacred on the spot, with those in the army – mostly already separated into unarmed labour battalions – also killed. At the Dardanelles and in Arabia, Armenian soldiers continued to fight in the Ottoman army. Removal from the west included the men and some of the deportees went by train. Women and children from central and eastern Asia Minor endured starvation, mass rape and enslavement on their marches.

In certain places, in particular the province of Diyarbekir under governor Reşid, removal amounted to the massacre of men, women and children even before they reached the provincial boundaries. On 28 September 1915, Reşid sent a telegram to the Minister of the Interior, proudly stating that he had removed 120,000 Armenians from his province.[51] On 19 October a friend named Halil Edib, vice-governor of the district of Mardin in the province of Diyarbekir, telegraphed his congratulations for the *kurban bayramı* (religious holiday), saying, 'I kiss your hands, you who have gained us the six [eastern] provinces and you have opened to us access to Turkestan [a key pan-Turkist

49 PA-AA/R14086, 1915–06–17-DE-003. English translation on the website www.armenocide.de

50 PA-AA/R14086, 1915–07–07-DE-001.

51 General Directorate of the State Archives (ed.), *Armenians in Ottoman Documents*, p. 105.

term] and to the Caucasus.'[52] The authorities of the province of Diyarbekir treated *all* Christians in a similarly murderous manner.

As early as 26 October 1914, Talat had ordered the governor of Van to remove the Christian Syriac population in Hakkâri near the Persian border. He considered this population unreliable, and wanted to disperse it among a Muslim majority in western provinces. He could not, however, implement this early policy of removal and dispersal in autumn 1914,[53] and did not transform it into a general policy of removal-cum-extermination as in the case of the Armenians. Compared to Armenian policy, indeed, centralised Syriac policy remained little articulated. In June 1915 the regime nevertheless applied a policy of destruction against the Syriac enclave in Hakkâri and also against villages near Midyat that reacted against Reşid's anti-Christian extermination. The German officer Scheubner-Richter, a member of the unit involved, considered the Syriac struggle to be 'a not unjustified defence by people who feared meeting the same fate as most Armenians'.[54] The villagers were ordered to submit to deportation. The Ottoman army could not defeat Azakh, but in the case of Hakkâri, two-thirds of about 100,000 Syriacs perished, while the others managed to escape to Russian-held territory.

Irrespective of the precise position of Talat about the Syriac future, the way in which Ottoman forces attacked the Syriac population in the provinces of Van and Diyarbekir and in northern Persia amounted to genocide.[55] Rather like the Romanies in relation to the European Jews under Nazi rule, the Syriacs / Assyro-Chaldeans were not at the centre of the perpetrating state's agenda, but nevertheless were widely killed when encountered. An authority in this area, David Gaunt presents statistics to the effect that 250,000 Syriacs were massacred or killed in fighting out of a pre-war population of 563,000 in the Ottoman Empire and Persia, though it is clear that precise figures are

52 Cited in Nejdet Bilgi, *Mehmed Reşid [Şahingiray], Hayatı ve Hâtıraları* (Izmir: Akademi Kitabevi, 1997), p. 29. For more on Halil Edib, see Uğur Ü. Üngör, 'Center and periphery in the Armenian genocide: the case of Diyarbekir province', in Hans-Lukas Kieser and Elmar Plozza (eds.), *Der Völkermord an den Armeniern, die Türkei und Europa* (Zurich: Chronos Verlag, 2006), pp. 71–88, here p. 73.

53 Order transliterated and translated in Gaunt, *Massacres*, p. 447; Hilmar Kaiser, 'Genocide at the twilight of the Ottoman Empire', in Donald Bloxham and A. Dirk Moses (eds.), *The Oxford Handbook of Genocide Studies* (Oxford University Press, 2010), pp. 365–85, here p. 371.

54 Paul Leverkühn, *Posten auf ewiger Wache: Aus dem abenteuerreichen Leben des Max von Scheubner-Richter* (Essen: Essener Verlagsanstalt, 1938), p. 83.

55 Gaunt, *Massacres*, p. 188; Kévorkian, *Le génocide*, p. 463.

impossible to obtain.[56] Most Christians, Armenians and Syriacs were massacred in, or removed from, the eastern provinces from spring 1915.

Several hundred thousand destitute Armenian deportees arrived in Syria in the summer and autumn of 1915. Most of the survivors were not resettled, as had been promised, but isolated in camps and starved to death according to rules followed by the Ministry of Interior that their local or regional demographic proportion must not exceed 2, 5 or 10 per cent.[57] Those who nevertheless survived were massacred in 1916. Ali Fuad, the governor of Der Zor, who had helped the deportees to make a new life, was replaced in July 1916 by the hardliner Salih Zeki, who organised the killings. According to an Ottoman source, 192,750 deportees concentrated near Der Zor, among them many children, were killed in the second half of 1916.[58] Only recently have scholars published witness accounts of the extreme horror of this 'second phase of the genocide' (in the phrase of Raymond Kévorkian) and studies on limited efforts to help the victims.[59]

The major group of survivors were 100,000–150,000 Armenians whom the CUP triumvir Jemal Pasha settled in southern Syria, converting them to Islam. A number of the survivors worked as forced labourers in military factories.[60] The destruction of the Ottoman Armenian community was symbolically completed on 11 August 1916, when the Armenian community's National Constitution (*Nizâmnâme*) of 1863 – the backbone of a 'menacing' Armenian dynamism according to the official news agency Millî – was abolished, and with it the Tanzimat principle of equality-cum-plurality.[61]

In contrast to the Hamidian massacres in the 1890s, conversion only warranted survival in 1915–16 if the Ministry of Interior permitted it according to the demographic rationale that underlay its vision of Turkish sovereignty in Asia Minor. Conversion of religious identity and confession of faith was

56 Gaunt, 'The Ottoman treatment of the Assyrians', p. 245.

57 Dündar, *Crime of Numbers*, pp. 113–19; and Akçam, *The Young Turks' Crime*, pp. 242–63.

58 Raymond Kevorkian, 'L'extermination des Arméniens par le régime jeune-turc (1915–1916)', in *Encyclopédie en ligne des violences de masse*, (22 March 2010), consulted 24 August 2012: www.massviolence.org/L-extermination-des-Armeniens-par-le-regime-jeune-turc-1915, 57.

59 Aram Andonian, *En ces sombres jours*, trans. Hervé Georgelin (Geneva: Métis Presses, 2007); Hilmar Kaiser, *At the Crossroads of Der Zor: Death, Survival, and Humanitarian Resistance in Aleppo, 1915–1917* (Princeton, NJ: Gomidas Institute, 2002); and Hans-Lukas Kieser, 'Beatrice Rohner's work in the death camps of Armenians in 1916', in Jacques Sémelin, Claire Andrieu and Sarah Gensburger (eds.), *Resisting Genocide: The Multiple Forms of Rescue* (New York: Columbia University Press, 2011), pp. 367–82.

60 Kévorkian, *Le génocide*, pp. 832–9.

61 See André Mandelstam, *Le sort de l'Empire Ottoman* (Lausanne and Paris: Librairie Payot, 1917), p. 284.

secondary to this rationale; or, as the governor of Trabzon put it at the beginning of July 1915, 'an Armenian converted to Islam will be expelled as a Muslim Armenian'.[62] This policy was a clear break with Muslim religious and imperial tradition, and so conversion with survival in Anatolia was a sensitive issue for the Ministry of Interior, which resolutely pursued its goal while trying to manage Muslim sensibilities and realities in the provinces. In contrast to some military doctors in the CUP reputed to be atheists, Talat was a practising Muslim.[63] During the main period of removal from July to October 1915, he prohibited conversion with few exceptions.[64]

Concerning the death toll, still the most reliable of the widely varying figures is that more than half of the nearly 2 million Ottoman Armenians alive in 1914 were killed in 1915–16. An important contribution to the discussion on the extent of the killings was the publication in 2008 of Talat's notebook, complete with demographic figures. Talat considered the Ottoman Armenian population in pre-1915 Asia Minor to be 1.5 million, of which he claimed to have removed more than 1.1 million.[65] According to the statistics of the Armenian Patriarchate, the Ottoman Armenian pre-war population numbered slightly more than 2 million. Raymond Kévorkian, who has worked on detailed Armenian demography across the genocide period, estimates that two-thirds of about 2 million Ottoman Armenians were killed, that is, approximately 1.3 million people.[66]

Beside 'Jemal's Armenians', few deportees had been able to escape and reach Aleppo. More important was the earlier escape to Erzincan and Erzurum, occupied by the Russian army in 1916. Thousands of Armenians had found refuge among the Alevis in mountainous Dersim in 1915 and were able to cross the Russian lines in 1916. Others had fled beyond the Eastern Front and returned with the advancing Russian army, which retreated after the October Revolution in November 1917. Unable to stop the return of Young Turkish rule, Armenian militias on the retreat committed massacres against Muslims, including the Alevi population, which did not support them then in

62 German consul in Trabzon, Bergfeld, to the Reichskanzler on 9 July 1915, PA-AA/R14086.

63 Hasan Babacan, *Mehmed Talât Paşa, 1874–1921* (Ankara: Türk Tarih Kurumu, 2005), p. 48.

64 Akçam, *The Young Turks' Crime*, pp. 296–301.

65 Murat Bardakçı (ed.), *Talât Paşa'nın evrâk-ı metrûkesi* (Istanbul: Everest, 2008), p. 109.

66 Kevorkian, 'L'extermination', p. 57.

that region.[67] By this time, such massacres were only one manifestation of a much wider set of inter-communal crimes committed. The fluctuation of the Caucasus/eastern Anatolian front and the infrastructural devastation of the region created tremendous insecurity for all – though again in particular for the Armenian population, among which were hundreds of thousands of refugees from Asia Minor.

The Treaty of Brest-Litovsk of 3 March 1918 allowed the relaunch of pan-Turkist schemes and raised the spectre of further Armenian extermination. Russia lost a huge part of her western Empire to Germany, but also, as in Article 4, the north-eastern corner of Asia Minor that it had acquired in the Berlin Treaty in 1878. In the eyes of the independent Social Democrats in the German Reichstag, this treaty threatened the Armenians hitherto under Russian protection in the Caucasus. The German Foreign Office confirmed in June 1918 the advance of Ottoman troops far beyond the agreement of Brest-Litovsk. More than a million people were in danger, according to Matthias Erzberger, by then a leader of the democratic opposition in the Reichstag.[68] He added that Talat's promise of protection was worthless. Enver's uncle, General Halil (Kut), in fact openly threatened to annihilate the Armenians even in Caucasian Armenia.[69]

The resolution of the world war on the Western European, southern Balkan and Syrian fronts prevented a further Ottoman advance in the Caucasus. The Republic of Armenia, declared on 28 May 1918, hoped to regain a part of north-eastern Anatolia via post-war diplomacy, but the related Treaty of Sèvres of August 1920 was not implemented. Armenia was then involved in wars with both Georgia and Azerbaijan, the latter particularly marked by anti-civilian violence by Armenian as well as Azeri forces. Soviet troops finally prevented eastern Armenia from being crushed by the Turkish nationalist forces that again advanced towards Erevan in 1920. In southern Asia Minor, around 150,000 Armenian refugees, who had resettled in Cilicia after 1918, fled when French forces retreated in 1921.[70]

67 Ahmet Refik, *İki komite, iki kitâl*, pp. 47–82; Kieser, *Der verpasste Friede*, p. 396; and Richard G. Hovannisian, *The Republic of Armenia* (Berkeley, CA: University of California, 1971), pp. 20–5.

68 Erich Matthias (ed.), *Der interfraktionelle Ausschuss 1917/18*, 2 vols. (Düsseldorf: Droste, 1959), vol. II, p. 410.

69 Hamit Bozarslan, 'L'extermination des Arméniens et des juifs: quelques éléments de comparaison', in Hans-Lukas Kieser and Dominik Schaller (eds.), *Der Völkermord an den Armeniern und die Shoah* ('The Armenian genocide and the Shoah') (Zurich: Chronos Verlag, 2002), pp. 322–3; and Kévorkian, *Le génocide*, pp. 859–76.

70 Kévorkian, *Le génocide*, pp. 913–19.

The price of 'success'

While visiting Berlin in August 1918, Talat, now Grand Vizier as well as Minister of the Interior and of Finance, realised that the war was lost, but consoled himself that 'we have given Anatolia the form of a national home and suppressed the elements of subversion and discord'.[71] This would be the basis for the future of that region. In contrast to the elites of the other empires collapsing in the 1910s, the Young Turks anticipated and successfully prepared the elements of a future that would preserve their group's hold on power. Despite their defeat, and with the exception of a few top leaders lost to the cause, the Young Turks formed the political, military and bureaucratic elite during the Greco-Turkish War and in the Republic of Turkey founded in 1923. Genocide thus successfully served the political project of an exclusively Turkish national home (*Türk Yurdu*) in Asia Minor. The founders of the nation-state, both the cohort under Talat Pasha in the 1910s and the cohort under Mustafa Kemal Atatürk in the interwar period, preserved the hegemony of Turkish-speaking Sunni Muslims who had been politically predominant in the Ottoman Empire. Until the end of the Cold War, their master narrative of modern Turkish renewal against tremendous odds largely influenced international historiography, along the way suppressing research on Young Turk crimes against humanity.[72] That intellectual situation has now changed markedly.

The Young Turks' worldview was more ethno-religious and cultural than the Nazis' more biological and ethno-racial ideology, though both were social Darwinist in character.[73] In both cases, young imperial elites and (would-be) saviours of empire traumatically had lived through and witnessed the loss of power, prestige, territory and homes in their youth. Driven by the *angst* of ruin, they succeeded in establishing a single-party regime that allowed them to implement revolutionary policies of change, including the expulsion and extermination of domestic 'enemy' groups. The removal of the Armenians was the most systematically murderous episode in an evolving campaign of demographic engineering in Turkey from 1913 onwards. With few exceptions,

71 Quoted in Muhittin Birgen, *İttihat ver Terakki'de on sene: İttihat ve Terakki neydi?* (Istanbul: Kitap Yayınevi, 2006), p. 460. Birgen was the chief-editor of *Tanin* and a personal counsel of Talat.

72 Bloxham, *The Great Game of Genocide*, Part 3; Hans-Lukas Kieser, 'Armenians, Turks, and Europe in the shadow of World War I: recent historiographical developments', in Kieser and Plozza (eds.), *Der Völkermord an den Armeniern, die Türkei und Europa*, pp. 43–60.

73 For comparative approaches see the bibliographical essay to this chapter below.

all Anatolian Christians were also excluded from the Turko-Muslim national struggle for Asia Minor after 1918 and, both demographically and culturally, from the construction of the new Republic of Turkey. The presumption that certain populations were inherently problematic by virtue of their identity ultimately underpinned a 'successful' model for eliminating the issue of minorities through forced resettlement. This rationale was condoned by Western diplomacy in the 1923 Treaty of Lausanne, with Britain in particular using 'population exchange' as a way of washing its hands of a demographic problem it had such a hand in creating by its earlier support of the Greek army of occupation and then by the policy of 'pacification' in Anatolia.

Behind the sanitised rhetoric of 'population exchange' lay hideous human realities, not least because for the vast majority of Ottoman 'Greeks' to whom the language of exchange was applied, the Treaty of Lausanne was just confirmation of a fait accompli. Only 190,000 were transferred in the sense meant, of the up to 1.25 million Christians – mainly 'Greek' Orthodox Christians from western Anatolia and the Pontus – who left Asia Minor for Greece, most of whom were quite literally fleeing for their lives. The Greek occupying presence in western Anatolia from May 1919 had served to further Athenian and Anglo-French geopolitics, but its use as a counterweight to Kemal's revived nationalist movement led to full-scale war in 1921–2. The Greek army and its collaborators committed numerous massacres against civilian populations and destroyed infrastructure vital to the life of many, especially in the scorched-earth retreat, but they met a foe that was at least as ruthless and ultimately, in its success, even more violent. The Turkish nationalist army drove the Greek forces back to the sea, and with them swathes of the remaining Christian population, murdering large numbers of them in the process and others through forced labour. A further mass exodus of terrorised Christians occurred after the conclusion of the war, but before the period scheduled for the (allegedly) orderly 'transfer'. Some 356,000 Muslims were 'transferred' in the other direction across the Aegean, often in terrible conditions. Like many of the Christian arrivals in Greece, these Muslims found themselves alienated by their new surroundings and with little in common with their co-religionists – thus giving the lie to the essentialism that had so shaped their fates.

Lausanne replaced the Treaty of Sèvres (itself a settlement that might well have entailed the ethnic cleansing of Muslims from within the borders of new states created in the fringes of Anatolia) and tacitly endorsed the logic of Young Turk policy even if not all its manifestations. Military 'facts' created new political realities. At once revisionist and avant-garde, the 'Lausanne paradigm' provides one bridge from a Wilhelmine Germany, on the whole deeply embarrassed by the genocide by its junior partner, to a Nazi Germany that endorsed and adopted multiple genocides in the Second World War.

A non-genocidal Ottoman decade would have required Ottoman neutrality in 1914 as well as the Young Turks' will to continue Ottoman reform and to build up Asia Minor together with the Ottoman Christians. Instead, they pursued a maximalist, war-related desire of imperial restoration and even pan-Turkist expansion as well as the ideal of Asia Minor as a Turkish home. Once they had been frustrated about the first, they turned to their second goal and opted for unprecedented violence against fellow citizens. Ottoman neutrality might have drastically shortened the First World War and thus even might have forestalled the Bolshevik Revolution.[74] For this counterfactual course to have played out, the CUP would have had to heed the advice of prudent people like CUP member Cavid Bey, instead of activists like Enver Pasha or prophets of world war and world revolution like Alexander Helphand-Parvus.

Counterfactuals demonstrate that contemporaries had choices. In the case of the CUP in 1915–16, the choices are evident. In the face of overwhelming evidence it is no longer intellectually viable for historians to doubt that genocide took place in Anatolia during the First World War. Here is one of the most terrible chapters in the history of a conflict, the character and dimensions of which changed the nature of warfare.

74 M. Şükrü Hanioğlu, 'The Second Constitutional Period, 1908–1918', in Reşat Kasaba (ed.), *The Cambridge History of Turkey*, vol. IV: *Turkey in the Modern World* (Cambridge University Press, 2008), pp. 62–111, here p. 94.

23

The laws of war

ANNIE DEPERCHIN

It was not a failure of law which led to the Great War. On the contrary, the conflict was framed by law from its outbreak to its conclusion, despite various violations of the rules of war. Such a paradoxical situation demands explanation. From the middle of the nineteenth century the international laws of war were framed slowly and patiently. Despite these developments, on the eve of the First World War these laws were still incomplete and fragile. Although they were broken in a generalised way between 1914 and 1918, the laws of war nonetheless remained a constant point of reference in the 'lawful war' (*guerre du droit*) in which all the warring nations believed they were engaged. As a result, at the end of the war this concept appeared as part of a peace claimed by the Allies to be a victory of law and justice. They thereby created for the first time a set of propositions in both penal and civil law concerning the responsibilities of states at war.

The slow gestation of the international laws of war

Most states regulated the behaviour of combatant troops in operation well before the First World War, with laws applicable to the armed forces grouped in codes which condemned forms of conduct considered undesirable. Killing outside combatant action and pillage, for example, were generally forbidden in the aim not of humanising war but of assuring military discipline. They did not constitute a universal set of laws of war applicable to all potential belligerents.

Approaches

The determination to suppress violence as the way to settle differences between nations is the ultimate aim of the laws of war. This concept must be retained in any analysis of the evolution of international law, through a mixture of idealism and pragmatism. This pacifist aim is anchored in two lines

Helen McPhail translated this chapter from French into English.

of approach which are not mutually exclusive. The first can be defined as 'compassionate' because it arises from sensitivity to the sufferings caused by wars; this is mainly the approach of pacifists following the line of Bertha von Suttner, who in 1889 asserted in *Die Waffen nieder* ('Lay down your arms') that war is a crime. The second approach, the rationalist approach, arose from consideration of the cost of modern warfare in terms of lives and destruction, lessons learned from the wars of the second half of the nineteenth century. Although the latter approach was to be reflected judicially in the theories of natural law, according to which certain elements of law are universal (because they are born of rationality and human sociability), the former created the energy which made it possible to put such principles into concrete form. From this fusion of approaches emerged an international code of the laws of war which arose out of the braiding together of incomplete standards dictated by the urgent need to take action to limit sufferings and those norms which, more systematically, attacked the root of the problem: war itself, which must be eradicated.

Whatever the nature of norms, their force required their formal implementation among nations. In effect, their development shows that even if nations ended up accepting a corpus of law, with more or less conviction, its effectiveness was not so much a function of compromise as of their recognition (or not) of the supremacy of international law. In order to understand how the Great War affected law, a fundamental legal question must be addressed: how to justify the superiority of these norms over the will of nations? If the Treaties of Westphalia in 1648, signed to bring an end collectively to the Thirty Years' War, the first 'European war', were the foundation on the international scale of recognition of the equality and sovereignty of nations, how could international law assert itself over them?

The basic question: does international law apply to states?

In this respect, judicial thinking drew very extensively on the seventeenth-century work of Grotius in his *On the Law of War and Peace* (1625). In this he defined natural law as consisting of 'the principles of sound reasoning which make us recognise that an action is morally honest or dishonest according to the match or necessary mismatch it has with the reasonable or sociable nature of Man'. In other words, natural reasoning imposes rules on human relations outside all social authority. International law combined with natural law is not the creation of nations: it precedes them and through their powers of reasoning, states discover it. Emmerich de Vattel took the concept forward: his *Law of Nations*, published in English in 1758, declared rules to be unconditionally obligatory which until then had been considered certainly beneficial, but still not compulsory.

In the middle of the nineteenth century the idea developed that the progress of a state in the eyes of civilisation was measured by its capacity to proscribe violence. Enlightened minds, sensitive to the human suffering inescapable in war, threw themselves into the struggle against war, which was less and less seen as the normal way to settle conflicts when diplomacy – in other words, politics – had failed to resolve them.

The struggle was initially undertaken very pragmatically, in the setting of the battlefield where the distress of the wounded was inescapable. It was driven by the forceful energy of Henry Dunant and was the outcome of an interview with Napoleon III, which by chance took place on the battlefield of Solferino in 1859. As a result of seeing the butchery (40,000 men dead and wounded) and the wholly inadequate practical help for the sufferings of the soldiers of both sides, Dunant devoted the rest of his life to ensuring that the wounded were deemed to have rights, whatever their nationality. On 22 August 1864 the first international Convention was signed by twelve nations; other nations would join later. The twelve met at the invitation of the Swiss federal government, as proposed by organisations set up by Dunant to provide aid for wounded soldiers. This Convention 'for the improvement of the condition of soldiers wounded during combat' was a decisive turning point in the evolution of the law. From that time on, efforts in the struggle against war turned to the development of written norms which nations undertook to respect. No superior authority had developed these norms or could observe their implementation; still, the idea grew stronger despite its controversial character that, according to the maxim *pacta sunt servanda* ('laws which must be obeyed'), the engagements freely undertaken by states had the strength of law. Such undertakings established an international law constraining nations, as would happen under a supranational law drawn up by an institution placed above them.

Nonetheless, the legal application of this theory was difficult to implement because, although nations could see that international law represented an ideal which it was right to support in the light of their own particular interests, they were generally reluctant to accept its constraint in practice. In consequence, for each nation war took on the character of an exercise of free will, not open to legal interpretation if applied and still less to sanction, if not. The law must restrict itself to informing belligerents as to how war was to be declared and ended, what rules must be respected in the conduct of hostilities and how the rights of neutrals should be respected, without approaching the question of knowing when – or why – it was legitimate to go to war. Leaving aside questions of the legitimacy of war, it was left to natural law and its moral approach to the problem to decide whether or not a particular war was justifiable.

Acceptance of these norms occurred through the exchange of documents by delegates authorised to do so in international conferences. The ever-increasing number of their undertakings added further weight to the move towards a degree of universality. From then on, any nation which failed to respect rules of which the content and text had been discussed and accepted collectively found itself in danger of being deemed outside the circle of civilised states. This was an outcome wanted by no one; hence the importance of the choice of questions to appear on conference agendas. Indeed, these protocols took on added importance, because by limiting the freedom of action of states in war in certain respects, they pointed towards regulation to come.

The development of the Treaties of Westphalia evidently enabled the establishment of a balance of the advantages conceded to each state, as well as a collective approach to problems, which represented the best way to limit conflict. In 1868 the personal initiative of the Tsar took this objective further, in establishing the regular convening of meetings as part of the customary framework for nations to discuss the limitations of weaponry. The conference that he called at St Petersburg ended not with a convention signed by all the states, but with a shared declaration which dealt only with the banning of one weapon, 'any projectile weighing less than 400 grammes which would be explosive or charged with a fulminant or inflammable materials'. The result may seem very modest. It must, however, be remembered that fear of bullets, designed to explode within the body, was a central obsession for the military at the time. If it was not a revolution in the limitation of weapons, which was the desired result, it was nonetheless a matter of importance. Weaponry was one of the most sensitive issues on the table, and the very considerable progress represented by this shared declaration on this particular topic has not been properly emphasised. Nor has the range of signatures assembled: with the exception of Brazil, they were all European and represented virtually all the belligerents in a potential European war. The conference also showed that preliminary reflection on matters of doctrine would enable national representatives to be more effective in the necessarily limited period of their meetings. It was to this need that eleven professors of law wished to respond when they met at Ghent in 1873. Acting entirely on their own initiative, they decided to found the Institute of International Law. The following year, once more on the initiative of the Tsar, a first effort in thinking about collective regulation was tried out at the Brussels Conference. Again, this did not result in a collective undertaking, because the object of the conference was purely to deliberate on the Russian proposal, which was submitted as a working basis for discussion. The instructions of the governments were very precise in this respect. As a result the conference agreed a text in the form of a structured 'Project for an international declaration on the laws and customs of war', consisting of fifty-six articles supported by comments from the delegates on points of disagreement.

The final protocol was signed on 27 August 1874. As much in the subjects which it approached (ways of harming the enemy, sieges and bombardment, spies, prisoners of war and, above all, questions linked to occupation and the nature of being a belligerent) as in the search for a precise formula for the presentation of the text, this conference established the future laws of war. Its work inspired the jurists of the Institute of International Law. At their congress in Oxford, on 9 September 1880, they published the *Manual of the Laws and Customs of War on Land*, in the form of a small code designed to make it easier for each nation to disseminate knowledge of the laws of war among the military. It aroused interest and discussion, but was in no way made obligatory, for this would have required a clear political will. This determination emerged at the conference that met at The Hague in 1899, where the *Manual* was used as the working basis of deliberations. Twenty-six powers sent delegates to the conference, jurists and military experts, and signed the final act. The corpus that developed included conventions, declarations and proposals which the states agreed formally to activate thereafter.

From the common declaration to the congress was a step of great significance, particularly in the context of a multi-lateral convention through which nations committed themselves in relation to each other. Their number gave force to the total sum of signatures, to the extent of perhaps creating a form of transcendence in relation to the sovereignty of nations. At the same time, some sensitive subjects had been debated, not least the law applicable to occupied territories. The considerable contribution of the Institute of International Law in the construction of the emerging legal structure was honoured by the award of the fourth Nobel Peace Prize in 1904.

Nonetheless this structure remained unfinished, and its completion was the object of a second conference which met at The Hague in 1907, on the initiative of the United States. The intention was to address the question of war, the source of all suffering, which preceding conferences had sought to cut back to the roots and eliminate. The question took this form: how could nations be prevented from turning to war to settle their differences? The judicial tool of arbitration, instituted in 1899, provided the solution which, they believed, must now be rendered obligatory and therefore effective.

Eight years after the first conference to which the title of 'peace conference' had been applied, forty-four nation-states – that is, the great majority at the time, including a number of non-European powers – placed their signature at the foot of the convention. One wonders if the scale of the feat was grasped at the time: forty-four nations had agreed to rules which would restrict their action in war by reference to specific protocols and norms.

Work continued thereafter, despite difficulties, and the task was certainly not over. Many questions remained in suspension, and the norms elaborated had to be made explicit. For this ongoing project, a Peace Palace was built at The Hague and inaugurated in 1913. Another conference was proposed there, to be held in 1914 or 1915.

On the eve of war: an incomplete and fragile legal framework

To avoid war: arbitration and its limitations

What the delegates wanted to see emerging from the conferences at The Hague was the abolition of war. Ideally, when a dispute arose between them, nations would submit to jurisdiction to settle the points at issue and thus spare the suffering war entailed in all its forms. In other words, it was a matter of transposing the existing mode of settling litigation which already existed in domestic law to the international level. Arbitration then seemed the most suitable way to proceed because it was the most straightforward to set up. The principle was accepted in 1899 and a permanent Court set up in the following year. Between 1900 and 1907, however, it adjudicated in only four cases. This was a modest total in relation to the international tensions and great crises that escaped its intervention, for example in Tangier in relation to Morocco, because that was resolved at an international conference (Algeciras, 1906). The 1907 Peace Conference at The Hague therefore adopted as its chief objective the development of international arbitration.

In 1914, four methods were open to the nations concerned for the peaceful resolution of conflicts: good offices, mediation, an international commission of enquiry and international arbitration. The two first procedures had more to do with diplomacy than with justice, since they consisted in reconciling opposing claims and pacifying resentment before it could endanger peace.

The international commission of enquiry must allow light to fall impartially on facts which were presented by the nations in opposition to each other. Nothing prevented this commission from adopting the role of conciliator, but the limitation of its competence to disputes which did not engage either honour or the essential interests of the parties quite sharply circumscribed its opportunities to intervene. The 1907 Convention stipulated that the Court of Arbitration, now to be known as the Special Court of Arbitration, must be accessible at all times. Nonetheless, no jurisdiction had existed which was available to nations in disagreement. The Court consisted of the permanent list of potential arbitrators (four names specified for six years by each signatory nation) from which, in a case of crisis, the states concerned were invited to select two arbitrators (only one of whom was of their own nationality). They in turn were to designate the President of the Court who would try the case in question. The Court must be set up within two months. During this time, recourse to arbitration being consensual, the states in dispute must draw up a case for arbitration, setting out the point at issue to be settled and the timing for instruction, or for presenting the full argument in writing. The case then came to trial and the judgement notified to the nations in dispute, which undertook to execute it in good faith; no appeal was envisaged.

The originators aimed at a procedure which would inevitably prevail through its flexibility and impartiality; but as often happened with an aim to provide a maximum of guarantees, this mechanism was onerous and lengthy to put into action compared to the urgency of and popular attention to international crises requiring rapid settlement. Further, it proved impossible to reach consensus on making arbitration compulsory. In addition, for those states using arbitration as a delaying tactic, military mobilisation was authorised in parallel with the legal proceedings. This possibility, combined with the optional nature of arbitration, meant that the chances of a judicial settlement of the point at issue were remote. In fact, the Special Court of Arbitration tried only eleven cases between 1907 and 1914. The nations in conflict did not turn to it in the Agadir Crisis in 1911, nor to prevent the Balkan wars of 1912–13. Moreover, after Agadir, the French President Poincaré proposed a conference in London to avoid the conflict extending into Europe – proof that, on the eve of the Great War, recourse to arbitration in an important crisis had not yet entered political custom. To think that it might be possible to avoid war was no more than a pious hope; and it was better to return to the rules on the conduct of war in order to limit the damage and suffering of those caught up in it.

Limiting the cruelties and hardships of war: regulating its conduct

The written and agreed legal corpus on the conduct of war was extended rapidly over the five decades between the first Geneva Convention in 1864 and the outbreak of the First World War. The Geneva Convention for the Amelioration of the Condition of the Wounded and Sick in Armies in the Field, dated 6 July 1906, was agreed after the convention signed at The Hague on 29 July 1899 and before the second Hague Convention of 18 October 1907. Most of the regulations concerning the conduct of war on land had been established in 1899, and the 1907 conference was arranged in part to make progress in the regulation of war at sea. This effort opened the way to the signing of eight conventions dealing with various features of this aspect of warfare:

Convention VI: *The Status of Enemy Merchant Ships at the Outbreak of Hostilities*
Convention VII: *The Conversion of Merchant Ships into Warships*
Convention VIII: *The Laying of Automatic Submarine Contact Mines*
Convention IX: *Bombardment by Naval Forces in Time of War*
Convention X: *Adaptation to Maritime War of the Principles of the Geneva Convention* (concerning the wounded)
Convention XI: *Certain Restrictions with Regard to the Exercise of the Right of Capture in Naval War*
Convention XII: *The Creation of an International Prize Court*
Convention XIII: *The Rights and Duties of Neutral Powers in Naval War*

Overall, the judicial corpus of The Hague after 1907 was supposed to protect prisoners, occupied populations – personally, and their possessions – and combatants, in the case of war either on land or at sea. The use of certain weapons was forbidden: apart from the explosive bullets which had been in question since 1868, in particular this included gas in various forms and projectiles launched from any kind of flying device. The use of other weapons was regulated, such as the laying of underwater mines. According to the principle inherited from the Enlightenment, with conflicts concerning only the nations actually at war, neutrals should not suffer any consequences except in relation to Conventions V and XII, relating respectively to the duties of the Powers and of neutral persons in cases of war on land and at sea.

To complete the legal structure relating to maritime warfare, a conference in London in 1909 concluded on 26 February with a protocol. Discussions continued the following year and concluded, on 19 September 1910, with a

Fig. 24.1 Soldiers of the French Empire in a German prisoner-of-war camp, 1917.

Fig. 24.2 French African soldier transported to a German casualty clearing centre for the evacuation of the wounded, 1914.

Fig. 24.3 Indian soldier signing up for military service with his thumb print.

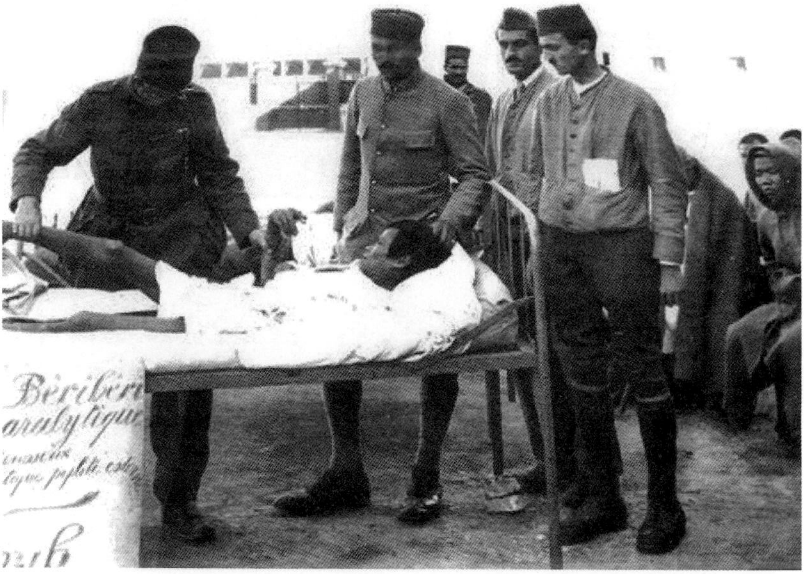

Fig. 24.4 Egyptian physicians treat an Asian labourer for beri-beri.

Fig. 24.5 Postcard of a black French soldier with a white nurse.

Fig. 24.6 Dying Serbian soldier, Isle of Vido, near Corfu.

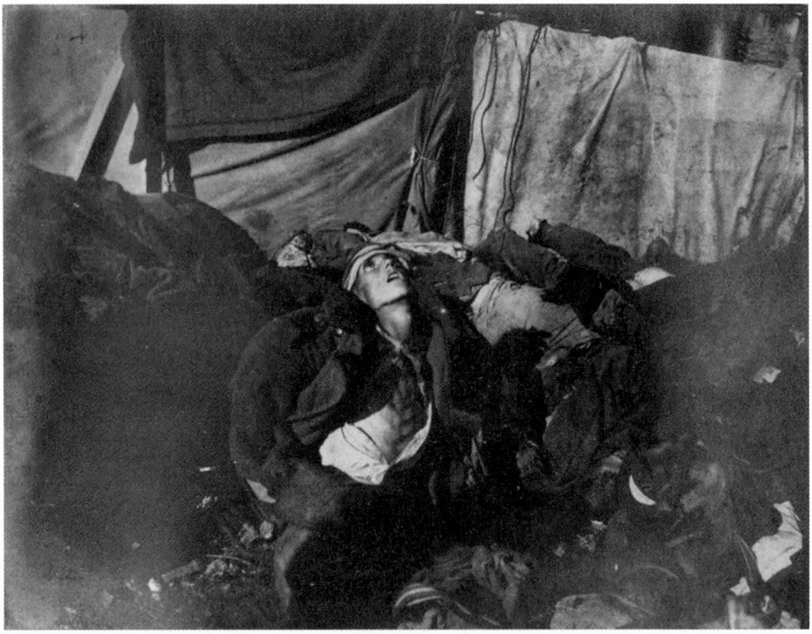

Fig. 24.7 *Charon's barque*, Isle of Vido, Corfu.

Fig. 24.8 A Jewish family in a field, Volhynia.

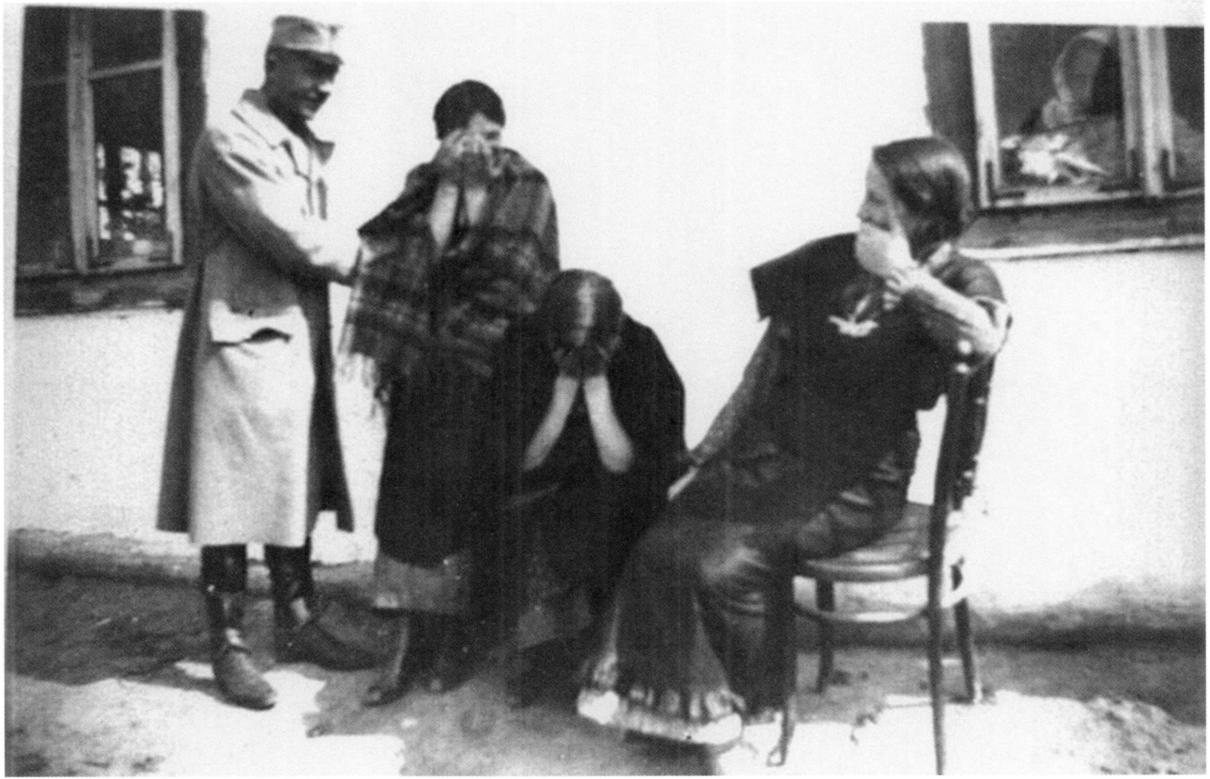

Fig. 24.9 Jewish prostitutes, Volhynia.

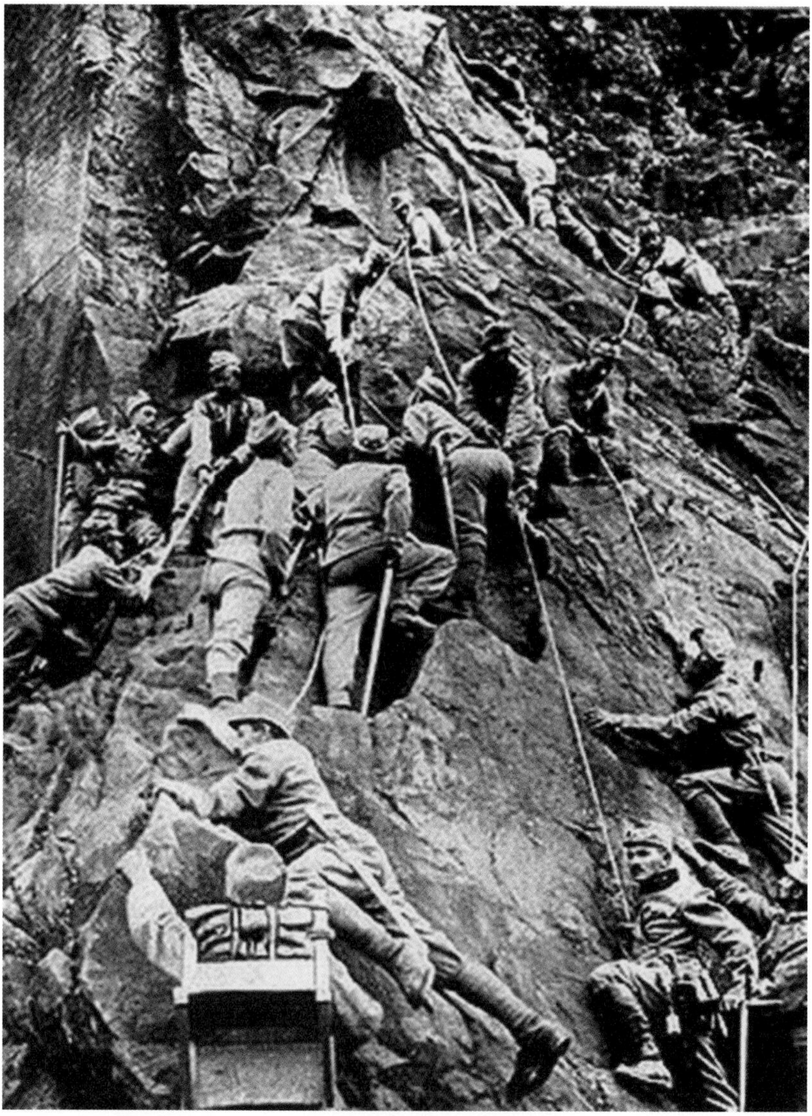

Fig. 24.10 Austro-Hungarian mountain troops in the vertical war on the Italian Front.

Fig. 24.11 The white war, the Kosturino Ridge on the Macedonian front.

Fig. 24.12 All quiet on the Eastern Front, Volhynia.

Fig. 24.13 Destroyed village on the Eastern Front, Volhynia.

Fig. 24.14 Airplane hauled by horses, Volhynia.

Fig. 24.15 HMS *Inflexible*, near the Falkland Islands, 1914.

Fig. 24.16 A Japanese cruiser off the coast of Vancouver, British Columbia, 1917.

Fig. 24.17 Horses stuck in the mud, Western Front.

Fig. 24.18 Passchendaele, 1917.

Fig. 24.19 The uncanny: part of a horse in a tree.

Fig. 24.20 Horses bringing provisions and supplies to soldiers on the Western Front.

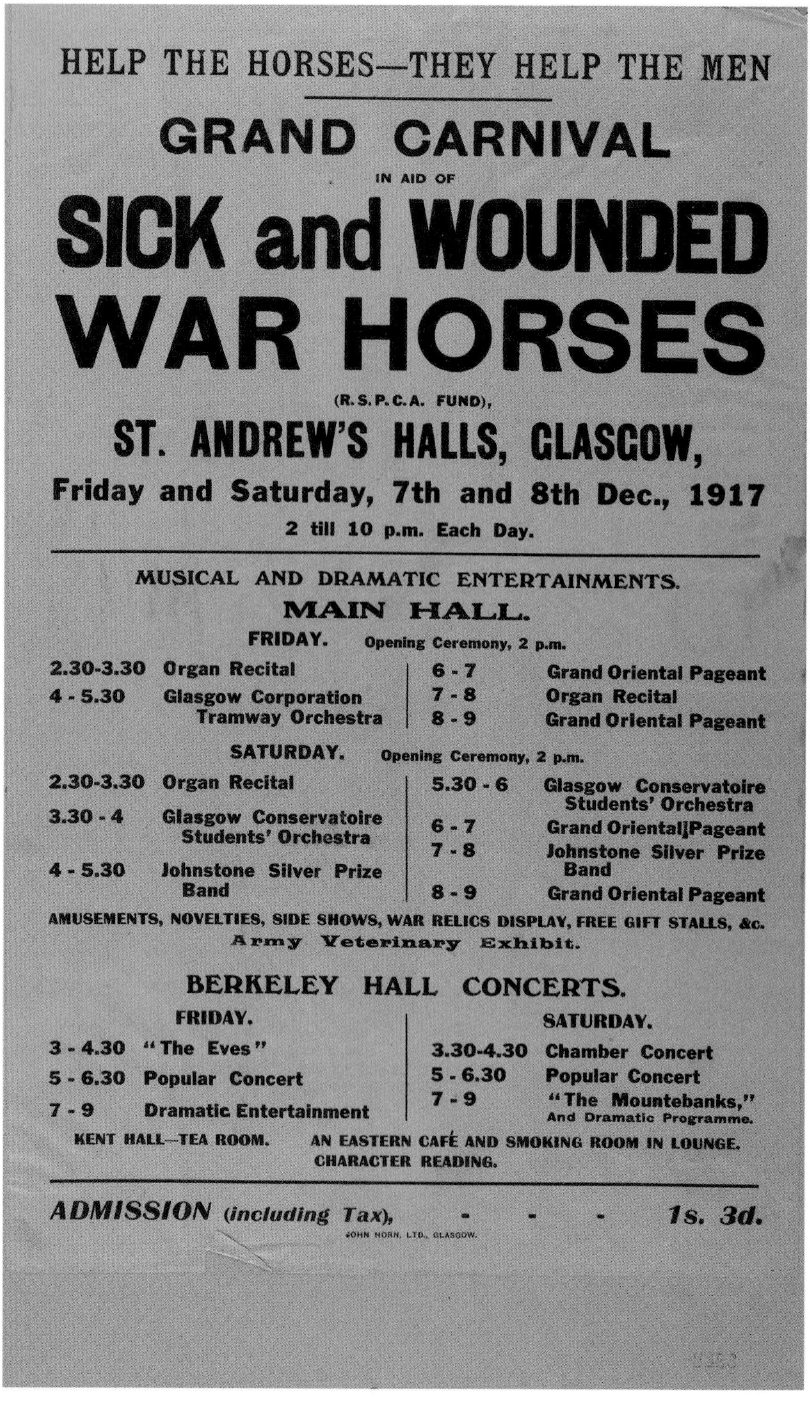

HELP THE HORSES—THEY HELP THE MEN

GRAND CARNIVAL

IN AID OF

SICK and WOUNDED WAR HORSES

(R. S. P. C. A. FUND),

ST. ANDREW'S HALLS, GLASGOW,

Friday and Saturday, 7th and 8th Dec., 1917

2 till 10 p.m. Each Day.

MUSICAL AND DRAMATIC ENTERTAINMENTS.

MAIN HALL.

FRIDAY. Opening Ceremony, 2 p.m.

2.30-3.30	Organ Recital	6 - 7	Grand Oriental Pageant
4 - 5.30	Glasgow Corporation Tramway Orchestra	7 - 8	Organ Recital
		8 - 9	Grand Oriental Pageant

SATURDAY. Opening Ceremony, 2 p.m.

2.30-3.30	Organ Recital	5.30 - 6	Glasgow Conservatoire Students' Orchestra
3.30 - 4	Glasgow Conservatoire Students' Orchestra	6 - 7	Grand Oriental Pageant
4 - 5.30	Johnstone Silver Prize Band	7 - 8	Johnstone Silver Prize Band
		8 - 9	Grand Oriental Pageant

AMUSEMENTS, NOVELTIES, SIDE SHOWS, WAR RELICS DISPLAY, FREE GIFT STALLS, &c.

Army Veterinary Exhibit.

BERKELEY HALL CONCERTS.

FRIDAY.		SATURDAY.	
3 - 4.30	"The Eves"	3.30-4.30	Chamber Concert
5 - 6.30	Popular Concert	5 - 6.30	Popular Concert
7 - 9	Dramatic Entertainment	7 - 9	"The Mountebanks," And Dramatic Programme.

KENT HALL—TEA ROOM. AN EASTERN CAFÉ AND SMOKING ROOM IN LOUNGE.
CHARACTER READING.

ADMISSION** (including Tax),* - - - ***1s. 3d.

JOHN HORN, LTD., GLASGOW.

Fig. 24.21 Poster announcing a Grand Carnival in aid of sick and wounded war horses, December 1917.

Fig. 24.22 A broken-down tank near Passchendaele, 1917.

Fig. 24.23 Flame-throwers on the Eastern Front.

Fig. 24.24 Gas attack on the Western Front, I.

Fig. 24.25 Gas attack on the Western Front, II.

Fig. 24.26 French soldiers with gas masks.

Fig. 24.27 Mules and soldiers wearing gas masks.

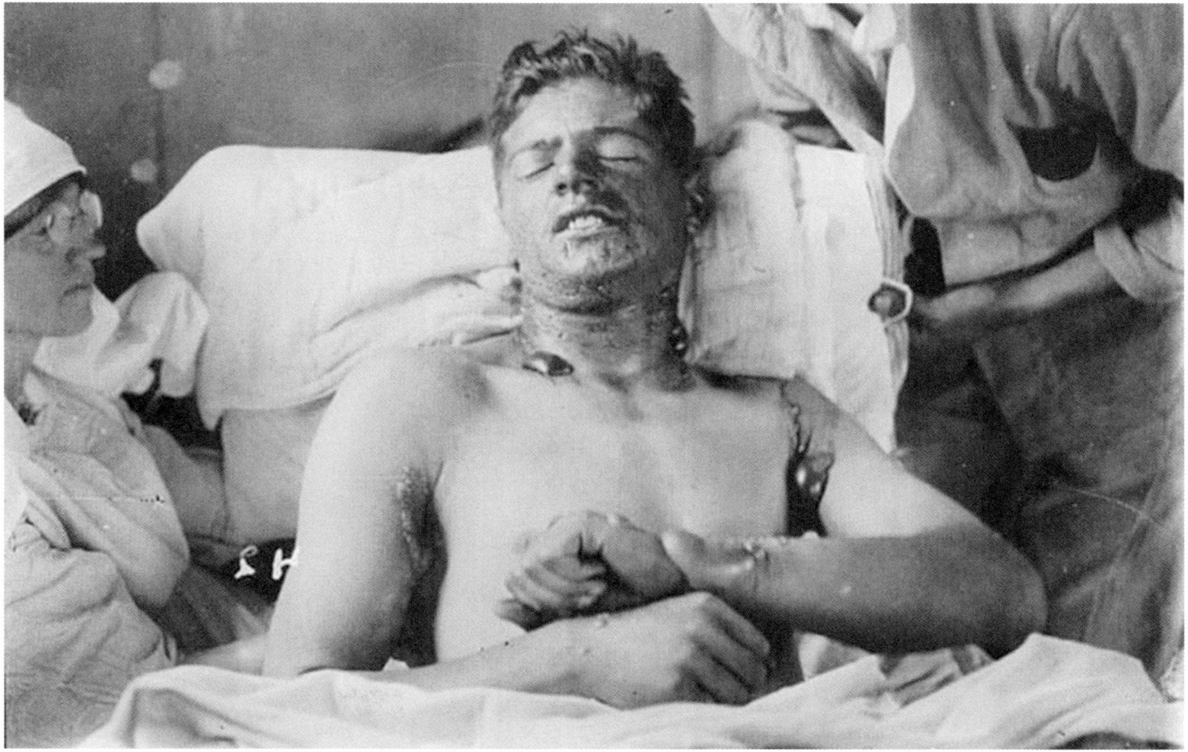

Fig. 24.28 A soldier wounded by mustard gas.

Fig. 24.29 Children who survived the Armenian genocide, Erevan, 1919.

Fig. 24.30 American aid for the survivors of the Armenian genocide, 1919.

Fig. 24.31 Food aid carried by a camel column for victims of the famine in Russia.

specific convention on the establishment of the International Prize Court, instituted during the 1909 conference. There was much more to be done in this field, but it is important not to underestimate these achievements.

Those who had laboured long to establish this immense body of law could legitimately feel cautiously satisfied: there were regulations framed for all the domains that could be affected by war. And yet these pacts required ratification and then implementation. The Russian delegate at the two conferences at The Hague, Fyodor Fyodorovich Martens, was keenly aware of the gaps in these documents. In order to proscribe zones of illegality, he had the somewhat extraordinary idea of including a paragraph in the preamble to the final act of the conference, which became immortalised under the name of 'the Martens clause':

> Until a more complete code of the laws of war has been issued, the High Contracting Parties deem it expedient to declare that, in the cases not included in the Regulations adopted by them, the inhabitants and the belligerents remain under the protection and rule of the principles of the law of nations, as they result from the usages established among civilised peoples, from the laws of humanity and the dictates of the public conscience.[1]

Thus the principles of natural law in the form of 'the laws of humanity', understood here in the sense of collective morality as of personal ethics, and the customs of war, applied in all matters that had not been the object of written agreed norms. This is a staggering extension of the position, well beyond the political thinking of the states who signed the Hague accords. Although jurists had no illusions as to the constraining power of these principles, the reference made to them in an act signed by the great majority of nations proclaimed a future, soon to arise, when an infringement of the laws of war would remove the offender from the limited danger of moral sanction alone and expose it to legal sanction.

Obstacles to the effectiveness of international law

The effectiveness of the international laws of war came up initially against material obstacles. The first was the question of the sanctions risked by a state and individuals in violation of its provisions. The introduction at conventions of sanctions in the event of violation of the laws of war made the nations hesitate to ratify them, and so the question did not figure on the conference

1 'Préambule de la Convention concernant les Lois et Coutumes de la guerre sur terre conclue à La Haye le 29 juillet 1899', in Ministère des Affaires étrangères, *Documents diplomatiques: Conférence internationale de la Paix* (Paris: Imprimerie nationale, 1900).

agendas in 1899 and 1907. Nonetheless, the various conventions contained plenty of references to the responsibilities of those who violated any specific clause. In respect of nations at war, the sanction introduced in 1907, on the initiative of Germany, to Article 3 of Convention IV (on the laws and customs of war on land), as developed in the Regulations annexed, provided that, 'A belligerent party which violated the provisions of the said Regulations shall, if the case demands, be liable to pay compensation. It shall be responsible for all acts committed by persons forming part of its armed forces.' So strongly did they wish to believe in the law that jurists saw in this provision an important innovation, extending beyond the real possibilities which it offered. In fact, how could it be envisaged that a victim – a wounded combatant or prisoner of war, an inhabitant of an occupied region – could take legal action against the nation responsible for his situation? This might be conceivable in theory, but in practice the difficulties in the way of activating this responsibility can easily be imagined. Located in the Convention itself, this Article was expected to sanction all the regulations which followed, and notably the obligation for each signatory nation to give instructions to its troops to apply the laws of war effectively. Yet as war loomed, a number of nations, including Germany, had still not conformed to this obligation, since the sanction provided in the Convention would have to be applied by someone; the question was, who? By whom, indeed, could it be put into operation and how?

The absence of a legal power sanctioning violations of law and of an executive power to enforce the execution of decisions was a second material obstacle to the effectiveness of accepted norms. Immediately before the war of 1914, nations were already cooperating over the form of international administration assuring the application of conventions which regulated relations between states in civil matters. Certain of these, concerning free circulation on rivers (Commission for the Navigation of the Rhine in 1815, Commission of the Danube in 1856), unions or offices were set up in services such as the International Telegraph Union (1865), the Universal Postal Union (1888), the Railways Union (1890), the International Office of Public Health (1904) or the International Office of Public Hygiene (1907). These ventures reinforced the notion of a 'society of nations' located above the nations themselves. Although the expression 'Society of Nations' figured in the text of 1907, in that case it reflected only the awareness of a growing interdependence between what were then termed civilised nation-states.

Legal thinking in this field ripened gradually, for example in the foundational thinking of Léon Bourgeois. The first French delegate at the two conferences at The Hague, in his book *Solidarité* (1896), and above all in

Pour la Société des Nations (1910), Bourgeois proposed the introduction of a tribunal of nations which would be given the task of watching over respect of international law. If this structure had existed at the time of the First World War, it would have required some means of coercion to be effective, in other words armed force. All this presupposed a degree of coordination of international relations which did not yet exist.

The way in which the laws of war were received nationally may have constituted another obstacle to their implementation; the reaction of politicians and the armed forces to the adoption of the regulations is indicative of deep-rooted attitudes rendering remote the chances of their application in the case of war. At the political level, each nation agreed to make an effort to 'humanise' war, but on condition that the norms adopted would not interfere with its security or impede its victory. At the Brussels conference in 1874, the first conference assembled on the general theme of the laws and customs of war, the nations' ambivalence was perceptible behind their delegates' behaviour. They feared that their representatives, carried away by the collective dynamic, might overstep the limits of their instructions. Each government reminded its delegates that the conference must only reflect on the proposal of a convention submitted by Russia, without deciding on its adoption, since any decisive vote was excluded. It would revert afterwards to the nations to validate the project or otherwise. This project, the outcome of a consensus which was implicit, was indeed no longer known as a 'draft convention', but rather a 'draft declaration' to be interpreted with the delegates' reservations included in the protocols of the sessions. As indicated by the final protocol, the delegates undertook only a 'conscientious enquiry' which would, they hoped, be useful for the future.

At The Hague in 1899, as in 1907, all contributions from national delegates, who held the status of plenipotentiaries, expressed their caution over certain norms. Their instructions were very precise, particularly on subjects which ran counter to national interests. In this context, historians often refer to the German attitude, expressed in 1899 by Colonel Gross von Schwarzhoff, in connection with the regulation of war on land. On the laws and duties of occupiers and occupied people, for example, the German attitude (fresh with the memory of the *francs-tireurs*, or snipers, of the Franco-Prussian War in 1870) was rooted in the logic of the occupier, and pushed for the adoption of regulations which favoured the occupier rather than the occupied. This was evident at the 1907 conference, where the regulations were to be spelled out more precisely. General Marschall von Bieberstein opposed Article 44, which forbade compulsion in order to obtain military information from the occupied population.

On the other hand, very little attention has been paid to the British attitude when it came to regulating maritime warfare. This regulation, proposed by the United States in 1856 at the Paris Conference, was not considered because of its rejection by Great Britain. In 1899 it was again put aside due to British objections that it was not part of the formal conference agenda. But it can be observed, perhaps through a sort of 'conference magic' that the British stance evolved with time. In the course of these conferences they finally accepted that interests seen as vital would be the object of discussions. The 1907 Conference therefore approached the topic of maritime warfare (two of the four commissions were working on this theme), although Great Britain still expected to frame the regulations in such a way that their meaning would suit her own interests. In British eyes, its island setting made the naval dimension of warfare crucial: its coasts must be protected and the sea kept clear of the enemy. The question of neutral nations' use of the sea was studied very closely, together with the capture of shipping and merchandise, entailing debate on contraband and blockade in wartime. It was all the more difficult to gain consensus on these points in that the doctrinal attitudes taken by the British differed materially from those of the continental nations, which were also unable to reach agreement between themselves. Most of the nations wished for the inviolability of neutral and enemy private property of ships and merchandise in transit to be recognised as corresponding to the ban on pillage in war on land. Britain, however, saw the law of capture as essential to its national defence, and wanted the prohibition of war contraband suppressed and its own rules of blockade to be imposed. The British conceded that to be effective a blockade must be legal, but the condition of an effective blockade was more easily fulfilled under the British doctrine than under continental doctrines, with the result of immobilising fewer ships. On the question of war contraband, agreement was obtained on absolute contraband (a list of goods unequivocally applicable to the war effort), thanks to the efforts of the special committee constituted to settle these problems, but consensus was not achieved on the list of relevant contraband goods. With the divergences remaining too substantial, questions of blockade and war contraband were finally postponed to the next conference, with the wish expressed that this meeting would develop a regulation relating to the laws and customs of war at sea analogous to that of war on land. The discussion was taken up again at the conferences held in London in 1909 and 1911, and the International Prize Court, the first supranational tribunal in history, was instituted to act as an appeal court on decisions handed down by the national jurisdictions on prizes. The text for this was not ratified, notably by Great Britain. The international conventions were not in fact framed for direct national application: to acquire legal force they must be ratified and domestic laws brought into line with international dispositions. On the eve of the war, by different means, Britain, like Germany, succeeded in escaping norms which were inconvenient, or in bending those which had been adopted to the meaning which favoured them.

Ignorance of the law was no excuse. But what scope could the international laws of war have if only jurists and, perhaps, politicians, were familiar with them? In order for the law to have a chance of being applied where and as it should be, the armed forces must be fully conversant with it. Francis Lieber was the first to spell out this point. His *Instructions for the Government of the Armies of the United States in the Field*, issued on 24 April 1863, assembled the principles of the laws and customs of war then in operation in a text of 157 articles which became known as 'The Lieber Code'. It was very soon being read far beyond American frontiers, notably in judicial circles, and spurred the move from customary laws of war to written laws. Manuals of international law appeared in France, the Netherlands and Russia by 1877, for the use of officers in the army on land. But it was precisely the pragmatic vision of the Lieber Code which inspired the Institute of International Law to issue its *Manual of the Laws of War*, known as the *Oxford Manual*, in 1880; later, in 1913, this extended to the *Manual of Maritime War*. It was to serve as a model for the directives which nations must give their troops, and we can see over the ensuing years how the rules of the laws of war gradually entered military training instructions. In Spain, for example, the 'Regulation for Field Service, 5 January 1882' contained a section devoted to human rights and the laws of war, including the points debated at the Brussels Conference in 1874. In Britain, the *Manual of Military Law*, written by Lord Thring in 1883 for the use of officers – without being official in the strict meaning of the term – was published under the auspices of the War Office and contained a chapter devoted to the 'Customs of War'. In 1890, Portugal added to its 'Interim Regulation on Field Service' a section devoted to law in a time of war. The same occurred in Italy with its 'Regulations on Field Service' of 16 September 1896. Although in France the 1893 edition of the *Manual of International Law for the Use of Army Officers* indicated the rules for good conduct during hostilities, they lacked the official element that would have made them enforceable. To take the law forward and to harmonise behaviour, Article 1 of the Convention of 1899 therefore required nations to instruct their armed land forces to conform to the recently adopted regulation on the laws and customs of war on land. The place of this Article, the first to be signed under the Act, shows that the negotiators assessed the extent to which the application of the regulations adopted was affected by their diffusion. This Article could also have been placed last to achieve a logical extension of the negotiations, but the aim was to show clearly that the humanisation of war began with the nations' determination to make it happen.

The Russian jurist, Fyodor Fyodorovich Martens, Russian delegate to Brussels and then The Hague, deplored the failure to press hard enough for the adequate integration of the norms of constraint and enforcement laid down in 1899, and regretted that this obligation had not been combined with a time-scale for its formal application. In France, the 1899 Conventions had been ratified swiftly (by a presidential decree of 28 November 1900) and reached the Minister for War six months later, but military instructions were not issued to implement its clauses. It should not be surprising, given the efforts of the Tsar to develop them, that it was in Russia that this integration was carried out officially and promptly. The Imperial *Prikaz* no. 409 of 14/27 June 1904, ordered the placing of the instructions on the laws and customs of war as an annex to the 'Regulation on Field Service and Instructions for Detached Combat in all Forms'. The first section was addressed to officers (forty-four articles in seven chapters), the second presented eleven articles in a very simple and paternalist manner, addressing the ordinary soldier in familiar style to tell him what he should do and avoid; it was closer in spirit to the Ten Commandments than to the laws of war.

In the period after the 1899 conference, a virtually complete silence on international law characterised the instructions given to the armed forces in both Germany and Austria-Hungary. The edition on field service in the German army of 1 January 1900 remained silent on the laws of war, apart from the already well-established clauses of the Geneva Convention of 1864 in the section devoted to health services. This was precisely the tenor of the Austro-Hungarian regulation of 15 March 1904. In fact a course of state law (*Rechtslehre*), designed for the use of officers in the Academies of Vienna and Leipzig, was published on the orders of the War Ministry in 1899, but although the laws of war were dealt with here in its fourth section, this was very theoretical in form compared to the much more important section on national law.

But it was above all the publication in 1902 of the *Kriegsbrauch im Land Kriege* ('The laws of continental war') by the historical section of the German High Command, in a collection of studies prepared for officers, which provoked anxiety in international legal circles. The nature of written law was denied to the laws of war, presented as having only a moral and optional nature. Deprived of legal power, only the fear of reprisals could guarantee its application, in other words the enemy's use of force. Further, the High

Command warned officers against humanitarian tendencies which for decades had degenerated into what they termed 'a sensitivity if not sentimentality', and announced that in war, 'true humanity often dwelt in the straightforward use of its forms of severity'.

For the German High Command, a conflict throughout its duration suspended the law because the military imperatives to ensure victory rendered its application impossible. The manual referred to the declarations of St Petersburg and Brussels, but ignored the norms set out and accepted by Germany in 1899. This led the French jurist, Alexandre Mérignhac, to conclude, at the end of an article published in 1907: 'What a formidable question-mark this mentality poses for those who, French or others, will have dealings with Germany in future wars!'[2]

War, and laws put to the test

The 'legal war'

The war began with a flagrant violation of law by Germany, that respecting the neutrality of Belgium and Luxembourg. France and Great Britain immediately located that breach in a wider legal framework: by failing to respect the Treaty of London (19 April 1839) and the Fifth Hague Convention of 1907, Articles 1, 2 and 10, Germany had flouted all international law. These belligerent acts provoked Great Britain to enter the war, and Germany was expelled from the ranks of civilised nations. The German government was well aware of what was at stake. On 3 August 1914 the German ambassador to Paris, Wilhelm von Schön, delivered the official declaration to the French Foreign Office. Knowing that German troops were about to cross Belgium, he anticipated events and declared it to be a legitimate violation of neutrality because French aviators had begun by flying over Belgian territory that same morning. It was known later, as admitted by Germany, that this was not true.[3] Indeed, the German government acknowledged the violation. In his speech in the Reichstag on 4 August, Chancellor Bethmann Hollweg declared: 'Our troops have occupied Luxemburg, perhaps already trodden Belgian soil. This is contrary to the prescriptions of international law . . . This illegal action – I

2 A. Mérignhac, 'Les théories du Grand Etat-major allemand sur les "Lois de la guerre continentale"', *Revue générale de droit international public*, 14 (1907), p. 239.

3 Belgian Foreign Office (ed.), *Livre gris*, no. 21 (Berne: Wyss, 1915); and L. Renault, 'Les premières violations du Droit des Gens par l'Allemagne (Luxembourg et Belgique)', in *L'œuvre internationale de Louis Renault 1843–1918* (Paris: Éditions Internationales, 1920), vol. III, p. 407.

speak openly – we shall seek to repair this illegal action which we are committing as soon as our military goal is achieved.'[4]

When the Chancellor addressed the British ambassador in Berlin, Sir Edward Groschen, on the same day, he managed to aggravate Germany's situation, asserting that it was inconceivable that Britain should enter a war purely because of one word: 'Neutrality' – a treaty being no more than 'a scrap of paper'. The Allies rose up at what they considered to be monumental cynicism, and the legal debate then opened between jurists of both sides. In his speech to the Reichstag, the Chancellor had acknowledged the violation, but justified it under the theory of necessity: 'Sirs, we are under the necessity to defend ourselves and necessity knows no law . . . France could wait; but we could not! An attack on our flanks on the lower Rhine could have been fatal to us . . . Faced with such a threat as this, you do what you can.'[5]

On the legal level, necessity is a justifying fact, that is a material or moral constraint (the *Nostand* concept) which may, by explaining a form of conduct, remove all moral responsibility – but did it, even so, constitute the right (the *Notrecht* concept) to commit an illicit action? For the Allies, the response was negative, because to accept the contrary would be to accept the arbitrary nature of force. In German doctrine, it was positive. The stakes of the debate were very important: it was a matter of determining how far a norm could be violated without the transgressor being declared *ipso facto* responsible.

The German doctrine can be explained by the influence of the Hegelian hierarchy of values to the domain of law, in which any conflict of interests is solved through the comparison of the values in question, the least important being sacrificed. During the war, the jurist Josef Kohler in his leaflet *Not kent kein Gebot* ('Necessity knows no law') undertook to demonstrate the existence of a law of necessity (and not of fact), applying a rule in German public law to international law: if a right of property is in danger, the owner who violates the property of another engages neither his criminal nor his personal responsibility (Articles 54 CP and 904 BGB). States therefore possessed the right, derived from the right of sovereignty, to preserve their integrity by means of war, an essential interest which was superior to the right of neutrality: when the legal organisation does not supply the means to resolve the conflict, the law must bend and give way to the victor: 'factum valet'. This analysis explains why the German delegates maintained so strongly that these rules on the conduct of war must be taken to their limit: to the extent that the necessities of war allow. It was said later that there was proof of German

4 Renault, 'Les premières violations', p. 419. 5 *Ibid.*

premeditation: in reality, they encountered no opposition on this point during the conferences, perhaps out of ignorance of the consequences of the German legal doctrine. During the war, the latter deployed ingenuity in assimilating state need (*Staatnotwendigkeit*) and strategic or military need (*Kriegsnotwendigkeit*) to the necessities of the war.

The great Belgian jurist, Charles de Visscher, maintained in vain that this showed confusion of policy and law, that the specific internal interests of a belligerent do not constitute a right and therefore cannot be upheld against other nations; Germany, like the Allies on their side, was convinced that it was undertaking the war by right. Germany found itself forced to violate Belgian neutrality because it was the only way in which to break its encirclement. Its survival (Germany's right to integrity recognised by international law) took precedence over the Belgian right to neutrality. Bethmann Hollweg's speech to the Reichstag on 4 August 1914 was thus self-explanatory, and it becomes simpler to understand the allusion, disastrous at the level of media interpretation, to 'scraps of paper'.

The conduct of war: legitimate defence and reprisals

The legal debate was equally intense concerning the generalised violation of civilian rights which was part of the German invasion after the unconstrained violation of Belgian and Luxembourger neutrality. All the belligerents clothed their own transgressions of the law in legal justifications – in other words: how did they escape from the law while still claiming to respect it?

Legitimate defence and reprisals constituted the justifications adopted by both sides in the war. Legitimate defence was based on an immediate and proportionate reaction to an act of aggression, and underlay German defence after the events at Louvain on 25–27 August 1914. To the Allies, the destruction by fire of part of the town and the execution of civilians became symbolic of the 'German atrocities' perpetrated in Belgium and the north and east of France. These stirred up indignation, particularly among other neutrals, whose opinion had to be 'managed'.

Not surprisingly, the German and Belgian versions of events were completely at odds with each other. The Belgians considered that the laws of war had been violated, and the Germans, who saw themselves as victims of snipers, maintained that this same right authorised legitimate defence in the form of the destruction of houses from which they had been fired on and the execution of civilians found in them. Shortly thereafter, Belgium and France (decree of 23 September 1914) named commissions of enquiry charged with amassing proof of questionable German activities (some 6,500 executions of civilians, destruction and looting on a grand scale) with the intention of bringing those responsible to trial at the end of the war. Reports were issued (eleven reports for the entire war in France), and the practice of appointing commissions of enquiry stretched to the Eastern Front (the Kristov Commission in Russia, for example).

There is some reason to affirm that the laws of war were violated everywhere and by all the warring nations. Germany felt obliged to publish a White Book on 10 May 1915, under the title, *The Conduct of the War by the Belgian People in Violation of International Law*, based on an enquiry undertaken among German soldiers and Belgian eyewitnesses. The Grey Book, entitled *Response to the German White Book*, written from an enquiry of the French Ministry for Foreign Affairs and the Belgian Minister of Justice, appeared in 1916 to refute its conclusions.

The violation of the laws of war was not limited to the war on land. From October 1914 the leaders of the German war fleet expressed their commitment to unrestricted submarine warfare. The opinion of Admiral von Pohl was identical to that of the general staff in 1904: 'The more energetic the war, the sooner the end and the less the sacrifice of wealth and human lives.'[6] But the reluctant Bethmann Hollweg did not give way until 1915, when the effects were felt of the blockade operated by the British: the waters of Great Britain and Ireland were declared a war zone, and any enemy warship or merchant ship which ventured into them would do so at its own risk. For Germany, the submarine war was justified by the right to reprisals because the blockade as practised by Britain contravened international law. If indeed the reprisals infringed the law in harming the innocent, it was in response to a previous violation and with the aim of stopping it.

The neutral nations also condemned the blockade. The risk of the capture of shipping and merchandise – seizures almost always justified by the captor state's national jurisdiction – now extended to the risk of their destruction by submarines, as in the case of the *Lusitania* on 7 May 1915. After a period of calm, the intensification of the blockade in 1916 was countered by the return of unlimited submarine warfare in February 1917, justified this time by necessity. As expressed by Ludendorff, it was a matter of national life or death: 'Our situation created in respect of the German people a military duty to practise it.'

In practice, reprisals provoked a series of infringements of the law, with each belligerent invoking a previous violation to justify its actions. The

6 Philippe Masson, 'La guerre sous marine', in Jean-Jacques Becker and Stéphane Audoin-Rouzeau (eds.), *Encyclopédie de la Grande Guerre* (Paris: Bayard, 2004), p. 438.

diplomatic note sent by the French government to all the representatives of the powers in Paris on 14 August 1914, illustrates clearly how the spiralling violations of the law began in the thinking of belligerents, and for the French, it moved beyond the original infraction of violating Belgian neutrality: 'The French government . . . maintains all reservations as to the reprisals which it might be led to undertake against an enemy so little concerned with a given promise.'[7] Each warring nation believed in its own status as the victim of an initial violation on the part of the enemy. In certain cases the fear of reprisals no doubt limited practices that ran counter to conventions, notably in relation to prisoners of war, but reprisals served above all as justification; under this heading they contributed to the brutalisation and totalisation of the war.

Peace under the law: sanctions and frustration

Once the war ended, the legal task was that of creating a peace which, because of its just foundations, would ensure that war would never again be possible. The laws of peace which American President Wilson stood for represented a peace without victory, that is without territorial acquisitions, and recognised the law of nations. Its principles were proclaimed in the Fourteen Points, which served as a contractual basis for the signature of the Armistice on 11 November 1918. For the Allies, the laws of peace presupposed in the first place a just peace, responding to the sufferings of the populations who were the victims of Germany and its allies. Those responsible must be specified and bear the consequences of their conduct in the treaties which would lay down the terms of their responsibility. From the Entente powers' perspective, Germany was designated as bearing the principal, if not the exclusive, responsibility; under the pretext that it had placed itself outside the law by failing to respect treaties, it was not admitted to negotiate the peace terms.

The question of responsibility was central to the Paris Conference which opened in January 1919, and it proved to be legally delicate. On their desks the plenipotentiaries found a memorandum entitled 'Examen de la responsabilité pénale de l'empereur Guillaume II d'Allemagne'. At the request of Clemenceau it had been drawn up by the Dean of the Faculty of Law in Paris, Fernand Larnaude, in collaboration with Louis de la Pradelle and two professors of criminal law, A. Le Poittevin and M. Garçon. For the first time in history, a head of state had to take responsibility for a war that his country was accused of having provoked. But the legal tools were lacking to make this case,

7 Ministère des affaires étrangères, *Livre jaune*, no. 157.

and the jurists, who were not blinded by patriotism, knew this, since the question of responsibility was posed at the very beginning of the war. In effect, the crime of aggression did not exist, and nor did the category of 'war crime' itself.

The German jurist Johann Casper Bluntschli was the first to have used the expression 'war crime', in his publication *Das moderne Völkerrecht der civilisirten Staten*,[8] in relation to the snipers of the Franco-Prussian War of 1870, but the term had no normative status. On the eve of the Great War, the question of responsibility did not appear central to jurists, who wrote little on the topic. The Swiss jurist Gustave Moynier focused his thoughts on how to condemn, through an international legal institution, only the infractions of the Geneva Convention. At the time of the Balkan wars the jurists had picked up the many violations of international law with respect to the wounded; but the Balkan peoples, being considered semi-barbarians, who must be helped to evolve under the guardianship of more advanced nations, were not seen by these condescending jurists as belonging to the nations subject to international law, an attribute of civilisation.

It is also true that the reports on these violations (notably the Carnegie reports) did not engage minds at the time of their publication shortly before the outbreak of the First World War. In 1908 a French magistrate, Jacques Dumas, proposed a synthesis in the *Revue générale de droit international public*. In this analysis, violations could be open to four types of sanction: moral (the judgement of international opinion, notably in the case of a refusal to submit to arbitration); material (as in retaliation and reprisals, in the form of a peaceful blockade, making the war itself serve the law which would change its nature); civil sanctions (i.e., reparations: it introduced the principle of proportionality to the damages suffered); and penal sanctions in respect of politicians. Wisely, it abstained from specifying the legal foundations of these sanctions. His analysis is interesting because it prefigures the approach of many others to this question during and after the war, an approach marked by the influence of French jurists. But for the time his conclusion was optimistic; in a fine example of positive belief, he wrote that:

> above all these sanctions floats still that which we name despite the fact that no text names it, the force of opinion. It is not wrong to say that the undertakings made at The Hague by all the powers worthy of the name find

8 Johann Caspar Bluntschli, *Das moderne Völkerrecht der civilisirten Staten* (Nördlingen: C. H. Beck, 1872), pp. 358–9.

> themselves from now on guaranteed against a large number of risks, perhaps even against the great majority.[9]

Specifically, however, Dumas did not stop there. The hypothesis of the violation of the laws of war had been foreseen in the conventions, with the sanction provided for in the form of an indemnity to be paid by the contravening state to the nation-victim of the violation. There was no question of a fine – in other words, a penal sanction – but of responsibility of a civil nature. Further, neither the amount nor the mode of calculation was indicated, nor indeed the authority which would enforce these decisions. In these circumstances, it may be concluded that only violations attributable to a conquered state would be sanctioned, and probably in the form of the lump sum indemnity which, traditionally, victors imposed on their conquests through peace treaties. This sanction, introduced at the request of the German delegate, nourished the theory of premeditation: the supposition that Germany would have tried in advance to evade the consequences of its responsibility in the knowledge that it would violate the law. Examination of the minutes of sessions of the two conferences equally invite the consideration that Germany in fact saw itself as the victim of behaviour which terrified it: the disloyal attitude of the occupied civilian populations. At the penal level, the obvious legal conclusion was that violations of the laws of war were based on national laws and their jurisdiction. During the war, at a moment when the 'German atrocities' raised the question of responsibility, the great French internationalist, Louis Renault, came to the same conclusion.

At the legal level, everything was thus said well before the end of the war. Given the state of international law, sanctioning the responsibility of the leaders and of direct authors of infractions of the rights of non-combatants, was illusory. No precise norm existed before the facts (which is the requirement in penal law, being restrictive in its interpretation and by virtue of the principles of non-retroactivity), nor were there international tribunals in existence entitled to judge them.

However, at its heart, as if to show that the question was central, the Treaty of Versailles contained a sequence of Articles (numbers 227 to 229) which, under the heading of 'Sanctions', established an *ad hoc* victors' justice. These reflected the legal embarrassment of the Allies. They are well known. Wilhelm II, accused of offending against the moral and sacred authority of treaties, would be judged by an international Allied tribunal. Those

9 J. Dumas, 'Les sanctions du droit international d'après les conventions de La Haye de 1899 et de 1907', *Revue générale de droit international public*, 15 (1908), p. 580.

responsible for violations of the laws of war would be extradited in order to be tried by the Allies' national military tribunals, which would be of mixed national composition when the crimes concerned several states. The outcome is also well known: the Netherlands refused to extradite Wilhelm II, who was to die in exile at Doorn. The Allies disagreed over the composition and extent of the lists of guilty men to be supplied by Germany. Finally, in January 1920, taking all lists together, some 850 people, included a number of great names from the German political, military and scientific worlds, were called for, particularly by the French, the Belgians (three-quarters of the accused), the British, the Italians and Yugoslavia. The Weimar government refused their extradition, which was not surprising: it is extremely rare for a state to extradite its nationals and a fortiori in the context of the indignation aroused in Germany by the publication of the Allied demand.

A compromise was found, which had been proposed by Germany some months earlier: in order to avoid aggravating the situation of the fragile Weimar Republic, those responsible would be judged in Germany by the High Court of Leipzig. Forty-five people appeared to answer for crimes seen as symbolic of the German conduct of the war. The briefs and bills of indictment were developed by the Allies (eleven for France, fifteen for Belgium, seven for Great Britain, twelve for Italy, Poland, Romania and Yugoslavia). The crimes with which the forty-five were charged principally concerned ill-treament of prisoners. The massacre of civilians was the most substantial of the accusations from Belgium (Andenne-Seilles) and France (Nomény, Jarny), the naval criminality of the submarine war in those from Great Britain (particularly the torpedoing of the hospital ships *Dover Castle* and *Llandovery Castle*) and, to a lesser extent, Italy. France also registered its belief that the execution of wounded men on the battlefield (the Stenger case) constituted a war crime. The great majority of these crimes were committed at the beginning of the war.

The prosecutor was unwilling to sustain most of these accusations, and the Court released most of the accused. Six men were convicted but received very light sentences and were acclaimed by the public, while the representatives of foreign delegations were harassed and left the town. The case provoked a diplomatic incident between France and Germany and illustrated the limits of national justice in the repression of war crimes.

Immediately after the Leipzig cases, the Supreme Council decided to set up a commission dealing with what were termed the 'guilty men of the war'. Representatives of the legal worlds of France, Great Britain, Belgium and Italy met to consider the result of the Leipzig proceedings. Their task was to present proposals on the individuals claimed by the Allied governments under Article 228 of the Treaty of Versailles, and on the lines of conduct to be observed in the application of this clause of the treaty. Its conclusions, handed down on 7 January 1922, were not in any way surprising: the verdicts of the Leipzig Court were not satisfactory. Certain of the accused were acquitted when they should have been found guilty, and the sentences of those condemned were deemed inadequate.

The commission favoured the continuation of the cases before Allied national jurisdictions better able to render justice. The German government was again required, as in 1920, to hand over the accused men to the Allied Powers. At the refusal of the German government, the Allies rejected extradition and retained the right to try criminals *in absentia*. The French government felt that British solidarity with its Allies was cooling, in particular with France, over how to pursue the cases. Aware that extradition of those charged was politically unattainable, it sought a solution which would offer public opinion the necessary reassurance. The concept was then tried in France and in Belgium until 1925, of cases of trials *in absentia* on a large scale before military courts, at the end of which the accused were convicted.

Overall, however, no one – neither victors nor vanquished – was satisfied with the legal treatment of the war. The former had achieved nothing but a parody of justice, while for the latter the responsibility imposed by the victors on them was seen as flagrantly unjust. This popular resentment helped give birth to a nationalist, and then a national-socialist campaign to reverse the verdict, in law and then in battle.

Still the legal history of the conflict was important. For the first time in history the outcome of a war was followed by a search for moral and legal responsibility for its ravages. No doubt the immaturity of the legal system, and above all the political inability – amply fed by war cultures – to exceed national perceptions of their own suffering during the war, help account for the incomplete legal resolution of the First World War. Nonetheless, by 1918 war itself was no longer seen as a normal way to settle a conflict between nations, and not all kinds of conduct in waging it were acceptable any longer.

It is important here to include another facet of the search for justice in wartime and after: the legal moves towards sanctioning Turkey for what we now term the Armenian genocide. This crime could have been seen solely as an internal matter for the Turks, open to criticism, no doubt, but not involving any international sanction for acts of war. However, Article 230 of the Treaty of Sèvres signed with Turkey stated that its authors must take responsibility before an international Allied court. This provision of the treaty would not be applied. The Turkish government had moved ahead to judge those responsible in cases where the principal accused could the more easily be condemned to death because they were tried and convicted *in absentia*. One man was actually executed for violating Turkish military law. And yet, in extending the field of protective norms to all civilians on the basis of their status as human beings, the Treaty of Sèvres stepped beyond the laws of war and was the first stage of the road leading to the proscription of crimes against humanity. In the Geneva accords of 1926, war was set outside the law, introducing the category of the crime of aggression.

Although legal tools have evolved little, a further threshold was crossed at the end of the Second World War. At Nuremburg the Allies, favoured by an admittedly different context, boldly created a retroactive criminal law and an *ad hoc* jurisdiction to try those who from then on were legally war criminals. From that time the idea has been accepted that a war which breaks out, whether international or civil, will trigger legal consequences for those responsible. The shadow of the Great War is still with us today.

24

Visual essay: Global war

JAY WINTER

Picturing war

Roland Barthes established a useful framework in which to understand the power of photographs with multiple meanings and with affective force. He distinguished between the 'studium', or common knowledge, and the 'punctum', or the arresting detail or aspect of a photograph that gives it enduring power. The 'studium' is something we 'perceive quite familiarly as a consequence of my knowledge, my culture; this field can be more or less stylized, more or less successful, depending on the photographer's skill or luck, but it always refers to a classical body of information'.[1] In other words, a photograph can confirm what we already know, or in the case of propaganda, what we are supposed to know.

Photography, though, has the power to escape from conventional limits. Photos may 'say' something which its creator or sponsor did not want to say or did not want us to see. Usually this escape from received wisdom or from a message we are supposed to receive is made possible by a visual detail or facet of the photograph which makes it odd, uncanny, puzzling. This act of breaking through the official surface of war photography happens in an instant, and at times, without our realising it happens. We reach, in Barthes's language, the *punctum*, the piercing of conventional imagery. When that happens, 'The second element will break (or punctuate) the *studium*. This time it is not I who seek it out (as I invest the field of the *studium* with my sovereign consciousness), it is this element which rises from the scene, shoots out of it like an arrow, and pierces me.'[2]

War photography is a vast terrain of images which describe what we are supposed to see, the *studium*, and the *punctum*, what arrests us in a striking and

1 Roland Barthes, *Camera Lucida: Reflections on Photography*, trans. Richard Howard (New York: Hill & Wang, 1981), pp. 25–7.
2 *Ibid.*, p. 27.

sometimes alarming manner. In this photographic essay, I try to point out the power of photographs to convey global war not as convention but as unusual, out of the ordinary, strange. I do so in three sets of images. Each group shows the vast sweep of the war, its tendency to move millions of men in unlikely encounters across the world, and to create new weapons to injure and to kill the enemy.

First, a caveat: there is a major debate about the propriety of showing photographs of dead bodies; it occurred during the 1914–18 war too. C. E. W. Nevinson had one of his realistic paintings of a dead British soldier censored, and displayed it in London with the tag 'Censored' completely covering the body in question. Military censors were similarly vigilant. Is this stance one of respect for the dead, or rather of sanitisation of the war? We use such photos here, in part because soldiers, and in this case doctors, took them and displayed them in their own photo albums for viewing after the war. But we also use them to pose the question as to the limits of war photography itself. Does an image of a dead soldier reproduced show disrespect for the dead? Does using such photographs incline us on the slippery slope to voyeurism? Or do such images bring back the landscape of battle in an unadulterated form? Each reader will have to make up her mind on these questions.

A world at war

Much of transnational history focuses on population movements, refugee flows and the transport of labour around the world. The Great War was probably the largest moment of displacement to date in global history, and it occurred over a short time and after a thirty-year period of out-migration from Europe to the Americas and the Antipodes, numbering perhaps 30 million people. The numbers on the move in the 1914–18 conflict were greater still. There were 70 million men in uniform fighting usually at a considerable distance from home, and assisting them were millions of white and non-white labourers.

The ethnic, racial and national mix of war was of staggering dimensions. The illustrations show Africans from all over the continent in a German prisoner-of-war camp, with their nationalities displayed as a key (Fig. 24.1). The encounter between this wounded Senegalese soldier and a German medical orderly on a French battlefield shows what imperial and transnational warfare was all about (Fig. 24.2). So does the modern laying on of hands by a British soldier, signing on this Indian recruit by fingerprint (Fig. 24.3). The need for medical care brought together this Egyptian doctor and a Vietnamese labourer suffering from beri-beri (Fig. 24.4). Those beyond help included Muslim soldiers buried in graveyards all over Europe. The African contribution to the defence of France was saluted in popular culture too, sometimes in racial stereotypes, but at other times (Fig. 24.5), with literally a touching affection.

The unlikely juxtapositions of war were captured by soldiers themselves, some of whom produced photo albums for their families and perhaps also for their own reminiscence. One French physician, Dr Beurrier, captured in photos his time on the Isle of Vido, dealing with the sick and wounded opposite the town of Corfu. His self-portrait opens his portfolio of photographs, many of which show dying or dead Serbian soldiers, with whom he had to deal daily (Fig 24.6). One he entitled 'Charon's barque' (Fig. 24.7); it shows the steady gaze of the physician on our frail remains. A thousand miles away, in Volhynia on the Eastern Front, a Jewish physician from Vienna, Bernhard Bardach, found himself in contact with a very different group of his co-religionists. The poor Jews of the Pale of Settlement had little in common with Bardach, a painter as well as a photographer. He photographed them at prayer (Fig. 24.8) from a cultural distance. Examining Jewish prostitutes for venereal disease in this remote part of what is now western Ukraine was an unlikely destination for a Viennese doctor (Fig. 24.9). Note the woman in the window on the right looking at prostitutes shielding their faces from the camera.

The second facet of the world war which photographs highlight is the sheer variety of landscapes of battle that soldiers and sailors faced for fifty months of combat. If we shift our optic away from the Western Front, we can see vastly different topographies. In Fig. 24.10, we see a Hungarian mountain corps unit scaling the sheer cliff faces of the Italian Front. The freezing terrain of the 'white war' is evident in Fig. 24.11. It shows the white war on the Kosturino Ridge on the Macedonian front. Evacuating the wounded from this terrain was extremely difficult, both here and on the Austrian Italian Front. The Eastern Front was huge; to describe its variety is impossible, since its length would describe a line extending from Scotland to Morocco. Still Dr Barbach gives us some sense of its endlessness in his photographs (Fig. 24.12), and also of the devastation which attended fighting in villages and towns all over what is now Poland and the Ukraine (24.13).

The air war created new possibilities and new vistas in which fighting took place. Bardach caught the mix of old and new in his photograph of horses dragging an airplane to a destination on the Eastern Front (Fig. 24.14). The global reach of the naval war was truly extraordinary. HMS *Inflexible* started the war in the Mediterranean, and helped sink two armoured cruisers during the Battle of the Falklands in 1914. In Fig. 24.15 we see her rescuing German sailors after the battle. In 1915 she shelled the Dardanelles, but was damaged by enemy fire. Back in service in 1916, she took part in the Battle of Jutland in 1916. Nothing could better illustrate the global character of the war than Fig. 24.16, showing a Japanese cruiser in protective duty off the coast of Vancouver.

Mud was the colour of much of the combat terrain of the Western Front, and mud was the colour of the men forced to fight there. In Figs. 24.17 and 24.18 we can see the odd character of a landscape resembling the dark side of the moon after a celestial flood. Horses sunk to their chests and men dwarfed by mountains of mud described a kind of war difficult to convey and even more difficult to endure. The 'puncta' in photographs of the Western Front arise from uncanny mixtures of the ordinary and the surreal. Fig. 24.19 shows half a horse in a tree, and in many instances, the suffering of animals brought out the humanity of soldiers, who could express emotion about horses more easily at times than about men (Fig. 24.20). It is not at all surprising that there were charitable events at home to collect money for sick and injured horses; they were an integral part of the most industrialised war in history (Fig. 24.21), not at all made redundant by the selective appearance of the tank (Fig. 24.22), more readily accepted in Allied armies than by the Central Powers.

The third way in which photographs can introduce us to the radically new character of the First World War is by showing the extent to which the deployment of new weapons and new tactics challenged the laws of war. Flame-throwers (Fig. 24.23) were chemical weapons, but much more radical weapons were introduced early in the war. Under pre-war international protocols, the use of poison gas weapons was deemed illegal. Starting in 1915, all armies developed stockpiles of such weapons and deployed them. First came chlorine, then phosgene and then mustard gas, and they all added to the horrors of the battlefield, without changing the strategic balance in any sector. Their effectiveness depended more on the wind direction (Figs. 24.24–24.25) than on gas masks and other counter-measures hastily adopted for men and animals alike (Figs. 24.26 and 24.27). Medical photographs showed the ravages caused by these weapons (Fig. 24.28), and helped the case for outlawing them after 1918.

The treatment of civilians was just as worrying, in that military and paramilitary operations in 1915 and after tore up the laws of war. Those laws were trampled on in the case of the abuse and murder of Jewish communities in Galicia by retreating Russian forces, and by the deportation and murder of perhaps 1 million Armenians in Anatolia, ordered by the ruling Ottoman Turkish triumvirate. Photographic evidence – some gathered by outraged German soldiers and physicians in Turkey – enables us to see the aftermath of genocide (Figs. 24.29 and 24.30). Photographs also open up the world of humanitarian aid throughout Eastern Europe and the Middle East, which was another element of the global war (Fig. 24.31). Transnational generosity extended to many groups of refugees, those who had lost everything and were on the move by the millions during and after the war.

Photography is part of the essential documentation of war. Its strength is to have captured moments – moments of horror or wonder, or just a sense of the uncanny mix of the familiar and the bizarre. The portability of the camera created vast private archives, enabling us to escape from official photography, and to have a glimpse of the enormous character of war from the standpoint of the observer, the person captivated by the detail of a photograph, the *punctum*, the shock of recognition at seeing not clichés and stereotypes, but traces of the strange face of war itself.

Bibliographical essays

1 Origins

Volker R. Berghahn

There are innumerable studies on the larger and deeper origins of the First World War, some of which are being mentioned in this chapter and also in the next one by Jean-Jacques Becker and Gerd Krumeich. While James Joll's volume, discussed in the Introduction to Chapter 1 above, continues to provide a good starting point, the more so since Richard Wetzel has updated the first edition, the following passages contain a number of additional titles that readers may find helpful as they try to understand the complexities of the subject. The annotations follow the thematic structure of the text.

Domestic politics and foreign policy

Those interested in the interaction of domestic politics and foreign-policy making may wish to start with Dietrich Geyer, *Russian Imperialism* (New Haven, CT: Yale University Press, 1987). The classic work in this interaction in the case of Germany is Eckart Kehr, *Economic Interest, Militarism and Foreign Policy* (Berkeley, CA: University of California Press, 1977). This perspective is being continued in Hans-Ulrich Wehler, *The German Empire, 1871–1918* (Leamington Spa: Berg, 1985). For the French case: Gerd Krumeich, *Armaments and Politics in France on the Eve of the First World War* (Leamington Spa: Berg, 1984) and Alfred Cobban, *A History of Modern France* (London: Penguin, 1963), especially the chapters on the Republic's attempts to stabilise the political system in the 1870s and 1880s. On the pressures exerted increasingly by national movements, see Paul M. Kennedy and Anthony Nicholls (eds.), *Nationalist and Racialist Movements in Britain and Germany before 1914* (London: Macmillan, 1981).

Imperialism

For an anthology on imperialism that contains a number of essays trying to conceptualise this phenomenon for the modern period, see Roger Owen and Bob Sutcliffe (eds.), *Studies in the Theory of Imperialism* (London: Longmans, 1972). On British colonialism it is still worthwhile to consult John Gallagher and Ronald Robinson, *Africa and the Victorians* (London and New York: Macmillan, 1961), not only because they discuss the interaction between the metropole (London) and the periphery (in this case the Sudan), but also because they introduced the distinction between an earlier 'informal imperialism' and a later 'formal' one that involved direct occupation and administration. On Belgian colonialism see Adam Hochschild's study, discussed in the text. On German colonialism, in addition to Isabel Hull's book (discussed in the text) and Sebastian Conrad (in the notes), see also Helmut Bley, *Namibia under German Rule* (Hamburg: LIT-Verlag, 1996).

Culture

The classic study on high culture is Carl Schorske, *Fin-de-siècle Vienna: Politics and Culture* (New York: Knopf, 1980). Unfortunately this is not a comprehensive study of Austro-Hungarian culture but a collection of essays. But if the reader begins with Schorske's really quite wonderful first essay on the 'Ringstrasse' in the optimistic days of the mid century, the later essays on the growing pessimism and sense of decadence are all the more intriguing. On the German side, see Fritz Stern, *The Politics of Cultural Despair* (Garden City, NY: Doubleday, 1965). The study by Edward R. Tannenbaum (cited in the text) is invaluable because it deals both with high culture and the avant-garde as well as with popular culture in pre-1914 Europe more widely.

Armaments and war preparations

Here again are quite a number of relevant studies, some of which have already been mentioned in the text and notes. Next to Samuel R. Williamson's and Volker R. Berghahn's, three other studies that appeared in the same Macmillan series on the Origins of the First World War are by John Keiger (on France), Zara Steiner (on Britain) and Dominic Lieven (on Russia). Indispensable still: Fritz Fischer, *War of Illusions* (New York: W. W. Norton, 1975). But contrast with Konrad H. Jarausch's biography of Reich Chancellor Bethmann Hollweg (*The Enigmatic Chancellor* (New Haven, CT: Yale University Press, 1972). He examines the localisation argument. Important also: Annika Mombauer, *Helmuth von Moltke and the Origins of the First World War* (Cambridge University Press, 2001); Robert Evans and Hartmut Pogge von Strandmann (eds.), *The Coming of the First World War* (Oxford: Clarendon Press, 1988), F. R. Bridge, *The Habsburg Monarchy among the Great Powers, 1815–1918* (New York: Berg, 1990); Manfred Boemecke *et al.* (eds.), *Anticipating Total War* (New York: St Martin's Press, 1996); Paul M. Kennedy (ed.), *The War Plans of the Great Powers, 1880–1914* (London: Allen & Unwin, 1979) and *The Rise of the Anglo-German Antagonism, 1860–1914* (Atlantic Highlands, NJ: Ashfield Press, 1987). Finally, because this anthology is also concerned with problems of pre-1914 political culture: Holger Afflerbach and David Stevenson (eds.), *An Improbable War?* (New York: Berghahn, 2007).

2 1914: Outbreak

Jean-Jacques Becker and Gerd Krumeich

Never have the origins of a war precipitated a debate as important and enduring as that on the outbreak of the First World War. It has been political, ideological and historiographical in character. There have been so many different strands to this debate that it is difficult to distinguish between polemics and history.

In the 1920s, the central issue in the debate on war origins was the question of 'responsibilities'. This matter became central from the moment the German government signed the Versailles Treaty which affirmed that Germany was solely and totally responsible for the war. In the early days, the key participants were less historians than journalists, retired military men and intellectuals of more or less good faith. A good guide to this phase is Annika Mombauer, *The Origins of the First World War: Controversies and Consensus* (London: Longman, 2002). What is striking is that this polemical moment also provided the occasion for the publication of studies, more political than historical, which went beyond the debate over 'responsibility'.

Reflections on what happened in July 1914 reached a level which merits the admiration of historians today. Three historians stand out: Bernadotte Schmitt, Pierre Renouvin and Jules Isaac. On this phase of the debate see: Jacques Droz, *Les causes de la Première guerre mondiale: essai d'historiographie* (Paris: Éditions du Seuil, 1973); and the more recent interpretation of Annika Mombauer, *The Origins*, pp. 78–118. On Pierre Renouvin, see the historiographical study on the war by Jay Winter and Antoine Prost, *The Great War in History: Debates and Controversies, 1914 to the Present* (Cambridge University Press, 2005) (the French version appeared under the title *Penser la Grande guerre* (Paris: Éditions du Seuil, 2004)). A remarkably complete and influential essay is that of Samuel R. Williamson and Ernest R. May, 'An identity of opinion: historians and July 1914', *Journal of Modern History*, 79 (2007), pp. 335–87.

Following the first generation of First World War historians was the Italian journalist and political figure, Luigi Albertini, whose study of 'July', published in Italian in 1942–3, was based not only on all available sources but on interviews with former leaders still alive. See his *Origins of the War of 1914*, trans. Isabella M. Massey, 3 vols. (London: Oxford University Press, 1952–7). This study is still alive in today's debates, though few acknowledge it. Albertini had the merit of establishing with as great a degree of precision as possible the chronology of diplomatic moves on all levels. His aim was to establish who knew what and when. To be sure, this cannot account for everything; it cannot establish how various moves were interpreted, and neglects that which was neglected at the time, but it is an indispensable aid against anachronism.

Albertini's scholarship was not well known – it appeared in English translation only in the 1950s – but we hear its echoes in the violent controversy arising from the publication in 1961 of Fritz Fischer's *Griff nach der Weltmacht* (Düsseldorf: Droste, 1964), which caused a sensation in Germany and in the international scholarly community. Fritz Fischer aimed to show that Germany wanted the war long before she provoked it in 1914. This was a war which seemed to be necessary for her to become a world power, or more precisely, a dominant world power. Contrary to prior claims, Fischer did not find many new sources on the basis of which he analysed the July 1914 crisis. What he did was to read through his personal optic a series of well-known and long-established documents. He owed much to the research of Albertini. Useful on the international dimensions of the Fischer controversy are Mombauer, *Origins*, pp. 127ff. and Winter and Prost, *The Great War*, pp. 468ff.

There was one new source which fuelled the 'Fischer debate' in the 1970s. It was the diary of Kurt Riezler, principal secretary of the German Chancellor, Bethmann Hollweg. This document was known to exist, but had been held privately in the family ever since. Mombauer, *Origins*, pp. 155–60, is useful on this source.

The Fischer thesis on sole German responsibility for the outbreak of war in 1914 requires a comparative analysis of the actions of each of the belligerents, accomplished by historians in an impressive list of books on individual countries and the origins of the war. These studies modified considerably our understanding of the July crisis. For this moment in scholarship, see Marc Trachtenberg, 'The coming of the First World War: a reassessment', in Trachtenberg, *History and Strategy* (Princeton University Press, 1991), pp. 47–99.

With the arrival of research on 'mentalities' in the 1960s and 1970s, there occurred a real paradigm change in approaches to this topic. Now historians of the twentieth century followed Bloch and Febvre in trying to understand the structures of feeling and thought of contemporaries in 1914. The first to do so was the British historian, James Joll, in his inaugural lecture at the London School of Economics in 1968. His theme was 'the unspoken assumptions' of the leaders of 1914, and his views can be followed in the 1968 edition of his inaugural lecture published by the London School of Economics in pamphlet form. The task of the historian, Joll said, was both difficult and unavoidable. It was 'to re-create the whole climate of opinion within which political leaders in the past operated, and to discover what were the assumptions in the minds of ordinary men and women faced with the consequences of their ruler's decisions' (p. 13). Joll later developed a new paradigm concerning the 'mood of 1914'. In his pioneering work on the Great War he showed that the decisions of July 1914 rested on sentiments formed earlier, and that the war they unleashed was one that was beyond their imagination at the time. On Joll's ideas, see Williamson and May's essay in the *Journal of Modern History*, cited above. Joll's view does not preclude detailed analysis of decisions taken and of responsibilities on different levels for the outbreak of the war. Instead its advantage is the avoidance of anachronism, of using our perspective to judge that of others, a practice which Marc Bloch termed a mortal sin in history.

Other historians reached conclusions similar to Joll at roughly the same time, though most recognise that it was Joll who led the way. This was particularly true in the case of Wolfgang Mommsen, who had played an important role in the Fischer controversy, and whose reflections on the 'topos of inevitable war' in the minds of the German leadership appeared in 1980 and was soon translated into several other languages. See his two essays: 'Die deutsche Kriegszielpolitik 1914–1918: Bemerkungen zum Stand der Diskussion', in Walter Laqueur and George L. Mosse (eds.), *Kriegsausbruch 1914* (Munich: Nymphenburger, 1967), pp. 60–100; and 'The topos of inevitable war in Germany in the decade before 1914', in Volker R. Berghahn and Martin Kitchen (eds.), *Germany in the Age of Total War* (London: Croom Helm, 1981), pp. 23–45.

Similarly pathbreaking was the work of Jean-Jacques Becker, *1914, Comment les Français sont entrés dans la guerre* (Paris: Presses de la Fondation Nationale des Sciences Politiques, 1977), on public opinion in France at the moment of the outbreak of the war, which permitted the historical study of the genesis of the *union sacrée*. Later, Richard Hamilton and Holger Herwig brought together a series of essays on *Decisions for War, 1914–1917* (New York: Cambridge University Press, 2004), where they moved in a different direction, setting aside questions of social structure or mentalities, to concentrate solely on 'the men on the spot', the men who took the decisions. They disclosed 'that the decision makers . . . sought to save, maintain, or enhance the power and prestige of the nation' (p. 20). It is evident that such a framework, subtly, perhaps subconsciously, reintroduces the notion of 'mentalities', in which social-Darwinian notions informed beliefs on the need to defend the nation.

It is striking that the mix of military plans and political decisions little concerned historians of responsibility for the war. To be sure, everyone knew there was a Schlieffen Plan, but the older historiography never established when and to what extent this plan was decisive in framing concrete decisions. These scholars were content to describe pre-mobilisation and mobilisation, partial and general in the last days of July. The best synthesis is still Steven E. Miller *et al.* (eds.), *Military Strategy and the Origins of the First World War* (Princeton University Press, 1991), and especially the chapter in this collection written by Marc Trachtenberg, 'The meaning of mobilization in 1914', pp. 195ff.

The puzzle of mobilisation was also at the heart of the work of the French scholar Jules Isaac, for whom the German decision during the crisis was marked by a degree of incoherence, responsibility for which he attributed to General Moltke. On this point, see Isaac's *Un débat historique: 1914, le problème des origines de la guerre* (Paris: Rieder, 1933), p. 157. This matter is significant, and suggests that we can find the key, and perhaps the decisive key, to Russian, German and French decisions in considerations of military 'necessity'. The research of Gerhard Ritter on German militarism (see his monumental *The Sword and the Sceptre: The Problem of Militarism in Germany*, vol. III: *The Tragedy of Statesmanship: Bethmann Hollweg as War Chancellor 1914–1917* (London: Allen Lane, 1972)) helped establish the validity of this interpretation. This view was further fortified by the work of Volker Berghahn, whose analysis of the July crisis distinguishes political, economic, military and intellectual factors (see his *Germany and the Approach of War in 1914*, 2nd edn (Basingstoke: Macmillan, 1993)). Last but not least, the important work of David Stevenson on armaments before the Great War concludes with a chapter on the 'militarization of diplomacy' during the July crisis: see his *Armaments and the Coming of War: Europe 1904–1914* (Oxford University Press, 1996), pp. 366ff.

To what extent can one say that military opinion prevailed in the war crisis? With respect to France, the question remains open and acute. Were Poincaré, President of the Republic, and Paléologue, French ambassador to Russia, primarily worried about preserving the Franco-Russian alliance, or were they prepared to risk everything to honour military accords? This latter position is that of Gerd Krumeich, *Armaments and Politics in France on the Eve of the First World War* (Leamington Spa: Berg, 1984); see also his 'Raymond Poincaré dans la Crise de Juillet 1914', in *La politique et la guerre (Mélanges Jean-Jacques Becker)* (Paris: Éditions Noêsis, 2002), pp. 508–18. Or did they have their own considerations facing a Germany worried for years about encirclement, real or imagined? This is the thesis of Stefan Schmidt, *Frankreichs Außenpolitik in der Julikrise 1914* (Munich: R. Oldenburg Verlag, 2009). John Keiger's synthesis (*France and the Origins of the First World War* (London: Macmillan, 1983)) leaves these questions open. But, as M. B. Hayne has shown in *The French Foreign Office and the Origins of the First World War 1898–1914* (Oxford: Clarendon Press, 1993), it is essential to recognise that there is no evidence of military pressure placed on French political leaders during the July crisis. In the case of Russia, we are much less well informed. There is research still to be done on the real impact of military planning on political decisions, a question on which there is still no consensus today. On this point, see Sean McMeekin, *The Russian Origins of the First World War* (Cambridge, MA: Harvard University Press, 2011), whose views are questioned by Volker Berghahn in Chapter 1 of this volume; and Keith Neilson, 'Russia', in Keith Wilson (ed.), *Decisions for War, 1914* (London: UCL Press, 1995), pp. 97–120.

Nevertheless, the research of Holger Afflerbach and of Annika Mombauer has given us much on which to interpret the correlation between military and political decisions. They have shown that the German military elite played a much larger role in the decisions taken in the July crisis than we have thought until now. See Holger Afflerbach, *Falkenhayn: Politisches Handeln und Denken im Kaiserreich* (Munich: R. Oldenbourg Verlag, 1994); Annika Mombauer, 'A reluctant military leader? Helmuth von Moltke and the July Crisis of 1914', *War in History*, 6:4 (1999), pp. 417–46; see also her essay on the 'July Crisis' in her book *Helmuth von Moltke and the Origins of the First World War* (Cambridge University Press, 2001). To be sure, Fischer and his students wrote of German 'militarism' and on the desire among the war party to impose its views on the political leadership. But Mombauer goes further in saying: 'It is striking to what extent military concerns and reasoning had become common currency, accepted without question by civilians and determining their decision making' (Mombauer, 'Reluctant military leader', p. 421). The views of Hew Strachan move in the same direction. See his 'Towards a comparative history of World War I: some reflections', *Militärgeschichtliche Zeitschrift*, 67 (2008), pp. 339–44. Mombauer shows striking similarities between the long-term, pessimistic attitude of Moltke, the Chief of the Imperial General Staff, and that of Bethmann Hollweg. Doubting time and again that Germany could win a quick and decisive victory, Moltke still told everyone within hearing range that Germany had to go to war and 'the sooner the better'. Wolfgang Mommsen had come to a similar interpretation of German thinking in the July crisis; see his essay on 'The topos of inevitable war'. Mombauer and Stig Förster separately showed that many German military leaders did not believe a war would be short and victorious; so much for the 'short war illusion' of which other historians spoke when looking at the war crisis. For Förster's formulation, see his 'Der deutsche Generalstab und die Illusion des kurzen Krieges 1871–1914: Metakritik eines Mythos', *Militärgeschichtliche Mitteilungen*, 54 (1995), pp. 61–98. The problem remains to determine the extent to which a phobia about 'encirclement' was the decisive element in the war crisis of 1914.

This point brings us back to the beginning of this bibliographical essay. Joll invited historians to think about what kind of war the leaders of 1914 were capable of imagining. It is in this domain that there remains much work still to be done. Cataclysms of the order of Verdun or the Somme could not have been in their minds, even if we find – from Moltke to Bethmann Hollweg or from Bebel to Sasonov – fears of the eventual destruction of Europe, a kind of seven years' war, in the terms Bebel used in 1911, entailing the destruction of millions of young men in a future war. In reflecting on the writings of actual military leaders both before and during the July crisis on the war or wars to come, we do not find a hint of what later would unfold on the battlefields of the Great War. It is in this kind of terrain that we can see why Jean-Baptiste Duroselle termed the Great War as 'incomprehensible' (see his *La Grande guerre des Français: 1914–1918: l'incompréhensible* (Paris: Perrin, 1994)). The war prepared for in 1914, the war undertaken in 1914, was utterly remote from the war Europe and the world had to live through from 1915 to 1918. To chart the difference between the war imagined and the real war to come is a kind of 'counterfactual history', a task which still awaits us.

Finally, there is the brilliantly told and abundantly documented study of Christopher Clark, *The Sleepwalkers: How Europe Went to War in 1914* (London: Allen Lane, 2012). While masterful, it tells an anti-Fischer tale with a bias against Serbia and towards Austria–Hungary and Germany, whose decision-makers vanish from the narrative at decisive moments in 1914.

3 1915: Stalemate

Stéphane Audoin-Rouzeau

The historiography of the First World War has rarely defined its chronology year by year. Many studies of this kind have encountered difficulties as a result, particularly in relation to 1915, caught as it is between 1914, with the outbreak of war and the first major operations, and 1916, the year of the great battles of materiel. This second year of the war is thus frequently isolated within studies that are wider in theme or national interest, and which consider the totality of the war. Such examples are not followed here. The choice of works cited below represents a selection among studies in which the year 1915 is seen as central.

For a rare study of 1915 as a whole, see Lyn Macdonald, *1915: The Death of Innocence* (London: Headline, 1993). A recent study adopts the *problématique* of the years 1914–15 as a fundamental turning point, treating 1915 in depth from a new perspective: John Horne (ed.), *Vers la guerre totale: le tournant de 1914–1915* (Paris: Tallandier, 2010). (Note in particular the substantial general introduction.)

At the narrative level, the chapters dealing with the military history of 1915 can be consulted in two major studies: John Keegan, *The First World War* (London: Hutchinson, 1998) and Hew Strachan, *European Armies and the Conduct of War* (London: Allen & Unwin, 1983).

The following general work, apart from its structure, picks out clearly certain key events of 1915, at least from the British point of view, both on the home front and on the battlefields. The point of view is narrative and analytical, but the chapters are short: Trevor Wilson, *The Myriad Faces of War: Britain and the Great War, 1914–1918* (Cambridge: Polity Press, 1986). (See in particular Parts 2, 3 and 5, for the military aspects and Part 4 for the home front.)

Certain military aspects of the year 1915 have been the subject of specific studies, notably Gallipoli: George Cassar, *The French and the Dardanelles: A Study of the Failure in the Conduct of War* (London: Allen & Unwin, 1971); Kevin Fewster, Vecihi Basarin and Hatice Basarin, *Gallipoli: The Turkish Story* (London: Allen & Unwin, 2003); Jenny Macleod, *Reconsidering Gallipoli* (Manchester University Press, 2004); and Victor Rudenno, *Gallipoli: Attack from the Sea* (New Haven, CT: Yale University Press, 2008).

The year 1915 is also very evident in a work which is fundamental on matters relating to the Eastern Front, both in its military aspects and the home front: Norman Stone, *The Eastern Front, 1914–1917* (London: Penguin, 1998).

By reason of the date of Italy's entry into the war, 1915 is a strong presence in Antonio Gibelli, *La grande guerra degli italiani, 1915–1918* (Milan: Sansoni, 1998).

On the use of gas, 1915 was a decisive period, well studied in the two following works: L. F. Haber, *The Poisonous Cloud: Chemical Warfare in the First World War* (Oxford: Clarendon Press, 1986); Olivier Lepick, *La Grande Guerre chimique, 1914–1918* (Paris: PUF, 1998).

On matters concerning civilian populations and the different forms of assault that they suffered in 1915, historiography has recently been very considerably enhanced. On the occupations during the 'long 1915' in a comparative study, a fundamental synthesis can be found in Sophie de Schaepdrijver, 'L'Europe occupée en 1915: entre violence et exploitation', in Horne (ed.), *Vers la guerre totale*, pp. 121–51.

On refugees in the Russian Empire, a crucial question in 1915, see Peter Gatrell, *A Whole Empire Walking: Refugees in Russia during the First World War* (Bloomington, IN: Indiana University Press, 1999.)

On Russian anti-Semitic acts of violence: Peter Holquist, 'Les violences de l'armée russe à l'encontre des Juifs en 1915: causes et limites', in Horne (ed.), *Vers la guerre totale*, pp. 191–219.

On the 'battle of words' which, very particularly in 1915, took over from the 'German atrocities' of 1914, see a fundamental book: John Horne and Alan Kramer, *German Atrocities, 1914: A History of Denial* (New Haven, CT and London: Yale University Press, 2001).

On the German blockade in 1915: Paul Vincent, *The Politics of Hunger: The Allied Blockade of Germany, 1915–1919* (Athens, OH: Ohio University Press, 1985); Gerd Krumeich, 'Le blocus maritime et la guerre sous-marine', in Horne (ed.), *Vers la guerre totale*, pp. 175–90.

On the vital question of the Armenian genocide, the following stand out: Arnold Toynbee, *Armenian Atrocities: The Murder of a Nation* (London: Hodder & Stoughton, 1915) (the great report by the British historian, then aged 26, which was published in November 1915 and which was the first book on the genocide); Donald Bloxham, *The Great Game of Genocide: Imperialism, Nationalism and the Destruction of the Ottoman Armenians* (Oxford University Press, 2005); Raymond Kévorkian, *Le génocide des Arméniens* (Paris: Odile Jacob, 2006); Taner Akçam, *A Shameful Act: The Armenian Genocide and the Question of the Turkish Responsibility* (New York: Metropolitan Books, 2006); Vahakn Dadrian, *The History of the Armenian Genocide: Ethnic Conflict from the Balkans to Anatolia to the Caucasus* (Providence and Oxford: Berg, 1995); and Yves Ternon, *Les Arméniens: histoire d'un génocide* (Paris: Éditions du Seuil, 1996).

Two studies of the economic mobilisation examine a significant development in 1915: R. J. Q. Adams, *Arms and the Wizard: Lloyd George and the Ministry of Munitions, 1915–1916* (London: Cassell, 1978); and L. H. Siegelbaum, *The Politics of Industrial Mobilization in Russia, 1914–1917: A Study of the War Industry Committee* (London: Macmillan, 1984).

On the scientific and technological mobilisation in 1915, an essential synthesis can be found in Anne Rasmussen, 'Sciences et techniques: l'escalade', in Horne (ed.), *Vers la guerre totale*, pp. 97–117.

4 1916: Impasse

Robin Prior

For those with French, the appropriate volumes of the official history, *Les Armées Françaises dans la Grande Guerre* (Paris: Imprimerie nationale, 1922–39) with their massive supplements of documents, are indispensable. For the Germans the Reichsarchiv, *Der Weltkreig 1914 bis 1918*, vol. x is good on detail, less reliable on interpretation.

It is sad to report that there are few modern studies of Verdun written by the French. The best book is still therefore Alistair Horne, *The Price of Glory: Verdun 1916* (London: Macmillan, 1963), although its frequent references to so-called parallel events in the Second World War make it somewhat anachronistic. To English readers it is still essential. Ian Ousby, *The Road to Verdun* (London: Jonathan Cape, 2002) is an attempt to integrate the battle into wider French society. It does not always succeed. Anthony Clayton, *Paths of Glory: The French Army 1914–1918* (London: Cassell, 2003) has chapters on Verdun. It is a brave attempt at an overview of the French but must be used with care as some of its very basic facts are wrong. Malcolm Brown, *Verdun 1916* (Stroud: Tempus, 1999) is, as might be expected, strong on the experiences of the individual soldier. David Mason, *Verdun* (Moreton-in-the Marsh: Windrush, 2000) is a useful summary. Its place of publication seems weirdly appropriate. Georges Blond, *Verdun* (London: Andre Deutsch, 1965) is one of the few French studies of the battle to have been translated. It is well worth study. I found the Michelin Guide, *Verdun and the Battles for its Possession* (Clermont Ferrand, 1919) useful to grasp the topography of the battlefield.

Pétain, because of later events, has received much attention. Nicholas Atkin, *Pétain* (London: Longman, 1997) and Richard Griffith, *Marshal Pétain* (London: Constable, 1970) are balanced accounts. Pétain's version, *Verdun* (London: Elkin Mathews & Marrot, 1930) is also more balanced in its appraisal of the battle than might be thought. In French, Guy Pedroncini, *Pétain: le soldat et la gloire, 1856–1918* (Paris: Perrin, 1989) is the essential work. Of the other French generals there is virtually nothing in English. Joffre, *The Memoirs of Marshal Joffre*, 2 vols. (London: Geoffrey Bles, 1932) are as devoid of insight as was Joffre himself in 1916. For another view of the political dimensions of the French war effort see J. C. King, *Generals and Politicians: Conflicts between France's High Command, Parliament and Government* (Berkeley, CA: University of California Press, 1951). A more modern study of French strategy is provided in Robert Doughty's *Pyrrhic Victory: French Strategy and Operations in the Great War* (Cambridge MA: Harvard University Press, 2005).

On the German side, Falkenhayn's *General Headquarters 1914–1916 and its Critical Decisions* (London: Hutchinson, 1919) must be read with forensic care. Much more reliable is Crown Prince Wilhelm, *My War Experiences* (London: Hurst & Blackett, 1922). Robert Foley, *German Strategy and the Path to Verdun* (Cambridge University Press, 2005) is an excellent account of the development of attrition. More generally there is Ian Passingham, *All the Kaiser's Men: The Life and Death of the German Army on the Western Front 1914–1918* (Stroud: Sutton, 2003).

For the Somme, the starting point for English-speaking readers must be Sir John Edmonds, *Military Operations: France and Belgium 1916*, volume I, and Captain Wilfrid Miles who wrote volume II. They were published by Macmillan in 1932 and 1938 respectively and are far more critical of Haig's generalship than might be thought.

There are many studies of the battle. Robin Prior and Trevor Wilson, *The Somme* (New Haven, CT and London: Yale University Press, 2005) is one of the most recent. For a different perspective, Gary Sheffield's *The Somme* (London: Cassell, 2003) is recommended. Peter Hart's *The Somme* (New York: W. W. Norton, 2008) is strong on the personal experiences of the soldiers. A. H. Farrar-Hockley, *The Somme* (London: Batsford, 1964) is an older study with many insights. Peter Liddle, *The 1916 Battle of the Somme: A Reappraisal* (London: Leo Cooper, 1992) doesn't reappraise much of interest. William Philpott, *Bloody Victory* (London: Little, Brown, 2009) is a useful reminder that the French also took part in the battle. In what sense the Somme can be seen as a British victory is more problematic. Elizabeth Greenhalgh's chapter on the Somme in her book *Victory Through Coalition* (Cambridge University Press, 2005) is a more judicious treatment.

There have been (too?) many studies of Haig. The definitive published version of his *War Diaries and Letters 1914–1918* is edited by Gary Sheffield and John Bourne (London: Weidenfeld & Nicolson, 2005). John Terraine's *Douglas Haig: The Educated Soldier* (London: Cassell, 1963) still has merit, although it glosses over Haig's failings. Denis Winter's *Haig's*

Command (London: Viking, 1991) is too full of conspiracy theories to be taken seriously. Duff Cooper's *Haig*, 2 vols. (London: Faber & Faber, 1935–6) was useful until editions of Haig's diaries appeared and demonstrated how selectively Duff Cooper had used them. Sir John Davidson's *Haig: Master of the Field* (London: Nevill, 1953) fails to convince. Gary Sheffield's *The Chief: Douglas Haig and the British Army* (London: Aurum Press, 2011) presents a viewpoint different from my own.

A series of battlefield guides to the Somme published by Leo Cooper and written by diverse hands should not be neglected. There are far too many to mention individually here, but they often contain remarkable insights into the terrain and difficulties thrown up by sections of the battlefield.

On the artillery, Jackson Hughes's tragically unpublished thesis, 'The Monstrous Anger of the Guns: British Artillery Tactics on the Western Front' (PhD thesis, University of Adelaide, 1994) should be consulted. The British official history, Martin Farndale, *History of the Royal Regiment of Artillery: The Western Front* (London: Royal Artillery Institution, 1986) is almost worthless for the Somme. Much better is the unpublished draft history by Brigadier Anstey, languishing in the Artillery Institution Archives in Greenwich. Lawrence Bragg *et al.*, *Artillery Survey in the First World War* (London: Field Survey Association, 1971) is essential for those trying to come to grips with the technical side of the subject.

The chapters on the Somme in Winston Churchill's *World Crisis* (London: Thornton Butterworth, 1923) have been too heavily criticised. Much material was supplied to him by James Edmonds, and his dissection of the casualties of the Somme is as good a study as can be found. I discuss it in *Churchill's 'World Crisis' As History* (London: Croom Helm, 1983). Lloyd George's *War Memoirs* must be read with caution and in conjuction with Andrew Suttie, *Rewriting the First World War: Lloyd George, Politics and Strategy* (Basingstoke: Palgrave Macmillan, 2005).

The memoir literature is too detailed to deal with here. John Bickersteth (ed.), *The Bickersteth Diaries* (London: Leo Cooper, 1996) is particularly harrowing. Martin Middlebrook, *The First Day on the Somme* (London: Allen Lane, 1971) is a kind of collective memoir. It enjoys a classic status but almost all of Middlebrook's military judgements can be called into question.

5 1917: Global war

Michael S. Neiberg

This bibliography avoids general histories that cover the entire war in an effort to focus on the main events of 1917. The following three volumes are dedicated exclusively to the year and have the added advantage of looking at the problem globally: Jean-Jacques Becker, *1917 en Europe: l'année impossible* (Brussels: Éditions Complexe, 1997); Ian F. W. Beckett (ed.), *1917: Beyond the Western Front* (Leiden: Brill, 2009); and Peter Dennis and Jeffrey Grey (eds.), *1917: Tactics, Training, and Technology* (Canberra: Army History Unit Press, 2007).

The American entry and first year of the war for the United States are the subject of a number of books. Grotelueschen is particularly valuable for the military aspects. Kennedy is a classic and Keene is most appropriate for a student audience. These all provide a good introduction to the topic: Justus Doenecke, *Nothing Less than War: A New History of America's Entry into World War I* (Lexington, KY: University Press of Kentucky, 2011);

Mark Grotelueschen, *The AEF Way of War: The American Army and Combat in World War I* (Cambridge University Press, 2007); Jennifer D. Keene, *World War I: The American Soldier Experience* (Lincoln, NE: University of Nebraska Press, 2011); David Kennedy, *Over Here: The First World War and American Society* (New York: Oxford University Press, 1980); and David Trask, *The AEF and Coalition Warmaking, 1917–1918* (Lawrence, KS: University Press of Kansas, 1993).

There is less scholarly attention to the events of 1917 in Russia than one might suppose. There is even less attention to the events of the Eastern Front in that year. McMeekin offers a recent analysis based on exhaustive primary work in numerous archives. Liulevicius offers a provocative and compelling thesis. All of these are useful: W. Bruce Lincoln, *Passage Through Armageddon: The Russians in War and Revolution* (New York: Simon & Schuster, 1986); Vejas Liulevicius, *War Land on the Eastern Front: Culture, National Identity and German Occupation in World War I* (Cambridge University Press, 2000); Sean McMeekin, *The Russian Origins of the First World War* (Cambridge, MA: Harvard University Press, 2011); and Allan K. Wildman, *The End of the Russian Imperial Army*, 2 vols. (Princeton University Press, 1980–7).

Perhaps not surprisingly, there is much more scholarship about events on the Western Front in 1917. There remains considerably more debate about British strategy and the Passchendaele campaign than about most other battles that year. Smith's book is one of the best on the events of this crucial year. It focuses on one French division as a way of explaining the mutinies that followed the Nivelle offensive. There is still no definitive biography of Nivelle himself. See the following: Martin Kitchen, *The Silent Dictatorship: The Politics of the German High Command under Hindenburg and Ludendorff, 1916–1918* (London: Croom Helm, 1976); Guy Pedroncini, *Les Mutineries de 1917* (Paris: PUF, 1967); Robin Prior and Trevor Wilson, *Passchendaele: The Untold Story* (New Haven, CT: Yale University Press, 1996); Leonard V. Smith, *Between Mutiny and Obedience: The Case of the French Fifth Infantry Division during World War I* (Princeton University Press, 1994); Tim Travers, *How the War Was Won: Command and Technology in the British Army on the Western Front 1917–1918* (London: Routledge, 1992).

The Italian Front has received increased scholarly attention of late. So, too, has the Middle Eastern front, although much of the discussion there is on the post-war political ramifications of the Balfour Declaration (issued in 1917) and the secret Sykes-Picot Agreement of 1916. The former famously promised British support for a Jewish homeland after the war while the latter divided the region into British and French spheres of influence. Studies of the Italian and Ottoman Fronts include: George Cassar, *The Forgotten Front: The British Campaign in Italy, 1917–1918* (London: Hambledon, 1998); Edward Erickson, *Ottoman Army Effectiveness in World War I: A Comparative Study* (London: Routledge, 2007); Elie Kedourie, *England and the Middle East: The Destruction of the Ottoman Empire, 1914–1921* (London: Bowes & Bowes, 1956); Mario Morselli, *Caporetto 1917: Victory or Defeat?* (London: Routledge, 2001); and Jan Karl Tannenbaum, *France and the Arab Middle East, 1914–1920* (Philadelphia: American Philosophical Society, 1978).

Finally, several historians have turned their attention to the experience of non-British units on the Western Front in this year. For Canada especially, 1917 was a critical year. Australia and New Zealand, although more commonly identified with Gallipoli, in fact suffered more casualties at Passchendaele. See the following for a guide to this part of the war: Tim Cook, *Shock Troops: Canadians Fighting the Great War, 1917–1918* (Toronto: Viking

Canada, 2008); Glyn Harper, *Massacre at Passchendaele: The New Zealand Story* (Auckland: HarperCollins, 2000); Geoffrey Hayes, Andrew Iarocci and Mike Bechtold (eds.), *Vimy Ridge: A Canadian Reassessment* (Waterloo, ON: Wilfrid Laurier University Press, 2007; and the still classic study by Bill Gammage: *The Broken Years: Australian Soldiers in the Great War* (Canberra: Australian National University Press, 1974).

6 1918: Endgame

Christoph Mick

Histories of the Great War include chapters on 1918, but often they are tagged on almost as an afterthought. Many important economic, social and cultural transformations had already begun before 1918 and were not completed by the time the war ended. In November 1918 the war on the Western Front was over but it still continued in large parts of Eastern Europe, and peace treaties with the Central Powers were only signed in 1919. The year 1918 is therefore, in many ways, a year of transition. As many important publications on the war and the immediate post-war period are discussed in other bibliographical essays of this volume, I will – with a few exceptions – be focusing on literature which is specifically dedicated to the year 1918.

The battles of the Marne and the Somme, of Verdun, Ypres and Passchendaele have traditionally attracted greater attention by historians than the German spring offensives or the Allied victories in the summer and autumn of 1918. This has only changed in the last few years. In 1999, an edited volume was published in Germany which gives an excellent overview of the ongoing discussions about the military, political, social, economic and cultural history of the last year of the Great War: Jörg Duppler and Gerhard Paul Gross (eds.), *Kriegsende 1918: Ereignis, Wirkung, Nachwirkung* (Munich: R. Oldenbourg Verlag, 1999).

A comprehensive history of 1918 was published by David Stevenson. The book covers all theatres of war and also includes chapters on morale, the home fronts, the war economy and submarine and naval warfare: David Stevenson, *With our Backs to the Wall: Victory and Defeat in 1918* (London: Allen Lane, 2011).

Two excellent studies discuss the military and (Martin Kitchen) political aspects of the German offensives: Martin Kitchen, *The German Offensives of 1918* (Stroud: Tempus, 2005); and David T. Zabecki, *The German 1918 Offensives: A Case Study in the Operational Level of War* (Abingdon: Routledge, 2006).

The best overview of the events on the Italian Front, which includes seventy pages on the year 1918, is Mark Thompson's *The White War: Life and Death on the Italian Front, 1915–1919* (London: Basic Books, 2008).

An indispensable work on the domestic situation in Austria-Hungary in 1918, which also covers the situation in Germany, is Holger H. Herwig, *The First World War: Germany and Austria-Hungary 1914–1918* (London: Edward Arnold, 1997).

German historiography after the Second World War has been more interested in the transition from the 'silent dictatorship' of Hindenburg and Ludendorff to the democratic Weimar Republic than in the spring offensives and subsequent German defeat. The question whether post-war Germany would have had a better chance of developing into a peaceful and democratic nation if there had been more transformation and less continuity, or whether the opposite is true, is still hotly debated. The leaders of the two social democratic parties in particular have come in for a lot of criticism. Could they have done more to disempower the old elites, to hold them accountable for the defeat and to achieve greater democracy and more social justice? For this discussion see Bruno Thoss, 'Militärische Entscheidung und politisch-gesellschaftlicher Umbruch: Das Jahr 1918 in der neueren Weltkriegsforschung', in Duppler and Gross (eds.), *Kriegsende 1918*, pp. 17–40.

Scott Stephenson analyses the curious fact that the soldiers on the Western Front remained disciplined up to the very end and only rarely participated in soldiers' councils and the German revolution: Scott Stephenson, *The Final Battle: Soldiers of the Western Front and the German Revolution of 1918* (Cambridge University Press, 2009).

The work by Deist still offers the best concise discussion of the reasons for the German military collapse: Wilhelm Deist, 'The military collapse of the German Empire: the reality behind the stab-in-the-back myth', *War in History*, 3 (1996), pp. 186–207.

A comprehensive discussion of the fatal role of the 'stab-in-the-back' myth during the Weimar Republic is provided in Boris Barth's *Dolchstoßlegende und politische Desintegration: Das Trauma der deutschen Niederlage im Ersten Weltkrieg 1914–1933* (Düsseldorf: Droste, 2003).

Two new political biographies of leading figures of the Third OHL have been published in recent years. Manfred Nebelin argues that Ludendorff, and not Wilhelm II, was the link between Bismarck and Hitler, stating that Ludendorff's views were closer to those of Hitler than to Bismarck's ideas. See Manfred Nebelin, *Ludendorff: Diktator im Ersten Weltkrieg* (Munich: Siedler, 2011). Wolfram Pyta argues against the view that Hindenburg was just a figurehead: Wolfram Pyta, *Hindenburg: Herrschaft zwischen Hohenzollern und Hitler* (Munich: Siedler, 2009).

The First World War plays a key role in many national narratives. As the British Expeditionary Force was in itself a supranational army, it should not come as a surprise that historians with different national backgrounds tend to focus on the important contribution of their respective national units for victory. A good overview of such 'national histories' of the war is given in the essays of the following edited volume: Ashley Ekins (ed.), *1918 – Year of Victory: The End of the Great War and the Shaping of History* (Titirangi, Auckland: Exisle, 2010).

American historians tend to stress the contribution of the American Expeditionary Force while British and French historians often highlight the naivety and inexperience of American officers and soldiers, the organisational deficits and the unnecessarily high casualty rates. A discussion of this is given in Meleah Ward, 'The cost of inexperience: Americans on the Western Front, 1918', in Ekins (ed.), *1918 – Year of Victory*, pp. 111–43.

The 'blame game' which was played during the war between British and French military commanders continues in historiography. Many historians of British military history tend to follow the argument put forward by Sir Douglas Haig that the BEF did not receive sufficient support from the French army during the Michael and Georgette offensives. They often marginalise the French contribution to stopping the German offensives and ignore the fact that it was the French army's defensive victory in Champagne and the success of the subsequent counter-offensive which helped turn the tide. Historians of French military history depict British generals as incompetent and often panicking. According to their interpretation the BEF had to be bailed out by the French. All historians are agreed that the soldiers themselves were extremely resilient. In 1918, not only soldiers of the BEF, but also French, Italian, German and Austro-Hungarian soldiers kept on fighting and pushing themselves to the limits of their physical and mental endurance.

Different opinions about who contributed most to repulsing the German offensives and the subsequent victories are discussed in (and expressed by) the following essays (all in Ekins (ed.), *1918 – Year of Victory*): Robin Prior, 'Stabbed in the front: the German defeat in 1918', pp. 27–40; Gary Sheffield, 'Finest hour? British forces on the Western Front in 1918: an overview', pp. 41–63 and Elizabeth Greenhalgh, 'A French victory, 1918', pp. 95–110. An ongoing debate among historians of British military history is the question of the 'learning curve' of the BEF. Did General Headquarters and the generals learn from the failed offensives of 1916 and 1917 or not? Gary Sheffield in particular argues that the failure of the German spring offensive and the following victories is evidence enough that there was a steep 'learning curve', and that Haig and Co. were not 'donkeys' who led 'lions' (the British soldiers) as many critics believed, a view still shared by a considerable part of the British public: Gary Sheffield, *Forgotten Victory: The First World War: Myths and Realities* (London: Headline, 2001).

The Treaties of Brest-Litovsk and Bucharest do not feature much in histories of the Great War. Monographs on the peace treaties and on German and Austrian occupation policies in the region are usually published by historians of Eastern Europe, not by historians of the Great War.

One exception is David Stevenson, who discusses the political context of the peace treaties and the armistice in chapter 5 of his book: *The First World War and International Politics* (Oxford University Press, 1988).

The classic study on German war aims in Eastern Europe and the political context of the Treaty of Brest-Litovsk is given in Winfried Baumgart, *Deutsche Ostpolitik 1918: Von Brest-Litowsk bis zum Ende des Ersten Weltkrieges* (Vienna and Munich: R. Oldenbourg Verlag, 1966).

The best book on the German occupation policy and one which also discusses the cultural dimensions and post-war implications of German rule in Eastern Europe (focusing mostly on Lithuania) is Vejas Gabriel Liulevicius, *War Land on the Eastern Front: Culture, National Identity and German Occupation in World War I* (Cambridge University Press, 2000).

For German policy in and towards Ukraine, see Frank Grelka, *Die ukrainische Nationalbewegung unter deutscher Besatzungsherrschaft 1918 und 1941/42* (Wiesbaden: Harrassowitz, 2005) and Włodzimierz Mędrzecki, *Niemiecka interwencja militarna na Ukrainie w 1918 roku* (Warsaw: Wydawnictwo, 2000).

7 1919: Aftermath

Bruno Cabanes

The study of the aftermath of the Great War covers three specific fields of research. To begin with, the historians associated with the Historial de la Grande Guerre (the Museum of the Great War) in Péronne, Somme, have studied the war's traumatic memory and the impact the conflict had on violence in the twentieth century. Secondly, the history of international relations has been significantly revitalised in recent years, as illustrated by Zara Steiner's standard work, *The Lights that Failed: European International History, 1919–1933* (New York: Oxford University Press, 2005). Lastly, transnational history has addressed the global problems of the 1920s – humanitarian crises, refugees, the development of networks of experts and the international recognition of new human rights and new standards. Stéphane Audoin-Rouzeau and Christophe Prochasson (eds.), *Sortir de la Grande Guerre* (Paris: Tallandier, 2008) offers a ground-breaking overview of the transition from war to peace, with its chapters on each belligerent country in the wake of the war.

On Woodrow Wilson and Wilsonianism, see Arno J. Mayer, *Politics and Diplomacy of Peacemaking: Containment and Counterrevolution at Versailles, 1918–1919* (New York: Knopf, 1967); Thomas J. Knock, *To End All Wars: Woodrow Wilson and the Quest for a New World Order* (Princeton University Press, 1995); Francis Anthony Boyle, *Foundations of World Order: The Legalist Approach to International Relations (1898–1922)* (Durham, NC: Duke University Press, 1999); Erez Manela, *The Wilsonian Moment: Self-Determination and the International Origins of Anticolonial Nationalism* (Oxford and New York: Oxford University Press, 2007); Leonard V. Smith, 'The Wilsonian challenge to international law', *Journal of the History of International Law*, 13 (2011), pp. 179–208.

For a study of the workings of the Peace Conference, see Margaret Macmillan, *Paris 1919: Six Months that Changed the World* (New York: Random House, 2003). For a critical reading of the Treaty of Versailles, see Manfred F. Boemeke *et al.* (eds.), *The Treaty of Versailles: A Reassessment after 75 Years* (Cambridge University Press, 1998). See also Gerd Krumeich (ed.), *Versailles 1919: Ziele, Wirkung, Wahrnehmung* (Essen: Klartext Verlag, 2001).

On veterans of the Great War, see Stephen R. Ward (ed.), *The War Generation: Veterans of the First World War* (Port Washington, NY: Kennikat Press, 1975); Antoine Prost, *Les anciens combattants et la société française, 1914–1939* (Paris: Presses de la Fondation des Sciences Politiques, 1977); and Bruno Cabanes, *La victoire endeuillée: la sortie de guerre des soldats français (1918–1920)* (Paris: Éditions du Seuil, 2004).

On veterans' pacifism, see Norman Ingram, *The Politics of Dissent: Pacifism in France, 1919–1939* (Oxford University Press, 1991); Sophie Lorrain, *Des pacifistes français et allemands pionniers de l'entente franco-allemande, 1871–1925* (Paris: L'Harmattan, 1999); Andrew Webster, 'The transnational dream: politicians, diplomats and soldiers in the League of Nations' pursuit of international disarmament, 1920–1938', *Contemporary European History*, 14:4 (2005), pp. 493–518; and Jean-Michel Guieu, *Le rameau et le glaive: les militants français pour la S.D.N.* (Paris: Presses de Sciences Po, 2008).

On disabled veterans, see Robert Weldon Whalen, *Bitter Wounds: German Victims of the Great War, 1914–1939* (Ithaca, NY: Cornell University Press, 1984); Joanna Bourke, *Dismembering the Male: Men's Bodies, Britain and the Great War* (University of Chicago Press, 1996); Sophie Delaporte, *Les gueules cassées: les blessés de la face de la Grande Guerre* (Paris: Éditions Noêsis, 1996); David A. Gerber (ed.), *Disabled Veterans in History* (Ann Arbor, MI: University of Michigan Press, 2000); Deborah Cohen, *The War Come Home: Disabled Veterans in Britain and Germany, 1914–1939* (Berkeley, CA: University of California Press, 2001); Jeffrey S. Reznick, 'Prostheses and propaganda: materiality and the human body in the Great War', in Nicholas J. Saunders, *Matters of Conflict: Material Culture, Memory and the First World War* (London and New York: Routledge, 2004), pp. 51–61; Sabine Kienitz, *Beschädigte Helden: Kriegsinvalidität und Körperbilder 1914–1923* (Paderborn: Schöningh, 2008); Marina Larsson, *Shattered Anzacs: Living with the Scars of War* (University of New South Wales Press, 2009); and Beth Linker, *War's Waste: Rehabilitation in World War I America* (University of Chicago Press, 2011).

On the memory of the Great War, see Annette Becker, *Les monuments aux morts: mémoire de la Grande Guerre* (Paris: Errance, 1988); Jay Winter, *Sites of Memory, Sites of Mourning: The Great War in European Cultural History* (Cambridge University Press, 1995); and Daniel J. Sherman, *The Construction of Memory in Interwar France* (University of Chicago Press, 1999).

On the return to private life and on gender, see Mary Louise Roberts, *Civilization Without Sexes: Reconstructing Gender in Postwar France, 1917–1927* (University of Chicago Press, 1994); and Bruno Cabanes and Guillaume Piketty (eds.), *Retour à l'intime au sortir de la guerre* (Paris: Tallandier, 2009).

On war widows and orphans, see Joy Damousi, *The Labour of Loss: Mourning, Memory and Wartime Bereavement in Australia* (Cambridge University Press, 1999); Olivier Faron, *Les enfants du deuil: Orphelins et pupilles de la nation de la Première Guerre mondiale* (Paris: La Découverte, 2001); Stéphane Audoin-Rouzeau, *Cinq deuils de guerre: 1914–1918* (Paris: Éditions Noêsis, 2001); Virginia Nicholson, *Singled Out: How Two Million British Women Survived Without Men After the First World War* (New York: Oxford University Press, 2008) and Erica A. Kuhlman, *Of Little Comfort: War Widows, Fallen Soldiers and the Remaking of the Nation After the Great War* (New York University Press, 2012).

On the creation of international organisations, see Susan Pedersen, 'Back to the League of Nations', *American Historical Review*, 112:4 (2007), pp. 1091–117; Sandrine Kott, 'Une "communauté épistémique" du social? Experts de l'I.L.O. et internationalisation des politiques sociales dans l'entre-deux guerres', *Genèses*, 2:71 (2008), pp. 26–46; Gerry Rodgers, Eddy Lee, Lee Swepston and Jasmien Van Daele (eds.), *The International Labour Organization and the Quest for Social Justice, 1919–2009* (Ithaca, NY: Cornell University Press and Geneva: International Labour Office, 2009); Jasmien Van Daele *et al.* (eds.), *ILO Histories: Essays on the International Labour Organization and its Impact on the World in the Twentieth Century* (Bern: Peter Lang, 2010) and Isabelle Moret-Lespinet and Vincent Viet (eds.), *L'Organisation internationale du Travail* (Rennes: PUR, 2011).

On human rights in the wake of the Great War, see Barbara Metzger, 'Towards an international human rights regime during the inter-war years: the League of Nations' combat of traffic in women and children', in Kevin Grant *et al.* (eds.), *Beyond Sovereignty: Britain, Empire, and Transnationalism, c. 1880–1950* (Basingstoke: Palgrave Macmillan, 2007), pp. 54–79; Antoine Prost and Jay Winter, *René Cassin* (Paris: Fayard, 2011); and Bruno Cabanes, *The Great War and the Origins of Humanitarianism* (Cambridge University Press, 2014).

On the question of minority groups, see Carol Fink, *Defending the Rights of Others: The Great Powers, the Jews, and International Minority Protection* (Cambridge University Press, 2004); and Tara Zahra, 'The "minority problem": national classification in the French and Czechoslovak borderlands', *Contemporary European Review*, 17 (2008), pp. 137–65.

On refugees, see Michael Marrus, *The Unwanted: European Refugees in the Twentieth Century* (Oxford University Press, 1985) and Claudena M. Skran, *Refugees in Inter-War Europe: The Emergence of a Regime* (Oxford: Clarendon Press, 1995). See also Philippe Nivet, *Les réfugiés français de la Grande Guerre, 1914–1920* (Paris: Economica, 2004); Nick Baron and Peter Gatrell (eds.), *Homelands: War, Population, and Statehood in Eastern Europe and Russia, 1918–1924* (London: Anthem Press, 2004); Catherine Gousseff, *L'exil russe: la fabrique du réfugié apatride* (Paris: CNRS Éditions, 2008); and Annemarie H. Sammartino, *The Impossible Border: Germany and the East, 1914–1922* (Ithaca, NY: Cornell University Press, 2010).

On refugees in the Near East, the standard work is Dzovinar Kévonian, *Réfugiés et diplomatie humanitaire: les acteurs européens et la scène proche-orientale pendant l'entre-deux-guerres* (Paris: Publications de la Sorbonne, 2004). See also Keith David Watenpaugh, 'The League of Nations' rescue of Armenian genocide survivors and the making of modern humanitarianism, 1920–1927', *American Historical Review*, 115:5 (2010), pp. 1315–39.

On the violence of the immediate post-war period, see George Mosse, *Fallen Soldiers: Reshaping the Memory of the World Wars* (New York: Oxford University Press, 1990). For a critical evaluation of Mosse's book, see Antoine Prost, 'The impact of war on French and German political cultures', *Historical Journal*, 37:1 (1994), pp. 209–17; John Horne (ed.), 'Démobilisations culturelles après la Grande Guerre', *14–18: Aujourd'hui–Today–Heute*, 5 (Paris: Éditions Noêsis, 2002), pp. 49–53; Peter Gatrell, 'War after the war: conflicts, 1919–1923', in John Horne (ed.), *A Companion to the First World War* (Chichester and Oxford: Wiley-Blackwell, 2010), pp. 558–75; and Robert Gerwarth and John Horne, 'The Great War and paramilitarism in Europe, 1917–23', *Contemporary European History*, 19:3 (2010), pp. 267–73.

8 The Western Front

Robin Prior

There is no one book which covers the Western Front as a whole, which given the diverse source material and the size of the archival record, is not surprising. Readers will have to turn to the bibliographies of particular years in this volume or as a point of entry start with some of the general books on the Great War listed here. All contain considerable sections on the Western Front.

General histories which cover the Western Front in some detail, are David Stevenson, *Cataclysm: The First World War as Political Tragedy* (New York: Basic Books, 2004), an excellent modern study, and Hew Strachan, *The Oxford Illustrated History of the First World War* (Oxford University Press, 1998). Strachan's *The First World War*, vol. 1: *To Arms* (Oxford University Press, 2001) should be consulted for the early development of the Western Front. When completed this will be a definitive study. S. Tucker's *The Great War 1914–18* (London: UCL, 1998) is a rather neglected good modern overview. *The First World War* by Robin Prior and Trevor Wilson (London: Cassell, 1999) has many chapters on the Western Front, as does Trevor Wilson's *The Myriad Faces of War: Britain and the Great War, 1914–1918* (Cambridge: Polity Press and Oxford: Blackwell, 1986). John Keegan's *The First World War* (London: Hutchinson, 1998) is surprisingly hard going. Niall Ferguson, *The Pity of War* (London: Basic Books, 1998) is in itself a pity. It demonstrates the danger of historians moving into areas about which they know little. So does J. Mosier, *The Myth of the Great War: A New Military History of World War I* (London: HarperCollins, 2001). It is certainly a new history of something. Whether that something is the Great War is more problematical. Gerard Groot, *The First World War* (London: Palgrave Macmillan, 2001) adds little. More interesting is A. Millett and W. Murray (eds.), *Military Effectiveness*, vol. 1: *The First World War* (London: Allen & Unwin, 1988). This contains many shrewd judgements on why some powers fared better than others on the Western Front. Marc Ferro, *The Great War 1914–1918* (London: Routledge, 1973) is a treatment of the war from a Marxist perspective. It is rather a historical curiosity now. Other studies are now too old to recommend. Anyone who thinks C. R. M. F. Cruttwell's *A History of the Great War 1914–1918* (Oxford:

Clarendon Press, 1936) has anything to offer has not read it recently. All A. J. P. Taylor's *War By Timetable* (London: Macdonald, 1969) proves is what nonsense an eminent historian can get away with. His *The First World War: An Illustrated History* (London: Penguin, 1966) should be read for the captions on the photographs but for nothing else. A sound illustrated history is J. Winter, *The Experience of World War I* (London: Macmillan, 1988). B. H. Liddell Hart, *History of the First World War* (or other various titles) (London, 1932) tries to demonstrate that the Western Front was the last place in which the war should have been fought. The presence there of the German army presents a problem for this thesis. Holger Herwig, *The First World War: Germany and Austria-Hungary 1914–1918* (London: Edward Arnold, 1997) is worth reading for the chapters on the Western Front from the point of view of the Central Powers. John Terraine's *The Western Front, 1914–1918* (London: Hutchinson, 1970) is very biased towards Haig. Robin Prior and Trevor Wilson have dealt with one commander's experiences between 1914 and 1918 in *Command on the Western Front: The Military Career of Sir Henry Rawlinson* (Oxford: Blackwell, 1992).

More specialised studies on aspects of the Western Front are Paddy Griffith, *Battle Tactics of the Western Front: The British Army's Art of Attack, 1916–18* (New Haven, CT and London: Yale University Press, 1994). 'Art' might be pitching it a bit high. S. Bidwell and Dominick Graham, *Fire-Power: British Army Weapons and Theories of War 1904–45* (London: Allen & Unwin, 1982) should not be neglected for its chapters on the technical side of fighting on the Western Front. John Terraine's *White Heat: The New Warfare* (London: Sidgwick & Jackson, 1982) has some useful chapters on the Western Front. Guy Hartcup, *The War of Invention: Scientific Developments 1914–1918* (London: Brassey's, 1988) is an interesting but slightly superficial book on an important subject. On one particularly nasty aspect of the war of invention, L. F. Haber, *The Poisonous Cloud: Chemical Warfare in the First World War* (Oxford: Clarendon Press, 1986) is particularly important. Tim Travers, in his *The Killing Ground: The British Army, the Western Front, and the Emergence of Modern Warfare* (London: Allen & Unwin, 1987), sometimes confuses the historiography of the war with its history. Bruce Gudmundsson, *Stormtroop Tactics: Innovation in the German Army 1914–1918* (Westport, CT: Praeger, 1989) fails to explain why such an innovative army lost the war. It is still, however, essential reading on German battle tactics. The same praise and criticism can be directed at Timothy Lupfer, *The Dynamics of Doctrine: the Changes in German Tactical Doctrine during the First World War* (Fort Leavenworth, KS: Combat Studies Institute, 1981). M Samuels, in his *Command or Control? Command, Training, and Tactics in the British and German Armies 1888–1918* (London: Frank Cass & Co., 1995), demonstrates that the German army must have emerged victorious from the Great War. Some Germans believed it at the time but no historians should believe it now. Altogether more important is G. C. Wynne, *If Germany Attacks: The Battle in Depth in the West* (London: Faber & Faber, 1940). Note the date of publication, which overshadowed the appearance of this important volume. E. D. Brose, *The Kaiser's Army: The Politics of Military Technology in Germany During the Machine Age 1870–1918* (Oxford University Press, 2001) has many useful insights from the German perspective of the Western Front. R. Chickering and S. Förster (eds.), *Great War, Total War: Combat and Mobilization on the Western Front 1914–1918* (Cambridge University Press, 2000) is a useful volume of essays. B. Rawling's *Surviving Trench Warfare: Technology and the Canadian Corps 1914–1918* (University of Toronto Press, 1992) has implications for trench warfare that extend beyond the Canadians. Charles Messenger's *Trench Fighting, 1914–1918* (London: Pan, 1973) is a popular but useful account. It should be studied by anyone wishing to know about the nature of trench warfare. On the logistics of the Western Front, Ian Brown's *British Logistics on the Western Front 1914–1919* (Westport, CT: Praeger, 1992) is a good study of a neglected area. Martin van Creveld has also dealt with some logistical aspects of the Western Front in his *Supplying War: Logistics from Wallenstein to Patton* (Cambridge University Press, 1977).

9 The Eastern Front

Holger Afflerbach

The most important single book on the Eastern Front is Norman Stone's *The Eastern Front* (London: Hodder & Stoughton, 1975). Stone has excellent and detailed knowledge and understanding of the events on the German, Austro-Hungarian and Russian sides, and his book is indispensable as a guide to military events on the Eastern Front. He focuses mainly on the shortcomings of Russian generals and of Russian military organisation and administration. Dennis Showalter offers a short and useful overview on the Eastern Front in 'War in the East and Balkans, 1914–18', in John Horne (ed.), *A Companion to World War I* (Chichester: Wiley-Blackwell, 2010), pp. 66–81. A very useful collected volume on 'the forgotten Front' was edited by Gerhard Gross, *Die Vergessene Front: Der Osten 1914/15: Ereignis, Wirkung, Nachwirkung* (Paderborn/Munich/Vienna/Zurich: Schöningh, 2006). This work takes a comprehensive approach to events, not limiting its analysis to military developments only, and it is regrettable that it stops in 1915.

The operational history of the Eastern Front fills many substantial volumes. The chapters of the official German history of the war, *Der Weltkrieg 1914–1918: die militärischen Operationen zu Lande. Bearbeitet im Reichsarchiv*, 14 vols. (Berlin: E. S. Mittler, 1925–44; vols. XIII–XIV new edn, Koblenz, 1956), as well as the relevant parts of *Oesterreich-Ungarns letzter Krieg, 1914–1918*, 15 vols. (Vienna: Verlag der Militärwissenschaftlichen Mitteilungen, 1931–8), cover the events in much detail. The Reichsarchiv published several volumes on single battles (*Schlachten des Weltkriegs in Einzeldarstellungen*, for example on Tannenberg or Gorlice). More a collection of sources than memoirs in the normal sense of the word, is Franz Conrad v. Hötzendorf, *Aus meiner Dienstzeit 1906–1918*, 5 vols. (Vienna: Rikola, 1921–5). Very useful is Manfried Rauchensteiner, *Der Tod des Doppeladlers: Österreich-Ungarn und der Erste Weltkrieg* (Graz/Vienna/Cologne: Styria Verlag, 1993), covering events on the Austrian fronts, and Holger Herwig, *The First World War: Germany and Austria-Hungary, 1914–1918* (London: Edward Arnold, 1997). See also Gary Shanafelt: *The Secret Enemy: Austria-Hungary and the German Alliance* (New York: Columbia University Press, 1985). On Russia, see Allan Wildman, *The End of the Russian Imperial Army*, 2 vols. (Princeton University Press, 1980–7) and William Fuller, *The Foe Within: Fantasies of Treason and the End of Imperial Russia* (Ithaca, NY: Cornell University Press, 2006).

An in-depth modern analysis of the events on the Eastern Front has to offer solutions to the problem of multi-ethnicity and sources in at least ten different languages. That alone makes a comprehensive analysis of the fighting which looks at events from a 'transnational' viewpoint very difficult. The role of army and command structures is important and a comparison tempting. For the German side, Holger Afflerbach, *Falkenhayn: Politisches Handeln und Denken im Kaiserreich* (Munich: R. Oldenbourg Verlag, 1994), offers a discussion of the strategic questions on the Eastern Front from 1914–16. A full-scale comparison (Gross (ed.), *Die Vergessene Front*, is a very good start) has to deal with the fighting and the experience of the soldiers, with weaponry and problems of equipment, supply and logistics. Much work is needed before the events in the East will be covered as well as those on the Western Front (see Robin Prior, Chapter 8 in this volume).

The fate of POWs (Alon Rachamimov, *POWs and the Great War: Captivity on the Eastern Front* (Oxford and New York: Berg, 2002) has recently attracted some attention, and so have the consequences of military advance and retreat, scorched earth politics and plundering of the civilian population. Of particular importance here is Peter Gatrell, *A Whole Empire Walking: Refugees in Russia during World War I* (Bloomington, IN: Indiana University Press, 2005). Vejas Gabriel Liulevicius, *War Land on the Eastern Front: Culture, National Identity and German Occupation in World War I* (Cambridge University Press, 2000), is a beginning, but deals more with German occupation than with the views of the inhabitants of these 'war lands'.

The role of public memory and remembrance – 'a Fussell of the Eastern Front' – is missing, though a beginning has been made (Karen Petrone, *The Great War in Russian Memory* (Bloomington, IN: Indiana University Press, 2011)). Doing this in a multi-national, comparative way would be an extremely challenging task.

10 The Italian Front

Nicola Labanca

In many general histories of the First World War, the military history of the Italian Front has long been neglected. Still, in recent years, some historians have returned to this theme. See, for instance, Hew Strachan (ed.), *The Oxford Illustrated History of the First World War* (Oxford University Press, 1998); John Keegan, *The First World War* (New York: A. Knopf-Random House, 1999); Ian F. W. Beckett, *The Great War, 1914–1918* (Harlow: Longman, 2001); Stéphane Audoin-Rouzeau and Jean-Jacques Becker (eds.), *Encyclopédie de la Grande Guerre, 1914–1918: histoire et culture* (Paris: Bayard, 2004); and David Stevenson, *Cataclysm: The First World War as Political Tragedy* (New York: Basic Books, 2004). But even here, accurate references are often not available or are imprecise.

The Italian side of the story is largely ignored in literature written for the general public too. No serious recent single book on Italian participation in the war is available in a language other than Italian. A notable and recent exception is Mark Thompson's *The White War: Life and Death on the Italian Front, 1915–1919* (New York: Basic Books, 2009). When an Italian translation of the *Encyclopédie de la Grande Guerre* by Audoin-Rouzeau and Becker was published (*La prima guerra mondiale*, ed. Antonio Gibelli (Turin: Einaudi, 2007)), a number of new articles, written by Italian historians, were introduced, presumably for the Italian readership. The Italian story, therefore, remains apart from the general history of the war.

More complex is the question about the nature and range of Austrian publications on the Italian Front. There is much in the fundamental work by the Canadian historian Holger Herwig, *The First World War: Germany and Austria-Hungary 1914–1918* (London: Edward Arnold, 1997), and in the German language, of course, Austrian books are fully available. (Now even in French: see the recent Max Schiavon, *L'Autriche-Hongrie dans la Première Guerre mondiale: la fin d'un Empire* (Paris: Soteca, 2011)). But even these works do not always help readers to understand the imperial and multi-ethnic complexities of the Austrian Dual Monarchy / Empire. We need to know in more detail the story of Slovenians, Croatians, Serbs and Czechs under and against Austria during the war – something that many recent general histories of the Habsburg Empire do not provide.

All this means that international appreciation of the two wars (Austrian, Italian) fought on the Italian Front still rests on old knowledge, not always revised by recent research. All this said – and denounced – in the last decades important and new studies have become available. The old gap between local–traditional and international–new research is already a thing of the past.

The best place to start for an understanding of the Austrian side is Manfried Rauchensteiner, *Der Tod des Doppeladlers: Österreich-Ungarn und der Erste Weltkrieg* (Graz: Styria Verlag, 1993); for a starting point on the Italian side, the best is Mario Isnenghi and Giorgio Rochat, *La grande guerra 1914–1918* (Florence: La nuova Italia, 2000).

Historiographical debates are on-going. For Austria, see Günther Kronenbitter, 'Waffenbrüder: Der Koalitionskrieg der Mittelmächte 1914–1918 und das Selbst-bild zweier Militäreliten', in Volker Dotterweich (ed.), *Mythen und Legenden in der Geschichte* (Munich: Ernst Vögel, 2004), pp. 157–86; and Hermann J. W. Kuprian, 'Warfare – Welfare: Gesellschaft, Politik und Militarisierung Österreich während des Ersten Weltkrieges', in Brigitte Mazohl-Wallnig, Hermann J. W. Kuprian, Gunda Barth-Scalmani (eds.), *Ein Krieg, zwei Schützengräben: Österreich-Italien und der Erste Weltkrieg in den Dolomiten 1915–1918* (Bozen: Athesia, 2005). And for Italy see Antonio Gibelli, *La grande guerra degli italiani 1915–1918* (Milan: Sansoni, 1998); Giovanna Procacci, 'La prima guerra mondiale', in Giuseppe Sabbatucci and Vittorio Vidotto (eds.), *Storia d'Italia,* vol. IV: *Guerre e fascismo* (Rome-Bari: Laterza, 1997); and Bruna Bianchi, *La follia e la fuga: nevrosi di guerra, diserzione e disobbedienza nell'esercito italiano, 1915–1918* (Rome: Bulzoni, 2001).

A good 'point of contact' with on-going studies at the national level may be found in collective, edited books. For Austria see the already quoted Mazohl-Wallnig, Kuprian, Barth-Scalmani (eds.), *Ein Krieg, zwei Schützengräben*; and Hermann J. W. Kuprian and Oswald Überegger (eds.), *Der Erste Weltkrieg in Alpenraum* (Innsbruck: Wagner, 2011). For Italy the most recent and impressive collection is Mario Isnenghi and Daniele Ceschin (eds.), *La Grande Guerra: dall'Intervento alla 'vittoria mutilata'* (Turin: Utet, 2008) (being the third volume of a five-volume series edited by Mario Isnenghi on *Italiani in guerra: Conflitti, identità, memorie dal Risorgimento ai nostri giorni* (Turin: Utet, 2008–10), ranging from the Risorgimento up to today).

The best available literatures, by Rauchensteiner and Isnenghi–Rochat and new research alongside them, have revised and superseded the first narratives and official histories of the war: Österreichischen Bundesministerium für Heereswesen und vom Kriegsarchiv (ed.), *Österreich-Ungarns letzter Krieg, 1914–1918* (Vienna: Verlag der Militärwissenschaftlichen Mitteilungen, 1930–8); and Ministero della guerra, Comando del corpo di stato maggiore, Ufficio storico, *L'esercito italiano nella grande guerra (1915–1918)* (Rome, 1927–88).

Among many topics most researched in the last decades, the debate on the consent/dissent of soldiers has attracted some attention in Austria and in Italy, but probably less than in other countries. This happened for different reasons: in Austria because of the relative advance of studies in the field of 'new military history' in the last two decades; in Italy – on the contrary – because the subject had already been deeply studied between the end of the 1960s and the 1970s (actually it was *the* point of rupture of the new studies on the First

World War in respect of the old 'patriotic' historiography and tradition), so that nowadays it does not sound so exciting to young scholars. In any case see, for Austria, the most important review article is by Oswald Überegger, 'Vom militärischen Paradigma zur "Kulturgeschichte des Krieges"? Entwicklungslinien der österreichischen Weltkriegsgeschichtsschreibung zwischen politisch-militärischer Instrumentalisierung und universitärer Verwissenschaftlichung', in Oswald Überegger (ed.), *Zwischen Nation und Region: Weltkriegsforschung im interregionalen Vergleich: Ergebnisse und Perspektiven* (Innsbruck: Wagner, 2004), pp. 63–122. Two different approaches to the Italian war may be found in Giovanna Procacci, *Soldati e prigionieri italiani nella Grande Guerra*, con una raccolta di lettere inedite (Rome: Editori Riuniti, 1993); and Mario Isnenghi, *La tragedia necessaria: da Caporetto all'Otto settembre* (Bologna: Il Mulino, 1999). An interesting new point of view is in Federico Mazzini, 'Cose de laltro mondo: una contro-cultura di guerra attraverso la scrittura popolare trentina, 1914–1920' (PhD thesis, University of Padua, 2009).

Another important topic, not by chance, is about 'borderlands', regions that suffered (and changed) borders because of the war. This is the case of Trieste, and even more of the Trentino. A very important chapter of this story is that of inhabitants of the Trentino, who during the war mainly fought on the Austrian side – of course, obliged by Austrian conscription – but were sent by Austria to fronts far away from the Italian one. A vocal minority of '*irredentisti*' volunteered in the Italian army. Some of the most innovative research comes from this regional approach. In Austria, Innsbruck University (alongside Vienna and Graz) is the central force. In Italy, much of this complex 'border story' has been studied by a wonderful network of historians from Rovereto and Trento, first grouped in an extremely interesting review, *Materiali di lavoro*. They produced a number of interesting publications, and now work in and around a network of historical museums in that region. Somehow in the middle, at Bozen/Bolzano, Süd Tirol/Alto Adige, another very active inter-regional/international network is grouped around the review *Geschichte und region/ Storia e regione*.

11 The Ottoman Front

Robin Prior

Serious readers should start with the Official History of each of the three main campaigns discussed here. These are for Palestine: George McMunn and Cyril Falls, *Military Operations: Egypt and Palestine,* vol. I: *From the Outbreak of War with Germany to June 1917* (London: HMSO, 1928) and Cyril Falls, *Military Operations: Egypt and Palestine,* vol. II: *From June 1917 to the End of the War* (London: HMSO, 1930); for Gallipoli: Cecil Aspinall-Oglander, *Military Operations: Gallipoli*, 2 vols. (London: Heinemann, 1929–32); and for Mesopotamia: F. J. Moberley, *Military Operations: Mesopotamia*, 4 vols. (London: HMSO, 1923–7). The Australian official history, Henry S. Gullett, *The Australian Imperial Force in Sinai and Palestine* (Sydney: Angus & Robertson, 1944), though rather romantic on the Light Horse, is more readable than its British equivalents.

More digestible reading on the Palestine campaign can be found in Anthony Bruce, *The Last Crusade: The Palestine Campaign in the First World War* (London: John Murray, 2002). This is the best modern study of the campaign. General Archibald Wavell, *The Palestine Campaign* (London: Constable, 1928) is an excellent book and has stood the test of time well. David Woodward, *Hell in the Holy Land: World War I in the Middle East* (Lexington, KY:

University Press of Kentucky, 2006) tells the story from the viewpoint of the ordinary soldier, but has some shrewd remarks on the strategy and tactics of the campaign. Matthew Hughes's *Allenby and British Strategy in the Middle East 1917–1919* (London: Frank Cass & Co., 1999) is a clear account of the finalities in Palestine. Unfortunately, there is no similar study of Archibald Murray's strategy and tactics. Alec Hill, *Chauvel of the Light Horse* (Melbourne University Press, 1978) is one of the best studies of any commander in the Middle East.

On Lawrence of Arabia it is difficult to know where to start. Some authorities regard Lawrence's *Seven Pillars of Wisdom* essential reading and a modern classic. I am not one of them, but there are many editions always in print. A more modern (and moderate) study is Lawrence James, *The Golden Warrior: The Life and Legend of Lawrence of Arabia* (London: Weidenfeld & Nicolson, 1990).

It is also difficult to know where to begin on Gallipoli. The author of this chapter has written a study, *Gallipoli: The End of the Myth* (New Haven, CT and London: Yale University Press, 2009), which even he thinks will do no such thing. I find C. E. W. Bean's volumes of the Australian official history virtually unreadable. There is, however, a great deal of information to be gleaned from them. Tim Travers, *Gallipoli 1915* (Stroud: Tempus, 2001) is particularly strong on the historiography of the campaign. Alan Moorehead, *Gallipoli* (London: Hamish Hamilton, 1956) is superbly written but desperately out of date. Robert Rhodes James, *Gallipoli* (London: Batsford, 1965) was the standard study for many years. It should now be treated with caution for the author's orientalist views of the Turks, his strange views on the Australians and his ludicrous optimism on the prospects of the campaign. Nigel Steel and Peter Hart, *Defeat at Gallipoli* (London: Macmillan, 1985) is a fine study of the soldiers during the campaign. Michael Hickey, *Gallipoli* (London: John Murray, 1995) doesn't add much. There are no studies of the Gallipoli commanders – Hamilton, Birdwood, Hunter-Weston – that can be recommended. John Lee has written *A Soldier's Life: General Sir Ian Hamilton* (London: Macmillan, 2000). Only those interested in the development of military hagiography should read it. George Cassar, *The French and the Dardanelles* (London: Allen & Unwin, 1971) holds the field in this area, although it is more about politics than military operations. Eric Bush, *Gallipoli* (London: Allen & Unwin, 1975), written by one who was there, but long after the event, is still worth reading, as is Cecil Malthus, *Anzac: A Retrospect* (Auckland: Whitcombe & Tombs, 1965). Jenny Macleod, *Reconsidering Gallipoli* (Manchester University Press, 2004) is a first rate investigation into the ever-growing and increasingly baffling Anzac Myth. On the naval side, Keyes's memoirs (*The Fight for Gallipoli: From the Naval Memoirs of Admiral of the Fleet, Sir Roger Keyes Baron, 1872–1945* (London: Eyre & Spottiswoode, 1941)) are self-serving to the point of desperation and cannot be recommended. Nor can almost anything else about the naval aspect of the operation. Readers can seek out the Report by the Mitchell Committee in AWM 124 in the Australian War Memorial, Canberra. It is by far the most analytical study of the naval failure.

On the Turkish side, the Turkish General Staff have rendered into a kind of English, *A Brief History of the Canakkale Campaign in the First World War* (Ankara, 2004). Edward Erikson is owed a debt of gratitude by anyone trying to come to grips with the Ottoman army. His *Ordered to Die: A History of the Ottoman Army in the First World War* (Westport, CN: Greenwood Press, 2001), although perhaps too glowing about the fighting power of the Turkish army, is essential. I find him totally unconvincing on the prospects of the naval attack.

On Mesopotamia the point of departure for many years has been A. J. Barker, *The Neglected War: Mesopotamia 1914–1918* (London: Faber & Faber, 1967). It must now give way to Charles Townshend, *When God Made Hell* (London: Faber & Faber, 2010). Its subtitle is too long to be given here, but it is a superb study of the military and political aspects of the campaign. It corrects many myths, especially regarding Townshend (the author is not a relative). The other Charles Townshend should not be neglected. His *My Campaign in Mesopotamia* (London: Thornton Butterworth, 1922), despite its shrill tone, makes a reasonable case. Ronald Millar, *Kut: Death of an Army* (London: Secker & Warburg, 1969) is good on the great siege. Russell Braddon's book on the same subject (*The Siege* (London: Jonathan Cape, 1969)) retains not a shred of credibility after the dissection it receives by the modern Charles Townshend. There are no modern studies of the careers of the other Mesopotamian generals. Nixon and Maude seem to have fallen into an historiographical crevasse. Wilfred Nunn's *Tigris Gunboats* (London: Melrose, 1932) is useful, although the author has no conception of the weirdness of the events described. Alexander Kearsey, *A Study of the Strategy and Tactics of the Mesopotamian Campaign 1914–1917* (London: Gale & Polden, 1934), is full of military insight, as is Elie Kedourie, *England and the Middle East: The Destruction of the Ottoman Empire, 1914–1921* (London: Bowes & Bowes, 1956). Its conclusions should be read in the light of my conclusions in this chapter. Peter Sluglett, *Britain in Iraq: Contriving King and Country, 1914–1932*, 2nd edn (New York: Columbia University Press, 2007) puts the whole political scene in perspective. Also good on the politics of the campaign is Paul Davis, *Ends and Means: The British Mesopotamian Campaign and Commission* (London and Toronto: Associated University Presses, 1994).

12 The war at sea

Paul Kennedy

One begins, as usual, with the official histories and then next, in deference, with the memoir literature of the leading participants in what was called 'the Great War at Sea'. By comparison with the magnificent, scholarly and vibrant official histories of the Second World War, these ones make for poor, apologetic and dull reading. The plain reason is this: that the official histories of the loser navies have little to say except that they did their best under impossible circumstances; while those of the winners seek to explain why their demonstration of naval mastery was nonetheless far less than expected and desired. For the lesser naval powers, this was not such a psychological problem, for what could the official historians of Austria-Hungary and Italy do but point to their country's geopolitical constraints, and then agreeably turn to a detailed discussion of minor operations in the Adriatic? (Hans Sokol's *Oesterreich-Ungarns Seekrieg* (Zurich: Amalthea-Verlag, 1933) is a nice exception.) Almost the same dilemma presented itself to the French historians: the Royal Navy held the North Sea and Channel, the Mediterranean was friendly waters and the great French struggle was on land. The US navy wished to present its naval contribution as epic, and a stepping-stone to greater things, but a battleship squadron at Scapa Flow and tentative beginnings at anti-U-boat warfare were really not so thrilling.

It was only in Britain and Germany that post-mortems on the war at sea provoked interest and great controversy, because in each country so much was at stake. In Germany the issue was not so much about whether the High Seas Fleet had done well – it had performed very competently under bad geopolitical and numerical circumstances. It was, rather, whether the overall Tirpitzian strategy of a 'Fleet Against England' had made any sense at all or whether, the next time around, the Fatherland should break out via Norway, as it was to do in 1940. The German official naval history prefers not to discuss that matter. In Britain, and for reasons described in the main chapter text, the debate was much more existential, which meant that as fine a historian and strategic thinker as Sir Julian Corbett could make no impact through the *History of the Great War: Naval Operations*, vols. I and II (London: Longmans, Green and Co., 1921), when the Admiralty insisted that it was to be their official account and analysis of things, not his – Beatty's interference here is inexcusable. The end result is thousands of pages, and lots of sketches of, say, the Fifth Battle Squadron turning to the left in the Jutland mists.

The memoir literature is even worse; at least the official histories give many incontestable facts. One looks in vain for an equivalent to Grant's *Memoirs* of the American Civil War, or to General William Slim's *Defeat into Victory* (on the 1942–5 Burma Campaign), perhaps the best war memoir ever. No matter whose autobiographies one reads – Scheer's, Hipper's, Sims's, Jellicoe's, Beatty's, Bacon's and so on – together with those of their dutiful interwar biographers, the critical general reader is dulled by their incapacity to step outside their own shoes and be brutally objective. One approaches Filson Young's *With Beatty in the North Sea* (London: Cassell, 1921) with the same dull feeling as one approaches the dentist. Vice-Admiral Dewar's *The Navy from Within* (London: Victor Gollancz, 1939) is like a fresh breeze by comparison. Perhaps we should not expect that much; autobiographies of Second World War air force generals have much the same mind-numbing effect.

There is one bright light here. It is the various volumes of the extraordinary and precious editions of *The Navy Record Society* (London, annually, since 1893). There is nothing like this set of unadulterated and reprinted original documents in the world, with at least a dozen edited volumes that pertain to the naval dimensions of the First World War – central command, regional operations, intelligence, Anglo-American naval relations, the private papers of Fisher, Jellicoe, Beatty and Keyes. But they are what they are: raw, wonderful documents. They need their interpreters.

Even the most navy-focused historians would agree that the older, generalist, 'Blue Water' writers – one thinks here of Richard Hough's *The Great War at Sea, 1914–1918* (Oxford University Press, 1983) and Geoffrey Bennett's *Naval Battles of The First World War* (London: Batsford, 1968) – are hopeless. There is not a critical bone in their bodies. All of them are happiest when discussing naval actions, few though they were. All of them conclude by stating that, at the end of the day (sic), sea-power was decisive. The evidence provided is limp.

Mahan told us, the navalists assert, that sea power was all-important. The war came after Germany invaded Belgium in August 1914. Sea power was applied. Ergo, it was decisive, because Germany finally lost. Battleship actions were hard to find between 1914 and 1918 but, still, the economic blockade prevailed. That's all one needed to know. Even military historians, as in Basil Liddell Hart's *The Real War: 1914–1918* (London: Faber & Faber, 1930), buy into that. Those far-off, distant ships ground the enemy into shreds. Obviously, the present author is deeply sceptical of this presumption.

The best single-volume history of the war at sea is Paul Halpern's wonderful *A Naval History of World War I* (Annapolis, MD: Naval Institute Press, 1994). This scholar's coverage of all the belligerent navies – of Austria-Hungary, the British Empire, France, Germany,

Japan, Italy, Russia and the United States – and his terrific bibliography are a godsend to scholars, and supplant hundreds of earlier works. Here is the forest as a whole, not the individual trees or branches. And the maps are great. But it ends, abruptly, with the surrender of the High Seas Fleet to the Allied navies in the Firth of Forth on 21 November 1918. 'The naval war was over', Halpern concludes (p. 449). There are no reflections, no summation, no attempt to draw up a balance-sheet from someone who is undoubtedly the most knowledgeable naval historian of the First World War.

There are finely grained studies of naval expenditures, technology, global strategy, logistics and all those vital, hitherto-neglected fields, but it seems to this critic that the deeper these superb scholars (I include Nicholas Lambert, Jon Sumida, James Goldrick, Barry Gough and Greg Kennedy in this pantheon) dig into the archives, the less chance they have of looking at the naval war as a whole, and of seeing it in the overall context of the First World War, let alone the whole sweep of Western military–technological history since the coming of the steam engine, the railway and the aeroplane. Even the magnificent five-volume history by my former mentor, Arthur J. Marder, *From the Dreadnought to Scapa Flow* (Oxford University Press, 1961–70, 1978), shows how a very fine historian can become a prisoner of the Admiralty archives.

One single recent work stands out in breaking the mould, and that is Andrew Gordon's *The Rules of the Game: Jutland and British Naval Command* (London: John Murray, 1996), because it enters into the mental universe of those naval leaders who found 1914–18 naval warfare so difficult to understand. Yet it is an exception. One wonders why this branch of history has become so sterile and inward-looking over the past decades, and why we seem to have lost track of the broader principles clearly delineated in such works as Admiral Sir Herbert Richmond's *Statesmen And Sea Power* (Oxford: Clarendon Press, 1946), which itself reaches back to the great Julian S. Corbett's *Some Principles of Maritime Strategy* (London: Longmans, 1911). Sea power is best understood not as exciting battlefleet exchanges or arcane fire-control techniques, but as control of the Great Commons. Apart from the frightening German U-boat actions against Allied shipping in 1917, soon to be countered by convoys, this was not a problem, at least, nothing like as scary as the years from 1941 to 1943. And the short-ranged High Seas Fleet was never a problem after Jutland.

The best brief analysis of what still needs to be done is by the fine Australian scholar, James Goldrick, in 'The need for a New Naval History of the First World War', Corbett Paper No.7 (Corbett Centre for Maritime Studies, Kings College London, 2011), but even he does not appreciate the cruel fact that the First World War was not a good war for the influence of sea power upon history. He suggests instead more research on naval logistics, manpower, communications . . . But what doth that availeth if young historians come out with a deep study (say, on naval mines) and can't answer the basic questions: 'So what?' How does maritime history affect the great subject of History itself? Only last year (2012) did Nicolas A. Lambert's book *Planning Armageddon: British Economic Warfare and the First World War* (Cambridge, MA: Harvard University Press, 2012) rise above this tunnel vision.

This author 'had a crack' at this issue almost forty years ago, in *The Rise and Fall of British Naval Mastery* (London and New York: Allen Lane, 1976). There is, alas, little that has been published since that time which addresses the big problem of sea power's relative impotence in this terrible, world-shattering war. J. H. Hexter once divided historians into 'splitters' and 'lumpers'. So far, the historiography of the war at sea between 1914 and 1918 definitely belongs to the splitters. It is time for some lumping.

13 The air war

John H. Morrow, Jr.

The best overarching works on the air war of 1914–18 are John H. Morrow Jr.,'s exhaustive volume, *The Great War in the Air: Military Aviation from 1909 to 1921* (Tuscaloosa, AL: University of Alabama Press, 2009 [reprint of the original edition published by the Smithsonian Institution Press in 1993]) and Lee Kennett's shorter and more anecdotal study, *The First Air War, 1914–1918* (New York: Free Press, 1991).

French military aviation, despite its signal importance in the First World War, has not received the attention it merits. The most important work on the subject remains the relevant chapters in the official volume by Charles Christienne *et al.*, *Histoire de l'aviation militaire française* (Paris: Charles Lavauzelle, 1980), which the Smithsonian Institution Press published in English under the title *A History of French Military Aviation* in 1986.

German military aviation receives due attention in John Morrow's consecutive works, *Building German Air Power, 1909–1914* (Knoxville, TN: University of Tennessee Press, 1976) and *German Air Power in World War I* (Lincoln, NE: University of Nebraska Press, 1982). Douglas H. Robinson's book, *The Zeppelin in Combat: A History of the German Naval Airship Division, 1912–1918* (London: Foulis, 1962) traces the dramatic and ill-fated history of the German naval airship campaign against England.

The history of British air power in the First World War has received the most attention in the literature in English, starting with the only official history to see the light of day after the war, Sir Walter Raleigh's and H. A. Jones's six-volume work, *The War in the Air* (Oxford: Clarendon Press, 1922–37). More recent popular and informative studies include Denis Winter's illuminating book, *The First of the Few: Fighter Pilots of the First World War* (London: Penguin, 1982) and Peter H. Liddle's anecdotal work, *The Airman's War 1914–18* (Poole, Dorset: Blandford, 1987). For a fine study of wartime air policy, the reader should see Malcolm Cooper's work, *The Birth of Independent Air Power: British Air Policy in the First World War* (London: Allen & Unwin, 1986). For a study of early Italian aviation, see Piero Vergnano's book, *Origins of Aviation in Italy, 1783–1918* (Genoa: Intyprint, 1964).

Richard P. Hallion's book, *Rise of the Fighter Aircraft, 1914–1918* (Annapolis, MD: Nautical & Aviation Publishing Co., 1984), offers a fine study of fighter, or pursuit aviation. Authors have devoted much attention to the warplanes of 1914–18 but little to the important history of the engines that are the heart of those aircraft: see the relevant chapters of Herschel Smith's *A History of Aircraft Piston Engines* (Manhattan, KS: Sunflower University Press, 1986 [1981]). Curators of the National Air and Space Museum published the following outstanding volume on the air war based on the Museum's outstanding exhibit on the First World War: Dominick A. Pisano, Thomas J. Dietz, Joanne M. Gernstein and Karl S. Schneide, *Legend, Memory, and the Great War in the Air* (Seattle: University of Washington Press, 1992).

Some of the books written by and about the fighter pilots of 1914–18 have become classics: Cecil Lewis's autobiographical study, *Sagittarius Rising* (Barnsley: Frontline Books, 2009 [1936]); V. M. Yeates's novel based on his wartime experience, *Winged Victory* (London: Buchan & Wright, 1985 [1936]); Edward Mannock's diary, *Edward Mannock: The Personal Diary of Maj. Edward 'Mick' Mannock*, introduced and edited by Frederick Oughton (London: Spearman, 1966); Manfred von Richthofen's memoir, *The Red Fighter Pilot*

(St Petersburg, FL: Red & Black, 2007 [1918]); James T. B. McCudden's memoir, *Flying Fury* (London: John Hamilton, 1930 [1918]); Eddie V. Rickenbacker's *Fighting the Flying Circus* (New York: Doubleday, 1965 [1919]); and John M. Grider's *War Birds: Diary of an Unknown Aviator*, ed. Elliot White Springs (Garden City, NY: Sun Dial Press, 1938). Adrian Smith has written perhaps the sole analytical study of these legendary aces in his book, *Mick Mannock, Fighter Pilot: Myth, Life, and Politics* (Basingstoke: Palgrave Macmillan, 2001).

Two more recent studies of First World War aviation are Peter Hart's books, *Bloody April: Slaughter in the Skies over Arras, 1917* (London: Cassell, 2007) and *Aces Falling: War above the Trenches, 1918* (London: Phoenix, 2009). Such books demonstrate the continuing power of First World War aviation to fire the imagination of another generation of readers.

14 Strategic command

Gary Sheffield and Stephen Badsey

Command remains an under-studied aspect of military history. In part, this is because of problems of definition. Leadership and command are related but not identical concepts. A seemingly promising title, John Keegan, *The Mask of Command* (New York: Viking, 1987) actually deals mainly with leadership. Martin van Creveld, *Command in War* (Cambridge, MA: Harvard University Press, 1985) is one of the few books to deal specifically with command. It retains its value, although it is showing its age; in particular, van Creveld's chapter on the British army on the Somme needs to be read in conjunction with more recent work on the subject. See also G. D. Sheffield (ed.), *Leadership and Command: The Anglo-American Military Experience since 1861* (London: Brassey's, 2002 [1997]).

Work on strategic command in the First World War is similarly patchy. Three collections of essays, Peter Paret *et al.* (eds.), *Makers of Modern Strategy from Machiavelli to the Nuclear Age* (Princeton University Press, 1986); Williamson Murray, MacGregor Knox and Alvin Bernstein (eds.), *The Making of Strategy: Rulers, States and War* (Cambridge University Press, 1994); and especially Roger Chickering and Stig Förster (eds.), *Great War, Total War: Combat and Mobilization on the Western Front 1914–18* (Cambridge University Press, 2000) contain material of relevance. Richard F. Hamilton and Holger H. Herwig (eds.), *War Planning 1914* (Cambridge University Press, 2010) is also very useful. Alliance command issues for either side are presently under-researched, but a good starting place for the Anglo-French alliance is Elizabeth Greenhalgh, *Victory Through Coalition: Britain and France during the First World War* (Cambridge University Press, 2005). For the war at sea, see Paul G. Halpern, *A Naval History of World War I* (Annapolis, MD: Naval Institute Press, 1994) and Andrew Gordon, *The Rules of the Game: Jutland and British Naval Command* (London: John Murray, 1996).

Some major figures in the Central Powers command hierarchy have been well served by historians: see Lawrence Sondhaus, *Franz Conrad von Hötzendorf: Architect of the Apocalypse* (Boston, MA: Humanities Press, 2000); and Annika Mombauer, *Helmuth von Moltke and the Origins of the First World War* (Cambridge University Press, 2000). Holger Afflerbach's biography, *Falkenhayn* (Munich: R. Oldenbourg Verlag, 1996) has yet to be translated into English. This should be read in conjunction with Robert T. Foley's important book, *German Strategy and the Path to Verdun* (Cambridge, 2005), which takes issue with some of Afflerbach's findings.

British grand strategy and military strategy are well dealt with in two books by David French: *British Strategy and War Aims 1914–16* (London: Allen & Unwin, 1986) and *The Strategy of the Lloyd George Coalition 1916–1918* (Oxford University Press, 1998). Those interested in key British strategic commanders may consult a number of useful books, including George H. Cassar, *Kitchener's War: British Strategy from 1914–16* (Dulles, VA: Brassey's, 2004); Richard Holmes, *The Little Field Marshal: A Life of Sir John French* (London: Cassell, 2005 [1981]); David R. Woodward, *Field Marshal Sir William Robertson: Chief of the Imperial General Staff in the Great War* (Westport, CT: Praeger, 1998). Douglas Haig remains intensely controversial. For two very different views, see J. P. Harris, *Douglas Haig and the First World War* (Cambridge University Press, 2009) and Gary Sheffield, *The Chief: Douglas Haig and the British Army* (London: Aurum Press, 2011).

For Italy, there is some background material in John Whittam, *The Politics of the Italian Army* (London: Croom Helm, 1977) which deals with the pre-1915 period. Mark Thompson, *The White War* (London: Faber & Faber, 2008) is an excellent recent survey of Italy's war that contains much relevant material. The US commander John J. Pershing can be approached through Donald Smythe, *Pershing: General of the Armies* (Bloomington, IN: Indiana University Press, 2007 [1986]). French commanders are much better served: see Robert A. Doughty, *Pyrrhic Victory: French Strategy and Operations in the Great War* (Cambridge MA: Harvard University Press, 2005) and Elizabeth Greenhalgh, *Foch in Command* (Cambridge University Press, 2011). Guy Pedroncini has written extensively on Pétain, e.g., *Pétain: le soldat et la gloire, 1856–1918* (Paris: Perrin, 1989). Edward J. Erickson's work, which draws on Ottoman material and modern Turkish studies, has transformed Western knowledge of the Ottoman army. Although not primarily concerned with the strategic level, his *Ottoman Military Effectiveness in World War I: A Comparative Study* (London: Routledge, 2007) contains much of interest.

Of the vast number of operational studies, only a handful can be mentioned. These include David T. Zabecki, *The German 1918 Offensives: A Case Study in the Operational Level of War* (Abingdon: Routledge, 2006); Robin Prior and Trevor Wilson, *Command on the Western Front: The Military Career of Sir Henry Rawlinson, 1914–18* (Oxford: Blackwell, 1992); Graydon A. Tunstall, *Blood on the Snow: The Carpathian Winter War of 1915* (Lawrence, KS: University Press of Kansas, 2010); Holger H. Herwig, *The Marne 1914: The Opening of World War I and the Battle that Changed the World* (New York: Random House, 2009); Richard DiNardo, *Breakthrough: The Gorlice-Tarnow Campaign, 1915* (Santa Barbara, CA: Praeger, 2010); and Dennis E. Showalter, *Tannenberg: Clash of Empires, 1914* (Washington, DC: Brassey's, 2004 [1991]).

15 The imperial framework

John H. Morrow, Jr.

Two general studies of the First World War that take a global or imperial approach are John H. Morrow, Jr.'s *The Great War: An Imperial History* (London and New York: Routledge, 2004) and Hew Strachan's study, *The First World War* (London: Penguin, 2005). Avner Offer's *The First World War: An Agrarian Interpretation* (Oxford: Clarendon Press, 1989) offers penetrating insights into the global nature of the war from an agrarian perspective.

For an understanding of the origins of the war within the context of imperialism, John A. Hobson's classic, *Imperialism* (Ann Arbor, MI: University of Michigan Press, 1965 [1902]) remains an indispensable starting point. On a related topic, D. P. Crook's book, *Darwinism, War and History: The Debate over the Biology of War from the 'Origins of Species' to the First World War* (Cambridge University Press, 1994), focuses on the contribution of Darwinism to the bellicose and imperialist atmosphere leading to war. An insightful work on the stress that empire imposed on Great Britain is Aaron L. Friedberg's *The Weary Titan: Britain and the Experience of Relative Decline, 1895–1905* (Princeton University Press, 1986). Pre-war British plans to wreck the German economy employing Britain's unique global power are the subject of Nicholas A. Lambert's tome, *Planning Armageddon: British Economic Warfare and the First World War* (Cambridge, MA: Harvard University Press, 2012). Sean McMeekin's invaluable study, *The Russian Origins of the First World War* (Cambridge, MA: Harvard University Press, 2011), exemplifies how an imperial perspective prevents simplistic attempts to blame a single power for the First World War. The role of the policies of the Ottoman Empire in the war's origins has received thorough attention only in Mustafa Aksakal's monograph, *The Ottoman Road to War: The Ottoman Empire and the First World War* (Cambridge University Press, 2008).

Some of the best works on imperialism concern France, which, alongside Britain, brought its colonial subjects to Europe to fight and work. Richard S. Fogarty's book, *Race and War in France: Colonial Subjects in the French Army, 1914–1918* (Baltimore, MD: Johns Hopkins University Press, 2008), is the latest and most comprehensive of works that include *From Adversaries to Comrades in Arms: West Africans and the French Military, 1885–1918* (Waltham, MA: African Studies Association, 1979) by Charles J. Balesi, *Memoirs of the Maelstrom: A Senegalese Oral History of the First World War* (Portsmouth, NH: Heinemann, 1999) by Joe Lunn and Tyler Stovall's path-breaking article on race in wartime France, 'The color line behind the lines: racial violence in France during the Great War', *American Historical Review*, 103:3 (1998), pp. 737–69. Guoqi Xu's fascinating book, *Strangers on the Western Front: Chinese Workers in the Great War* (Cambridge, MA: Harvard University Press, 2011) sheds light on a hitherto ignored group of workers in France.

In regard to Britain and India, the former's most significant imperial possession, see Philippa Levine's article on race and gender in Britain, 'Battle colors: race, sex, and colonial soldiery in World War I', *Journal of Women's History*, 9:4 (1998), pp. 104–30; David Omissi's informative and moving edited collection of the letters of Indian soldiers, *Indian Voices of the Great War: Soldiers' Letters, 1914–1918* (London: Macmillan, 1999); and Richard J. Popplewell's book on British intelligence operations in and about India, *Intelligence and Imperial Defense: British Intelligence and the Defense of the Indian Empire, 1904–1924* (London: Frank Cass & Co., 1995).

On the war in Africa, see the general studies, *The Great War in Africa, 1914–1918* (New York: W. W. Norton, 1986) by Byron Farwell, and Melvin Page (ed.), *Africa and the First World War* (New York: St Martin's Press, 1987). The revelatory monograph by Mahir Saul and Patrick Royer, *West African Challenge to Empire: Culture and History in the Volta-Bani Anticolonial War* (Athens, OH: Ohio University Press, 2001), examines a significant rising against the French in West Africa. Melvin Page's book, *The Chiwaya War: Malawians and the First World War* (Boulder, CO: Westview Press, 2000) and James J. Mathews's article, 'World War I and the rise of African nationalism: Nigerian veterans as catalysts of political change', *Journal of Modern African Studies*, 20:3 (1982), pp. 493–502, shed light on developments in British colonial Africa.

For readers interested in the military history of difficult British campaigns against the Ottomans, see Charles Townsend, *Desert Hell: The British Invasion of Mesopotamia* (Cambridge, MA: Harvard University Press, 2011) and Peter Hart, *Gallipoli* (Oxford University Press, 2011). On the all-important topics of the Ottoman Empire and the Middle East, see Michael A. Reynold's book, *Shattering Empires: The Clash and Collapse of the Ottoman and Russian Empires, 1908–1918* (Cambridge University Press, 2011) and David Fromkin's readable study, *A Peace to End All Peace: The Fall of the Ottoman Empire and the Creation of the Modern Middle East* (New York: Henry Holt, 1989). Finally, the unique horror and harbinger of an even more monstrous Holocaust, the Armenian genocide, receives due attention in two recent books: Raymond Kévorkian, *The Armenian Genocide: A Complete History* (London: I. B. Tauris, 2011); and Tamer Akçam, *The Young Turks' Crime against Humanity: The Armenian Genocide and Ethnic Cleansing in the Ottoman Empire* (Princeton University Press, 2012).

16 Africa

Bill Nasson

The volume of writing about Africa and 1914–18 still remains comparatively modest. Addressing the impact of the war on the entire continent entails paying attention to a literature on weighty general themes of empire and colonialism, and taking account of a wide spectrum of military, political, social, economic, religious, cultural and ethnic and racial dynamics. For here the war was both an external European imposition and a conflict shaped by the impulses of varied African societies.

At an introductory world war level, although many histories of 1914–18 either ignore Africa or barely touch it, a few of the more recent which seek to place the continent in a wider picture are Jay Winter and Blaine Baggett, *The Great War and the Shaping of the 20th Century* (London: BBC Books, 1996); John H. Morrow, Jr., *The Great War: An Imperial History* (New York: Routledge, 2005); Michael S. Neiberg, *Fighting the Great War: A Global History* (Cambridge, MA: Harvard University Press, 2006); and William Kelleher Storey, *The First World War: A Concise Global History* (Lanham, MD: Rowman & Littlefield, 2009).

For Africa overviews, see the special 'World War I and Africa' issue of the *Journal of African History*, 19:1 (1978); Michael Crowder, 'The First World War and its consequences', in A. Adu Boahen (ed.), *Africa under Colonial Domination, 1880–1935*, UNESCO General History of Africa, vol. VII (Berkeley, CA: University of California Press, 1985), pp. 283–311; M. E. Page (ed.), *Africa and the First World War* (New York: St Martin's Press, 1987); David Killingray, 'The war in Africa', in Hew Strachan (ed.), *The Oxford Illustrated History of the First World War* (Oxford University Press, 1998), pp. 191–212; and Hew Strachan, *The First World War in Africa* (Oxford University Press, 2004).

On West Africa, see Michael Crowder and Jide Osuntokun, 'The First World War and West Africa, 1914–1918', in J. F. Ade Ajayi and Michael Crowder (eds.), *History of West Africa*, 2 vols. (London: Longman, 1974), vol. II, pp. 484–513. On the British colonial side, there is Akinjide Osuntokun, *Nigeria in the First World War* (Harlow: Longman Ibadan History Series, 1979). For French colonies, there are excellent studies of soldiering experience in

Marc Michel, *L'appel a l'Afrique: contributions et réactions a l'effort de guerre en A.O.F. (1914–1919)* (Paris: Publications de la Sorbonne, 1982); Myron Echenberg, *Colonial Conscripts: The Tirailleurs Senegalais in French West Africa, 1857–1960* (Portsmouth, NH: Heinemann, 1991); and Joe Lunn, *Memoirs of the Maelstrom: A Senegalese Oral History of the First World War* (Oxford: James Currey, 1999).

On East and Central Africa there are both appraisals and more specialised local and thematic studies. A first-rate guide is Bruce Vandervort's historiographically assured 'New light on the East African theater of the Great War: a review essay of English-language sources', in Stephen M. Miller (ed.), *Soldiers and Settlers in Africa, 1850–1918* (Amsterdam: Brill, 2009), pp. 287–305. For military campaigning and the totality of the war's effects, see Melvyn E. Page, *The Chiwaya War: Malawians and the First World War* (Boulder, CO: Westview Press, 2000); Edward Paice, *Tip & Run: The Untold Story of the Great War in Africa* (London: Weidenfeld & Nicolson, 2007); R. Anderson, *The Forgotten Front: The East African Campaign, 1914–1918* (Stroud: Tempus, 2004); and Anne Samson, *Britain, South Africa and the East African Campaign, 1914–1918* (London: Frank Cass & Co., 2006). A perceptive recent depiction of Africans under German command is Michelle Moyd, '"We don't want to die for nothing": *askari* at war in German East Africa, 1914–1918', in Santanu Das (ed.), *Race, Empire and First World War Writing* (Cambridge University Press, 2011), pp. 53–76.

Modern specialist literature on North Africa is notably sparse, and for insights readers should consult histories of the region as well as of affected countries, such as Dirk Vanderwalle, *A History of Modern Libya* (Cambridge University Press, 2006); and Robert O. Collins, *A History of Modern Sudan* (Cambridge University Press, 2008).

On southern Africa, see Simon E. Katzenellenbogen, 'Southern Africa and the war of 1914–18', in M. R. D. Foot (ed.), *War and Society* (London: Longman, 1973), pp. 161–88; N. G. Garson, 'South Africa and World War I', *Journal of Imperial and Commonwealth History*, 8:1 (1979), pp. 92–116; Albert Grundlingh, *Fighting Their Own War: South African Blacks and the First World War* (Johannesburg: Ravan, 1987); and Bill Nasson, *Springboks on the Somme: South Africa in the Great War, 1914–1918* (Johannesburg: Penguin, 2007).

On war-related rebellions and uprisings, see George Shepperson and Thomas Price, *Independent African: John Chilembwe and the Nyasaland Native Uprising of 1915* (Edinburgh University Press, 1967); Sandra Swart, '"A Boer and his gun and his wife are three things always together": republican masculinity and the 1914 rebellion', *Journal of Southern African Studies*, 24:2 (1998), pp. 116–38.

17 The Ottoman Empire

Mustafa Aksakal

For the pre-war international context, see Nazan Çiçek, *Turkish Critics of the Eastern Question in the Late Nineteenth Century* (London: I. B. Tauris, 2010); Michael A. Reynolds, *Shattering Empires: The Clash and Collapse of the Ottoman and Russian Empires, 1908–1918* (Cambridge University Press, 2011); and Donald Bloxham, *The Great Game of Genocide: Imperialism, Nationalism, and the Destruction of the Ottoman Armenians* (Oxford University Press, 2005).

On social conditions, see Yiğit Akın, 'The Ottoman Home Front during World War I: Everyday Politics, Society, and Culture' (unpublished PhD thesis, Ohio State University,

2011); Melanie Tanielian, 'The War of Famine: Everyday Life in Wartime Beirut and Mount Lebanon (1914–1918)' (unpublished PhD thesis, University of California, Berkeley, 2012); Part I in Elizabeth Thompson, *Colonial Citizens: Republican Rights, Paternal Privilege and Gender in French Syria and Lebanon* (New York: Columbia University Press, 2000); and Yavuz Selim Karakışla, *Women, War and Work in the Ottoman Empire: Society for the Employment of Ottoman Muslim Women, 1916–1923* (Istanbul: Ottoman Bank Archive and Research Centre, 2005).

On conscription and the lives of soldiers, see Mehmet Beşikçi, *The Ottoman Mobilization of Manpower in the First World War: Between Voluntarism and Resistance* (Leiden: Brill, 2012); Yücel Yanıkdağ, 'Educating the peasants: the Ottoman army and enlisted men in uniform', *Middle Eastern Studies*, 40:6 (2004), pp. 91–107, and his *Healing the Nation: Prisoners of War, Medicine and Nationalism in Turkey, 1914–1939* (Edinburgh University Press, 2013). On disease, see Hikmet Özedmir, *The Ottoman Army, 1914–1918: Disease and Death on the Battlefield*, trans. Saban Kardaş (Salt Lake City, UT: University of Utah Press, 2008). For operational history, see Edward J. Erickson, *Ordered to Die: A History of the Ottoman Army in the First World War* (Westport, CT: Greenwood Press, 2001) and his *Gallipoli: The Ottoman Campaign*, 1915–1916 (Barnsley: Pen & Sword, 2010).

For the Committee of Union and Progress – the party in power – see M. Şükrü Hanioğlu, *Preparation for a Revolution: The Young Turks, 1902–1908* (Oxford University Press, 2001); Nader Sohrabi, *Revolution and Constitutionalism in the Ottoman Empire and Iran* (Cambridge University Press, 2011); M. Naim Turfan, *Rise of the Young Turks: Politics, the Military and Ottoman Collapse* (London: I. B. Tauris, 2000); and Erik J. Zürcher, *The Young Turk Legacy and Nation-Building: From the Ottoman Empire to Atatürk's Turkey* (London: I. B. Tauris, 2010). On economic conditions and war financing, see Zafer Toprak, *İttihad-Terakki ve Cihan Harbi: Savaş Ekonomisi ve Türkiye'de Devletçilik, 1914–1918* (Istanbul: Homer Kitabevi, 2003).

On intervention, see Handan Nezir Akmeşe, *The Birth of Modern Turkey: The Ottoman Military and the March to World War I* (London: I. B. Tauris, 2005); F. A. K. Yasamee, 'The Ottoman Empire', in Keith Wilson (ed.), *Decisions for War, 1914* (Abingdon: Routledge, 1995); and Mustafa Aksakal, *The Ottoman Road to War in 1914: The Ottoman Empire and the First World War* (Cambridge University Press, 2008).

On local and regional politics, imperial citizenship and nationalism, see Hasan Kayalı, *Arabs and Young Turks: Ottomanism, Arabism, and Islamism in the Ottoman Empire, 1908–1918* (Berkeley, CA: University of California Press, 1997); Abigail Jacobson, *From Empire to Empire: Jerusalem Between Ottoman and British Rule* (Syracuse University Press, 2011); Michelle U. Campos, *Ottoman Brothers: Muslims, Christians, and Jews in Early Twentieth-Century Palestine* (Stanford University Press, 2011); Janet Klein, *The Margins of Empire: Kurdish Militias in the Ottoman Tribal Zone* (Stanford University Press); and Kamal Madhar Ahmad, *Kurdistan during the First World War*, trans. Ali Maher İbrahim (London: Saqi Books, 1994).

On ethnic violence, deportations and Armenians, see Ryan Gingeras, *Sorrowful Shores: Violence, Ethnicity, and the End of the Ottoman Empire, 1912–1923* (Oxford University Press, 2009); Uğur Ümit Üngör, *The Making of Modern Turkey: Nation and State in Eastern Anatolia, 1913–1950* (Oxford University Press, 2011); and Ronald Grigor Suny, Fatma Müge Göçek and Norman M. Naimark (eds.), *A Question of Genocide: Armenians and Turks at the End of the Ottoman Empire* (Oxford University Press, 2011). On statistics, see Fuat Dündar, *Crime of*

Numbers: The Role of Statistics in the Armenian Question (1878–1918) (New Brunswick, NJ: Transaction Publishers, 2010).

On the press and propaganda, see Thomas Philipp, 'Perceptions of the First World War in the contemporary Arab press', in Itzchak Weisman and Fruma Zachs (eds.), *Ottoman Reform and Muslim Regeneration* (London: I. B. Tauris, 2005); Gottfried Hagen, *Die Türkei im Ersten Weltkrieg: Flugblätter und Flugschriften in arabischer, persischer und osmanisch-türkischer Sprache aus einer Sammlung der Universitätsbibliothek Heidelberg* (Frankfurt am Main: Peter Lang, 1990); and Erol Köroğlu, *Ottoman Propaganda and Turkish Identity: Literature in Turkey during World War I* (London: I. B. Tauris, 2007).

For first-hand accounts, see Salim Tamari, *Year of the Locust: A Soldier's Diary and the Erasure of Palestine's Ottoman Past* (Berkeley, CA: University of California Press, 2011); Ian Lyster (ed.), *Among the Ottomans: Diaries from Turkey in World War I* (London: I. B. Tauris, 2011); and Hanna Mina, *Fragments of Memory: A Story of a Syrian Family*, trans. Olive Kenny and Lorne Kenny (Northampton: Interlink Books, 2004 [1975]).

On memory and continued effects, see Olaf Farschid, Manfred Kropp and Stephan Dähne (eds.), *The First World War as Remembered in the Countries of the Eastern Mediterranean* (Würzburg: Ergon Verlag and Orient-Institut Beirut, 2006); Fatma Müge Göçek, *The Transformation of Turkey: Redefining State and Society from the Ottoman Empire to the Modern Era* (London: I. B. Tauris, 2011); and Michael Provence, 'Ottoman modernity, colonialism, and insurgency in the Arab Middle East', *International Journal of Middle East Studies*, 43 (2011), pp. 205–25.

18 Asia

Guoqi Xu

The field of Asia and the Great War is largely a virgin land, and we still do not have a rigorous treatment of this topic from a comparative perspective. What we do have are uneven studies of the topic related to individual Asian nations.

On China, Guoqi Xu's *China and the Great War: China's Pursuit of a New National Identity and Internationalization* (Cambridge University Press, 2005 [2011]) provides a general history of China and the war from an international history perspective. Guoqi Xu's *Strangers on the Western Front: Chinese Workers in the Great War* (Cambridge, MA: Harvard University Press, 2011) studies the long-ignored but important journey of 140,000 Chinese workers from their homes in Asia to the Western Front during the Great War, and the roles they played in the histories of both Asia and the world.

On Japan, Frederick Dickinson's *War and National Reinvention: Japan in the Great War, 1914–1919* (Cambridge, MA: Harvard University Press, 1999) is an excellent study of the war's impact on Japanese political development and her role in the war. For Japan's 'racial equality' clause in the Paris Peace Conference negotiations, see Naoko Shimaz, *Japan, Race and Equality: The Racial Equality Proposal of 1919* (London: Routledge, 2009).

The scholarship on India and the Great War seems to be relatively extensive. Yet an authoritative volume on India and the war has not yet emerged. For personal perceptions and observations on the war, see David Omissi, *Indian Voices of the Great War* (London: Palgrave Macmillan, 1999) and DeWitt C. Ellinwood, *Between Two Worlds: A Rajput Officer in the Indian Army, 1905–1921, Based on the Diary of Amar Singh* (Lanham, MD: Hamilton,

2005); Santanu Das's, 'Indians at home, Mesopotamia and France, 1914–1918: towards an intimate history', in Santanu Das (ed.), *Race, Empire and First World War Writing* (Cambridge University Press, 2011), brings a fresh and new perspective into our understanding of the history of India and the Great War.

Scholars have just turned their attentions to the study of Vietnam and the Great War. Most scholars in this field focus on its colonial aspects. A good example is Richard Fogarty, *Race and War in France: Colonial Subjects in the French Army, 1914–1918* (Baltimore, MD: Johns Hopkins University Press, 2008) which has an excellent discussion of Vietnamese labourers in France during the Great War. Kimloan Hill's work is an important step forward. See her book *Coolies into Rebels: Impact of World War I on French Indochina* (Paris: Les Indes Savantes, 2011), based on her doctoral dissertation, and her articles 'Strangers in a foreign land: Vietnamese soldiers and workers in France during World War I', in Nhung Tuyet Tran and Anthony Reid (eds.), *Viet Nam: Borderless Histories* (Madison, WI: University of Wisconsin Press, 2006), pp. 256–89, and 'Sacrifices, sex, race: Vietnamese experiences in the First World War', in Das (ed.), *Race, Empire and First World War Writing*, pp. 53–69.

On Asia and the post-war Peace Conference, the best book is Erez Manela, *The Wilsonian Moment: Self-Determination and the International Origins of Anticolonial Nationalism* (New York: Oxford University Press, 2007), which has excellent discussions on China, India and Korea and their roles and interests in the post-war world order.

19 North America

Jennifer D. Keene

There are no transnational North American histories of the First World War. National histories predominate, while histories focused on international relations focus heavily on Woodrow Wilson's vision of a new world order.

David Mackenzie (ed.), *Canada and the First World War: Essays in Honour of Robert Craig Brown* (University of Toronto Press, 2005) contains a series of excellent essays by leading scholars that challenge older interpretative paradigms of the war's impact on Canada. Desmond Morton, *Marching to Armageddon: Canadians and the Great War, 1914–1919* (Toronto: Lester & Orpen Dennys, 1989) is the classic study of Canada's war. Robert Craig Brown and Ramsey Cook, *Canada, 1896–1921: A Nation Transformed* (Toronto: McClelland & Stewart, 1974) contains five chapters dealing with the First World War which offer perhaps the best synthetic overview to date. In considering the entire span of US-Canadian relations, John Herd Thompson and Stephen J. Randall, *Canada and the United States: Ambivalent Allies*, 4th edn (Athens, GA: University of Georgia Press, 2008) view the First World War as a turning point. On Canadian commemorative practices, see Jonathan Vance, *Death So Noble: Memory, Meaning, and the First World War* (Vancouver: UBC Press, 1997). Tim Cook's two volumes on the Canadian military trace the evolution in tactics, strategy and fighting prowess over the course of the war: *At the Sharp End: Canadians Fighting the Great War 1914–1916* (Toronto: Viking, 2007) and *Shock Troops: Canadians Fighting the Great War, 1917–1918* (Toronto: Viking, 2008). Timothy Winegard explores the experiences of native peoples within Canada in *Indigenous Peoples of the British Dominions and the First World War* (Cambridge University Press, 2011) and *For King and Kanata: Canadian Indians and the First World War* (Winnipeg: University of Manitoba Press, 2012).

Excellent overviews of America's war effort include David M. Kennedy, *Over Here: The First World War and American Society* (New York: Oxford University Press, 1980); Robert H. Zieger, *America's Great War: World War I and the American Experience* (Oxford: Rowman & Littlefield, 2000); and Robert H. Ferrell, *Woodrow Wilson and World War I, 1917–1921* (New York: Free Press, 2001). For more insight into the home front, civil rights and mobilisation, see Christopher Capozzola, *Uncle Sam Wants You: World War I and the Making of the Modern American Citizen* (New York: Oxford University Press, 2008); Jennifer D. Keene, *Doughboys, the Great War and the Remaking of America* (Baltimore, MD: Johns Hopkins University Press, 2001); and Chad L. Williams, *Torchbearers of Democracy: African American Soldiers in the World War I Era* (Chapel Hill, NC: University of North Carolina Press, 2010). Recent work on the American combat experience includes Edward G. Lengel, *To Conquer Hell: The Meuse-Argonne, 1918* (New York: Henry Holt, 2008) and Mark Grotelueschen, *The AEF Way of War: The American Army and Combat in World War I* (Cambridge University Press, 2007). Steven Trout traces the disjointed American memorialisation of the war in *On the Battlefield of Memory: The First World War and American Remembrance, 1919–1941* (Tuscaloosa, AL: University of Alabama Press, 2010).

Historians documenting America's evolving foreign relations during the war pay close attention to Mexico, but almost uniformly ignore relations with Canada. One exception is Kathleen Burk, *Britain, America and the Sinews of War, 1914–1918* (Boston: Allen & Unwin, 1985). Insightful discussions of America's evolving relationship with Mexico are found in John Milton Cooper, Jr., *Woodrow Wilson: A Biography* (New York: Knopf, 2009); N. G. Levin, *Woodrow Wilson and World Politics: America's Response to War and Revolution* (New York: Oxford University Press, 1968); Friedrich Katz, *The Secret War in Mexico: Europe, the United States and the Mexican Revolution* (University of Chicago Press, 1981); and Mark T. Gilderhus, *Pan American Visions: Woodrow Wilson in the Western Hemisphere, 1913–1921* (Tucson, AZ: University of Arizona Press, 1986). Akira Iriye, *The Cambridge History of American Foreign Relations*, vol. III: *The Globalizing of America, 1913–1945* (Cambridge University Press, 1993) considers how the war fits into America's gradual rise as a world power in the first part of the twentieth century.

20 Latin America

Olivier Compagnon

The effects of the Great War on Latin America form a complex and still developing field of historical research. Among recent attempts at synthesis are: Olivier Compagnon and Armelle Enders, 'L'Amérique latine et la guerre', in Stéphane Audoin-Rouzeau and Jean-Jacques Becker (eds.), *Encyclopédie de la Grande Guerre, 1914–1918* (Paris: Bayard, 2004), pp. 889–901, and Olivier Compagnon, '1914–18: the death throes of civilization: the elites of Latin America face the Great War', in Jenny Macleod and Pierre Purseigle (eds.), *Uncovered Fields: Perspectives in First World War Studies* (Leiden: Brill, 2004), pp. 279–95. This second article is an analysis of the reception of the conflict by the intellectual elites, and an evaluation of the war as a turning point in identity in the cultural history of contemporary Latin America.

For an earlier synthesis, see Bill Albert and Paul Henderson, *South America and the First World War: The Impact of the War on Brazil, Argentina, Peru and Chile* (Cambridge University

Press, 1988). There are other important national studies surrounding the question of intervention and the political effects of wartime developments. These three are important contributions: Francisco Luiz Teixeira Vinhosa, *O Brasil e a Primeira Guerra mundial* (Rio de Janeiro: IBGE, 1990). This is the most complete work on Brazil in the First World War, above all, founded on an analysis of diplomatic sources. See also Freddy Vivas Gallardo, 'Venezuela y la Primera Guerra mundial: de la neutralidad al compromiso (octubre 1914–marzo 1919), *Revista de la Facultad de Ciencias Jurídicas y Políticas*, 61 (1981), pp. 113–33, and Ricardo Weinmann, *Argentina en la Primera guerra mundial: neutralidad, transición política y continuismo económico* (Buenos Aires: Biblio, Fundación Simón Rodríguez, 1994). Weinmann's is an important work on Argentina and the Great War, with a focus in particular on the radical presidency of Hipólito Yrigoyen from 1916 on.

Many scholars have approached the impact of war on Latin America in terms of her economic history. The most complete presentation of the economic consequences of the conflict in this region is Victor Bulmer-Thomas, *La historia ecónomica de América latina desde la Independencia* (Mexico: Fondo de Cultura Ecónomica, 1998), chapter 6, pp. 185–228. Another notable study is Roger Gravil, 'Argentina and the First World War', *Revista de História* (27th year), 54 (1976), pp. 385–417. Here is a careful analysis of the economic consequences of the Great War in Argentina. Another contribution is Marc Badia I Miro and Anna Carreras Marin, 'The First World War and coal trade geography in Latin America and the Caribbean, 1890–1930', *Jahrbuch für Geschichte Lateinamerikas*, 45 (2008), pp. 369–91. On Peru, see Victor A. Madueño, 'La Primera Guerra mundial el desarrollo industrial del Perú', *Estudios Andinos*, 17–18 (1982), pp. 41–53. And on Central America, see Frank Notten, *La influencia de la Primera Guerra Mundial sobre las economías centroamericanas, 1900–1929: Un enfoque desde el comercio exterior* (San José: Centro de Investigaciones Históricas de América Central/Universidad de Costa Rica, 2012).

The British side of the story, with an emphasis on economic issues, is the focus of Philip A. Dehne, *On the Far Western Front: Britain's First World War in South America* (Manchester University Press, 2009). Based on British archives, this is a study of relations between Great Britain and Latin America putting the accent on the economic stakes and supplying valuable data on the black lists. See as well Juan Ricardo Couyoumdjian, *Chile y Gran Bretaña durante la Primera Guerra mundial y la postguerra, 1914–1921* (Santiago: Editorial Andres Bello/Universidad Católica de Chile, 1986). And on expatriates to Uruguay, see Álvaro Cuenca, *La colonia británica de Montevideo y la Gran Guerra* (Montevideo: Torre del Vigia Editores, 2006).

Others with European origins were mobilised too. See Emilio Franzina, 'La guerra lontana: il primo conflitto mondiale e gli italiani d'Argentina', *Estudios migratiorios latinoamericanos*, 44 (2000), pp. 66–73, and Franzina, 'Italiani del Brasile ed italobrasiliani durante il Primo Conflitto Mondiale (1914–1918)', *História: Debates e Tendências*, 5:1 (2004), pp. 225–67. These are two fundamental articles on the mechanisms of mobilisation at a distance among the substantial Italian community in Argentina and Brazil. Other groups are treated in Frederick C. Luebke, *Germans in Brazil: A Comparative History of Cultural Conflict During World War I* (Baton Rouge and London: Louisiana State University Press, 1987). This is a remarkable study of the communities of Germanic origin established in the northern states of Brazil between 1914 and 1918. See as well Hernán Otero, *La guerra e la sangre: Los franco-argentinos ante la Primera Guerra Mundial* (Buenos Aires: Sudamericana, 2009).

Cultural historians have entered this field as well. One Chilean poet's response to the war is the subject of Keith Ellis, 'Vicente Huidobro y la Primera Guerra mundial', *Hispanic Review*, 57:3 (Summer 1999), pp. 333–46. A brief study of the treatment of the war in 1914 and 1917 in two daily papers in Rio de Janeiro, the *Correio da Manha* and the *Jornal do Commercio* is available in Sydney Garambone, *A Primeira Guerra Mundial e a imprensa brasileira* (Rio de Janeiro: Mauad, 2003). See also Olivier Compagnon, *L'adieu à l'Europe: L'Amérique latine et la Grande Guerre (Argentine et Brésil, 1914–1939)* (Paris: Fayard, 2013).

On the political history of the war period and its aftermath, there are a number of useful studies. On Argentina, María Inés Tato has offered these interpretations of domestic political conflict and the war: 'La disputa por la argentinidad: rupturistas y neutralistas durante la Primera guerra mundial', *Temas de historia argentina y americana*, 13 (July–December 2008), pp. 227–50; 'La contienda europea en las calles porteñas: manifestaciones civices y pasiones nacionales en torno de la Primera Guerra Mundial', in María Inés Tato and Martin Castro (eds.), *Del Centenario al peronismo: dimensiones de la vida politica argentina* (Buenos Aires: Imago Mundi, 2010), pp. 33–63; and 'Nacionalismo e internacionalismo en la Argentina durante la Gran Guerra', *Projeto História*, 36 (June 2008), pp. 49–62.

On the press, we have: Patricia Vega Jiménez, '¿Especulación desinformativa? La Primera Guerra Mundial en los periódicos de Costa Rica y El Salvador', *Mesoamérica*, 51 (2009), pp. 94–122; and Yolanda de la Parra, 'La Primera Guerra Mundial y la prensa mexicana', *Estudios de historia moderna y contemporánea de México*, 10 (1986), pp. 155–76.

On the vexed question of relations with the United States and the war, a good place to start is Friedrich Katz, *The Secret War in Mexico: Europe, the United States and the Mexican Revolution* (University of Chicago Press, 1981). This is a classic study on diplomats, both European and North American, in Mexico in the double context of the revolution and the Great War. There are two older studies, still worth reading: Barbara Tuchman, *The Zimmermann Telegram* (New York: Dell Publishing Co., 1965); and Joseph S. Tulchin, *The Aftermath of War: World War I and U.S. Policy toward Latin America* (New York University Press, 1971), an old but still valuable decrypting of inter-American relations after the war.

On the League of Nations and Latin America, see Thomas Fischer, *Die Souveränität der Schwachen: Lateinamerika und der Völkerbund, 1920–1936* (Stuttgart: Franz Steiner, 2012). This is a complete and richly documented analysis of the Latin American presence in the League of Nations. The French side of the story is explored in Yannick Wehrli, 'Les délégations latino-américanes et les intérêts de la France à la Société des Nations', *Relations internationales*, 137:1 (2009), pp. 45–59.

21 Atrocities and war crimes

John Horne

The topic addressed in this chapter involves legal, cultural and military history. On the legal side, an indispensable history of international law and the conduct of war is Geoffrey Best, *Humanity in Warfare: The Modern History of the International Law of Armed Conflicts* (London: Weidenfeld & Nicolson, 1980). For the relevant texts, two useful collections are Adam Roberts and Richard Guelff (eds.), *Documents on the Laws of War*, 2nd edn (Oxford: Clarendon Press, 1989 [1982]) and Michael Reisman and Chris Antoniou (eds.), *The Laws of War: A Comprehensive Collection of Primary Documents on International Laws Governing*

Armed Conflicts (New York: Vintage, 1994). The proceedings of the Hague Peace Conferences of 1899 and 1907 may be found in James Brown Scott (ed.), *Texts of the Peace Conferences at The Hague, 1899 and 1907* (Boston and London: Ginn & Co., 1908). On the Leipzig war crimes trials in 1921, see *German War Trials: Report of Proceedings before the Supreme Court in Leipzig* (London: HMSO, 1921); James F. Willis, *Prologue to Nuremberg: The Politics and Diplomacy of Punishing War Criminals of the First World War* (Westport, CT and London: Greenwood Press, 1982); Annie Deperchin-Gouillard, 'Responsabilité et violation du droit des gens pendant la première guerre mondiale: volonté politique et impuissance juridique', in Annette Wieviorka (ed.), *Les Procès de Nuremberg et de Tokyo* (Brussels: Éditions Complexe, 1996), pp. 25–49; and Gerd Hankel, *Die Leipziger Prozesse: Deutsche Kriegsverbrechen und ihre strafrechtliche Verfolgung nach dem Ersten Weltkrieg* (Hamburg: Hamburger Edition, 2003). On the trials of perpetrators of the Armenian genocide in Constantinople, see Taner Akçam, *Armenien und der Völkermord: Die Istanbuler Prozesse und die türkische Nationalbewegung* (Hamburg: Hamburger Edition, 1996).

On the cultural meaning of 'atrocities' and the ways in which they designated the enemy as well as the crimes allegedly committed, see John Horne and Alan Kramer, *German Atrocities, 1914: A History of Denial* (New Haven, CT and London: Yale University Press, 2001). So far, there is no equivalent study for the Eastern Front, though for the Russian invasion of East Prussia, see Imanuel Geiss, 'Die Kosaken kommen! Ostpreußen im August 1914', in Geiss, *Das deutsche Reich und der Erste Weltkrieg*, 2nd edn (Munich: Piper, 1985 [1978]). On the allegations and reality of atrocities during the Austro-Hungarian invasion of Serbia, the best work is Jonathan Gumz, *The Resurrection and Collapse of Empire in Habsburg Serbia, 1914–1918* (Cambridge University Press, 2009), pp. 44–61. For the legality and reality of the protected status of the POW, see Heather Jones, *Violence against Prisoners of War in the First World War: Britain, France and Germany, 1914–1920* (Cambridge University Press, 2011).

Works that look at the interplay of the cultural construction of the enemy and the exactions against occupied civilian populations are, for the Western Front, the pioneering works of Annette Becker, *Oubliés de la Grande Guerre: humanitaire et culture de guerre: populations occupées, déportés civils, prisonniers de guerre* (Paris: Éditions Noêsis, 1998) and *Les cicatrices rouges, 14–18: France et Belgique occupées* (Paris: Fayard, 2010); and Sophie de Schaepdrijver, *La Belgique et la première guerre mondiale* (1997; translation from the Dutch, Brussels: Peter Lang, 2004); and for the Eastern Front, Vejas Gabriel Liulevicius, *War Land on the Eastern Front: Culture, National Identity and German Occupation in World War I* (Cambridge University Press, 2000). For a detailed contemporary study of the deportation of Belgian labour to Germany (written for the Belgian government in exile), see Fernand Passelecq, *Déportation et travail forcé des ouvriers et de la population civile de la Belgique occupée (1916–1918)* (Paris: PUF, 1928). An important essay on the applicability or otherwise of international law to the German occupations in Belgium and France is Annie Deperchin and Laurence van Ypersele, 'Droit et occupation: les cas de la France et de la Belgique', in John Horne (ed.), *Vers la guerre totale: le tournant de 1914–1915* (Paris: Tallandier, 2010), pp. 153–74.

On violence against home populations, see, for the Russian retreat in 1915, Peter Holquist, 'Les violences de l'armée russe à l'encontre des Juifs en 1915: causes et limites', in Horne (ed.), *Vers la guerre totale*, pp. 191–219, and Peter Gatrell, *A Whole Empire Walking: Refugees in Russia during the First World War* (Bloomington, IN: Indiana University Press,

1999), esp. pp. 15–97. The Armenian genocide is dealt with in Chapter 22 of this volume, but for its subordination to Great Power relations and the relative view taken of it by the Allies (compared to the greater vilification of Germany), see Donald Bloxham, *The Great Game of Genocide: Imperialism, Nationalism and the Destruction of the Ottoman Armenians* (Oxford University Press, 2005) and Annette Becker and Jay Winter, 'Le génocide arménien et les réactions de l'opinion internationale,' in Horne (ed.), *Vers la guerre totale*, pp. 291–313.

There is no satisfactory cultural history of the claims and counter-claims surrounding the Allied blockade and German submarine campaigns, but see Gerd Krumeich, 'Le blocus maritime et la guerre sous-marine', in Horne (ed.), *Vers la guerre totale*, pp. 175–90. On the moral and legal dimension of the air war, in addition to Best, *Humanity in Warfare*, see Christian Geinitz, 'The First German air war against noncombatants: strategic bombing of German cities in World War I', in Roger Chickering and Stig Förster (eds.), *Great War, Total War: Combat and Mobilization on the Western Front, 1914–1918* (Cambridge University Press, 2000), pp. 207–25.

Much of the discussion of 'propaganda' during the First World War still adopts the uncritical use of the term from the 1920s, itself a negative reaction against the supposed manipulation of minds during the Great War. For an attempt to think about constructions of 'truth' and 'falsehood' in the polarised circumstances of wartime, see John Horne, '"Propagande" et "vérité" dans la Grande Guerre', in Christophe Prochasson and Anne Rasmussen (eds.), *Vrai et faux dans la Grande Guerre* (Paris: Bayard, 2004), pp. 76–95.

The military and political context for each of the themes treated in this chapter is discussed elsewhere in this history, notably in Volume I: Chapter 12 (War at sea) and Chapter 13 (The air war); Volume II: Chapter 11 (Prisoners of war) and Chapter 18 (Blockade and economic warfare); and Volume III: Chapter 8 (Refugees and exiles), Chapter 9 (Minorities), Chapter 10 (Populations under occupation) and Chapter 11 (Captive civilians). Finally, for another overview from a somewhat different perspective, see Alan Kramer, 'Combatants and noncombatants: atrocities, massacres and war crimes', in John Horne (ed.), *A Companion to World War I* (Chichester and Oxford: Wiley-Blackwell, 2010), pp. 188–201.

22 Genocide

Hans-Lukas Kieser and Donald Bloxham

There is now an impressive scholarship based on extensive Ottoman documentation as well as Armenian and other primary sources. Raymond Kévorkian's *The Armenian Genocide: a Complete History* (London: I. B. Tauris, 2011) is a hugely detailed historical account of almost every aspect of the genocide. See also his analysis, including detailed timeline, 'The extermination of Ottoman Armenians by the Young Turk regime (1915–1916)', in the *Online Encyclopedia of Mass Violence* at www.massviolence.org. Taner Akçam's *The Young Turks' Crime Against Humanity: The Armenian Genocide and Ethnic Cleansing in the Ottoman Empire* (Princeton University Press, 2012) is the most recent of the author's book-length engagements with the topic. His and Vahakn N. Dadrian's *Judgment at Istanbul: The Armenian Genocide Trials* (New York: Berghahn, 2011) also contains much relevant evidence. Hilmar Kaiser has written many authoritative essays, including the primary-source-based overview, 'Genocide at the twilight of the Ottoman Empire', in Donald Bloxham and A. Dirk

Moses (eds.), *The Oxford Handbook of Genocide Studies* (Oxford University Press, 2010), pp. 365–85. Fuat Dündar's *Crime of Numbers: The Role of Statistics in the Armenian Question (1878–1918)* (New Brunswick, NJ: Transaction Publishers, 2010) looks at issues around the genocide from a demographer's perspective; his *İttihat ve Terakki'nin Müslümanları İskân Politikası, 1913–1918* (Istanbul: İletişim Yayınları, 2001) sheds light on aspects of demographic engineering and the historical context from the Balkan wars onwards. Uğur Ümit Üngör's *The Making of Modern Turkey: Nation and State in Eastern Anatolia, 1913–1950* (Oxford University Press, 2011) considers the fate of the Armenians based on a detailed case study of the Diyarbekir province. His and Mehmet Polatel's *Confiscation and Destruction: The Young Turk Seizure of Armenian Property* (London: Continuum, 2011), details the plunder of the victims. Hans-Lukas Kieser's *Der verpasste Friede: Mission, Ethnie und Staat in den Ostprovinzen der Türkei 1839–1938* (Zurich: Chronos Verlag, 2000), considers the genocide period and the background from the beginning of the Tanzimat reform period onwards.

Non-Armenian victim groups are considered in some measure in most of the above works. The fate of the Syriacs is the focus of David Gaunt's *Massacres, Resistance, Protectors: Muslim-Christian Relations in Eastern Anatolia during World War I* (Piscataway, NJ: Gorgias Press, 2006), and is treated in the second chapter of Üngör's *The Making of Modern Turkey*. Like Kieser's *Der verpasste Friede*, Üngör's work also considers Young Turk and then Kemalist policies of violence and assimilation against the Kurds. On continuities between the Young Turk regime and the later republican regime, see Erik J. Zürcher, *The Young Turk Legacy and Nation Building: From the Ottoman Empire to Atatürk's Turkey* (London: I. B. Tauris, 2010.)

On the international context, see Donald Bloxham, *The Great Game of Genocide: Imperialism, Nationalism, and the Destruction of the Ottoman Armenians* (Oxford University Press, 2005). Wolfgang Gust (ed.), *Der Völkermord an den Armeniern 1915/16: Dokumente aus dem Politischen Archiv des deutschen Auswärtigen Amts* (Springe: zu Klampen! Verlag, 2005) presents German diplomatic documents illustrating German responses and eyewitness accounts of the reality of the situation in Asia Minor. (Gust's website www.armenocide.net/ reproduces these documents and includes English translations.) Artem Ohandjanian's multi-volume edited collection, *Österreich-Armenien, 1872–1936: Faksimilesammlung diplomatischer Aktenstücke* (Vienna: Ohandjanian Eigenverlag, 1995) does much the same for the diplomatic records of the Dual Monarchy. For other key international diplomatic eyewitnesses, see Ara Sarafian (ed.), *United States Official Records on the Armenian Genocide 1915–1917* (London: Taderon Press, 2004). Amongst the plethora of contemporary accounts, especially detailed and systematic is Johannes Lepsius, *Der Todesgang des armenischen Volkes: Bericht über das Schicksal des armenischen Volkes in der Türkei während des Weltkrieges* (Potsdam: Tempelverlag, 1919).

Of a number of edited collections three merit particular mention: Ronald Grigor Suny, Fatma Müge Göçek and Norman M. Naimark (eds.), *A Question of Genocide: Armenians and Turks at the End of the Ottoman Empire* (New York: Oxford University Press, 2011); Hans-Lukas Kieser and Dominik Schaller (eds.), *Der Völkermord an den Armeniern und die Shoah/The Armenian Genocide and the Shoah* (Zurich: Chronos, 2002). Richard Hovannisian (ed.), *Remembrance and Denial: The Case of the Armenian Genocide* (Detroit, MI: Wayne State University Press, 1999) combines useful historical essays with studies of Turkish denial.

For attempts to put late Ottoman genocide and other cases discussed in the chapter into a wider context, see Kieser and Schaller (eds.), *Der Völkermord an den Armeniern und die Shoah*; Donald Bloxham, *The Final Solution: A Genocide* (Oxford University Press, 2009), and Mark Levene, *The Crisis of Genocide*, vol. I: *1912–1938* and vol. II: *1939–1953* (Oxford University Press, 2013).

On Russian violence towards minorities during the war, see Edward D. Sokol, *The Revolt of 1916 in Russian Central Asia* (Baltimore, MD: Johns Hopkins University Press, 1954); Eric Lohr, *Nationalising the Russian Empire: The Campaign against Enemy Aliens during World War One* (Cambridge, MA: Harvard University Press, 2003); Peter Gatrell, *A Whole Empire Walking: Refugees in Russia during the First World War* (Bloomington, IN: Indiana University Press, 1999); Alexander V. Prusin, *Nationalizing a Borderland: War, Ethnicity, and Anti-Jewish Violence in East Galicia, 1914–1920* (Tuscaloosa, AL: University of Alabama Press, 2005); and Peter Holquist, 'Les violences de l'armée russe à l'encontre des Juifs en 1915: causes et limites', in John Horne (ed.), *Vers la guerre totale: le tournant de 1914–1915* (Paris: Tallandier, 2010), pp. 191–219. Holquist's essay in Suny *et al.* (eds.), *A Question of Genocide*, compares Russian wartime policy towards Transcaucasian Muslims with Ottoman policy towards Armenians. For important remarks on context, see Michael A. Reynolds, *Shattering Empires: The Clash and Collapse of the Russian and Ottoman Empires, 1908–1919* (Cambridge University Press, 2011).

On the other episode considered in this chapter, see Mahir Şaul and Patrick Yves Royer, *West African Challenge to Empire: Culture and History in the Volta-Bani Anticolonial War* (Athens, OH: Ohio University Press, 2001).

Material related to the chapter as a whole is considered in this history in Volume I: Chapter 17 (Ottoman Empire) and Chapter 21 (Atrocities and war crimes); Volume II: Chapter 23 (The wars after the war); and Volume III: Chapters 8–11 (in the section 'Populations at risk').

23 The laws of war

Annie Deperchin

Consultation of the official documents is the best way to approach the laws of war and to understand the stages of their development and the difficulties encountered. The debates on various questions can be studied in these texts: *Actes de la Conférence de Bruxelles de 1874: Sur le projet d'une convention internationale concernant la Guerre* (Paris: Librairie des Publications législatives, 1874); Ministère des Affaires étrangères, *Deuxième Conférence internationale de la Paix 1907: Documents diplomatiques* (Paris: Imprimerie nationale, 1908); Ministère des Affaires étrangères, *Conférence internationale de la Paix 1899: Documents diplomatiques* (Paris: Imprimerie nationale, 1908).

To understand legal reasoning on the laws of war, there is an old work, but one which has lost none of its relevance. It deals with the evolution of the laws in all their dimensions from 1864 to 1899 and draws up the account of how lawyers dealt with the wars of its period: F. de Martens, *La paix et la guerre* (Paris: A. Rousseau, 1901).

On the violations of the laws of war and their legal treatment, two recent works are helpful. In English, there is an important study by two Irish historians, focusing on the opening stages of the war, but with an analysis dealing with violations of the law and how societies responded to them: John Horne and Alan Kramer, *German Atrocities 1914: A History of Denial* (New Haven, CT and London: Yale University Press, 2001). In German, from a specialist in the contemporary laws of war and giving a full judicial approach to the Leipzig cases, there is Gerd Hankel, *Die leipziger Prozesse: Deutsche Kriegsverbrechen und ihre strafrechtliche Verfolgung nach dem Ersten Weltkrieg* (Hamburg: Hamburger Edition, 2003).

Index

Cumulative index for Volumes I, II, and III.